THE JEWS OF ARAB LANDS

THE JEWS OF ARAB LANDS

A HISTORY AND SOURCE BOOK

NORMAN A. STILLMAN

PHILADELPHIA · 5739–1979

THE JEWISH PUBLICATION SOCIETY OF AMERICA

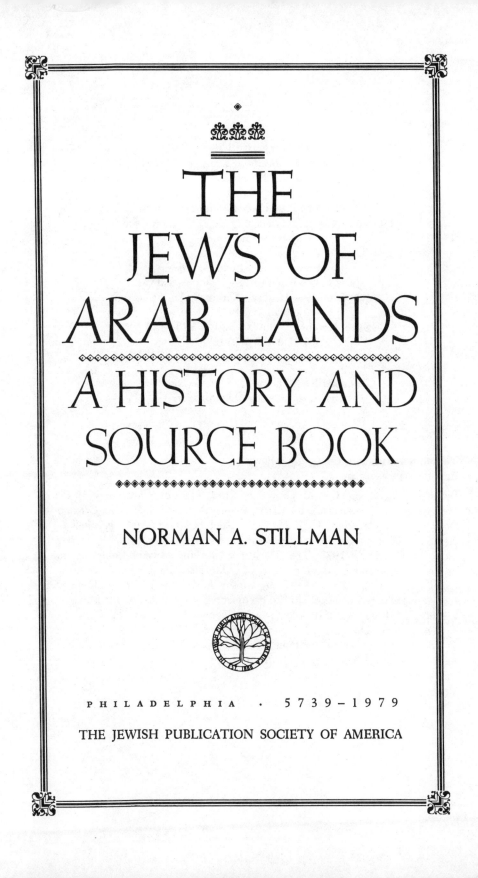

Manufactured in the United States of America
Library of Congress Cataloging in Publication Data
Main entry under title:
The Jews of Arab lands.
Bibliography: p. Includes index.
1. Jews in Arab countries—History—Sources.
2. Arab countries—History—Sources. I. Stillman, Norman A., 1945–
DS135.A68J48 909′.04′924 78–70078
ISBN 0–8276–0116–6

Designed by Adrianne Onderdonk Dudden
Endpaper maps by Quentin Fiore

The author wishes to thank the following publishers for permission to quote from the sources listed:

By permission of the Oxford University Press, for *The Chronology of Bar Hebraeus,* vol. 1, translated by E. A. Wallis Budge (1932), and *Ottoman Documents on Palestine, 1552–1615,* by Uriel Heyd © 1960; reprinted by permission of Princeton University Press, *Letters of Medieval Jewish Traders,* by S. D. Goitein © 1973; The Regents of the University of California, reprinted by permission of the University of California Press, for *Ibn Kammuna's Examination of the Three Faiths* by Moshe Perlmann © 1971; Union of American Hebrew Congregations, for documents from *The Jew in the Medieval World,* edited by Jacob R. Marcus (Atheneum, 1975), SUNY Press, for revised portions of "Aspects of Jewish Life in Islamic Spain," in *Aspects of Jewish Culture,* edited by Paul Szarmach © 1978; *The Wiener Library Bulletin,* for translation by David Littman of Alliance Israélite Universelle Paris archives documents in *Bulletin* 28.

To my master and teacher
S. D. GOITEIN
who inspired me with
his own interest in
Jews and Arabs

CONTENTS

PREFACE xv
NOTE ON STYLE xxi
CHRONOLOGICAL TABLE xxiii
LIST OF ILLUSTRATIONS xxix

PART ONE ✱ *HISTORY*

1 THE FIRST ENCOUNTER: MUḤAMMAD AND THE JEWS 3

2 UNDER THE NEW ORDER: MIDDLE-EASTERN JEWRY IN THE FIRST THREE CENTURIES OF ISLAM 22

3 THE BEST YEARS: MEDITERRANEAN JEWRY IN THE ISLAMIC HIGH MIDDLE AGES 40

Ifrīqiya (Tunisia) 42

Egypt 46

Spain 53

The Best Years in Retrospect 61

4 THE LONG TWILIGHT: THE JEWS OF ARAB LANDS IN THE LATER MIDDLE AGES 64

The Mamluk Empire 67

North Africa (The Maghreb) 76

The Arab Provinces of the Ottoman Empire 87

5 THE DAWN OF MODERN TIMES: THE JEWS OF ARAB LANDS IN THE NINETEENTH CENTURY 95

EPILOGUE 108

PART TWO ⌘ SOURCES

1 THE FIRST ENCOUNTER: MUḤAMMAD AND THE JEWS 113

Muḥammad's First Jewish Convert 113
Muḥammad's Ordinance for Medina 115
Muḥammad's Jewish Adversaries in Medina 119
"Mukhayrīq Is the Best of the Jews" 121
The Affair of the Banū Qaynuqāᶜ 122
The Assassination of Kaᶜb b. al-Ashraf 124
The Brothers Muḥayyiṣa and Ḥuwayyiṣa 128
The Raid against the Banu 'l-Naḍīr 129
The Extermination of the Banū Qurayẓa 137
Muḥammad and the Jews of Khaybar 145
The Koran on the Treatment of the People of the Book 149
Some Koranic Pronouncements on the Jews 150

2 UNDER THE NEW ORDER: MIDDLE-EASTERN JEWRY IN THE FIRST THREE CENTURIES OF ISLAM 152

Jews Aid the Arabs in the Conquest of Hebron 152
The Christians and Jews of Ḥimṣ Prefer the Arabs to the Byzantines 153
ᶜUmar Permits the Jews to Return to Jerusalem 154
Jews Aid the Muslim Conquerors of Spain 156
The Pact of ᶜUmar 157
How the Jizya Is to be Collected and from Whom 159
Islamic Protectionism: Tariffs for Muslims and Non-Muslims 162
The Itinerary of the Radhanite Jewish Merchants 163
The First Jews' Oath in Islam 165
The Caliph al-Mutawakkil and the Ahl al-Dhimma 167
Why the Muslim Masses Prefer Christians to Jews 169
More of the Same 170
The Installation of the Exilarch 171

A Shiᶜite View of the Exilarchate 176
A Caliphal Proclamation of Appointment for a New Gaon 178
A Christian and a Jewish Notable Pay Their Poll Tax 180
The Appointment of Daniel b. Samuel to the Gaonate 181
The Appointment of Eli b. Zachariah to the Gaonate 182

3 THE BEST YEARS: MEDITERRANEAN JEWRY IN THE ISLAMIC HIGH MIDDLE AGES 183

A Letter Mentioning the Appointment of the First Nagid in Tunisia 183
The Death of the First Nagid 186
A Synagogue Accused of Being in Violation of Islamic Law Is Vindicated in Court 189
The Jews of Fustat Raise Money to Pay the Taxes of Their Brethren in Jerusalem 192
A Sick and Destitute Fugitive from the Poll Tax Collector Seeks the Aid of a Jewish Courtier 194
A Charity List 195
A Fatimid Caliph Steps Into a Dispute Between Rabbanites and Karaites in the Holy Land 198
Christian and Jewish Officials in the Fatimid Empire 200
The Caliph al-Ḥākim Protects the Jews from the Wrath of the Populace 201
A Petition to a Court Jew in Fatimid Egypt 204
A Lament for the Jews of Palestine during the Bedouin Rampages of 1024 205
The Assassination of Abū Saᶜd al-Tustarī 207
A Report on a Compound of Buildings Dedicated as a Charitable Trust of the Jewish Community 208
Ḥasday b. Shaprūṭ Makes Spanish Jewry Independent from the Authority of Baghdad 210
Samuel and Joseph Ibn Naghrēla 211
A Poetical Attack on the Jews of Granada 214
The Fall of the Jewish Vizier of Granada 217

A Medieval Curriculum of Advanced Jewish and Secular Studies 226
From the Autobiography of a Jewish Apostate 229
Maimonides' Epistle to the Jews of Yemen 233
Forced Conversion of the Jews of Aden 247
The Self-styled Caliph Is Assassinated and the Forced Converts of Aden Return to Judaism 249
Obadiah the Proselyte on the Treatment of the Jews of Baghdad under al-Muqtadī 251
Benjamin of Tudela's Description of Baghdadi Jewry 252
The Murderer of a Jew and His Wife Is Punished 254

4 THE LONG TWILIGHT: THE JEWS OF ARAB LANDS IN THE LATER MIDDLE AGES 255

A Document of Protection (Dhimma) Attributed by the Jews to Muḥammad 255
A Retort to Muslim Traditions Concerning Jews and the Bible 259
A Jewish Philosopher on Islam and Why Some Dhimmīs Convert to It 261
The Fall of the Ilkhanids' Jewish Vizier 262
An Italian Jew's Impression of Cairo in the Late Fifteenth Century 264
The Jews' Oath in Mamluk Egypt 267
The Charge of Appointment for a Nagid in Mamluk Egypt 269
Instructions to a Market Inspector on the Supervision of Dhimmīs 271
Al-Malik al-Ṣāliḥ's Decree against the Dhimmīs 273
Some Jewish Anecdotes from an Anti-Dhimmī Treatise 275
Traveling Incognito with a Mamluk Caravan 277
The Condition of the Jews in Jerusalem in the Early Sixteenth Century 278
The Rise and Fall of a Family of Court Jews 279

The Fall of Ibn Baṭash Spells Catastrophe for Moroccan Jewry 281
A Flemish Scholar's Observations on the Jews of Merinid Fez 287
Portrait of a Jewish Physician by His Muslim Pupil 288
Damascene Jewry in 1522 289
An Italian Jew Describes the Revival of Safed under the Ottomans 290
Don Joseph Attempts to Rebuild Tiberias as a Jewish City 293
An Order for the Deportation of the Jews of Safed to Cyprus 295
The Sultan Rescinds the Order of Deportation 296
The Jews of Safed Seek Redress from the Ottoman Sultan for Persecution by Local Officials 298
The Ottoman Sultan Orders a New Census of the Jews of Safed for Tax Purposes 299
An Order from the Sultan to Investigate Reports of Illegally Built Synagogues in Safed 300
Firman Confirming the Confiscation of the Naḥmanides Synagogue in Jerusalem 301
"The Murder Is to Our Detriment, Yet We Have to Pay the Blood Price" 303
The Lot of the Jews in Early ʿAlawid Morocco 304
Vigilante Justice for a Jew in Eighteenth-Century Algiers 305
A Jew is Appointed Moroccan Public Minister to the English Court 306
A Jewish Emissary from Morocco Asks to Present His Credentials to the British Secretary of State 307
The Tetouan Pogrom of 1790 308
A Moroccan Account of the Same Incident 309
The Widow of a Moroccan Jewish Dragoman Petitions the King of England 310
The Manners and Customs of Moroccan Jewry 312

The Jews of Marrakesh 315
The Recruitment of a Jewish Interpreter in Tangier 317
Aleppan Jewry in the Eighteenth Century 318
The Jewish Community of Sanʿa in the Late Eighteenth Century 322

5 THE DAWN OF MODERN TIMES: THE JEWS OF ARAB LANDS IN THE NINETEENTH CENTURY 324

Cairene Jewry in the First Half of the Nineteenth Century 324
The Jewish Quarter of Jerusalem 328
The Synagogues and Schools of Jerusalem in the 1830s 329
A Glimpse of a Wealthy Jerusalem Jewish Family 332
A Visit with the Chief Rabbi of Jerusalem 334
The Jewish Community of Tiberias in the Early Nineteenth Century 336
Agitation against the Jews of Safed 340
A German Orientalist Is Caught in an Attack upon the Jews of Safed 342
The Jewish Settlers in Masqat 347
A Famous Jewish Traveler Visits His Brethren in Aden 349
The Home of a Wealthy Damascene Jew 353
A British Consul Assesses the General Feeling toward Jews and Christians in the Levant 354
A British Consul's General Observations on the Jews of Palestine 356
The Khaṭṭ-i Humayun 357
A Muslim View of the Khaṭṭ-i Humayun 361
A Petition for the Establishment of the First Hebrew Journal in Palestine 362
Jewish Merchants in Haifa Petition to Keep Their Synagogue Open 364
The Ashkenazi Jews of Palestine Establish Separate Butchers 365

Jewish Merchants of Gibraltar Seek Exemption from the Moroccan Dress Code for Dhimmīs 367

The Jews of Mogadore Pay Their Poll Tax 368

A Moroccan Jewish Merchant Aids in the Redemption of British Captives from the Corsairs 370

A Decree in Favor of Moroccan Jewry 371

Iraqi Jews in the India Trade 374

Baghdadi Jews in the Service of British Merchants 375

The Jews of Baghdad Meet English Missionaries 377

Jewish and Christian Inhabitants Join in the Defense of al-Jazira Against the Kurds 384

A Rabbi Is Accused of Disrespect to Muḥammad 385

An Anti-Jewish Incident Is Prevented by a Zealous Turkish Official 388

A Dispute Over the Custody of Ezekiel's Tomb 389

A Plea for Aid in the Damascus Affair 393

A Report on the Treatment of Jewish Prisoners in the Damascus Affair 396

The British Consul in Egypt Tries to Intercede for The Accused in the Damascus Affair 399

Montefiore and Crémieux Appeal to Muḥammad ʿAlī 400

The Ottoman Sultan Issues a Firman Condemning The Blood Libel 401

The Prussian Consul Tries to Intercede for the Jews of Damascus 403

Instructions from H.B.M.'s Ambassador to Constantinople Regarding Jews Seeking British Protection 405

A Libyan Jew Tries to Regain Lost British Protection 406

A Resident Jew Is Appointed Austrian Consular Representative in Tripoli, Libya 409

A Report to the Alliance Concerning the Pillage of the Jewish Quarters on the Tunisian Island of Djerba 410

Tunisian Jewry Complains to the Alliance Israélite Universelle 411

A Diplomatic Incident over the German Naturalization of Some Tunisian Jews 413
A Description of the Jews of Tunis Shortly before the French Takeover 416
A Sabbath among the Jews of Port Said 423
A Report on Blood Libels in Damanhur, Egypt 426

BIBLIOGRAPHY 429

Abbreviations of Journals and Encyclopedias 431
Archival and Manuscript Sources 431
Selected Published Works 433

INDEX 453

PREFACE

With the advent of Islam and the great Arab conquests of the seventh and eighth centuries of this era, a new world order was established stretching from India and Central Asia in the east to Morocco and Spain in the west. The majority of world Jewry at that time came under Arab rule. The Jews soon adopted the language of their conquerors, and along with the other peoples of this vast empire, took part in creating a new and vibrant civilization, medieval Islam, which enjoyed the most advanced material culture since the heyday of Rome. In the scientific and intellectual spheres, this civilization was to remain unsurpassed until the Renaissance in Europe. It would continue to evoke the admiration, wonder, and envy of Europeans long after it had been eclipsed.

Jewish culture itself developed and flourished during the Islamic High Middle Ages (ca. 850–1250). This was the period that saw the veritable crystalization and formulation of Judaism as we know it today. During this time, the Babylonian Talmud gradually became the constitutional foundation of Diaspora Judaism, the synagogue service and the prayerbook text took on their familiar form, Jewish theology was systematized, Jewish law codified, and Hebrew language and literature underwent its greatest revival prior to its rebirth in modern times.

By the end of the thirteenth century, however, the center of historical gravity had shifted northward and westward to Europe. So too had the major centers of Jewish population and creativity. Most of the countries of the Arab world came under the rule of non-Arab military dynasties that imposed a Middle Eastern brand of feudalism upon their domains. The general cultural level and the socioeconomic conditions of Arabic-speaking Jewry stagnated and declined with the decay of the Muslim world and the concomitant rise of the West. This does not mean that Jewish life there was at that time totally barren and sterile. Even during the long centuries of torpor, there were creative impulses that bore fruits. Furthermore, at certain points of osmosis, such as port towns and trading centers, there were enterprising individuals who mediated between the respective economies and cultures of East and West. Nevertheless, for the overwhelming majority of Jews in Arab lands, there was a marked decline in the quality of their life throughout the late Islamic Middle Ages (ca. 1250–1800).

As Europe began its inexorable intrusion into the Muslim East during the nineteenth century, it was the Jews, together with members of other minorities, who were among the first to embrace—to a greater or a lesser degree—Western culture and Western values. Profound changes began to overtake their traditional way of life, and their position in Muslim Arab society was radically altered.

The twentieth century marked an entirely new chapter in the history of the Jews of Arab lands. Colonialism and imperialism in various forms came, conquered, and went. Conflicting Jewish and Arab nationalisms came into being and set out upon a collision course. Today, few Jews remain in the Arab world. The vast majority of those who left are now in the State of Israel. An entirely new generation, whose native language is Hebrew rather than Arabic and whose culture is Israeli, has grown up with its strong Western orientation.

I deliberately chose not to extend the scope of this book beyond the third quarter of the nineteenth century, preferring to leave off at the dawn of a new era in the history of the Jews of Arab lands. The latest era, which has been marked by a rapid concatenation of events leading to the mass exodus of the Jews from the Arab world, deserves to be treated separately and at length.

This book therefore deals with the Jews of Arab lands before the metamorphosis that occurred in this century. It aims to present a historical tableau of the Jewish experience in the traditional Arab world from the rise of Islam to the last quarter of the nineteenth century, when the forces of change were already well under way in most of the Middle East and North Africa. Because of the enormous temporal and geographical span to be dealt with here, such a tableau can only be painted with broad brushstrokes. A basic problem in presenting such a sweeping panorama is how to avoid "a schematic image which nowhere was a reality."[1]

Yet another problem in attempting any assessment of the history of the Jews of Arab lands is the intensity of feelings aroused by the topic itself. The nature of the Jewish experience under Islam, generally, and in the Arab world, particularly, has been subject to widely varying assessments. These range from the popular "golden age" school to a revisionist "persecution and pogrom" approach. The present conflict in the Middle East with all its ramifications has made the topic of the historical relations between Jews and Arabs a favorite theme for apologists on both sides. Fortunately, it has also been a subject of investigation for more dispassionate students of history. But with the exception of S. D. Goitein's *Jews and Arabs*,[2] most of these studies have comprised highly specific monographs aimed primarily at other scholars, and they have dealt almost exclusively with intellectual, rather than social, history. In *Jews and Arabs,* Goitein achieved a happy balance between scholarly and popular presentation and between intellectual and socioeconomic content. The book remains the best general introduction to the cultural interaction (or symbiosis, as Goitein terms it) between Arabs and Jews during the classical period of Islamic civilization.

Between Goitein's introduction and the specialized monographs, there has remained a considerable gap. This gap has been all the more formidable because most of the sources for a history of the Jews of Arab lands are written in one of several Near Eastern languages and scripts, which are read only by a small circle of scholars in the West. Relatively little has been translated into English or any other Western languages. The lack of primary materials in English translation has been noted by scholars and educators. In a recent bibliographical essay, Mark R. Cohen wrote: "A major desideratum for the purposes of college-level instruction is a collection of translated sources devoted exclusively to the Jews in the Islamic world."[3]

The present book aims at filling these gaps in some measure. As the problem was twofold, the book was conceived in two parts. Part

1 S. D. Goitein, "Jewish Society and Institutions under Islam," in *Jewish Society Through the Ages,* ed. H. H. Ben Sasson and S. Ettinger (New York, 1971), p. 172.

2 3rd ed. (New York, 1974).

3 Mark R. Cohen, "The Jews under Islam: From the Rise of Islam to Sabbatai Zevi," in *Bibliographical Essays in Medieval Jewish Studies,* vol. 2 (New York, 1976), p. 173.

One consists of five chapters that offer a survey of Jewish social history in the Arab world and that at the same time provide the framework for the sources presented in Part Two. The second part is a kind of mirror image of the first. It is divided into five sections corresponding to the chapters in Part One. Thus, I have tried to present the reader with a picture of sufficient breadth and sweep, on the one hand, and, on the other, the elements of fine detail as found in the sources themselves. Indeed, it is the sources that have been allotted the lion's share in this book. They form their own colorful mosaic alongside the synthetic tableau. Most of the material in Part Two has been translated from Arabic and Hebrew, some from Aramaic, Persian, and Turkish, and the rest from various European languages. Most of the translations are my own, although in several cases I have included translations by others. There is also some material from English-language sources.

The importance of the sources presented in Part Two lies not so much in whatever concrete facts or hardcore data they may contain. Some do offer precise, quantitative information. Unfortunately, sources of this sort, especially from earlier periods, are few. The real value of much of the source material presented here is that it speaks with the voices of the participants in this historical drama or, at least, in the voices of firsthand observers. Many of the texts translated here came from published works; however, many of the readings were also drawn from hitherto unedited archival materials from Middle Eastern and European archives and manuscript collections. Through these sources, which include historical narratives, literary works, official documents, and personal correspondence, we see how Arabs and Jews viewed each other and how they related to one another. From the Jewish sources, we also get some idea—and this is no less important—of how the Jews viewed themselves. The reports of occasional visitors from outside the Arab world offer yet another perspective. So too, do the extensive European diplomatic and consular records from the eighteenth and nineteenth centuries.

Some of the sources are downright contradictory vis-à-vis others. This is to be expected. History, like beauty, is frequently in the eye of the beholder. Many of the sources reflect the biases of the individual writers and of the community they represented. For example, the report of the downfall of the Ilkhanids' Jewish vizier Sa^{c}d al-Dawla (see pp. 262–63) gives no indication at all of the great vision and administrative skill of this talented individual. The writer Gregory Bar Hebraeus, who was a Christian polemicist, was primarily interested in showing the justified humiliation and degradation of the Jews. But these biases are themselves historical "facts" reflecting spiritual and social realities. Still, these documents are in many cases raw material that need interpretation. Most of the sources have been well annotated with footnotes. The subject matter and the historical context of the source material are referred to throughout the text and footnotes in Part One, which is itself interpretative.

I realize that in addressing this book to both an academic and a general readership I run the risk of satisfying neither. However, I have tried like Koheleth "to find acceptable words, honestly written, expressing truth" (Eccles. 12:10).

This book could not have been researched or written without the generous support and good will of numerous individuals and institutions. It is my pleasant duty to acknowledge their assistance.

I am deeply indebted to Professor Bernard Lewis for his continuous encouragement and counsel. He graciously read the entire manuscript, which has benefited from his suggestions and criticisms.

Thanks are due also to Professors Theodore Rabb, Yosef Hayim Yerushalmi, and David Biale, each of whom read part of the manuscript and made valuable comments. Professor Rabb was particularly helpful in establishing contacts for me in London.

My mentor, Professor S. D. Goitein, discussed this project with me at every stage. Whatever training I have as an Arabist and as a historian of the Jews of the Islamic world must be credited to him. My profound indebtedness is indicated by dedicating this book to him.

My teacher and friend, the late Professor Richard Ettinghausen, made several suggestions for possible illustrations and kindly provided me with the photograph of the Turkish shadow puppet in illustration 5.

Mrs. Rachelle Moore and the staff of the State University of New York at Binghamton Interlibrary Loan Office cheerfully processed over 1,000 requests for books and periodicals not available to me in Binghamton. She took a personal interest in this project and did everything possible to expedite my requests. Thanks are also due to my graduate assistants at Binghamton: Christopher Ferguson, Charles Williams, and Joan Creatura, for a variety of services. My colleague, Dr. Samuel Morell, on several occasions aided me in tracing down elusive talmudic references.

Mr. Maurice Woolf, Mr. Allan Gossels, and the staff of the

Public Records Office were all extremely helpful to me during my research visit in London. Dr. Stefan Reif, Director of the Taylor-Schechter Genizah Research Unit, University Library, Cambridge, graciously facilitated my receiving a photocopy of an important manuscript.

In Rabat, my work was made easier by the kindness of Prof. Germain Ayache; Dr. Abdelhadi Tazi, Directeur du Centre Universitaire de la Recherche Scientifique; and Mr. Abderrahman El Fasi, Directeur de la Bibliothèque Royale.

In Vienna, I was shown every courtesy by Herr Professor Dr. Richard Blass, Director of the Haus-, Hof- und Staatsarchiv, and by his efficient staff.

My own university has been most supportive of my research. I was granted Release Time during the Spring of 1977 and a Title F Leave during the Spring of 1978. Financial aid for my research came from the SUNY Research Foundation and also from the Anti-Defamation League of B'nai B'rith. Some of the material for this book was collected in conjunction with another research project funded by the National Endowment for the Humanities, the Social Science Research Council, and the SUNY Foundation. To all these institutions my sincere thanks.

I would be remiss in not acknowledging the unflagging support of The Jewish Publication Society of America and its editor, Mr. Maier Deshell. My grateful thanks are also extended to Mrs. Frances Noyes of the JPS editorial staff. Tirelessly, and with unfailing good spirits, she guided the manuscript from the copy editing stage to the final printing.

It is customary for an author to conclude his acknowledgments with thanks to his wife—usually for taking care of the children and being "a helpmate fit for him." My case is special. This book was originally planned as a joint effort by us both. However, my wife and colleague, Yedida, had several other important research commitments and had to see her own book through the press. She was thus unable to join me in this project. Nevertheless, she helped me translate several Arabic and Hebrew documents in Part Two and was always ready with her advice, criticism, and comment. The verses from Proverbs 31 on the "Woman of Valor" recited by me each Friday evening in her honor are not mere rote as far as I am concerned.

Norman A. Stillman
Binghamton, N.Y.

NOTE ON STYLE

Foreign terms are always explained or translated at their first occurrence and are italicized throughout. The transcription of Arabic names and words follows the system employed in the *Encyclopaedia of Islam,* new edition, with the usual exception made by most English-speaking Arabists of *j* for *dj* and *q* for *ḳ*. Place names are given in their familiar English forms and without diacritical marks.

Hebrew and Aramaic words have been transcribed according to a simple, standardized system that is on the whole compatible with the Arabic transcription. Common biblical Hebrew names are rendered in the accepted English forms. Most of the translations of biblical passages are my own. Occasionally, I have used the translation of *The Holy Scriptures* (Philadelphia: Jewish Publication Society, 1956).

Total consistency seemed impossible in the case of Ottoman Turkish words and names. In general, purely Turkish words appear in the orthography adopted by the Republic of Turkey, whereas proper names and some common terms appear in their Arabic form.

Most of the documents in Part Two are unabridged. In those instances where minor deletions have been made, I have indicated the ellipses with the usual system of points. A full line of points indicates a major deletion; however, deletions at the end of paragraphs have not been indicated. Parentheses are usually used for interpolations, which I have made for clarification of the reading, although they may also indicate parenthetical remarks in the texts themselves. In several instances, I have made slight revisions in the punctuation and spelling within a document in order to bring these into line with standard modern usage. Most of the archaisms of spelling, punctuation, and style have been left untouched so as not to detract from the period flavor.

The few abbreviations used in the text are mostly self-evident. For readers not familiar with Hebrew or Arabic, the abbreviation *b.* between two personal names indicates "son of" or "daughter of." The unabbreviated forms (Ibn, Ben, Bint, Bat) are used when the first name is omitted. The various Hebrew titles of respect (Rav, Rabbi, Rabbenu) are all abbreviated R.

N. A. S.

CHRONOLOGICAL TABLE

70	Fall of the Second Temple
132–35	Revolt of Bar Kokhba
ca. 425	Redaction of the Babylonian Talmud
517–25	Dhū Nuwās, Jewish king in Yemen
571	Probable birth of Muḥammad
ca. 610	Muḥammad receives his first revelations
622	Muḥammad's *Hijra* from Mecca to Medina
624	Muslim victory over the Meccans at Badr; expulsion of the Banū Qaynuqā^{c}
625	Muslim defeat at Mount Uḥud; expulsion of the Banu l-Naḍīr
627	Muslims repel Meccans at the battle of the Trench; extermination of the Banū Qurayẓa
628	Muḥammad attacks and subjects the Jewish oasis of Khaybar
630	Mecca surrenders to Muḥammad
632	Muḥammad dies; Abū Bakr, first caliph
634–44	Caliphate of ^{c}Umar b. al-Khaṭṭāb; Jews exiled from the Hijaz
633–38	Arabs conquer Syria and Iraq
639–42	Arabs conquer Egypt
651	Death of Yezdegird III, last Sasanian shah; one of shah's daughters given to Jewish Exilarch Bustanay
656	Murder of Caliph ^{c}Uthmān; first civil war in Islam
658	R. Isaac Gaon of Pumbeditha and thousands of Jews welcome Caliph ^{c}Alī into Firuz-Shapur
661–750	Umayyad Caliphate

711–12	Muslims conquer Spain, receive widespread Jewish support
717–20	Caliphate of ᶜUmar b. ᶜAbd al-ᶜAzīz; hardening of attitude toward *dhimmīs*
750–1258	Abbasid Caliphate
762	Baghdad founded; rise of Middle Eastern bourgeoisie
ca. 767	Anan b. David founds Karaite sect
813–33	Caliphate of al-Ma'mūn; beginning of Hellenistic renaissance in Islam
909	Fatimid caliphate established in North Africa; flourishing Jewish center in Qayrawan
916	Death of Neṭīra, founder of a great Jewish banking house in Baghdad
928–42	Saᶜadya Gaon of Sura: translates the Bible into Arabic; redacts the first standard prayerbook; writes the first systematic work of Jewish theology
929	Umayyad prince of Spain assumes title of caliph
969	Fatimid conquest of Egypt
973	Fatimid caliph enters the new capital, Cairo; rise of Egyptian Jewry
975	Death of Ḥasday b. Shaprūṭ, the great patron of Jewish letters in Spain
1007–19	Persecution of Christians by Fatimid Caliph al-Ḥākim
1012–19	Persecution of Jews by al-Ḥākim
1015	Abraham b. ᶜAṭā' becomes first *nāgīd* in Qayrawan
1027	Samuel b. Naghrēla becomes first *nāgīd* in Granada
1038–56	Samuel b. Naghrēla is vizier of the Berber king of Granada
1047	Assassination of Jewish courtier Abū Saᶜd al-Tustarī in Cairo
1050–57	Banū Hilāl Bedouin ravage Ifrīqiya
1066	Assassination of Joseph ha-Nagid; massacre of the Jews of Granada
1085	Christians recapture Toledo
1090	Almoravids conquer Muslim Spain; Jewish quarter of Granada destroyed a second time
1096–99	First Crusade
1099–1187	Latin Kingdom of Jerusalem
ca. 1139	Judah ha-Levi, Jewish poet laureate of Spain, completes final draft of *The Kuzari,* glorifying rabbinic Judaism and rejecting philosophy
1140	Judah ha-Levi leaves Spain for Egypt and Palestine
1147–60	Almohads conquer the Maghreb and much of

	Islamic Spain; widespread massacres and forced conversions of Jews
1165	Maimonides family emigrates to Palestine
1171	End of the Fatimid Caliphate; Moses Maimonides becomes leader of Egyptian Jews for several years
1171–1250	Ayyubid Dynasty established in Egypt and Syria by Saladin
1180	Moses Maimonides completes his great law code, the *Mishneh Torah*
1187	Saladin defeats Crusaders at the Horns of Hattin; fall of the Latin Kingdom of Jerusalem
1190	Moses Maimonides completes *Guide of the Perplexed,* synthesizing Judaism and Aristotelianism
1198–1202	Forced conversion of Jews in Yemen and Aden under self-styled Caliph al-Malik al-Muᶜizz Ismāᶜīl; Maimonides writes *Epistle to the Yemenites*
1204	Death of Moses Maimonides; leadership of Egyptian Jewry becomes hereditary within the Maimonides family
1237	Death of Abraham Maimonides, Moses' son and successor
1250–1517	Mamluk Empire in Egypt, Syria, and Palestine
1258	Baghdad captured by the Mongols under Hülagü; end of Abbasid Caliphate and beginning of Ilkhanid dynasty; no distinction between Muslim and *dhimmīs*
1260	Mamluks turn back the Mongols at Ayn Jalut
1291	Assassination of Saᶜd al-Dawla and other Jewish officials of the Ilkhanids; anti-Jewish riots in Iraq
1301, 1354, 1419	Crackdown on *dhimmīs* in the Mamluk Empire; strict enforcement of the Pact of ᶜUmar
1391	Jewish refugees from Catalonia and Majorca arrive in Tunisia and Algeria
1438	First *mellāḥ* established in Fez
1453	Ottomans capture Constantinople; demise of the Byzantine Empire
1465	Revolt brings down the Merinid Dynasty in Morocco; Ibn Baṭash, Jewish vizier, slain; massacre of the Jews in Fez and throughout the country
1492	Expulsion of Jews and Moors from Spain
1497	Expulsion of Jews from Portugal
1517	Ottomans conquer the Mamluk Empire; usher in a period of Jewish economic and cultural revival in the Levant; widespread messianic anticipation

1523	Adventurer David Reubeni arrives in Palestine, claiming to be a prince from a distant Jewish kingdom
1538	Jacob Berab and scholars in Safed try to revive ancient rabbinical ordination
ca. 1560	Doña Gracia and Don Joseph Nasi begin rebuilding of Tiberias as a Jewish center
1569–72	Isaac Luria teaches kabbalah in Safed
1574–95	Reign of Murad III; reintroduction of the sumptuary restrictions for *dhimmīs*
1575	Death of R. Joseph Karo, author of the *Shulḥān ᶜArūkh* in Safed
1577	Hebrew printing press established in Safed—first press east of Constantinople and west of China
1586	Naḥmanides Synagogue, the oldest synagogue in Jerusalem, confiscated by the Muslim authorities
1639	Iraq permanently recaptured by Ottomans from the Persians
1665	False messiah Sabbatay Ṣevi appears in Gaza and is widely accepted by Jews the world over
1666	Apostasy of Sabbatay Ṣevi in Adrianople; beginning of a period of socioeconomic and intellectual decline for Middle Eastern Jewry
1683	Failure of the Ottoman siege of Vienna; beginning of a series of Turkish defeats in Europe
1699	Treaty of Karlowitz marks decline of Ottoman power in Europe
1798–1801	Napoleon occupies Egypt
1805–48	Muḥammad ᶜAlī independent ruler of Egypt under nominal Ottoman suzerainty; introduction of European-style reforms in administration, military, and economy
1830	France invades Algeria
1831–40	Egyptian occupation of Syria and Palestine; non-Muslims benefit, especially Syrian Christians
1836	Beginning of regular British steamship service to Egypt and Syria
1839	Khaṭṭ-i Sherif improves civil status of *dhimmīs* in Ottoman Empire; Britain occupies Aden
1840	Damascus Affair; Montefiore and Crémieux appear before Muḥammad ᶜAlī and Sultan ᶜAbd al-Majīd; beginning of organized European Jewish efforts on behalf of oriental Jewry

1856	Khaṭṭ-i Humayun grants equality to Ottoman non-Muslims
1857	Batto Sfez, Tunisian Jew, executed for blasphemy against Islam ᶜAhd al-Amān improves civil status of Tunisian Jewry
1860	Alliance Israélite Universelle founded in Paris; 5,000 Christians massacred in Syria
1862	First Alliance school opened in Tetouan
1864	Montefiore procures edict of toleration for Jews from the Moroccan sultan; the edict is soon after revoked; Alliance schools opened in Tangier, Damascus, and Baghdad
1867	Alliance school opened in Jerusalem
1869	Suez Canal opened
1870	Mikveh Israel agricultural school opened by the Alliance outside Jaffa; the Crémieux Decree grants Algerian Jews French citizenship
1881	French occupation of Tunisia
1882	Britain occupies Egypt; first European and Yemenite Jewish agricultural colonists in Palestine
1883	Tunisia declared a protectorate of France

LIST OF ILLUSTRATIONS

following p. 90

1. "Old Jewish Castle" of Marḥab in Khaybar
2. A Geniza letter written by a fugitive from the poll tax collector in eleventh-century Egypt
3. The traditional "House of Maimonides" in Fez
4. The remains of the Naḥmanides Synagogue in Jerusalem, confiscated from the Jews in 1598
5. Turkish shadow puppet of a Jewish peddler
6. Doña Gracia Nasi, patroness of Ottoman Jewry, from a portrait medal by Pastorino de Pastorini, 1553
7. The mystical prayer book known as *Siddūr ha-Arī*. Moroccan ms. dated 1790
8. Carpet page from the *Second Leningrad Bible*
9. Carpet page from *Ōṣerōt Ḥayyīm* (Treasures of Life) by R. Isaac Luria, ha-Arī. Moroccan ms. dated 1760
10. Street in the Mellāḥ of Fez
11. Entrance to the Mellāḥ of Sefrou (Morocco), once the most crowded Jewish quarter in Morocco, now totally devoid of Jews
12. A typical side street in the Gāᶜ al-Yahūd (Jewish Quarter) of Sanᶜa, Yemen
13. Inside a synagogue in Sanᶜa (early twentieth century)
14. The Ben Gualid (Walīd) Synagogue in Tetouan, Morocco
15. Entrance to the Mellāḥ of Tetouan (founded in 1807)
16. An Algerian Jew depicted in a late eighteenth-century etching

following p. 316

17. Jazzār Pasha passes judgment on a criminal while his Jewish adviser,

Ḥayyīm Farḥī (with patched eye and amputated nose), stands nearby holding a list of accusations. Early nineteenth century
18. A street in the Jewish quarter of Old Jerusalem
19. A well-to-do Jewish family at home on Mount Zion, ca. 1840
20. Scene in the Elijah the Prophet Synagogue, Jerusalem, nineteenth century
21. A Jewish moneylender in Jerusalem, nineteenth century
22. A Jewish couple in Jerusalem, 1873
23. A Jewish woman in Tiberias, nineteenth century
24. Beiruti Jews, nineteenth century
25. Courtyard of a wealthy Jewish household in Damascus, nineteenth century
26. A Jewish woman of Aleppo wearing the headdress and false tresses of a married woman, nineteenth century

following p. 392

27. Sir Moses Montefiore presenting a petition on behalf of Moroccan Jews to Sultan Muḥammad IV in Marrakesh, February 1, 1864
28. David Sassoon, founder of the Bombay banking house, in his native Iraqi costume, ca. 1864
29. Well-to-do Iraqi Jew and his wife, nineteenth century
30. The tomb of the Prophet Ezekiel at al-Kifl, Iraq
31. The rabbis of Baghdad, twentieth century
32. Jewish woman of Rabat veiled in the traditional *ḥayk,* early twentieth century
33. Moroccan Jewish bride, from a portrait by Delacroix
34. The martyrdom of Sol Hatchuel (Lalla Suleika), from a painting by Alfred Dehodencq
35. R. Moses Serusi, Tripolitanian scholar, author of *Va-Yeshev Moshe,* late nineteenth or early twentieth century

PART ONE

HISTORY

1

THE FIRST ENCOUNTER

Muḥammad and the Jews

Jews had been living in the Arabian Peninsula centuries before the birth of the Prophet of Islam. The dates and circumstances surrounding their arrival are shrouded in legend, and even the most valiant attempts at reconstructing the history of this very early period as, for example, Charles Cutler Torrey has tried to do, are sheer speculation.[1] The Jewish communities in the advanced urban civilizations of ancient South Arabia most likely date back to biblical times. The legendary encounter between Solomon and the Queen of Sheba (Arabian Saba') attests to the antiquity of Israelite-Arabian contacts.[2] This was the Arabia Felix of classical geographers, a land of incense and spices and a way station on the routes to eastern Africa, on the one hand, and India and the Orient, on the other.

Jewish settlers had already established themselves in the oasis communities of northern Arabia by the latter part of the Second

[1] Charles C. Torrey, *The Jewish Foundation of Islam* (New York, 1933). Like most scholars Torrey accepts the likelihood of an Israelite presence in Southern Arabia from Solomonic times. He hypothesizes that large-scale Hebrew settlement in Northern Arabia begins under the neo-Babylonian king Nabonidus (555–538), pp. 10–27. Other noteworthy works of this sort include: R. Dozy, *Die Israeliten zu Mekka von Davids Zeit bis ins funfte Jahrhundert unserer Zeitrechnung* (Leipzig, 1864); D. S. Margoliouth, *The Relations between Arabs and Israelites prior to the Rise of Islam* (London, 1924); H. Z. [J. W.] Hirschberg, *Yisrā'ēl ba-ᶜArāv* (Tel Aviv, 1946); Y. Ben Ze'ev, *Ha-Yehūdīm ba-ᶜArāv* (Jerusalem, 1957).

[2] 1 Kings 10:1–10 and 2 Chron. 9:1–9, 12. Isa. 60:6 mentions "The caravan of camels. . . . All coming from Sheba; They shall bring gold and frankincense."

Temple period. Although this area was not as culturally felicitous as the southern region, it was not by any means totally an Arabia Deserta. Jews could find a livelihood in date-growing, caravan commerce, and in the crafts. Their ranks must have been swelled by refugees who fled Judea after the rebellions against Rome collapsed in a sea of blood in 70 and 135 C.E. By the time Muḥammad was born, sometime around the year 571, Jews were not only to be found in considerable numbers in Arabia but were well integrated into the life and culture of the peninsula.[3] Like their pagan neighbors, the Jews spoke Arabic, were organized into clans and tribes, and had assimilated many of the values of desert society. They formed alliances and participated in intertribal feuds. The odes of the pre-Islamic Jewish poet al-Samaw'al b. ᶜAdiyā' reflect the same rugged ethos of *muruwwa,* or manly virtues, as expressed in countless poems by non-Jewish Arabs.[4] Jewish influence in Arabia was significant enough that for a short time Judaism was adopted by the royal house of the Yemenite kingdom of Ḥimyar under Yūsuf Asᶜar Dhū Nuwās (ruled ca. 517–25), who was killed while trying to repel an overwhelming Ethiopian invasion.[5] Although the spiritual influence of the Jews was strong in pagan Yemen, they themselves probably constituted a relatively small proportion of the population.

Despite their high degree of assimilation into Arabian society, Jews were still viewed as a separate group with their own peculiar customs and characteristics. Arab poets of the pre-Islamic period (assuming that a substantial part of the poetry attributed to them is genuine) occasionally refer to Jewish religious practices, and the Koran frequently mentions such typical Jewish institutions as the Sabbath, *kashrut,* and the Torah.[6] The daily language spoken by Jews among

[3] The most thorough examination of the evidence for a Jewish presence in Arabia during this period is in Hirschberg, *Yisrā'ēl ba-ᶜArāv,* pp. 29–137.

[4] Samaw'al's dīwān has been edited by H. Z. [J. W.] Hirschberg, *Der Dīwān des as-Samauàl ibn ᶜAdijā'* (Krakow, 1931). An example of al-Samaw'al's poetry in English translation may be found in A. J. Arberry, *Arabic Poetry: A Primer for Students* (Cambridge, 1965), pp. 30–32. For the pre-Islamic Arab ideal of *muruwwa,* see Ignaz Goldziher's classic essay "Muruwwa and Dīn," in his *Muslim Studies,* vol. 1, trans. C. R. Barber and S. M. Stern (London, 1967), pp. 11–44.

[5] Hirschberg, *Yisrā'ēl ba-ᶜArāv,* pp. 75–111; idem, "Yūsuf 'Asᶜar Yath'ar Dhū Nuwās" (Masrūq), *EJ* 16: 897–900; M. R. Al-Assouad, "Dhū Nuwās," *EI*² 1: 243–45.

[6] Examples of such references are brought by D. S. Margoliouth, *Arabs and Israelites,* p. 73; Ilsa Lichtenstadter, "Some References to Jews in Pre-Islamic Arabic Literature," *PAAJR* 10 (1940): 185–94; Hirschberg, *Yisrā'ēl ba-ᶜArāv,* pp. 112–16. The Sabbath is mentioned in the Koran in Suras 2:65/61;

themselves with its admixture of Aramaic and Hebrew words seemed to the Arabs a dialect all its own. Some of these Aramaic terms and concepts, however, passed unnoticed into the speech of Arabs at large. So too, religious ideas, ethical notions, and homiletic lore were disseminated among the pagan Arabs who came into close contact with Jews.[7] The same could be said with regard to the Christians of Arabia who, like the Jews, formed a distinct religious community while at the same time being highly assimilated.

The young man Muḥammad had probably met many Jews and Christians. His hometown of Mecca was a great mercantile entrepôt situated along the caravan route linking Yemen in the south with Byzantine Egypt and Syria-Palestine to the northwest and the Sasanian Empire to the northeast. According to Muslim tradition,[8] Muḥammad had on more than one occasion accompanied caravans into Syria and had seen the piety of the Syriac monks, which made a deep and lasting impression upon him. He also encountered Christians and Jews in Arabia. The trade route to Syria passed through the Wādi 'l-Qurā (Valley of Villages), which had a large Jewish population. Farther north, on the fringes of the Byzantine territory, were Christian Arab tribes. So too, in northeastern Arabia on the border of Iraq, which was the administrative center of the Sasanian Empire, were large numbers of Christian Arabs. Those Jews and Christians with whom Muḥammad came into closest contact were merchants, either in Mecca itself, or at one of the annual fairs, such as the one held in nearby ᶜUkāẓ.

Some of the merchants whom Muḥammad encountered probably acted as amateur missionaries, who in addition to their commercial activities spread the message of the one God. These self-appointed missionaries most certainly did not preach fine points of dogma or theology, but rather emphasized the moral and ethical essentials of monotheism to their pagan Arab listeners. Despite some obvious ex-

---

4:47/50; 4:154/153; 7:163; 16:124/125. Jewish dietary laws are referred to in Sura 3:93. The Torah is mentioned no less than a dozen times, as for example, Sura 3:3.

[7] Regarding *al-yahūdiyya,* or "Jewish speech," see Gordon D. Newby, "Observations about an Early Judaeo-Arabic," *JQR* n.s. 41 (1970): 212–21; see also Torrey, *The Jewish Foundation of Islam,* pp. 47–53; and Hirschberg, *Yisrā'ēl baᶜArāv,* pp. 200–2. The two major studies on loanwords (particularly Aramaic loanwords) in old Arabic are: Siegmund Fraenkel, *Die aramäischen Fremdwörter im Arabischen* (Leiden, 1886; reprint ed., Hildesheim, 1962); and A. Jeffrey, *The Foreign Vocabulary of the Qur'ān* (Baroda, 1938).

[8] Ibn Hishām, *Sīra,* vol. 1, pp. 180–83 and 188; Eng. trans. pp. 79–81 and 82. (For the complete citation of both these works, see the following note.)

ternal differences between Christians and Jews, the message they preached seemed surprisingly the same. To wit, there is but one God, the Creator of heaven, earth, and all that is therein, Who has in His mercy and loving-kindness revealed to man what is required of him, and Who on the Last Day will call all souls before His great judgment seat, rewarding the righteous with eternal bliss and damning the sinner to everlasting torment. The code of conduct enjoined by these preachers was also striking in its sameness—"thou shalt not murder," "thou shalt not steal," "thou shalt not commit adultery," "oppress not the widow, the orphan, the stranger, or the indigent." As merchants, they also emphasized the obligation to maintain fair weights and measures and to be honest in business dealings.

The time was ripe in Arabia for this kind of proselytizing. There was a spiritual malaise in the peninsula not unlike that of the Mediterranean world in late antiquity. The traditional Arab paganism and polydemonism had become sterile and unsatisfying to many. The townspeople were becoming culturally and morally more sophisticated. Many freelance seekers of God, called *ḥanīfs* in Arabic tradition, set off on a pilgrim's progress toward monotheism without accepting either Judaism or Christianity. Some of these more sensitive souls were inspired with the belief that they had been chosen like the prophets of old to bring the Divine message to their own people.

One such soul was Muḥammad b. ᶜAbd Allāh b. ᶜAbd al-Muṭallib of the Hashemite clan of the tribe of Quraysh in Mecca.[9] What differentiated him from other *ḥanīfs,* would-be prophets, and warners was the fact that he was a great religious genius. Muḥammad seems to have been particularly impressed by the preachers' frequent references to a book or scroll as divine authority. These missionaries would hold their scripture in hand, citing verses in the original language and then translating them into broken Arabic. The moral lessons cited were often driven home by picturesque homiletic tales. Muḥammad eventually came to the profound religious conclusion that just as God was

[9] The traditional biography of Muḥammad is Ibn Hishām's recension of Ibn Isḥāq's *al-Sīra al-Nabawiyya,* 2 vols. (Cairo, 1955); *The Life of Muhammad,* abridged Eng. trans. A. Guillaume (Karachi, 1955). There are numerous accounts of Muḥammad's life by Western scholars. Among the most significant are: Frants Buhl, *Das Leben Muhammeds,* German trans. H. H. Schaeder (Heidelberg, 1930); Tor Andrae, *Mohammed the Man and his Faith,* trans. T. Menzel (New York, 1955); W. Montgomery Watt, *Muhammad at Mecca* (Oxford, 1953); idem, *Muhammad at Medina* (Oxford, 1956); Maurice Gaudefroy-Demombymes, *Mahomet* (Paris, 1956); Maxime Rodinson, *Mohammed* (New York, 1974); Leone Caetani, *Annali dell' Islam,* vols. 1–2 (Milan, 1905–7); and Rudi Paret, *Mohammed und der Koran* (Stuttgart, 1957).

one, so was His message, which He had revealed to different peoples at different times in their own language. He began to wonder why God in His infinite mercy had not yet bestowed His saving word upon the Arab people who until now had been astray in night and were, therefore, condemned to perdition. How long were his people to remain in ignorance? Who would bring them God's heavenly scripture in their own language?

Muḥammad was, we are told, given to meditations and night vigils,[10] inspired perhaps by the ascetic examples of anchorite monks who could be found here and there throughout the Syrian and Arabian deserts, or perhaps by the pious *ḥanīfs,* or even by Judeo-Christian sects such as the Ebionites. During one such vigil on a lonely mountainside not far from Mecca the answer to his question came: "Recite in the name of your Lord Who created . . ."[11] It was he who had been chosen. He was about forty years of age at the time. Like most good prophets, Muḥammad was not entirely prepared for his theophany. He doubted his sanity. But soon he became convinced that God—Allah—had spoken to him through the angel Gabriel and was revealing to him a message in "clear Arabic." His sincerity convinced others. His first converts were members of his immediate household—his wife Khadīja, his adopted son Zayd b. Ḥāritha, and his cousin ᶜAlī, who lived with them. Soon he began to meet with some success amongst his fellow Meccans. Even those, and they were the majority, who were not swayed by his preaching looked upon him as a man with spiritual powers. After all, he spoke in rhymed prose and swore strange oaths by natural phenomena, just like the *kāhins* (soothsayers) and *shāᶜirs* (poets) who received their inspiration from the *jinn* (spirits). However, when Muḥammad's message of imminent judgment before Allah came to its ultimate conclusion in a total rejection of traditional Arab paganism, then Muḥammad began to meet with stiff, hardcore opposition. Mecca was the leading religious center of pagan Arabia, and its shrine, the Kaᶜba, was the object of an important annual pilgrimage. The religious and economic interests that he threatened were too great. His opponents accused him of being mad. They claimed that he was merely spouting words taught to him by others:

Those who do not believe have said, "This is nothing but a lie which he has invented. Other people have helped him with it." They have come

[10] Ibn Hishām, *al-Sīra al-Nabawiyya,* vol. 1 (Cairo, 1955), p. 235; Eng. trans., p. 105. For an interesting psychohistorical treatment of Muḥammad's retreats into meditation, see Rodinson, *Mohammed,* pp. 69–83.

[11] Sura 96:1.

forth with injustice and falsehood. They have also said, "Fables of the ancients which he has copied. They are dictated to him morning and evening."[12]
We know that they say, "It is only a mortal who teaches him." But the speech of him to whom they refer is foreign, while this is clear Arabic language.[13]

A period of ostracism and some persecution against the Prophet and his followers ensued. Finally, Muḥammad decided that the climate in Mecca was too inhospitable for continuing his mission there. In September 622, after having looked into the possibility of going to other towns, Muḥammad emigrated to the oasis community of Yathrib, also known as Medina, which lay about 250 miles to the north. For later Muslims, the year of the *Hijra* (Emigration) marks the beginning of the Islamic Era. And here, an entirely new phase of history begins.

For all intents and purposes, the story of Muslim-Jewish relations begins with Muḥammad's arrival in Medina. Prior to the *Hijra,* he had met individual Christians and Jews who had come to Mecca on business, as well as during his own travels. It has long been debated whether Muḥammad's principal monotheist informants were Jews or Christians. Abraham Geiger in the nineteenth century was the first to argue cogently for Jewish teachers.[14] This view predominated until the 1920s when Tor Andrae and Richard Bell made strong cases for Christian mentors.[15] More recently, S. D. Goitein has advanced very convincing arguments in favor of sectarian Jewish influences.[16] Unfortunately, our sources, which are exclusively Muslim and from a much later period, are silent on this point, and all of the arguments have of necessity been based on the contents of the suras revealed to Muḥammad in Mecca.[17] Be that as it may, it is indisputably clear that

[12] Sura 25:4–5.

[13] Sura 16:103/105.

[14] *Was hat Mohammed aus dem Judenthume aufgenommen?* (Baden, 1833); *Judaism and Islam,* Eng. trans. F. M. Young (Madras, 1898; reprint ed., with a Prolegomenon by Moshe Pearlmann, New York, 1970).

[15] Tor Andrae, *Der Ursprung des Islams und das Christentum* (Uppsala and Stockholm, 1926); *Les Origines de l'Islam et le Christianisme,* J. Roche, French trans. (Paris, 1955); Richard Bell, *The Origin of Islam in its Christian Environment* (London, 1926).

[16] S. D. Goitein, "Who were Muḥammad's Chief Teachers?" *Gotthold E. Weil Jubilee Volume* (Jerusalem, 1952) [Heb.]; idem, *Hā-Islām shel Muḥammad* (Jerusalem, 1956); idem, *Jews and Arabs,* 3rd ed. (New York, 1974), especially chap. 4, pp. 50–61.

[17] The problems inherent in attempting to identify Muḥammad's "sources" on the basis of the contents of the Koran have been pointed out by Julian

in Medina, Muḥammad came into daily face-to-face contact with a large, organized Jewish community. The encounter did not prove to be an auspicious one.

The fertile oasis of Yathrib had been settled by Jewish agriculturalists centuries before Muḥammad's arrival. The arabicized Aramaic by-name of the place, al-Madīna (the district), probably was given to it by the Jews themselves.[18] They formed the majority of the population and were organized in tribes. The three most important were the Banū 'l-Naḍīr, the Banū Qurayẓa, and the Banū Qaynuqāᶜ. The first two were priestly tribes known as *al-kāhinān* (the two Kōhanīm) and Banū Hārūn (sons of Aaron). Medina was also inhabited by two large confederations of pagan Arabs—the Banū Aws and the Banū Khazraj. They had settled there sometime during the fifth century, having emigrated from southern Arabia after the catastrophic bursting of the Ma'rib Dam. A long struggle for dominance ensued in which the Naḍīr and Qurayẓa sided with the Aws, while Qaynuqāᶜ allied itself with the Khazraj. Both sides were exhausted by the conflict, and it is in light of this that we must understand the invitation extended to Muḥammad by the Medinese.

Muḥammad's reputation had already begun to spread through western Arabia. Several Medinese had been converted to his new faith while visiting Mecca for the pilgrimage and enthusiastically proselytized among their own people upon their return. At the very time that Muḥammad was seeking a new home, members of both the Aws and Khazraj decided to invite him to come to Medina as its chief magistrate, who would provide much needed leadership in the strife-torn community by virtue of his spiritual gifts. His function was to be similar to that of the *ḥakam,* the wise neutral arbiter of intertribal disputes. The negotiations were delicate and involved two meetings near Mecca, at a pass called al-ᶜAqaba. At the second meeting, in June 622, seventy-five Medinese accepted Islam and swore allegiance to the Prophet, pledging to defend him as one of their own. Even traditional Muslim sources have noted that the readiness of the Medinese to accept Islamic monotheism was conditioned by their longtime association and familiarity with Jews.[19]

Obermann, "Islamic Origins: A Study in Background and Foundation," in *The Arab Heritage,* ed. N. Faris (Princeton, 1944), pp. 58–120.

18 The traditional Muslim explanation that the name al-Madīna is derived from Madīnat al-Nabī (the town of the Prophet) is rejected by most Western scholars.

19 Thus, for example, Ibn Hishām, *Sīra,* vol. 1, p. 468; Eng. trans., p. 197.

The Jews had no part in inviting Muḥammad to Medina, and no Jews were present at the ᶜAqaba negotiations. Yet the potential awkwardness of their presence in Medina under the new order was obvious to all. Fealty to the Prophet and his cause meant the dissolution of other bonds and alliances, and according to the laws of the desert, those not protected by alliances have no rights. Thus, it was clear to all concerned that eventually the Jews would have to go.[20]

Most modern historians in the West have argued that Muḥammad came to Medina expecting to be accepted by the Jews there, and when he was rejected by them, he turned against them in pique, driving out two tribes and exterminating the third. The distinguished British scholar W. Montgomery Watt even goes so far as to speculate that "had the Jews come to terms with Muḥammad instead of opposing him . . . they might have become partners in the Arab empire and Islam a sect of Jewry."[21] These notions do not give Muḥammad much credit either as a student of religion or as a politician. He would have been incredibly naïve to believe that the Jews would accept his new faith. He must have been aware that Jews did not recognize Christians, nor did Christians recognize Jews, nor did members of the different Christian sects recognize each other. Why then would they recognize him? On the other hand, he may have expected that the Jews of Medina would concede the validity of his mission to the Arab people. The God-fearing Gentiles had been granted a certain degree of acceptance by Jews in the hellenistic world, and those on the road to monotheism were probably still encouraged. There is internal evidence in the Koran for the view that Muḥammad was encouraged in his mission to the pagans of Mecca by his monotheist mentors. If Goitein is correct in surmising that these mentors in Mecca were sectarian Jews, then the fierce antagonism shown to the Prophet by the Medinese Jews is all the more understandable because it stems from the bitter conflict within Jewry at that time between the forces of orthodoxy and sectarianism.[22] The Jewish opposition to Muḥammad was certainly in part

[20] Ibid., p. 442; Eng. trans., p. 203. The passage is extremely revealing. While one of the Medinese is pledging loyalty to Muḥammad on behalf of all the rest, another interrupts and says: "O Apostle of Allah, there are bonds between us and those men—referring to the Jews—which we are about to sever. Could it be that after we have done so, when Allah will have made you triumphant, that you would return to your own people and forsake us?" According to the *Sīra,* Muḥammad smiled and said, "Nay, blood is blood, and unavenged blood is unavenged blood. I belong to you and you to me." (My translation differs somewhat from Guillaume's.)

[21] Watt, *Muhammad at Medina,* p. 219.

[22] Goitein, *Jews and Arabs,* p. 67.

political, although this does not seem to have been the predominant factor as some have suggested. For had the Jewish tribes of Medina been motivated by "the idea of exerting a considerable political influence over the oasis as a whole,"[23] they would have put up a united front against the political threat.

When Muḥammad arrived in Medina in September 622, his position was, naturally, rather precarious. Neither he nor his fellow emigrants from Mecca were in the best of financial circumstances. Not all of the people of Medina were wholehearted supporters of Muḥammad by any means. (These nonenthusiasts, some of whom may even have been opponents, have been dubbed with the uncomplimentary epithet of the Hypocrites by Muslim tradition.) He, therefore, had to proceed with some discretion until he could consolidate his position.

One of Muḥammad's first acts was the promulgation of a document that outlined the relationships between the various groups in Medina. This document looks like a covenant for the governance of the community and, thus, has been dubbed by many scholars the Constitution of Medina. To a certain extent it was a constitution, but in reality was only an interim step and was soon abandoned by Muḥammad when he had no further need of it. The document (which is translated in Part Two of this book) is a masterpiece of *clair-obscur*. It is an eloquent testimony to Muḥammad's political foresight and diplomatic skill. The document confirmed the Jews as members of the Medinese community with certain rights and responsibilities. This status, however, was granted only as long as the Jews did not act wrongfully. The vagueness of this qualification was to provide Muḥammad with a legal avenue for changing their status at a later date.

The Jewish scholars of Medina must have been particularly irksome to Muḥammad. It was bad enough that they rejected his prophethood, but this, as already indicated, was understandable in a sense even to Muḥammad. That they openly contradicted what he had to say was worse. And that they ridiculed what seemed to them his glaring errors in relating biblical and midrashic narratives was unforgivable. The learned Jews attacked him on the level at which he was most vulnerable and at the time in which he could do least about it. His experimentation with certain Jewish pietist practices such as the fast of Yom Kippur (called in Arabic ᶜAshūrā') and prayer toward Jerusalem made no impression upon these rancorous opponents.[24] There was little

[23] Rodinson, *Mohammed,* p. 160.

[24] Most modern biographers of Muḥammad have explained the temporary

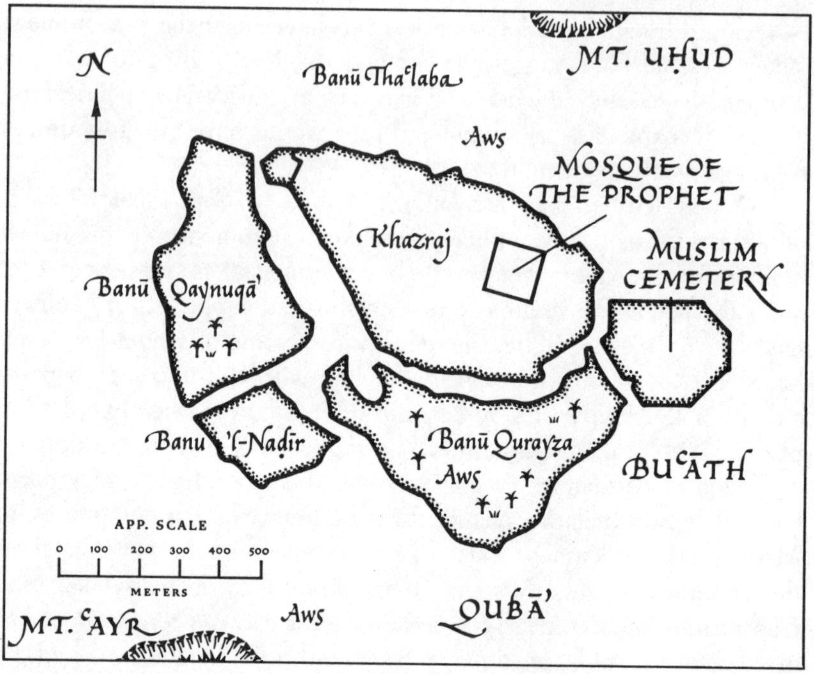

The Tribes in Medina at the Time of Muḥammad

Muḥammad could do to them at this time except to continue with his own preparations for the war against Mecca and await the changes in circumstance when he would be able to punish those who had wronged him. He also became increasingly convinced during this period that the Jews' rejection of him was because of pride and contumacy. As he knew with an unshakable religious certainty that his revelations were true, he came to the logical conclusion that whatever the Jews were citing to contradict him must be false. He may already have heard sometime in the past the common Christian accusation that the Jews had corrupted the text of their Scriptures. In this, he may have been abetted by the Jewish renegade ʿAbd Allāh b. Salām. Like

adoption of these customs as attempts to win over the Jews or, at the very least, as concessions to them. Goitein's explanation seems more plausible: "He was inspired in Medina by Jewish rites and laws for the same reason which induced him in Mecca to incorporate in the Koran the stories of the Bible along with the religious tenets and ethical concepts of 'the Possessors of the Book.' He believed that all these aspects of religion were instituted by God and therefore worthy of emulation." *Studies in Islamic History and Institutions* (Leiden, 1966), pp. 4ff. The specific question of the ʿAshūrā' fast is discussed by Goitein in *Studies*, pp. 94–99.

so many Jewish converts to Islam and Christianity in the Middle Ages, ᶜAbd Allāh proved his zeal for his new faith by exposing the falseness of his former coreligionists who in their stubbornness denied or suppressed those signs in their sacred texts that foretold the coming of Muhammad or Jesus, as the case may be.

The Muslims' first significant victory over the Meccans at Badr in 624 was just the sort of turning point Muḥammad had been waiting for. He now had the power and the prestige to begin moving against his enemies in Medina. Two pagan poets, one an old man, the other a woman with an infant at her breast, were assassinated for having written satirical verses about him. Shortly thereafter, he turned upon the weakest of the three Jewish tribes, the Banū Qaynuqāᶜ, whose members were mainly craftsmen and artisans. After a short siege the Qaynuqāᶜ surrendered unconditionally. Muḥammad's position was still not so firmly established that he could act with complete impugnity, and when the Khazrajī chieftain ᶜAbd Allāh b. Ubayy demanded that mercy be shown his former clients, the Prophet had to acquiesce. ᶜAbd Allāh b. Ubayy thus earned himself a place in Islamic tradition as the arch-hypocrite, and the Jews of Qaynuqāᶜ were able to leave Medina with some of their possessions. They eventually made their way to Adhriᶜāt in Syria.[25]

No historian has failed to notice the fact that the other two Jewish tribes did not come to the aid of their brethren. Clearly, the Jews did not grasp the nature of the conflict. It probably seemed to them to be a tribal and political affair of the traditional Arabian kind with which they were familiar, rather than a religious one. Besides, the Qaynuqāᶜ had been on the opposing side of the Naḍīr and Qurayẓa during the old Aws-Khazraj struggles. Even the assassination of Kaᶜb b. al-Ashraf, who was a chieftain of the Banu 'l-Naḍīr, did not fully change the Jews' perception of things. After all, Kaᶜb had written verses satirizing Islam and insulting Muslim womanhood. Retaliation for such a slight to a group's honor was perfectly consistent with the heroic norms of Arab society in that period. Kaᶜb was an Arab, through his father, as well as a Jew, through his mother. The new dimensions of the conflict were still not clear, but the Jews began to feel uneasy.

The defeat of the Muslim army at Mount Uḥud on March 23, 625, weakened Muḥammad's position somewhat. He needed a victory now to regain the lost prestige. Already some of his missionaries had

[25] The biblical Edrei, modern Derᶜa. It is today a Syrian frontier post on the border with Jordan.

been murdered by Bedouin tribesmen. He decided, therefore, to attack the Naḍīr. Like the Qurayẓa and the smaller Jewish clans, they had not come to the Prophet's aid at Uḥud because the battle took place on the Sabbath. They could barely conceal their satisfaction with the Muslim's defeat. Furthermore, they were wealthy and occupied some of the best land in Medina, while the Muslims were in difficult financial straits at the time. Muḥammad had already had unpleasant experiences trying to collect contributions or obtain loans from the Jews. On one such occasion Abū Bakr, a close companion of the Prophet, had been given the mocking retort: "We are not in need of Allah, whereas He seems to be in need of us. . . . We are rich compared to Him."[26]

Muḥammad had no difficulty in finding a *casus belli*. On the basis of a divine revelation, he accused the Naḍīr of plotting against his life and ordered them to leave Medina. Expecting support from the Qurayẓa and from ᶜAbd Allāh b. Ubayy and his partisans, they decided to resist the eviction decree. When the aid they had counted upon failed to materialize, they surrendered on the condition that they be allowed to leave with all their movable goods, except their arms.

Humility was never a virtue in old Arabian society, and the Naḍīr decided to go into exile with their heads held high. They departed for the Jewish oasis of Khaybar in an impressive caravan of 600 camels, which paraded through the heart of Medina to the music of pipes and timbrels. Their women unveiled their faces to flaunt their renowned beauty and sported all their finery. It is clear from all of the poetry composed upon the occasion that the Arabs were duly impressed—perhaps overly so. Two years later, the men of Naḍīr lost their lives, their wealth, and their women when the Muslims took Khaybar.

The lands of the Banu 'l-Naḍīr were divided among the Emigrants, who till then had no patrimony of their own in their adopted home and who were for the most part beholden to the Medinese Helpers for their livelihood. The Prophet's own share of land made him financially independent. The booty formed the basis for the new Muslim state treasury.

There remained only one important Jewish tribe in Medina—the Banū Qurayẓa. They must have been in a state of serious alarm by this time but were incapable of taking any action on their own. According to Muslim tradition, Kaᶜb b. Asad, the Quraẓī chieftain, had made a treaty with Muḥammad. This seems doubtful, however, and is prob-

[26] Ibn Hishām, *Sīra,* vol. 1, p. 559; Eng. trans., p. 263.

ably the invention of later Muslim writers who wished to justify the harsh punishment that was meted out to the Qurayẓa.[27] When the Meccans and their Bedouin allies moved toward Medina in 627, the Qurayẓa contributed to the defense effort by supplying spades, picks, and baskets for the excavation of the defensive trench along the exposed northern side of the oasis.[28] During the brief siege of Medina, the Qurayẓa remained in their forts in a state of armed neutrality. Although they never committed any aggressive acts, their loyalty was questionable, for they allowed themselves to be approached by the enemy, who sought to win them over. The emissary from the besiegers was Ḥuyayy b. Akhṭab, a chieftain of the exiled Naḍīr who, according to some Muslim traditions, was the mastermind of the entire operation. This sort of parleying was quite common in Arabian warfare. Muḥammad himself attempted to buy off the Ghaṭāfān and Fazāra, the Bedouin allies of the Meccans.

The Qurayẓa were supposedly won over to the enemy, but they never could agree upon a course of action because they did not trust the Meccans entirely. In the end they did nothing. That they did nothing was of no account, for from the Muslim point of view, they had "sinned in their hearts."

The very day the besieging army turned away from Medina, Muḥammad attacked the Banū Qurayẓa. The Jewish tribe held out for twenty-five days. When all hope was gone they sought to surrender on the same terms as had the Naḍīr. This time the Prophet intended to make an example of them. He still could not act with complete disregard of public opinion. The degree of the Qurayẓa's treason was by no means clear. Muḥammad had previously spared the Banū Qaynuqāᶜ at the request of their former allies the Khazraj. Many Awsites were now pleading that their former confederates be shown mercy. Always the master politician, Muḥammad stepped aside and appointed Saᶜd b. Muᶜādh to pass judgment upon them. Saᶜd was a devout Muslim and a chieftain of the Aws, who was dying of wounds received during the siege against the Qurayẓa. Saᶜd took the hint and condemned the adult males to death and the hapless women and children to slavery. Muḥammad then declared that this was none other than Allah's decision. Actually, it is clear from the Muslim sources that the Qurayẓa's fate had been decided even before their surrender. One of Muḥammad's emissaries, Abū Lubāba, who had advised the Qurayẓa to give up, had

27 Ibid., vol. 2, p. 220; Eng. trans., p. 453.

28 al-Wāqidī, *Kitāb al-Maghāzī,* vol. 2, ed. M. Jones (London, 1966), p. 445.

to perform penance for hinting to the Jews what their real fate would be.[29]

The men of Qurayẓa were beheaded in the central marketplace of Medina, and their bodies thrown into large open trenches. Only two or three saved their lives through conversion. Between 600 and 900 men were slain. The slaughter of so many men was an extremely impressive act that enhanced Muhammad's prestige throughout Arabia. Here was a man to be reckoned with. He was now absolute master in Medina. Some historians, such as Tor Andrae, H. Z. Hirschberg, and Salo Baron, have censured Muhammad's savage treatment of the Jews of Qurayẓa.[30] W. Montgomery Watt, on the other hand, has offered as strong an apologetic defense of Muḥammad's conduct on this occasion as might be expected from any devout Muslim.[31] Neither blame nor vindication are in order here. We cannot judge the treatment of the Qurayẓa by present-day moral standards. Their fate was a bitter one, but not unusual according to the harsh rules of war during that period. As Rudi Paret has observed, Muḥammad had to be more concerned with adverse public opinion when he had some date palms cut down during the siege of the Naḍīr than when on a given day he had some 600 or more Jews put to the sword.[32]

At that time Medina was not altogether devoid of Jews. There still remained a few individual Jews and some small, marginal clans that had not belonged to any of those principal Jewish tribes. These few individuals posed no threat whatsoever to Muḥammad and so were left unmolested for a while. Eventually, however, they were forced to sell their properties and leave the area.[33]

[29] Ibid., pp. 506–7; Ibn Hishām, *Sīra,* vol. 2, pp. 236–37; Eng. trans., p. 462.

[30] Andrae, *Mohammed,* p. 155; Hirschberg, *Yisrā'ēl ba-ᶜArāv,* p. 146; Baron, *Social and Religious History of the Jews,* vol. 3, p. 79.

[31] "The Condemnation of the Jews of Banū Qurayẓah: A Study in the Sources of the Sīrah," *Muslim World* 42 (1952): 160–71.

[32] The proverbial words of the poet Zuhayr sum up the harsh ethos of the age: "He that does not harm others, will himself be harmed." See *Sharḥ al-Muᶜallaqāt al-Sabᶜ lil-Zawzanī* (Beirut, n.d.), p. 121. The slaughter of adult males and the enslavement of women and children were common practice throughout the ancient world. See, for example, Deut. 20:13–14, where the Israelites are enjoined to mete out such treatment to their enemies. See also the famous tragedy of the Melians in Thucydides, *The Peloponnesian War,* trans. Crawley (New York, 1951), p. 337. For Paret's observation, see his *Mohammed und der Koran* (Stuttgart, 1957), p. 112.

[33] Most historians accept the fact that some Jews remained in Medina after the elimination of the three great Jewish tribes. The early Muslim sources occasionally mention *en passant* those Jews who remained, as for example, Ibn

Muḥammad had not forgotten the enmity the Jews had shown him. Neither had he forgotten that many members of the Naḍīr were now comfortably resettled in Khaybar. The Jews of this rich oasis must have clearly understood the danger they were in. Ḥuyayy b. Akhṭab had gone from Khaybar with his son to join the Meccan and Bedouin forces besieging Medina at the time of the Battle of the Trench. He had been killed after having fought alongside the Banū Qurayẓa. Another chieftain, Abu 'l-Rāfiᶜ b. Abi 'l-Ḥuqayq, was assassinated in bed by some of Muḥammad's henchmen, who had stolen into Khaybar at night, aided by a Muslim who spoke the Jewish dialect of Arabic.[34]

The Jews were anxious to ward off any calamity and were willing to enter into negotiations with the strongman of Medina. Muḥammad sent emissaries to Khaybar inviting the war chief of the Naḍīr, a man by the name of Usayr (Yusayr) b. Zārim, to come to Medina to parley. Usayr set off with thirty companions and a Muslim escort. Suspecting no foul play, the Jews went unarmed. On the way, the Muslims turned upon the defenseless delegation, killing all but one who managed to escape. "War is deception," according to an oft-quoted saying of the Prophet.[35]

There was consequently no doubt in Khaybar that all-out war was inevitable. The Jews of Khaybar joined in a defense alliance with their coreligionists in the Fadak oasis and with several Bedouin tribes. For a while Muḥammad made no move, and the Jews of Khaybar felt the

---

Saᶜd, *Kitāb al-Ṭabaqāt al-Kabīr,* vol. 2, pt. 1, ed. E. Sachau et al. (Leiden, 1909), p. 77. What became of them is not at all clear. The scenario which Hirschberg has put together from some rather vague references in the *ḥadīth* literature seems most plausible. See Hirschberg, *Yisrā'ēl ba-ᶜArāv,* pp. 146–47 and 303, nn. 68–69, and the sources cited there. One such *ḥadīth* is in al-Bukhārī, *al-Jāmiᶜ al-Ṣaḥīḥ,* bk. 34 (Kitāb al-Buyūᶜ), Bāb 107, in the edition of M. Ludolf Krehl (Leiden, 1864), vol. 2, p. 41.

34 Ibn Saᶜd, *Kītāb al-Ṭabaqāt al-Kabīr,* vol. 2, pt. 1, p. 66; al-Wāqidī, *Kitāb al-Maghāzī,* vol. 1, ed. Marsden Jones, p. 392. Ibn Hishām, *Sīra,* vol. 2, pp. 273–75, relates the assassination, but makes no mention of ᶜAbd Allāh b. ᶜAtīk's ability to speak (*yarṭunu*) the Jewish dialect.

35 Ibn Saᶜd, *Ṭabaqāt,* vol. 2, pt. 1, pp. 66–67; al-Wāqidī, *Kitāb al-Maghāzī,* vol. 2, pp. 566–68; Ibn Hishām, *Sīra,* vol. 2, pp. 618–19, where his name is given as al-Yusayr b. Rizām (according to Ibn Isḥāq) and Ibn Rāzim (according to Ibn Hishām). For problems in the chronology of the assassinations of Abu 'l-Rāfiᶜ and Yusayr due to variants in the sources, see Watt, *Muhammad at Medina,* pp. 212–13. For the Prophet's remark that war is deception (*khudᶜa*), see al-Bukhārī, *Ṣaḥīḥ,* bk. 56 (Kitāb al-Jihād), Bāb 157, ed. Krehl, vol. 2, p. 254. This *ḥadīth* appears in several other canonical collections.

immediate danger of a Muslim attack was averted. The respite was only temporary.

Muḥammad advanced in force against Khaybar in May 628. The timing could not have been better. The Jews were not expecting the attack and were unprepared for an extended siege. The Muslims had been disappointed by the Prophet's recent abortive attempt to make a pilgrimage to Mecca and by his signing a truce with the Quraysh at al-Ḥudaybiyya. They needed a victory to raise their spirits. Furthermore, it was clear from the circumstances surrounding the incident at al-Ḥudaybiyya that most of the Bedouin were still not closely tied to the Umma (the Muslim community). Muḥammad needed to show them that it was worth their while to be allied to his cause.

The Jews of Khaybar put up a fierce resistance to the Muslims. The lesson to be learned from the fate of their Medinese coreligionists had not been lost upon them. Muḥammad was forced to fight it out with them, fortress by fortress. In the meantime, he was able to buy off the Khaybarīs' Bedouin allies and prevent any reinforcements from coming to the assistance of the besieged. The Jews of Khaybar were finally forced to surrender, but were able to do so on terms—except, that is, for the Naḍīr, who were given no quarter. In return for their personal safety and the right to retain their homes and property, the Khaybarīs agreed to pay the Umma one-half of their annual date harvest. The terms were burdensome, but not unusually harsh. Oasis dwellers customarily paid (and in many places still pay) "protection money" in the form of a share of their produce to neighboring Bedouin. As Salo Baron has noted, "this practice, far from being considered at that time a sign of political weakness, was freely indulged in also by the great Byzantine and Persian empires to secure peace from many unruly neighboring tribes."[36]

The settlement made with the Jews of Khaybar was repeated with those of Fadak and the oases of the Wādi 'l-Qurā.[37] These agreements became significant as legal precedents for the treatment of Jews and Christians in the later Islamic state. Once subdued and made tribute bearers, they were to be shown tolerance. Muslim sources differ on the details of the Khaybar treaty.[38] One important clause that

[36] Salo Wittmayer Baron, *A Social and Religious History of the Jews*, vol. 3 (New York and Philadelphia, 1957), p. 79.

[37] al-Balādhurī, *Futūḥ al-Buldān* (Cairo, 1959), p. 47; Eng. trans. Philip Hitti, *The Origins of the Islamic State* (New York, 1916; reprint ed., Beirut, 1966), p. 57.

[38] Compare Ibn Hishām, *Sīra*, vol. 2, p. 356; Eng. trans., pp. 524ff.; al-

is common to most of the versions states that the Jews might remain in their homes only as long as the Muslims permitted, but could be expelled whenever the Umma saw fit to do so. Such a stipulation seems highly unlikely and is certainly a later interpolation inserted to justify the expulsion of Jews from the Hijaz under the Caliph ᶜUmar (634–44). It is clear that the Jews had been kept on because of their valuable skills in agriculture. During the caliphate of ᶜUmar, when the great conquests of the Middle East were taking place, vast numbers of prisoners of war were brought into Arabia as slaves. Many of these were peasant villagers. The Jewish labor force was no longer necessary; neither were the Jews at that time strong enough to force any concessions from the Umma. The Khaybarī Jews spread throughout the Middle East after their expulsion, many of them settling in Palestine. They were able to maintain their own distinct identity until at least the twelfth century. In later times they became popular figures in Arabic folklore.[39]

The submission of Khaybar and the Jewish oases of the northern Hijaz produced the effect Muḥammad desired. His power, prestige, and influence waxed ever greater. Bedouin tribes, who until this time had sat upon the sidelines, flocked to his banner. Eighteen months after the conquest of Khaybar, Mecca surrendered peacefully, and its citizens accepted Islam. The surrender of Ṭā'if, Mecca's rival city, soon followed. Muḥammad had become the undisputed master of the Hijaz. Soon delegations from all over Arabia were coming to Medina to sign treaties acknowledging the supremacy of Allah's apostle. Many tribes requested missionaries to teach them and their brethren the new faith.

The Jews and Christians of Yemen in the south, and of Yamama, Nejd, and Bahrayn in the east, began to pay tribute to the new overlord. This tribute, called *jizya,* a word that probably indicated "compensation,"[40] was not originally the poll tax it was to become in later Islamic times, although it also had this meaning in Muḥammad's lifetime. The early treaties made between Muḥammad and the Jews of Maqnaᶜ on the Gulf of Aqaba or the Christians of Najran in Yemen clearly show that the initial *jizya* was in the form of an annual percentage

---

Balādhurī, *Futuḥ al-Buldān,* p. 39; Eng. trans., p. 46; Ibn Saᶜd, *Ṭabaqāt,* vol. 2, pt. 1, pp. 82ff.; and al-Wāqidī, *Kitāb al-Maghāzī,* vol. 2, p. 690.

39 For folk traditions concerning the Khaybarī Jews, see Itzhak Ben-Zvi, *The Exiled and the Redeemed,* trans. I. Abbady (Philadelphia, 1957), pp. 167–208.

40 It is perhaps an Aramaic loanword. For the most recent discussion of the origin of this term, see Geo Widengren, "The Status of the Jews in the Sasanian Empire," *Iranica Antiqua* 1 (1961):153–54.

of produce and a fixed quantity of goods.[41] The payment of the *jizya* tribute by Jews and Christians received divine sanction in the autumn of 630, when the koranic verse was revealed that enjoined the Muslims to fight against the peoples of the Book "until they pay the *jizya* out of hand, and have been humbled" (Sura 9:29). The injunction was clear and unequivocal, even if the precise nuances of the Arabic phraseology were somewhat hazy. The non-Muslim was to be subjugated. He was to be made a tribute bearer, and he was to be humbled. Just how he was to be humbled was to be more explicitly defined as time went on. But the basis for his position in Muslim Arab society was permanently established by the eternal word of Allah.

In 632, Muḥammad set the precedent of making the *jizya* a poll tax. In his instructions to his representative in Yemen, he wrote:

> Any Jew or Christian who embraces Islam, sincerely and of his own accord, and practices the Islamic religion, is to be considered one of the Believers. He is to have the same rights and the same duties as they. However, no one who belongs to either Christianity or Judaism is to be dissuaded from it. Every adult, male or female, freeman or slave, must pay a dinar of full weight or its equivalent in garments. Whoever fulfills that has the protection of Allah and His Apostle. Whoever withholds that is the enemy of Allah, His Apostle, and the Believers altogether.[42]

W. Montgomery Watt has questioned the authenticity of these instructions, suspecting that they had been altered by Muslim historians to "reflect the practice of a period later than Muḥammad's lifetime."[43] However, since this universal poll tax of one dinar on all adults of both sexes was not the practice in later Islamic times, it seems highly unlikely that such a document, which differs considerably from eventual Islamic law, would be attributed to none other than the Prophet himself. It has been preserved in the *Sīra* and other early sources precisely because of its authenticity. Although later Muslim rulers were to depart from the specifics of this document, they faithfully maintained its spirit. The general guidelines for the treatment of the People of the Book were firmly established. When the Arabs went on to conquer their vast empire, they had clear proof through koranic text and had the administrative procedures of the Prophet himself to fall back upon.

[41] Ibn Saᶜd, *Ṭabaqāt,* vol. 1, pt. 2, p. 28; al-Balādhurī, *Futūḥ al-Buldān,* pp. 81ff; Eng. trans., pp. 93ff.

[42] Ibn Hishām, *Sīra,* vol. 2, p. 596; Guillaume's Eng. trans., pp. 647ff., differs somewhat from my own.

[43] Watt, *Muhammad at Medina,* p. 128.

In the same year that he established the poll tax, Muḥammad died after a brief illness. A period of instability followed. Some Arabs broke their ties to the Umma. Religious reformers and would-be prophets in other parts of the peninsula who had been overshadowed during Muḥammad's lifetime now tried to duplicate his success. Some Jews and Christians hoped to throw off the yoke of subjection.[44] It took nearly one year to reestablish Muslim hegemony throughout Arabia. These local conflicts, known in Islamic tradition as the Wars of Ridda (Apostasy), formed the backdrop for the great conquests that were to follow immediately, almost as a coincidental outcome. Soon the entire Middle East with its enormous Christian, Jewish, and Zoroastrian populations would be under Muslim Arab rule. A new phase in the history of the Jews of soon-to-be-expanded Arab lands was about to commence.

[44] See Ibn Hishām, *Sīra,* vol. 2, p. 665; Eng. trans., p. 689.

2

UNDER THE NEW ORDER

Middle-Eastern Jewry in the First Three Centuries of Islam

The decade and a half following Muḥammad's death witnessed one of the most amazing conquests in world history. During that short span of time the entire Middle East was overwhelmed by invading Arab hordes. The two leading world powers, the Byzantine and Sasanian empires, lost the majority of their territories. In fact, the Persian Empire, which had played a dominant role in western Asia for a thousand years, collapsed entirely. So great was the trauma that Persian, for all intents and purposes, disappeared as a written language for the next three centuries. With the exception of the Iranian Plateau and Armenia, all of these newly conquered provinces were to become the very heartlands of the expanded Arab world.

The Arabs were facilitated in their conquests by several important factors. Byzantium and Sasanian Iran were in a state of military exhaustion. Both had been greatly weakened by the many wars between them—the last of which had dragged on from 602 to 628 C.E. Both had suffered from internal political and religious strife. Furthermore, there was no great affection for either of the regimes from their Near Eastern subjects. The Monophysite majority of Egypt and Syria considered themselves oppressed under Greek Orthodox rule. The Jews who had been persecuted by the Byzantines for generations were now undergoing particularly trying times. They had openly sided with the Persian enemy who had invaded in 614 and had occupied Syria, Palestine, and Egypt for the next fifteen years. The Jews were now considered a "fifth column." The emperor Heraclius, who was desperately trying to reunite his badly fraying empire, ordered their forcible conversion to Christianity sometime around 633.[1] Heraclius engendered even more disaffection that year when in an attempt to economize, he decided to forego payment of the annual protection money to the Bedouin of the Negev and Sinai deserts, who acted as irregular troops and who were a buffer against the Arabian Peninsula.

The Jews and Nestorian Christians of the Persian Empire, though not entirely alienated from the state, had suffered brief persecutions in the late sixth century and were probably tired of the political and economic instability of the late Sasanian period.[2]

In addition to all of these factors that facilitated the Arab conquests may be added a strong wave of messianic expectation, which affected Jews and Christians alike. In fact, among the few written Jewish sources for the period are apocalyptic works such as the *Sēfer Eliyāhū* (Book of Elijah), which was written on the eve of the Arab invasion of the Middle East, and the *Nistārōt shel Rabbī Shimᶜōn b. Yōḥay* (Secrets of R. Simeon b. Yoḥay), which though dating from the following century incorporates materials dating back to the Muslim conquests.[3] Many saw the Arab invasion as a visitation from God upon the wicked kingdom of Edom (the metaphor for Christian Byzantium).

In some cities and towns the Jews, Samaritans, and Monophysite Christians openly collaborated with the invaders. In Emesa (called by the Arabs, Ḥimṣ), the local Jews and Christians barred the gates of their city before the Byzantine army. In Hebron and Caesarea, the Muslims were able to penetrate the defenses with the aid of Jewish collaborators.[4] Seventy years later, during the Muslim invasion of

[1] For a survey of Jewish history in the Byzantine Empire from the fifth to seventh centuries, see Salo Wittmayer Baron, *Social and Religious History of the Jews,* vol. 3 (New York and Philadelphia, 1957), pp. 4–24. The precise date of the order of forced conversion is not known. Ibid., p. 24, places it in 632 C.E. F. E. Peters, *Allah's Commonwealth* (New York, 1973), p. 38, places it in 634. It seems most likely that this decree was issued shortly before the Arab invasion.

[2] The most detailed study of the Jews in the late Sasanian period is Jacob Neusner, *A History of the Jews in Babylonia V: Later Sasanian Times* (Leiden, 1970). See especially pp. 125–32.

[3] Both of these works are edited with introduction and notes in Yehuda Ibn Shemuel (Kaufmann) ed., *Midreshē Ge'ulla* (Jerusalem and Tel Aviv, 1953), pp. 31–48 and 162–98, respectively. Two other apocalyptic treatises closely associated with these are the *Pereq Eliyāhū* (ibid., pp. 49–54) and the *Tefillat Rabbī Shimᶜōn b. Yōḥay* (ibid., pp. 254–86). The last is translated and analyzed by Bernard Lewis, "An Apocalyptic Vision of Islamic History," *BSOAS* 13, pt. 2 (1950): 308–38.

[4] For Ḥimṣ, see al-Balādhurī, *Futūḥ al-Buldān,* ed. R. M. Riḍwān (Cairo, 1959), p. 143 (trans. in Part Two below, p. 153); for Hebron, see "Canonici Hebronensis Tractatus de inventione sanctorum patriarchum Abra-

Spain, the Jews rose up en masse in armed revolt against their Visigothic persecutors, and in city after city were organized by the overextended Muslims into garrisons.[5]

The widespread and almost total Jewish alliance with the Muslim forces invading Spain in 711 seems to have been a very special case in the history of the Islamic conquests. The invasion of the Middle East was not by any means a joyous, liberating experience. There was a great deal of death and destruction. The inhabitants of towns taken by storm were either killed or led into captivity, and their property was forfeited.

Not everyone welcomed the invaders. The tales told by Jewish refugees from Medina and the Hijaz must have made many uneasy. Most Jews in the Byzantine provinces remembered only too well how they had been betrayed by their Persian allies only a few years earlier. The Palestinian Jewish community had had to pay dearly for their close cooperation with the Persians after the Byzantine reconquest. The majority of Jews, therefore, watched the Arab conquest from the sidelines. There is one instance, that of Gaza, where the Jews actually may have fought alongside the Byzantine troops, who were badly outnumbered by the Arabs, in a vain attempt to defend the city.[6]

As the Arabs conquered town after town and region after region, they were increasingly faced with the problem of how to deal with their new subjects. The victors suddenly found themselves a tiny minority in a vast empire inhabited by Christians, Jews, and Zoroastrians. There were a series of precedents from Arabia with regard to the treatment of non-Muslims to fall back upon. The Jews of Khaybar and the oases of northern Arabia paid a fixed percent of their annual crops. The Christians and Jews of Yemen paid a poll tax and were required to furnish certain services to the Muslim community. Despite the lack of uniformity in these precedents, the general tenor and intent were in accordance with Sura 9:29, which enjoins the Muslims to

---

ham, Ysaac et Jacob," *Recueil des historiens des croisades: historiens occidentaux,* vol. 5 (Paris, 1895), p. 309 (trans. in Part Two below, p. 152); for Caesarea, see al-Balādhurī, *Futūḥ al-Buldān,* p. 146; Eng. trans., pp. 216ff.

[5] Anon., *Akhbār Majmūᶜa,* ed. Emilio Lafuente y Alcántara (Madrid, 1867), pp. 12–14 (trans. in Part Two below, p. 156). See also Ibn ᶜIdhārī, *al-Bayān al-Mughrib fī Akhbār al-Andalus wa 'l-Maghrib,* vol. 2, ed. G. S. Colin and E. Lévi-Provençal (Leiden, 1951), p. 12. For additional sources, including the Latin, see Eliyahu Ashtor, *The Jews of Moslem Spain,* vol. 1 (Philadelphia, 1973), pp. 407–9, nn. 1–15.

[6] See Baron, *Social and Religious History of the Jews,* vol. 3, p. 87 and p. 268ff., n. 17. The sources are not very clear on this point.

make unbelievers into humbled tribute bearers. As these various practices went back to the Prophet himself, they had the sanctity of being his *sunna* (practice).

There does not seem to be any uniformity in the stipulations imposed upon the conquered peoples. Later, Muslim sources projecting back the legal systems of their own time created the impression that all the conquered people paid a poll tax (*jizya*) and a land tax (*kharāj*). This anachronism was uncritically accepted by many scholars. Other scholars, seeing the confusion of terms in the earliest sources, concluded that the Arabs simply imposed a lump sum tribute everywhere they went and did not distinguish between the sources of tax revenues. Daniel Dennett and Frede Løkkegaard, working independently, have shown that the terms imposed upon the conquered peoples varied greatly depending upon the conditions surrounding their surrender.[7] Some of the early agreements clearly indicated a poll tax and/or land tax to be paid by the conquered population.

The capitulation that became the model for the treatment of Jews and Christians (and later, Zoroastrians) in the new empire was the document of surrender extended by the second caliph, ᶜUmar b. al-Khaṭṭāb (ruled 634–44) to the patriarch of Jerusalem, Sophronios.[8] Even if the text of this document, which has been preserved in later Arab histories, is not genuine, its general tenor is. The terms of this negotiated surrender became the basis of the so-called Pact of ᶜUmar, the theoretical treaty between the People of the Book and the Muslim state. Many of the provisions and restrictions of the pact were only elaborated with the passage of time, and it was probably redacted during the caliphate of ᶜUmar b. ᶜAbd al-ᶜAzīz (ruled 717–20), when there was a definite hardening in the attitude of Muslims toward non-Muslims.

The Pact of ᶜUmar was a writ of protection (*amān*, or *dhimma*) extended by Allah's community to their protégés (*ahl al-dhimma* or *dhimmīs*). In return for the safeguarding of life and property and the right to worship unmolested according to their conscience, the *dhimmīs* had to pay the *jizya* and the *kharāj*. They were to conduct themselves

[7] Daniel C. Dennett, *Conversion and the Poll Tax in Early Islam,* Harvard Historical Monographs, vol. 22 (Cambridge, Mass., 1950); and Frede Løkkegaard, *Islamic Taxation in the Classic Period, with Special Reference to Circumstances in Iraq* (Copenhagen, 1950). Both are reprinted in a single volume entitled *Islamic Taxation: Two Studies* (New York, 1973).

[8] The text of this document is given in al-Ṭabarī, *Ta'rīkh al-Rusul wa 'l-Mulūk* [*Annales*], Prima Series, vol. 5, ed. M. J. de Goeje et al. (reprint ed., Leiden, 1964), pp. 2405–6.

with the demeanor and comportment befitting a subject population. They were never to strike a Muslim. They were not to carry arms, ride horses, or use normal riding saddles on their mounts. They were not to build new houses of worship nor repair old ones. They were not to hold public religious processions (including funeral processions), nor pray too loudly. Naturally, they were not to proselytize. They had to wear clothing that distinguished them from the Arabs. This last prescription was easy enough to observe at first, as Arabs and non-Arabs did not dress alike anyway. Later, however, as a general Islamic fashion began to develop throughout the empire, this meant that *dhimmīs* had to wear badges or specially dyed outer garments.

Certain provisions of the pact applied only to the early years of Arab military occupation and eventually fell into desuetude. These included the obligation to provide hospitality to Arab troops, to come forth with military intelligence, and not to harbor any spies. By the same token, other provisions were added to the pact when the Arabs became permanent settlers living side by side with their *dhimmī* subjects. These provisions included the prohibition against *dhimmīs* building homes higher than Muslim homes, adopting Arabic names and titles, studying the Koran, or selling fermented beverages. Furthermore, *dhimmīs* were to be restricted from government service. In other words, at least in theory, *dhimmīs* were to be permanent outsiders with no real part in the Muslim Arab *civitas Dei.*[9]

Many of these restrictions and their highly ramified refinements were probably inspired by the discriminatory legislation against Jews that was already in force in the Byzantine lands conquered by the Arabs. The actual application was frequently less harsh in the Arab world during the early Middle Ages than in Byzantium, but the spirit was very much the same. Many restrictions of the pact were difficult to enforce in the early Islamic centuries. As we have already noted, the Arabs were a minority in their own empire. Most men of fighting age were engaged in various sorts of military duties—policing their vast territories, expanding the borders of the empire, or fighting each other in the sectarian or intertribal conflicts that plagued the first century of Islam. The occupying forces settled mainly in their own encampments, separate from the main centers of native population.

[9] The best studies of the Pact of ᶜUmar and its later ramifications are: A. S. Tritton, *The Caliphs and their Non-Muslim Subjects: A Critical Study of the Covenant of ᶜUmar* (reprint ed., London, 1930); Antoine Fattal, *Le Statut légal des non-musulmans en pays d'Islam* (Beirut, 1958); and Claude Cahen, "Dhimma," *EI*² 2:227–31.

They did this in order to preserve their own separate identity and not to be absorbed among the masses of their subjects. Much of the local administration was left in the hands of the native civil servants, who were more experienced in such matters. The local officials, in town, looked to the leaders of the individual religious communities to collect the taxes due from their coreligionists. Such a system of benign neglect allowed for a considerable degree of internal autonomy within the various religious communities.

The Jewish and Christian polities were, on the whole, able to look after themselves rather well under these conditions, as they already possessed a communal organization molded in the Greco-Roman civil tradition. On the other hand, Zoroastrianism, which was intimately bound up with the fallen Sasanian state, lost its very *raison d'être* and rapidly declined into insignificance.

The Jews were psychologically better able to adapt to the new facts of life created by the Arabs' conquest than were either the Christians or Zoroastrians. They had already been a subject people for over five centuries. The rabbis had given them a concept of Jewishness that was independent of physical territory or political sovereignty. Their God was still the God of history, and they were still His chosen people. They were in *gālūt* (exile), and it was simply not yet over. The victories of the Arabs over the empires of Byzantium and Iran only proved how ephemeral were the kingdoms of men.

It was probably easier for the Jews to adapt to the new order economically as well as psychologically. The tax burden imposed upon them along with all *dhimmīs* under Islam was not much different from the discriminatory taxes paid to their former overlords. For the Christians of the Byzantine Empire and the Zoroastrians of Iran, however, the trauma was much worse (though not for the Christians of the Persian Empire, whose status was comparable to that of the Jews). They had suddenly gone from being members of the dominant faith to the status of inferior—albeit tolerated—subjects. The tax burden they now shouldered was considerably heavier than before. It is understandable in light of these factors that the majority of Christians and Zoroastrians—and, of course, a significant number of Jews—converted to Islam over the next century and a half. Escape from oppressive taxation and social inferiority was certainly a great inducement to conversion. Large numbers of converts (*mawālī*) flocked to the Arab garrison towns to reap the benefits of their new status and to provide the conquerors with goods and services. Many *mawālī* were sorely disappointed when they discovered they were not to be permitted to go from being tribute bearers to pension receivers by the ruling Arab military elite. Eventually, however, there were enough converts to undermine totally the old tax base and necessitate fundamental changes in the economic system of the empire.

The Middle East underwent tremendous upheavals and far-reaching social changes during the first two centuries of the Islamic era. These changes profoundly affected every segment of the population, including the Jews. Unfortunately, the details of this process of transformation are by no means clear due to the lack of sources from the period when these changes were actually taking place. This is particularly true with regard to the fortunes of the Jewish communities in the newly expanded Arab world, "since at that time very little was written by Jews on any subject, and still less has come down to us."[10] Furthermore, the Arab historians of a somewhat later date when looking back over this important period of Islamic history had far more pressing concerns than presenting the internal histories of the minorities within their empire.

But even though the specific course of events in Jewish life during these decisive years remains obscure, the outcome is eminently clear. During this time large numbers of Jews in the Islamic East, and particularly in Iraq where the majority resided, gradually changed over from the agrarian way of life depicted in the Talmud to a more cosmopolitan one. The transformation was by no means immediate. For the first two generations of Arab rule, all movement within the Dār al-Islām was severely restricted for a variety of reasons. Not least among these was military security. Another important consideration was ensuring that taxes were not evaded. (Even in later more liberal times a receipt for taxes paid was the traveler's basic passport.) A third reason of no less importance was to maintain the agricultural labor force that produced food and such necessary raw materials as cloth fibers and oil for lamps. The *jizya* and *kharāj* were a crushing burden for the non-Muslim peasantry who eked out a bare living in a subsistence economy. The hardship and oppression endured by the people who worked the land led not only to large-scale conversions but also eventually to a mass flight from the villages to the cities. The authorities tried to staunch the flow, but this became increasingly difficult as sectarian and civil strife diverted the attention and energy of the Arabs during the later years of the Umayyad Caliphate, which finally fell in 750.[11]

[10] Baron, *Ancient and Medieval Jewish History*, ed. Leon A. Feldman (New Brunswick, N.J., 1972), p. 79.

[11] The maltreatment of the peasantry, their flight to the cities, and the

The downfall of the Umayyads was brought about in part by the rise of a new middle class and the state's increasing inability to maintain the traditional military system. By the third Islamic century (the ninth century of the Common Era) Jews were taking part along with the masses of *mawālī* and *dhimmīs* in shaping what S. D. Goitein has designated "the bourgeois revolution."[12] This event combined the development of Islamic urbanism, the flowering of a cultural renascence that drew heavily upon the Hellenistic intellectual and scientific heritage, and the dramatic growth of a mercantile economy and the business arts that is usually referred to by socioeconomic historians as the Commercial Revolution.

The Umayyads had ruled their empire from the environs of Damascus. Their successors, the Abbasids, had their power base in the eastern territories and had no wish to settle in Syria. The rich province of Iraq became the center of their caliphate. In 762, al-Manṣūr, the second ruler of the dynasty, founded a new capital, Madīnaṭ al-Salām (the City of Peace—that is, earthly paradise) on the west bank of the Tigris not far from the ruins of the Persian imperial seat of Ctesiphon. The new metropolis incorporated several ancient settlements, the most important of which was the village of Baghdad, which through popular usage eventually gave its name to the entire city.

The establishment of the Abbasid capital in Iraq was to have profound consequences for all the Jews of Arab lands. Iraq was ancient Babylonia—Jewish Bāvēl. It was already the foremost center of world Jewry two centuries before the Arab conquest. It possessed two great seats of Jewish learning, the venerable academies of Sura and Pumbedītha. It had produced the Babylonian Talmud, which was to become the constitutional foundation of later medieval Jewish life. It also boasted having at its head a putative descendant of the last king of Judah, a scion of the House of David, the exilarch (*rēsh gālūthā*). Prior to the advent of Islam, the exilarch had served as the governor of the Jews living within the Sasanian realm. He was more or less the counterpart of the patriarch (*nāsī*) in earlier Byzantine Palestine. When the Arabs invaded Iraq and Iran, they recognized and confirmed the authority of the Jewish exilarch and the Nestorian catholicos over their respective congregations.

---

attempts to send them back are all amply documented in Islamic sources. See, for example, al-Mubarrad, *Kitāb al-Kāmil,* vol. 1, ed. W. Wright (Leipzig, 1864), p. 286; al-Ṭabarī, *Annales,* Secunda Series, vol. 2, p. 1122; and Abū Yūsuf, *Kitāb al-Kharāj* (Cairo, A. H. 1382), pp. 105–6.

[12] S. D. Goitein, *Jews and Arabs* (New York, 1974), pp. 7 and 100.

The conquerors singled out Exilarch Bustanay b. Ḥaninay for particular honor because he was considered to be a descendant of King David, whom they revered as a prophet. According to Jewish tradition, Bustanay was given the captive daughter of one of the last Sasanian shahs for a wife.[13] The gesture was clearly to emphasize his own noble lineage and the esteem that he held in the eyes of Muslims. After all, Caliph ᶜAlī (ruled 656–61) gave another Persian princess to his own son Ḥusayn, who was the grandson of the Prophet Muḥammad. Bustanay must have rendered the conquerors important services and apparently, along with the catholicos, acted as a trusted adviser on native affairs. After Bustanay's death sometime around 680, his sons by Jewish wives attempted to repudiate the offspring of the Persian princess, claiming she had never been properly manumitted and thus her issue were merely slaves of their father's household. Despite the fact that the three sons of the princess were declared legitimate, their status was questioned intermittently for years.[14] Not until several generations later did any of their descendants attain the exilarchate. It was perhaps because of the frequent politics and intrigue within the exilarch's house that the office never achieved the actual ecumenical authority over the Jews of the Islamic world that some historians, most notably Salo Baron, have posited for it.[15]

When the Abbasids rose to power in Iraq in 750, the exilarchate took on increased significance to be sure. The exilarch was now close to the seat of caliphal power. He was accorded considerable dignity at the court of a dynasty that prided itself on its own noble lineage, going back to al-ᶜAbbās, the Prophet's uncle. There was no other Jewish figurehead comparable to the exilarch. The office of the Palestinian patriarch had been dissolved three centuries earlier by the Emperor Theodosius. Thus, at the Abbasid court, at least, the exilarch came to be recognized as the leading representative of the Jews residing within their vast empire, which stretched from the Indus River to the Atlantic Ocean. He certainly represented his people's interests in the halls of power and was the obvious authority to be consulted on Jewish affairs. His actual administrative authority over the Jews outside Iraq and Persia, however, was probably token at best. Still, the mere exis-

[13] She was the daughter either of Khosroes II or Yezdegird III (most likely the latter).

[14] All of the data on Bustanay are analyzed in Hayyim Tyckoczynski, "Bustānay Rōsh ha-Gōla," *Devir* 1 (1923): 145–79. See also Baron, *A Social and Religious History of the Jews,* vol. 3, pp. 89 and 270, n. 20.

[15] Baron, *Social and Religious History of the Jews,* vol. 5, pp. 5–13, especially p. 7.

tence of a Jewish prince—even if he was only a figurehead who was shown respect by the Gentiles—was a source of self-esteem for all Jews and a proof of the biblical prophecy that "the sceptre shall not depart from Judah" (Gen. 49:10). The Spanish traveler Benjamin of Tudela, who visited Baghdad in the second half of the twelfth century, describes with obvious pride and some hyperbole the reception of Exilarch Daniel b. Ḥasday at the court of the caliph at a time when the authority of both was at a low ebb.[16] If the exilarchs ever enjoyed any real authority over distant Jewish communities, it was probably during the first fifty years of the Abbasid Caliphate, when the rule of that dynasty extended over much of the Dominion of Islam.

Sometime during the first half of the ninth century, ecumenical Jewish leadership became increasingly associated with the persons who headed the Babylonian academies (Hebrew, *yeshīvōt;* Aramaic, *methīvāthā*) of Sura and Pumbedītha. At the end of the sixth century, the respective heads of these institutions took on the title of Rēsh Methīvath Ge'ōn Yaᶜaqōv (the Head of the Academy of the Pride of Jacob). This grandiloquent title was contracted by later generations to *gaon.* In their own days the *geonim* were usually referred to as "our Masters, the Heads of the Academies." Even before Islamic times, they had great followings within Babylonia. The head of the Pumbedītha Academy, R. Isaac, is reported to have welcomed the Caliph ᶜAlī into Firuz-Shapur at the head of 90,000 Jews in 658.[17]

The *geonim* were the great propagators and expounders of the Babylonian Talmud, which they sought to make the constitutional framework for the entire Jewish community. The spread of Talmudic Judaism out of Iraq was not an instantaneous process but extended over a long period of time. As it spread, so did the prestige and influence of the *geonim* and their schools. Throughout the eighth and ninth centuries, the renown of the *geonim* grew to the point that they were recognized by their coreligionists the world over as the highest authorities on Jewish law, which encompassed all aspects of Jewish life. As the great rabbinic scholar Louis Ginzberg succinctly put it: "The Babylonian Amoraim [expounders of the Mishna during the third through sixth centuries] created a Talmud; the Geonim made it 'The Talmud.' "[18]

[16] The passage is translated in Part Two below, pp. 252–54.

[17] Sherira Gaon, *Iggeret [From the Gaonic Period. 2: The Epistle of R. Sherira Gaon, arranged in two versions, originating from Spain and France, with variae lectiones from all the Mss. and Geniza fragments in the world],* ed. Benjamin M. Lewin (Haifa, 1921), p. 101 [in Heb.].

[18] Louis Ginzberg, *Geonica,* vol. 1 (reprint ed., New York, 1968), p. 73.

The *geonim* based their claims to legitimate and preeminent leadership upon the contention that they were the sole possessors of the living, authoritative, rabbinic tradition that went back to the Saboraim, the Amoraim, the Tannaim, the men of the Great Assembly, and ultimately back to Moses himself. For most Jews the *geonim* "reigned" (*mālekhū*), and their authority was supreme because it interpreted Divine Law from which there is no appeal. Their decisions frequently bore the admonition: "This is the *halakha* (religious law) and there is no moving from it."[19]

The Jewish communities of the wider Islamic Diaspora sent donations as well as queries (*she'eltōt*) on law, ritual, and textual exegesis to the academies. The great influence of the *geonim* was exerted through their responsa (*teshūvōt*), or authoritative legal opinions. In order to facilitate the flow of correspondence back and forth, as well as the donations that were the lifeblood of the academies, a network of representatives of the academies developed throughout the Islamic world during the ninth and tenth centuries. By the eleventh century the system was well established. The men who represented the academies in the local Jewish communities were not infrequently alumni of the institutions. They were entrusted with the task of collecting communal contributions and queries and forwarding them to Iraq. As great distances had to be traversed, there were intermediaries living between the communities and the academies who facilitated the transfer of correspondence in either direction.[20]

Not all Jews accepted the geonic authority, especially the small but numerous sectarian groups of eastern Iran. The most serious challenge to the *geonim* came from the fundamentalist Karaite schism, which denied the authenticity of the rabbinic oral tradition and accepted only the Bible as the principal source of Jewish law. The movement began in the second half of the eighth century with ᶜAnan b. David, a disappointed candidate for the exilarchate. It became a force to be reckoned with in the ninth and early tenth centuries, when

[19] *Kākh halākha ve-ēyn lāzūz minnah.*

[20] For a study of one such individual who functioned as an intermediary, see my articles "Quelques renseignements biographiques sur Yōsēf Ibn ᶜAwkal, médiateur entre les communautés juives du Maghreb et les Académies d'Irak," *REJ* 132, fasc. 4 (October–December, 1973), pp. 529–42; and "Joseph Ibn ᶜAwkal: A Jewish Communal Leader in Eleventh Century Egypt," *The Eleventh Century*, ed. Stanley Ferber and Sandro Sticca, Acta of the Center for Medieval and Early Renaissance Studies, State University of New York at Binghamton, vol. 1 (Binghamton, N.Y., 1974), pp. 39–50. For a broad discussion of the ties between the Geonim and the local communities, see Goitein, *A Mediterranean Society*, vol. 2 (Berkeley and Los Angeles, 1971), pp. 8–13.

it had some of its best intellectual leadership among men such as Benjamin al-Nehāwandī and Daniel al-Qūmisī. The Karaites attracted and absorbed some of the various smaller sectarian groups. These "protestants" of Judaism began as a movement with pronounced ascetic tendencies. Within a few centuries of the founding of their sect, they counted among their number some of the wealthiest Jewish merchants of the Middle East.

The Karaites were not the only Jews in the Islamic world who were not under the diocesan authority of the Babylonian *geonim*. There were Rabbanite Jews who followed the rites and customs of the ancient and venerable academy of Tiberias in Palestine. Little is known about the Palestinian Academy prior to the tenth century. Ever since the dissolution of the patriarchate, the heads of the Tiberian Academy had served as both spiritual and secular leaders of Palestinian Jewry. It is not known exactly when they assumed the title of *gaon* in imitation of their Babylonian counterparts. It would seem that this took place sometime after 969 when Palestine became part of the empire of the Fatimids, who were Shiᶜite counter-Caliphs.[21]

The influence of the Palestinian gaonate outside of the Holy Land was limited. The congregations under its jurisdiction were all in the former Byzantine provinces of Egypt and North Africa. The Palestinian gaonate also maintained ties with the Jews of Byzantium and Italy. To these distant lands were sent special envoys who delivered sermons, answered some of the religious queries on the spot, and collected the contributions for the academy.[22]

From the second half of the eighth century on, the Palestinian Academy found itself increasingly overshadowed by its sister institutions in Iraq. The influence of the Babylonian academies was becoming strong even within Palestine itself. The advent of the Abbasid Caliphate, the centralization of power in Iraq, and the rise of a new cosmopolitan civilization throughout the Islamic imperium all contributed to the growing importance of the Babylonian *geonim* and to their academies as the institutions of central Jewish authority.

The new freedom of movement that began in the late eighth century and continued for more than three hundred years greatly facilitated the spread of Babylonian authority. The travel restrictions in force under the Umayyads disappeared under the Abbasids. With a

[21] Concerning the Palestinian Academy and the authority of its leadership, see Simha Assaf, *Teqūfat ha-Ge'ōnīm ve-Sifrūtāh* (Jerusalem, 1955), pp. 91–101.

[22] Ibid., pp. 104–5.

bustling international commerce centered in Baghdad and Basra, people traveled to and fro, east and west. Some of the Iraqi Jewish merchants who came to the western provinces of the empire began to settle there temporarily or permanently. In so doing, they helped to disseminate further the Judaism of the Babylonian Talmud. At the same time they were extending the authority of the *geonim* of Sura and Pumbedītha. A genuine population movement westward occurred during the civil wars that plagued Iraq during the second half of the ninth century and the first half of the tenth century. By the end of the tenth century nearly every major city in Syria, Palestine, Egypt, and, most probably, North Africa had a Babylonian as well as a Palestinian congregation.[23]

The rise of a vigorous Jewish mercantile class in the Muslim East was perhaps the single most important socioeconomic factor underlying the predominance of Babylonian Jewry as a whole. In early Abbasid times Jews began taking a significant role in a burgeoning international trade. Jewish merchants from the district of Rādhān (later called Jūkhā) around Baghdad extended their operations as far east as China and as far west as Spain.[24] The rapidly expanding commerce necessitated the development of banking, a profession in which Jews were prominently represented as well, although they certainly did not come to dominate it after a stage of initial Christian preeminence, as Louis Massignon has supposed.[25] A few Jews actually did attain the highest ranks in the world of commerce and finance from time to time, but these were the exceptions and not the rule. The discriminatory tariff of 5 percent levied on the goods of *dhimmī* merchants at this time when the Muslims were paying 2.5 percent was to ensure the

[23] Syria: Damascus, Aleppo, Palmyra; Palestine: Ramle and Baniyas; Egypt: Fustat, Alexandria, al-Mahalla. See Goitein, *Mediterranean Society*, vol. 2, pp. 6 and 519ff., nn. 2–3, and the sources cited there. There is no concrete evidence for the existence of synagogues for both rites in the towns of the Maghreb. However, it seems most likely that the case was no different there than that of the Levant, for we know that many eastern Jews settled in North Africa and that there were congregations there that accepted the religious authority of Babylon.

[24] Convincing arguments for the identification of Rādhān with Jūkhā or Sawād Baghdād have been made by Moshe Gil, "The Rādhānite Merchants and the Land of Rādhān," *JESHO* 17, pt. 3 (1974): 299–328. The famous passage from Ibn Khurradādhbe describing the itinerary of the Rādhānites is translated in Part Two below, pp. 163–64.

[25] L. Massignon, "L'influence de l'Islam au moyen âge sur la fondation et l'essor des banques juives," *Bulletin des Etudes Orientales de l'Institut Français de Damas* 1 (1931): 3–12. Most of the state bankers mentioned in the Arabic sources seem to have been Christians.

primacy of the Muslim merchant class through what would be called today a "most favored trading status."[26] Of course, the overwhelming majority of Jews pursued humble trades and occupations, eking out a bare livelihood like the rest of the Middle Eastern masses.

The Jewish mercantile elite formed the backbone of the religious leadership, a situation that had its parallel in the Muslim community at the time. Between the years 788 and 798, for example, the gaonate of Pumbedītha was held by Rādhānites.[27] The intimate bond between the scholars and the merchants was not an entirely new phenomenon. The leaders of the Babylonian academies had been recruited from the ranks of the merchants long before the Arab conquest.[28] However, as the merchant class expanded and increased in power economically and politically, there arose in ninth- and tenth-century Baghdad a lay plutocracy that played the dominant role in Jewish comunal life.

The Abbasid capital provided the ideal setting for the growth, development, and political activities of an influential Jewish merchant class. F. E. Peters has given a vivid description of the atmosphere of the Baghdadi melting pot:

> Intellectually, commercially, and circumstantially, Baghdad inherited within the *Dār al-Islām* the role played by Alexandria in the old Hellenic *oikoumene*. Turbulent, cosmopolitan, invincibly successful, given more to scholarship and trade than to piety, the unrivaled center of arts and letters and the seat of the secular and religious power in Islam, Baghdad had, like its Egyptian counterpart, no past. Its present was frequently unruly, since rich and poor, Arab, Iranian, and Turk, Shiᶜite and traditionalist, Christian and Jew, scholar, merchant and soldier rubbed shoulders within the walls.[29]

It was in Baghdad that the new plutocracy made itself felt in Jewish affairs in ways that affected the larger Diaspora. When a new exilarch was to be chosen, the decision was taken at a meeting of elders in the home of a merchant prince such as Neṭīra (d. 916), the founder of a great banking establishment and himself a *novus homo* who was

[26] The passage from Abū Yūsuf's handbook on taxation is translated in Part Two below, pp. 159–61.

[27] Gil, "The Rādhānite Merchants," p. 322.

[28] There are numerous talmudic references to scholars, including the heads of academies, involved in trade, especially the lucrative silk trade. See Goitein, "Baᶜayōt Yesōd be-Histōriyya ha-Yehūdīt," *Proceedings of the Fifth World Congress of Jewish Studies*, vol. 2 (Jerusalem, 1972), pp. 101–6, and in particular the references on pp. 102–3.

[29] F. E. Peters, *Allah's Commonweath* (New York, 1973), p. 143.

never referred to with the usual patronymic, as if he had no father worth mentioning.[30]

The positions taken by such men in Jewish communal matters were frequently decisive. Because of their influence in Muslim court circles as *jahbadhs*, or government bankers, they could make or break even a prince of the exile. Such was the case when a dispute broke out between Exilarch Mar ᶜUqba and the *gaon* of Pumbedītha, R. Judah b. Samuel. It was the intervention of Neṭīra and his father-in-law Joseph b. Phinehas that resulted in ᶜUqba's banishment in 909 to Kirmanshah in Iran.[31] It was due to the protection of the Sons of Neṭīra and the Sons of Aaron (Aaron b. Amram had been Joseph b. Phinehas's business partner) that the famous Saᶜadya was able to maintain himself as *gaon* of Sura for two full years after having been deposed by Exilarch David b. Zakkay in 930. The ultimate reconciliation between Saᶜadya and Ben Zakkay was brought about through the good offices of the wealthy Bishr b. Aaron in 937.[32] One cannot fail to note that in several of the examples cited here, we see the merchant-bankers joining in common cause with the rabbinical scholars against the House of David. The elite of wealth and intellect was asserting itself against the elite of aristocratic birth. A similar phenomenon was occurring in the contemporary Muslim community. Throughout the ninth and tenth centuries, the newly Arabized Persians and others of *mawālī* extraction were asserting themselves in society. The affluent bourgeoisie was eagerly engaged in the pursuit not only of wealth, but of the religious and Hellenic sciences—that is, of religious and social status.

The ties that bound the merchants and the scholars were numerous. Neṭīra had sent his son Sahl to the Pumbedītha Academy, where he became a devoted disciple of Saᶜadya, who taught there before

[30] Concerning this man and the sources referring to him, see Walter J. Fischel, *Jews in the Economic and Political Life of Mediaeval Islam* (reprint ed. with new Introduction, New York, 1969), pp. 34–44. See also Abraham David, "Netira," *EJ* 12: 999–1000. An extensive Arabic passage on Neṭīra and his sons has been edited with Hebrew translation by Alexander Harkavy, "Netira und seine Söhne," in *Abraham Berliner Festschrift*, vol. 1 (reprint ed., Jerusalem, 1969), pp. 34–43.

[31] Nathan ha-Bavlī in A. Neubauer, ed., *Mediaeval Jewish Chronicles and Chronological Notes*, vol. 2 (Oxford, 1895), pp. 78–79. See Salo Baron's reconstruction of these events in his *A Social and Religious History of the Jews*, vol. 5, pp. 10–11, and his assessment of Nathan ha-Bavlī's account in *Ancient and Medieval Jewish History*, pp. 104–8.

[32] Nathan ha-Bavlī in Neubauer, *Mediaeval Jewish Chronicles*, vol. 2, p. 82.

assuming the gaonate of Sura.[33] In a letter to his coreligionists in Egypt written shortly after his accession to the gaonate in 928, Saᶜadya offers to bring to the attention of the Jewish court bankers any matters requiring their intercession with the authorities:

Whenever you have any request or petition for the government, please bring it to our attention so that we may then inform the heads of prominent houses in Baghdad among whom we live, such as the Sons of Neṭīra and the Sons of Aaron (may the memory of their departed fathers be blessed, etc.). They will procure a response from the Ruler for you with the help of the Lord our Fortress. Follow this procedure, and do not deviate from it.[34]

The merchants not only sent their sons to study at the academies, but often went there themselves. Jacob b. ᶜAwkal, the founder of a great merchant house in tenth-century Fustat, had studied at Pumbedītha with Sherira Gaon (d. 1006). The enthusiastic alumnus became the representative of the academy in Egypt.[35] The entire worldwide network of intermediaries and representatives of the academies consisted of merchants and men of substance who had the means to facilitate the flow of correspondence and monies. Funds destined for the academies often came in the form of *suftajas,* bills of exchange resembling the modern cashier's check, which were drawn on Baghdadi banking houses.[36] Substantial sums were involved. For example, the annual revenue for the Sura *gaon* in the tenth century was 1,500 dinars. For the sake of comparison, the cost of living for a middle-class family in Iraq at that time has been estimated at about 240 dinars a year.[37]

The reader should not lose sight of the fact that the highly developed Jewish communal organization, which has only been briefly described here, operated within the context of the Islamic state. There

[33] Harkavy, "Netira und seine Söhne," *Berliner Festschrift,* vol. 1, p. 38 (Ar. text), p. 40 (Heb. trans.).

[34] The Hebrew text of this passage is given in Fischel, *Jews,* p. 34, where Louis Ginzberg's translation is quoted. My own rendering differs somewhat.

[35] See Stillman, "Quelques renseignements biographiques sur Yōsēf b. ᶜAwkal," *REJ* 132: 538.

[36] Fischel, *Jews,* pp. 17–21, especially pp. 18ff. Concerning the *suftaja* and other instruments of payment, see Goitein, *Mediterranean Society,* vol. 1, pp. 242–46.

[37] Eliyahu Ashtor, *Histoire des prix et des salaires dans l'Orient médiéval* (Paris, 1969), p. 62. Baron, *Ancient and Medieval Jewish History,* p. 412, n. 48, is not altogether correct in referring to the revenues of Sura as "relatively insignificant." His comparisons are with the fabulous wealth of some of the greatest men of the age.

was a considerable degree of internal autonomy to be sure, for this was the nature of Muslim society and, indeed, of all medieval societies where corporate, national identities were essentially religious. In medieval Christian Europe too "extensive Jewish self-government was universally accepted as the necessary and welcome complement to recognized religious disparity."[38]

Muslim authorities were concerned above all that taxes be paid and that *dhimmī* subjects acknowledge in a variety of ways, some more and some less humiliating, the dominion of Islam. As long as the non-Muslims complied, they were accorded a good measure of internal self-rule. However, even in the conduct of their own communal affairs, they were not entirely free of government supervision and, at times, downright interference.

Both the *geonim* and the exilarchs who were chosen within the community had to be approved by the government. Their formal assumption of office came only upon receipt of a caliphal proclamation and a letter of appointment. A writ of approval continued to be absolutely necessary for all principal leaders of Jewish communities (*nāgīd, shaykh al-Yahūd, ḥākhām bāshī,* and others) in Muslim lands down to modern times.[39] The document not only confirmed the rights and privileges of the official but also the restrictions of his own and his communities' *dhimmī* status.

The Muslim authorities could and did block the appointment of religious leaders within the *dhimmī* communities. The Chalcedonian Orthodox patriarchates of Alexandria, Antioch, and Jerusalem frequently went unoccupied because of caliphal opposition.[40] That this

[38] Baron, *The Jewish Community: Its History and Structure to the American Revolution,* vol. 1 (reprint ed., Westport, Conn., 1972), p. 208. On a broader plane, Gustave E. von Grunebaum has discussed the "essential kinship of thought and sentiment" shared by the Latin, Byzantine, and Muslim worlds. See his *Medieval Islam,* 2d ed. (Chicago, 1962), pp. 1–63.

[39] Examples of such documents are translated in Part Two below, pp. 178–79 and pp. 269–70. No examples of a letter of appointment for an Exilarch have survived. It was probably similar to the ones issued to the Nestorian Catholicos. For the latter, see A. von Kremer, "Zwei arabische Urkunden," *ZDMG* 7 (1853): 219–33. The same text with some revisions and an English translation is given in H. F. Amedroz, "Tales of Official Life from the 'Tadhkira' of Ibn Hamdun, etc.," *JRAS* n.v. (1908): 447ff. and 467ff. Another writ is given by A. Mingana, "A Charter of Protection Granted the Nestorian Church in A.D. 1138, by Muktafi II, Caliph of Baghdad," *Bulletin of the John Rylands Library, Manchester* 10 (1926): 127–33.

[40] Demetrios J. Constantelos, "The Moslem Conquests of the Near East as Revealed in the Greek Sources of the Seventh and the Eighth Centuries," *Byzantion* 42, pt. 2 (1972): 336, 345–47.

church was singled out for particularly harsh treatment at times is understandable, as it was the official church of the Byzantine enemy. But other churches, including the anti-Byzantine Nestorian and Coptic, suffered interference. The Umayyad Caliph ᶜAbd al-Malik is alleged to have imprisoned the Nestorian patriarch Khanishu and to have appointed a rival in his stead.[41] Two exilarchs and at least one candidate for the office are reported to have been put to death by the Muslim authorities. These extreme cases were exceptional and the circumstances surrounding them not entirely clear.[42]

Disputes within the community and rivalries for office were open invitations to government involvement. The outcomes in such controversies in the end were often decided by the Muslim authorities in favor of the faction paying the highest bribes. Aaron b. Sarjado is reported to have paid 60,000 dirhams in order to facilitate Saᶜadya's forced retirement during the conflict with Ben Zakkay, and even this sum was apparently not enough at first.[43]

Quite understandably, it was a generally accepted principle within the Jewish community to avoid involving the Muslim authorities in internal Jewish affairs. This principle was violated in many instances, but on the whole it was adhered to. After all, it was clear to everyone that the gentile state did not have the best interests of its Jewish subjects at heart, nor could it be expected to. The Jews like all other *dhimmīs* enjoyed extensive communal autonomy precisely because the state did not care what they did so long as they paid their taxes, kept the peace, and remained in their place.

[41] Ibid., p. 346, citing Bar Hebraeus, *Chronicon Ecclesiasticum,* Sect. II, 27, ed. J. B. Abbeloos and Th. J. Lamy, vol. 3 (Paris and Rome, 1877), pp. 130–32.

[42] Two of the deaths are reported in Jewish sources. Nathan ha-Bavlī reports the execution of the candidate for the Exilarchate in ca. 941, who was accused of having blasphemed Muḥammad (in Neubauer, *Mediaeval Jewish Chronicles,* vol. 2, pp. 82–83). Ibn Daud mentions the tragic end of the Exilarch Hezekiah b. David (d. ca. 1058), who was imprisoned and tortured after having been denounced by informers to the authorities. See Abraham Ibn Daud, *The Book of Tradition (Sefer Ha-Qabbalah),* ed. and trans. Gerson D. Cohen (Philadelphia, 1967), p. 44 (Heb. text); p. 61 (Eng. trans.). The great Muslim historian al-Ṭabarī relates the tale of an Exilarch who was put to death by the last Umayyad Caliph Marwān II (ruled 744–50) for having given him a magic mirror which showed him displeasing things. See Ṭabarī, *Annales,*Tertia Series, vol. 1, pp. 165–66. The passage is translated in Ignaz Goldziher, "Notes et mélanges: Renseignement de source musulmane sur la dignité de Resch-Galuta," *REJ* 8 (1884): 123–24. There may be a historical kernel of truth to this obviously legendary account.

[43] Nathan ha-Bavlī, in Neubauer, *Mediaeval Jewish Chronicles,* vol. 2, p. 80.

3

THE BEST YEARS
Mediterranean Jewry in the Islamic High Middle Ages

Medieval Islamic civilization flowered and matured between the years 900 and 1200. At the very time that the empire of the Arabs was fragmenting politically into autonomous and semiautonomous regions, a certain degree of cultural unity was achieved. This was the classical period—"the Renaissance of Islam" (to use Adam Mez's phrase). Commerce flourished; so did arts and letters and the Hellenic sciences. Greek learning had been translated into Arabic and was a profound cultural force. Its influence could be felt in both religious and secular thought. The overall tenor of the age was *laissez faire,* both economically and intellectually. Muslims and non-Muslims all had a share in the general prosperity, for there was plenty to go around. Often, the extreme implications of the *dhimmīs'* status could be conveniently ignored. Sectarian controversies within each of the three religious communities were frequently of more concern than were interfaith disputes.[1]

Islam during this period became a distinctive and refined religious system. In a parallel development, Judaism evolved and crystallized in many respects into the religious civilization we know today. The

[1] The classic portrait of Islamic civilization at this period is Adam Mez, *Die Renaissance des Islams* (Heidelberg, 1922); Eng. trans. Salahuddin Khuda Bakhsh and D. S. Margoliouth, *The Renaissance of Islam* (Patna, 1937). For a survey of the Hellenic corpus received by the Arabs, see Franz Rosenthal, *The Classical Heritage in Islam,* trans. Emile and Jenny Marmorstein (Berkeley and Los Angeles, 1965); Richard Walzer, *Greek into Arabic* (Cambridge, Mass., 1962); and F. E. Peters, *Allah's Commonwealth* (New York, 1973), pp. 266–543.

synagogue service and ritual in general became more standardized through the prayerbooks of Rav ᶜAmram (written ca. 860) and Saᶜadya (written ca. 940). *Halakha,* the framework of law that governs every aspect of Jewish life, was progressively systematized during these centuries through gaonic responsa, talmudic commentaries, and finally near the end of the period, through a growing trend toward codification, of which the first great attempt was Moses Maimonides' *Mishne Torah* (completed in 1180). The classic works of Jewish philosophy beginning with Saᶜadya's *Book of Beliefs and Opinions* (written ca. 936) and culminating in Maimonides' *Guide of the Perplexed* (written in 1190) were composed during this period. Hebrew philology, lexicography, and grammar were all firmly established, laying the foundation not only for such biblical exegesis of high scholarly standards as Abraham b. Ezra's (written between 1140 and 1164), but also for a veritable renascence of the Hebrew language as an artistic medium. The finest Hebrew poets since the Prophets and Psalmists wrote sublime verses whose beauty still stirs the heart today. Probably at no other time in the thirteen hundred years of Jewish history under Islam were the Jews as thoroughly assimilated into the general cultural milieu of the Arabic-speaking world.[2]

The Islamic High Middle Ages witnessed the rise of vibrant and increasingly independent centers of Jewish life outside Iraq in the countries of the Mediterranean Basin. Three principal Jewish communities came into prominence at this time—Egypt, Ifriqiya (modern Tunisia), and Spain. Each of these regions had contained a considerable Jewish population even before this period. It was only at this time, however, that they became clearly visible and historically articulate.

There are several reasons for the new visibility of these Mediterranean communities. Not least among these was the decline of Iraq. For the first century and a half of Abbasid rule, the economic and cultural epicenter of the Islamic world lay in the east. All roads led to Baghdad, and all civilization radiated from it to the peripheries of the empire. Even the early rise of autonomous and semiautonomous provinces (such as Umayyad Spain in 756, Aghlabid Ifriqiya in 800, and Tulunid Egypt in 868) had not really changed this fact of Baghdadi cultural preeminence. But the progressive political strife and civil disorder that plagued Iraq from the late ninth century on did

[2] See the general cultural survey in S. D. Goitein, *Jews and Arabs* (New York, 1974), pp. 125–211; also Abraham S. Halkin, "The Judeo-Islamic Age: The Great Fusion," in *Great Ages and Ideas of the Jewish People,* ed. Leo W. Schwartz (New York, 1956), pp. 213ff.

bring about a perceptible decline in Baghdadi leadership. One of the consequences was a steady flow of people to the west. This population movement resulted in what would be called today a minor "brain drain." Not only intellectuals, but artisans and other talented individuals moved westward into the more stable lands bordering the Mediterranean.[3]

Another factor that contributed to the development of the Mediterranean Jewish communities was the rise in the tenth century of independent caliphates in North Africa and Spain.

IFRIQIYA (TUNISIA)

In 909, the first Shiᶜite counter-caliphate was declared in Ifriqiya by the Fatimid branch of the Ismaᶜili sect. The first ruler, ᶜUbayd Allāh, was proclaimed Mahdī, the Islamic messianic figure, in addition to being the infallible Imām. The new state was dynamic and aggressive. It was clearly bent upon universal domination. It declared its intention before all the world by the symbolic act of establishing its new fortified capital al-Mahdiyya (the city of the Mahdī) on the Tunisian coast. The symbolic declaration was clear. Ever since the age of the Arab conquests, all of the capitals of Muslim territories had been founded inland, usually on the border between the desert and the sown. The early Muslims had for the most part turned their backs on the Mediterranean, which was Baḥr al-Rūm (the Byzantine Sea). The Fatimids now made it into an important Islamic artery of communication and transportation.

The Fatimid Empire began to expand both to the east and west, almost from the moment of its founding. Ifriqiya became "the hub of the Mediterranean," the halfway point on both the Spain-to-Egypt sealane and the trans-African caravan route. Mahdiyya developed into a great commercial depot and a zone of contact with European traders from the city-states of neighboring Italy.[4]

[3] For evidence in the Cairo Geniza documents on this migration, see S. D. Goitein, *Mediterranean Society,* vol. 1 (Berkeley and Los Angeles, 1967), pp. 30 and 400, n. 2.

[4] S. D. Goitein, "La Tunisie du XIe siècle à la lumière des documents de la Geniza du Caire," *Etudes d'Orientalisme dédiées à la mémoire de Lévi-Provençal* (Paris, 1962), pp. 559–79; expanded Eng. trans., "Medieval Tunisia—The Hub of the Mediterranean," in idem, *Studies,* pp. 308–28. See also idem, *Mediterranean Society,* vol. 1, passim.

The Shi^cite faithful, who until now had been forced to keep their beliefs secret, flocked into Ifriqiya. So did many other Muslims and non-Muslims—men of talent and ambition who sensed opportunity awaiting them under the new regime.[5] One such man was Ya^cqūb b. Killis, a Jew recently converted to Islam, who still maintained close ties with his former coreligionists. He was brought to the attention of Caliph al-Mu^cizz by some court Jews. He had already had a varied career. Born in Baghdad, he moved to the Levant, where he became the Representative of the Merchants (*Wakīl al-Tujjār*), which was an important and highly respected office in Ramle. Just before coming to Ifriqiya, he had served the Ikhshidid ruler in Egypt. He soon made himself useful to his new masters by helping to plan the conquest of Egypt, which had been their primary goal for sixty years. When Egypt did indeed fall to the Fatimid general Jawhar in 969, Ibn Killis was sent to reorganize the province, which had sunk into a state of chaos. Together with Jawhar, he prepared Egypt to become the center of the greater Fatimid Empire. He brilliantly revamped the financial structure of the country and instituted a significant reform of the currency.[6] In 973, the Fatimid caliph and his entire court moved into Cairo, the newly constructed seat of government alongside Fustat. The ascendancy of Egypt was about to begin.

The Jews of Ifriqiya had prospered during the sixty years of Fatimid occupation. The heterodox Fatimids showed relatively more tolerance toward their *dhimmī* subjects than had most Islamic rulers. Perhaps this was due in part to the fact that the majority of the Fatimid subjects in North Africa, and later in Egypt, were orthodox Muslims who were by and large unfriendly to their Isma^cili overlords. Furthermore, the Isma^cilis were not bound to the exoteric letter of Islamic law, for they believed that the Koran had an esoteric inner meaning. Finally, because the Imām was infallible, he could act as he chose toward his non-Muslim subjects—or toward any of his subjects for that matter—without any interference from the religious scholars.

The Fatimids did not impose the discriminatory tariffs for *dhimmīs* prescribed by orthodox Muslim law. They appear to have had

[5] Many of these newcomers were looked upon as "carpetbaggers" by the indigenous population. See, for example, Ibn ^cIdhārī, *Kitāb al-Bayān al-Mughrib fī Akhbār al-Andalus wa 'l-Maghrib*, vol. 1, ed. G. S. Colin and E. Lévi-Provençal (Leiden, 1948), pp. 182–83. See also Georges Marçais, *La Berbérie musulmane* (Paris, 1946), pp. 138–42; and n. 3 above.

[6] The career of Ibn Killis is treated at length in Walter J. Fischel, *Jews in the Economic and Political Life of Mediaeval Islam* (New York, 1969), pp. 45–68.

even fewer qualms than most Islamic rulers in employing nonbelievers in the civil service. Jewish merchants prospered in the generally liberal economic atmosphere of this free-trade zone. North African businessmen (some of whom had originally come from the Middle East) dominated the trade of the Islamic Mediterranean area, and after the Fatimid conquest of Egypt, they assumed the leading role in the trade with India as well. These enterprising merchants continued to play a major role along the Spain-to-India trade route for centuries. Many of them settled in Egypt, which had become the new center of gravity after 969, while maintaining offices in Ifriqiya.[7] Still more transferred to Egypt in the wake of the devastating Bedouin invasions that overwhelmed Ifriqiya between 1050 and 1057.

The combined factors of general prosperity and official tolerance toward non-Muslims in Fatimid Ifriqiya provided a salubrious climate for the growth and development of a strong and vital Jewish community. The largest concentration of Jews was in Qayrawan, the traditional capital of the province and leading city in all the Maghreb. Throughout the greater part of the tenth and eleventh centuries, the Jewish community of Qayrawan was the outstanding major spiritual and intellectual center of Jewry outside of Iraq. The "sages of Qayrawan" were noted in Hebrew literature for both their religious and secular learning.[8] In the latter category, certainly the most famous figure was the physician and neoplatonic philosopher Isaac Israeli (d. 950). His Arabic works were translated into Hebrew and Latin and were studied for centuries in medieval and renaissance Europe, where he was dubbed the *eximius monarcha medicinae*.[9] Isaac's pupil Abū Sahl Dūnash b. Tamīm (d. ca. 960), also a physician and philosopher of note, earned himself a reputation in the field of Hebrew grammar and philology and was the author of a commentary on the popular mystical treatise *Sēfer ha-Yeṣīra* (The Book of Creation).[10]

[7] For a detailed portrait of one such merchant house, see N. A. Stillman, "The Eleventh-Century Merchant House of Ibn ᶜAwkal (A Geniza Study)," *JESHO* 16, pt. 1 (1973): 15–88.

[8] The pioneer study on the sages of Qayrawan that though outdated has never been superseded is Samuel Poznanski, "Anshē Qayrawān," *Festschrift zu Ehren des Dr. A. Harkavy* (St. Petersburg, 1908), pp. 175–220. Many of the interstices in Poznanski's work are filled in by H. Z. [J. W.] Hirschberg, *A History of the Jews in North Africa*, vol. 1 (Leiden, 1974), pp. 298–361. However, for caveats that must be kept in mind when using Hirschberg's book, see N. A. Stillman, "Recent North African Studies in Israel: A Review Article," *IJMES* 8, no. 3 (July, 1977): 406–7.

[9] Alexander Altmann and S. M. Stern, *Isaac Israeli: A Neo-Platonic Philosopher of the Early Eleventh Century* (London, 1958).

[10] Georges Vajda, *Introduction à la pensée juive du Moyen Age* (Paris,

The Jewish community of Qayrawan took the greatest pride in its religious scholarship. The city boasted two *yeshivot.* One of these schools was founded in the late tenth century by a scholar of Persian extraction, R. Jacob b. Nissīm Ibn Shāhīn (d. 1006/7). Throughout the first half of the eleventh century the institution was headed by his son Nissīm b. Jacob (d. 1062). Both father and son were correspondents of the Babylonian *geonim.* It was in answer to a series of questions from R. Jacob that Sherira Gaon wrote his famous "Epistle," which is one of the major sources for the history of the Babylonian gaonate. R. Nissīm was probably the greatest of the "sages of Qayrawan." Among his many works are a very important commentary on the Talmud and a book of didactic and entertaining tales entitled *The Book of Comfort.*[11]

Qayrawan's other institution of higher learning was the *yeshiva* of Ḥushiel b. Elḥanan (d. early eleventh century), an Italian scholar who had come to North Africa during the eleventh century and introduced new approaches to the study of *halakha.* R. Ḥushiel's son and successor, R. Ḥananel (d. 1057), was one of the most celebrated medieval Jewish scholars. He is best known for his commentary on the entire Babylonian Talmud, which enjoyed wide circulation throughout Europe during the Middle Ages but has survived only in part down to the present.[12]

The Jews of Qayrawan possessed a strong, hierarchal communal organization that they patterned after that of Baghdad. The Iraqi scholar Nathan ha-Bavlī, who settled in Qayrawan sometime after 950, wrote his account of Baghdadi Jewry at the request of the Qayrawanese who were looking to the Babylonian model of self-government. The Jews of Qayrawan were not seeking to break away from the diocesan authority of Baghdad as has been suggested by Baron,[13] but rather they were seeking to adopt a suitably sophisticated structure for their com-

---

1947), pp. 68–70; Poznanski, "Anshē Qayrawān," p. 190; Hirschberg, *The Jews in North Africa,* vol. 1, pp. 101, 151, and 309.

[11] Hirschberg, *The Jews in North Africa,* vol. 1, pp. 327–39. The text of *The Book of Comfort* has been edited by Julian Obermann, *Studies in Islam and Judaism: The Arabic Original of Ibn Shahin's Book of Comfort* (New Haven, 1933), and it has recently been translated by William M. Brinner, *An Elegant Composition Concerning Relief after Adversity* (New Haven, 1977).

[12] Hirschberg, *A History of the Jews in North Africa,* vol. 1 (Leiden, 1974), pp. 322–24; Poznanski, "Anshē Qayrawān," pp. 194–98.

[13] Salo Wittmayer Baron, *A Social and Religious History of the Jews,* vol. 6 (New York and Philadelphia, 1958), pp. 213–14. See also ibid., vol. 5, pp. 39–40.

munity, which had evolved rapidly and was no longer a provincial backwater.

The recognized head of the Jewish community before the Muslim authorities was usually some distinguished citizen who also served at the court in some capacity. Until the early eleventh century, this function was probably filled by the official who was known as the *rōsh ha-qehillōt,* or head of the congregations (that is, of Fatimid North Africa). This honorific title was borne by individuals in the Levant and apparently signified different offices at various times and in various places.[14] In 1015, the leader of Tunisian Jewry, Ibrāhīm b. ᶜAṭā', who was court physician to the Zirid governors Bādis and al-Muᶜizz, and who was himself the son of a *rōsh ha-qehillōt,* had the illustrious title of Negīd ha-Gōla (Prince of the Diaspora or *nāgīd*) conferred upon him by Hay Gaon in recognition of his outstanding services both to his community and to the Pumbedītha Academy. Ibn ᶜAṭā' was, in the parlance of modern fundraisers, "a big giver" to Jewish causes in general.[15] The title of *nāgīd* was borne by the successive heads of Tunisian Jewry throughout most of the eleventh century.[16]

EGYPT

The closest ties bound the Jewish communities of Ifriqiya and Egypt after 969. The two Jewries were now part of the same empire. As mentioned above, many North African Jews, and Near Easterners who had only recently settled in North Africa, came to Egypt with the Fatimids. These emigrants usually remained in close contact with friends, relatives, and business associates in Ifriqiya. S. D. Goitein has noted that at this time "a large part, if not the majority of the Jews in

[14] On the various uses of this title, see Goitein, *Mediterranean Society,* vol. 2, pp. 75–77.

[15] Ibn ᶜAṭā' appears as one of the two biggest givers on a list of contributors to the Babylonian Academies from sometime between 1007 and 1013. See Goitein, "The Qayrawan United Appeal for the Babylonian Yeshivoth and the Emergence of the Nagid Abraham Ben-ᶜAta'," *Zion* 27, nos. 3–4 (1962): 156–65, especially 160–61.

[16] The most thorough treatment of the subject of the office of the *nāgīd* and its origins is in Goitein, *Mediterranean Society,* vol. 2, pp. 23–40. Goitein's study renders obsolete all the earlier theories entertained by historians. A Geniza letter mentioning the appointment of Ibn ᶜAṭā' as the first *nāgīd* is translated in Part Two below, pp. 183–85.

Egypt, were immigrants or the descendants of such."[17] Many merchants commuted back and forth quite frequently between Fustat-Cairo and Qayrawan-Mahdiyya, traveling in the spring and autumn by ship and in the winter and summer by caravan.

The two Jewries maintained important administrative ties. Fustat and Qayrawan were connecting links in the chain of communication that bound the Jewish communities of the entire western Islamic world with the spiritual centers in Palestine and Iraq. The ties between Fustat and Qayrawan went beyond those of family, business, and matters connected with the gaonic academies. There were also intellectual ties. Scholars in both cities corresponded with one another. R. Ḥushiel, for example, exchanged letters with R. Shemarya b. Elḥanan (d. 1011), the founder of a *yeshiva* in Fustat and the religious leader of Egyptian Jewry.[18]

The Egyptian Jewish community quickly outstripped its North African counterpart during the eleventh century in size, wealth, and political influence, although not in scholarship. The transferal of the Fatimid court to Cairo marked the beginning of the eclipse of Ifriqiya, which gradually was slipping back into provinciality for a variety of reasons, technological as well as geopolitical. The devastating Bedouin invasions of the mid-eleventh century only hastened the process of decline.

We know more about Egyptian Jewish society at this time than we do about any other Jewish community of the Middle Ages, whether in Christian Europe or the Muslim world, thanks to the fortuitous discovery of an enormous cache of documents in a Fustat synagogue at the end of the nineteenth century. These are the so-called Cairo Geniza documents. This vast collection of letters, business accounts, legal documents, and all sorts of public and private records, as well as literary works, originated not only in Egypt, but from all over the lands of the Mediterranean and along the route to India. It is Egyptian society, however, that is reflected in the greatest detail.[19]

Egypt had a very sizable Jewish population during the eleventh

[17] Goitein, "Jewish Society and Institutions under Islam," in *Jewish Society Through the Ages,* ed. H. H. Ben Sasson and S. Ettinger (New York, 1971), p. 174.

[18] A letter from R. Ḥushiel replying to R. Shemarya has been preserved in the Cairo Geniza. See Solomon Schechter, "Geniza Specimens: A Letter of Chushiel," *JQR* 11 (1899): 643–50.

[19] The story of the Geniza's discovery is told in Goitein, *Mediterranean Society,* vol. 1, pp. 1–28, where a full introduction is given. See also Norman Golb, "Sixty Years of Genizah Research," *Judaism* 6 (1957): 3–16.

and twelfth centuries. Over ninety cities, towns, villages, and hamlets with Jewish inhabitants are known.[20] Fustat had a Rabbanite Jewish community numbering some 3,600 souls.[21] In addition, there were the much smaller Karaite community and a small congregation in nearby Cairo, bringing the total Jewish population in the capital to well over 4,000.

The Jews of Egypt in the first hundred years of Fatimid rule had no national official recognized by the government as the chief authority and representative of the entire Jewish community comparable to the *nāgīd* in Ifriqiya. For, when the Fatimids took Palestine shortly after conquering Egypt, they recognized the head of the Tiberian Academy, which was now located in Ramle, the capital of the province, as the highest Jewish authority in their realm; however, they in no way hindered Jews of the Babylonian rite from seeking the spiritual guidance of their own *geonim* in Iraq.

The highest Jewish legal authority in Egypt was a representative of the Palestinian Academy, who was called the *rāv rōsh,* or chief scholar. The first holder of this office was a *ḥāvēr,* or fellow, of the Palestinian Academy by the name of Ephraim about whom almost nothing is known.[22] Throughout the first quarter of the eleventh century, the position of *rāv rōsh* was occupied successively by a father and son, Shemarya b. Elḥanan, who has already been mentioned, and Elḥanan b. Shemarya (d. ca. 1025).[23] After R. Elḥanan's death, it

[20] See Norman Golb, "The Topography of the Jews of Medieval Egypt," *JNES* 24 (1965): 251–70, and *JNES* 33 (1974): 116–48.

[21] This estimate is based on a list of welfare recipients from around the year 1026, which indicates that there were approximately 350 households on the Rabbanite communal rolls (TS 24.76). Using Goitein's ratio of one donor for every four welfare recipients, as well as his estimate of 2.5 persons per well-to-do family, we come to a figure of around 3,660 souls for the entire Rabbanite population. See Goitein, *Mediterranean Society,* vol. 2, pp. 139–40, 438–39, and 469, Table 1. Ashtor's estimate of only 1,500 is valid for the period after 1201–2, when the Jewish community had been decimated by plague and famine. See Eliyahu Ashtor, "Prolegomena to the Medieval History of Oriental Jewry," *JQR* n.s. 50 (1959): 56–57; and also idem., "Some Features of the Jewish Communities in Medieval Egypt," *Zion* 30, nos. 1–2 (1965): 63–64 [Heb.], where Ashtor argues the validity of his calculations for this earlier period as well.

[22] He is mentioned in a single Geniza manuscript, TS 20.96. Even the name of his father is not yet known.

[23] For more data on these men, see the index in Jacob Mann, *The Jews in Egypt and in Palestine under the Fātimid Caliphs,* 2 vols. in one, with Preface and Reader's Guide by S. D. Goitein (New York, 1970); Shraga Abramson, *Ba-Merkāzīm uva-Tefūṣōṭ bitqūfat ha-Ge'ōnīm* (Jerusalem, 1965) pp. 105–73; S. D. Goitein, "Shemarya b. Elḥanan: With Two New Auto-

seems that the *rāv rōsh*'s office fell into desuetude and that the chief *dayyānīm* (judges) of the Palestinian Jews acted as communal leaders for all the Rabbanites of Egypt. It was not until around 1065 that there finally appeared an officially recognized Jewish leader for all of Egypt. The formal Arabic title of this dignitary was *ra'īs al-Yahūd* (head of the Jews). In Hebrew he was referred to as *nāgīd*. This new post arose in the last third of the eleventh century, when the Palestinian gaonate was on the wane, weakened by internal rivalries. The loss of Palestine to the Seljuq Turks in 1071, together with other factors, caused the Fatimids to turn increasingly inward and Egyptocentric. Thus, a Jewish community under local leadership was desirable from the point of view of Fatimid policy. Independence from the Palestinian gaonate also must have looked attractive to the Jews of Egypt, for the prestige of the institution had been seriously tarnished by unseemly and highly divisive squabbles. The gaonate lost even more of its aura of venerability when it went into exile outside of the Holy Land, first in Tyre and later in Damascus.[24]

The function of the *ra'īs al-Yahūd* seems to have evolved slowly over the next two centuries until finally his powers and responsibilities were well defined in the administrative handbooks of the Mamluk Period (1250–1517).[25] Mark R. Cohen has hypothesized that the office of the *ra'īs al-Yahūd* developed along parallel lines with changes in the Coptic patriarchate at that time. In Cohen's view, the recognition extended the *ra'īs al-Yahūd* by the government probably came as part of a conscious policy of centralization instituted by Egyptian strongman Badr al-Jamālī, who was vizier from 1074 to 1094.[26] This hypothesis makes good sense. Unfortunately, the details of the development of the headship of the Jews are still not altogether clear.

Like so many of the top echelon communal offices in the medieval Islamic world, the position of *ra'īs al-Yahūd* tended from its inception to be dominated by a single family. Three of the first four occupants of the office were members of a family of court physicians—Judah b.

---

graphs," *Tarbiz* 32, no. 3 (1963): 266–72; idem, "Elḥanan b. Shemarya as Communal Leader," *Joshua Finkel Jubilee Volume* (New York, 1973).

[24] Goitein, *Mediterranean Society*, vol. 2, pp. 23–30. See also Mark Robert Cohen, *The Origins of the Office of Head of the Jews ("Ra'īs al-Yahūd") in the Fatimid Empire: The Period of the House of Mevorakh b. Saadya, ca. 1064 to 1126*, unpublished doctoral dissertation (New York, Jewish Theological Seminary of America, 1976).

[25] An example of a charge of office given a Ra'īs al-Yahūd by the Mamluk authorities is translated in Part Two below, pp. 269–70.

[26] Cohen, *Head of the Jews*, pp. 110–39.

Sa^cadya (ca. 1064–78), Mevorakh b. Sa^cadya (ca. 1078–82 and 1094–1114), and Moses b. Mevorakh (1112–ca. 1126). Their sixty-year rule was interrupted for a little over a decade between 1082 and 1094, when David b. Daniel, an ambitious member of the House of David and a disappointed aspirant to the Palestinian gaonate, was able to usurp the headship of the Jews for himself. From the late twelfth to the early fifteenth centuries, the position was handed down in dynastic succession from the great Moses Maimonides to his descendants.

Many of the Jewish communal officials in Egypt were connected in some way or other with government. The Fatimids and their successors, the Ayyubids (1171–1250), employed *dhimmīs* in their administrations far beyond their proportion in the general population. Not a few non-Muslims even made it into the ranks of the royal entourage and were thus known as *aṣḥāb al-khila*^c, or "those who wear the robes of honor."[27] One should not attribute the large number of *dhimmīs* in government service merely to benign tolerance of the rulers or to the faculty of overcompensation frequently exhibited by members of a minority, although these were factors to be sure. Careers in government, which were fraught with danger, were not that attractive to the majority of people, and since the economy was booming there were ample opportunities, as well as physical security, in the thriving marketplace. Furthermore, the prevalent attitude toward government service among many pious Muslims at this time was decidedly negative, an attitude not shared by Jews.[28] In spite of all this, the overwhelming majority of government personnel were still Muslims and not Jews or Christians. Naturally, the highest offices of the realm such as the vizierate of state were normally reserved for Believers. There are two or three notable exceptions of Christians who wielded the power of a vizier, sometimes bearing the title and sometimes not. Those individuals of Jewish birth who achieved this exalted office, such as Ya^cqūb b. Killis, Ḥasan b. Ibrāhīm al-Tustarī, and Ṣadaqa b. Yūsuf al-Fallāḥī, had all converted to Islam prior to their appointment.[29]

[27] On "robes of honor," see N. A. Stillman, "Khil^ca," *EI*² 5:6–7. For more on Jewish courtiers, see Goitein, *Mediterranean Society*, vol. 2, pp. 345–54; also Fischel, *Jews*, pp. ix–xvi.

[28] See Goitein, *Studies in Islamic History and Institutions* (Leiden, 1966), pp. 197–213, where the attitudes toward government in Islam and Judaism are compared.

[29] For sources on the career of Ibn Killis, see n. 6 above; for Ḥasan al-Tustarī, see Ibn Muyassar, *Ta'rīkh Miṣr* [*Annales d'Egypte*], ed. Henri Massé (Cairo, 1919), p. 32; for Ibn al-Fallāḥī, see al-Suyūṭī *Husn al-'Muḥāḍara fī Akhbār Miṣr wa 'l-Qāhira,* vol. 2 (Cairo, 1968), p. 201.

The one Jewish courtier who did scale the pinnacles of power in Fatimid Egypt during the thirties and forties of the eleventh century was the merchant prince and purveyor to the court Abū Saᶜd Ibrāhīm al-Tustarī.[30] He became a power behind the throne when his former Sudanese slave girl, whom he had sold to the palace harem, became Queen Mother and acting regent for her son al-Mustanṣir, who succeeded to the caliphate in 1036 while still a small boy. The Queen Mother relied upon her onetime master as her confidant and most trusted agent. Abū Saᶜd had the power to make and break viziers—a power that in fact he exercised. Abū Saᶜd's violent end in 1047 was a rather typical denouement for the career of a man in high government office at that time, be he Jew, Christian, or Muslim. Still, part of the agitation that finally brought him down pandered to anti-Jewish sentiments. Some popular verses of anti-Jewish satire that were disseminated prior to Abū Saᶜd's downfall ran as follows:

> The Jews of this time have attained
>   their utmost hopes and have come to rule.
> Honor is theirs, wealth is theirs too,
>   and from them come the counsellor and ruler.
> People of Egypt, I have good advice
>   for you—Turn Jew, for Heaven itself
>   has become Jewish![31]

These lines were favorites with writers who wished to point out that a Jew had risen too high and his coreligionists were becoming "uppity."[32]

There is no doubt that non-Muslims in government frequently extended patronage in a variety of ways to members of their own confession. Their dignity and status made them pillars of their own congrega-

30 Abū Saᶜd's career is traced in detail in Fischel, *Jews*, pp. 68–89.

31 Ibn Muyassar, *Ta'rīkh Miṣr*, pp. 61–62; al-Suyūṭī, *Ḥusn al-Muḥāḍara*, vol. 2, p. 201. Goitein, *Mediterranean Society*, vol. 2, p. 374, has shown that the last verse may contain a punning allusion to Abu Saᶜd.

32 The Persian historian al-Waṣṣāf also cites these verses when referring to the Saᶜd al-Dawla, the Jewish physician and vizier of the Mongol Il-Khān Arghūn (*Ta'rīkh-i Waṣṣāf* British Museum Add. 23517, f. 202a), cited in Fischel, *Jews*, p. 111. Al-Waṣṣāf, however, has an additional verse:

> Yet wait and you shall hear
> their torments cry
> And see them fall and
> perish presently

(after the translation in Fischel).

tions. Many court Jews in Fatimid and Ayyubid Egypt served in communal posts as well. Even when they did not hold any official positions within the Jewish community, they used their influence and good offices in the circles of power to aid and protect their coreligionists. Jewish courtiers were eulogized as defenders of their people from "enemies, foes, ill-wishers, accusers, and calumniators."[33]

There are many letters in the Geniza that were written to courtiers seeking their intercession with the authorities on behalf of an individual or an entire community. In one pathetic letter, a poor, sick fugitive from the poll-tax collector beseeches a Jewish official in some branch of government service to use his influence to get him temporarily listed as a missing person.[34] In another letter, the Jews of Tripoli, Lebanon, petition Abū Naṣr Faḍl (Ḥesed) al-Tustarī, the brother of Abū Saᶜd, to help them obtain government permission to rebuild their synagogue, which had been destroyed during the anti-*dhimmī* persecutions of the mad caliph al-Ḥākim (1007–21).[35] The Tustaris were Karaites, but possessed a stronge sense of Jewish communal feeling, and came to the aid of Rabbanites as well as Karaites. Even the *geonim* of Palestine and Iraq were wont to correspond with them on matters pertaining to the Jewish commonweal.[36] The Tustaris are praised frequently in the Geniza for their efforts on behalf of their fellow Jews. This sort of *esprit de corps,* which ignored sectarian lines, was typical of Egypt but all too rare in other countries of Jewish settlement.[37]

The Jewish community of Egypt in the High Middle Ages was affluent, influential, and on the whole stable and secure. It was well organized. In short, it was bourgeois but not particularly creative in the spiritual or intellectual spheres. The Jews of Egypt were pious and hardworking, and they took care of the less fortunate among them through admirable social services.[38] They were generous in supporting

[33] Mann, *Jews,* vol. 2, pp. 11–12.

[34] Translated in Part Two below, p. 194.

[35] Translated in Part Two below, p. 204.

[36] Correspondence with Solomon b. Judah: Mann, *Jews,* vol. 2, p. 78; with Hay Gaon: idem, *Texts and Studies in Jewish History and Literature,* vol. 1, with an Introduction by Gerson D. Cohen (New York, 1972), p. 118.

[37] For other examples of this kind of cooperation between members of the two sects in Egypt, see Goitein, *Mediterranean Society,* vol. 2, pp. 53–54, 96, 110, 299. On the other hand, the Karaites and Rabbanites in Palestine were frequently at loggerheads. See, for example, the document pertaining to a sectarian dispute in the Holy Land, translated below, p. 198. For the persecution of Karaites by Rabbanites in Spain, see N. A. Stillman, "Aspects of Jewish Life in Islamic Spain," in Paul E. Szarmach, ed., *Aspects of Jewish Culture in the Middle Ages* (Albany, 1979), p. 66 and the sources cited there.

[38] On the charitable institutions of Egyptian Jewry, see Goitein, *Mediter-*

Jewish institutions at home and in the spiritual centers of Palestine and Iraq. There were some men of learning among them, none truly outstanding, and even some of these had come from elsewhere. It is true that the greatest Jewish mind of the entire Middle Ages, Moses Maimonides, spent over half his life—and the most productive part, at that—in Egypt between 1168 and 1204. However, he arrived there a grown man and a scholar of some renown, the product of the most unique Jewish community of the Middle Ages—the Jewish community of Islamic Spain.

SPAIN

No medieval civilization has captured the imagination of Westerners more than that of Moorish Spain. Even in medieval Christian Europe the very name of Cordova evoked visions of dazzling splendor. The German nun Hroswitha (ca. 940–ca. 1002) from her cell in the abbey at Gandersheim described the Moorish capital as "a fair ornament . . . illustrious because of its charms and also renowned for all resources."[39] Washington Irving's popular book *The Alhambra* (published in 1832) only fed the fire of Andalusian romanticism.

The German Jewish historians of the nineteenth century, such as Heinrich Graetz, Leopold Zunz, and Moritz Steinschneider, who pioneered in the field of modern Judaic Studies, or as they called it *Die Wissenschaft des Judentums* (The Science of Judaism), were also brought under Spain's enchanted spell. As intellectual historians they were particularly impressed by the rich and original literature in Hebrew poetry and Judeo-Arabic philosophy created by Spanish Jews. Henceforth, it became commonplace to refer to the Golden Age of Spain, a notion borrowed from classical literary history. The scholars of the *Wissenschaft des Judentums* school were also struck by Andalusian Jewry's high degree of cultural assimilation—a consum-

---

ranean Society, vol. 2, pp. 91–143. Compare N. A. Stillman, "Charity and Social Service in Medieval Islam," *Societas* 5, no. 2 (Spring 1975): 105–15. On the sober and rather jejune religiosity of Egyptian Jews at this period, see Goitein, "Religion in Everyday Life as Reflected in the Documents of the Cairo Geniza," in *Religion in a Religious Age,* ed. S. D. Goitein (Cambridge, Mass., 1974), pp. 3–17.

39 Hroswitha, *The Passion of Saint Pelagius,* vss. 12–18, cited in Von Grunebaum, *Medieval Islam: A Study in Cultural Orientation,* 2d ed. (Chicago, 1962), p. 57.

mation they devoutly wished for European Jewry in their own day.[40] They pointed with pride to the part played by Spanish and Provençal Jews in the translation process, which brought the fruits of medieval Islamic Hellenism into Europe.[41] Finally, they were impressed by the important and conspicuous role played by some Jewish individuals in the political life of Muslim Spain.

The Arabs called Spain al-Andalus. It was an isolated provincial enclave on the western frontier of the Islamic world with no distinctive culture of its own until the tenth century. Its demography was more heterogeneous than anywhere else in the Dār al-Islām. The Arabs themselves formed only a small minority of the population, which included Berbers, Muslims of native Spanish stock who were called Muwallads, Mozarabic Christians, Slavs who were brought in large numbers as military slaves, Blacks who were also imported as slaves, and, of course, Jews.

The Jews were a relatively small group in this ethnic mix. Eliyahu Ashtor has estimated that they were probably never more than a little over half a percent of the total Iberian population. However, they formed a considerable segment of the urban populace—overall, about 6 to 10 percent, and in some towns and cities as much as 15 to 20 percent.[42] It was also in the major urban centers of the southern half of the peninsula that the Arabs were settled, and it was there that Hispano-Arabic culture developed.

The Jews kept a relatively low profile during the first two hundred years of Arab rule, for although they had actively collaborated with the Muslim invaders of Visigothic Spain, they simply became part of the subject population when the province was organized under caliphal authority and integrated into the Islamic legal and social system.

Like Ifriqiya and Egypt, Spain embarked upon a course of national assertion and self-realization in the tenth century. This period began with the declaration of an independent caliphate by the Umayyad

[40] Cf. for example Heinrich Graetz, *History of the Jews,* vol. 3 (Philadelphia, 1946), p. 41: "The Jewish inhabitants of this happy peninsula [Iberia] contributed by their hearty interest to the greatness of the country, which they loved as only a fatherland can be loved"; and again, ibid., p. 235: "The cultured Jews of Andalusia spoke and wrote the language of the country as fluently as their Arab fellow-citizens, who were as proud of the Jewish poets as the Jews themselves."

[41] The classic work on this subject is still Moritz Steinschneider, *Die hebraïschen Übersetzungen des Mittelalters und die Juden als Dolmetscher* (Berlin, 1893).

[42] Eliyahu Ashtor, "The Number of the Jews in Moslem Spain," *Zion* 28 (1963): 34–56, conclusions on pp. 55–56 [Heb.].

prince ᶜAbd al-Raḥmān III in 929. It is during his reign that we see the sudden development of a flourishing, creative, and highly independent Jewish community in Spain.

This sudden efflorescence of Andalusian Jewry was in no small measure linked to the rise of a remarkable physician, diplomat, and statesman, Ḥasday b. Shaprūṭ (905–75). He was a court physician and trusted adviser to the caliphs ᶜAbd al-Raḥmān III and al-Ḥakam II (961–76). On several occasions Ḥasday was charged with delicate diplomatic negotiations with the Christian kingdoms of the North and with the Byzantine Empire.

Because of his position as the leading Jewish courtier in the caliphate, Ḥasday acted as the secular head of the Spanish Jewish community. According to Jewish sources, he bore the princely Hebrew title of *nāsī*.[43] As was customary for a courtier or man of rank (wealth in such cases is a corollary), Ḥasday was a patron of the arts and sciences. As the leading Jew of al-Andalus, he naturally felt it his duty to be Maecenas to his own brethren. His personal secretary, Menaḥem b. Sarūq was a poet, philologist, and author of the first Hebrew-Hebrew dictionary.[44] Under Ḥasday's patronage the North African-born poet Dūnash b. Labrāṭ, Menaḥem's rival, pioneered in the composition of Hebrew poetry employing Arabic metrics. Dūnash's innovation set the trend that was to become standard for medieval Andalusian Hebrew poetry.[45]

Ḥasday's tenure as *nāsī* marks a turning point in the communal as well as cultural history of Andalusian Jewry. Under his leadership the Jewish community of Spain made a decisive break from the authority of the Babylonian academies. The twelfth-century chronicler and

[43] Ibn Daud, *The Book of Tradition (Sēfer ha-Qabbalah)*, ed. and trans. Gerson D. Cohen (Philadelphia, 1967), p. 49 (Heb. text); p. 67 (Eng. trans.). This title did not indicate Davidic descent as it did in the Middle East at that time. Concerning the *nāsīs* of the House of David, see Goitein, *Mediterranean Society*, vol. 2, p. 19.

[44] This dictionary is usually referred to as *Ha-Maḥberet* (The Composition Book) although its original title was probably *Sēfer Pitrōnīm* (The Book of Solutions). It is edited by Z. H. Filipowski, *Antiquissimum Linguae Hebraicae et Chaldaicae Lexicon a Menahem Ben Saruk* (London, 1854).

[45] The best introductions to Andalusian Hebrew prosody are: A. Mirsky, "ᶜArkhē ha-Shīrā hā-ᶜIvrīt bi-Sfārād," in *The Spanish Heritage*, vol. 1, ed. Richard Bennet (New York, 1971), pp. 186–268; Jefim Schirmann, *ha-Shīrā hā-ᶜIvrīt bi-Sfārād uve-Prōvāns*, vol. 1 (Jerusalem and Tel Aviv, 1960–61), pp. xxiii-lv; and ibid., vol. 4, pp. 701–37. See also Shalom Spiegel, "On Medieval Hebrew Poetry," in *The Jews: Their History, Religion, and Culture*, vol. 2, ed. Louis Finkelstein (Philadelphia, 1949), pp. 528–66, which however deals mainly with themes and includes the poetry from other lands as well.

apologist Abraham b. Daud attributes this secession to the fortuitous arrival in Cordova of the Italian scholar R. Moses b. Ḥanokh as the prisoner of Spanish pirates in 972. According to Ibn Daud, R. Moses was redeemed and soon recognized because of his great erudition as the *rāv rōsh* of the Spanish Caliphate. He established his own *yeshiva* in Cordova and began to issue responsa for all legal and ritual queries.[46]

R. Moses is one of Ibn Daud's four scholarly captives, three of whom are supposed to have established new independent schools, each in a different Mediterranean land. The story has been deliberately cloaked in romance in order to show the hand of Divine Providence in Jewish history.[47] However, it is clear from a careful assessment of Jewish and non-Jewish sources that the moving force behind this break with the gaonic authorities was none other than Ḥasday himself.

Ḥasday, it would seem, had a grand vision of Spain as a leading seat of world Jewry. He carried on an extensive correspondence with foreign Jewish communities. He imported Hebrew books and attracted foreign scholars to Spain. The rise of R. Moses b. Ḥanokh as chief scholar and the ensuing break with Iraq were clearly part and parcel of Ḥasday's program for an independent Andalusian Jewry. This is confirmed by the Muslim writer Ṣāᶜid al-Andalusī and from geonic correspondence preserved in the Geniza.[48]

Andalusian Jewry remained under the secular leadership of a *nāsī* and the religious authority of a *rāv rōsh* until the collapse of the Cordova Caliphate in 1009, when Islamic Spain was divided into the numerous principalities of the so-called Party Kings (that is, Arab, Berber, Slav, and so forth). The Jewish community was now as fragmented as was the entire body politic. Many people were uprooted, and there was a good deal of movement from place to place. For a time the Jewish community, like Andalusian society, remained in a state of flux.

[46] See p. 55, n. 43 above (G. Cohen, Eng. trans., p. 64f.).

[47] The aim of Ibn Daud has been discussed at length by Gerson D. Cohen, "The Story of the Four Captives," *PAAJR* 29 (1960–61): 55–131.

[48] The passage from Ṣāᶜid al-Andalusī is translated below in Part Two, p. 210. The Geniza letter in question is from Hay Gaon to R. Jacob b. Nissīm in Qayrawan. In it Hay complains that R. Ḥanokh b. Moses, the son and successor of R. Moses b. Ḥanokh, had ignored the correspondence sent to him by Hay's father, Sherira Gaon. See TS 20.100, 11.23–25, ed. in Mann, *Texts,* vol. 1, p. 121. I have presented a more detailed analysis of Ḥasday and his role in the break with Babylon in my essay "Aspects of Jewish Life in Islamic Spain," in *Aspects of Jewish Culture in the Middle Ages,* ed. Paul E. Szarmach (Albany, 1979), pp. 57–62. For the most detailed biography of Ḥasday, see Ashtor, *The Jews of Moslem Spain,* vol. 1, pp. 155–227.

The loss of political unity did not signal a cultural decline. On the contrary, Andalusian civilization flowered during the period of the Party Kings (1009–90). Each court tried to the best of its ability to recreate in miniature the splendor of Cordova. Men of diverse talents were drawn into the service of local rulers. The political, ethnic, and social fragmentation of Andalusian society offered Jews an extraordinary opportunity for government service, and there arose a relatively significant class of Jewish courtiers. These men were not merely the usual physicians, purveyors, clerks, and petty bureaucrats found in other Islamic countries at the time. They also included such high-ranking administrators as Yequtiel b. Ḥasan (d. 1039) in Saragossa and Abraham b. Muhājir (d. ca. 1100) in Seville. The attainment of rank and political power were an express part of the Jewish upper-class ethos.[49]

No office, except that of the ruler, seemed out of the reach of a talented and ambitious Jew. In the Berber kingdom of Granada, the viziership of state was held by the Jew Samuel b. Naghrēla for over three decades until his death in 1056. Because of his exalted political station, Samuel was unquestionably the highest ranking Jewish courtier in all of Spain. In recognition of his special status, he took on the title of *nāgīd* around the year 1027. It was probably bestowed upon him by Hay Gaon, who, it will be recalled, bestowed the honor upon Ibrāhīm b. ᶜAṭā' in Ifriqiya a dozen years earlier. However, this is nowhere documented. It may even be that Samuel b. Naghrēla arrogated the title for himself, for he never suffered from false modesty. In one of his poetical meditations he asks himself, "Are you capable of properly praising God?" He at once replies, "I am the David of my generation."[50]

Samuel ha-Nagid was the quintessential representative of the Andalusian Jewish courtier. He was a soldier and politician, an outstanding talmudic scholar, a patron of the arts, and was himself one of the four greatest masters of medieval Hebrew poetry. His personality

[49] Gerson Cohen has suggested that perhaps the Jewish courtiers had visions of a surrogate messianic age in al-Andalus, which they might bring about by political domination. See his comments in his edition of Ibn Daud, *Sefer ha-Qabbalah*, pp. 278–89. However, see my caveats in "Aspects of Jewish Life in Islamic Spain," pp. 64–65.

[50] Samuel ha-Nagid, *Divan Shmuel Hanagid*, ed. Dov Jarden (Jerusalem, 1956), p. 33, vs. 38; also in Schirmann, *ha-Shīrā hā-ᶜIvrīt*, vol. 1, p. 111. For a succinct biography of the Nagid, see Schirmann, "Samuel Hannagid, the Man, the Soldier, the Politician," *Jewish Social Studies* 13, no. 2 (April 1951): 99–126.

was a perfect blend of the tripartite pride in the purity of language, lineage, and religion that characterized the Jewish and the Arab upper classes.

The upper echelon of Andalusian Jewish society exhibited a marked sense of elitism—not only with regard to their fellow Jews in Spain, but with regard to their coreligionists abroad. The poet and critic Moses b. Ezra (d. after 1135) unabashedly declares that the reason for the superiority of Hebrew *belles lettres* in Spain over anywhere else in the Diaspora is due to the fact that the Andalusian Jews were none other than the descendants of the people of Jerusalem who surpassed all other Israelites "in the purity of language and the tradition of legal science."[51]

The importance of this linguistic pride cannot be overemphasized. Ever since the rise of Islam, the Arabs had considered their poetry and rhetoric to be their greatest cultural heritage. This notion was so ingrained in Islamic society, and in Spain the Jews had assimilated these cultural values to such a degree, that even a Jew like Moses b. Ezra could write:

Because the Arab tribes excelled in their eloquence and rhetoric, they were able to extend their dominion over many languages and to overcome many nations, forcing them to accept their suzerainty.[52]

The flowering of Hebrew poetry in Spain must be understood as an emphatic assertion of Jewish secular or national culture's equality with the Arabic. The poet and translator Judah al-Ḥarīzī (d. ca. 1235) states quite candidly that he composed his *Taḥkemōnī,* which is patterned after the highly esteemed *Maqāmāt* of al-Ḥarīzī, in order "to show the power of the Holy Language to the Holy People."[53]

Traditionally minded Muslims in Spain found the proud bearing of the Jewish patricians to be nothing short of hubris and an affront to Islam. The fawning panegyrics of Samuel ha-Nagid's nominally Muslim poet, al-Munfatil, who in one poem went so far as to suggest that his brethren should kiss the Jewish vizier's hands as they would the black stone of the Kaᶜba, must have been repugnant if not blasphemous to true Believers.[54] A critical treatise on the Koran that was

[51] Moses B. Ezra, *Sēfer Shīrat Yisrā'ēl (Kitāb al-Muḥāḍara wa'l Mudhākara)*, Hebrew trans. B. Halper (reprint ed., Jerusalem, 1966–67), p. 62.

[52] Ibid., p. 53.

[53] al-Ḥarīzī, *Taḥkemōnī,* ed. Y. Toporovsky (Tel Aviv, 1952), p. 12.

[54] Henri Pérès, *La Poésie andalouse en arabe classique* (Paris, 1953), pp.

attributed to the *nāgīd* provoked a scathing retort from the great Muslim scholar ᶜAlī b. Ḥazm. Ibn Ḥazm expressed the deeply rooted resentment felt by devout Muslims throughout the country when he advised the Party Kings:

Let any prince upon whom Allah has bestowed some of His bounty take heed. . . . Let him get away from this filthy, stinking, dirty crew beset with Allah's anger and malediction, with humiliation and wretchedness, misfortune, filth, and dirt, as no other people has ever been.[55]

The depth of anti-Jewish sentiment can also be seen from the rabble-rousing poetry of Abū Isḥāq of Elvira who called for the overthrow of Samuel's son and successor, Joseph ha-Nagid. "And do not spare his people," Abū Isḥāq added, "for they have amassed every precious thing!"[56] Joseph was assassinated in a popular uprising against him on December 30, 1066, the eve of the Sabbath. His body was crucified upon the city's main gate. On the following morning a mob went on a rampage in the Jewish quarter of Granada, slaughtering its inhabitants and razing the quarter to the ground.[57]

The Jewish community of Granada was reestablished sometime later, but was destroyed again with great loss of life when the city was sacked by the Almoravids in 1090.

The Jewish elite in most of the other cities of Muslim Spain managed to maintain their accustomed life-style throughout the remainder of the eleventh century and the first half of the twelfth century. Their position, however, was gradually eroding. The relentless pressure of the Christian Reconquista progressively polarized Andalusian society and resulted in a hardening of Muslim religious attitudes. This polarization became even sharper when most of what remained of al-Andalus was incorporated into the Almoravid Empire

---

269ff. This poem is a remarkable piece of sycophancy, even considering its genre. Al-Munfatil goes on to say that he openly professes the religion of the Sabbath in front of the Nagid, and continues to profess it secretly among his fellow Muslims. It is surprising that Pérès and, after him, others should actually take these lines seriously.

[55] The translation is from Moshe Perlmann, "Eleventh-Century Andalusian Authors on the Jews of Granada," *PAAJR* 18 (1948–49), p. 283. The entire text of Ibn Ḥazm's retort is edited in Emilio García-Gomez, "Polémica religiosa entre Ibn Hazm e Ibn al-Nagrila," *al-Andalus* 4 (1936): 1–28.

[56] The entire poem is translated below in Part Two, pp. 214–16.

[57] The murder of the *nāgīd* and the bloodbath that followed are graphically depicted by Ashtor, *The Jews of Moslem Spain*, vol. 2. (Heb. edition), pp. 116–17. Ashtor's description is based on the Arabic and Hebrew sources that are given in ibid., p. 363, n. 281.

after 1090. There followed a steady decline of Jews in the civil service. There were still some peripheral court figures, but none with the power or the prestige of the Ibn Naghrēlas and their ilk.

Most of the Jewish upper class seems to have remained remarkably complacent during this lengthy twilight. Their political position had declined, but so had the power of Islamic Spain. Their culture had lost none of its brilliance. Andalusian Jewry could still be justifiably proud of its religious scholarship. The *yeshiva* founded by the great talmudist Isaac al-Fāsī (d. 1103) continued to flourish under his pupil Joseph b. Megash (d. 1141). The art of Hebrew poetry rose to new heights of polished perfection in the verses of Judah ha-Levi (1075–1141), who in his own lifetime was acknowledged the poet laureate of Spanish Jewry.

Jewish civilization in Muslim Spain still showed all the vital life signs, but there was a deep-seated malaise in the Jewish community. One sure sign of the anxiety of the times was outbreaks of apocalyptic messianism. One such incident occurred in Cordova sometime between 1110 and 1115, when people began to acclaim a certain Ibn Arieh as the Messiah. The rabbinic and courtly elite quickly stepped in and had the would-be Messiah flogged and excommunicated before the entire congregation.[58] Another wave of millenarianism swept through the Jewish communities of Spain and also Morocco in 1130. Many people, including Judah ha-Levi, believed that the dominion of Islam would pass away in that year.[59] They were sorely disappointed when 1130 came and went.

The failure of apocalyptic messianism cast many into doubt and despair. Judah ha-Levi went through such a crisis of faith, but he recovered from it with a new, deeper sense of spiritual certainty. He had become an ardent proto-Zionist, and in a stirring cycle of poems, referred to as the "Songs of Zion," he expressed his yearning to return to his ancestral homeland. The yearning for Zion was nothing new in medieval Hebrew poetry; however, in his philosophical dialogue *The Kuzari* he went even further and totally rejected the ethos of Andalusian Jewish culture. *The Kuzari* was a glorification of rabbinic Judaism and an unabashed statement of nationalism, very much in the modern sense of the word. The perfect Jewish life, according to ha-Levi, was

[58] The incident is related by Maimonides in his *Epistle to the Jews of Yemen,* translated below in Part Two, pp. 233–46.

[59] Schirmann, *ha-Shīrā hā-ᶜIvrīt,* vol. 2, p. 480. In Fez, the entire Jewish community was brought to the brink of ruin preparing for the coming of the Messiah. See the account in Maimonides, *Epistle,* below, pp. 243–44.

possible only in the Land of Israel. In other words, Spain was no substitute for Zion, the Andalusian civilization of which they were so proud was vanity, and all the efforts of the Jewish upper class to obtain power and prestige at gentile courts were for naught.[60] It was a waste of time to transplant Andalusian Jewry in the Christian kingdoms of northern Spain. Israel's exile under Muslim or Christian rule was in the end equally bitter.

Judah ha-Levi's compatriots understood perfectly well what he was saying. Judging from the reaction of his Spanish contemporaries, most did not agree. Ha-Levi, however, took his verses seriously. In spite of his age, the dangers in going to Crusader-held Palestine, and the protestations of his friends, Judah ha-Levi left Spain for Egypt and proceeded from there to Palestine, where he died in July 1141.[61]

By 1172, almost all of Islamic Spain came under the control of the Almohads, fanatic sectarian Berbers from the Ante Atlas mountains of Morocco. The Almohads tolerated neither Jews nor Christians within their empire. There were mass conversions of Jews to Islam. Many fled over the frontier into Christian Spain, while others made their way to the more tolerant Muslim East. Ayyubid Egypt and Syria offered a haven to Andalusian refugees. Jewish life in the little that was left of Islamic Spain ceased to exist altogether.

THE BEST YEARS IN RETROSPECT

It is not mere coincidence that the flowering of Jewish culture in the Arab world should occur at the very time that Islamic civilization was at its apogee. Classical Islamic civilization was not Islam the religion, although the latter was an essential component. Islamic civilization was an amalgam of cultural elements that included Islamic religion, Arabic culture with its strong pre-Islamic roots, Greek humanism, and subtle remnants of the ancient heritage of the Near East. For a few brief centuries, Greek humanism and Islam's own universal tendencies combined with a dynamic mercantile economy to produce a relatively open society in which more often than not Muslims and non-Muslims could participate, if not on an entirely equal footing, at

[60] See Judah ha-Levi, *The Kuzari,* bk. 5, para. 25.

[61] Some historians have doubted whether ha-Levi actually reached Palestine. On the basis of Geniza letters, it is now certain that he at least reached Tyre. See Goitein, "The Biography of Rabbi Judah ha-Levi in the Light of the Cairo Geniza Documents," *PAAJR* 28 (1959): 41–56.

least with near equality in those spheres of activity that were not specifically religious, particularly in the marketplace, in certain scientific and intellectual circles and, to an extent, in the civil service.

The Muslim majority felt secure enough and was sufficiently prosperous not to be overly concerned with enforcing the humility of its *dhimmī* neighbors. Muslims and non-Muslims lived in close propinquity, for there were no ghettos at this time. Most Jews and Christians lived in their own quarters near their houses of worship, but these neighborhoods were rarely exclusively Jewish or Christian.[62]

Day-to-day contacts between Muslims and non-Muslims were on the whole amicable. There are many examples of Muslims, Christians, and Jews in joint business ventures. Intimate social relationships, however, were rare. One's religious community was the principal arena for social life and activity. Furthermore, there was a tenuousness in the cordiality of interfaith relationships. The non-Muslim could never entirely disembarrass himself of his *dhimmī* status. There was no lack of preachers and religious reformers to remind Muslims and non-Muslims alike that the Pact of ᶜUmar was being violated. Where the infractions were minor, the preaching had little effect. But there were limits. The Muslim community's sense of propriety could be deeply offended when *dhimmīs* rose too high or became too conspicuous in government service. As was already noted above, the results could be disastrous both for the *dhimmī* official and for his coreligionists.

The fall of a Jewish courtier was a cause of deep anxiety for his brethren until the storm had passed. Three months after the assassination of Abū Saᶜd al-Tustarī in Cairo, a Jewish merchant in Qayrawan wrote to an Egyptian friend:

> The couriers have brought news that has left us stunned. I pray God will cause us to hear news that will set our hearts at rest and console everyone, namely that Abū Naṣr (Abu Saᶜd's brother) is still alive. May He place him within the bounds of safety. May He not expose him to any mishap. This will be a comfort to all, and it will calm our hearts for your sake.[63]

The position of a Jewish community could also become precarious

[62] For the testimony of the Cairo Geniza, see Goitein, *Mediterranean Society*, vol. 2, pp. 289–93. Concerning the Jewish "quarters" in Spain, see Ashtor, *Jews of Moslem Spain*, vol. 1, pp. 291–354. As in the Middle East, these were not compulsory ghettos, but rather neighborhoods where the majority of the population was Jewish.

[63] TS 20.180, 11. 7–9 (Nahray 172). The pronoun "your" in "your sake" (Ar., *jihatikum*) is in the plural, indicating the writer's concern for the addressee and for all Egyptian Jews. The entire letter is translated in Goitein, *Letters of Medieval Jewish Traders* (Princeton, 1973), pp. 149–53. Goitein's translation of this particular passage differs slightly from my own.

in times of civil strife, famine, or other catastrophe. Times of crises brought popular religious frenzy to its height. The Jews were a small, defenseless minority whose status as infidels and humble tribute bearers was defined by Islamic law.

Anti-Semitism, that is, "the hatred of Jews qua Jews," did exist in the medieval Arab world even in the period of greatest tolerance. The Jews had a code word for this judeophobia in their Arabic. It was *sin'ūth,* a Hebrew word meaning *hatred,* but understood as referring to Jew-hatred. The problem was by no means rampant, and it was more serious in some places than in others. It seems to have been endemic in Alexandria, which had a history of unpleasant Jewish-gentile relations going back to antiquity.[64]

Outright persecution of Jews or non-Muslims in general was rare, but there was always that uncertain possibility. At the whim of the ruler, the harshest interpretations of the sumptuary laws could be strictly enforced, as suddenly happened during the reign of al-Ḥākim. Al-Ḥākim, however, was a religious maniac who went far beyond even the strict interpretation of the Pact of ^{c}Umar in his treatment of non-Muslims.[65]

Even in the best of times, *dhimmīs* in all walks of life and at every level of society could suddenly and rudely be reminded of their true status. The *nāgīd* Ibrāhīm b. ^{c}Aṭā', who was the personal physician of Zirid Amir al-Mu^{c}izz b. Bādīs, was publicly insulted while bearing a message from his royal master to the great Maliki scholar Abū ^{c}Imrān al-Fāsī. Abū ^{c}Imrān was furious; he had mistaken the *nāgīd* for a Muslim because he was not wearing a Jewish badge. The zealous *faqīh* (jurist) stained the Jew's turban on the spot and then sent him packing. The humiliated Jewish courtier sought redress from his patron, the amir, but was rebuffed. As the ruler observed, it was a good lesson "showing the power of Islam and the veneration inspired by the Muslim scholars."[66]

It would be unfair to overemphasize the insecurity of the Jews of Arab lands during the period that has been surveyed in this chapter, but it would be equally unfair to ignore it. Islamic tolerance was a two-sided coin. For the most part, it was the brighter, more humane side that prevailed throughout the Islamic High Middle Ages.

[64] For instances of anti-Semitism, see Goitein, *Mediterranean Society,* vol. 2, pp. 278–83.

[65] For an enumeration of impositions, see M. Canard, "al-Ḥākim bi-Amr Allāh," *EI*^{2} 3: 77–78.

[66] Hady Roger Idris, "Deux Maîtres de l'école juridique kairouanaise sous les Zīrīdes (XIe siècle): Abū Bakr b. ^{c}Abd al-Raḥmān et Abū ^{c}Imrān al-Fāsī," *AIEO* 13 (1955): 55–56.

4

THE LONG TWILIGHT

The Jews of Arab Lands in the Later Middle Ages

The spiritual, social, and economic climate of the Muslim world underwent a profound transformation during the course of the thirteenth century. Islamic civilization was on the defensive everywhere. The Crusaders had intruded into the Middle East and remained for nearly two centuries (1098–1291). Most of Spain was lost to the armies of the Reconquista. By 1264, only Granada remained under Muslim rule. All of Sicily had submitted to the Normans by the close of the eleventh century. The coast of North Africa was ravaged by Europeans from the opposite shores of the Mediterranean from the mid-eleventh century onwards. The Mongol horde swept across Asia during the thirteenth century and into the Muslim East, leaving a path of devastation in its wake. On February 10, 1258, Hülagü Khān took Baghdad after a brief siege, executed Caliph al-Mustaᶜṣim along with many members of his family, and put an end to the caliphate.

The secular and humanistic tendencies of Hellenism, which until this period had been predominant cultural forces in Islamic society, began to wane; at the same time the Islamic religious element in its most rigid form began to wax ever stronger. Non-Arab soldier castes ruled the successor states to the caliphate. The political, social, and economic order they imposed might be called with some justification an oriental brand of feudalism. The dynamic mercantile economy of the High Middle Ages stagnated. The currency was debased from years of gold outflow. Muslim society closed in upon itself within popular religious brotherhoods, trade guilds, and state monopolies.

Economically, the non-Muslim minorities became increasingly marginal. Numerically, they became smaller as well.

Institutionalization was the order of the day. Society became highly stratified, the foreign military elite being at the top, followed by the religious functionaries, civil servants, the Muslim bourgeoisie, the native Muslim masses, and finally the *ahl al-dhimma* (people of the pact). The frustration of the Muslim Arabs, who were themselves now a subject population, was eased somewhat by the clearly inferior status to which the *dhimmīs* were relegated.

The state-controlled *madrasas,* or Islamic institutions of higher learning, produced religious scholars who were trained in accordance with an approved curriculum. Many of the *madrasa* graduates went on to careers in the state bureaucracy. They began to squeeze the *dhimmīs* out of the civil service with the passage of time.

The presence of a cadre of officials trained in Islamic orthodoxy ensured the application of religious law in many areas. This was particularly true with regard to the *ahl al-dhimma.* The laws of *ghiyār,* or "differentiation," were enforced throughout the later Middle Ages with greater consistency than in earlier times and with increasing vigor.

The process of Jewish economic decline and social isolation was by no means instantaneous, nor did it occur at the same rate in the various Islamic states. There were even temporary bright spots on this generally gloomy tableau. For the Jews of Iraq and Iran, for example, the second half of the thirteenth century was a period of unusual freedom and opportunity. The early Mongol *īl-khāns,* who ruled Iraq and Iran, were pagans. They did not recognize the distinction between *dhimmī* and Muslim. They were hostile to Sunni Islam for political reasons, but openly showed favor to Shiᶜites, Christians, and Jews, much to the chagrin of the orthodox Muslim majority. Little wonder that the Christians joyously greeted the Mongols when they marched into Damascus in 1259.[1]

Jewish and Christian officials served in the Mongol administration. The apogee of Jewish influence came during the reign of Arghūn Khān (1284–91). Under his patronage, the Jewish physician and scholar Saᶜd al-Dawla became vizier of the entire Ilkhanid state in 1289. Saᶜd al-Dawla was an accomplished linguist who could speak Mongolian and Turkish in addition to Persian and Arabic. He became

[1] Bertold Spuler, *The Muslim World, A Historical Survey, II: The Mongol Period,* trans. F. R. C. Bagley (Leiden, 1960), p. 20.

Arghūn's closest confidant. He appointed many Jews including his own relatives to positions of importance in the administration. Nepotism then as now was a time-honored Middle Eastern practice.[2]

Only a few years before Saᶜd al-Dawla's accession to power, the Jewish oculist and philosopher Saᶜd b. Kammūna (d. 1285) had written a comparative study of Judaism, Christianity, and Islam entitled *An Examination into the Inquiries of the Three Faiths.*[3] The publication of such a book in Arabic would have been unthinkable when Islam was the ruling faith. It is an eloquent testimony to the change in the legal position of non-Muslims while the Ilkhanid dynasty remained pagan.

The rapid rise of the Jews under the Mongols was followed by an even more rapid fall. Popular sentiment had been building up against the non-Muslims for nearly three decades. A riot broke out in Baghdad in 1284, after a sermon was preached against Ibn Kammūna's audacious book, which contained passages critical of Islam. The Jewish philosopher had to flee the city and was condemned to death in absentia in order to appease the mob.[4]

This manifestation of the passions stirred up by one Jew's rather dispassionate essay on comparative religion was but a foreshadowing of things to come. In 1291, Saᶜd al-Dawla and his Jewish associates were murdered while Arghūn Khān lay on his own deathbed. The elimination of the Jewish vizier was a signal for a purge of Jewish officials throughout Iraq and Iran. Anti-Jewish riots erupted everywhere. Some Jews saved themselves by embracing Islam, although they later were able to return to their former faith.[5]

The unalloyed joy of the Muslim populace at the downfall of the Jews was expressed by the preacher Zayn al-Dīn ᶜAlī b. Ṣāᶜid in a biting Arabic satire that opens with the lines:

We praise Him in Whose name the heavens turn.
Those Jewish apes have been destroyed.

[2] For the biography of Saᶜd al-Dawla, see Walter J. Fischel, *Jews in the Economic and Political Life of Mediaeval Islam* (New York, 1969), pp. 90–114.

[3] The Arabic text has been edited by Moshe Perlmann, *Saᶜd B. Manṣūr Ibn Kammūna's Examination of the Inquiries into the Three Faiths* (Berkeley and Los Angeles, 1967). Perlmann has also made a complete, annotated translation, an excerpt from which appears in Part Two below, pp. 259–61.

[4] The incident is reported by the Baghdadi chronicler Ibn al-Fuwaṭī, *al-Ḥawādith al-Jāmiᶜa wa'l-Tajārib al-Nāfiᶜa,* ed. M. Jawād (Baghdad, 1932), pp. 441–42.

[5] Fischel, *Jews,* pp. 111–17 and the sources cited there.

Their Sa^cd al-Dawla ("Fortune of the Dynasty") has had an unlucky conjunction,
And they have been disgraced and exposed!

and ends with a refutation of the poet who once had said "Turn Jew, for Heaven itself has become Jewish."[6]

The Jews and Christians of Iraq and Iran soon returned to their traditional *dhimmī* status when the Ilkhanid dynasty became Muslim once and for all in 1295.[7] For the rest of the Islamic Middle Ages the lot of Iraqi Jewry was more consistent with that experienced by their brethren in other Arab lands.

The Arab world west of Iraq was divided into several feudal military states from the middle of the thirteenth century until the Ottoman takeover of the Middle East and much of North Africa in the sixteenth century. The largest and by far the most important of these feudal states was the Mamluk Empire, which comprised Egypt, part of Libya, Syria, Palestine, and western Arabia. The Maghreb was divided into three principal Berber kingdoms, whose borders were continually expanding and contracting in their rivalries with one another. These states corresponded roughly to the modern national divisions of Northwest Africa—with the Ḥafṣids in Tunisia, the Zayyanids in Algeria, and the Merinids in Morocco. Jews lived in all of these domains, and despite local variations, their social and economic status was on the whole quite similar.

THE MAMLUK EMPIRE

The Mamluk Empire contained the remnant of what had been the most important Jewish community at the close of the Islamic High Middle Ages. The Jewish community of Egypt, which was the heart of the Mamluk domain, was still relatively prosperous and well organized when the Mamluks came to power in 1250.

The Mamluk state was ruled by a military elite of Turkish-speaking former slaves who were originally imported into Egypt to serve in the Ayyubid army. After their accession to power in 1250, the Mamluks continued to replenish their numbers by importing slaves

[6] The entire poem is published with a translation in Edward G. Browne, *A Literary History of Persia III: The Tartar Dominion (1265–1502)* (Cambridge, 1964), pp. 34–36. See the poem to which Zayn al-Dīn is referring, above, p. 51.

[7] Spuler, *The Mongol Period,* pp. 35–36.

from the Caucasus. The Mamluks ensured their grip upon the Levant when they turned back the Mongols from Syria and Palestine in 1260. Despite the enmity between the Mamluk and Ilkhanid empires, their feudal systems were remarkably alike. Most of the land in the Middle East was broken up into fiefs, which were held by the foreign military class.[8] This made for a generally uniform socioeconomic picture throughout the region.

There was a significant difference, as far as the Jews were concerned, during the first half-century of Mongol and Mamluk rule. The Mamluks were Muslims who portrayed themselves as defenders of the faith against Christian Crusaders and pagan Mongols. To emphasize their Islamic legitimacy, the Mamluk Sultan Baybars (ruled 1260–77) gave refuge to the survivors of the Abbasid house and established a puppet caliphate in Cairo that lasted until the Ottoman conquest in 1517. The Mamluks curried the favor of the *ᶜulamā'*, the Muslim scholarly class, which in Islam is somewhat analogous to a clergy. In such an atmosphere the discriminating aspects of the *dhimmīs'* status could hardly be ignored.

The trend toward stricter enforcement of the *dhimma* code had already begun under the Ayyubids who ruled Egypt and Syria from 1171 to 1250. By the end of Ayyubid rule, most Jews wore a distinguishing mark on their turbans and cloaks, and most Christians wore a special outer belt. Much of the time, members of the *dhimmī* upper class were still able to evade the requirement, which was considered a mark of humiliation as well as differentiation. Periodic decrees were the way Islamic rulers reminded the upper-class *dhimmīs* that they should pay for their exemption, which they did.[9]

Under the Mamluks, the sumptuary laws were taken more seriously than in earlier periods. After all, as the Mamluks did not allow the native Arabs to dress like Mamluks or ride horses as they did, they were not going to permit nonbelievers to dress like Believers. The reimposition of the dress code over a number of years was not an indication of any great tolerance in the interim. Medieval regimes were woefully inefficient when compared with modern totalitarian states in controlling the daily lives and actions of their subjects. Decrees of

[8] Ibid., p. 57. For a more detailed, but not entirely convincing, comparison, see A. N. Poliak, "The Influence of Chingiz-Khān's Yāsa upon the General Organization of the Mamlūk State," *BSOAS* 10 (1940–42): 862–76; and idem, "Some Notes on the Feudal System of the Mamlūks," *JRAS* n.v. (1937): 97–107.

[9] S. D. Goitein, *Mediterranean Society*, vol. 2 (Berkeley and Los Angeles, 1971), pp. 287–88.

many sorts had to be reissued from time to time to demonstrate official resolution. The same held true for medieval Christian Europe, where the coercive power of the state was also limited. The imposition of the Jewish badge, which was enjoined by the Fourth Lateran Council in 1215, took many years to implement and was nowhere enforced with any consistency until the fourteenth or fifteenth centuries.[10]

In 1301, the Mamluk authorities took serious measures to crack down upon transgressors of the Pact of ᶜUmar and introduced a number of new requirements. Henceforth, non-Muslims had to wear identifying colored turbans—blue for Christians, yellow for Jews, red for Samaritans.[11] The decree of 1301 forbade *dhimmīs* to build homes higher than those of their Muslim neighbors. Vigilante mobs took action to enforce the new regulation and tore down the upper stories of *dhimmī* homes and shops. They even lowered the benches on which customers sat in front of *dhimmī* shops. A number of churches and synagogues were vandalized and razed, although the Chief Qāḍī later ruled that this last action was justified only if it could be proven that the sanctuaries were built after the advent of Islam.[12]

Nine years later, the Mamluk council of state considered the possibility of once again allowing the *dhimmī* upper class to be exempted from the requirement of wearing colored turbans in order to raise money for the exchequer. The proposal was rejected, however, at the urging of the famous Ḥanbalite theologian and jurist Aḥmad b. Taymiyya.[13]

In 1354, Sultan al-Malik al-Ṣāliḥ issued a new decree reiterating the Pact of ᶜUmar and adding new sumptuary regulations. Because it had become fashionable to wear large turbans, Jews and Christians

[10] See Bernhard Blumenkranz, "Badge, Jewish," *EJ* 4: 63–70. See also Yitzhak Baer, *A History of the Jews in Christian Spain*, vol. 1 (Philadelphia, 1971), p. 116.

[11] L. A. Mayer, *Mamluk Costume: A Survey* (Geneva, 1952), p. 65, where the date is given as 1300.

[12] See the passage from al-Maqrīzī translated in Bernard Lewis, ed. and trans., *Islam from the Prophet Muhammad to the Capture of Constantinople II: Religion and Society* (New York, 1974), pp. 229–32. See also E. Strauss [–Ashtor], *A History of the Jews in Egypt and Syria under the Rule of the Mamlūks*, vol. 1 (Jerusalem, 1944), pp. 86–87, and vol. 2 (Jerusalem, 1951), p. 220 [Heb.].

[13] Ibn Kathīr, *al-Bidāya wa 'l-Nihāya*, vol. 14 (Cairo, 1939), pp. 53–54, where it says that the Jews were willing to return to wearing plain turbans with a distinguishing mark or badge and were willing to pay the incredible sum of 700,000 dinars per annum in addition to the *jizya* for that privilege. A translation of this passage may be found in Bernard Lewis, *Islam: Religion and Society*, vol. 2 (New York, 1974), pp. 232–33.

were now limited in the size of their headdress. No more than ten ells of winding cloth could be used. *Dhimmī* women were now ordered to appear in public only in enveloping wraps dyed the same identifying color as their menfolks' turbans. *Dhimmī* males were henceforth to wear a distinctive metal neck ring when visiting the public baths, so that even undressed they could not be mistaken for Muslims. *Dhimmī* females were to be barred from bathing with Muslim women altogether. Apparently Muslim women were considered more susceptible than Muslim men to the deleterious influence of nonbelievers. Special bathhouses were to be built to accommodate the women of the *ahl al-dhimma*. Anti-*dhimmī* riots broke out in Cairo and elsewhere similar to the mob violence that erupted in the wake of the decree of 1301.[14]

A new group of Mamluks who were mainly of Circassian origin took control of Egypt in 1382. Their accession to power did not result in any improvement in the situation of non-Muslims. Quite to the contrary, the prevailing attitude toward *dhimmīs* was more severe than ever. Religious passions were easily kindled.

In 1419, the Coptic patriarch was summoned to Sultan al-Malik al-Mu'ayyad's court, and there was compelled to remain standing while Muslim scholars delivered lengthy anti-Christian diatribes. At the same time, a Christian scribe who had been in the service of the vizier was whipped and displayed naked in the streets of Cairo. All this was in retaliation for the subjection of Muslims in the Christian kingdom of Abyssinia.[15]

Anti-Christian sentiment diffused into anti-*dhimmī* sentiment. The *muḥtasib* (market inspector) of Cairo issued a proclamation "emphasizing and intensifying"—in the words of the chronicles—the regulations for *dhimmīs*.[16] Their turbans were to be reduced now to seven ells of cloth. The sleeves of their robes were to be of narrow cut because wide sleeves were a mark of respectability. They could no longer ride even on donkeys within the cities (horses and mules had

[14] The decree of al-Malik al-Ṣāliḥ is translated in Part Two below, pp. 273–74. See also Mayer, *Mamluk Costume*, p. 66, and Strauss [–Ashtor], *Jews under the Mamlūks*, vol. 2, p. 220, where other sources with further details are cited.

[15] al-Maqrīzī, *Kitāb al-Sulūk li-Maᶜrifat Duwal al-Mulūk*, vol. 4, pt. 1, ed., S. ᶜAbd al-Fattāḥ ᶜAshūr (Cairo, 1972), pp. 493–94; also Ibn Taghrī Birdī, *al-Nujūm al-Zāhira fī Mulūk Miṣr wa l-Qāhira*, vol. 6, ed. W. Popper (Berkeley, 1933), p. 398; Eng. trans., idem, *History of Egypt: 1382–1422 A.D.*, University of California Publications in Semitic Philology (UCPSP) 17 (Berkeley and Los Angeles, 1957), p. 67.

[16] Ibn Taghrī Birdī, *Nujūm*, vol. 6, p. 400; Eng. trans., UCPSP 17, p. 69.

been prohibited them long before).[17] The Mamluk historian Ibn Taghrī Birdī noted that the *dhimmīs* "felt themselves hard pressed and made every effort to obtain the cancellation of the order, but they did not attain their goal."[18] The same writer only a few lines earlier remarked that nothing was more meritorious in Allah's sight than exalting the authority of Islam and debasing that of the unbelievers.[19] The popular sentiment against non-Muslims must have been intense at the time of the proclamation of 1419. The contemporary historian al-Maqrīzī observed that many *dhimmīs* ceased going to the public baths and would no longer let their women appear in the marketplaces.[20]

Anti-*dhimmī* decrees were issued periodically throughout the fifteenth century. Most merely repeated or revised in some slight way the customary sumptuary laws. For example, the permissible size for a *dhimmī* turban fluctuated back and forth between seven and ten ells of fabric.

One decree that stood out as truly unusual was made by Sultan Jaqmaq in 1448. The new decree prohibited Jewish and Christian physicians from treating Muslim patients.[21] This was a momentous reversal. The medical profession in the Muslim world had always been notably nonsectarian. Jews and Christians had made outstanding contributions to Islamic medicine, and they were given honorable mention in the medieval Arabic biographies of physicians. The medical profession had been perhaps the single most important avenue of advancement for non-Muslims in Islamic society. It was noted in the preceeding chapter that many court Jews were physicians.

There had always been some pious opposition to *dhimmīs* practicing medicine on Muslims, but it was never taken seriously. Almost every caliph from al-Manṣūr onward had had non-Muslim physicians among his doctors. Jaqmaq's decree is indicative not only of the decline of the position of non-Muslims in the later Islamic Middle Ages, but also of the waning esteem for Hellenic science and its practitioners. Only two centuries earlier in Egypt, the Muslim poet Ibn Sanā' al-Mulk could sing the praises of the Jewish physician Moses Maimonides, namely:

17 al-Maqrīzī, *Sulūk,* vol. 4, pt. 1, p. 495; Mayer, *Mamluk Costume,* p. 67.

18 Ibn Taghrī Birdī, *Nujūm,* vol. 6, p. 400; Eng. trans., UCPSP 17, p. 69. al-Maqrīzī, *Sulūk,* vol. 4, pt. 1, p. 495, says the same.

19 Ibn Taghrī Birdī, *Nujūm,* vol. 6, p. 399; Eng. trans., UCPSP 17, p. 68.

20 al-Maqrīzī, *Sulūk,* vol. 4, pt. 1, p. 495.

21 Ibn Taghrī Birdī, *Nujūm,* vol. 7, p. 160; Eng. trans., UCPSP 19, p. 109.

I consider Galen's medicine for the body only,
While Abū ᶜImrān's [that is, Maimonides']
is for the body and soul.
Were he to treat Time with his wisdom,
He would surely cure it of the disease of ignorance.[22]

Between Ibn Sanā' al-Mulk's time and that of Jaqmaq, a great deal of anti-*dhimmī* propaganda had come into circulation, some of which was aimed directly at infidel physicians.[23] Polemical treatises of the thirteenth and fourteenth centuries, such as al-Jawbarī's *Kashf al-Asrār* (Unveiled Secrets) and al-Wāsiṭī's *Radd ᶜalā Ahl al-Dhimma* (Refutation of the People of the Pact), contained horror stories concerning *dhimmī* physicians and Muslim patients.[24] In one anecdote, al-Wāsiṭī has none other than Maimonides himself admit that the blood of Gentiles is licit for Jews.[25] Religious handbooks of the period, such as Ibn al-Ḥājj's *Madkhal al-Sharᶜ al-Sharīf* (Introduction to the Noble Religious Law), echo these attitudes.[26] The motif of the malevolent *dhimmī* doctor—especially the Jewish doctor—became widespread in later Arabic literature.[27]

The decree against non-Muslim doctors was but one of a number of innovative anti-*dhimmī* measures taken in the Mamluk period. Sometime during the thirteenth or fourteenth centuries, a humiliating Jews' oath was reintroduced after a moratorium of over half a millennium. The oath did allow the Jew to give testimony before a Muslim court, but it was purposely worded to be degrading and even ludicrous. It consisted of a detailed self-imposed curse in which the Jew renounced all that he held sacred should his witness prove false. The

[22] Ibn Abī ᶜUṣaybiᶜa, *ᶜUyūn al-Anbā' fī Ṭabaqāt al-Aṭibbā*, ed. Nizār Riḍā (Beirut, 1965), p. 582.

[23] See Moshe Perlmann, "Notes on Anti-Christian Propaganda in the Mamlūk Empire," *BSOAS* 10 (1940–42): 843–61; idem, "Asnawī's Tract Against Christian Officials," *Ignace Goldziher Memorial Volume*, vol. 2, ed. S. Löwinger et al. (Jerusalem, 1958), pp. 172–208; idem, "Notes on the Position of Jewish Physicians in Medieval Muslim Countries," *Israel Oriental Studies* 2 (1972): 315–19.

[24] An extract from al-Wāsiṭī is translated in Part Two below, pp. 275–76. For a highly interesting excerpt from al-Jawbarī, see Perlmann, "Jewish Physicians," *Israel Oriental Studies* 2: 316–17.

[25] Translated in Part Two below, p. 276.

[26] Ibn al-Ḥājj, *al-Madkhal*, vol. 4 (Cairo, 1960), pp. 114–22.

[27] See Norman A. Stillman, "Muslims and Jews in Morocco: Perceptions, Images, Stereotypes," *Proceedings of the Seminar on Muslim-Jewish Relations in North Africa* (New York, 1975), p. 19.

tone and intent of the Mamluk oath for Jews is reminiscent of the notorious oath *More Judaico* in Europe.[28]

The last one hundred years or more of Mamluk rule weighed heavily upon all of the subjects of the empire—Muslim and non-Muslim. There was continual violence and lawlessness. The once-thriving economy was in shambles, and the currency so debased that copper coins came to replace silver dirhams. The population had been substantially depleted by the Black Death and the recurrent epidemics of plague that ravaged Egypt and Syria from the mid-fourteenth century on. The general tax burden was normally oppressive and at times crushing.[29]

Non-Muslims could draw little comfort from the ecumenical suffering. Their lot was even worse than that of the Muslim population, both socially and economically. The systematic and minutely detailed discrimination of *dhimmīs* had a visibly debilitating effect. Large numbers of Copts and Jews, especially among the professional classes who found the institutionalized humiliation too burdensome, converted to Islam. One can detect a definite sense of ill will in the Arabic chronicles of the period directed toward these neo-Muslims, many of whom were employed by the government.[30]

The outright persecution of non-Muslims in the Mamluk Empire was not constant. There were periods of respite between the discriminatory decrees, the outbreaks of violence against *dhimmī* persons and property, and the special exactions levied above and beyond the *jizya*. The social climate, on the other hand, was continually inhospitable. There was an omnipresent air of hostility toward the "infidels." The

[28] The texts of the earlier and the Mamluk Jews' oath are translated in Part Two below, pp. 165–66 and 267–68, respectively. For the Jews' oath in Europe, see Isaac Levitats, "Oath More Judaico or Juramentum Judaeorum," *EJ* 12: 1302–3, where the text of one such oath is given.

[29] On the decline of the economy, see William Popper, *Egypt and Syria under the Circassian Sultans, 1382–1486 A.D.: Systematic Notes to Ibn Taghrī Birdī's Chronicles of Egypt* (continued), UCPSP 16 (Berkeley and Los Angeles, 1957), pp. 41–123; also Eliyahu Ashtor, *Histoire des prix et des salaires dans l'Orient médiéval* (Paris, 1969), pp. 267–449 and 539–53. Concerning the demographic and economic effects of the Black Death and subsequent plagues, see Michael W. Dols, *The Black Death in the Middle East* (Princeton, 1977), pp. 143–302. For a brief summary of the oppression of the Circassian period, see Stanley Lane-Poole, *A History of Egypt in the Middle Ages* (reprint ed., London, 1968), pp. 325–50.

[30] See, for example, Ibn Taghrī Birdī, *Nujūm*, vol. 6, pp. 586–87; Eng. trans., UCPSP 18, pp. 23–24; also ibid., vol. 7, p. 722; Eng. trans., UCPSP 23, p. 56.

non-Muslim communities were under severe stress, which over time weakened the social fabric even though they continued to maintain their autonomous institutions under the leadership of the patriarch in the case of the Christians and the *ra'īs al-Yahūd* in the case of the Jews. European travelers and pilgrims did not fail to notice the social decay. Friar Félix Fabri, who visited Egypt in 1483, was deeply shocked by the predominance of Christian prostitutes and pimps in Alexandria. He even goes so far as to praise the "Saracens" for not reducing their own daughters to prostitution, although, he notes with pious horror, they did maintain brothels for "ephebes."[31]

The travelers' reports on the Jewish community at this time also indicate serious social decline. R. Obadiah da Bertinoro, who emigrated to Palestine via Egypt in 1487, mentions Jewish officials selling off ritual ornaments, Torah scrolls, and codices from the synagogues of Cairo and Jerusalem to foreign Jews and even Gentiles. The beadle of the venerable Ben Ezra Synagogue in Fustat sold its Torah scroll for 100 dinars and promptly converted to Islam. The elders of the Jewish community in Jerusalem are singled out as being rapacious and corrupt.[32] R. Obadiah also reports widespread poverty and a lack of charity toward the Jewish poor, which is quite the reverse of the situation in the Fatimid and Ayyubid periods, when the social services of the Egyptian Jewish community were highly developed.[33]

Many of the local Jewish communities described by R. Obadiah and others had dwindled into insignificance. Meshullam da Volterra, who visited Egypt and the Holy Land in 1481, mentions that there were only sixty Jewish families left in Alexandria.[34] R. Obadiah writing just six years later puts the number of Alexandrian Jewish families at only about twenty-five.[35] Meshullam estimates approxi-

[31] Félix Fabri, *Voyage en Egypte de Félix Fabri, 1483,* vol. 2, trans. Jacques Masson (Paris, 1975), pp. 704–7.

[32] R. Obadiah Jare da Bertinoro, Letter from Jerusalem to his father (1488), in Avraham Yaari, *Letters from the Land of Israel* (Ramat Gan, 1971), pp. 122–24 [Heb.]. Eng. trans. in *Jewish Travellers: A Treasury of Travelogues from 9 Centuries,* ed. Elkan Nathan Adler (reprint ed., New York, 1966), pp. 229–31.

[33] R. Obadiah da Bertinoro, in Yaari, *Letters,* pp. 121–22; Adler, *Travellers,* p. 228–29.

[34] Meshullam b. Menaḥem da Volterra, *Massā^c Meshullam me-Vōlterra be-Ereṣ Yisrā'ēl be-Shnat 5241 (1481),* ed. A. Yaari (Jerusalem, 1948), p. 48.

[35] R. Obadiah da Bertinoro, in Yaari, *Letters,* p. 115; Adler, *Travellers,* p. 161. R. Obadiah cites Alexandrian Jews who could remember when their community numbered 4000 (!) households. Although the figure itself is fantastic, it does show an awareness of the acute depopulation of Egyptian Jewry.

mately 800 Jewish households for Cairo, and R. Obadiah about 700.[36]

The arrival of exiles from Spain at the end of the fifteenth century and the beginning of the sixteenth century infused new blood into the anemic Jewish communities of the Mamluk Empire. Emigrants from Sicily, Italy, and North Africa also began to come into Egypt, Palestine, and Syria at this time. These new immigrants were to play a significant role in the partial revival of Levantine Jewry after the Ottoman conquest.[37]

It is unlikely that any Jews mourned the passing of the Mamluk regime. Most of them looked toward the Ottomans as liberators, although they were in no position to render any assistance to them in the conquest.

The Jewish experience under the Mamluks in many respects paralleled that of their brethren in medieval Christian Europe. In both cases, the Jews were extended "general sufferance with severe limitations."[38] In both cases, too, the Jews lived within an atmosphere of progressively heightening religious consciousness and cultivated contempt. There were significant differences to be sure. The Jews of Mamluk Egypt, Palestine, and Syria were occasionally subject to violent popular outburts, but these never turned into massacres such as occurred in the wake of the Crusades. Furthermore, as oppressive as Jewish life was under the Mamluks, there was at least one mitigating factor not to be found in most of Europe. In the Mamluk Empire, the Jews were not the only infidels. The Copts more frequently and more immediately took the brunt of anti-*dhimmī* persecution. Although, as we have already observed, any persecution of the Copts could rapidly spill over onto the Jews as well.

In contemporary North Africa, however, there were no native Christians to absorb some of the Muslim hostility against nonbelievers. As we shall see subsequently, the parallels with medieval Christian Europe were even stronger in the Maghreb during this period.

36 Meshullam, *Massāᶜ*, p. 57; Adler, *Travellers,* p. 171; R. Obadiah, in Yaari, *Letters,* p. 119; Adler, *Travellers,* p. 225. Meshullam gives 800 as the figure for the Rabbanites only; however, it is most likely that he has confused this number with the total Jewish population, including Karaites and Samaritans.

37 See Strauss [–Ashtor], *Jews under the Mamlūks,* vol. 2, pp. 438–547.

38 Salo Wittmayer Baron, *Social and Religious History of the Jews,* vol. 9 (New York and Philadelphia, 1965), p. 5. Baron uses this phrase to describe the policy of the church in medieval Europe. Oddly enough, he probably would not agree with the comparison between the Mamluk Empire and Latin Christendom (see ibid., vol. 2, pp. 171–72).

North African Jewry was just emerging from a traumatic century of Almohad rule at about the time the Mamluks were coming to power in Egypt. Most of the urban Jewish population from Tunisia to Morocco had outwardly professed Islam during the height of the Almohad terror. Those communities that resisted were put to the sword. Their memory was immortalized by the Andalusian poet Abraham b. Ezra in a celebrated lament.[39] As such mass conversions under extreme duress were clearly suspect, the Almohad authorities treated the neo-Muslims much like *dhimmīs,* forcing them to wear distinguishing clothing and severely limiting their civil rights. The Almohad caliph Ya^cqūb al-Manṣūr (ruled 1184–99) rationalized this persecution with the remark:

If I were sure of the sincerity of their Islam, I would let them mix with the Muslims . . . , and if I were sure of their unbelief, I would kill their men, enslave their offspring, and declare their property spoils for the Muslims. But I am uncertain about their case.[40]

The Almohad period was a definite aberration in the history of the Jews of Arab lands, or of any Muslim countries for that matter. The forced conversion of Jews was extremely rare, since the overwhelming majority of Muslims accepted the koranic dictum: "There is no compulsion in religion" (Sura 2:256). The few instances of the forcible conversion of Jews to Islam—and there are no more than half a dozen over a period of thirteen centuries—all occurred under heterodox fanatics. The most recent case took place in Meshed, Iran, in 1839.[41]

[39] David Kahana, *R. Avraham b. ᶜEzra* (Warsaw, 1894), pp. 140–43. The poem has been reprinted many times.

[40] al-Marrākushī, *al-Muᶜjib fī Talkhīṣ Akhbār al-Maghrib* [The History of the Almohades], ed. Reinhart Dozy, 2d ed. (reprint ed., Amsterdam, 1968), p. 223.

[41] It is immaterial whether this famous koranic verse is a call to religious tolerance, or as Rudi Paret has recently suggested, an expression of resignation in the face of obdurate unbelief. The end result is the same. See Rudi Paret, "Sure 2,256: lā ikrāha fī d-dīni. Toleranz oder Resignation?" *Der Islam* 45 (1969): 299–300; and idem, *Der Koran: Kommentar und Konkordanz* (Stuttgart, 1971), pp. 54–55.

The forced converts of Meshed remained crypto-Jews until well into the twentieth century, when most returned to Judaism. See W. J. Fischel, "Qehillat hā-Anūsīm be-Fāras," *Zion* 1 (1935): 38–74; also I. Ben-Zvi, "Two Documents Concerning the Forced Converts of Meshed," *Zion* 4 (1938): 250–57 [Heb.].

Maghrebi Jewry emerged from the Almohad period spiritually and numerically impoverished. Most of the Jewish intellectual leadership had fled to the more tolerant Islamic East, like the Maimonides family, or had accepted martyrdom, like R. Judah b. Shushan. The Jews became the *dhimmīs* par excellence in North African society, for no native Christian population seems to have survived the Almohad persecution.

It is nearly impossible to draw any composite picture of Jewish life for all of North Africa during the post-Almohad period. The historical experience of the Jews varied considerably in each of the three kingdoms.

The Jews of Ḥafṣid Tunisia enjoyed the most tranquility of any Maghrebi Jewish community at this time. There is a great irony in this, for the Ḥafṣids considered themselves the legitimate heirs of Almohadism. The Tunisian Jews kept a relatively low profile, were never too conspicuous in public life, and in general conformed in their behavior and comportment to what was expected of a protected people. The *jizya* was collected and the laws of differentiation observed, but without the special rigor of the Mamluk Empire.[42]

The Jews in the Zayyanid kingdom of Tlemcen, in what is today Algeria, also led a peaceful and rather undistinguished existence during the thirteenth and fourteenth centuries. The level of Jewish culture improved immeasurably after 1391, when a large number of Sefardic refugees arrived in the wake of anti-Jewish disturbances in Spain and the Balearic Islands. Under the leadership of men like R. Isaac b. Sheshet Perfet and R. Simon b. Ṣemaḥ Duran, Algeria became the Jewish spiritual center of the entire Maghreb.[43] The Jews of Ḥafṣid Tunisia and Zayyanid Algeria maintained particularly strong ties, and the *minhag* (customary practice) of the rabbis of Algiers was adopted by the Jews of Tunisia as well.

The relative security and calm of Algerian and Tunisian Jewish life in the late Middle Ages stands in marked contrast to the prevailing situation in most of the Arabic-speaking lands from Iraq to Morocco.

[42] The most detailed account of the Jews in Ḥafṣid Tunisia is to be found in Robert Brunschvig, *La Berbérie Orientale sous les Ḥafṣides des origines à la fin du XVe siècle,* vol. 1 (Paris, 1940), pp. 396–430. See also H. Z. [J. W.] Hirschberg, *A History of the Jews in North Africa,* vol. 1 (Leiden, 1974), pp. 458–80.

[43] Concerning these men and their reforms, see Abraham M. Hershman, *Rabbi Isaac ben Sheshet Perfet and His Times* (New York, 1943), and Isidore Epstein, *The Responsa of Rabbi Simon b. Ẓemaḥ Duran as a Source of the History of the Jews in North Africa* (London, 1930).

The Jews of the Further Maghreb, as Morocco was called in medieval Arabic, underwent a very different historical experience than did their coreligionists in neighboring Algeria and Tunisia. In many respects, this experience conformed more to the rhythms of Jewish life in the Middle East with important regional variations. The course of Moroccan Jewish social history was marked by tremendous polarities of tolerance and intolerance, assimilation and isolation, and security and insecurity. It is a significant history because until modern times, Morocco had boasted the largest Jewish community by far in North Africa and, indeed, in the entire Islamic Diaspora.

As Almohad rule disintegrated, Moroccan Jews began openly to reestablish their communities throughout the major towns and cities of the country. The new Merinid dynasty was not at all ill disposed toward the Jews. The Merinids were Muslims, but showed none of the zeal for religious reform that was the very *raison d'être* of their predecessors, the Almohads. Islamic idealism was simply not a determinant factor in their political program. The Muslim population, on the other hand, had been profoundly affected by the militant reform spirit of the Almohads and, before them, the Almoravids. Their deep religiosity was now channeled into strict Malikism and popular pietist movements. The contrasting religious outlooks of the Merinids and their subjects laid the foundations for later tension. From the beginning, the Merinids probably felt themselves to be outsiders in the cities of Morocco. They were nomadic Zenāta Berbers from the southeastern part of the country and had little in common with the Arab bourgeoisie. Because of their essential alienation from the general population, the Merinids established their seat of government in a new administrative quarter, al-Madīna al-Bayḍā' (later simply called New Fez) outside the walls of Old Fez.[44]

The Merinids were not averse to appointing Jews to high positions within their administration. The Sultan Yūsuf b. Yaᶜqūb (ruled 1286–1307) had several Jewish courtiers from the Waqqāṣa family, one of whom, Khalīfa the Elder, was his majordomo.[45] The latter's cousin,

[44] To this day, New Fez (*Fās Jedīd*) has a much less urbane atmosphere than Old Fez (*Fās al-Bālī*). Concerning this city, see Roger Le Tourneau, *Fez in the Age of the Marinides,* trans. Besse Alberta Clement (Norman, Okla., 1961).

[45] Ibn Khaldūn, *Kitāb al-ᶜIbar,* vol. 7 (Bulaq, A.H. 1284, pp. 232–33); al-Nāṣirī, *Kitāb al-Istiqṣā' li-Akhbār Duwal al-Maghrib al-Aqṣā,* vol. 3 (Casablanca, 1954), pp. 80–81 (based mainly on the account in Ibn Khaldūn). Ibn al-Aḥmar, *Rawḍat al-Nisrīn,* ed. and trans. C. Bouáli and G. Marçais (Paris, 1917), p. 17 (text), p. 69 (trans.), where the family name is given as Ruqqāṣa.

Khalīfa the Younger, served the Sultan Abu 'l-Rabīᶜ Sulaymān (ruled 1308–10) in several unspecified offices.[46] The last Merinid ruler, ᶜAbd al-Ḥaqq b. Abī Saᶜīd (ruled 1421–65), raised a Jew named Aaron b. Baṭash to the vizierate during the final year of his reign.[47]

The presence of a few Jews at the Merinid court ought not to be interpreted, as David Corcos has done, as indicating any widespread Jewish economic power in Morocco at that time, or any particular affinity between the Zenāta Berbers and the Jews.[48] The Merinids employed Jews in their service because of the latter's extreme vulnerability and, hence, according to Islamic political psychology, dependability. It is for this same reason that Muslim rulers in the East had for centuries depended upon Turkish guards, black slaves, and eunuchs in various capacities. As the Jews were a very marginal component of Moroccan society, they had no power base. They therefore offered no threat. They were considered totally dependant upon their masters, for they could expect no sympathy among the Muslim masses.

Just how vulnerable the Jews actually were can be seen from their transferal to a special quarter in New Fez next to the *dār al-makhzan* (government administrative center). The Jews were brought to the *mellāḥ,* as such quarters came to be called in Morocco, in 1438.[49] The removal of the Jews from Old Fez came in the wake of anti-Jewish disturbances that broke out when a rumor circulated that the Jews had poured wine into the lamp reservoirs of a mosque.[50] The accusation has its parallel in the Host desecration with which Jews were frequently charged in Europe at that period. The unlikely nature of the crime was perfectly consistent with the negative stereotype of Jews in the Moroccan popular imagination.[51] This was not, however,

---

For a discussion (sometimes fanciful) of the possible etymologies of this name, see David Corcos, "The Jews of Morocco under the Marinides," *JQR* n.s. 55 (1964–65): 139–40, n. 118.

[46] Ibn Khaldūn, *ᶜIbar,* vol. 7, p. 239; al-Nāṣirī, *Istiqṣā',* vol. 3, p. 100; Ibn al-Aḥmar, *Rawḍat al-Nisrīn,* p. 19 (text), p. 71 (trans.).

[47] The story of Ibn Baṭash as related by ᶜAbd al-Bāsiṭ is translated in Part Two below, pp. 281–86.

[48] Corcos, "Jews of Morocco," *JQR* n.s. 55 (1965): 77 passim; idem, "Jews of Morocco," *JQR* n.s. 54 (1964): 271–77.

[49] The quarter was originally called Ḥimṣ after the city in Syria. On the etymology of the word *mellāḥ,* see Maurice Gaudefroy-Demombynes, "Marocain mellāh," *JA* 11, sér. 3 (1914): 651–58.

[50] This is the reason given by Rabbi Abner ha-Ṣarfatī (nineteenth century) in his chronicle *Yaḥas Fās.* See Y. D. Semah, "Une chronique juive de Fès: Le 'Yahas Fès' de Ribbi Abner Hassarfaty," *Hespéris* 19, fasc. 1–2 (1934): 91.

[51] For a detailed discussion of the popular images of Jews, see N. A.

the first anti-Jewish riot in Merinid Fez. On March 10, 1276, a massacre began when it was rumored that a Jew had acted improperly toward a Muslim woman. The disorder was halted only by the appearance on the scene of Sultan Yaᶜqūb b. Yūsuf. Once again, this was an offense completely in keeping with popular stereotypes.[52]

The eventual removal of the Jews to the *mellāḥ* was meant for their own protection. The *juderías* of medieval Aragon and Castile were similarly located near royal citadels and fulfilled much the same function.[53] The Flemish priest and missionary, Nicholas Clenardus, who spent a year in Fez between 1540 and 1541, wrote to a friend that he purposely chose to live in the *mellāḥ* rather than in the Christian *funduq* in Old Fez for reasons of security. As a priest, he was subject to all kinds of abuse by Muslims in the streets. He added that the Jews detested Christians as much as Muslims but were—quite understandably—"less audacious."[54]

The *mellāḥ* of Fez became the prototype of the Moroccan ghetto. Despite the fact that it was founded for the protection of the Jews and not as a punishment, the Jewish sources make it quite clear that the Jews themselves viewed their confinement to the *mellāḥ* to be a tragedy, "a sudden and a bitter exile."[55] It only increased their sense of isolation and marginality. The *mellāḥs* of the other towns of Morocco,

---

Stillman, "Muslims and Jews in Morocco: Perceptions, Images, Stereotypes," *Proceedings of the Seminar on Muslim-Jewish Relations in North Africa,* pp. 13–27, especially pp. 18–21.

[52] Ibn Abī Zarᶜ, *Rawḍ al-Qirṭās,* French trans. A. Beaumier (Paris, 1860), p. 459, Spanish trans. A. Huici Miranda (Valencia, 1918), p. 327, relates the event in detail but does not give the cause. The allegation is found in anon., *al-Dakhīra al-Saniyya fī Ta'rīkh al-Dawla al-Marīniyya,* ed. Mohamed Bencheneb (Algiers, 1921), p. 186. The sexual motif which is implicit here is discussed in N. A. Stillman, "Muslims and Jews in Morocco," p. 20. For parallels and variants, see the notes there.

[53] See Yitzhak Baer, *A History of the Jews in Christian Spain,* vol. 1 (Philadelphia, 1971), pp. 49–50.

[54] The passage from Clenardus's letter is translated in Part Two below, p. 287.

[55] Jacob Toledano, *Nēr ha-Maᶜarāv: Hū Tōledōt Yisrā'ēl be-Mārōqqō* (Jerusalem, 1911), p. 44, citing unspecified chroniclers. Also ha-Ṣarfatī, *Yaḥas Fās,* in Semah, "Une chronique juive," *Hespéris* 19: 91. David Corcos's attempt to rehabilitate the Mellāḥ from its negative image as a ghetto is unconvincing, although he does make some valid points. See Corcos, "Les Juifs au Maroc et leurs mellahs," *Zakhor le-Abraham: Mélanges Abraham Elmaleh,* ed. H. Z. [J. W.] Hirschberg (Jerusalem, 1972), pp. xiv-lxxviii. On this tendency to idealize the Moroccan past among some emigrants, see N. A. Stillman, "The Moroccan Jewish Experience: A Revisionist View," *The Jerusalem Quarterly* 9 (1978): 112.

all of which were established later under the Saᶜadians (1550–1650) and the ᶜAlawids (1666 to the present), were founded with the express intent of ostracism rather than protection. The later legendary etymology of the word *mellāḥ* as a place where Jews originally salted the heads of executed criminals for public display emphasizes the outcast connotation that was attached to it.

The Fez *mellāḥ* did not always fulfill its protective function very well. On May 14, 1465, its inhabitants were almost entirely exterminated by the rebels who brought down the Merinid dynasty. The attack upon the Jews of Fez, according to the contemporary Egyptian traveler ᶜAbd al-Bāsiṭ, touched off a wave of similar massacres throughout the country.[56] The most immediate cause of this general uprising was the appointment of a Jew, Aaron b. Baṭash, to the vizierate. Up until this time the Merinid sultans had always been able to stem any popular dissatisfaction with their Jewish courtiers by the simple expedient of executing the official. The few Jewish courtiers who are known to us from the Arabic sources were, in fact, all put to death by the rulers they served—"and the dynasty was cleansed of their filth," as the chroniclers usually commented.[57] ᶜAbd al-Ḥaqq tried this traditional method, but found it to no avail. He had gone beyond all acceptable bounds in appointing a *dhimmī* to such an office as the vizierate. The downfall of Aaron b. Baṭash, like the downfalls of Joseph ha-Nagid in Granada and Saᶜd al-Dawla in the Ilkhanid Empire, spelled disaster for the entire Jewish community.

Moroccan Jewry began to recover from the pogroms of 1465 under the Waṭṭāsids (1472–1554). The ranks of the Jewish community swelled with the arrival of waves of refugees from Spain and Portugal after 1492. The newcomers were for the most part economically and culturally superior to the native Jewish population to whom they condescendingly referred as *forasteros* (strangers) or *berberiscos* (Berbers, or natives). The Sefardic scholarly mercantile elite was quick to dominate Jewish communal life in Morocco.[58]

The Waṭṭāsid sultans employed some of the well-connected immigrants as commercial and diplomatic go-betweens with the Portuguese crown (and to a lesser extent with Spain). Men such as R. Abraham b. Zamiro of Safi, and Jacob Rosales and Jacob Rute of Fez, were

56 Translated in Part Two below, pp. 281–86.

57 For example, Ibn Khaldūn, *ᶜIbar*, vol. 7, p. 233.

58 Corcos, "Moroccan Jewry in the First Half of the 16th Century," *Sefunot* 10 (1966): 53–111 [Heb.]. H. Z. [J. W.] Hirschberg, *A History of the Jews in North Africa*, vol. 1 (Leiden, 1974), pp. 410–14.

as much agents of Portugal as of Morocco.[59] The Waṭṭāsids, and later the Saᶜadians, also took into their service some Jewish artisans and technicians who possessed strategic military skills.[60] These men were employed in much the same spirit as Christian mercenaries. Most were not considered to be truly government officials with any administrative authority over Muslims. They were, therefore, not too obnoxious to the Moroccan masses.

Not all of Morocco was under native Muslim control in the early sixteenth century, and with the exception of *conversos,* who sought to return openly to their former faith, most of the Jewish newcomers seem to have preferred living in the Portuguese-held coastal towns rather than the Islamic interior. They joined in the defense of these enclaves against Muslim attacks and sought to withdraw with the Christian colonists when the Portuguese had to evacuate.[61] The reasons for this interesting preference are both social and economic. The Portuguese were notably tolerant toward the Jews in their African possessions long after the issuance of the Edict of Expulsion of 1497 and the establishment of the Inquisition in 1540. Furthermore, the ports were probably the most active mercantile entrepôts of the period, and artisans were not excluded by the Islamic guilds that existed in the major towns of the interior.

Jewish life in the Muslim interior was dominated by the Sefardic plutocracy that continued to maintain control of Moroccan Jewry until modern times. Each local community had a *nāgīd,* or *shaykh al-Yahūd,* who was appointed by the government. The chief figure in the larger Jewish community was the *nāgīd* of the capital, who was invariably a court Jew. For several generations, beginning in ca. 1538, the office was held by members of the Rute family.

Those Jews who served the Waṭṭāsids, various local chieftains, and later the Saᶜadians, were a privileged few. Like most men who moved in court circles, a considerable gap separated them from the rest

[59] A great deal of revealing documentation of their activities is to be found in *Les sources inédites de l'histoire du Maroc: Archives et bibliothèques du Portugal,* ed. Pierre de Cenival, David Lopes, and Robert Ricard, first series, 5 vols. (Paris, 1934–51). See also Yosef Hayim Yerushalmi, "Professing Jews in Post-Expulsion Spain and Portugal," *Salo Wittmayer Baron Jubilee Volume,* ed. Saul Lieberman, with Arthur Hyman (Jerusalem, 1975), pp. 1023–58.

[60] See, for example, *Sources inédites—Portugal,* vol. 3, pp. 220–23; also Hirschberg, *Jews in North Africa,* vol. 1, pp. 418–19 and 428–29.

[61] Jews helped in the defense of Safi in 1510—Robert Ricard, *Les Portugais au Maroc* (Rabat, 1937), p. 62. Jews were evacuated from Azzemour to Arzila in 1541—*Sources inédites—Portugal,* vol. 3, pp. 352–55. Numerous examples may be found in *Sources inédites* of similar instances.

of the population. Some were concerned communal leaders, whereas others were as oppressive and overbearing with their coreligionists as any courtier might be.[62] Life was probably not easy for anyone outside the ruling elite in Morocco. For the average Jew, however, life was even more difficult, certainly more complex.

Throughout the later Middle Ages and into early modern times, the laws governing Jews in Morocco were among the most strictly applied in all the Arab world. By the end of the fifteenth century, a considerable body of juridical opinion concerning the restrictive treatment of Jews had already built up, as can be seen from the *Kitāb al-Mi^cyār al-Mughrib* (The Marvelous Touchstone), a voluminous collection of Maghrebi *fatwās,* or legal opinions, edited by Aḥmad al-Wansharīsī, who died in Fez in 1508.[63]

The discriminatory laws for non-Muslims were in actuality considerably harsher than most of those found in the theoretical literature. Throughout the principal towns and orthodox religious centers of Morocco, the koranic injunction to humble the *dhimmī* was understood in the most literal sense. The sumptuary laws were not only enforced but were given a specifically Moroccan twist. In addition to wearing distinguishing black garments that were the very opposite of the Believers' white, Jews were compelled to walk barefoot in the streets of some towns. In others, this last indignity only applied when a Jew passed by a mosque. Almost nowhere were Jews allowed to wear normal footgear when walking outside the *mellāḥ.* In Fez, from the early sixteenth century on, the prescribed shoes for Jews were sandals of straw.[64]

The very strictly applied laws of differentiation were due in no small measure to the rising sociopolitical importance of charismatic

62 An example of the latter was Moses Abūṭām, who served the Wāṭṭsid Bū Ḥassūn (d. 1554). See Toledano, *Nēr ha-Ma^carāv,* pp. 64–65. Samuel Romanelli, who visited Morocco in the late eighteenth century, noted that Jews who served at court and rose to high positions were often as arrogant as anyone else in authority. See his *Massā' ba-^cArāv,* ed. Jefim [Ḥayyim] Schirmann in *Ketāvīm Nivḥārīm* [Selected Writings of Samuel Romanelli] (Jerusalem, 1968), p. 110.

63 The full title is *al-Mi^cyār al-Mughrib wa 'l-Jāmi^c al-Mu^crib ^can Fatāwī ^cUlamā' Ifrīqiya wa 'l-Andalus wa 'l-Maghrib* (Fez, A.H. 1314–15), 12 vols. Partially translated by Emile Amar, "La pierre de touche," *Archives Marocaines,* vols. 12–13 (Paris, 1908–9), where the sections dealing with the treatment of *dhimmīs* are vol. 12, pp. 231–65, and vol. 13, pp. 30–36.

64 For a discussion of the Pact of ^cUmar in its Moroccan form, see Jane Satlow Gerber, "The Pact of ^cUmar in Morocco: A Reappraisal of Muslim-Jewish Relations," in *Proceedings of the Seminar on Muslim-Jewish Relations in North Africa* (New York, 1975), pp. 40–50.

religious leaders throughout Morocco during the waning years of the Merinid dynasty. The inability of the Waṭṭāsids to dislodge the Portuguese from the Moroccan coast and, indeed, their relatively close relations with the Christians through Jewish intermediaries only enhanced the prestige of the *Shorfa* (class. Ar., *shurafā'*), the descendants of the Prophet, and the *Murabṭīn* (class. Ar., *murābiṭūn*), Sufi holy men whom the Europeans called marabouts. The proliferation of these populist, charismatic figures and their rivalries and conflicts may have been a cause of severe political fragmentation in Morocco until the advent of the ᶜAlawid dynasty. But nonetheless, they set the spiritual tone of the age, and it was a bellicose tone fired by the zeal of *jihād* (holy war) against the Christian incursions. This is the period in Moroccan history that Henri Terrasse has dubbed *"la Crise Maraboutique."*[65] Both the Saᶜadians and the ᶜAlawids accepted the religious ideals and—no less important—the norms of this heroic, if anarchic, age. Their legitimacy as national leaders was based on their being both *Shorfa* and *Mjāhdīn* (class. Ar., *mujāhidūn*), the Islamic equivalent of Crusaders. Such an atmosphere was understandably not very conducive to the lenient interpretation of the restrictive laws governing nonbelievers within their society.

Jewish life throughout much of Morocco changed very little during the Sharifan period. There are numerous descriptions of Moroccan Jewry by European visitors to Morocco from the sixteenth to nineteenth centuries. They are remarkably consistent in the picture they present. They bear ample witness to the highly ritualized degradation of the Jews in the major towns and cities. One of the more common indignities suffered by Jews was having stones thrown at them in the streets by Muslim children. This was a time-honored custom in many parts of the Arab world, and though bothersome, was rarely dangerous since there was usually no malicious intent.[66]

On the whole, Moroccan Jews accepted their enforced humility philosophically. They considered it, after all, to be part of the burden of a people in exile, and they adhered punctiliously to the restrictions

[65] Henri Terrasse, *Histoire du Maroc,* vol. 2 (Casablanca, 1950), pp. 143–56.

[66] On the stoning of Jews by Moroccan children, see the passage from G. Mouette, translated in Part Two below, pp. 304–5. This custom in Yemen is discussed by Goitein, *Jews and Arabs* (New York, 1974), p. 76. I myself have seen youngsters throw stones and in other ways harass Jews in Morocco on more than one occasion. My colleague Dr. Judith Goldstein informs me that she has witnessed such stone-throwing while doing fieldwork among the Jews of Yazd, Iran. (Oral communication on May 17, 1976.)

imposed upon them. Nowhere in the Arab chronicles of the later Middle Ages do we read of members of the Moroccan Jewish elite violating the Pact of ᶜUmar with any show of ostentation. There was no need in Morocco to reintroduce periodically the sumptuary laws, as had been the case in the Mamluk Empire.

Moroccan Jews took refuge from the harsher realities of their life in the fervor of their religiosity. There were strong currents of kabbalistic mysticism, messianism, and religious Zionism in Moroccan Judaism.[67] There was an important Maghrebi Jewish community in Palestine from the sixteenth century on.[68] A considerable number of Moroccan Jews also found solace from the vicissitudes of their existence in *maḥya,* their potent anise-flavored brandy. Like their Yemenite brethren, Moroccan Jews were hard drinkers.[69] Many travelers to both countries commented on the widespread alcoholism. The parallel is not at all fortuitous. For these two countries were by far the strictest in the Arabic-speaking world in their interpretation and implementation of the laws pertaining to *dhimmīs,* who in both instances were exclusively Jews.

The pariah status of the Jews was not without some economic compensations. Excluded from many trades by the Islamic guilds, Moroccan Jews, like their Ashkenazic counterparts in medieval Europe, performed certain necessary economic functions that were religiously reprehensible to the non-Jewish majority. As in Europe, many moneylenders in Morocco were Jewish. The Jews also had the virtual monopoly on jewelry-smithing and the spinning of fine metallic thread used in the brocade industry.[70] This was because in Maliki

[67] For a very general treatment of North African mysticism, see André Chouraqui, *Between East and West: A History of the Jews in North Africa,* trans. Michael M. Bernet (New York, 1973), pp. 104–12. On the spread of Sabbatianism into the Maghreb, see Gershom Scholem, *Sabbetai Ṣevi: The Mystical Messiah (1626–1676)* (Princeton, 1973), pp. 640–51 and 894–99.

[68] See Nathan Slouschz, "La colonie des Maghrabim en Palestine, ses origines et son état actuel," *Archives Marocaines* 2 (1904): 229–57; Meir Benayahu, "The History of the Connections of Moroccan Jewry with Palestine," *Sinai* 35 (1954): 317–40 [Heb.].

[69] On alcoholism among the Yemenites, see Erich Brauer, *Ethnologie der Jemenitischen Juden* (Heidelberg, 1934), pp. 110–12. Most of the reports on alcoholism among the Moroccans are from the nineteenth century, but there is no reason to assume that the phenomenon was new. See, for example, J. E. Budgett Meakin, "The Jews of Morocco," *JQR* 4 (1892): 381.

[70] On Jews in banking and moneylending in Morocco, see Haim Bentov, "Jewish Artisans in Fez during the 17th and 18th Centuries," *Sefunot* 10 (1966): 437, 447–48, and 471–472 [Heb.]; Haïm Zafrani, *Les Juifs au Maroc: vie sociale, économique et religieuse* (Paris, 1972), pp. 178–88, where

Muslim eyes the fashioning of gold and silver objects for sale above and beyond the intrinsic value of the metal itself was akin to usury. Furthermore, metalworking of any kind had negative magical connotations in Moroccan superstition.

A number of Sefardic Jews in the major ports and some towns of the interior played a significant role in Moroccan commerce from the late Middle Ages to modern times. This was because of a combination of their linguistic skills and close familial and business contacts with Jews abroad. Naturally, only a small minority of Moroccan Jews were engaged in such lucrative activities. The majority were artisans and petty tradesmen. Within the confines of the *mellāḥ,* they formed their own guilds and professional associations.[71]

It should be remembered that in spite of the generalized, restrictive trends described here, Moroccan Jews were never as severely limited in their pursuit of occupations as were the Jews in medieval and early modern Europe. Jews could and did enter into joint business ventures with Muslims. Even after the founding of the various *mellāḥs,* there were always many Jews who worked in the Muslim *madīna.*[72] Some Jews traveled into the Berber hinterlands under guarantees of protection and provided services to the tribesmen as peddlers, jobbers, and agents.[73] In the south of the country on the fringes of the Sahara, there were even Jewish agricultural settlements that probably dated back to antiquity.[74]

Although the economic life of the Jews in late medieval Morocco was certainly less restricted than in Europe, there were nevertheless

---

there is a discussion of the theoretical legal aspects, but little actual data; Leland Bowie, "An Aspect of Muslim-Jewish Relations in Late Nineteenth-Century Morocco: A European Diplomatic View," *IJMES* 7, no. 1 (January 1976): 7–15. On Jews in jewelry-smithing and metallurgy, see Bentov, "Jewish Artisans in Fez," pp. 425–31 and 448–449; Zafrani, *Les Juifs au Maroc,* pp. 163–66; M. Vicaire and R. Le Tourneau, "L'Industrie du fil d'or au Mellah de Fès," *Bulletin Economique du Maroc,* 3 (1936): 185–90; and idem, "La fabrication du fil d'or à Fès," *Hespéris* 24 (1937): 67–88.

[71] See Haim Bentov, "Jewish Artisans in Fez," pp. 421–23; Haïm Zafrani, *Les Juifs au Maroc,* pp. 168–69.

[72] See Gerber, "The Pact of ᶜUmar in Morocco," *Muslim-Jewish Relations in North Africa,* p. 44, for Fez; for Sale, see Kenneth L. Brown, *People of Salé: Tradition and Change in a Moroccan City* (Manchester, 1976), p. 42.

[73] See N. A. Stillman, "Muslims and Jews in Morocco," *Muslim-Jewish Relations in North Africa,* p. 25 and the sources cited there in n. 41; also Allan R. Meyers, "Patronage and Protection: Notes on the Status of Jews in Precolonial Morocco," unpublished paper presented at the Association for Jewish Studies Meeting, Boston, Mass., on December 18, 1977.

[74] Zafrani, *Les Juifs du Maroc,* pp. 172–76 and the sources cited there.

strong parallels in other aspects of life. This is particularly striking in the social isolation of the Jews and their ritualized degradation. Their continual vulnerability to violence in both settings was also similar. The situation of the Jews in most of the Arab lands east of Morocco was to some degree less oppressive—at least, less consistently so. Whatever changes that for better or for worse affected most of Arabic-speaking Jewry as a result of the Ottoman conquests, these changes failed to reach Morocco. For the majority of Moroccan Jews, the twilight of the later Middle Ages was to continue well into the nineteenth century, and for some, into the second decade of the twentieth century.

THE ARAB PROVINCES OF THE OTTOMAN EMPIRE

The Ottoman conquest of much of the Middle East and North Africa during the sixteenth century brought about, for a brief period of time, a general amelioration of Jewish life in Arab lands. As far as the non-Muslim population was concerned, Ottoman rule was far less oppressive than that of the Mamluks in Egypt and Syria or the Safavid Persians in Iraq.

The Ottomans had already provided a haven for large numbers of Jewish refugees from the Iberian Peninsula for nearly three decades before subjugating the Arab territories to the south. The Sultan Bayezid II (1481–1512) welcomed the talented Sefardim into his realm and issued firmans to his provincial governors specifying the terms of Jewish settlement and ensuring the protection of the newcomers.[75] Bayezid and his courtiers are said to have considered Ferdinand of Spain a fool for impoverishing his own kingdom while enriching theirs.[76] Some of the Sefardic immigrants were skilled in the art of manufacturing weapons and helped the Turks to produce their own cannon and powder. The victory of Selim the Grim (1512–20) over

[75] M. Franco, *Essai sur l'histoire des Israélites de l'Empire Ottoman depuis les origines jusqu' à nos jours* (Paris, 1897), pp. 37–38. For an example of the terms of settlement, see Nicoara Beldiceanu, "Un acte sur le statut de la communauté juive de Trikala," *REJ* 40 (1972): 129–38.

[76] The remark about Ferdinand is attributed to Bayezid's courtiers by R. Eliyahu b. Elqana Capsali, *Seder Eliyahu Zuta*, vol. 1, ed. Aryeh Shmuelevitz et al. (Jerusalem, 1975), p. 240; and to Bayezid himself by Imanuel Aboab, *Nomologia o discursos legales compuestos* (Amsterdam, 1629), p. 195. The attribution in either case ought to be taken "with a grain of salt."

the Mamluks in Syria-Palestine in 1516 and in Egypt in 1517 was in no small measure because of the superiority of Ottoman fire power, which was already well developed before the arrival of the Jews.

The Jewish refugees from the expulsions of 1492 and 1496 were soon followed by Marranos fleeing the terror of the Inquisition. In the Ottoman Empire, they could openly return to Judaism. One former Marrano, Samuel Usque, described "the great nation of Turkey" to his brethren as:

> a broad expansive sea which our Lord has opened with the rod of His mercy. . . . Here the gates of liberty are always wide open for you that you may fully practice your Judaism.[77]

There had been some Jewish immigration into the Levant during the last years of Mamluk rule. Most of the refugees from Spain and Portugal who had moved into the Eastern Mediterranean preferred—quite understandably—to settle in Ottoman Greece or Turkey. After 1517, however, large numbers began taking up residence in Egypt, Syria and, especially, Palestine because of its religious and national significance.

The fall of Byzantium in 1453 had already reawakened Jewish messianic expectations. The hope of Israel's redemption was again aroused around the time of Selim's conquests. R. Abraham b. Eliezer ha-Levi, a Spanish exile in Jerusalem, wrote that the signs heralding the End of Days would occur sometime during the 1520s and that the Messiah himself would appear in 1530 or 1531.[78] The arrival of the adventurer David Reubeni in the Holy Land in 1523, claiming to be a prince from a Jewish kingdom in Ethiopia, added fuel to the messianic fervor.[79] The fact that the prophecies of redemption remained unfulfilled did not put an end to messianic speculation. It only caused

[77] Samuel Usque, *Consolation for the Tribulations of Israel,* trans. Martin A. Cohen (Philadelphia, 1965), p. 231.

[78] R. Abraham's predictions were made in his commentary on *The Prophecy of the Child Naḥman b. Pinḥas.* See Itzhak Ben-Zvi, *Eretz-Israel under Ottoman Rule: Four Centuries of History,* 2d ed. (Jerusalem, 1966), p. 155 [Heb.]. Concerning R. Abraham and his works, see Gershom G. Scholem, "The Cabbalist Rabbi Abraham Ben Eliezer Halevi," *Kirjath Sepher* 2, nos. 2 and 4 (1925): 101–41 and 269–73 [Heb.]; also idem, "Chapters from the History of Cabbalistical Literature, 9: New Researches on R. Abraham b. Eliezer Halevi," *Kirjath Sepher* 7, no. 1 (1930): 149–65 [Heb.].

[79] The "diary" attributed to Reubeni is published in Adolf Neubauer, *Medieval Jewish Chronicles,* vol. 2, pp. 133–223; and an abridged English translation in Adler, *Jewish Travellers,* pp. 251–328. His stay in Palestine is described on pp. 143–48 (text); 260–67 (trans.).

renewed attempts at computing the arrival of the messianic era, or—in the language of the kabbalists—"determining the End." The ardor for messianism was finally dampened after the mass hysteria and subsequent disappointment in the Jewish world created by the appearance of the false messiah Sabbatay Ṣevi in Gaza in 1665, and his apostasy in Adrianople in 1666. Until the debacle of Sabbatianism, the messianic dream remained a vital energizing force among Palestinian Jews.[80]

The Jewish population of the Holy Land swelled during the first fifty years of Ottoman rule. By the mid-sixteenth century, the number of Jews in Palestine had reached approximately 10,000.[81] The Jewish population of Jerusalem increased by about 50 percent between the years 1533 and 1553.[82] Most of the settlers were Sefardim, but by no means all of them. Some came from Italy and others from northern and eastern Europe. Jerusalem, Tiberias, and above all Safed became centers of Jewish spiritual and economic activity.

Safed became the foremost Jewish town in Palestine during these years. It was the seat of a burgeoning textile industry in which the Jews appear to have played a major role.[83] Safed also became the adopted home for some of the leading Jewish scholars of the age—men such as R. Jacob Berab (d. 1546), who tried to reestablish the ancient rabbinical ordination and reconstitute the Sanhedrin, and his successor and disciple R. Joseph Karo (d. 1575), whose *Shulḥān ᶜArūkh* remains to this day the most authoritative handbook of Jewish law among both Ashkenazim and Sefardim. Devotees of Jewish mysticism flocked to Safed. The most famous of all the kabbalists, R. Isaac Luria, "the Godly Lion," taught his esoteric doctrines there from 1569 until his death in 1572. A Hebrew printing press was established in Safed

80 The authoritative study of Sabbatay Ṣevi, his movement, and its repercussions throughout the Jewish world is Scholem, *Sabbatai Ṣevi.* On the messianic spirit in sixteenth-century Palestine, see Ben-Zvi, *Eretz-Israel under Ottoman Rule,* pp. 155–68 passim.

81 Lewis, *Notes and Documents from the Turkish Archives: A Contribution to the History of the Jews in the Ottoman Empire* (Jerusalem, 1952), p. 10.

82 Ibid., pp. 7–8; Ben-Zvi, *Eretz Israel under Ottoman Rule,* pp. 161–62.

83 Shmuel Avitsur, "Safed—Center of the Manufacture of Woven Woolens in the Fifteenth Century," *Sefunot* 6 (1962): 41–69 [Heb.]. Despite its title, this article deals mainly with the sixteenth century. See also Yaᶜaqov Kenaᶜani, "Ha-Ḥayyīm ha-Kalkaliyyīm be-Ṣfāt ūve-Svivōtēhā be-Mē'ā ha-Shesh ᶜEsre ve-Ḥaṣī ha-Mē'ā ha-Shevaᶜ ᶜEsre," *Zion* o.s. 6 (1933–34): 195–201; Ben-Zvi, *Eretz-Israel under Ottoman Rule,* pp. 172–73; Lewis, *Notes,* pp. 13–15; and the documents translated in Part Two below, pp. 290–92 and 293–94.

by Eliezer and Abraham Ashkenazi in 1577. It was in operation for a decade and was the first press of any kind east of Constantinople and west of China.[84]

Bold projects for developing the Holy Land were conceived by Jewish courtiers in Constantinople. Doña Gracia Mendes and her nephew Don Joseph Nasi undertook the rebuilding of Tiberias, which had fallen into ruin as a Jewish city. In 1558 or 1559, Doña Gracia received a patent from Sultan Sulaymān the Magnificent, leasing to her the town of Tiberias for a sum of 1,000 cruzados per annum. In the years that followed, the walls of Tiberias were rebuilt, a *yeshiva* was founded, and letters were sent out to various Italian Jewish communities, inviting people to settle in the newly revived town. The plan to restore Tiberias as a Jewish center had messianic overtones, as there was an ancient tradition that the Messiah would appear there. The restoration scheme may well have had more practical motives also. Even while he was still a nominal Christian in Italy, Don Joseph had proposed the idea of a Jewish commonwealth that would be a refuge for any and all persecuted Jews. After the death of Don Joseph in 1579, the town was leased to another Sefardic courtier, Solomon Ibn Yaᶜīsh, who continued building and development for a time. Don Solomon's son Jacob actually went to settle there.[85]

The prosperity and relative security of the sixteenth century was enjoyed by Jews in most of the Arab provinces of the Ottoman Empire. In each province, Jews lived their own independent communal life. The communities themselves were subdivided according to ethnic groups that included Mustaᶜrabīm (or Moriscos), as the native Arabic-speaking Jews were called, Sefardim, Maghrebis, Italians, and, in some places, Ashkenazim. At this early period there was as yet no centralized millet system (see below, p. 97) in the Ottoman Empire, although later historians have tended to project it back anachronistically.[86]

[84] There is a considerable body of literature on the intellectual and spiritual life of Safed. The best survey in English is still Solomon Schechter's "Safed in the Sixteenth Century: A City of Legists and Mystics," in his *Studies in Judaism*, 2d ser. (Philadelphia, 1945), pp. 202–306. See also Ben-Zvi, *Eretz-Israel under Ottoman Rule*, pp. 176–87. See also Naphtali Ben-Menaḥem, "A Bibliography of Publications on Safed," *Sefunot* 6 (1962): 475–500, where 504 works on Safed are cited.

[85] Concerning the Tiberias project, see Cecil Roth, *The House of Nasi: The Duke of Naxos* (Philadelphia, 1948), pp. 97–135; and J. Braslavsky, "Jewish Settlement in Tiberias from Don Joseph Nasi to Ibn Yaish," *Zion* 5, no. 1 (1940): 45–72 [Heb.]. See also the passage translated in Part Two below, pp. 293–94.

[86] This point has been argued convincingly by Benjamin Braude, "The

1. "Old Jewish Castle" of Marḥab in Khaybar
H. St. John Philby, *The Land of Midian* (London: Ernest Benn Ltd., 1957)

2. A Geniza letter written by a fugitive from the poll tax collector in eleventh-century Egypt
(ULC Or 1081 J 13)

3. *The traditional "House of Maimonides" in Fez*

Hayyē ha-Yehūdīm be-Marōqqō, (Israel Museum Catalogue No. 103, Jerusalem, 1973)

4. *The remains of the Naḥmanides Synagogue in Jerusalem, confiscated from the Jews in 1598*

Izhak Ben-Zvi, *Eretz-Israel under Ottoman Rule* (Jerusalem: Ben-Zvi Institute, 1966)

5. *Turkish shadow puppet of a Jewish peddler*

Hellmut Ritter, *Karagös,* 2d series (Istanbul, 1941). Courtesy of Richard Ettinghausen, Metropolitan Museum of Art, New York

6. *Doña Gracia Nasi, patroness of Ottoman Jewry, from a portrait medal by Pastorino de Pastorini, 1553*

7. *The mystical prayer book known as* Siddūr ha-Arī. *Moroccan ms. dated 1790*
Israel Museum Catalogue No. 103

TOP RIGHT:
8. *Carpet page from the* Second Leningrad Bible

BOTTOM RIGHT:
9. *Carpet page from* Ōṣerōt Ḥayyīm *(Treasures of Life) by R. Isaac Luria, ha-Arī. Moroccan ms. dated 1760*
Israel Museum Catalogue No. 103

ספר
אוצרות חיים
יצחק לוריא אשכנזי זלה״ה
וברכה
כמוהר״ר חיים ויטל זלה״ה
הארי זלה״ה
יעקב צמח זלה״ה
תהלות
ואמלא
אשרי
הרשם

10. Street in the Mellāḥ of Fez

H. Z. Hirschberg, *Me-Ereṣ Mevō ha-Shemesh* (Jerusalem: Ha-Histadrūt ha-Ṣiyyonit, 1957)

TOP RIGHT:

11. Entrance to the Mellāḥ of Sefrou (Morocco), once the most crowded Jewish quarter in Morocco, now totally devoid of Jews

Photo by Yedida K. Stillman

BOTTOM RIGHT:

12. A typical side street in the Gāᶜ al-Yahūd (Jewish Quarter) of Sanᶜa, Yemen

Carl Rathjens, *Jewish Domestic Architecture in Sanᶜa, Yemen* (Jerusalem: Israel Oriental Society, 1957)

13. Inside a synagogue in San^{c}a (early twentieth century)

Eugen Mittwoch, ed., *Aus dem Jemen: Hermann Burchardts letzte Reise durch Südarabien* (Leipzig: n.p., n.d.)

TOP RIGHT:

14. The Ben Gualid (Walīd) Synagogue in Tetouan, Morocco

Photo by Yedida K. Stillman

BOTTOM RIGHT:

15. Entrance to the Mellāḥ of Tetouan (founded in 1807)

H. Z. Hirschberg, *Me-Ereṣ Mevō ha-Shemesh* (Jerusalem: Ha-Histadrūt ha-Ṣiyyōnīt, 1957)

16. An Algerian Jew depicted in a late eighteenth-century etching
Courtesy of the L. A. Mayer Memorial Institute for Islamic Art, Jerusalem

There was no conscious general policy toward Jews or non-Muslims. Whatever policies there were, were basically ad hoc and rather liberal. With the exception of enforcing the *jizya,* there was little that was traditionally Islamic in the early Ottoman treatment of *dhimmīs.* The Turkish attitude toward non-Muslims at this time, as Gibb and Bowen have pointed out, "was far from being conventionally Moslem."[87] There were occasional examples of Jews being mistreated by local authorities, sometimes at the instigation of religious fanatics. However, most difficulties with the local authorities could be referred to the Jewish courtiers in Constantinople, who frequently interceded at the Porte (Ottoman court) on behalf of their coreligionists.

The sixteenth century was a brief interlude of brightness in the long twilight of the late Islamic Middle Ages for the Jews of Arab lands. The shadows again began appearing toward the end of the century. The administrative abilities of Ottoman rulers began to decline. This was most keenly felt in the provinces, where corruption, inefficiency, and frequent disorder were commonplace. With the disciplined control of Constantinople slipping, the position of the Jews became more tenuous. R. David Ibn Abī Zimra (d. 1573), the chief Jewish scholar in Egypt, had written in the heyday of Ottoman rule that "the spilling of Jewish blood [by members of the non-Jewish populace] is not common because they fear the authority of the government."[88] Perhaps no Jewish communities in the Ottoman Arab provinces suffered more than did those in Palestine from the breakdown of strong central authority. Arab uprisings and a series of natural catastrophes left Safed, Tiberias, and other formerly thriving Jewish settlements utterly depopulated.

The Sublime Porte was not by any means entirely powerless as the decline set in, but Jews found that they had less access even to the

---

Ottoman State and Non-Muslim Communities, 1500–1700: The Myth of the Jewish Millet," unpublished paper delivered at a conference on Aspects of Jewish Life under Islam, Ohio State University, Columbus, May 16–17, 1976; in Shaul Shaked, *Aspects of Jewish Life under Islam,* forthcoming, and idem, "Myths of the Pre-Tanzimat Millet System," a paper delivered at the Princeton Millet Conference, June 1978.

[87] H. A. R. Gibb and Harold Bowen, *Islamic Society and the West: A Study of the Impact of Western Civilization on Moslem Culture in the Near East,* vol. 1, pt. 2 (London, 1965), p. 209.

[88] The passage is quoted in the original Hebrew-Aramaic in Israel M. Goldman, *The Life and Times of Rabbi David Ibn Abi Zimra* (New York, 1970), p. 235, n. 60. A freer English translation is given by Goldman in the same work, p. 156.

halls of dwindling power. There were still Jewish courtiers in the seventeenth century, but none enjoyed the stature and, more importantly, the influence of men like Joseph Nasi, Solomon Ibn Yaᶜīsh, or Moses and Joseph Hamon in the preceding period.

Another important factor that contributed to the overall decline of Ottoman Jewry was the growing tendency toward religious conservatism in Istanbul and a concerted effort to emphasize the Islamic nature of the society.[89] In such an atmosphere, the social and political status of the Jews—and of all *dhimmīs*—declined. Their economic position, however, was less affected by the Islamic normalization, for their international contacts, their linguistic abilities, and their talents amply compensated for their social disabilities.

The laws of differentiation were reinstated to mark the *dhimmīs'* essential otherness. Murād III (1574–95) was the first sultan to reintroduce the sumptuary restrictions, which had long been ignored. He forbade the wearing of silks by *dhimmīs* and ordered them to wear a special high, conical hat, or *boneta,* rather than the turban. He is supposed to have originally ordered in a moment of extreme pique the wholesale massacre of the Jews in his realm, and it was only at the intervention of his mother and the grand vizier that he rescinded the decree.[90] If Murād did indeed issue such an order, it was probably for the purpose of raising money, for he could be sure that substantial sums would be paid for him to revoke it.

Beginning with Murād's reign, the prohibition against synagogue construction and repair was strictly enforced. In 1584, an investigation was ordered to determine the legality of the numerous synagogues in Safed. The exact outcome of the investigation is not known, although several years later the number of synagogues in the town had been reduced by one-third. In 1856, the venerable Naḥmanides Synagogue in Jerusalem, which had been in continual use for over three centuries, was permanently confiscated and turned into a warehouse.[91]

The restrictions on synagogues were frequently circumvented by establishing conventicles in private homes. This is the reason for so many of the small synagogues in the Arab world to this day being named after individuals or families. If denounced to the authorities, these makeshift meeting rooms could be closed down and their con-

[89] See Karl Binswanger, *Untersuchungen zum Status der Nichtmuslime im osmanischen Reich des 16. Jahrhunderts, mit einer Neudefinition des Begriffes "Dimma"* (Munich, 1977), pp. 165–99.

[90] Franco, *Israélites de l'Empire Ottoman*, p. 72.

[91] See the documents translated in Part Two below, pp. 300–2.

tents made liable to confiscation unless sufficient bribes were paid. This state of affairs continued well into the nineteenth century and was one of the most typical and consistent forms of harassment endured by Jews in the Ottoman Empire and, in fact, in all Muslim lands.[92]

The seventeenth, eighteenth, and nineteenth centuries were oppressive years for most of the inhabitants of the Middle East. The ruling Turkish minority treated the average Arab Muslim almost as contemptuously as they did the *dhimmīs*. Each of the religious communities cordially detested one another. Religious tensions ran as high as at any period in Muslim history, including perhaps even the period of the Crusaders. The Islamic Ottoman state was declining on the world scene, while Christian European power was on the rise.

The native economy stagnated during these centuries and came to be dominated by Europeans through the institution of the capitulations, or *imtiyāzāt,* which may be considered to a certain degree as the mercantile forerunner of modern colonialism. The great majority of Jews, like the rest of the Middle Eastern masses, were reduced to poverty or subsistence level. There were always some who prospered. The European trading companies conducted much of their business in the Levant with the help of local Christian and Jewish agents. *Dhimmīs* were still predominant in the reprehensible professions such as moneylending, moneychanging, tax farming, and collecting customs duties. But, as in earlier periods, these people represented only a small fraction of the total *dhimmī* population and were, for better or for worse, the dominant elite in their respective communities. There was also a special class of Jews from European countries who came to the Levant as protected foreign nationals and were, therefore, spared many of the inconveniences—not to mention the indignities—of *dhimmī* status. These *francos,* or *franjīs,* as they were called by the local Jews, contributed to the native Jewish communities, but were not really part of them. In any case, their numbers were insignificant.[93] A few native Ottoman Jews shared the privileges of the *francos*. These were the *beratlıs*. They were the possessors of special patents (Turk., *berāt*) that were granted them in return for various services to European

[92] See, for example, the document translated in Part Two below, p. 364; and also H. Z. [J. W.] Hirschberg, "The Oriental Jewish Communities," in A. J. Arberry, *Religion in the Middle East: Three Religions in Concord and Conflict,* vol. 1 (Cambridge, 1969), pp. 153–55, especially p. 154.

[93] Concerning the Francos, see Alexander Lutzky, "The 'Francos' and the Effect of the Capitulations on the Jews in Aleppo," *Zion* 6, no. 1 (1940): 46–79. [Heb.]. See also below Part Two, p. 318.

commercial and diplomatic representatives, or which they purchased outright. There were many more Christian *beratlıs* than Jewish ones, and within the Jewish community the *beratlıs* constituted a tiny fraction of the population.[94]

By the dawn of the nineteenth century, the condition of most of the Jews in the Ottoman provinces was not much different from what it had been before the conquest of Selim the Grim, four hundred years earlier.

[94] See Bernard Lewis, "Beratli," *EI*² 1:1171.

5

THE DAWN OF MODERN TIMES

The Jews of Arab Lands in the Nineteenth Century

The Muslim world and all of its peoples underwent a veritable metamorphosis during the course of the nineteenth century. This profound transformation, which was both social and political, began in different places at different times. The rate of change varied here and there and in some regions may have seemed imperceptible even as the century was drawing to a close. Nevertheless, the forces of change were at work undermining many of the traditional foundations upon which the Middle Eastern social and political order was based. The causes for change were both internal and external, but the prime factor was undoubtedly the impact of an ascendant Europe upon the economic, political, and cultural life of the Islamic world. This metamorphosis is still not complete, and much of the social disorientation that has accompanied it is still manifest today.

No native group in the nineteenth century benefited more from European interference into Middle Eastern affairs than did the *dhimmīs*. They were quick to see that increased European influence and penetration meant a weakening of the traditional Islamic norms of society, and hence could only better their own position. *Dhimmīs* accepted the outward trappings of westernization earlier and with greater ease than did most Muslims. The small, *dhimmī* mercantile elite had for centuries maintained close ties with European economic interests in the Islamic world. *Dhimmīs* eagerly sought the protection of European powers through the latter's consular agents, who, under the capitulations, had extraterritorial authority in the Ottoman Empire, Morocco, and other Islamic states. *Dhimmī* merchants who were able to travel to British India, French Algeria, or Europe itself frequently returned home as naturalized foreign subjects, safely removed from the confines of the legal system of their native land.

For their part, the European powers openly espoused the cause of non-Muslims, or more particularly Christians, in the Ottoman Empire. They were motivated in this both by genuine moral sentiments and by blatant imperialistic designs. The fact that at first the European powers were interested almost exclusively in the local Christians is immaterial as far as the Jews (whose cause was frequently espoused by the British) were concerned, for Islamic law did not distinguish between Christians and Jews as *dhimmīs*. Most improvements, therefore, in the legal position of Christians were enjoyed by Jewish subjects of the Porte as well.

The first formal move toward improving the legal position of non-Muslims in the Ottoman Empire was the promulgation by Sultan ᶜAbd al-Majīd I of the Khaṭṭ-i Sherif of Gülhane (Noble Rescript of the Rose Chamber) on November 3, 1839. The Khaṭṭ-i Sherif was a programmatic enumeration of reforms that affected the individual subjects of the Ottoman state. It echoed many of the libertarian ideals that had been voiced in the French Declaration of the Rights of Man fifty years earlier. The most significant aspect of the decree as far as *dhimmīs* were concerned was that it granted civil equality to non-Muslims, namely:

> These imperial concessions are extended to all of Our subjects. They will enjoy them irrespective of to whatever religion or sect they may belong. We are according, therefore, complete security to the inhabitants of the Empire with regard to their lives, their honor, and their fortunes even as it is required by the sacred text of our law.[1]

It took some forty years to implement the reforms promised by the Khaṭṭ-i Sherif in Turkey itself. In the Arab provinces of the Ottoman Empire, the decree went almost unnoticed and, in any case, had little practical effect. Many of the local pashas and begs were feudal lords in their satrapies and did not share the outlook of the *tanzimatçılar* (reformers) in Constantinople headed by the progressive-minded Muṣṭafā Rashīd Pasha.[2]

[1] E. Engelhardt, *La Turquie et le Tanzimat ou histoire des réformes dans l'Empire Ottoman depuis 1826 jusqu'à nos jours,* vol. 1 (Paris, 1882), p. 260. The full official French text of the decree is given in ibid., pp. 257–61.

[2] A good, up-to-date survey of the Tanzimat era and the men who made it may be found in Stanford J. Shaw and Ezel Kural Shaw, *History of the Ottoman Empire and Modern Turkey,* vol. 2 (Cambridge, 1977), pp. 55–272.

ᶜAbd al-Majīd had to reiterate the goals and sentiments of the Khaṭṭ-i Sherif on February 18, 1856, in a new reform decree, the Khaṭṭ-i Humayun (Imperial Rescript).[3] The Khaṭṭ-i Humayun went even further in stipulating the rights of non-Muslims. Henceforth, abusive and derogatory references to non-Muslims were to be banned from official usage. The common appellation for the *dhimmī* populace, *raᶜāyā*—a word meaning "grazing cattle"—was dropped from official documents. The Khaṭṭ-i Humayun accorded non-Muslims the right to repair sanctuaries and communal buildings and indirectly guaranteed their right to build new houses of worship with the approval of the Porte.

The new edict also called for reorganization of the religious communities on a national basis. In keeping with the spirit of the Tanzimat, they were to be constitutionally organized with lay and religious governing bodies. This particular reform in effect led to the creation by imperial fiat of the well-known millet system, whereby each individual non-Muslim religious community in its entirety became an officially recognized autonomous body whose members were represented to the state through designated communal leaders. The first steps toward creating the Jewish millet as a recognized, legal entity had already been taken by the Ottoman authorities in the two decades preceding the promulgation of the Khaṭṭ-i Humayun when the office of *ḥākhām-bāshī*, or chief rabbi, was created, first in Constantinople and later in other major cities.

One of the more conspicuous marks of the new civil equality for Ottoman non-Muslims was the abolition of the *jizya*, which since early Islamic times had been understood as a symbol of *dhimmī* humiliation. In its place was imposed a new tax, the *bedel-i askeri* (military substitution tax), which fell upon non-Muslims who were now liable for military conscription. The *bedel-i askeri* remained in force until 1909, when any form of monetary payment in lieu of military service was abolished.[4]

The Khaṭṭ-i Humayun was followed by a series of Provincial Reform Laws that aimed at modernizing the administration of the

[3] The full French text is given in Engelhardt, *La Turquie et le Tanzimat*, vol. 1, pp. 263–70. An abridged translation is given in Part Two below, pp. 357–60. For the effects of the Tanzimat in the Levant, see Moshe Maᶜoz, *Ottoman Reform in Syria and Palestine, 1840–1861: The Impact of the Tanzimat on Politics and Society* (Oxford, 1968).

[4] Engelhardt, *La Turquie et le Tanzimat*, vol. 1, pp. 126–27; M. Franco, *Israélites de l'Empire Ottoman* (Paris, 1897), p. 146; Shaw and Shaw, *Ottoman Empire and Modern Turkey*, vol. 2, p. 100.

Ottoman provinces where, as previously mentioned, the spirit of the Tanzimat was least in evidence. This reform legislation also dealt specifically with the civil rights of non-Muslims, specifying that they should be represented on advisory councils at the *vilayet* (province), *sanjaq* (subprovince), and *kaza* (district) levels. The inclusion of non-Muslims on advisory councils was not entirely new. The process had already begun a few years earlier. For example, as of 1840, a Jew sat on the fourteen-man municipal council of Jerusalem. The Provincial Reform Laws, however, standardized the process of including non-Muslims in provincial civil affairs, although their role was—to say the least—a very limited one.[5]

Reforms in the civil status of non-Muslims were introduced in the wake of the Turkish Tanzimat in Tunisia, which was an autonomous tributary state of the Ottoman Empire. The ruler of Tunisia, Muḥammad Beg (1855–59), under pressure from the European consuls issued a decree in 1857 that reflected the spirit of the Khaṭṭ-i Sherif and the Khaṭṭ-i Humayun. The ᶜAhd al-Amān (Covenant of Security) proclaimed, among other things, the equality of Tunisian Jews (there were no native Christians although there were many foreign residents) with Muslims before the law and guaranteed their persons, their property, and their honor. Although it did not abolish discriminatory taxation, the ᶜAhd al-Amān promised a progressive lightening of the tax burden. The Tunisian decree did not go as far as the Turkish reforms, and its language was more traditionally Islamic. Even so, it still stirred up a considerable degree of popular resentment.[6]

Like Tunisia, Egypt in the nineteenth century was an autonomous state that was nominally a province of the Ottoman Empire. Its pasha,

[5] Itzhak Ben-Zvi, *Eretz-Israel under Ottoman Rule,* 2d ed. (Jerusalem, 1966), p. 350 [Heb.]; Franco, *Israélites de l'Empire Ottoman,* p. 150. Extracts from the Provincial Reform Laws are given in Engelhardt, *La Turquie et le Tanzimat,* vol. 1, pp. 271–76.

[6] Excerpts from the text of the *ᶜAhd al-Amān* relating to Jews or non-Muslims generally are given in David Cazès, *Essai sur l'histoire des Israélites de Tunisie: depuis les temps les plus reculés jusqu'à l'établissement du protectorat de la France en Tunisie* (Paris, 1889), pp. 152–56. Cazès refers to the edict as "la Constitution," whereas most writers referred to it as "le Pacte Fondamental." Both are correct since in Ottoman usage the concept of a constitution was expressed by *qānūn asāsī,* or "fundamental law." See also H. Z. [J. W.] Hirschberg, *A History of the Jews in North Africa,* vol. 2, pp. 146–47 [Heb.]; Jamil M. Abun-Nasr, *A History of the Maghrib,* 2d ed. (Cambridge, 1975), pp. 264–65. The best study on the vicissitudes of Tanzimat reforms in Tunisia is André Raymond, "La France, la Grande-Bretagne et le problème de la réforme à Tunis (1855–1857)," *Etudes Maghrébines: Mélanges Charles-André Julien* (Paris, 1964), pp. 137–64.

Muḥammad ᶜAlī (1805–49), had introduced numerous administrative and economic reforms, some of which were well in advance of those in Turkey. The general physical security and well-being of his Jewish and Christian subjects improved under his rule and that of his successors. Despite heavy taxation, the economic position of non-Muslims in Egypt became progressively stronger throughout the century with the growth of a Western-oriented economy. The legal and social status of Egyptian Jewry, on the other hand, improved but little until the last two decades of the century. Civil equality was only granted in 1882 under the Khedive Tawfīq, and that was after the establishment of the British Occupation.[7]

The civil advances made by the Jews in the Ottoman Empire, its tributary states, and in Algeria (which had been under French rule since the 1830s),[8] stirred the desire for some form of emancipation among the urban Jewish elite in Sharifan Morocco. Moroccan Jewry, it will be recalled, lived under one of the most oppressive *dhimma* systems of the later Islamic Middle Ages, comparable only to that of Yemen and Iran. As mentioned in the preceding chapter, this system remained in force throughout Morocco for most of the nineteenth century, and in some places continued well into the twentieth century.

Toward the end of the year 1863, the noted British philanthropist and Jewish leader Sir Moses Montefiore set out for Morocco with a delegation of British Jews, including Haim Guedalla, who was of Moroccan descent and was related to Sir Moses by marriage. The delegation had the full backing of the British government and was given diplomatic support. One of the aims of the mission was to obtain from Sultan Muḥammad IV (ruled 1859–73) a decree that in some measure would improve the legal and social position of Morocco's Jews and, at the very least, indicate the sultan's intent to protect them from widespread abuse. The memorandum presented to Mawlāy Muḥammad requested that the Jews "enjoy the benefits" of other Moroccan subjects. It did not specify anything as far-reaching as the Khaṭṭ-i Sherif or the Khaṭṭ-i Humayun, but did mention firmans obtained by Sir Moses from ᶜAbd al-Majīd in 1840 and ᶜAbd al-ᶜAzīz in 1863, and

[7] See Jacob M. Landau, *Jews in Nineteenth-Century Egypt* (New York, 1969), pp. 16–20. See also the passages in Part Two below, pp. 324–27 and 423–27.

[8] The process of the emancipation of Algerian Jewry is not discussed here at all. For a succinct survey, see André N. Chouraqui, *Between East and West: A History of the Jews of North Africa,* trans. Michael M. Bernet (New York, 1973), pp. 141–57; also Hirschberg, *The Jews of North Africa,* vol. 2, pp. 77–88 [Heb.].

thus indirectly alluded to the Tanzimat reforms. It is clear from the account in the Sharifan historian al-Nāṣirī that the allusions were clearly understood despite the guarded language.[9] The Sultan was not willing to grant anything resembling emancipation to his Jewish subjects. However, he expressed his sympathy with the humanitarian goals of Sir Moses' mission. On February 5, 1864, Mawlāy Muḥammad issued a *dahir* (class. Ar., *ẓahīr*), or royal decree, declaring his intention to treat his Jews with complete justice as was due any Moroccan subject and to protect them from all oppression. The language of the *dahir* was in complete accordance with Islamic tradition, albeit in the best sense. It made no concessions vis-à-vis the legal status of the Jews. From the Moroccan point of view, the *dahir* was already too much of a concession that gave the Jews wrong ideas. According to al-Nāṣirī, the Jews "became arrogant and reckless, and they wanted to have special rights under the law." The sultan quickly issued a second decree after the English mission had departed, clarifying his initial *dahir* to the point of nullifying it. The *dahir* of February 5, 1864, was a dead letter. Morocco would have no part in Tanzimat-style reforms at this time.[10]

Legal emancipation had merely been put off for another fifty years, when it would be imposed from without. Meanwhile, other forces were at work to improve the condition of the Jews of Morocco and other Arab lands—most notably the newly formed Alliance Israélite Universelle.

The Alliance was founded in Paris in 1860 and was the first international Jewish organization of its kind. Its goals were clearly stated in the first article of *Les Statuts de l'Alliance Israélite Universelle:*

1. to work everywhere for the emancipation and moral progress of Jews;
2. to lend effective assistance to those who suffer because of their being Jews;
3. to encourage every publication appropriate to achieving this result.[11]

The Alliance sought to carry out its program through diplomatic and educational activities, and it was in the latter sphere that it was most effective in achieving—to use Narcisse Leven's phrase—"l'éman-

[9] The passage from al-Nāṣirī is translated in Part Two below, pp. 371–73.

[10] For the circumstances surrounding Sir Moses' mission to Morocco, see Hirschberg, *The Jews in North Africa,* vol. 2, pp. 306–12 [Heb.]; also Chouraqui, *Between East and West,* pp. 172–73.

[11] André N. Chouraqui, *Cent ans d'histoire: l'Alliance Israélite Universelle et la renaissance juive contemporain (1860–1960)* (Paris, 1965), pp. 412, 415.

cipation par l'instruction."[12] The work of the Alliance was never limited exclusively to the Arabic-speaking or the wider Islamic world, but from the very beginning, the major focus of its educational endeavors was in the Ottoman Empire and in North Africa.

The first Alliance school was founded in Tetouan in 1862. Its curriculum combined religious and modern secular instruction in Hebrew, French, and the language of the country. The Tetouan school became the model for those that followed. In 1864, two Alliance schools were opened in Tangier, one in Damascus, and another in Baghdad. In 1867, the Jerusalem school opened its doors to students, and in 1870, the Mikveh Israel Agricultural School was established on 650 acres of land near Jaffa. By the end of the century, Alliance elementary and secondary schools had been established in most of the major towns and cities that had Jewish communities, from Morocco to Iran.[13] The Alliance educational network produced cadres of westernized Middle Eastern Jews who now had a distinct advantage of opportunity over the largely uneducated Muslim masses as the Middle East and the Maghreb were drawn ineluctably into the modern world economic system. Together with the rapidly evolving native Christians who benefited from missionary schools, they came to have a place in the economic life of the Muslim world that was far out of proportion to their numbers or their social status in the general population. Their western ties and their economic success were deeply resented by the Muslim majority. It was this conspicuous overachievement on the part of some *dhimmīs* that would contribute to their undoing as a group in the twentieth century with the rise of nationalism in the Arab world.

It is a great irony that during the nineteenth century, which was the very period when the legal and economic position of the Jews was improving throughout the Arab world, the physical security of Jewish persons and property was quite precarious and in many places was actually declining. This insecurity was in part because of a general deterioration of the forces of law and order in most Arab lands. Egypt, with its strong central government established by Muḥammad ʿAlī, was the notable exception to this rule. Outside Egypt, town and village dwellers were frequently the victims of pillage and rape at the hands of marauding tribesmen or rebellious troops. Anyone or any group was

[12] Narcisse Leven, *Cinquante ans d'histoire: l'Alliance Israélite Universelle (1860–1910),* vol. 2 (Paris, 1920), pp. 7–8.

[13] For the history of the Alliance schools in the Middle East, see Leven, *Cinquante ans,* vol. 2, pp. 10–272 and 289–332. A map indicating the Alliance schools from Morocco to Iran is given by Chouraqui, *Cent ans,* pp. 448–49.

considered fair game by extortionate provincial governors and local officials. Non-Muslims, however, were especially vulnerable because of their traditionally weak social position.

Jewish accounts of abuse or oppression at this period were naturally concerned with their own predicament and usually did not go into detail on the plight of others. Thus the distinction between attacks against Jews as Jews and attacks against them as weak and defenseless townspeople is often blurred. The widespread insecurity and misrule that characterized life in much of the nineteenth-century Arab world led a number of scholars—particularly those dealing with Morocco—to conclude that the Jews were really no worse off than anyone else outside the ruling class.[14] Judging the relative security or insecurity of one group vis-à-vis others in nineteenth-century Arab societies is, of course, difficult, but as far as Morocco is concerned, the evidence clearly indicates that this judgment is seriously mistaken.[15] There were periodic incidents of anti-Jewish violence that were often inspired by populist religious reformers. Some anti-Jewish riots in late nineteenth-century Morocco had socioeconomic rather than religious causes, but this does not change their specifically anti-Jewish tone.[16]

At the other end of the Arab world in Iraq, both Jews and native Christians lived in a continual state of insecurity throughout the nineteenth century. The situation was worst in the *vilayet* of Mosul, which comprised all of northern Mesopotamia. The region was frequently in turmoil due to the unruliness of the Kurdish tribes. Jews and Christians suffered additional hardships by virtue of their being non-Muslims. They were subject to physical abuse by Turks, Arabs, as well as Kurds. The British consul in Mosul, Charles Rassam, writing to his nation's ambassador in Constantinople in 1841, described the

[14] See, for example, Hirschberg, *Jews in North Africa,* vol. 2, p. 208 [Heb.]; Lawrence Rosen, "Muslim-Jewish relations in a Moroccan City," *IJMES* 3, no. 4 (October 1972): 447; Stuart Schaar, "Conflict and Change in Nineteenth Century Morocco" (Ph.D. diss., Princeton University, 1965), p. 166; see also Schaar's remarks in *Muslim-Jewish Relations in North Africa* (New York, 1975), pp. 29–31, particularly p. 31. For a more cautious assessment of the situation of Jews in the Ottoman Arab provinces, see Shimon Shamir, "Muslim-Arab Attitudes Toward Jews: The Ottoman and Modern Periods," in *Violence and Defense in the Jewish Experience,* ed. Salo W. Baron and George S. Wise (Philadelphia, 1977), p. 197.

[15] See Norman A. Stillman, "The Moroccan Jewish Experience: A Revisionist View," *The Jerusalem Quarterly* 9 (1978):121.

[16] See Leland Bowie, "An Aspect of Muslim-Jewish Relations in Late Nineteenth-Century Morocco," *IJMES* 7, no. 1 (January 1976): 14–15.

Jews of the *vilayet* as being "subject to tyranny of the worst kind."[17] Reports on the treatment of Christians contain more of the same.[18]

In Baghdad, the large, well-to-do Jewish community was subjected to perpetual official oppression during the governorship of Dā'ūd Pasha (ruled 1817–31) and his religious adviser, Mulla Muḥammad, who was called by the Jews *al-mōsēr* (the Informer). Toward the end of Dā'ūd Pasha's despotic rule, many Jews fled the province seeking refuge in Iran, Masqat, India, and even Australia. Among the refugees were members of the famous Sassoon clan.[19]

The relations between Muslims and non-Muslims in Baghdad—as indeed in most of Iraq—remained tense throughout the nineteenth century and into the twentieth. There were numerous anti-Jewish and anti-Christian riots, some limited and some on a large scale. The mere rumor of one was enough to throw the *dhimmī* communities into a panic.[20]

Jews and Christians were especially vulnerable to accusations that they had blasphemed against Muḥammad or that they had once converted to Islam and thereafter apostasized. Capital punishment was called for in either case. There were many instances of Jews being accused of blasphemy or apostasy in Iraq during the second half of the nineteenth century. Friendly *wālīs* (governors), just *qāḍīs* (judges), and British consuls sometimes intervened to see that justice was done. However, as late as 1876, a Jew was beaten and hanged outside the city gates because of a charge of blasphemy.[21] This problem was not unique to Iraqi Jewry. Jews everywhere in the Muslim world were in danger of such accusations whenever they had a falling out with a Muslim or tried to collect a bad debt. In 1834, for example, Sol Hatchuel, a fourteen-year-old girl from Tangier, was executed in Morocco, having been charged with accepting Islam, which she de-

17 Public Records Office (London), FO 195/228.

18 For example, ibid., letter from Rassam to British Ambassador Sir Stratford Canning in Constantinople, dated July 29, 1843.

19 David Solomon Sassoon, *A History of the Jews in Baghdad* (Letchworth, England, 1949), pp. 123–27; also Abraham Ben-Jacob, *A History of the Jews of Iraq: From the End of the Gaonic Period (1038 C.E.) to the Present Time* (Jerusalem, 1965), pp. 103–5 and 114–15 [Heb.].

20 See, for example, the document in Part Two below, p. 388.

21 Ben-Jacob, *The Jews of Iraq*, p. 143, where more examples are cited in n. 9 [Heb.]. See also the consular correspondence concerned with one such incident in Part Two below, pp. 385–87. For a survey of Islamic legal questions, see A. Turki, "Situation du ⟨⟨Tributaire⟩⟩ qui insulte l'Islam au regard de la doctrine et de la jurisprudence musulmanes," *Studia Islamica* 30 (1969).

nied.[22] In 1857, a Tunisian Jew, Batto Sfez, was accused of blasphemy. Despite the intervention of the European consular corps in Tunis, Sfez was executed.[23] There seem to have been more reports of such incidents from Iraq, however, than from any other Arab country at that time.

The Jews of Syria lived a generally more secure existence than did their brethren in Iraq during the nineteenth century. Tensions between the religious and ethnic communities of Syria ran deep. On the whole, the Christians seem to have borne the brunt of periodic Muslim or Druze violence. The reason for this was that the Christians were a much larger and more conspicuous minority than the Jews. They had strong ties with European economic interests in the Levant. They had profited more than any group during the occupation of Ibrāhīm Pasha (ruled 1833–40), Muḥammad ʿAlī's son. In addition to this, the militancy of the Maronites in Mount Lebanon and their bloody struggles with the Druze often spilled over into Syria proper, with dire consequences for the Syrian Christians who became the victims of Druze or Muslim reprisals. The most notorious example of anti-Christian persecution of this sort was the massacre of some 5,000 Christians in Damascus in 1860.[24]

The Syrian Christians, for their part, harbored a deep antipathy for the Jews, who were a weaker minority than themselves. Although they had no empathy for the Muslims either (or for members of the different Christian sects), they shared a common heritage with the Arab Muslim and, despite their social disabilities, considered themselves part of Arab culture and society. In fact, it was the Syrian Christians who created the renascence of Arabic language and literature known as the *Nahḍa* (Revival) in the second half of the nineteenth century.

The Syrian Christians shared not only the Arabs' traditional contempt for the Jew but also European anti-Semitic notions, which were imported by French traders and missionaries. The Eastern churches had always maintained that the Jews were deicides and were a people

[22] Hirschberg, *The Jews in North Africa,* vol. 2, pp. 304–5 [Heb.]. Sol Hatchuel became a popular saint and her tomb in Fez an object of pilgrimage. See L. Voinot, *Pèlerinages judéo-musulmans du Maroc* (Paris, 1948), pp. 50–51.

[23] Cazès, *L'histoire des Israélites de Tunisie,* pp. 150–51; Hirschberg, *The Jews in North Africa,* vol. 2 p. 145 [Heb.]; Leven, *Cinquante ans,* vol. 2, pp. 103–4.

[24] In the aftermath of these persecutions the Christians turned on the Jews. See the document translated in Part Two below, pp. 403–5.

cursed by God, but they did not have in their storehouse of anti-Jewish lore such typically European horror stories as the desecration of the Host or the blood libel. The belief that Jews kidnapped and sacrificed Christian children was current among the Christians of Aleppo in the 1750s and may have already been in circulation at the beginning of the seventeenth century.[25] This particular prejudice does not seem to have had any detrimental consequences as far as the Jews were concerned until the nineteenth century.

The first serious blood libel in the Arab world was the so-called Damascus Affair of 1840. This affair was touched off by the disappearance of an Italian Capuchin friar and his native servant in Damascus on February 5, 1840. The local Christians, supported by the French Consul Ratti-Menton, accused the Jews of having murdered the two men in order to obtain their blood for the coming Passover. A Jewish barber was arrested and made a "confession" under torture, implicating seven leading members of the community in the crime. All were arrested and tortured. Two died under examination, one saved himself by embracing Islam, and the others "confessed." Sixty-three Jewish children were taken hostage by the pasha in order to force their parents to reveal the whereabouts of the martyrs' blood. The entire Damascene Jewish community was in a state of panic.

News of the trials and the confessions spread throughout the Levant and were believed by Muslims as well as Christians. The community in Damascus became subject to mob violence, and there were reprisals against Jews in other parts of the province.

The Damascus Affair became a *cause célèbre* among European and American Jews as well as among liberal Gentiles. The governments of England and Austria also intervened on behalf of the Jews in order to embarass the French, who were their rivals in the region and who exercised great influence at the court of Muḥammad ᶜAlī, whose domain included Syria at the time. In May 1840, the Austrian consul in Alexandria persuaded Muḥammad ᶜAlī to issue an order to

[25] Alexander Russell, *The Natural History of Aleppo,* vol. 2, 2d ed. (London, 1756), p. 74. There are several examples of the blood libel appearing in Turkey itself in the fifteenth and sixteenth centuries, but it does not seem to have taken root there or to have spread into the Arab provinces. See Uriel Heyd, "Ritual Murder Accusations in 15th and 16th Century Turkey," *Sefunot* 5 (1961): 137–49 [Heb.]; also Abraham Galanté, *Documents officiels turcs concernant les Juifs de Turquie: Recueil de 114 lois, reglements, firmans, bérats, ordres, et décisions de tribunaux* (Istanbul, 1931), pp. 157–58; Salomon A. Rosanes, *Histoire des Israélites de Turquie et de l'Orient,* vol. 2 (Sofia, 1937–38), pp. 283–85 [Heb.].

his governor in Damascus to protect the Jewish community there from any further mob violence. In August, a deputation of British and French Jews led by Sir Moses Montefiore and Adolphe Crémieux went to Egypt to intercede on behalf of the accused. After nearly three weeks of negotiations, Muḥammad ᶜAlī ordered the release of the prisoners, although he refused to reopen the investigation or declare them officially innocent. The deputation went on to Constantinople, where three months later it was able to procure from the Turkish sultan, ᶜAbd al-Majīd, a firman explicitly denouncing the blood libel.[26]

The Damascus Affair was only the beginning. The blood libel became firmly established in the popular imagination of the Levant and accusations of attempted or actual ritual murder were leveled against Jews throughout the century in Syria, Palestine, and Egypt. In 1844, Muslims in Cairo accused the Jews of murdering a Christian for his blood. This time, however, Muḥammad ᶜAlī quickly stepped in to prevent any violence and to see that justice was done.[27] Three years later, the blood libel was raised against the Jews in the Lebanese village of Dayr al-Qamar by local Maronites, and in that same year the Greek Orthodox in Jerusalem accused the Jews there of attempting to murder a Christian child for ritual purposes.[28] Neither of these incidents ended in tragedy, but later outbreaks of the blood libel did result in localized persecutions, especially in Egypt, during the last decades of the nineteenth century.[29]

Modern post-Enlightenment anti-Semitism seems to have made very little headway in the Arab world during the nineteenth century. The earliest examples of modern anti-Semitic literature in the European

[26] Documentation on the Damascus Affair, including a translation of the Sultan's firman, is given in Part Two below, pp. 393–402. For additional documentation, see Albert M. Hyamson, "The Damascus Affair—1840," *Transactions of the Jewish Historical Society of England* 16 (1945–51): 47–71. See also A. J. Brawer, "Damascus Affair," *EJ* 5: 1249–52 and the bibliography cited there.

[27] Jacob M. Landau, *Jews in Nineteenth-Century Egypt* (New York, 1969), p. 31.

[28] Eliyahu Ashtor, "Syria: From the Arab Conquest," *EJ* 15: 645; James Finn, *Stirring Times, or Records from Jerusalem Consular Chronicles of 1853 to 1856,* vol. 1 (London, 1878), pp. 107–10.

[29] Landau, *Jews in Nineteenth-Century Egypt,* pp. 38–39, 182–83, 199–200, 203–4, 215–17, 298–99. See also idem, "Ritual Murder Accusations and Persecutions of Jews in 19th Century Egypt," *Sefunot* 5 (1961): 417–60, where incidents that occurred between the years of 1870 and 1892 are discussed in detail and where references to the blood libel in neighboring countries are also given, as for example, in Damascus in 1890 (ibid., p. 422). See also Part Two below, pp. 426–27.

mold did not make their appearance until the last three decades of the century among Syro-Lebanese Christians, who were under strong French cultural influence. Most of these early anti-Semitic works were published in Beirut and were translations of European tracts. One such book, Najīb al-Ḥājj's *Fi 'l-Zawāya Khabāya, aw Kashf Asrār al-Yahūd* (Clandestine Things in the Corners, or Secrets of the Jews Unmasked) was merely an adaptation of Georges Corneilhan's *Juifs et opportunistes.*[30]

Anti-Jewish literature developed slowly at first and was confined to a limited circle of westernized Christian intellectuals in Syria and Egypt. The influence of this literature was negligible. Modern anti-Semitism was still too new and too palpably foreign an ideology even for most educated Arabs at this time. Nevertheless, these early works laid the foundation for a much more extensive literature of this genre in the twentieth century when a radical change took place in the general attitude of the Arabs toward Jews.

The beginnings of anti-Semitism in the Arab world may be seen as part of the struggle of one partially emancipated minority—the Christians—to protect itself against the economic competition of another partially emancipated but less assimilated minority—the Jews. The vast majority of Muslim Arabs did not yet perceive the Jews as an economic or political threat. This would come in the twentieth century with the confrontation of opposing Jewish and Arab nationalisms.

[30] See N. A. Stillman, "New Attitudes toward the Jew in the Arab World," *Jewish Social Studies* 37, nos. 3–4 (Summer–Fall 1975): 197–204, where the development of modern anti-Semitic literature in Arabic is discussed.

EPILOGUE

The history of the Jews of Arab lands is only a few centuries shorter than the entire post–Second Temple Diaspora. It is not an easy history to summarize or interpret. The time span is long—almost a millennium and a half. The geographical expanse is immense—during the Middle Ages, stretching across three continents with diverse regional cultures and, in later times, covering an area only slightly contracted.

In the history of any complex civilization there are elements of unity as well as diversity. As we have seen in the preceding chapters, the single most important element of unity and social stability within the Arab world has been Islam itself. One must keep in mind that Islam, like Judaism, has always been much more than a religion. For the Muslim, throughout the centuries surveyed in this book, it has been an all-embracing way of life. Equally important, Islam has since its inception been a polity whose citizens were the Believers, and in the earliest years, these were synonymous with the Arabs. Like many other societies, Islam made provisions for those living under its aegis who were not full-fledged members of the body politic—in this case, the "protected peoples," or *dhimmīs*.

It was Islam, therefore, that established the framework within which the dominant society related to its tolerated subjects. The history of the Jews of Arab lands must be viewed within this framework. For Islam was the principle underlying factor affecting the Arab's perception of the Jew, his attitude towards him, and ultimately, his treatment of him.

This social system had many positive as well as negative aspects. Jews, along with other *dhimmīs,* were guaranteed their lives, their property, and the right to worship as they chose (within certain limits). They were allowed a great deal of internal communal autonomy, and they were also granted a considerable measure of economic opportunity. In return for these benefits, they had to accept an inferior status with certain legal and social disabilities. The system was by no means uniform throughout time and place, and it could be interpreted more or less strictly. During periods of economic, political, and social stability, the interpretation and application tended to be more liberal. Conversely, in times of stress, they tended to be harsher and more restrictive. However, as in any society based upon the defined superiority of one group and inferiority of another, the seeds were sown for the eventual debasement and abuse of the inferior group. As was observed, the later Islamic Middle Ages, which continued well into the nineteenth century in much of the Arab world, was marked by a general decline of the non-Muslim population and its progressive degradation. There were exceptions to this trend, as for example, during the seventeenth-century revival following the Ottoman conquest of the Levant. But the overall trend was one of definite social decline.

Small wonder, then, that in the early modern period many non-Muslim subjects in the Islamic world were only too eager to link their destinies to the forces of European mercantilism and imperialism. They had little reason to be loyal to their traditional masters. Little wonder, also, that they were eager to embrace European culture. They had never been entirely part of the dominant native culture, although they had come close to it during the High Middle Ages at the time of the Hellenistic renaissance in Islam.

The civil emancipation extended under European pressure to the non-Muslims of the Ottoman Empire during the nineteenth century proved to be a mixed blessing for the Jews in the Arab provinces. Their legal and economic position clearly improved. However, with the deterioration of Ottoman control, there was in many places a breakdown in law and order, and Jewish lives and property were frequently more vulnerable than before emancipation. In granting equality to *dhimmīs,* the Ottoman state greatly diminished its Islamic legitimacy in the eyes of many of its Muslim subjects, especially in the Arab provinces.

The Ottoman reforms set in motion other forces that in the long run would contribute to the undoing of the Jews of Arab lands. The large, newly emancipated, and more assimilated Christian minority in the Levant came into fierce economic competition with the Jews. The Christians found a secular bond between themselves and the Arab Muslims who were disaffected from the Ottoman regime. This was at first the bond of Arabic culture and, later, Arab nationalism. The Jews for the most part were not attracted by either (Iraqi Jewry was a notable exception, at least as far as Arabic culture was concerned). As a result, they would find themselves even more isolated as a group in the emerging Arab nations of the twentieth century. In their struggle with the Jews, the Levantine Christians also helped to introduce and disseminate Western anti-Semitism in the Arab world. Although their efforts did not meet with too great a success at first, they laid the foundations for the widespread anti-Jewish propaganda that developed in that part of the world during the first half of the twentieth century and flowered in the wake of the Arab-Israeli conflict.

PART TWO

SOURCES

1

THE FIRST ENCOUNTER
Muḥammad and the Jews

MUHAMMAD'S FIRST JEWISH CONVERT
(622)

Ibn Isḥāq stated: The following is part of the story of ᶜAbd Allāh b. Salām concerning him and his conversion as told to me by one of his relatives.

He was a rabbi and a scholar. He said: "When I heard about the Apostle of Allah—may Allah bless him and grant him peace—I realized from his description, his name, and his time that he was the one whom we had been expecting. I was delighted by that, but kept silent until the Apostle of Allah came to Medina. When he alighted in Qubā'[1] among the Banū ᶜAmr b. ᶜAwf, a man came to announce his arrival. I was working at the time on top of one of my palm trees, and my aunt Khālida b. al-Ḥāritha was sitting below. When I heard the news of the Apostle's arrival I cried, 'Allah is most great!' Hearing this, my aunt said to me, 'By Allah, had you heard that Moses the son of Amram were coming, you could not have been more excited!'

I answered her, 'Indeed, aunt, he is by Allah Moses' brother and follows his religion. He has been sent with the same mission.'

She asked, 'O nephew, is he the prophet who we have been told will be sent at this very time?'

'Yes,' I replied.

[1] A suburb of Medina, where the first mosque had been founded by the earliest Emigrants and the Helpers before Muḥammad's arrival.

'Then it is so,' she said.

Then I went to the Apostle of Allah—may Allah bless him and grant him peace—and accepted Islam. Afterwards, I returned home and ordered the members of my household to convert as well, which they did."

He went on: "I concealed my conversion from the Jews. I then came to the Apostle and said to him, 'O Apostle of Allah, the Jews are a people given to falsehood. I would like you to take me into one of your apartments and hide me from them. Then ask them about me so that they will tell you how I am regarded among them before they learn of my conversion. For if they know about it already, they would slander and denounce me.'

So the Apostle of Allah—may Allah bless him and grant him peace—took me into one of his apartments, and they came before him. They spoke with him and asked him questions. He in turn asked them, 'What kind of a man is al-Ḥuṣayn b. Salām[2] among you?'

'He is our chief and the son of our chief, our rabbi and our leading scholar,' they replied.

As they finished speaking, I came out in front of them and said, 'O Jews, fear Allah and accept what he has sent you! For by Allah, you surely know that he is the Apostle of Allah.' You will find him foretold in the Torah both by his name and his description. I bear witness that he is the Apostle of Allah. I believe in him. I declare him to be true. And I acknowledge him.'

'You lie!' they cried, and went on to slander me.

Then I said to the Apostle of Allah—may Allah bless him and grant him peace, 'Did I not tell you, o Apostle, that they were a slandering, treacherous, lying, and immoral people?'

I now proclaimed my conversion to Islam and the conversion of my household. My aunt Khālida b. al-Ḥāritha converted too, and what a goodly conversion that was."

Ibn Hishām, *al-Sīra al-Nabawiyya,* vol. 1
(Cairo, 1955), pp. 516–17.

[2] His name prior to his conversion. See above, p. 12ff., and below p. 120.

MUHAMMAD'S ORDINANCE FOR MEDINA

The Apostle of Allah—may Allah bless him and grant him peace—drew up a document between the Emigrants[1] and the Helpers,[2] in which he made a pact and a convenant with the Jews, confirming them in their religion and their possessions, and he stipulated certain conditions for them and imposed certain duties upon them:

In the name of Allah, the Merciful, the Beneficent.

This is a document from Muḥammad the Prophet, between the Believers and Muslims of Quraysh and Yathrib and whoever follows them and are attached to them and strives with them. They are a single community in the face of all other men.[3]

The Emigrants of Quraysh shall pay the bloodwit among themselves according to their Custom. They shall redeem their captives with kindness and justice among the Believers.

The Banū ᶜAwf shall give priority[4] to paying the bloodwit for their own in accordance with their custom. Each sub-clan shall ransom its captives with kindness and justice among the Believers.

This applies also to the Banū Sāᶜida, the Banu 'l-Ḥārith, the Banū Jusham, the Banu 'l-Najjār, the Banū ᶜAmr b. ᶜAwf, the Banu 'l-Nabīt, and the Banu 'l-Aws.[5]

The Believers are not to forsake any destitute individuals among them, but are to give him the means, as is considered proper, to pay for ransom or bloodwit.

A Believer may not become the ally of a client of another Believer against the latter.

The God-fearing Believers shall be against whoever does injustice, whoever seeks power or oppression, or sin, or enmity, or corruption among the Believers. Every man's hand shall be against him, even if he is the son of one of them.

[1] Ar., *muhājirūn* (Muḥammad's followers from Mecca who came with him to Medina).

[2] Ar., *anṣār.* The term given to Muḥammad's Medinese followers. Apparently this term was not in use at this early time since, in the document itself, Muḥammad has to mention each tribe.

[3] Moshe Gil has suggested reading *min dūni 'l-nās* as "they are no longer individuals." See M. Gil, "The Constitution of Medina: A Reconsideration," *Israel Oriental Studies* 4 (1974): 49–50.

[4] Reading with Gil (op. cit., p. 51), *al-awlā,* and not *al-ūlā* (previous).

[5] The first five tribes mentioned belong to the confederation of Khazraj. The last three belong to the other great Medinese confederation of Aws.

A Believer shall not kill a Believer for the sake of an unbeliever, nor shall he aid an unbeliever against a Believer.

Allah's protection is one; He grants protection even to the least among them.[6] The Believers are responsible for one another in the face of all other men.

Any Jew who follows us shall have aid and comfort. Such a Jew shall not be oppressed nor his enemies aided against him.[7]

The peace of the Believers is one. No Believer shall conclude a separate peace from another Believer fighting in the Path of Allah.[8] Rather it should be for all equally. . . .

The Believers should avenge each other's blood when it is spilled in the Path of Allah.

Verily, the God-fearing Believers are under the best and most correct guidance.[9]

No polytheist shall grant protection to the goods or person of a member of Quraysh, nor intervene in his behalf against a Believer.

Whoever wrongfully kills a Believer—where the evidence is clear—shall be subject to retaliation unless the next of kin of the murdered man is satisfied (with bloodwit). The Believers shall be against him as a group, and they have no choice but to take action against him.

It is not permissible for a Believer who has acknowledged what is in this document, and who believes in Allah and the Last Day, to aid a wrong-doer[10] or to give him shelter. Should anyone aid or shelter him, then Allah's curse and wrath will be upon him on the Day of Resurrection, and no compensation or atonement will be accepted from him.

Whenever you dispute over anything, the matter is to be referred to Allah, Almighty and Exalted, and to Muḥammad.

The Jews shall lay out funds along with the Believers as long as they are at war.

[6] Accepting Gil's suggestion (op. cit., pp. 53–54) to have Allah as the implied subject of the phrase *yujīru ᶜalayhim adnāhum*. The other possible reading here is: "Even the least of them may extend protection to a stranger on their behalf." Thus, Alfred Guillaume, *The Life of Muhammad* (Lahore, 1968), p. 232; and W. Montgomery Watt, *Muhammad at Medina* (Oxford, 1956), p. 222.

[7] Gil (op. cit., p. 63) believes that this means those Jews who accept Islam. Goitein, on the other hand, contends that this does not refer to converts but to the Jews residing in Medina. See S. D. Goitein, *Hā-Islām shel Muḥammad* (Jerusalem, 5716/1956), p. 201.

[8] Ar., *sabīl Allāh* was the idiom at this time for "holy war."

[9] The implication of this passage is that it would be best if all the people of Medina were Muslims.

[10] The word used here for "wrong-doer" is *muḥdith* or "innovator."

The Jews of the Banū ᶜAwf are a community with the Believers.[11] The Jews have their religion, and the Muslims have theirs. This applies to their clients and themselves, except those who act wrongfully and sin, for they bring destruction upon themselves and their households.

The same applies to the Jews of the Banu 'l-Najjār as to the Jews of the Banū ᶜAwf, and so too for the Jews of Banu 'l-Ḥārith, Banū Sāᶜida, Banū Jusham, Banu 'l-Aws, and Banū Thaᶜlaba, except those who act wrongfully and sin, for they bring destruction upon themselves and their households.

The same applies to the Jafna clan of the Thaᶜlaba and to the Banū Shuṭayba.[12]

Faithfulness is the best protection against sin!

The clients of Thaᶜlaba are as themselves. The familiars of the Jews are as themselves.[13]

None of them shall go out to war[14] without Muḥammad's permission, but he will not be held back from avenging a wound. However, whoever acts rashly in killing brings death upon himself and his household, unless it is against someone who has done wrong, for this is acceptable to Allah.

The Jews are responsible for their expenses, and the Muslims for theirs. Each, however, must aid the other against anyone who attacks one of the parties of the document. Sincerity and good counsel should obtain between them. Faithfulness is the best protection against sin!

A man is not to be held guilty for his ally's conduct. Aid should be given to a person who is wronged.

The Jews shall lay out funds along with the Believers as long as they are at war.[15]

The valley of Yathrib is an inviolate perserve for the adherents of this document.

The protégé is like oneself, as long as he does no harm and sins not.

[11] These Jews are said to form a community (Ar., *umma*) with the Believers, because they are the clients of Muslim tribes.

[12] Jafna seems to have been a Jewish clan, and the Banū Shuṭayba were closely associated with Jews, if not possibly Jewish themselves. See Gil, op. cit., pp. 61–62 and the sources cited there.

[13] The "familiars of the Jews" (Ar., *biṭānat al-Yahūd*) are apparently small pagan groups under their protection.

[14] Gil (op. cit., p. 62) believes *lā yakhruj minhum aḥad* is an interdiction against their leaving the city without permission. However, this does not seem to fit into the context of the following sentences.

[15] This repetition of an earlier clause seems to indicate that it was very important to Muḥammad for the Jews to share in the expenses of his military operations.

No woman shall be given protection except with her family's consent.

Should any incident or quarrel arise between the adherents of this document which may cause disturbance, it should be referred to Allah, Almighty, and Exalted, and Muḥammad, the Apostle of Allah.

Allah is pleased with what is in this document which is most pious and righteous.

No protection is to be afforded to the Quraysh and those who help them.

The adherents of this document must aid one another against anyone who attacks Yathrib.

If they (the Jews) are called to make peace and maintain it, they must do so. And if they call upon the Believers for the like of this, it is within their rights, except where one is fighting for the sake of the Faith. . . .[16]

The Jews of al-Aws, both their clients and themselves, are considered in the same condition as the people of this document with pure faithfulness from the people of this document. Faithfulness is the best protection against sin!

No one acquires anything except for himself. Verily, Allah is over the very true and upright contents of this document. This document does not protect the evildoer and sinner. He who goes out to war is safe, and he who remains in Medina is safe, unless he does wrong or sins. Allah is protector of the righteous and God-fearing, and Muḥammad is Allah's Apostle.

Ibn Hishām, *al-Sīra al-Nabawiyya,* vol. 1
(Cairo, 1375/1955), pp. 501–4.

[16] Julius Wellhausen was surprised that Muḥammad would allow the Jews to conclude a separate peace which could be binding upon the Muslims. However, Muḥammad has left himself a convenient escape clause, since every war of the Believers could be considered "for the sake of the Faith." See Wellhausen, *Skizzen und Vorarbeiten,* vol. 4 (Berlin, 1889), p. 72.

Ibn Isḥāq states that at that time the Rabbis of the Jews began to manifest their hostility toward the Apostle of Allah—may Allah bless him and grant him peace. They did it out of jealousy, envy, and malice because Allah Exalted had conferred distinction upon the Arabs by choosing him as His messenger from amongst them. They were joined by some men from the Aws and Khazraj who had remained in their paganism. These were the hypocrites who clung to the faith of their fathers which was marked by polytheism and denial of the resurrection. However, when Islam appeared and their people united under it, they were forced to pretend to have accepted Islam. But they accepted only to protect themselves from being killed, while remaining hypocrites in secret. Thus they felt inclined toward the Jews because they belied the Prophet—may Allah bless him and grant him peace—and because they strove against Islam.

It was the Rabbis of the Jews who would question the Apostle of Allah and harass him. They brought to him abstruse questions in order to confuse the truth with falsehood. Portions of the Koran were revealed concerning them and their questions. Although a few queries concerning what is permitted and forbidden were asked by the Muslims themselves.

(These are the names of those Jews:)

From the Banu 'l-Naḍīr there were: Ḥuyayy b. Akhṭab[1] and his brothers Abū Yāsir and Judayy; Sallām b. Mishkam; Kināna b. al-Rabīᶜ b. Abi 'l-Ḥuqayq; Sallām b. Abi 'l-Ḥuqayq; Abū Rāfiᶜ al-Aᶜwar, who was killed by the companions of the Apostle of Allah at Khaybar; al-Rabīᶜ b. al-Rabīᶜ b. Abi 'l-Ḥuqayq; ᶜAmr b. Jaḥḥāsh; Kaᶜb b. al-Ashraf, who was from the Ṭayyi' of the Banū Nabhān clan, and whose mother was from the Banu 'l-Nāḍīr;[2] al-Ḥajjāj b. ᶜAmr, an ally of Kaᶜb b. al-Ashraf; and Kardam b. Qays, also an ally of Kaᶜb.

From the Banū Thaᶜlaba b. al-Fiṭyawn there were: ᶜAbd Allāh b. Ṣūriyā al-Aᶜwar—there was no one in the Hijāz in his time more learned in the Torah; Ibn Ṣalūbā; and Mukhayrīq, who had been their rabbi, but later converted to Islam.[3]

From the Banū Qaynuqāᶜ there were: Zayd b. al-Laṣīt—according to some his name was Ibn al-Luṣīt; Saᶜd b. Ḥunayf; Maḥmūd b. Sayḥān; ᶜUzayr b. Abī ᶜUzayr;[4] ᶜAbd Allāh b. Ṣayf—according to some his

[1] He is the father of Muḥammad's "Jewish wife" Ṣafiyya. Concerning Ḥuyayy and his daughter, see below, pp. 129–36.

[2] According to Muslim tradition, he was one of the Prophet's greatest enemies in Medina. For his assassination, see below, pp. 124–27.

[3] See his story below, p. 121.

[4] Not ᶜUzayz b. ᶜUzayz as in the Arabic text, p. 514.

name was Ibn Ḍayf; Suwayd b. al-Ḥārith; Rifā^{c}a b. Qays; Pinḥāṣ; Ashyā^{c}; Nu^{c}mān b. Aḍa; Baḥrī b. ^{c}Amr; Sha's b. ^{c}Adī; Sha's b. Qays Zayd b. al-Ḥārith; Nu^{c}man b. ^{c}Amr; Sukayn b. Abī Sukayn; ^{c}Adī b. Zayd; Nu^{c}mān b. Abī Awfā; Abū Anas; Maḥmūd b. Daḥya; Mālik b. Ṣayf, whose name according to some was Ibn Ḍayf; Ka^{c}b b. Rāshid; ^{c}Azar; Rāfi^{c} b. Abī Rāfi^{c}; Khālid; Azār b. Abī Azār, whose name was Āzir b. Āzir according to some sources; Rāfi^{c} b. Ḥāritha; Rāfi^{c} b. Ḥuraymila; Rāfi^{c} b. Khārija; Mālik b. ^{c}Awf; Rifā^{c}a b. Zayd b. al-Tābūt;[5] and ^{c}Abd Allah b. Salām b. al-Ḥārith, who was their rabbi and chief scholar.[6] His name was originally al-Ḥuṣayn, but when he became a Muslim, the Apostle of Allah—may Allah bless him and grant him peace—gave him the name ^{c}Abd Allāh.

From the Banū Qurayẓa there were: al-Zubayr b. Bāṭā b. Wahb; ^{c}Azzāl b. Shamwīl; Ka^{c}b b. Asad, who had negotiated a treaty on behalf of the Banū Qurayẓa which was broken in the Year of the Parties (627);[7] Shamwīl b. Zayd; Jabal b. ^{c}Amr b. Sukayna; al-Nahhām b. Zayd; Qardam b. Ka^{c}b; Wahb b. Zayd; Nāfi^{c} b. Abī Nāfi^{c}; Abū Nāfi^{c}; ^{c}Adī b. Zayd; al-Ḥārith b. ^{c}Awf; Kardam b. Zayd; Usāma b. Ḥabīb; Rāfi^{c} b. Rumayla; Jabal b. Abī Qushayr; and Wahb b. Yahūdhā.

From the Jews of Banū Zurayq, there was Labīd b. A^{c}ṣam. It was he who cast a spell upon the Apostle of Allah—may Allah bless him and grant him peace—so that he was unable to have sexual relations with his wives.[8]

From the Jews of Banū Ḥāritha, there was Kināna b. Ṣūriyā.

From the Jews of Banū ^{c}Amr b. ^{c}Awf, there was Qardam b. ^{c}Amr.

And from the Jews of Banu 'l-Najjār, there was Silsila b. Barhām.

These then were the Rabbis of the Jews, men whose malice and enmity was aimed at the Apostle of Allah and his companions. They raised questions and stirred up mischief against Islam in order to extinguish it—the two exceptions to this being ^{c}Abd Allāh b. Salām and Mukhayrīq.

Ibn Hishām, *al-Sīra al-Nabawiyya,* vol. 1
(Cairo, 1955), pp. 513–16.

[5] This is a rather odd name. *Tābūt* in Arabic means "ark" (from Heb., *tēvā*).

[6] Renegades are invariably presented by their new coreligionists as great scholars of their former faith. ^{c}Abd Allāh, like many Jewish apostates in medieval Christian Europe, saw it his duty to expose whatever the Jews had "suppressed" in their scriptures. See his story above, pp. 113–14.

[7] This treaty was supposedly concluded with Muḥammad and kept with Ka^{c}b. It was torn up during the Meccans' siege of Medina. Several names appearing here seem to be variants of the Quraẓīs mentioned in the account of the extermination of their tribe given below. See below, p. 143.

[8] The spell that rendered Muḥammad impotent supposedly lasted for one year. The commentator al-Suhaylī argues that this is a genuine tradition.

"MUKHAYRIQ IS THE BEST OF THE JEWS"

Ibn Isḥāq stated: what follows is from the story of Mukhayrīq:

He was a learned rabbi. He was a wealthy man, too, possessing much property in date palms. He recognized the Apostle of Allah—may Allah bless him and grant him peace—by his description and by what he found in his scholarship. However, he was accustomed to his own religion, and this held him back, until the Battle of Uḥud (625) which fell upon the sabbath.

He said, "O Jews, by Allah you know full well that you are duty bound to aid Muḥammad."

"But today is the sabbath," they answered.

"You have no sabbath!" he said.

Then he took up his weapons and went out to join the Apostle of Allah—may Allah bless him and grant him peace—at Uḥud. He charged those of his people whom he left behind, saying, "If I am killed this day, my property is to go to Muḥammad to use as Allah directs him." During the battle, he fought until he was killed.

According to what I have been told, the Apostle—may Allah bless him and grant him peace—used to say, "Mukhayrīq is the best of the Jews."

The Apostle took his property. The bulk of the alms he distributed in Medina came from it.

Ibn Hishām, *al-Sīra al-Nabawiyya,* vol. 1
(Cairo, 1955), p. 518.

Meanwhile, the affair of the Banū Qaynuqā[c] took place. It is considered one of the military exploits of the Apostle of Allah—may Allah bless him and grant him peace. This is the story.

The Apostle of Allah—may Allah bless him and grant him peace—assembled them in the market of Qaynuqā[c]. Then he said to them, "O Jews, beware lest Allah bring down upon you vengeance like that which has descended upon the Quraysh. Accept Islam, for you know that I am a prophet who has been sent. You will find that in your scriptures and Allah's covenant with you."

"O Muḥammad," they replied, "you seem to think that we are your people. Do not delude yourself because you have till now encountered people with no knowledge of war and thus have gained advantage over them. By Allah, if we should go to war with you, you will surely learn that we are men!"

Ibn Isḥāq related that he was informed by a freedman of Zayd b. Thābit's family on the authority of either Sa[c]īd b. Jubayr or [c]Ikrima, on the authority of Ibn [c]Abbās, that the following verses were revealed concerning the Banū Qaynuqā[c]:

> Say to those who disbelieve—You will be defeated and gathered into Hell, and what an evil resting place that is! You already had a sign in the two parties that met in battle. One party fought on the path of Allah, while the other disbelieving seemed to see them as though double with their eyes. Allah strengthens with His aid whom He wills. Lo, there is a lesson in that for men of insight. (Sura 3:12–13/10–11)

The "two parties" refer to the participants at the Battle of Badr (624), namely, the companions of the Apostle of Allah—may Allah bless him and grant him peace—and the Quraysh.

Ibn Isḥāq continued: [c]Āṣim b. [c]Umar b. Qatāda informed me that the Banū Qaynuqā[c] were the first Jews who violated the agreement between them and the Apostle of Allah—may Allah bless him and grant him peace, and they went to war with him between Badr and Uḥud.

Ibn Hishām adds: [c]Abd Allāh b. Ja[c]far b. al-Miswar b. Makhrima mentioned on the authority of Abū [c]Awn that the cause of the Qaynuqā[c] affair was that an Arab woman had come with some merchandise to the market of the Banū Qaynuqā[c]. She sat down next to a goldsmith there. Then they began urging her to unveil her face, which she refused. The goldsmith moved close to the hem of her garment and tied it behind her back. When she got up her privities were exposed. They laughed at her, and she screamed. Then a Muslim jumped upon the goldsmith who was Jewish and killed him. Then the Jews overwhelmed the Muslim and killed him. The family of the slain Muslim called upon their coreligionists for help against the Jews. The Muslims were furious, and thus there was bad blood created between them and the Banū Qaynuqāᶜ.

(Ibn Isḥāq's narrative now continues:) So the Apostle of Allah—may Allah bless him and grant him peace—besieged them until they surrendered unconditionally.

ᶜAbd Allāh b. Ubayy b. Salūl[1] stood up for them with him after Allah had delivered them into his power, and said, "O Muḥammad, deal kindly with my clients." (For they were allies of the Khazraj.)

But the Apostle of Allah—may Allah bless him and grant him peace—was slow to respond, so he said again, "Muḥammad, deal kindly with my clients." At this, he turned away from him, so ᶜAbd Allāh stuck his hand into the collar of the Apostle's coat of mail.[2]

"Unhand me!" the Apostle said to him. His face became dark with rage. "Woe unto you, unhand me!"

"No, by Allah," came the answer, "I will not let you go until you deal kindly with my clients. Four hundred men without coats of mail, and three hundred with, protected me from all manner of men.[3] Are you going to cut them down in a single morning? By Allah, I am a man who fears the changes of circumstances."

"They are yours," replied the Apostle of Allah—may Allah bless him and grant him peace.

During the time that the Apostle had besieged them, he placed Bashīr b. ᶜAbd al-Mundhir in charge of Medina. The entire siege lasted fifteen days.

Ibn Hishām, *al-Sīra al-Nabawiyya,* vol. 2
(Cairo, 1955), pp. 47–49.

[1] He was one of the leading men of Medina. He goes down in Muslim history with the unsavory distinction of being the chief of the Hypocrites (Ar., *munāfiqūn*), those Medinese who did not accept Islam and the Prophet wholeheartedly.

[2] Ibn Hisham adds here that the name of this coat of mail was *dhāt al-fuḍūl.* As is the case with many other heroic figures, tradition has given appropriate names to his weapons and garments.

[3] Ar., *min al-aḥmar wa 'l-aswad* (literally, "from the red and the black").

Ibn Isḥāq stated: this is the story of Kaᶜb b. al-Ashraf.

After the defeat of the enemy at Badr (624), Zayd b. Ḥāritha came to the people of the Lower Quarter (of Medina) and ᶜAbd Allāh b. Ruwāḥa to the people of the Upper Quarter bearing the good news. The Apostle of Allah—may Allah bless him and grant him peace—had sent them to the Muslims of Medina to proclaim the victory of Allah Almighty and Exalted and the slaying of the polytheists.

According to ᶜAbd Allāh b. al-Mughīth, ᶜAbd Allāh b. Abī Bakr, ᶜĀṣim b. ᶜUmar, and Ṣāliḥ b. Abī Umāma, each of whom told me part of this story, Kaᶜb b. al-Ashraf, a member of the Banū Nabhān branch of the Ṭayyi', whose mother was of the Banu 'l-Naḍīr, exclaimed: "Is it true? Did Muḥammad really kill those whom these two men have named? Those were the nobles of the Arabs and the kings of men. By Allah, if Muḥammad has indeed struck down these people, then it were better to be buried in the earth than to walk upon it!"

When the enemy of Allah was sure of the news, he departed and went to Mecca. He stayed with al-Muṭallib b. Abī Wadāᶜa b. Ḍubayra al-Sahmī, whose wife ᶜĀtika b. al-ᶜĪṣ b. Umayya took him in and entertained him. He in turn began to agitate against the Apostle of Allah—may Allah bless him and grant him peace—and he composed verses in which he wept for those of Quraysh whose bodies were cast into the pit after Badr.[1]

Then Kaᶜb returned to Medina where he wrote erotic poetry about the Muslim women in order to offend them. At this, the Apostle of Allah—may Allah bless him and grant him peace—said, "Who will take care of Ibn al-Ashraf for me?"[2]

"I shall," answered Muḥammad b. Maslama, the brother of the Banū ᶜAbd al-Ashhal. "I will kill him."

"Do it then, if you can," he said.

So Muḥammad b. Maslama returned home and remained three days, neither eating nor drinking except what was absolutely necessary to maintain life. When this was reported to the Apostle of Allah—may Allah bless him and grant him peace—he summoned him and asked, "Why have you given up food and drink?"

"O Apostle of Allah," he replied, "I gave my word to you and do not know whether or not I can fulfill it."

He answered, "It is only incumbent upon you to try."

[1] At this point, there follow two and one-half pages of verses in the Arabic text, which we have omitted here.

[2] Ar., *man lī bi-'bn al-Ashraf*.

"O Apostle of Allah," he said, "we shall have to tell lies."

"Say what seems best to you, for in this you are at liberty to do that."

So Muḥammad b. Maslama plotted his murder together with Silkān b. Salāma b. Waqsh, who was called Abū Nā'ila, who was a member of the Banū ᶜAbd al-Ashhal and the milk-brother[3] of Kaᶜb b. al-Ashraf, with al-Ḥārith b. Aws b. Muᶜādh, also of Banū ᶜAbd al-Ashhal, and with Abū ᶜAbs b. Jabr of the Banū Ḥāritha. They sent Silkān (Abū Nā'ila) to the enemy of Allah Kaᶜb b. al-Ashraf before they themselves came to him. He went and talked with him for some time, and they recited verses to one another. (Abū Nā'ila would often recite poetry.)

Then he said, "Woe is me,[4] o Ibn al-Ashraf. I have come with a matter I want to tell you, but wish you to keep secret for me."

"I shall do that," Kaᶜb replied.

The other went on, "This man's coming has brought upon us a terrible trial. The Arabs have become our enemy. They shoot at us with a single bow.[5] They have cut the roads for us so that our families perish, our lives have become strained, and we find ourselves and our households in distress.

"By Allah," Kaᶜb replied, "did I not keep telling you, Ibn Salāma, that this affair would turn out as I have said?"

Silkān then said to him, "I would like you to sell us food. We shall put up security and be faithful to you. You in turn will deal generously in this."

"Will you give me your women as security?"[6]

"How can we give our womenfolk as security, when you are the most vigorous man in Yathrib and one of the best scented?"[7]

"Will you give me your sons as security, then?"

"Surely you wish to shame us! I have some friends who are of the same mind as I am, and I would like to bring you to them so that you can sell to them on good terms. We shall offer you enough arms to make a good pledge." (Silkān's purpose here was that he should not object when they came with weapons.)

"Weapons are a good security," Kaᶜb said.

[3] Milk-brotherhood (Ar., *riḍāᶜ or riḍāᶜa*), a kind of foster brotherhood resulting from being suckled together, was considered to be a close bond of relationship among the pre-Islamic Arabs.

[4] The Arabic text has *wayḥaka* (literally, "woe unto you"). The sense, however, seems to be as we have translated.

[5] That is, they are united against us.

[6] This line and the following retort are not in Ibn Isḥāq's narrative. Ibn Hishām adds it at the end of the paragraph.

[7] Reading *wa-aᶜṭaruhum* instead of *wa-aᶜṭawhum*, which is clearly a misprint in the Arabic text (p. 55, next to last line).

So Silkān returned to his companions and told them his news. He ordered them to take their arms. Then they hurried off, joining him later at the house of the Apostle of Allah—may Allah bless him and grant him peace.

The Apostle walked with them as far as Baqīᶜ al-Gharqad.[8] Then he sent them on their mission, saying, "Go in Allah's name. O Allah, help them." Then the Apostle of Allah—may Allah bless him and grant him peace—returned to his house.

It was a moonlit night. They proceeded until they reached his castle where Abū Nā'ila called out to him. Now it so happened that Kaᶜb was only recently married. He jumped up in his bed sheet, but his wife held on to the end of it and said, "You are a man at war. Those in a state of war do not go out at this hour."

He replied, "It is Abū Nā'ila. Had he found me sleeping, he would not have awakened me."

But she said, "By Allah, I can detect evil in his voice!"

"If a warrior is called, he must answer even if it is for a stabbing," said Kaᶜb.

With that, he went down and chatted with them for a while. Then Abū Nā'ila said, "Would you like to walk with us, Ibn al-Ashraf, to Shiᶜb al-ᶜAjūz[9] so we can talk there for the rest of the night?"

"If you wish," he replied.

So they went out walking. They had been going some time when Abū Nā'ila ran his hand through the hair of his temples. Then he sniffed his hands and said, "I never smelled a better scent than I have tonight."

They walked on a while, and he did the same thing again so that he would be put at ease. On they walked, and again he did it, but this time he grabbed his sidelock and cried, "Strike the enemy of Allah!" With this, they struck at him, but their swords clashed over him with no effect.

Muḥammad b. Maslama recalled later, "When I saw our swords were of no avail, I remembered a dagger attached to my sword[10] and I drew it. The enemy of Allah had already cried out with such a scream that there was not a castle around in which a fire was not lit. So I thrust it into his groin and bore down upon it until I reached his genitals, whereupon the enemy of Allah fell."

"Al-Ḥārith b. Aws b. Muᶜādh had been hit and was wounded either in

[8] This bramble-covered field became the first Islamic cemetery in Medina two years after this incident. See A. J. Wensinck and A. S. Bazmee Ansari, "Baḳīᶜ al-Gharḳad," *EI*² 1: 957–58.

[9] This was a ravine behind Medina. See Yāqūt, *Muᶜjam al-Buldān,* vol. 3, ed. F. Wüstenfeld (Leipzig, 1868), pp. 295–96.

[10] Ar., *fa-dhakartu mighwalan fī-sayfī.*

the head or the foot by one of our own swords. We made away until we had passed the Banū Umayya b. Zayd, the Banū Qurayẓa, and Buᶜāth, and had reached the Ḥarrat al-ᶜUrayḍ.[11]

Our companion al-Ḥārith b. Aws lagged behind us, having lost much blood. We waited for him for some time. Finally, he reached us, following our tracks. We carried him and brought him to the Apostle of Allah—may Allah bless him and grant him peace—as the last part of the night was waning. He was standing in prayer. We greeted him, and he came out to us. Then we told him how we had killed Allah's enemy. He spat upon our companion's wound. Then he went in again, and we returned to our families."

"The Jews were terrified by our attack upon Allah's enemy. And there was not a Jew there who did not fear for his life."

Ibn Hishām, *al-Sīra al-Nabawiyya,* vol. 2 (Cairo, 1955), pp. 51–57.

[11] A *ḥarra* is an area covered with black volcanic stone, of which there are many in the vicinity of Medina. Al-ᶜ-Urayḍ is another name for the wadi of Medina. Thus, the Ḥarrat al-ᶜUrayḍ was apparently some spot in the wadi. See L. Veccia Vaglieri, "Ḥarra," *EI*² 3: 226–27; and Yāqūt, *Muᶜjam al-Buldān,* vol. 3, pp. 661–62.

THE BROTHERS MUHAYYISA AND HUWAYYISA

Ibn Isḥāq relates:

The Apostle of Allah—may Allah bless him and grant him peace—declared, "Kill any Jew who falls into your power. So Muḥayyiṣa b. Masᶜūd[1] fell upon Ibn Sunayna,[2] one of the Jewish merchants with whom his family had social and commercial relations and killed him. Ḥūwayyiṣa b. Masᶜūd was not a Muslim at this time. He was older than Muḥayyiṣa. When the latter had committed the murder, Ḥuwayyiṣa began beating him, saying, "What an enemy of Allah you are! Did you kill him when, by Allah, most of the fat on your belly came from his wealth?"

Muḥayyiṣa said that he answered, "By Allah, had he who commanded me to kill him commanded me to kill you, I would have cut off your head." This was the beginning of Ḥuwayyiṣa's becoming a Muslim.

"By Allah," he asked, "had Muḥammad commanded you to kill me, would you have done so?"

"Yes, by Allah, had he commanded me to strike off your head, I would have surely done it."

"By Allah," he exclaimed, "any religion that can bring you to this is indeed wonderful!" Thereupon Ḥuwayyiṣa converted to Islam.

Ibn Hishām, *al-Sīra al-Nabawiyya,* vol. 2
(Cairo, 1955), p. 58.

[1] In the Arabic text Ibn Hishām interjects here that "according to some his full name was Muḥayyiṣa b. Masᶜūd b. Kaᶜb b. ᶜĀmir b. ᶜAdī b. Majdaᶜa b. Ḥāritha b. al-Ḥārith b. al-Khazraj b. ᶜAmr b. Mālik b. al-Aws."

[2] Ibn Hishām injects here: "some say his name was Ibn Subayna."

THE RAID AGAINST THE BANU 'L-NADIR
(A.H. 3/625)

This took place in Rabīᶜ I, thirty-seven months after the Hijra of the Prophet—may Allah bless him and grant him peace.

I was told the following account by Muḥammad b. ᶜAbd Allāh, ᶜAbd Allāh b. Jaᶜfar, Muḥammad b. Yaḥyā b. Sahl, Ibn Abī Ḥabība, Maᶜmar b. Rāshid, and others whom I shall not name. Each told me part of the story:

ᶜAmr b. Umayya went from Bi'r Maᶜūna to Qanāt. There he met two men from the Banū ᶜĀmir. He asked them their pedigree and they gave it to him. He sat conversing with them till they fell asleep. Then he fell upon them and killed them. He then went to the Apostle. . . . He told him about the incident involving the two men. The Apostle of Allah—may Allah bless him and grant him peace—said, "You have done badly. Those men had a guarantee of protection from us."

"I did not know," replied the other. "I only saw them in their polytheism. Their people have done us harm through treachery." Now he had brought their spoils, and the Apostle of Allah—may Allah bless him and grant him peace—ordered him to set aside the spoils from the two men until he could send it back along with the bloodwit.

The Apostle of Allah—may Allah bless him and grant him peace—went to the Banu 'l-Naḍīr to ask their help in paying the bloodwit. It so happens that the Banu 'l-Naḍīr were the allies of the Banū ᶜĀmir. The Apostle went out on Saturday with a group of Emigrants and Helpers. He performed his prayers in the mosque of Qubā'[1] on the way. After that, he came to the Banu 'l-Naḍīr, finding them in their meeting.[2] He and his companions sat down. He addressed them, asking their help with the bloodwit for the two Kilābīs killed by ᶜAmr b. Umayya. They replied, "We shall do as you wish, o Abu 'l-Qāsim.[3] It is about time that you came to visit us. Do seat yourself and let us feed you." The Apostle of Allah—may Allah bless him and grant him peace—was reclining against the wall of one of their houses. Meanwhile, some of them withdrew to confer among themselves.

Ḥuyayy b. Akhṭab spoke, "O Jews, Muḥammad has come to you with

[1] Qubā' was a suburb of Medina. Muḥammad spent several days there after making his *Hijra.* It was there also that he laid the foundations for his first mosque. See Ibn Hishām, *al-Sīra al-Nabawiyya,* vol. 1 (Cairo, 1955), p. 494; Eng. trans. Alfred Guillaume, *The Life of Muhammad* (Lahore, 1968), p. 227.

[2] Perhaps al-Wāqidī is referring to their Sabbath service.

[3] This was Muḥammad's by-name (*kunyā*).

only a tiny group of companions. There are not even ten." (With him were Abū Bakr, ᶜUmar, ᶜAlī, al-Zubayr, Ṭalḥa, Saᶜd b. Muᶜādh, Usayd b. Ḥuḍayr, and Saᶜd b. ᶜUbāda.)[4] "Let us throw a stone at him from the roof of this house under which he is sitting and kill him. You will never find him more vulnerable than at this moment! If he is killed his companions will scatter. Those of the Quraysh who are with him will betake themselves to their sacred precinct (that is, Mecca). Those of the Aws and Khazraj here will remain your allies. Do not put off for a future day what you have been wanting to do. Now is the time!"

ᶜAmr b. Jiḥāsh spoke up. "I shall climb to the roof and drop a stone on him."

But Sallām b. Mishkam warned, "O my people, heed me now, disobey me in the future. By God, if you do this, it will be reported that we dealt treacherously with him. Indeed, this would be a violation of the treaty between us and him. Do not do this! By God, if you will not listen and carry out what you are seeking, then there will continue to be a remnant of this religion until the Day of Resurrection. The Jews will be exterminated, and his religion will triumph."

However, the stone was all ready to be thrown onto the Apostle of Allah—may Allah bless him and grant him peace. Just as it was about to be dropped, the Apostle received a revelation from heaven telling him what they were planning to do. He quickly got up as if he had some pressing need and set off toward Medina. His companions, who were sitting and chatting, thought that he had got up in order to take care of some need. But when they had waited for him in vain, Abū Bakr—may Allah be pleased with him—said, "We have no reason to stay here. The Apostle of Allah—may Allah bless him and grant him peace—has been sent off on some affair." So they got up to leave.

Ḥuyyay said to them, "Abu 'l-Qāsim has rushed away, and here we had wanted to entertain him and offer him food!" The Jews now regretted what they had done.

Kināna b. Ṣuwayrā' said to them, "Do you know why Muḥammad got up?"

"No, by God, we do not know, and neither do you," they retorted.

"On the contrary. By the Torah! I do indeed know. Muḥammad was informed of the treachery you were plotting. Do not deceive yourselves. By God, he is surely the Apostle of God. He would not have got up unless he had been informed of your plans. He is none other than the last of the prophets. You were hoping that he would spring from the Sons of Aaron,

[4] These were leading companions. They include no less than three of the first four caliphs (namely, Abū Bakr, ᶜUmar, and ᶜAlī).

but God has done as He wishes. From our books and from what we have learned from the Torah, which has not been changed or substituted, we know that his birthplace was to be Mecca and that he would emigrate to Yathrib [Medina]. The description of him does not differ one iota from that in our scripture. What he has brought you [Islam] is better than having him wage war against you. I can see you going into exile, your little ones screaming, your houses and property left behind. These are the basis of your distinction. Therefore, heed me in two courses of action. There is a third, but there is no good in it."

"What are the first two?" they asked.

"Accept Islam and join Muhammad. You will be assured of your property and your children. You will become the elite among his companions. Your property will remain in your possession and you will not have to leave your homes."

"We will not abandon the Torah and the Covenant of Moses," came the reply.

"Then he will send you a message ordering you to leave his city. However, he will not consider your blood or your wealth licit. Your property will remain yours. You will be able to sell it if you wish or to retain it."

"So be it," they said.

When the Apostle of Allah—may Allah bless him and grant him peace—returned to Medina, his companions followed him. . . . When they caught up with him they learned that he had just summoned Muḥammad b. Maslama. Abū Bakr asked him, "Why did you get up without telling us, o Apostle of Allah?"

"The Jews were plotting treachery. Allah informed me of it, and so I got up and left."

Muḥammad b. Maslama arrived, and the Apostle told him to go to the Jews of Banu 'l-Naḍīr and deliver this message: "The Apostle of Allah has sent me to tell you to leave his city."

When he came to them, he said, "The Apostle of Allah has sent me with a message for you, but I will not deliver it until I have reminded you of something which you know. I adjure you by the Torah which Allah revealed to Moses, do you recall that I once came to you before Muḥammad—may Allah bless him and grant him peace—had been sent on his prophetic mission. You had the Torah before you and you said to me, 'O Ibn Maslama, if you wish to dine, we shall entertain you, and if you wish to become a Jew, we shall convert you.' I answered you, 'Feed me, but do not make a Jew of me. By Allah, I shall never become a Jew.' You fed me from one of your bowls. By Allah, it looked as if it were of pearl. Then you said to me, 'Nothing keeps you from our religion other than the fact that it is the religion of the Jews. You seem to be seeking the religion of the

Ḥanīfs[5] about which you have heard. . . . The true Master of the Ḥanīf religion will come to you soon. He is very cheerful and very deadly. In his eye is a red tinge. He shall come from the direction of Yemen [i.e., from the South], riding an ass, wearing a *shamla,*[6] and content with a crust of bread. His sword will be hanging from his shoulder. He will not perform miracles. He will pronounce wise judgments as if he were from your own noble roots.[7] By God, there will be pillage, bloodshed, and mutilation in your town.' "

"Yes by God, we did say that to you," the Jews replied, "but it did not apply to him."

"I shall say no more about it," he said. "The Apostle of Allah has directed me to say to you: 'You have violated the treaty I concluded with you by plotting treacherously against me.' He bade me recount to you what you had been contemplating, how ᶜAmr b. Jiḥāsh climbed to the roof of the house in order to throw a stone."

They were dumbstruck, unable to utter a sound.

He concluded, "Leave my city. I shall grant you ten days. Whoever is seen after that will have his head struck off."

"O Muḥammad (Ibn Maslama), we never would have thought that a member of the Aws (their allies) would bring a message like this!"

"Hearts change," Muḥammad answered.

They took several days to make preparations. They sent for pack camels they had kept in reserve in Dhu 'l-Jadar,[8] and rented others from some people of the Ashjaᶜ tribe. While they were busy making preparations, a message was brought to them from Ibn Ubayy[9] by Suwayd and Dāᶜis: "Do not leave your homes and property. Stay in your fortresses. I have 2000 men with me from my people and the Arabs. They will join you in your fortifications and are prepared to die to the last man before he

[5] The Ḥanīfs in pre-Islamic Arabia were free-lance seekers of God. Al-Wāqidī seems to have the Jews using it in the koranic sense of pure monotheism. See W. M. Watt, "Ḥanīf," *EI*² 3: 165f.

[6] A simple wrap worn in Arabia at this time similar to an *izār*. See Yedida K. Stillman, "Libās," *EI*² 5 (in press).

[7] I am following Wellhausen's rendering here. The Arabic reads: *ka-annahu washījatukum hādhihi,* and as M. Jones points out in his footnote, is rather obscure. See Julius Wellhausen, *Muhammed in Medina: Das ist Vakidi's Kitab al-Maghazi in verkürzter deutscher Wiedergabe* (Berlin, 1882), p. 162: *als sei er von eurer eigenen edelsten Wurzel.* See also M. Jones, ed., *Maghāzī,* vol. 1, p. 367, n. 2.

[8] A pasture six miles from Medina near Qubā'. See Jones, *Maghāzī,* vol. 1, p. 367, n. 3.

[9] The leader of the so-called Hypocrites, see above, p. 123.

could reach you. The Qurayẓa will support you. Surely, they would never abandon you. Your allies from Ghaṭafān will also reinforce you."

Ibn Ubayy sent word to Kaᶜb b. Asad[10] that he should support his coreligionists. But Kaᶜb replied that no one from the Banū Qurayẓa would violate the treaty. As a result Ibn Ubayy despaired of any help from the Qurayẓa. He wanted the dispute between the Banu 'l-Naḍīr and the Apostle to be decided by war. He continued sending messages to Ḥuyayy until finally Ḥuyayy decided to send a message to Muḥammad informing him that they would not leave their homes nor their property, and let him do what he must. Ḥuyayy was depending upon the help promised by Ibn Ubayy.

Ḥuyayy said to his people, "Let us repair to our fortresses, bring in our cattle, and patrol our lanes. We shall transport rocks into our fortifications. We have enough food to last us a year and an unlimited water supply which cannot be cut off. Does anyone think that Muḥammad would besiege us an entire year? I hardly think so!"

Sallām b. Mishkam answered him, "By God, you are indulging in false hopes, Ḥuyayy. Heaven knows, I would certainly disassociate myself from you along with those Jews who heed me were it not for the fact that your authority would be weakened and you would be scorned. However, do not do this, Ḥuyayy, for by God, you know and we know with you that he is indeed the Apostle of God and that he is described in our literature. If we have not followed him because we begrudge the fact that prophecy has departed from the Sons of Aaron, then let us go and accept the guarantee of safe conduct he has offered us and leave his city."

. . . .

In the end, Ḥuyayy dispatched his brother Judayy to the Apostle of Allah—may Allah bless him and grant him peace—with this message: "We shall not leave our homes and property. Do what you will." He also ordered his brother to go to Ibn Ubayy and inform him of his message to Muḥammad and to bid him quickly fulfill his promise of aid. When Judayy came before the Apostle of Allah—may Allah bless him and grant him peace—he found him seated amongst his companions. He delivered his message, and the Apostle exclaimed, "Allah is most great!" The Muslims repeated the cry. Then he said, "The Jews have declared war!"

Judayy left and came to Ibn Ubayy who was seated in his house with a small group of his allies. Meanwhile, the Apostle's herald had already proclaimed his order to march on the Banu 'l-Naḍīr. Even as Judayy was

[10] The chief of the Qurayẓa. See below, p. 141.

sitting with ᶜAbd Allāh b. Ubayy and his allies, in came ᶜAbd Allāh b. ᶜAbd Allāh b. Ubayy. He put on his shirt of mail, picked up his sword, and went out to join the war party. Judayy b. Akhṭab realized when he saw Ibn Ubayy just sitting there in his house while his son was taking up arms that he could not hope for any assistance from him, so he hurried off to Ḥuyayy.

The Apostle of Allah—may Allah bless him and grant him peace—set out with his companions and performed the afternoon prayer in the territory of the Banu 'l-Naḍīr. When they saw the Apostle and his companions, they mounted the ramparts of the forts with arrows and stones. The Qurayẓa disassociated themselves from them and did not come to their aid with either arms or men. They kept far away.

When neither ᶜAbd Allāh, who just sat in his house, nor any of his allies showed up the next day, the Banu 'l-Naḍīr despaired of his aid. Sallām b. Mishkam and Kināna b. Ṣuwayrā' began speaking to Ḥuyayy, "Where is the help from Ibn Ubayy that you were claiming?"

What am I to do?" asked Ḥuyayy. "A massacre has been decreed for us!"

Saᶜd b. ᶜUbāda supplied the Muslims with dates while the Jews remained in their stronghold. The Apostle then ordered that their palm trees be cut down and burned. He appointed two of his companions, Abū Laylā al-Māzinī and ᶜAbd Allāh b. Salām,[11] to do the job. Abū Laylā cut down the variety known as *ᶜajwa,* while ᶜAbd Allāh b. Salām cut down the variety called *lawn.* . . . When the *ᶜajwa* palms were cut down the Jewish women began to tear their clothes, beat their cheeks, and wail. . . . Abū Rāfiᶜ Sallām screamed at them, "Even if our *ᶜajwas* are cut down here, we still have more in Khaybar."[12] But one old woman answered him, "He will do the same thing there." "God smite your mouth!" Abū Rāfiᶜ told her. "I have 10,000 warriors as my allies in Khaybar." When these words of Abū Rāfiᶜ's were reported to the Apostle, he smiled.

The Jews became anxious at the destruction of their *ᶜajwa* palms. Sallām b. Mishkam said to Ḥuyayy, "Our *ᶜadhq* palms are even more precious than the *ᶜajwa.* Once planted, they will not bear fruit for thirty years more if cut down."

So Ḥuyayy sent the following message to the Apostle of Allah—may Allah bless him and grant him peace: "O Muḥammad, you have forbidden corruption. Why then do you cut down palm trees? We shall give you whatever you ask, and we shall depart from your city."

[11] He was Muḥammad's first Jewish convert. See the story of his conversion above, pp. 113–14.

[12] This was the important Jewish agricultural settlement approximately ninety miles north of Medina. It too fell to Muḥammad. See below, pp. 145–49.

The Apostle replied, "I shall not consent to it today. However, depart with whatever your camels can carry except weapons."

Sallām said, "Accept the offer, damn you, before you are forced to accept worse terms!"

"What could be worse than this?" complained Ḥuyayy.

"That he take your offspring captive, kill your warriors, in addition to taking your property. Our property is the least consideration for us today if we compare it to slaughter and captivity."

Nevertheless, Ḥuyayy refused to accept the terms for one or two days. Seeing him hesitating like this, Yāmīn b. ᶜUmayr and Abū Saᶜd b. Wahb said to each other, "You know very well that he is the Apostle of Allah. Let us wait no longer and convert to Islam. We will then be guaranteed our lives and our property. So they went down by night, became Muslims, and thereby preserved their lives and their property.

Finally, the Jews surrendered on condition that they could take whatever their camels could carry excluding their weapons. Now that the Apostle of Allah had dislodged them, he said to Yāmīn,[13] "What do you think of your cousin ᶜAmr b. Jiḥāsh and the way he plotted to kill me?" (ᶜAmr was married to Yāmīn's sister al-Ruwāᶜ b. ᶜUmayr.)

Yāmīn answered, "I can take care of him for you, o Apostle of Allah." He then paid a man from Qays 10 dinars to assassinate ᶜAmr b. Jiḥāsh. (Some say he paid him 5 loads of dates.) The man lay in wait for him and killed him. Yāmīn came back to the Prophet—may Allah bless him and grant him peace—and informed him of the assassination which delighted him.

The Apostle of Allah had besieged the Banu 'l-Naḍīr fifteen days before ousting them from Medina. He appointed Muḥammad b. Maslama to supervise their departure. They complained that they had outstanding debts against people. The Apostle told them to hurry up and collect them. . . . Abū Rāfiᶜ Sallām b. Abi 'l-Ḥuqayq had lent Usayd b. Ḥuḍayr 100 dinars for one year. He settled with him for 80 dinars on his capital and absolved him from the rest.

During the siege the Jews had destroyed their houses which they were leaving behind. The Muslims had further ruined what was left behind and burned until the truce was called. The Jews loaded up their timbers and the lintels of their doors.

The Apostle of Allah—may Allah bless him and grant him peace—said to Ṣafiyya b. Ḥuyayy,[14] "If only you had seen me fastening the saddle for your maternal uncle Baḥrī b. ᶜAmr, and how I sent him on his way!"

[13] From this point on he is called Ibn Yāmīn in the text.

[14] She was to become the Prophet's "Jewish wife" after the fall of Khaybar. See below, p. 146.

They loaded up their women and children and departed via the territory of the Balḥārith b. al-Khazraj, and after that through the territory of the Jabaliyya, and then over the bridge. From there they went past the Muṣallā[15] and crossed the marketplace of Medina. Their women were decked out in litters wearing silk, brocade, velvet, and fine red and green silk. People lined up to gape at them. They passed by in a train one after the other, borne by 600 camels. . . . They went off beating tambourines and playing on pipes.

al-Wāqidī, *Kitāb al-Maghāzī*, vol. 1,
ed. Marsden Jones (London, 1966), pp. 363–75.

[15] A large outdoor prayer area.

THE EXTERMINATION OF THE BANU QURAYZA (A.H. 5/627)

The angel Gabriel appeared to the Apostle of Allah—may Allah bless him and grant him peace—at the time of the noonday prayer. As al-Zuhrī related to me, he wore a turban of silk embroidered with gold which covered his face. He rode a mule with a velvet brocade saddle. He asked, "Have you already put aside your arms, o Apostle of Allah?" He answered that he had, to which Gabriel replied, "The angels have not yet put aside their weapons, and I have just now returned from seeking out the enemy. Allah Almighty and Exalted commands you, o Muḥammad, to march against the Banū Qurayẓa. Indeed, I am on my way to them to shake their strongholds."

The Apostle of Allah—may Allah bless him and grant him peace—ordered a muezzin to call out to the people who hear and obey that they should not perform the afternoon prayer except on the territory of the Banū Qurayẓa. He then left Ibn Umm Maktūm in charge of Medina, according to Ibn Hishām.

The Apostle of Allah—may Allah bless him and grant him peace—sent ᶜAlī b. Abī Ṭālib ahead of him with his banner to the Banū Qurayẓa, and the people flocked to it. ᶜAlī marched forward until, as he drew near the fortifications, he heard them speaking about the Apostle in a despicable way. He turned back until he met the Apostle of Allah—may Allah bless him and grant him peace—on the road. He told him, "O Apostle of Allah, you must not come near these scoundrels!"

"Why?" he asked. "I think you must have heard them insulting me."

"Yes, I did."

"Had they seen me, they would not have said such things!" Then, when he drew near their fortifications, he called out, "O you brothers of apes, has Allah shamed you and brought down His vengeance upon you?"

"O Abu 'l-Qāsim," they called back, "you have never been a barbarian."

. . . .

The Apostle of Allah—may Allah bless him and grant him peace—besieged them twenty-five days[1] until his siege exhausted them and Allah cast terror into their hearts.

It so happened that Ḥuyayy b. Akhṭab[2] joined the Banū Qurayẓa in

[1] According to al-Wāqidī, it was a fortnight. See al-Wāqidī, *Kitāb al-Maghāzī*, vol, 2, ed. M. Jones (London, 1966), p. 496.

[2] The leader of the Banu 'l-Naḍīr. See above, pp. 129–35.

their fortress when the Quraysh and Ghaṭafān had turned back.[3] He did this in fulfillment of the agreement he had made with Kaᶜb b. Asad.

When they became certain that the Apostle was not going to turn away from them without a fight, Kaᶜb b. Asad spoke to them. "O Jews, you see the circumstances that have descended upon us. I shall propose three courses of action. Choose whichever you please. They are: 1) that we follow this man and testify to his truth, for by God, it is surely already clear to you that he is a prophet sent by God and that he is indeed the one whom you find mentioned in your scripture. This way you will insure your lives, your property, your children, and your wives."

But they replied, "We will never separate ourselves from the rule of the Torah, neither will we exchange it for another."

"If you refuse this course of action, 2) then let us slay our women and children. After that, we shall go out against Muḥammad and his companions as men with our swords drawn, having left no impediments behind us, and let God decide between us and Muḥammad. If we perish, we perish. At least we shall not have left behind us any offspring to worry about. If we should triumph, then by my life, we can certainly find other wives and children."

But they responded, "Should we kill these poor things! What good would life be after that?"

"If you refuse to accept this proposal of mine," he said, 3) "tonight is the sabbath eve, perhaps Muḥammad and his companions will feel secure from us at that time. Let us go down and it may be that we can take Muḥammad and his companions by surprise."

They countered, "We would be profaning our sabbath, and we would be doing none other that that which was done by those before us who were transformed into apes,[4] as you well know."

He exclaimed, "Not a man among you has spent a single night since the time his mother gave birth to him resolute against fate!"

Then they sent to the Apostle of Allah—may Allah bless him and grant him peace—requesting that he send Abū Lubāba b. ᶜAbd al-Mundhir to them that they might take counsel with him. He was a brother of the Banū ᶜAmr b. ᶜAwf, and they were allies of the Aws.[5] So the Apostle of Allah—may Allah bless him and grant him peace—sent him to them. When they saw him, the men rose up to greet him, while the women

[3] After failing to take Medina at the Battle of the Trench (March–April 627). This was the last great effort of the Quraysh of Mecca to quash Muḥammad and his new religion. The Ghaṭafān joined the attackers upon the urging of the Banu 'l-Naḍīr, in Khaybar, who promised them half the date harvest. See al-Wāqidī, *Kitāb al-Maghāzī*, vol. 2, p. 443.

[4] See Sura 2:65/61.

[5] The Banū ᶜAmr b. ᶜAwf were a clan of the Aws.

and children broke out crying in his face, and his heart softened toward them.

"Do you think we should surrender to Muḥammad's judgment, Abū Lubāba?" they asked.

"Yes," he replied, but made a sign with his hand toward his throat indicating that it would be slaughter. Abū Lubāba recalled later, "By Allah, my feet had not moved an inch from the spot when I realized I had betrayed Allah and His Apostle." With that, Abū Lubāba immediately left them. Instead of going to the Apostle of Allah—may Allah bless him and grant him peace—he went and tied himself to one of the pillars in the mosque, saying, "I shall not leave this place until Allah pardons me for what I have done." Then he promised Allah, "I shall not come to the Banū Qurayẓa ever again, nor shall I ever again be seen in a city in which I betrayed Allah and His Apostle."

When the news about him reached the Apostle of Allah—may Allah bless him and grant him peace—who had been waiting for him, he said, "If he had only come to me, I would have prayed that he be forgiven. However, since he acted as he did, I shall not free him from his place until Allah pardons him."

Yazīd b. ᶜAbd Allāh b. Qusayṭ told me that Abū Lubāba's pardon was revealed to the Apostle of Allah—may Allah bless him and grant him peace—at dawn while he was in the house of Umm Salama.[6] She later recalled, "I heard the Apostle laughing at dawn and asked him, 'why are you laughing, o Apostle of Allah?' 'May Allah cause you to laugh,' he replied, 'Abū Lubāba has been pardoned'. . . . When the Apostle passed him on his way to morning prayer, he set him free."

Thaᶜlaba b. Saᶜya, Usayd b. Saᶜya, and Asad b. ᶜUbayd converted to Islam on the night that the Banū Qurayẓa surrendered to the Apostle's judgment. They were members of the Banū Hadl, not Qurayẓa or al-Naḍīr—indeed, their pedigree was higher than that for they were part of the Banū Umm al-Qawm.

On that same night ᶜAmr b. Suᶜdā al-Quraẓī went out past the Apostle's guard which was under Muḥammad b. Maslama that evening. When Ibn Maslama spotted him, he called out, "Who is that?" And ᶜAmr b. Suᶜdā identified himself. It so happened that ᶜAmr had refused to join the Banū Qurayẓa in their treachery toward the Apostle of Allah—may Allah bless him and grant him peace—saying that he would never act treacherously toward Muḥammad. When Ibn Maslama recognized him, he exclaimed, "Please Allah, do not deprive me from removing the stumbling

[6] Each of the Prophet's wives had a separate hut along the east wall of the enclosure which was his residence. See K. A. C. Creswell, "Architecture," *EI*² 1: 609.

blocks of the noble." Then he let him go his way. He immediately set out and went until he came to the door of the Apostle's Mosque in Medina that night. After that he vanished, and no one knows to this very day where in the world he went. When his story was told the Apostle of Allah—may Allah bless him and grant him peace—he replied, "That man was saved by Allah on account of his faithfulness." Some people claim that he was tied with a rotten rope along with the others from the Banū Qurayẓa when they surrendered themselves to the Apostle's judgment, and that the rope was found thrown aside, no one knowing where he had gone. Concerning this, the Apostle said, "Allah knows best what really happened."

When it became morning, they surrendered to the judgment of the Apostle of Allah—may Allah bless him and grant him peace. Then the Aws jumped up and pleaded, "O Apostle of Allah, these are our clients, not those of the Khazraj, and you know well how you recently treated our brethren's clients." Now the Apostle of Allah—may Allah bless him and grant him peace—prior to the campaign against the Banū Qurayẓa had besieged the Banū Qaynuqāᶜ, who were allies of the Khazraj.[7] When they had surrendered to his judgment, ᶜAbd Allāh b. Ubayy b. Salūl asked him for them, and he gave them over to him. Therefore, when the Aws pleaded with him, he said, "Would you be satisfied, o People of Aws, if one of your own men were to pass judgment on them?"

"Certainly," they replied.

The Apostle of Allah—may Allah bless him and grant him peace—said, "Then it shall be left to Saᶜd b. Muᶜādh." Now the Apostle had put Saᶜd b. Muᶜādh in the tent of a woman of Aslam, named Rufayda, which was pitched inside his mosque.[8] She used to care for the wounded and personally see to those Muslims in need of attention. The Apostle had instructed his people, when the latter was struck by an arrow at the Battle of the Trench, to put him in Rufayda's tent until he could visit him soon after.

When the Apostle of Allah—may Allah bless him and grant him peace—appointed him as arbiter over the fate of the Banū Qurayẓa, his people came to him and lifted him onto a donkey on which they had placed a leather cushion for he was a handsomely corpulent man. Then they went with him to the Apostle. On the way they kept imploring him, "O Abū ᶜAmr,[9] deal graciously with your clients, for the Apostle has ap-

[7] See above, pp. 122–23.

[8] That is, in the large open court of the Prophet's residence that also served as the mosque of the early Muslim community in Medina. See J. Pedersen, "Masdjid," Shorter *EI*, p. 331.

[9] Saᶜd's *kunyā* or byname.

pointed you arbiter so that you might be gracious to them." As they continued to press him, he replied, "It is time for Saᶜd to ignore the censure of men for the sake of Allah."

Some of his tribesmen who were with him then returned to the quarter of the Banū ᶜAbd al-Ashhal and announced to them the impending death of the Banū Qurayẓa before Saᶜd had even arrived because of what he had been heard to say.

When Saᶜd reached the Apostle of Allah—may Allah bless him and grant him peace—the Apostle said, "Rise to greet your leader." The Emigrants of Quraysh said to themselves that the Apostle must be referring to the Helpers. The Helpers, on the other hand, thought the Apostle was including everyone, and so they got up and said, "O Abū ᶜAmr, the Apostle has appointed you arbiter over the fate of your clients so that you may pass judgment upon them."

"Will you accept as binding, by Allah's covenant and His Pact, the judgment upon them once I have given it?" They replied that they would. "And will it be binding upon one who is here," he said turning toward the Apostle, not mentioning him by name out of respect. The Apostle of Allah—may Allah bless him and grant him peace—answered yes. Saᶜd said, "My judgment is that the men be executed, their property divided, and the women and children made captives.

ᶜĀsim b. ᶜUmar b. Qatāda told me on the authority of ᶜAbd al-Raḥmān b. ᶜAmr b. Saᶜd b. Muᶜādh on the authority of Alqama b. Waqqāṣ al-Laythī that the Apostle said to Saᶜd, "You have judged them according to the verdict of Allah above the seventh heaven."

When they surrendered, the Apostle of Allah—may Allah bless him and grant him peace—had them imprisoned in Medina, in the quarter of Bint al-Ḥārith, a woman of the Banu 'l-Najjār. Then the Apostle went to the Market of Medina, which is its market to this day, and had trenches dug. After that, he sent for them and had them decapitated into those trenches as they were brought out in groups. The enemy of Allah, Ḥuyayy b. Akhṭab was among them, as was Kaᶜb b. Asad, the chief of the tribe. In all, they were about 600 or 700, although some say there were as many as 800 or 900. As they were being brought out in groups to the Apostle, they asked Kaᶜb, "O Kaᶜb, what do you think he will do with us?"

"Will you never understand? Can't you see that the summoner does not cease, and those who are led away from you do not return? By God, it is death!"

These proceedings continued until the Apostle of Allah—may Allah bless him and grant him peace—had finished them off.

Ḥuyayy b. Akhṭab, the enemy of Allah, was brought out with his hands bound behind his neck. He was wearing an embroidered robe, the color of rosebuds,[10] which he had torn from all sides with rents the size of fingertips so that it would not be taken as spoil. He looked at the Apostle of Allah—may Allah bless him and grant him peace—and said, "By God, I do not blame myself for opposing you. However, he who forsakes God will be forsaken." Then he drew near the people there and said, "There is no evil in God's command. God has ordained a book, a decree, and a slaughter for the Children of Israel." Then he sat down and was beheaded.

Muhammad b. Jaᶜfar b. al-Zubayr informed me on the authority of ᶜUrwa b. al- Zubayr that ᶜĀ'isha, the Mother of the Faithful, said, "Only one of their women was killed. By Allah, she was with me, talking with me and shaking with laughter, while the Apostle was killing her menfolk in the marketplace. Suddenly an unseen voice called her by name—'Where is so-and-so?' 'By God, I am here,' she cried. 'Woe unto you,' I said, 'what is wrong with you?' 'I am to be killed,' she said. 'What for?'—'For something I have done.' She was led away and beheaded."

ᶜĀ'isha used to say, "I shall never forget my amazement at her good spirits and copious laughter, when all the time she knew that she would be killed." (Ibn Hishām adds:) It was she who had thrown a millstone on Khallād b. Suwayd, killing him.

I was told by Ibn Shihāb al-Zuhrī that Thābit b. Qays b. al-Shammās came to al-Zabīr b. Bāṭā al-Quraẓī, who was called Abū ᶜAbd al-Raḥmān. Now al-Zabīr had spared Thābit's life before the advent of Islam. (One of al-Zabīr's sons told me that he had spared him at the Battle of Buᶜāth[11] when he had taken him prisoner, cut off his forelock, but then let him go.) Thābit came to him—he was already an old man—and asked him, "Do you recognize me, Abū ᶜAbd al-Raḥmān?"

"Would a man like me, not recognize a man like you?"

"I want to repay you for the kindness you showed me."

"The noble repays the noble."

Then Thābit b. Qays came to the Apostle of Allah—may Allah bless him and grant him peace—and said, "O Apostle of Allah, al-Zabīr once spared my life, I dearly want to repay him for it. Therefore, grant me his life."

"He is yours," the Apostle replied.

[10] Ar., *faqqāhiyya*: "a reddish color like that of roses when they blossom," *Lisān al-ᶜArab*, cited in the notes to Ibn Hishām, *al-Sīra al-Nabawiyya*, vol. 2, p. 241, n. 2.

[11] In this battle that took place ca. 617, on the territory of the Banū Qurayẓa, the Aws and their Jewish allies, the Banū Qurayẓa and Banu 'l-Naḍīr, defeated the other great Medinese confederation, the Khazraj. See C. E. Bosworth, "Buᶜāth," *EI*² 1: 1,283; and Yisrā'ēl Ben-Ze'ev, *Ha-Yehūdīm ba-ᶜArāv* (Jerusalem, 1957), pp. 87–94.

Then he went back to him and informed him that the Apostle had granted him his life.

"An old man with no family and no children—what use does he have for life?" retorted al-Zabīr.

Thābit returned to the Apostle and said, "By my father and my mother, o Apostle, grant me the lives of his wife and children."

"They are yours," he said.

He came and told him. But al-Zabīr said, "A household in the Hijaz without property! How can they survive like that?"

So Thābit went again to the Apostle and said, "What about his property?"

"It is yours," he replied.

Thābit returned and told him that the Apostle had granted him his property. Now he asked, "Tell me, Thābit, what has happened to him whose face was like a Chinese mirror in which the virgins of the tribe would look at themselves, Kaᶜb b. Asad?"

"He was killed."

"What about the lord of the desert and the sown, Ḥuyayy b. Akhṭab?"

"Killed."

"And what has become of our vanguard when we attacked and our rearguard when we retreated, ᶜAzzāl b. Samaw'al?"

"Killed."

"And what has become of the two assemblies, the clan of Banū Kaᶜb b. Qurayẓa and Banū ᶜAmr b. Qurayẓa?"

"They were taken out and killed."

"Then I ask, o Thābit, by the claim I have upon you, will you not let me join my people, for by God, there is no good in life after they are gone. I do not have the patience to wait even the time it takes to pour a bucket of water to join my loved ones." So Thābit came up to him and beheaded him.

When Abū Bakr the Righteous learned that he had said "to join my loved ones," he remarked, "By Allah, he will join them in the fire of Hell for all eternity!"

The Apostle of Allah—may Allah bless him and grant him peace—had commanded that every male who had attained puberty should be slain.

I was informed by Shuᶜba b. al-Ḥajjāj on the authority of ᶜAbd al-Malik b. ᶜUmayr that ᶜAṭiyya al-Quraẓī said, "The Apostle of Allah—may Allah bless him and grant him peace—had given orders that every male of the Banū Qurayẓa who had reached puberty should be slain. I was still a youth, and they discovered that I was not yet adolescent, so they let me go."

I was told by Ayyūb b. ᶜAbd al-Raḥmān b. ᶜAbd Allāh b. Abī Ṣaᶜṣaᶜa, brother of the Banū ᶜAdī b. al-Najjār, that Salmā b. Qays Umm al-Mundhir, the sister of Salīṭ b. Qays, who was one of the Apostle's maternal aunts, and who had prayed with him towards both *qiblas,*[12] and had acknowledged him with the allegiance of women, asked him to grant her the life of Rifāᶜa b. Samaw'al al-Quraẓī. He was already an adult and had taken refuge with her. He had been acquainted with her family previously. "O Prophet of Allah," she said, "by my father and mother, I appeal to you, grant me Rifāᶜa's life. He has already declared that he will pray as a Muslim and eat camel meat." So he turned him over to her, and she spared his life.

The Apostle of Allah—may Allah bless him and grant him peace—divided the property of the Banū Qurayẓa along with their wives and their children among the Muslims. On that day he announced the shares for both horses and men, and he took out the fifth for himself.[13] Each cavalryman got three shares—two for the horse and one for its rider. Each infantryman, having no horse, got a single share. There were thirty-six horses taken on the Day of the Banū Qurayẓa. They constituted the first spoils for which lots were cast and from which the fifth was taken. The allotments were made in accordance with established practice and what the Apostle had done, and this became the customary practice for raids.

After that, the Apostle of Allah—may Allah bless him and grant him peace—sent Saᶜd b. Zayd al-Anṣārī, brother of the Banū ᶜAbd al-Ashhal, with some of the female captives from the Banū Qurayẓa to Nejd, where he sold them for horses and arms.

The Apostle of Allah—may Allah bless him and grant him peace—chose for himself from their women Rayḥāna b. ᶜAmr b. Khunāfa, a woman of the clan of Banū ᶜAmr b. Qurayẓa. She remained with the Apostle until she died as his chattel. The Apostle offered to marry her and impose the veil on her, but she said, "No. Keep me as your chattel for that will be easier on both me and you." So he kept her that way. Now at the time of her capture, she resisted being converted to Islam, accepting nothing but Judaism. So the Apostle put her aside, and he was upset on account of that. But while he was in the company of his companions, he heard footsteps behind him and said, "This is surely Thaᶜlaba b. Saᶜya bringing me the good tidings that Rayḥāna has accepted Islam!" He approached him and said, "O Apostle of Allah, Rayḥāna has become a Muslim." This made him glad.

Ibn Hishām, *al-Sīra al-Nabawiyya,* vol. 2
(Cairo, 1955), pp. 233–45.

[12] That is, the two directions of prayer, Mecca and—for a short while—Jerusalem.

[13] The Koran (Sura 9:41) specifically states: "Know that whatever you take as spoils, one fifth is for Allah, for the Apostle and his kinsmen, for the orphan, the poor, and the wayfarer."

MUHAMMAD AND THE JEWS OF KHAYBAR
(A.H. 7/628)

Muḥammad b. Isḥāq stated: The Apostle of Allah—may Allah bless him and grant him peace—stayed in Medina upon returning from al-Ḥudaybiyya[1] during the month of Dhu 'l-Ḥijja and part of Muḥarram since the polytheists were overseeing the pilgrimage. Then he set out against Khaybar during the latter part of Muḥarram. (Ibn Hishām adds:) Numayla b. ᶜAbd Allāh was left in charge of Medina, and the standard was entrusted to ᶜAlī b. Abī Ṭālib[2]—may Allah be pleased with him. The banner was white.

(Ibn Isḥāq continued:) I was told by someone whom I do not suspect on the authority of Anas b. Mālik that whenever the Apostle of Allah—may Allah bless him and grant him peace—raided a people, he would not attack until it was morning. If he heard the call to prayer, he held back. If he did not hear it, he attacked.[3] We arrived in Khaybar at night, and so the Apostle spent the night there. When it became light, and he did not hear the call to prayer, he mounted up—and we with him. I rode behind Abū Ṭalḥa, and my foot touched against the Apostle's foot. We encountered some workmen from Khaybar coming out with their spades and baskets. When they saw the Apostle of Allah—may Allah bless him and grant him peace—and the troops, they exclaimed, "It is Muḥammad and the army with him!" Then they turned in flight. The Apostle of Allah shouted, "Allah is most great! Khaybar is destroyed! When we come down into a people's square, it is an ill-fated morning for those who have been warned!"

. . . .

The Apostle of Allah—may Allah bless him and grant him peace—seized the various properties one by one, and he conquered the fortresses in the same manner. The first to be captured was the fortress of Nāᶜim. Maḥmūd b. Maslama was killed there by a millstone which was thrown upon him from above. Next was al-Qamūṣ, the fortress of the Banū Abi

[1] About six weeks before the expedition against Khaybar, Muḥammad signed an agreement with the Quraysh at this spot on the edge of the sacred territory of Mecca. Among other things, Muḥammad agreed not to make the pilgrimage that year. Many of his followers were dismayed and disappointed. The raid against Khaybar was in part a consolation. See W. Montgomery Watt, "al-Ḥudaybiyya," *EI*² 3: 539.

[2] He was Muḥammad's cousin, son-in-law, and the fourth caliph.

[3] This is not as generous as it may seem at first, for only Muslims would make the call to prayer.

'l-Ḥuqayq. The Apostle of Allah—may Allah bless him and grant him peace—took some of them captive. Among those taken were Ṣafiyya b. Ḥuyyay b. Akhṭab and two cousins of hers. She had been the wife of Kināna b. al-Rabīᶜ b. Abi 'l-Ḥuqayq. The Apostle chose Ṣafiyya for himself. Now Diḥya b. Khalīfa al-Kalbī had asked the Apostle for Ṣafiyya, and so when he chose her for himself, he gave Diḥya her two cousins. The female captives from Khaybar were distributed among the Muslims.

Until this time, the Muslims ate the meat of domestic donkeys, but then the Apostle of Allah—may Allah bless him and grant him peace—arose and forbade the people to do several things which he enumerated.

ᶜAbd Allāh b. Abī Najīḥ informed me on the authority of Makḥūl that the Apostle of Allah—may Allah bless him and grant him peace—forbade four things that day: approaching pregnant captives sexually, eating the meat of domestic donkeys, eating the flesh of any beast of prey, and selling booty before it was properly distributed.

. . . .

When the Apostle of Allah—may Allah bless him and grant him peace—had taken nearly all their fortresses and had got possession of most of their property, he came to al-Waṭīḥ and al-Sulālim, which were the last fortresses of the people of Khaybar to be captured. The Apostle besieged them for approximately ten days. (Ibn Hishām adds:) The war-cry of the Apostle's companions at the battle of Khaybar was "O you who have been given victory, kill! kill!"

ᶜAbd Allāh b. Sahl b. ᶜAbd al-Raḥmān b. Sahl, brother of the Banū Ḥāritha, told me on the authority of Jābir b. ᶜAbd Allāh that the Jew Marḥab came out of their fortress fully armed and said:

> Khaybar knows that I am Marḥab
> A seasoned warrior fully armed
> Sometimes piercing, sometimes striking
> As when lions advance in rage.
> My inviolable sanctuary may not be approached.

He was saying, "Who will meet me in combat?"

The Apostle of Allah—may Allah bless him and grant him peace—then asked, "Who will take care of this man?"

"I shall take care of him for you," answered Muḥammad b. Maslama. "By Allah, I have the duty of an avenger who has not yet had satisfaction because my brother was killed yesterday."

"Go to him then," he said. "O Allah, help him against the other."

When the two approached each other, there was an old tree whose wood had become soft standing between them. Each of them began to take shelter from the other behind it. When one of them dodged behind it, the other would hack at it with his sword, until finally each one was exposed to the other. The tree had become like a man standing up erect. No branches were left on it. Then Marḥab attacked Muḥammad b. Maslama and struck at him. The latter protected himself with his shield. The sword cut into it and became stuck. Muḥammad b. Maslama struck him back and killed him.

Kināna b. al-Rabīᶜ, who had custody of the treasure of the Banu 'l Naḍīr, was brought before the Apostle of Allah—may Allah bless him and grant him peace. He questioned him concerning its whereabouts. He, however, denied knowing its location. Then one of the Jews came to the Apostle and told him, "I saw Kināna walking around in a certain ruin early each morning."

At this, the Apostle said to Kināna, "Do you know that if we find that you have it, I shall have you killed?"

"Yes," he replied.

The Apostle of Allah—may Allah bless him and grant him peace—ordered the ruin to be excavated, and part of the Banu 'l Naḍīr's treasure was dug up. So the Apostle questioned him about the rest, but he refused to hand it over. Then the Apostle ordered al-Zubayr b. al-ᶜAwwām, saying, "Torture him until you extract it from him." Al-Zubayr struck a fire with flint on his chest until he nearly expired. Then the Apostle gave him over to Muḥammad b. Maslama who cut off his head as part of his revenge for his brother Maḥmūd b. Maslama.

The Apostle of Allah—may Allah bless him and grant him peace—had besieged the people of Khaybar in their fortresses al-Waṭīḥ and al-Sulālim until they came to realize all was lost, and they entreated him to be lenient with them and to refrain from shedding their blood. This he agreed to do. The Apostle had already taken possession of all their property—al-Shaqq, Naṭāh, al-Katība, and all their fortresses—with the sole exception of what belonged to these two fortresses.

When the people of Fadak[4] heard about what happened to them, they sent to the Apostle of Allah—may Allah bless him and grant him peace—entreating him to be lenient with them too, and refrain from shedding their blood. They in turn would surrender all of their property to him. He

[4] This agricultural settlement was located not far from Khaybar, and like it was inhabited by Jews. After the death of Muḥammad, Fadak became a point of contention between Fāṭima, the Prophet's daughter, and Abū Bakr, the first caliph. She claimed that it had been left to her by her father, but Abū Bakr argued that its pious foundation was established by Muḥammad for charitable purposes. The dispute over who was entitled to the revenues of Fadak was to continue for nearly two centuries. See L. Veccia Vaglieri, "Fadak," *EI*[2] 2: 725–27.

agreed to this. Muḥayyiṣa b. Masᶜūd,[5] brother of the Banū Ḥāritha, was one of the intermediaries between them and the Apostle.

When the people of Khaybar had surrendered on these terms, they asked the Apostle of Allah—may Allah bless him and grant him peace—to employ them on their former property for half the produce. "We are more knowledgeable about that than you and are better cultivators. So the Apostle of Allah—may Allah bless him and grant him peace—made peace with them in return for fifty percent of their produce, adding, "On condition that we may expel you if and when we wish to expel you."[6] He made peace with the inhabitants of Fadak on the same terms. Thus, Khaybar became part of the communal spoils of the Muslims, whereas Fadak was exclusively for the Apostle of Allah—may Allah bless him and grant him peace—because they had not driven horses or camels against it.[7]

When the Apostle of Allah—may Allah bless him and grant him peace—had rested, Zaynab b. al-Ḥārith, Sallām b. Mishkam's wife, presented him with a roasted lamb. She had previously inquired as to which joint of lamb was the Apostle's favorite. When told it was the shoulder, she put a great deal of poison in it, poisoning the rest of the lamb as well. Then she brought it. When she had placed it before the Apostle of Allah—may Allah bless him and grant him peace—he took the shoulder and chewed a piece of it, but he did not swallow it. Bishr b. al-Barāʾ b. Maᶜrūr was with him, and also took a piece from it as did the Apostle. Now Bishr swallowed it, whereas the Apostle of Allah—may Allah bless him and grant him peace—spit it out and said, "This bone tells me that it is poisoned." Then he summoned her, and she confessed. "What brought you to do this?" he asked.

"You know very well what you have brought upon my people," she replied. "I thought to myself, if this man is only a king I shall be rid of him, and if he is a prophet, he will be informed [that the lamb was poisoned]."

At these words, the Apostle of Allah—may Allah bless him and grant him peace—let her off. Bishr died from what he had eaten.

Marwān b. ᶜUthmān b. Abī Saᶜīd b. al-Muᶜallā told me that the Apostle of Allah—may Allah bless him and grant him peace—said to Umm Bishr b. al-Barāʾ when she came to visit him during the illness from which

[5] Concerning him, see above, p. 128.

[6] This clause is most probably a later interpolation that was put in to justify the expulsion of the Jews from northern Arabia by Caliph ᶜUmar in 642.

[7] In Sura 17:64/66, the Muslims are enjoined to urge horse and foot against the unbelievers so as to "share in their wealth and children." Since Fadak surrendered without being attacked, there was no need to share the booty.

he was to die, "O Umm Bishr, this is the time in which I feel a deadly attack from what I ate with your brother at Khaybar."

Indeed, the Muslims consider the Apostle to have died a martyr in addition to the prophethood with which Allah had honored him.

Ibn Hishām, *al-Sīra al-Nabawiyya,* vol. 2 (Cairo, 1955), pp. 328–38.

THE KORAN ON THE TREATMENT OF THE PEOPLE OF THE BOOK

Fight against those to whom the Scriptures were given, who believe not in Allah nor in the Last Day, who forbid not what Allah and His apostle have forbidden, and follow not the true faith, until they pay the tribute out of hand, and are humbled.[1]

(Sura 9:29)

O you who believe! Take not the Jews and the Christians as friends. They are friends to one another. Whoever of you befriends them is one of them. Allah does not guide the people who do evil.

(Sura 5:51)

There is to be no compulsion in religion. Rectitude has been clearly distinguished from error. So whoever disbelieves in idols and believes in Allah has taken hold of the firmest handle. It cannot split. Allah is All-hearing and All-knowing.[2]

(Sura 2:256)

[1] I have translated the last phrase of this verse (Ar., *ḥattā yuᶜṭu 'l-jizyata ᶜan yadin wa-hum ṣāghirūn*) as later Muslims came to understand it. However, as noted in Part One above, p. 20, the precise nuances are hazy. The passage has been the subject of a lively scholarly debate over the past two and a half decades. For a convenient survey of the major arguments and their proponents, see Rudi Paret, *Der Koran: Kommentar und Konkordanz* (Stuttgart, 1971), p. 200.

[2] Concerning this interesting passage, see Part One above, p. 76, and the relevant literature cited there in n. 41.

. . . . ;

Wretchedness and baseness were stamped upon them (that is, the Jews), and they were visited with wrath from Allah. That was because they disbelieved in Allah's revelations and slew the prophets wrongfully.[1] That was for their disobedience and transgression.

(Sura 2:61)

Have you not seen those who have received a portion of the Scripture? They purchase error, and they want you to go astray from the path.

But Allah knows best who your enemies are, and it is sufficient to have Allah as a friend. It is sufficient to have Allah as a helper.

Some of the Jews pervert words from their meanings, and say, "We hear and we disobey,"[2] and "Hear without hearing," and "Heed us!"[3] twisting with their tongues and slandering religion. If they had said, "We have heard and obey," or "Hear and observe us," it would have been better for them and more upright. But Allah had cursed them for their disbelief, so they believe not, except for a few.

(Sura 4:44–46)

And for the evildoing of the Jews, We have forbidden them some good things that were previously permitted them,[4] and because of their barring many from Allah's way,

[1] The accusation that the Jews murdered prophets goes back to the New Testament and was a common theme in anti-Jewish polemics. See Matt. 23:29–38, Luke 11:47–51, and I Thess. 2:14–16; also Justin Martyr, *Dialogue with Trypho,* in Frank Ephraim Talmage, ed., *Disputation and Dialogue: Readings in the Jewish-Christian Encounter* (New York, 1975), p. 252.

[2] Ar., *samiᶜnā wa-ᶜaṣaynā.* The Jews of Medina may have mocked Muḥammad with a Hebrew play on words. "We hear and obey" in Hebrew (*shāmaᶜnū we-ᶜasīnū*) sounds the exact opposite in Arabic.

[3] According to Muslim tradition, the Believers would get the Prophet's attention by using this phrase (Ar., *rāᶜinā*). The Jews, however, turned it into a phrase of mockery by some mispronunciation, perhaps *rāᶜinnā* (our fool). See al-Bayḍāwī, *Anwār al-Tanzīl wa-Asrār al-Ta'wīl* (Jedda, n.d.), p. 22. They may have made some pun on the Hebrew word *raᶜ* (evil one).

[4] This argument also seems to come from a Christian source. The notion

And for their taking usury which was prohibited for them, and because of their consuming people's wealth under false pretense. We have prepared for the unbelievers among them a painful punishment.

(Sura 4:160–61)

The Jews say, "Ezra is the son of Allah,"[5] and the Christians say, "The Messiah is the son of Allah." Those are the words of their mouths, conforming to the words of the unbelievers before them. Allah attack them! How perverse they are!

They have taken their rabbis[6] and their monks as lords besides Allah, and so too the Messiah son of Mary, though they were commanded to serve but one God. There is no God but He. Allah is exalted above that which they deify beside Him.

(Sura 9:30–31)

The Jews say, "Allah's hands are fettered." Their hands are fettered, and they are cursed for what they have said! On the contrary, His hands are spread open. He bestows as He wills. That which has been revealed to you from your Lord will surely increase the arrogance and unbelief of many among them. We have cast enmity and hatred among them until the Day of Resurrection. Every time they light the fire of war, Allah extinguishes it. They hasten to spread corruption throughout the earth, but Allah does not love corrupters!

(Sura 5:64)

Indeed, you will surely find that the most vehement of men in enmity to those who believe are the Jews and the polytheists. But you will also surely find that the closest of them in love to those who believe are those who say, "We are Christians." That is because there are among them priests and monks, and because they are not arrogant.

(Sura 5:82)

---

was set forth in Syriac anti-Jewish polemical literature that all of the Mosaic code and the Levitical and Deuteronomic legislation was given to the Jews as a punishment for their idolatry. See Marcel Simon, *Verus Israël: Etude sur les relations entre Chrétiens et Juifs dans l'Empire Romain (135–425)* (Paris, 1964), pp. 114 and 180.

5 The origin of this strange charge is unknown. For possible explanations, see H. Z. [J. W.] Hirschberg, "Ezra in Islam," *EJ* 6: 1,106–7.

6 This accusation is also enigmatic. Perhaps Muḥammad was impressed by the deference paid by Jews and Christians to their scholars and religious leaders. Even so, the charge is unusual.

2

UNDER THE NEW ORDER

Middle-Eastern Jewry in the First Three Centuries of Islam

JEWS AID THE ARABS IN THE CONQUEST OF HEBRON

(638)

But when they (the Arabs) came to Hebron, they marveled at the strong and beautiful construction of its walls and that there was no opening by which they could enter it. Meanwhile, some Jews, who had remained under the Greeks in that region, came over to them and said: "Grant us security so that we would have a similar status amongst you, and may we be conceded the right to build a synagogue in front of the entrance (to the cave of Machpelah). If you will do this, we will show you where you should make a gateway."

And thus it was done.

"Canonici Hebronensis Tractatus de inventione sanctorum patriarchum Abraham, Ysaac, et Jacob," in *Sēfer ha-Yishūv*, vol. 2, p. 6.

THE CHRISTIANS AND JEWS OF HIMS PREFER THE ARABS TO THE BYZANTINES

Abū Ḥafṣ al-Dimashqī told me that Saᶜīd b. ᶜAbd al-ᶜAzīz told him, "I was informed as follows"—

When Heraclius gathered his troops against the Muslims, and the Muslims learned that they were advancing upon them to do battle at the Yarmuk, the Muslims gave back to the people of Ḥimṣ the tribute[1] which they had taken from them. They told them: "We are too preoccupied to aid and defend you. You are on your own."

But the people of Ḥimṣ replied: "We prefer your rule and your justice to the oppression and injustice under which we were formerly. And we shall surely repel Heraclius' army from the city, with the help of your governor."

Then the Jews rose up and said: "By the Torah, Heraclius' governor shall not enter the city of Ḥimṣ unless we are vanquished and utterly played out!"

Then they locked the gates and set guards over them. The people of the other cities which had surrendered to the Muslims, both Christians and Jews, did likewise, saying, "If the Byzantines and their followers[2] are victorious over the Muslims, we shall revert to our former state. If they are not, then we shall retain control of our own affairs as long as the Muslims maintain their forces.

When Allah caused the unbelievers to be defeated and granted victory to the Muslims, they opened the gates of their cities and sent out a festive welcome[3] with music, and they paid the tribute.

al-Balādhurī, *Futūh al-Buldān,* ed. Riḍwan Muḥammad Riḍwān (Cairo, 1959), p. 143; = edition of M. J. de Goeje (Leiden, 1866), p. 137.

[1] Ar., *kharāj,* used here in the sense of general tribute.

[2] "Their followers" are probably the Greek Orthodox Christians. Most of the native Christians were Monophysites.

[3] Ar., *wa-akhrajū 'l-muqallisīn.*

ᶜUMAR PERMITS THE JEWS TO RETURN TO JERUSALEM

So every Muslim who came was in town or valley, and there came with them a group of Jews. Then he (ᶜUmar) ordered them to sweep the holy place (the Temple site) and to cleanse it. ᶜUmar himself oversaw them at all times, and each time something was uncovered, he would ask the Jewish elders about the Rock, which was the Foundation Stone.[1] Finally, one of their scholars indicated the precise boundaries of the place, as a result of which, it was uncovered. He commanded that walls be built around the holy site and that a dome be constructed over the Foundation Stone, and that it should be gilded.[2]

After this, the Jews sent word to all the rest of the Jews in Palestine[3] to inform them of the agreement that ᶜUmar had made with them. The letter was sent back to them asking what would be the number of people who would be allowed to move to Jerusalem. So they came into ᶜUmar's presence and asked him, "How many people from the Jewish community will the Commander of the Faithful order to move to this city?" "What will your enemies (the Christians) say?" "Speak to them, and after that, I shall have the final word that will put an end to the dispute between you."

Then the Christian Patriarch and his entourage appeared, and ᶜUmar said to them, "I have made an agreement with the Jews concerning all. . . . Let there come here that number which you yourselves indicate." The Patriarch responded, "Let the number of those who come with their families and their children be fifty households." The Jews replied to this, "We shall not be less than two hundred households." They kept haggling over this until ᶜUmar commanded that there be seventy households—to which they agreed.

Then ᶜUmar said, "Where would you wish to live in the city?" "In the southern part," they replied. And that it is now the Market of the Jews. The aim of their request was to be near the Temple Mount and its gates, and likewise to be near the water of Silwan[4] for ritual bathing. The Commander of the Faithful granted this to them.

[1] Heb., *even shetiyya,* which is the stone in the Temple on which the Ark of the Covenant stood.

[2] The gilded dome here is an anachronism. The Dome of the Rock sanctuary was not erected until half a century after ᶜUmar, under the caliph ᶜAbd al-Malik.

[3] Ar., *al-Shām,* literally, "Syria," but was used by Jews also in the more particular sense of Palestine.

[4] That is, the biblical pool of Siloam or Shiloah.

Then seventy families moved from Tiberias and the area around it with their wives and children. They filled up the quarter with buildings the remains of which lasted for many generations. And after that . . .[5]

TS Arabic Box 6, f. 1, Judeo-Arabic text
published by Simha Assaf,
Meqōrōt u-Meḥqārīm be-Tōledōt Yisrāʼēl
(Jerusalem, 1946), pp. 20–21.

[5] Unfortunately, the text breaks off here.

JEWS AID THE MUSLIM CONQUERORS OF SPAIN
(EARLY EIGHTH CENTURY)

Mughīth entered Cordova's municipal palace and occupied[1] it. Then he went out the next day and besieged the uncircumcised who had taken refuge in the cathedral. Mughīth maintained the siege against the uncircumcised for three months until they were worn out by it. . . . Then he demanded their unconditional surrender as captives, and he had them beheaded. That church came to be known as the Church of the Captives.

He gathered the Jews of Cordova together and made them into a garrison over the city.[2] He occupied the citadel himself and gave the city to his men.

He wrote to Ṭāriq about the conquests he had made.

The troops that were sent toward Reiyo subdued it. It's uncircumcised took refuge into the impenetrable mountains. They then proceeded to join up with the force headed for Elvira, which they besieged and captured. On that very day, they gathered its Jews together. It had become their custom to gather the Jews in each town and set them as a garrison over the municipality. They would leave with them a party of Muslims, while most of the men would march on. They did this in Granada, Elvira, but not in Malaga or Reiyo, because they could not find any Jews in them.[3]

Anon., *Akhbār Majmūʿa,*
ed. Emilio Lafuente y Alcantara
(Madrid, 1867), pp. 12–14.

[1] Ar., *wa-dakhala Mughīth balāṭ Qurṭuba fa 'khtaṭṭahu.* For *ikhtaṭṭa* in the sense of "to occupy" or "to take possession of," see Reinhart Dozy, *Supplément,* vol. 1, p. 379b, where both examples are taken from this passage.

[2] Ar., *wa-jamaʿa yahūd Qurṭuba fa-ḍammahum ilayhā.* For *ḍamma* in the sense of "to form a garrison" or "to organize troops," see Dozy, *Supplément,* vol. 2, p. 12a, where all the examples are from Spanish Arabic sources.

[3] These last two paragraphs appear in the Arabic text immediately following the second sentence of paragraph one as a long interpolation. I have taken the liberty to rearrange them for better reading in English. There is a question whether the Muslims subdued the provinces of Reiyo and Murcia in southeastern Spain at this time. See Evariste Lévi-Provençal, *Histoire de l'Espagne Musulmane,* vol. 1 (Paris and Leiden, 1950), p. 23.

THE PACT OF ᶜUMAR
(SEVENTH CENTURY?)

ᶜAbd al-Raḥmān b. Ghanam[1] related the following: When ᶜUmar b. al-Khaṭṭāb—may Allah be pleased with him—made peace with the Christian inhabitants of Syria, we wrote him the following.

In the name of Allah, the Merciful, the Beneficent.

This letter is addressed to Allah's servant ᶜUmar, the Commander of the Faithful, by the Christians of such-and-such city. When you advanced against us, we asked you for a guarantee of protection for our persons, our offspring, our property, and the people of our sect, and we have taken upon ourselves the following obligations toward you, namely:

We shall not build in our cities or in their vicinity any new monasteries, churches, hermitages, or monks' cells. We shall not restore, by night or by day, any of them that have fallen into ruin or which are located in the Muslims' quarters.

We shall keep our gates wide open for passersby and travelers. We shall provide three days' food and lodging to any Muslims who pass our way.

We shall not shelter any spy in our churches or in our homes, nor shall we hide him from the Muslims.

We shall not teach our children the Koran.

We shall not hold public religious ceremonies. We shall not seek to proselytize anyone. We shall not prevent any of our kin from embracing Islam if they so desire.

We shall show deference to the Muslims and shall rise from our seats when they wish to sit down.

We shall not attempt to resemble the Muslims in any way with regard to their dress, as for example, with the *qalansuwa,*[2] the turban,[3] sandals, or parting the hair (in the Arab fashion). We shall not speak as they do, nor shall we adopt their *kunyas.*[4]

We shall not ride on saddles.

[1] He died in 697.

[2] The *qalansuwa* was a conical cap. See Reinhart Dozy, *Dictionnaire détaillé des noms des vêtements chez les Arabes* (Amsterdam, 1845), pp. 365–71.

[3] The turban (Ar., *ᶜimāma*) came to be considered the "crown of the Arabs" (Ar., *tāj al-ᶜarab*) and the "badge of Islam" (Ar., *sīmā al-Islām*). See Reinhart Dozy, *Dictionnaire des vêtements,* pp. 305–11; and W. Björkman, "Turban," *EI*[1] 4: 885–93.

[4] The Arabic byname, formed with *abū* (father of, or possessor of).

We shall not wear swords or bear weapons of any kind, or ever carry them with us.

We shall not engrave our signets in Arabic.

We shall not sell wines.

We shall clip the forelocks of our head.

We shall always adorn ourselves in our traditional fashion. We shall bind the *zunnār*[5] around our waists.

We shall not display our crosses or our books anywhere in the Muslims' thoroughfares or in their marketplaces. We shall only beat our clappers in our churches very quietly. We shall not raise our voices when reciting the service in our churches, nor when in the presence of Muslims. Neither shall we raise our voices in our funeral processions.

We shall not display lights in any of the Muslim thoroughfares or in their marketplaces.

We shall not come near them with our funeral processions.

We shall not take any of the slaves that have been allotted to the Muslims.

We shall not build our homes higher than theirs.

(When I brought the letter to ᶜUmar—may Allah be pleased with him—he added the clause "We shall not strike any Muslim.")

We accept these conditions for ourselves and for the members of our sect, in return for which we are to be given a guarantee of security. Should we violate in any way these conditions which we have accepted and for which we stand security, then there shall be no covenant of protection for us, and we shall be liable to the penalties for rebelliousness and sedition.

Then ᶜUmar—may Allah be pleased with him—wrote: "Sign what they have requested, but add two clauses that will also be binding upon them; namely, they shall not buy anyone who has been taken prisoner by the Muslims, and that anyone who deliberately strikes a Muslim will forfeit the protection of this pact."

Translated from al-Ṭurṭūshī,
Sirāj al-Mulūk (Cairo, 1289/1872), pp. 229–30.

[5] A kind of belt. See Dozy, *Dictionnaire des vêtements*, pp. 196–98.

HOW THE JIZYA IS TO BE COLLECTED AND FROM WHOM

(SECOND HALF OF THE EIGHTH CENTURY)

The *jizya* is required of all the *ahl al-dhimma* in the Sawād (the lower half of Iraq), Ḥīra, and the rest of the conquered lands, namely, the Jews, the Christians, Zoroastrians, Sabaeans, and Samaritans. The only exceptions are the Christians of the Banū Taghlib tribe and the people of Najran.[1] The *jizya* is incumbent upon all adult males, but not upon women and children. For the wealthy the tax is forty-eight dirhams,[2] for those of medium income twenty-four, and for the poor, the agricultural workers and manual laborers, twelve dirhams. It is to be collected from them each year. It may be paid in kind, for example, beasts of burden, goods, and other such things. These are to be accepted in accordance with their value. However, no animals not ritually slaughtered, no pigs, and no wine may be accepted in payment of the *jizya*. ᶜUmar b. al-Khaṭṭāb—may Allah be pleased with him—had already forbidden the acceptance of such things for the *jizya*. "Leave them to their owners," he said. "They, however, may sell them, and the proceeds from the sale may then be accepted from them." This kind of payment is permissible when it is easier for the tributaries. ᶜAlī b. Abī Ṭālib—may Allah honor him—used to accept large and small needles and would count their value toward their individual tribute, according to what I have learned.

The *jizya* is not to be collected from the indigent who receives alms, nor from a blindman who has no craft and no work, nor from any invalid receiving alms, nor from any cripple. However, it is to be collected from any invalid, cripple, or blindman with means. The same goes for those monks living in monasteries when they have means, but not from those who are mendicants supported by the alms of wealthy people.

The *jizya* is not collected from a Muslim, unless he converted after the completion of a calendar year, because the *jizya* was due from him at the time of his conversion and had become part of the tribute due to the entire Muslim community, and therefore should be collected from him. If, on the other hand, a man converts before the end of a given year—whether by a day or two, or by a month or two, more or less—no part of the *jizya* at all is to be collected from him since his conversion was prior to the end of that

[1] Najran was the Christian center of Yemen in early Islamic times and the seat of the Nestorian bishop. See above, pp. 19–20.

[2] At this time forty-eight dirhams were equal to four dinars. Thus, the graded poll tax was: 4, 2, and 1. This is an amazing precedent, as Muḥammad ordered a poll tax of "a dinar of full weight or its equivalent" in 632. See above, p. 20.

year. If a man dies before the *jizya* has been collected from him, or after only a part has been collected, another part remaining, it is not to be collected from his heirs, nor from his estate, since it is not reckoned as an outstanding debt, just as when a man converts still owing a portion of the *jizya* on his head, it is not collected.

The *jizya* is not to be exacted from an old man who cannot work and has no resources. Neither may anything be collected from anyone of unsound mind.

The *zakāt*[3] does not apply to the livestock of the *Ahl al-Dhimma*—that is, their camels, cattle, and sheep. This holds true for men and women equally.

No one of the *ahl al-dhimma* should be beaten in order to exact payment of the *jizya*, nor made to stand in the hot sun, nor should hateful things be inflicted upon their bodies, or anything of that sort. Rather, they should be treated with leniency. They should be imprisoned until they pay what they owe. They are not to be let out of custody until the *jizya* has been exacted from them in full. No governor may release any Christian, Jew, Zoroastrian, Sabaean, or Samaritan unless the *jizya* is collected from him. He may not reduce anyone's payment by allowing a portion to be left unpaid. It is not permissible for one person to be exempted and for another to have to pay. That cannot be done, because their lives and possessions are guaranteed safety only upon payment of the *jizya*, which is comparable to tribute money.[4]

With regard to collecting the *jizya* in the major cities, such as Baghdad, Kufa, Basra, and the like, it is my considered opinion that the Imām should entrust it to some man of integrity in each city, one of its good and trustworthy citizens, whose piety and fidelity can be depended upon. Assistants should be appointed for him who are to gather the adherents of the different faiths, namely the Jews, Christians, Zoroastrians, Sabaeans, and Samaritans, and collect from them in accordance with the classifications which I have already described: forty-eight dirhams from the well-to-do, such as the moneychanger, cloth merchant, the owner of an estate, merchant, the practicing physician, and anyone having a profession or a trade to live by. The *jizya* should be collected in accordance with their profession or commerce—forty-eight dirhams from the well-to-do and twenty-four from those with middle income. . . . Twelve dirhams are to be collected from such manual workers as tailors, dyers, shoemakers, and

[3] The *zakāt* was the so-called alms tax incumbent upon all Muslims. See Joseph Schacht, "Zakāt,'" *EI*[1] 4: 1,202–5; also Norman A. Stillman, "Charity and Social Service in Medieval Islam," *Societas* 5, no. 2 (Spring 1975): 106–7.

[4] Ar., *wa 'l-jizya bi-manzilati māl al-kharāj.*

cobblers, and those in similar occupations. When the tax has been collected by those in charge, it should be turned over to the Treasury.

As for collecting the *jizya* in the Sawād—you should instruct your agents who are in charge of collecting the *kharāj*[5] to send on their authority men whose piety and fidelity can be depended upon. These men should go to each village and order its headman to gather all its Jews, Christians, Zoroastrians, Sabaeans, and Samaritans. When this is done, they should collect the *jizya* from them according to the categories outlined above. . . . Should the village headman say, "I shall make an agreement with you on their behalf and will give you a lump sum for them," the collectors are to ignore his request, because the loss of *jizya* revenues from this would be very considerable. Let us suppose the village chief made an agreement to pay five hundred dirhams. There may be enough of the *ahl al-dhimma* to pay one thousand dirhams or more!

It is proper, O Commander of the Faithful—may Allah be your support—that you treat leniently those people who have a contract of protection from your Prophet and cousin, Muḥammad—may Allah bless him and grant him peace. You should look after them, so that they are not oppressed, mistreated, or taxed beyond their means. None of their property may be confiscated, except as required by law. It has been related that the Apostle of Allah—may Allah bless him and grant him peace—said: "Whoever oppresses a protégé or taxes him beyond his means, will have me as that man's advocate."[6]

Abū Yūsuf, *Kitāb al-Kharāj*
(Cairo, 1382/1962–63), pp. 122–25.

[5] *Kharāj* here is the land tax on conquered lands. See above, p. 25.

[6] This is not a canonical ḥadīth. Notice that it is cited without any chain of transmission (*isnād*).

ISLAMIC PROTECTIONISM: TARIFFS FOR MUSLIMS AND NON-MUSLIMS
(SECOND HALF OF THE EIGHTH CENTURY)

With regard to the collection of tariffs,[1] it is my considered opinion that you should appoint collectors who are men of probity and religion and command them not to act unjustly toward people in their dealings with them, not to oppress them, and not to collect more than is due from them.

You should order these customs agents to lump the various articles of merchandise together for a single evaluation. The duty is then to be collected—from Muslims at the rate of 2½ percent, from the *Ahl al-Dhimma* at the rate of 5 percent, and from foreigners from outside the Domain of Islam at the rate of 10 percent.[2] This applies to all merchandise which passes before the customs agent totaling 200 dirhams or more. However, nothing is collected if the total value is less than 200 dirhams. Likewise, if the total value comes to 20 mithqāls,[3] the duty is collected, but not if it is less.

ᶜUmar b. al-Khaṭṭāb established the tariffs. Thus, there is nothing improper in collecting them,[4] so long as people are not treated unjustly and no more is taken than is due.

Whatever is collected from a Muslim is to be used as *ṣadaqa* funds.[5] Whatever is collected from the *ahl al-dhimma* or from foreigners is to be used as *kharāj* funds. The same goes for the individual capitation tax collected from the members of the *ahl al-dhimma.*

Abū Yūsuf, *Kitāb al-Kharāj*
(Cairo, 1382/1962–63), pp. 132–33.

1 Ar., *ᶜushūr,* literally, "tithes."

2 See above, pp. 34–35 and 43–44.

3 The mithqāl was synonymous with the gold dinar.

4 Since these tariffs do not go back to the Prophet, there were obviously pietists who questioned their legality. Abū Yūsuf seems to be answering any such objections.

5 The *ṣadaqa* funds were those used for charitable purposes. They came from among other things the *zakāt* tax. See Norman A. Stillman, "Charity and Social Service in Medieval Islam," *Societas* 5, no. 2 (Spring 1975): 106–7.

THE ITINERARY OF THE RADHANITE JEWISH MERCHANTS

They speak Arabic, Persian, Greek, Frankish, Andalusian, and Slavonic. They travel from East to West and from West to East by both land and sea. From the West, they bring adult slaves, girls and boys, brocade, beaver pelts, assorted furs, sables, and swords. They sail from the Land of the Franks[1] on the Western Sea (the Mediterranean) and set out for al-Faramā (Pelusium).[2] There they transport their merchandise by pack animal to al-Qulzum,[3] which is twenty-five parasangs away.[4] At al-Qulzum they set sail for al-Jār[5] and Jidda,[6] after which they proceed to Sind,[7] India, and China. From China they bring musk, aloeswood, camphor, cinnamon, and other products obtained from those regions, as they make their way back to al-Qulzum. Then they transport it overland to al-Faramā, there setting sail on the Western Sea once again. Some go straight to Constantinople to sell their merchandise to the Byzantines, while others go to the capital of the king of the Franks and sell their goods there.

Sometimes they choose to take their merchandise from the Land of the Franks across the Western Sea to Antioch, and thence overland on a three-day journey to al-Jābiya,[8] from which they sail down the Euphrates to

[1] The land of the Franks does not necessarily mean France here. It may refer to the Frankish-ruled part of Italy. See Moshe Gil, "The Rādhānite Merchants and the Land of Rādhān," *JESHO* 17, pt. 3 (1974): 310.

[2] This is the Pelusium of antiquity. It was a port on the easternmost branch of the Nile, approximately twenty miles from the present Port Said. It was totally abandoned in the early Islamic Middle Ages. See Yāqūt, *Mu*ᶜ*jam al-Buldān,* vol. 3, ed. F. Wüstenfeld (Leipzig, 1868), pp. 882–84.

[3] The port of Qulzum (Gr., Klosma) was on the Red Sea at the mouth of the canal leading to the Nile. Like Faramā, it was abandoned by the time of Yāqūt. See E. Honigmann, "al-Ḳulzum," *EI*[1] 2: 1,114–15.

[4] The parasang was three Arabic miles, or six kilometers. See Walther Hinz, *Islamische Masse und Gewichte* (Leiden, 1955), p. 62.

[5] Al-Jār on the Red Sea coast of Arabia was the port of Medina. It was later replaced by Yanbuᶜ (Janbo). See A. Dietrich, "al-Djār," *EI*[2] 2: 454–55.

[6] Jidda to this day is the supply port of Mecca. See R. Hartmann and Phebe Ann Marr, "Djudda," *EI*[2] 2: 571–73.

[7] Sind is the Arabic name for the lower Indus River valley and delta. See T. W. Haig, "Sind," *EI*[1] 4: 433–35.

[8] A town in the Jawlān (Golan) region, about 80 kilometers south of Damascus. See H. Lammens and J. Sourdel-Thomine, "al-Djābiya," *EI*[2] 2: 360.

Baghdad, then down the Tigris to Ubulla.[9] From Ubulla they sail to Oman, Sind, India, and China—in that order.

. . . .

As for their overland itinerary—those of them that set out from Spain or the Land of the Franks can cross over to the Further Sūs,[10] go from there to Tangier, and then across to Ifrīqiya (Tunisia), Egypt, Ramle, Damascus, Kufa, Baghdad, Basra, Ahwaz, Fars, Kirman, Sind, India, and finally, China. Sometimes they take the route behind the Byzantine Empire through the Land of the Slavs to Khamlīj, the capital of the Khazars. Then they cross the Sea of Jurjān (the Caspian) toward Balkh and Transoxania. From there they continue to Yurt and Tughuzghuzz,[11] and finally to China.

Ibn Khurradādhbih, *al-Masālik wa 'l-Mamālik,*
ed. M. J. de Goeje (Leiden, 1889), pp. 153–55.

[9] Ubulla was a port in southern Iraq not far from Basra. See Yāqūt, *Muᶜjam al-Buldān,* vol. 1, p. 97; also Gil, "The Rādhānite Merchants," p. 309.

[10] There are a number of places in the Islamic world known as al-Sūs. However, the Further Sus (al-Sūs al-Aqṣā) normally indicated the Berber region of Southwest Morocco, which to this day is called the Sus. See Evariste Lévi-Provençal, "al-Sūs al-Aḳṣā," *EI*¹ 4: 568–70; also Prosper Ricard, *Maroc: Les Guides Bleus* (Paris, 1950), pp. 205–12.

[11] This is the Central Asian homeland of the confederation of Turkish tribes known as the Nine Clans (Toquz Oghuz, from which the Arabic Tughuzghuzz is derived). See Claude Cahen, "Ghuzz," *EI*² 2: 1,106–10.

THE FIRST JEWS' OATH IN ISLAM
(SECOND HALF OF THE EIGHTH CENTURY)

According to Muḥammad b. ᶜUmar al-Madāʾinī in his book *The Pen and the Inkwell,*[1] the first time that these oaths were created for people of the Jewish faith was during the time of al-Faḍl b. al-Rabīᶜ,[2] the vizier of Hārūn al-Rashīd. They were created by a secretary of his who had asked him, "How do you put a Jew under oath?"

Al-Faḍl replied, "I say to him":

If not (i.e. if you are not speaking the truth), then may you be separated from your God whom alone you worship and whom alone you profess. May you detest your religion which previously you had approved. May you repudiate the Torah. May you say that Ezra's ass rides Moses' camel. May you be cursed by 800 rabbis through the words of David and Jesus son of Mary. May you be transformed as the Sabbath-breakers were transformed into apes and pigs.[3] May you transgress what was ordained by Daniel, Ashloma,[4] and John. May you meet God with the blood of John the son of Zacharias on your hands. May you shatter Mt. Sinai into stones. May you beat the clapper[5] in the Temple. May the twelve tribes and the patriarchs, Israel, Isaac, and Abraham, wash their hands of you. May you immerse the Catholicos' beard in the baptismal font of the Christians. May you change your sabbath from Saturday to Sunday.

And if not (i.e., if you are not speaking the truth), then may Allah ordain that you meet that which comes out of the water on Friday night.[6] May Allah make your food pig's flesh, camel's tripe, and swine's entrails. May Allah cause Nebuchadnezzar to rule over you and your people a second time, killing the men of fighting age, enslaving the youth, and destroying the cities. May Allah reveal to you the hands that will seize the knees (of the patriarchs) of the tribes. May Allah punish you with every tongue you denied and every verse you

[1] Neither this writer nor his book are cited in Carl Brockelmann, *Geschichte der arabischen Literatur,* 2d ed. and Supplement (Leiden, 1937–49).

[2] He became the vizier of Hārūn al-Rashīd after the fall of the Barmacids in 803, and continued in that office under Hārūn's son al-Amīn (809–13).

[3] According to the Koran (Sura 2:65/61), the Jewish Sabbath-breakers were transformed into apes. Pigs, however, are not mentioned.

[4] I cannot identify this prophet.

[5] The clapper (Ar., *nāqūs*) is commonly used by Christians in the Middle East during services.

[6] Some demon apparently.

distorted. May you say that Moses was false and that he is in the Place of Ruin and the House of Deception. May you disavow "I am that I am, the Lord of Hosts, God Almighty."[7]

This oath is binding upon you and your descendants until the Day of Resurrection.[8]

al-Qalqashandī, *Ṣubḥ al-Aᶜshā,* vol. 13
(Cairo, 1293/1918), pp. 266–67.

[7] The Arabic has a transliteration of the Hebrew *ehiyeh ashēr ehiyeh [adōnāy] ṣeva'ōt ēl shadday.*

[8] For a later and more elaborate Jews' oath, see below, pp. 267–68.

THE CALIPH AL-MUTAWAKKIL AND THE AHL AL-DHIMMA

In that year (235/850), al-Mutawakkil ordered that the Christians and all the rest of the *ahl al-dhimma* be made to wear honey-colored *ṭaylasāns*[1] and the *zunnār* belts.[2] They were to ride on saddles with wooden stirrups, and two balls were to be attached to the rear of their saddles. He required them to attach two buttons on their *qalansuwas*[3]—those of them that wore this cap. And it was to be of a different color from the *qalansuwa* worn by Muslims. He further required them to affix two patches on the exterior of their slaves' garments. The color of these patches had to be different from that of the garment. One of the patches was to be worn in front on the breast and the other on the back. Each of the patches should measure four fingers in diameter. They too were to be honey-colored. Whosoever of them wears a turban, its color was likewise to be honey-colored. If any of their women went out veiled, they had to be enveloped in a honey-colored *izār*.[4] He further commanded that their slaves be made to wear the *zunnār* and be forbidden to wear the *minṭaqa*.[5]

He gave orders that any of their houses of worship built after the advent of Islam were to be destroyed and that one-tenth of their homes be confiscated. If the place was spacious enough, it was to be converted into a mosque. If it was not suitable for a mosque, it was to be made an open space. He commanded that wooden images of devils be nailed to the doors of their homes to distinguish them from the homes of Muslims.

[1] The word *ṭaylasān* designated different types of headcoverings in different periods. It was originally a hat and later, a shawl. At this period it was probably a cowl or hood. See Yedida K. Stillman, "Libās," *EI*² 5 (in press) and the sources cited there.

[2] This belt (from Gr., *zonarion*) was the distinguishing badge of Christians according to Muslim sumptuary laws. See Y. Stillman, "Libās," (in preparation). Reinhart Dozy, *Dictionnaire détaillé des noms de vêtements chez les Arabes* (Amsterdam, 1845), pp. 196–98, deals mainly with a different item by this name from Islamic Spain.

[3] The *qalansuwa* was a conical cap which came in a short and a long (like a mitre) form. See Dozy, *Dictionnaire des vêtements,* pp. 365–71.

[4] The *izār* was a large outer wrap resembling a bedsheet. It is still worn in many places throughout the Arab world. See Dozy, *Dictionnaire des vêtements,* pp. 24–38; also Y. K. Stillman, "Female Attire of Medieval Egypt: According to the Trousseau Lists and Cognate Material from the Cairo Geniza" (Ph.D. dissertation, University of Pennsylvania, 1972), pp. 46–50.

[5] This was originally a kind of belt worn by the Arab military. In some periods it was synonymous with the *zunnār*, however. See Dozy, *Dictionnaire des vêtements,* pp. 420–21, who knows it only as a belt of gold or silver; also Stillman, "Libās," (in press).

He forbade their being employed in the government offices or in any official business whereby they might have authority over Muslims. He prohibited their children studying in Muslim schools. Nor was any Muslim permitted to teach them. He forbade them to display crosses on their Palm Sundays, and he prohibited any Jewish chanting in the streets. He gave orders that their graves should be made level with the ground so as not to resemble the graves of Muslims. And he wrote to all his governors regarding this.

al-Ṭabarī, *Ta'rīkh al-Rusul wa 'l-Mulūk,* vol. 3,
ed. M. J. de Goeje et al. (Leiden, 1879), pp. 1389–90.

WHY THE MUSLIM MASSES PREFER CHRISTIANS TO JEWS

I shall begin by discussing the reasons why the Christians have come to be better liked by the masses than the Zoroastrians, and why they are considered by them to be more sincere than the Jews, closer in affection, less treacherous, less unbelieving, and deserving of a lighter punishment (at the Last Judgment). There are many reasons for this, and the causes are clear. Whoever investigates them will know them, and whoever does not will remain ignorant.

First, the Jews were the Muslim's neighbors in Yathrib (Medina) and elsewhere, and the enmity of neighbors resembles the enmity of relatives in intensity of power and in the persistence of rancor. Moreover, man will treat as an enemy someone he knows. He will turn against someone he sees, and he will be incompatible with someone who resembles him. He will observe the shortcomings of those with whom he mixes. Loathing and estrangement will be in direct proportion to the degree of prior love and intimacy. It is for this reason that the feuds between neighbors and relatives, among all people as well as the Arabs, have been longer and more intense in enmity. Thus, when the Emigrants became the neighbors of the Jews—after the Anṣār had already been for a long time their neighbors and partners in their settlement—the Jews began to envy them the blessings resulting from their faith[1] and the union they formed after their separation. They cast doubts in the mind of the common folk and tried to weaken their faith. They made common cause with the enemies and the envious. Then they went beyond mere backbiting and insinuating doubt to overt hostility. They gathered their cunning and dedicated themselves and their wealth to fighting them and to attempting to expel them from their homes. That struggle against them was prolonged, exhaustive, and it came increasingly into the open. Rancor built up, the hatred doubled, and the resentment was firmly established.

The Christians, on the other hand, due to the fact that they lived far away both from the place where the Prophet—may Allah bless him and grant him peace—received his call and from the place to which he emigrated, did not undertake to slander Islam, nor did they have a chance to stir up plots, nor unite for war. This, therefore, is the first reason why the hearts of Muslims are hardened toward the Jews, but inclined toward the Christians.

[1] That is, the material benefits that were coming to them as full-fledged members of the Umma.

Then there was the case of the Muslims who emigrated to Ethiopia[2] and were received well there, which made the Christians more endeared to the Muslim masses. The more the heart is softened toward one people, the more it is hardened toward their enemies. And the less they hated the Christians, the more they despised the Jews. It is human nature for a man to love whoever does him good or is the cause of it whether for the sake of Allah or not, whether intentional or by mere chance.

al-Jāḥiẓ, *al-Radd ᶜala 'l-Naṣārā,* ed.
Joshua Finkel (Cairo, 1926), pp. 13–14.

MORE OF THE SAME

One of the reasons why the masses respect them (the Christians) and the vulgar have affection for them is that among them are to be found government secretaries, attendants of kings, physicians of nobles, perfumers, and bankers; whereas, you will find a Jew only as a dyer, a tanner, a cupper, a butcher, or a tinker. So when the masses saw the Jews and Christians in this light, they imagined that the Jews' religion held the same place amongst the other religions as do their trades amongst the professions, and that their unbelief was the most contaminated even as they were the filthiest of peoples. The reason that the Christians are less hideous—though they certainly are ugly—is that the Israelite marries only another Israelite, and all of their deformity is brought back among them and confined within them. Foreign elements do not intermingle with them, and the virility found in other races is not crossbred into them. They have, therefore, not been distinguished either for their intelligence, their physique, or their cleverness. As the reader certainly knows, the same is the case with horses, camels, asses, and pigeons when they are inbred.

al-Jāḥiẓ, *al-Radd ᶜala 'l-Naṣārā,* ed.
Joshua Finkel (Cairo, 1926), pp. 17–18.

[2] During the period that Muḥammad and his followers were being persecuted in Mecca, some of the Muslims emigrated to Ethiopia. See, for example, Maxime Rodinson, *Mohammad* (New York, 1974), pp. 113–16.

THE INSTALLATION OF THE EXILARCH
(TENTH-CENTURY BAGHDAD)

R. Nathan ha-Kohen [ha-Bavlī] went on to describe the appointment of the Exilarch and how the people paid their allegiance to him at that time. It was as follows:

When there was a communal consensus on the appointment, the two Heads of the Yeshivot, together with their students, all the leaders of the congregation, and the elders, would gather in some prominent individual's house in Baghdad. He would be one of the greatest of that generation, such as Neṭira[1] or the like. The man in whose home they gather is singled out for honor by this and receives much praise. His standing is enhanced by this meeting of the leaders and elders in his home.

The community would gather in the main synagogue on Thursday. The Exilarch would be installed by the laying of hands. The shofar was sounded to let all the people know from the youngest to the eldest. And when everyone heard it, each of them would send him a gift—each according to his means. All the leaders of the congregation and the wealthy would send him fine clothes, jewelry, and gold and silver vessels—each as he saw fit. The Exilarch, for his part, would take great pains in preparing a feast for Thursday and Friday which included all kinds of food and drink, and all sorts of confections, such as various sweets.

When he arose on Saturday to go to the synagogue, many of the prominent members of the community would join him in order to accompany him there. At the synagogue a wooden dais has already been specially prepared for him. It was seven cubits in length and three in width.[2] It was entirely covered with fine fabrics of blue, purple, and crimson silk. Under the dais stood young men who had been chosen from amongst the leading families of the community. These young men were distinguished for their sweet, pleasant voices. They had to be well versed in all aspects of prayer.

Meanwhile, the Exilarch himself was hidden from sight together with the Heads of the Yeshivot. So at this time, while the youths were standing beneath the dais, there was no one at all sitting on it.

Then the Cantor would begin with the "Praised be He who spoke,"[3]

[1] Concerning this important Jewish notable who was a banker to the Abbasid court, see Walter J. Fischel, *Jews in the Economic and Political Life of Mediaeval Islam* (New York, 1969), pp. 34–44; and above, pp. 35–36.

[2] Approximately 4.66 meters x 2 meters assuming that the Hebrew cubit is being used to refer to the Arabic *dhirā*ᶜ *al-malik*. See Walther Hinz, *Islamische Masse und Gewichte* (Leiden, 1955), p. 59.

[3] The first prayer recited after the Preliminary Morning Blessings (*birkōt ha-shaḥar*) and the Mourners' Kaddish.

and the young men would answer in chorus at the end of each phrase with "Praised be He." When the Cantor chanted the Sabbath Psalm (Psalm 92), they respond with the refrain "It is good to give thanks unto the Lord." The entire congregation recited in unison the preliminary hymns.[4] When they had finished, the Cantor would stand up and begin the prayer "The soul of every living being shall praise You," and the choir of young men would respond after each phrase he had chanted "Shall praise You." They continued this way until they reached the first Sanctification[5] which the congregation would recite silently and the young men out loud. Immediately following this, the youths fell silent, and Cantor alone would continue until he had completed the prayer "Praised be Thou, o Lord, Who has redeemed Israel." Then all the people would rise for the Amidah.[6] When the Cantor comes to the Sanctification during the repetition before the Ark,[7] the chorus of young men repeat after "the Holy God" in a loud voice. The Cantor then finishes the prayer, and the congregation would sit down quietly.

When everyone was seated, the Exilarch would emerge from the place where he was hidden, and when the people saw him, they would all rise to their feet and remain standing until he was seated alone on the dais that had been set up for him. Next, the Head of the Sura Yeshiva would come out and take a seat on the dais after bowing to the Exilarch, who would return the bow. After him, the Head of the Pumbedītha Yeshiva emerges, bows, and sits to the Exilarch's left. Throughout all this, the people remain standing until all three have taken their seats—the Exilarch in the center, the Sura Gaon on his right, and the Pumbedītha Gaon on his left. An empty space remained between each of the Geonim and the Exilarch. Over his head was spread a canopy of precious fabric which was suspended by a cord of fine linen and purple.

At this point, the Cantor would lean his head under the canopy and bless the Exilarch with benedictions which had been specially composed for the occasion one or two days before. He would do this in a low voice which could only be heard by those seated on the dais and by the choir under it. As he is blessing him, the young men would respond in loud

[4] Aram., "verses of song," the selection of psalms and poetical biblical readings recited after the prayer "Praised be He who spoke."

[5] The first recitation of Isa. 6:3: "Holy, holy, holy is the Lord of hosts," and so on.

[6] The so-called "standing" prayer containing the *Shemona ᶜEsreh* (Eighteen Benedictions), recited first silently by the congregation, then repeated out loud by the cantor. It forms the essential core of the daily service.

[7] This second, longer sanctification begins with the prayer "We sanctify Your name on earth." It is recited facing the Ark.

chorus "Amen!" But the entire congregation remains silent throughout his blessing.

The Exilarch now begins the sermon, expounding on the Torah portion for that Sabbath. Or, he might give permission to the Sura Gaon to open with the sermon, and the Sura Gaon, in turn, would grant permission to the Pumbedītha Gaon. In this way, they show their deference to one another, until finally, the Head of the Sura Yeshiva begins. An interpreter who is standing near him passes his words on to the people.[8] He would deliver the sermon in an awe-inspiring manner with his eyes closed. He would envelop himself in his prayershawl which he pulled over his head and down to the brow. No one in the congregation would open his mouth, twitter, or say a word while he was speaking. Should he feel, however, that someone was talking, he would open his eyes, and fear and trembling would descend over the congregation. At the conclusion of the sermon, he would present a problem with the formula: "Indeed, you should study." A wise and learned elder would stand, give an answer, and then sit down again.

The Cantor now recited the Kaddish.[9] When he reached the words "in your lifetime and in your days," he would add "and during the lifetime of our Prince, the Exilarch"[10] before continuing with "and during the lifetime of all the House of Israel." Upon finishing the Kaddish, he again blessed the Exilarch, and after him the Heads of the Yeshivot. With the blessings completed, he now declares: "Such-and-such a city and its villages have contributed such-and-such a sum to the Yeshiva. He mentions all the cities that have sent contributions, and he blesses them. Next, he blesses those individuals who are responsible[11] for collecting the contributions and who look after them until they reach the Yeshivot.

The service now continues with the Cantor taking the Torah scroll from the Ark. After having called up the Kohen and the Levite, the Cantor brings the scroll down from the reader's pulpit over to the Exilarch. All the

[8] This interpreter may either have been translating the sermon from Aramaic to Arabic, or—and this seems more likely—he was a sort of human loudspeaker who passed on the speaker's words to the assembly. Such "repeaters" were found in the large mosques in Islam as well.

[9] The Aramaic doxology recited at the conclusion of various parts of the service.

[10] It was customary in the Middle Ages to insert special mention of the exilarch, the heads of the *yeshivot*, the *nāsī*, or a leading scholar in the Kaddish known as *Qaddīsh de-Rabbānān* (the scholar's Kaddish). This was done as a token of allegiance, just as in Islam, the caliph, sultan, or governor were regularly mentioned in the *khuṭba* (Friday sermon).

[11] See above, pp. 47–48.

people remain standing while the Exilarch has the Torah in his hands and reads from it. The Heads of the Yeshivot stand beside him. The Sura Gaon translates it after him. Then he gives the Torah scroll back to the Cantor who returns it to the Ark. After it is put back into the Ark, the Exilarch takes his seat, and everyone else sits down. Following the Exilarch, the Rēshē Kallōt read (from another scroll), followed by the students of the Geonim. The Geonim themselves, however, do not read from the Torah since others had been given precedence on this occasion.

When the *mafṭīr*[12] has finished the last portion, a prominent and wealthy individual standing near him would translate after him. This is a great honor and distinction for him. When he has finished, the Cantor again blesses the Exilarch by the Torah. All the readers who are experienced and qualified to conduct services stand around the Ark and say "Amen." He then blesses the two Geonim and returns the second Torah scroll to its place. Everybody prays the Musaf service[13] and goes out.

As the Exilarch departs, all the people accompany him to his house in a procession, going before and after him, singing his praises. The Heads of the Yeshivot, however, do not go with him. The Exilarch does not permit any of the scholars who have accompanied him to his house to leave until they have enjoyed at least seven days' hospitality. From that time on, he does not leave his house. People gather and pray with him there, be it on secular days, sabbaths, or holidays. If he does have to go out on some business, he rides in the litter of an official similar to that of the Caliph's ministers. He would be beautifully attired. Behind him would walk a train of as many as fifteen men. His servant would run after him. Should he happen to pass any Israelites, they would run up to him, touch his hands,[14] and greet him. As many as fifty or sixty people might do this both on his way to his destination and upon his return home. This is the custom. He would never go out without his entourage, just like any of the Caliph's ministers.

Whenever the Exilarch wishes to appear before the Caliph either to request something or simply to wait upon him, he asks the Caliph's viziers and servants who have regular entry to his court to speak to the Caliph, so

[12] The *mafṭīr* is the person who reads the concluding verses of the weekly Torah portion, followed by the Prophetic portion (Heb., *hafṭāra*).

[13] The "additional service" on Sabbaths and holidays, which follows the *shaḥarīt*, or "morning service."

[14] The Hebrew text reads *maḥazīqīm be-yādāv* (literally, "grasp his hands"). However, it is customary in the Middle East and North Africa merely to quickly touch or press the hand of a holy man or some other charismatic figure.

that he may grant him the permission to come into his presence.[15] The Caliph then grants the permission and orders the guards at the palace gate to admit him. When the Exilarch enters, the Caliph's slaves would run before him. He comes prepared with dinars and dirhams in his pocket to distribute to all those slaves who usher him in. He would continually be putting his hand into his bosom pocket and giving each and every one whatever God had ordained for him. They in turn treat him with honor and touch his hand until he comes into the presence of the Caliph and bows to him. The Caliph signals to one of his retainers who takes the Exilarch by the hand and seats him in the spot which the Caliph has indicated. The Exilarch then converses with the Caliph. The latter would ask after his health and his affairs, and the purpose of the visit. The Exilarch then requests permission to address him which is immediately granted. He then begins with praises and blessings formally prepared beforehand in which he eulogizes the Caliph's ancestors. He conciliates him with kind words until his request is granted and he is given what he has asked. The Caliph then commands that a decree be written to that effect, and the Exilarch retires, happily taking his leave.

From the "Report of Nathan ha-Bavlī," *Sēder ᶜŌlām Zūṭā*, in *Medieval Jewish Chronicles*, vol. 2, ed. Adolf Neubauer (Oxford, 1895), pp. 83–85.

15 This account is in contrast to that of Benjamin of Tudela (below, pp. 252–54). At the time of Nathan ha-Bavlī it would seem that the exilarch was not regularly received by the caliph, neither did he have automatic access to the court.

Then a group of Jews established the transmission from one generation to another of a testament.[1] They claim that this testament goes down to the descendants of David. They deem this testament to be in the possession of David's descendants, and they consider it an inheritance. They claim that a son inherits it from his father. These descendants of David are in Iraq and are called Exilarch.[2]

The Jews pay them one-fifth of their possessions and pay them for the redemption of their first-born sons, their cattle, and their beasts of burden. Whenever an ox is slaughtered, the Exilarch is brought 1 and 1/3 dirhams of full weight plus the price of the animal's liver. When a Jew gets married, he gives the Exilarch 4 dirhams of full weight. When any of them builds a house, he pays him likewise 4 dirhams. Once married, no one can divorce without his authorization or the authorization of his representative. And when a Jew divorces his wife, 4 dirhams of full weight are collected from him.

He is responsible for raising illegitimate Jewish children and those whose father is unknown until they are grown. When such a child grows up, he becomes his master. If he wills he can manumit him or sell him. It is they who bear him when he goes out of his house. They do not let him walk on foot.

It is said that the Jews are the property[3] of the Exilarchs. Their hands (that is, the Exilarchs') are longer than those of ordinary men so that they reach their knees when standing up straight. This is a deceitful lie!

Their title is Exilarch. They claim that Moses and Aaron will return to this world and that then they will have dominion over the Muslims. Every prophet sent by Allah among the Children of Israel who was not of

[1] This idea of the transmission of authority by means of a testament (Ar., *waṣiyya*) is typically Shiᶜite. The great emphasis placed by the exilarchs on their direct descent from David must have appealed to Shiᶜite notions of ᶜAlid legitimacy.

[2] The writer calls him *Rās al-Jālūt,* which is the Arabic equivalent of Aram., *Rēsh Galūthā.*

[3] The word used for property here is *fay',* which literally means "booty," but which in early Islamic times came to mean specifically conquered land that was dedicated to God and the Muslim community. The gist here is that the Jewish community is the exilarch's private trust. See Frede Løkkegaard, "Fay'," *EI*[2] 2: 869–70.

the Exilarchs or their descendants was accused of lying by them and was killed. For they said, "Were he a prophet, he would be an offspring of these or one of their descendants unto whom they have passed on their testament."

al-Qāsim b. Ibrāhīm, *al-Radd ᶜala 'l-Rawāfiḍ min Aṣḥāb al-Ghuluww*, Ar. text ed. Shlomo Pines in *REJ* 199–200 (1936): 71–72; Fr. trans. pp. 72–73.

A CALIPHAL PROCLAMATION OF APPOINTMENT FOR A NEW GAON[1]

On the ninth of Dhu 'l-Qaᶜda 605 (15 May 1209), he (the Caliph al-Nāṣir) appointed Ibn Hiba as Head of the Yeshiva of the Jews.[2] He issued his writ of appointment and handed it over to him. Ibn Hiba read it out to the Jews in the synagogue. Its text is as follows:

> In the name of Allah, the Merciful, the Beneficent, Praise be to Allah Whom thanks are due, Whose exalted authority is supreme, Whose state is mighty, Whose rule is perfect, Whose grace is far-reaching, Whose wisdom stands alone in loftiness. . . . Who guides with His perfect knowledge whomsoever He wills from amongst His creatures to the paths of Right Belief, Who causes the clouds of His bounty to pour forth on all who acknowledge His Lordship and recognize that in His truth He chose Muḥammad and his house from the noblest stock and the highest lineage, from the most highborn of the Arabs in dignity, of the most honored tribe, the most shining in noble deeds, and He sent him as a prophet to all mankind. . . . and He abrogated with His immaculate Sharīᶜa the earlier religions and laws. . . .
>
> Praise be to Allah Who has made as His Caliph on earth and His Deputy amongst mankind, the Imām who imposes obedience over the rest of men, al-Nāṣir li-Dīn Allāh, Commander of the Faithful and the Heir to the prophets who were sent in truth, etc. . .
>
> Since Daniel b. Elazar b. Hibat Allāh has petitioned that he be appointed Head of the Yeshiva of the Jews to fill the place of the deceased Elazar b. Hilāl b. Fahd, in accordance with the same rules and customs; and since it has come to be known how he is esteemed by the people of his sect, and what good qualities he possesses; and since he is worthy of that which he has petitioned by virtue of his good conduct amongst them and his impeccable demeanor, al-Nāṣir li-Dīn Allāh—may Allah Exalted maintain him in his high place—has ordained in a noble, sacred, mighty, pure, caliphal decree—may Allah increase its majesty extending throughout the public places[3] and cause it to be carried out in the four corners of the earth and the horizons; namely, that he shall be appointed Head of the Yeshiva of the

[1] Although this text and the three that follow it are all from the thirteenth century, they reflect the practices initiated in early Abbasid times. It is for this reason that they are given here.

[2] Daniel b. Elazer b. Hibat Allāh was *gaon,* or head of the *yeshiva* (Ar., *ra's al-mathība*), from 1209 until sometime before 1220. Very little is known about him.

[3] "The public places"—Ar., *al-riwāq* (literally, "the colonnade," or "the portico").

Jews in the manner of the abovementioned deceased, just as Ibn al-Dastūr[4] had also been Head of the Yeshiva. He is to have jurisdiction in all that the deceased had jurisdiction and authority over all places which customarily came under his authority. He is to have full right to administer freely therein. He may distinguish himself from his fellows and peers with attire permitted to those of his rank. It is proper that the Jewish communities and judges of Baghdad and the provinces of Iraq submit to that which he orders. They should have recourse to his word in the arbitration of their affairs, and they should act in accordance with it. They are to allow him the official privileges which were customary for his predecessors in this office in all places over which his administration extends without any opposition to him in this, as long as he acts in accordance with the stipulations of the Dhimma Contract in all that he does and in all that he orders, and as long as he is dutiful and attentive in obedience and in his obligation to seek the Caliph's Guardianship and to venerate him—if Allah Exalted wills it, for upon Him do we rely.

Written on the ninth of Dhu 'l-Qaᶜda 605. Praise be to Allah alone, and His blessings upon our Master the Prophet Muḥammad and his house. He is the seal of the prophets and the lord of prophetic messengers, who was chosen above all the rest of mankind together. Continuous blessing upon him until the Day of Judgment.

Ibn al-Sāᶜī, *al-Jāmiᶜ al-Mukhtaṣar,* vol. 9 (Baghdad, 1934), pp. 266–69.

[4] Samuel b. ᶜAlī Ibn al-Dastūr (d. 1194) was the most important *gaon* of the twelfth century. Shlomoh Zalman Havlin, "Samuel Ben Alī," *EJ* 14: 803–4.

A CHRISTIAN AND A JEWISH NOTABLE PAY THEIR POLL TAX

On the first day of Muḥarram 627 (20 November 1229), Muḥyi 'l-Dīn Abū ᶜAbd Allāh Muḥammad b. Faḍlān sat in the Bureau of the Poll Tax and exacted payment of the *jizya* from the *dhimmīs*. Each of them would stand before him individually until his *jizya* had been weighed. A receipt would be issued him while he was humiliated.[1] They were greatly distressed by this procedure.

It so happens that Abū ᶜAlī b. al-Masīḥī (a Christian) was chief physician. He enjoyed special privileges and had free access to the caliph's palace. He claimed to be ill, excused himself, and requested that his poll tax be received from his son. However, it was not accepted from the latter, and he had to appear and pay it.

Ibn al-Shuwayḥ,[2] the head of the Yeshiva of the Jews, went to Muḥyi 'l-Dīn's house one night and asked him to accept the poll tax from him. But he showed no regard for him and replied: "You cannot escape appearing at the Bureau in broad daylight and paying it there." He was quite strict about that and would excuse no one.

Ibn al-Fuwaṭī, *al-Ḥawādith al-Jāmiᶜa,*
ed. Musṭafā Jawād (Baghdad, 1932), p. 13.

[1] In accordance with Sura 9:29.

[2] He was born sometime before 1167 and died in 1247. He was the author of both secular and liturgical poetry. See Jefim Ḥayyim Schirmann, "Ibn Shuwayk, Isaac Ben Israel," *EJ* 8: 1202.

THE APPOINTMENT OF DANIEL B. SAMUEL TO THE GAONATE

In that year (645/1247–48), Daniel b. Samuel Ibn Abi 'l-Rabīᶜ was appointed Head of the Yeshiva. The Vizier Mu'ayyad al-Dīn Muḥammad b. al-ᶜAlqamī conveyed him before the Chief Qāḍī ᶜAbd al-Raḥmān b. al-Lamghānī, sat him before him, and said:

> I am appointing you leader of the adherents of your denomination[1] of the people of your religion which has been abrogated by the Muḥammadan religious law. You may lead them within the boundaries of their religion, command them in that which they are commanded by the religious law, forbid them that which they are forbidden by it. You are to judge between them in their conflicts and legal disputes in accordance with their religious law. Praised be to Allah for Islam.

Then he (Daniel b. Samuel) rose and put on his *ṭarḥa*[2] in the Qāḍī's antechamber. Then he set out on foot accompanied by a group of Jews and some retainers from the Office of the Vizier. A group from the common people blocked his way and sought to stone him, but the opportunity was denied them, and they were prevented from doing this. A group of them were seized. They were imprisoned and punished.

Ibn al-Fuwaṭī, *al-Ḥawādith al-Jāmiᶜa,* ed.
Muṣṭafā Jawād (Baghdad, 1932), p. 218.

[1] The word used here is *milla.* The denomination is the Rabbanite.

[2] The *ṭarḥa* was a large shawl worn over the head and shoulders. It was particularly associated in the Middle Ages with scholars and judges. It was more or less synonymous with the garment called *ṭaylasān.* See Reinhart Dozy, *Dictionnaire détaillé des noms de vêtements chez les Arabes* (Amsterdam, 1845), pp. 254–62.

THE APPOINTMENT OF ELI B. ZACHARIAH TO THE GAONATE

In that year (648/1250–51), Eli b. Zachariah, the Arbilī[1] Jew, requested that he be appointed Head of the Yeshiva of the Jews. This was granted. The Vizier conferred with him on this and conveyed him before the Chief Qāḍī. The latter seated him before him and after praising Allah and calling for His blessing upon Muḥammad, said to him:

> I am granting you the leadership over the people of your religious law which has been abrogated by the Law of Islam (may Allah cause it to last as long as Heaven and Earth endure). This is on condition that you arbitrate between those of them who bring their litigation before you. You are to command them to do that which they are commanded by their religion and to forbid them whatever they are forbidden by their religion.

Then he arose from the Chief Qāḍī's presence and put on his *ṭarḥa*[2] in his antechamber. He went out through the Bāb al-Nūbī. With him went a throng of Jews and attendants. He took with him his writ of appointment which was issued for him by the Vizier's Office.

Ibn al-Fuwaṭī, *al-Ḥawādith al-Jāmiᶜa,* ed.
Muṣṭafā Jawād (Baghdad, 1932), p. 248.

[1] He was from the town of Arbil (later Irbil) in northern Iraq, east of Mosul. This town had a Jewish community from the time of the Second Temple until 1951. See Eliyahu Ashtor, "Irbil," *EJ* 8: 1462–63.

[2] Concerning this shawl-like garment, see above, p. 181, n. 2.

3

THE BEST YEARS
Mediterranean Jewry in the Islamic High Middle Ages

A LETTER MENTIONING THE APPOINTMENT OF THE FIRST NAGID IN TUNISIA (1015)

May God give you a long life of strength and prosperity, O our great and noble Elder, and days filled with happiness and contentment. May He not deprive you of success, and may He be with you in this world and the world to come.

I am writing on the twenty-fifth of Kislev (December 1015), the day of the departure of the caravan—may God protect it. I have sent to you in it—may God be your support—an explanatory letter aside from this one. I gave it to our brother Abū ᶜImrān b. al-Majjānī[1]—may God protect him—and he put it in his bundle of papers. With him also is a letter for our brother Abū Ibrāhīm b. Sahl. Please see to it that it gets to him. I have previously described to you the tranquility here which followed the terrible anxiety, and our confidence which followed our dread. Indeed, this is due to God Almighty and Exalted, for he has granted the return of the Sultan (Bādīs b. al-Manṣūr) from the Maghreb safe and victorious, as well as the return of the Elder, my Master Abū Isḥāq the Nagid, along with him. At the time of their return from the Maghreb, a caravan had come from the East carrying a sealed bundle containing packets of letters from our Masters, the Heads of the Yeshivot.

[1] Abū ᶜImrān Mūsā b. al-Majjānī was the chief business agent of the addressee in Qayrawan. See Norman A. Stillman, "The Eleventh-Century Merchant House of Ibn ᶜAwkal," *JESHO* 16, pt. 1 (1973): 17 and 25–27.

I have apprised you in detail of the contents of our Master Hay's letters to the congregation and to us dignifying the Elder Abū Isḥāq—may God strengthen him—with the title "Nagid of the Diaspora." And he (the Nagid) summoned the people before his blessed seat and presented himself before them. Then he took up a collection (on behalf of the Yeshivot), and the people gave. This took place during this same month. We have not been able to collect all the money. However, it is being collected. We shall write to our Masters, the Heads of the Yeshivot, and send the letters along with the money to you in the last caravan of the season—God willing.

I have informed you . . . explained what happened with the Nagid of the Diaspora—may God strengthen him—and Ismāᶜīl b. Barhūn[2] with regard to the money from a previous collection which he entrusted to the latter two years ago and which he was to send to his brother Abu 'l-Khayr in Fustat that he might pass it on to you, so that you—may God be your support—might take care of it.[3] The money remained with him until the departure of the Nagid for the Maghreb. The Nagid ordered Ismāᶜīl to write to his brother to pass it on to you so that you could forward it to the Heads of the Yeshivot. And when the Nagid went, we asked for such a letter from Ismāᶜīl, but he refused, feeling that the Nagid would be a long time in the Maghreb. However, he was gone only two months and returned safe and victorious. And now again we have asked him to write to his brother so that the money would be passed on to you, and he insisted that he had written. But then, he said, "I have sworn never to send anything via Abu 'l-Faraj b. ᶜAwkal—may God protect him. However, I shall write my brother that this money belongs to the Elder, Abū Isḥāq the Nagid of the Diaspora. Do as he instructed you in his letter, and we shall be free of it!" So we said to him, "Write it then." He pledged with several oaths that he payed him in gold and silver coin totaling 200 dinars, of which 10 dinars are for the members of the Palestinian Yeshiva and the remainder for the members of the Iraqi Yeshivot. Our letter with the relevant information will reach you with the next caravan. We want to gather up all that is being collected now. It too shall reach you. We shall ascertain the total amount and shall write to you with regard to each individual and what he should receive.

I have already informed you in my more detailed letter which was

[2] He was a member of the Tahertis, a close-knit Jewish merchant family whose headquarters were in Qayrawan-Mahdiyya. For their family tree, see S. D. Goitein, "La Tunisie du XIe siècle à la lumière des documents de la Geniza du Caire," *Etudes d'Orientalisme dédiées à la mémoire de Lévi-Provençal* (Paris, 1962), p. 568, where Abu 'l-Khayr is identical with Mūsā.

[3] That is, see that it is properly transferred to the gaonic academies.

sent just prior to this one with a small company of travelers[4] that the letters of the Nagid will reach Abu 'l-Khayr instructing him that the money be passed on to you. In the letters is an authorization from the Nagid, validated in court, stating that he should forward nothing except through you. The Nagid has just now hastened and written a letter in his own hand to our brother Abu 'l-Khayr—may God shield him—reminding him of what had previously been sent to him via his brother quite a while ago and specifying what was sent in gold and what in silver. He further informed him of the rate of exchange and ordered him to convert everything into gold and to hand it over to you so that it should be in your possession until you receive the money collected this year. He also instructed him how it should be divided, and how much should be allotted to each of our Masters, the Heads of the Yeshivot. He admonished him to pass the money on to you alone. And he (Abu 'l-Khayr)—God willing—is one who would not disobey.

Our brother-in-law, their brother, Abu 'l-Faḍl, has arrived from Spain bringing with him the collection from there . . . for the Jerusalemites . . . and 30 for the Iraqis. We shall write to you regarding its division. He dealt with it solely for the sake of Heaven, and he devoted himself zealously to it until it arrived. May God reward him.

Please receive our best regards. . . . May the end be good.

To our great and chosen Elder, Abu 'l-Faraj—may God shield and preserve him—Joseph b. Jacob b. ᶜAwkal (may his soul find rest). May God be his Protector and Shepherd.

From Joseph and Nissīm, the sons of Berechiah (may his soul find rest).

Destined for Fustat—God willing.

Bodl. MS Heb. d 65, f. 9; Ar. text edited by Simḥa Assaf
in *J. N. Epstein Jubilee Volume*
(Jerusalem, 1950), pp. 179–84,
with Heb. trans. Re-edited by Norman A. Stillman
in *Hespéris-Tamuda* 13 (1972): 51–59, with Fr. trans.

[4] Ar., *rifqa.* Concerning this type of small caravan, which did not operate according to a set schedule, see Goitein, *Mediterranean Society,* vol. 1 (Berkeley and Los Angeles, 1968) pp. 277–78.

THE DEATH OF THE FIRST NAGID

(ELEVENTH-CENTURY TUNISIA)

O our great and chosen Elder—may God grant you a long life in blessing and happiness, may He ward off all misfortune, and may He bestow upon you success in all things.

We are writing to you, our brother, on the 8th of Marḥeshvan.[1] We are in a state ordained by the Creator Almighty and Exalted—"But He is at one with Himself, and who can turn Him? And what His soul desireth, even that He doeth."[2] We have been dealt a heavy blow, and we have suffered a great loss in our bereavement of our support, the support of all Israel. Our exalted Master, our Nagid, the Prince of the Diaspora, has passed away. Woe unto this calamity which has struck us, this disaster which has come upon us with his loss. Thus we say: "The Crown has fallen from our head; Woe unto us! for we have sinned."[3] Master, "our iniquities have turned away these things, and our sins have withheld good from us."[4] We are afraid and anxious, for we are left uncovered with him gone, as he was the protector of the community and its support. There is no doubt that God Almighty and Exalted has taken him from us for the bliss which has come to him and for the evil which has found us with him gone. As it is said of one such as he: "The righteous is taken away from the evil to come."[5]

Indeed, Master, the time is ripe for troubles. As to our position, I have already complained to you. It has been for a long time exposed and stripped naked of its elders. The shepherd is gone who guided it. This Nagid—may God have mercy upon him—was one who protected the community's welfare from those who would expose it and took good care of most of its affairs. When he departed, no one was left to take good care of matters and to protect our interests. But rather, we have become, as it is said: "For ye shall be as a terebinth whose leaf fadeth, and as a garden that hath no water."[6]

I am writing this letter to you on the day following his passing—may his soul find rest in Paradise. I do not know how to describe to you the state of affairs, nor am I able to give you any account of this affliction

[1] Corresponds to October–November or November–December.
[2] Job 23:13.
[3] Lam. 5:16.
[4] Jer. 5:22.
[5] Isa. 57:1.
[6] Isa. 1:30.

because it is more terrible than anything I might describe. It is as if we all became orphans bereaved of their parents, for the distinguished received much good from him—and the common folk even more. Now the poor and the destitute are utterly deprived of his protection. Now the enemy and the opponent have become arrogant toward us.[7] We do not know how our situation will turn out. Indeed, those who are far away from us (in the outlying areas and the provinces) feel his loss even more strongly than we, because the governors and officials are crushing them while they can find no one from whom to seek aid.

. . . .

We had thought along with him, Master, that on this past Sukkot we would gather together and look into the matter of our Masters, the Heads of Yeshivot. We intended to answer their letters and to investigate what had been detained in Fustat from reaching them. And there were other things we wished to look into so that we could bring the matter out into the open and clear it up.[8] But then fate descended upon him unawares, and he went to the Abode of Truth. "He has gone to rest and left us to sigh."[9] Perhaps, Master, I shall find a way afterwards when the darkness has lifted, and I shall write to you what I know and express what is within me and impart it to you, so that you may inform our Masters.

I cannot be blamed (for not taking care of the affairs of the Baghdad Yeshivot at this time). The affairs of the kingdom, O our brother, are in an extreme state of turmoil. Our city at this moment *is completely closed off, no one comes in or goes out.*[10] The place is ravaged by hunger and

[7] "The enemy and the opponent" (Ar., *al-ᶜadū wa 'l-makhālif*) are euphemisms for "Jew-baiter" or "anti-Semite." The Jews of the Arabic-speaking world frequently used the Hebrew *sōnē* ("hater" or "enemy") as a code word for this. In this particular period it seems that the Hebrew word *sin'ūt* was coined as a term for anti-Semitism. See S. D. Goitein, *Mediterranean Society,* vol. 2, p. 278; and Part One above, p. 63.

[8] The writers are referring to the annual donations sent by the communities of the Maghreb (as elsewhere) to the *yeshivot* in Iraq. As can be seen from the earlier letter of the Ben Berechiahs to Ibn ᶜAwkal (above, pp. 183–85) this was not the first time that there had been problems in the transferal of funds.

[9] This line of rhymed Hebrew may come from a longer dirge.

[10] *Sāgūr ū-mesugar ēyn yōṣē' ve-ēyn bā'*. A paraphrase of Josh. 6:1. In the biblical verse the two participles meaning "closed" are feminine, as cities in Hebrew are feminine; but in Arabic the word *balad* is masculine, and so the writers for the sake of agreement use the Hebrew masculine. The writers may have written this piece of intelligence in Hebrew as a security precaution just

drought. And just when there was a little rain, and people began to open their eyes, the judgment of God came upon this leader. And he was taken unto Him, leaving our position exposed and ruined . . .

The people of Gabes, too, have suffered severe hardship on account of the heavy payment that fell upon them during the time of the famine, leaving them stripped bare. Most of them are in our city at this time.[11]

The Further Maghreb, like Sijilmasa and other cities, is in chaos with people dead from hunger and sword. We live in great fear—may God make us secure from this dread.

I have already asked you several times to clarify for me the matter of the Gabesians' money, namely, the 100 dinars which they had sent with Abū Zikrī Judah and which should have reached you several years ago. There has been a good deal of correspondence and controversy since that time, and we do not know what became of it.[12] Please explain to me what you know of it, and whether any of it arrived or not. Would you also let me know what was sent with the sons of Barhūn, our in-laws[13]—may God protect them. I cannot write you any more than this now. . . .

Do you think you might be so kind as to send a letter or some news. Since you are gracious, do not leave me to my grief any longer, and do not deprive me of your customary kindness. I ask God to reunite us quickly under the best of circumstances. If I should find a way to write at the time of the next caravan after this, then it shall reach you. And if the situation should become even more oppressive, then we are depending upon you to inform our Masters of that which I have written to you and to convey my apology to them.

May God shield and preserve you. . . . And may the end be peace.

To our great Elder Abu 'l-Faraj—may God preserve him Joseph b. Jacob b. ᶜAwkal (may his soul find rest) God is his Protector and his Shepherd

From Joseph and Nissīm the sons of Berchiah (may his soul find rest)

Destined for Fustat
God willing

Geniza Document
Antonin 904, in *J. N. Epstein Jubilee Volume,*
S. Assaf, ed. (Jerusalem, 1950), pp. 184–85.

---

in case the letter should fall into the hands of the government secret service (*aṣḥāb al-akhbār*).

[11] It is not clear whether Jews specifically are meant here.

[12] See n. 8 above.

[13] These are the same Tahertī brothers who figure so prominently in the dispute mentioned in the Ben Berechiahs' earlier letter (above, pp. 183–85).

A SYNAGOGUE ACCUSED OF BEING IN VIOLATION OF ISLAMIC LAW IS VINDICATED IN COURT
(FIRST HALF OF THE ELEVENTH CENTURY)

Praised be to Allah, Lord of the universe.

In the name of Allah, the Merciful, the Beneficent.

This is a testimony in a case for which the truth has been established. Praised be to Allah alone.

The one who stands in need of exalted Allah, Ibrāhīm b. ᶜAlī al-Anṣārī, kissed the ground before the noble tribunal of the glorious Imam—may Allah make his dominion eternal and through it strengthen the Faith—and testified that the synagogue at the head of the Zuwayla Quarter, known as the Synagogue of the Rabbanite Jews, is modern, built only recently. The plaintiff requested from the noble tribunal that the matter be brought to our Master the Shaykh al-Islām, the Shāfiᶜī judge, that he may seek out who has authority over it, hear the complaint against him, and order the demolition of the aforementioned synagogue so that the triumph of right will result.

The qāḍī took the matter into consideration and issued a lofty order that the person in charge of the aforementioned synagogue be sought out.

Then there appeared the just elder, Abū ᶜImrān Moses b. Jacob b. Isaac al-Isrāʾīlī, the physician of His Majesty and Head of the Jewish community, Rabbanite, Karaite, and Samaritan. He came before the seat of judgment of our Lord the Chief Qāḍī and Chief Dāᶜī,[1] the Shāfiᶜī judge—may God extend His shadow over him. The plaintiff against him was the above-mentioned al-Burhānī Ibrāhīm. He charged that the synagogue in question was modern and of recent construction and that the defendant had unrightful control over it. He demanded that it be removed from his control.

In response to questioning, the aforementioned Moses replied that the synagogue was of ancient construction, that he exercised administrative control over it in accordance with Islamic law for a period of more than forty years, and that he had legal proof attesting to this.

Then our Lord the Chief Qāḍī and Chief Dāᶜī, the Shāfiᶜī judge—may Allah extend His shadow over him—asked the plaintiff al-Burhānī Ibrāhīm whether he had any proof to back up his accusation. He answered that he had no proof nor anything to support his contention. Next, the Chief Qāḍī and Chief Dāᶜī, the Shāfiᶜī judge, ordered the defendant Moses to produce the evidence he had which would substantiate his reply to the charges. He then produced the following witnesses: Bahāʾ al-Dīn b. Qāsim b. Mu-

[1] That is, he was also chief missionary or head of the Fatimid propaganda machine known as the Daᶜwa.

hannā', Ismāᶜīl b. Fakhr al-Dīn b. ᶜAbd al-Hādī, ᶜAlī b. Ḥāmid b. Ḥasan, known as Suwayd, the honorable Ḥājj Khaṭṭāb b. Naṣīr al-Dīn b. Mujāhid, known by the name of his grandfather, Fakhr al-Dīn b. Aḥmad Khālid, also known by the name of his grandfather, the Ḥājj Manṣūr b. Badr b. Naṣīr al-Dīn, known as "the Tall One," the eminent, honorable, and respected Shihāb al-Dīn b. al-Zaynī, Khiḍr b. Futayḥ, known by the name of his grandfather, the teacher Shaḥāta b. Muḥammad b. Ma'dhin, known by the name of his grandfather, the one who stands in need of exalted Allah, Sulaymān b. Ayyūb b. Muḥammad, known by the name of his father, and the Ḥājj Ramaḍān b. ᶜAlī al-Sandabīsī.

They testified before our Lord the Judge that they knew the synagogue known as the Synagogue of the Rabbanite Jews which stands at the head of the Zuwayla Quarter in a street known today as Darb al-Nabbādhīn. It is situated in accordance with the four cardinal directions as follows: the southern side is adjacent to the house of the just Elder Abū ᶜImrān Moses, the northern side is adjacent to the house known as that of Jacob, father of the aforesaid Moses, the eastern side adjoins the street in which it is located, and this is the front of the building and its main entrance. The western side adjoins the house known as the property of Isaac, grandfather of Moses. They were completely familiar with this structure, its boundaries, and its rights, with a lawful awareness which precludes ignorance. They further testified that the aforementioned synagogue was of ancient construction and not recently built. In addition to this, they also testified unanimously and in a sound and consistent narrative that the synagogue in question was a valid pious foundation,[2] considered to be from years gone by an inalienable pious foundation, authorized and verified as belonging to the Rabbanite Jews collectively and individually for their customary worship, and that it is under the supervision of whoever is Head of the Jewish communities. They also testified that the just Elder Abū ᶜImrān Moses, mentioned above, has been in control of said synagogue for a period of more than forty years prior to the present date, and that the synagogue's status as a pious foundation was ancient, going back more than two generations.

This was made known, and the witnesses testified to that effect under questioning by the judge. This was then affirmed by the Chief Qāḍī and Chief Dāᶜī Abū Muḥammad al-Qāsim on the basis of the testimony cited above as a valid substantiation—decisive, credible, and sufficient.

[2] Referred to in this document by the Islamic term *waqf*. In the Judeo-Arabic of the period it was most commonly referred to by the Hebrew *qōdesh*. See S. D. Goitein, *Mediterranean Society*, vol. 2, pp. 112–21, passim; and Moshe Gil, *Documents of the Jewish Pious Foundations from the Cairo Geniza* (Leiden, 1976).

He gave judgment in accordance with the facts and findings and made his decision compulsory. In all this, he rendered judgment after the contents of this document had been read out before him in the presence of the witnesses who have affixed their signatures to the bottom of this document, its contents having been verified, on this the 9th day of Shaᶜbān 429 (17 May 1038).

Witnessed by: Muḥammad b. ᶜAbd Allāh b. Muḥammad b. Rajā
Muḥammad b. Aḥmad b. ᶜĪsā al-ᶜUtbī
ᶜUmar b. ᶜAbd al-ᶜAzīz b. Khalaf

Manuscript from the Rabbanite archives of Cairo, Richard Gottheil,ed., in *JQR* 19 (1906–7), 472–78.

THE JEWS OF FUSTAT RAISE MONEY TO PAY THE TAXES OF THEIR BRETHREN IN JERUSALEM
(FIRST HALF OF THE ELEVENTH CENTURY)

Peace, peace be his allotment.
May his blessings from heaven above increase.
May he have salvation, mercy, and his prayers accepted.
May he find favor and lovingkindness and enlightenment
In the eyes of God and man, altogether.[1]
All these and more, may they be multiplied for him,
Our dear one, his glorious honor
The holy master and teacher, the Allūf and Rōsh Kalla[2]
The wise and understanding Sahlān b. Abraham . . .

Abundant greetings and blessings from the congregation of the City of the Great King (Jerusalem).[3] They recount your praise and testify to your strength on account of what you have done for us.

A letter from our envoy has arrived relating how you helped and aided him; how you encouraged the people to help their poor brethren time after time; and you informed them with touching words of their misery, their helplessness, and this heavy burden which has weighed like a yoke upon its inhabitants.

It is for this reason (that is, the collection of taxes), that the Arabs sit here as an imposition on the city, imposing officials and fixed payments upon its men, in return for which they (the Arabs) do not molest those of the House of Israel who come to seek atonement amongst its stones and pity in its dust; who come to circumambulate the gates of the Temple and to pray over them with upraised voices, reciting the *Qedūsha* and the

[1] Compare with Prov. 3:4.

[2] These are both titles of honor bestowed upon members and supporters of the Babylonian *yeshivot*. The first title may be loosely translated as "distinguished member," the second "head of the assembly." This latter title originally designated the seven leading scholars, each of whom was in charge of a row of nine others at the biannual assemblies (Heb., *kallōt*) of the *yeshivot* held during the months of Elul and Adar, when students came from far and wide to study tractates of the Talmud. These titles became the regular designations for representatives of the *yeshivot* in Egypt and elsewhere. See, for another example, Norman A. Stillman, "Quelques renseignements biographiques sur Yōsēf Ibn ʿAwkal, médiateur entre les Communautés juives du Maghreb et les Académies d'Irak," *REJ* 132, fasc. 4 (1973): 538.

[3] See Ps. 48:3.

Bārekhū;[4] and who come to ascend the Mount of Olives with song and to stand there on holidays facing the Shrine of the Lord, the place of the Divine Presence, His Footstool, and no one says a word to them. Now the heavy tax is a fixed levy, and we are but few in number. We have only enough to pay a small part of it. The remainder, we have to borrow at interest so that the pilgrims to the Holy City will not be threatened with tax notices. Thus, it is a duty for all Israel to support those who live in Jerusalem and to be a tent peg for them in time of need. Everyone who champions their cause will be entitled to share in their joy.

The Allūf's well-being and his reward will surely come from the Lord God of Israel. Abundant greetings and may you attain great salvation.

From Solomon the Younger, Head of the Yeshiva of the Pride of Jacob, on behalf of the Rabbanite community of the Holy City—may God re-establish it.

From the Cairo Geniza TS 13 J 11, f. 5,
Jacob Mann, ed., in *The Jews of Egypt and Palestine under the Fatimid Caliphs*,
vol. 2, p. 186.

[4] The *Bārekhū* is the prayer summoning the congregation to worship with which the morning and evening liturgy formally begins. The *Qedūsha* (sanctification) is the third blessing of the Eighteen Benedictions of the daily service.

A SICK AND DESTITUTE FUGITIVE FROM THE POLL TAX COLLECTOR SEEKS THE AID OF A JEWISH COURTIER

(ELEVENTH-CENTURY EGYPT)

This slave kisses the ground before his Master the Elder Abū Naṣr—may God Exalted preserve him, may He maintain his honored position, and make his happiness permanent.

O Master, do not ask about my condition which is one of sickness, infirmity, want, and excessive fear because of the search out for me by the tax officer[1] who is bearing down upon me. He is issuing warrants for my arrest[2] and has been sending them to detectives[3] who are on my trail. I am afraid that they will find my hiding place. If I fall into their hands, I shall surely die under the punishment or go to prison and die there.

Now I seek refuge in God—praised be He—and in you. Protect me! My deliverance and salvation will come from God through your hand—may God deliver you from all distress. You can accomplish this for me by asking Shams al-Dīn[4] to write a letter to the authorities in al-Maḥalla that they should register us as missing, for everyone says that my only chance of salvation is in being registered as missing.

Then, if God should ordain that some money will be found to pay my poll tax, let it be said that is for the fugitives,[5] since it is not for myself alone, but for me and my sons, as I am held responsible for their poll tax as well.

This calamity has struck me alone. I have submitted my case to God and to you. By the bread which y[ou feed me], and by the protection (you have given me) and by my upbringing,[6] may I be bound to God's countenance. May you have provision from God Exalted. May He never afflict you with distress.

I am in God's debt and in yours.

Peace.

Geniza Manuscript
ULC Or 1081 J 13

[1] Ar., *mushārif.*

[2] Ar., *riqā*ᶜ (literally, "notes").

[3] Ar., *lil-raqqāṣīn* (literally, "to the runners").

[4] The chief tax officer in Cairo.

[5] Ar., *al-hāribīn.* The writer is suggesting that if money is raised to cover his back taxes, it should be paid on his account so that when he and his sons emerged from hiding, they would not be considered fugitives.

[6] *bi-ḥaqq al-khubz alladhī t[u'khilunī] wa-ḥaqq al-jiwār wa 'l-tarbiya.*

A CHARITY LIST
(ELEVENTH-CENTURY EGYPT)

Outstanding Pledges for the Poll Tax (of the Poor)—Paid.[1]

The Elder Abu 'l-Khayr of the Street of the Burnishers	1 dinar
The Elder Abū Surūr Faraḥ	1 dinar
The Elder Abū Sa^{c}d b. al-Sukkarī[2]	1 dinar
The cousin of the preceding donor[3]	1½ dinar
The Elder Abū Manṣūr b. Ḥayyīm	2 dinar
The Elder Abū A^{c}lā b. al-Bahūdī	½ dinar
The Elder Abu 'l-A^{c}lā b. Sha^{c}yā	½ dinar
The Elder Abū Manṣūr al-Tustarī[4]	1 dinar
The Secretary whose office is in the Carpet Bourse	½ dinar
Ibn al-Tadmūrī	¼ dinar
The Elder Abu 'l-Ḥasan Sibā^{c}	½ dinar
The nephew of the preceding donor[5]	¼ dinar
Abū Sa^{c}d b. al-Qābisī	¼ dinar
Ibn al-Raffā	¼ dinar
Isḥāq Abū Faraḥ's boy	¼ dinar
Nissīm's brother-in-law	⅛ dinar
Ibn ^{c}Imrān the Physician	¼ dinar
Ibn Sahl the Preparer of Potions[6]	⅛ dinar
Ibn Mufarrij al-Abzārī[7]	⅛ dinar
Ibn Bushayr	½ dinar
The Elder Abu 'l-Ḥasan Ṣadaqa	½ dinar
The Elder Abū Zikrī b. Sighmār[8]	½ dinar

[1] This interpretation of the document follows that of S. D. Goitein, *Mediterranean Society,* vol. 2, pp. 473–74, and includes his corrections to the text of Gottheil and Worrell.

[2] Sukkarī is a sugar merchant. Here it seems to be a family name.

[3] Ar., *ibn ^{c}ammūh* (for *ibn ^{c}ammihi*).

[4] The brother of the "vizier" of the Fatimid dowager, Abū Sa^{c}d al-Tustarī, and the banker Abū Naṣr al-Tustarī, both of whom were murdered in 1048. See above, pp. 51–52 and below, p. 207.

[5] Ar., *ibn akhūh* (for *ibn akhīhi*).

[6] Ar., *al-sharābī.* It is not the "wine-dealer" as translated by Gottheil-Worrell, p. 69. See S. D. Goitein, *Mediterranean Society,* vol. 2, p. 581, n. 1.

[7] *Al-Abzārī* means "the seed merchant" and not "the man from Buzār" as in Gottheil-Worrell, p. 68, n. 32. It is not clear whether this is his family name or merely his profession.

[8] His full name is Abū Zikrī Judah b. Moses b. Sighmār. He was "the scion of a great family of scholars, judges, and merchants" (Goitein, *Mediterranean Society,* vol. 1, p. 158).

Abu 'l-Faraj Nissīm	½ dinar
Abū Zikrī b. Manasseh	¼ dinar
Abū Naṣr, the son of the professional mourner,[9] and his partner	½ dinar
Muṣā b. al-Majjānī[10]	⅛ dinar
Nissīm al-Maghribī	⅛ dinar
Abu 'l-Khayr the Moneychanger	2 qīrāṭs[11]
Abū ᶜImrān with the Police	⅛ dinar
Ibn Raḥmuh	¼ dinar
Abū ᶜImrān b. Ṣaghīr	¼ dinar
Abū ᶜImrān	¼ dinar
Abū Naṣr b. Mukhtār	¼ dinar
Abu 'l-Khayr the Proselyte[12]	¼ dinar
My Master the Elder Abū Manṣūr	½ dinar
Abū Saᶜd b. al-Qaṭā'if	½ dinar
Abū ᶜImrān b. al-Khayyāṭ[13]	¼ dinar
Abu 'l-Ḥayy	⅛ dinar
Abu 'l-Ḥusayn b. al-ᶜĀbid[14] and his brother-in-law Hiba together	the entire sum
And his (Abu 'l-Ḥusayn's) brother-in-law al-Faraj	¾ dinar[15]
Ṣadaqa of the Ṣaffayn[16]	¼ dinar
Ṣadaqa the Glazier	¼ dinar
Abu 'l-Ḥusayn the Goldsmith[17]	¼ dinar
Ṭayyibān	¼ dinar
Abu 'l-Ḥasan Ṣadaqa b. Simon	¼ dinar
The Elder Abū Isḥāq b. al-ᶜAssāl[18]	¼ dinar

[9] Ar.–Heb., *al-meqōnnēn.*

[10] A leading merchant of Qayrawan and the business partner of the great merchant prince Joseph b. ᶜAwkal. See Norman A. Stillman, "The Eleventh-Century Merchant House of Ibn ᶜAwkal," *JESHO* 16, pt. 1 (1973): 25–27, passim.

[11] The *qīrāṭ,* or carat, equalled 1/24 of a dinar and was usually a money of account.

[12] Ar.–Heb., *al-gēr.*

[13] Son of the tailor. Here a family name.

[14] The Pious.

[15] The text reads: *niṣf wa-rubᶜ* (a half and a quarter).

[16] The Ṣaffayn (the two rows) was an exchange in Fustat comparable to the *qayṣāriyya.* Its name indicates that it was probably a building with a colonnade. See S. D. Goitein, *Mediterranean Society,* vol. 1, p. 194.

[17] Ar. *al-dhahabī* is one of the numerous terms for people in the goldsmith's profession, which was highly specialized. See Goitein, *Mediterranean Society,* vol. 1, p. 108.

[18] Son of the honey-merchant. Here a family name.

Faraj b. Nahum	¼ dinar
Azhar b. Azhar	¼ dinar
The Elder Abū Isḥāq b. Ḥujjayj	¼ dinar
The Elder Abū Yūsuf b. al- . . .	¼ dinar
Khalaf the Oil Merchant[19]	⅛ dinar
Abū Surūr Faraḥ al-Maghribī	¼ dinar
Abū Mūsā Hārūn the Jahbadh[20]	¼ dinar

Geniza Document
Gottheil-Worrell XIII

[19] Ar., *al-zayyāt.*

[20] A *jahbadh* was a government banker who performed a variety of services: a "cashier (or treasurer), money changer, and accountant" (Goitein, *Mediterranean Society,* vol. 1 pp. 248ff.). See Walter J. Fischel, "Djabadh," *EI*[2] 2: 382–83.

A FATIMID CALIPH STEPS INTO A DISPUTE BETWEEN RABBANITES AND KARAITES IN THE HOLY LAND

A petition was submitted by the Rabbanite Jewish Community[1] to the Court of the Commander of the Faithful in which they requested that they be treated in accordance with the exalted document which had been issued on their behalf, to the effect that their rabbis should be enabled to fulfill the commandments of their faith and the customary usages of their ancestors in their houses of worship, and that they be free to serve their communities in Jerusalem, Ramleh, and other cities. Furthermore, that anyone be restrained who purposes to them that which is not in accordance with the justice of the Empire, or tries to impose upon them that which is contrary to established practice; that there be desistance from any opposition to the observance of their holidays and the performance of their rites on them; and that any of their opponents who try to alter this state of affairs be checked.

Therefore, the Commander of the Faithful has commanded that an open decree[2] be issued, in which it is stated that neither of the two Jewish communities, namely the Rabbanites and the Karaites, are to be allowed to interfere with each other. All the adherents of these two denominations should be enabled to follow the customary usages of their faith without any interference from the other denomination. The Karaites cannot be allowed to obstruct the way of Rabbanite communal leaders by keeping them away from the districts of Jerusalem and Ramle.[3] Businessmen of both communities should be allowed to follow their own customary usages, as they wish, with regard to the conduct of business[4] or abstention therefrom on their holidays.

Both communities should beware contravening this order. They should know that anyone who violates or trespasses will be severely punished as a restraint to them and a deterrent to others.

[1] *Mutarjama bi-jamāᶜat al-yahūd al-rabbāniyyīn* (literally, "The Rabbanite Jewish Community is inscribed on the heading [*tarjama*]").

[2] For a discussion of the Arabic term *manshūr* and its use in the Fatimid period for a particular class of documents, see S. M. Stern, *Fāṭimid Decrees* (London, 1964), pp. 85–90.

[3] Ramle is called here Palestine (*Filasṭīn*), since it was common then, as now, to refer to the capital of a country in Arabic by the name of the country. Thus, for example, Miṣr at that time indicated Fustat, just as Maṣr in colloquial Egyptian today indicates Cairo.

[4] *Al-bayᶜ wa 'l-shira*—literally, "buying and selling"—are to this day idiomatic for "carrying on business" or "carrying on one's affairs."

It was deemed necessary to write you . . . that you should exercise extreme care not to show any preference or partiality. You are to arrest anyone who contravenes this order and report the affair. Take cognizance of that which the Commander of the Faithful has apprised you, and act in strict accordance with it and with its intent—God willing.

Peace.

Geniza Document
TS 13 J 7, f. 29, ed. S. D. Goitein,
in *Journal of Jewish Studies* 5, no. 3
(1954): 123–25; re-ed. S. M. Stern,
Fāṭimid Decrees (London, 1964), pp. 32–34.

CHRISTIAN AND JEWISH OFFICIALS IN THE FATIMID EMPIRE

(TENTH–ELEVENTH CENTURIES)

It is said that he (the Caliph al-ᶜAzīz) appointed ᶜĪsā b. Nestorius the Christian as his secretary[1] and designated a Jew by the name of Menasseh[2] as his deputy in Syria. The Christians and Jews waxed proud because of these two and caused injury to the Muslims. Then the people of Fustat strengthened their resolve and wrote a complaint which they put into the hand of a doll which they made of paper. It read:

> By Him who has strengthened the Jews through Menasseh and the Christians through ᶜĪsā b. Nestorius, and who has humbled the Muslims through you, will you not expose the wrong that has been done to me?

They placed this doll with note in its hand in al-ᶜAzīz's path. When he saw it, he ordered it brought to him. After reading its contents and seeing the paper doll, he understood what was intended by this.

So he arrested both of them. He confiscated 300,000 dinars from ᶜĪsā and took a great sum from the Jew.

Ibn al-Athīr, *al-Kāmil fi 'l-Ta'rīkh,*
vol. 9, ed. Carl Johan Tornberg (Leiden, 1863), pp. 81–82.

[1] ᶜĪsā b. Nestorius—whether he possessed the title or not—was the vizier of the Fatimid Empire under al-ᶜAzīz and again later under al-Ḥākim, who eventually executed him.

[2] His full name was Menasseh b. Abraham Ibn al-Qazzāz. He was the civil governor in Damascus from 990–96. It is not known exactly what became of him after his arrest. On the basis of a poem written in honor of his son ᶜAdiya, it would seem that he died peacefully, perhaps in honorable retirement. His son and grandsons continued to hold distinguished positions in both the government bureaucracy and the Syrian Jewish community. See Jacob Mann, *The Jews in Egypt and Palestine under the Fatimid Caliphs,* reprint ed., vol. 1 (New York, 1970) pp. 19–22, passim; the poem is in Mann, *Jews,* ibid., pp. 12–13 (cf. ll. 11, 28–30).

THE CALIPH AL-HAKIM PROTECTS THE JEWS FROM THE WRATH OF THE POPULACE

This came to pass in the days of the caliph who is called our Lord al-Ḥākim bi-Amr Allāh, who reigned in the land of Egypt and ruled over the four corners of the land, whose dominion grew ever greater and mightier, whose throne was raised above that of his forefathers. He was only thirteen when he became caliph, yet he ruled over all the kingdom with magnanimity and wisdom. He had no need of any deputy or adviser. There were some who plotted against him and some who rose up in rebellion, but God cast them down beneath the soles of his feet, because he loved justice and hated corruption.[1] He appointed judges throughout the country and commanded them to judge fairly and with justice.

On the third day of Shevat, 4772 of Creation (31 December 1011), the Ḥazzan Putiel[2] was gathered to his eternal rest. The Jews came together to pay him honor. They carried his bier and passed through one of the streets on the way that leads to the cemetery. The Egyptian mob was stirred up against them, and they began to curse and stone them. They raged around them. Then they made false accusations against them and maligned them. They mocked and jeered them and sought to destroy them. They buzzed to one another and became arrogant. The governor sent his police and agents, and the qāḍī sent his messengers and couriers. They broke through the crowd surrounding the bier and encircled the funeral party. They began to drive them away and abuse them in the streets.

The Jews were terrified and ran for their lives. Some fled, some hid, and some paid bribes. Others were stripped of their clothes. Still others were thrown into prison and shackled hand and foot. In all, twenty-three were arrested and brought to two prisons. They suffered greatly, and passed the night hungry and thirsty. Some of their clothing was taken from them as payment for their jailers.

Among them was a member of the Jewish High Court, a poor, old, humble and God-fearing man, named Samuel b. Hoshaᶜna. He was the third ranking officer of the Palestinian Yeshiva.

They awoke the following day, the fourth of Shevat, and were taken out trembling with fear at the third hour of the day. They were dragged and shoved through the streets. Crowds of thousands gathered around

[1] Perhaps this is an oblique reference to the persecution of the Christians by al-Ḥākim, which was already at its height at this time.

[2] Perhaps a scribal error for the more common name Paltiel. See Jacob Mann, *Jews,* Second Supplement, p. 432, n. 1.

them in an uproar. The noise was shattering. Every Jew-baiter,[3] every vile and contemptible individual followed after them as they were dragged off to the place of execution. They were stripped naked and forced forward by the enraged mob so that they might all be killed at the same time.

They had only gone ten ells, when a herald called out with orders to bring them to the royal palace. Some of the police kept trying to drag them to the place of execution, while others pulled them toward the palace. The Caliph ordered that they should be conducted to the palace guardhouse. They suffered in their chains as if their very souls were in irons.

All of the congregation of Israel that lived in Egypt was greatly distressed. They hid in their homes and their cellars, unable to go in or out, for they dared not move about. The inhabitants of the city intended to despoil them and to massacre them, erasing any trace of them from the face of the earth. The Jews turned this way and that, but there was no one to help them.

So all the men, women, and children mourned, wept, and fasted—even the pregnant women and nursing mothers. Their terror grew as they could find no counsel and no answer to their plight. But then some of the poor Jews—men, women, and children—took heart, gathered up their courage, and were prepared to sacrifice their lives for their brethren. They rose up on the morning of the fifth and threw themselves down before the palace gate. They put dust on their heads, prostrated themselves, and cried out before God and said: "Save us, o lord Caliph!"

When their cry was heard by our lord the Caliph and he knew of their pain and suffering, he took pity upon them in their misery. God turned his heart so that he would spare them. For the Caliph's heart was in the hand of the Lord as streams of water "he turns it wherever He wills."[4] The falsehood of the accusers became known to him. It was said that there were close to two hundred of them, but that there was not among them a single person who could give testimony whatever. There were only four who could even give a doubtful testimony.

The Caliph ordered that the prisoners be released and their shackles removed. He further commanded that all their clothing be returned to them down to the last shoelace. And they did as he commanded. As they went out, they blessed the Caliph. They gathered around the gates of his palace and invoked more blessings upon him for a long life, a happy reign, that his armies should be strengthened, his troops aided, that all the lands

[3] Heb., *ᶜārīṣ,* literally "tyrant." Along with *sōnē* this is one of the many code words for what would today be called "anti-Semite."

[4] A paraphrase of Prov. 21:1.

of the East and West should be laid open in conquest[5] before him, and that all of his enemies should be utterly destroyed.

Their brethren who had hidden themselves went out to meet them, and they proceeded together through the streets, blessing the Caliph as they walked until they reached the Great Synagogue.[6] There they took out three Torah scrolls and gave thanks to God over and over. They blessed the Caliph again and recited the great Hallel.[7] And there was much rejoicing.

The leaders of the people summoned them together and ordained that they should fast and afflict themselves every year from the third day of the month of Shevat until the fifth . . . in remembrance of these miracles, to give thanks to our God, and to ask for abundant blessing upon our lord the Caliph.

from the *Megilla* of Samuel b. Hoshaᶜna,
ed. Jacob Mann, in *Jews,*
reprint ed. (New York, 1970), Second Supplement, pp. 433–35.

[5] *Ve-liftoaḥ lifānāv mizrāḥē hā-ᶜōlām u-maᶜarāvāv*. The entire phrase is an Arabism.

[6] That is, the Synagogue of the Palestinians. See S. D. Goitein, *Mediterranean Society,* vol. 2, p. 6.

[7] Psalm 136, which is recited on Sabbaths, festivals, and joyous communal occasions.

A PETITION TO A COURT JEW IN FATIMID EGYPT

To our great, righteous, lord and master, Ḥesed b. Sahl (Abū Saᶜd al-Tustarī), the elder, the mighty and honored minister—may our Rock preserve him and our God aid him; may our Creator bless him and may our Holy one support him; and may He cover him with the protection of His shadow.

We the entire congregation of Tripoli send our greetings to our Lord, the honorable Elder, and ask the Lord our God, Who hears the cry of the downtrodden, to grant you eternal life. We wish to inform your Excellency that we are in great distress because we have no place to pray. Everywhere else, the synagogues have been returned to the House of Israel—except in our town. The reason for this is that our synagogue was converted into a mosque. We are, therefore, petitioning our Master to show us kindness with an edict[1] from the Government permitting us to build for ourselves a synagogue—as has been done everywhere else—on one of our ruined properties on which servants of the ruler dwell without paying any rent. We may point out to our Lord that this very year the congregation in Jubayl[2] rebuilt their synagogue, and no Muslim said anything. We also wish to inform our Lord that we will pay an annual rent for the place to the Gentiles.

There is no need to mention that this is a matter which would be pleasing to God. Your welfare and blessings will increase forever. Selah.

May salvation come swiftly.

Unnumbered Geniza manuscript from the
Adler Collection of the Jewish Theological Seminary,
ed. Jacob Mann, in *Jews*, vol. 2, pp. 72–73.

[1] Called here *neshtavan* (a Persian loan word), which was the normal equivalent in the Hebrew of that period for Ar., *sijill*.

[2] This small port lies between Beirut and Tripoli on the site of the biblical Gebal (Gr., Byblos).

*A LAMENT FOR THE JEWS OF PALESTINE DURING THE BEDOUIN RAMPAGES OF 1024**

Weep, my brothers, and mourn
Over Zion, all of us together,
Like the mourning of Hadadrimmon[1]
And Josiah the son of Amon.

Weep for those tender, genteel ones
Who barefoot tread on thorns.
They draw water for Black slaves,
And they hew wood for them.

Weep for the man who was forced into slavery,
But was not prepared for it.
They told him, "Suffer and bear it!"
But he could not shoulder the burden.

Weep for men who must see
Their praiseworthy sons
Who are like fine gold[2]
Desecrated at the hands of Black slaves.

Weep for the blind who wander[3]
Through Zion, soiled
With the blood of pregnant women disemboweled[4]
And with the blood of old men and infants.

Weep for those pure ones who were made
Impure—forced to eat their abomination,
So that they should be made to forget the Covenant of
  their Rock,
And their Homeland, the place of their desire.

*In his edition of this lament, Schirmann attributes it to the time of the persecutions of al-Ḥākim (sometime after 1012). However, S. D. Goitein has pointed out that the poem deals only with Palestine and not with the Fatimid Empire as a whole, and that the incidents described of indiscriminate pillage, sodomy, rape, murder, and enslavement did not take place under al-Ḥākim. Such atrocities did occur during the Bedouin uprisings, which began in 1024 under the leadership of the Banū Jarrāḥ brothers. See Goitein, "The Time and Circumstances of the Lamentations of Joseph Ibn Abitur," *Yediot Bahaqirat Eretz-Israel Weatjqoteha* 28, nos. 3–4 (1964): 247–49 [Heb.].

[1] Zech. 12:11. Refers to the defeat of Josiah and his death at Megiddo at the hands of the Pharaoh Necoh (described in 2 Kings 23:29–30).

[2] Lam. 4:2.

[3] Lam. 4:14.

[4] Hos. 14:1.

Weep for the pure women
Who had been protected and kept from stain,
Who now by the Seed of Ham
Were in the pangs of pregnancy.

Weep indeed for the maidens
With their finely sculptured figures,[5]
Who became slaves to
The loathsome slavegirls.[6]

Weep bitterly and mourn too
For the synagogues which
Were broken into by ravening beasts,
And in them kites have gathered.[7]

Weep for those shattered people
Who have been gathered for a day of evil;
And also for the poor and penniless
Who have been oppressed and crushed.

Yea, weep for our living ones,[8]
No need to cry for our dead—
Since to be like them
Is always our desire.

Therefore, do not try,
My friend, to comfort me.
For those who were torn to pieces
In Zion and have no one to bury them.

Joseph b. Abītūr, "Qīna," in Ḥayyim Schirmann, *Ha-Shīra hāᶜIvrīt bi-Sfārād uve-Prōvāns,* vol. 1 (Jerusalem and Tel Aviv, 1961), pp. 64–65.

[5] Ps. 146:12.
[6] That is, the wives of the Bedouin warriors.
[7] Isa. 34:15.
[8] Jer. 22:10.

THE ASSASSINATION OF ABU SA^c^D AL-TUSTARI
(CAIRO, 1047)

There was a Jew, a dealer in gems, who was very intimate with the ruler (the Fatimid Caliph al-Mustanṣir). He was exceedingly wealthy. The royal house had complete confidence in him with regard to the purchase of precious stones.

One day, the royal troops fell upon this Jew and killed him. This having been done, they feared the ruler's wrath. They mounted up, twenty thousand strong, and went to the parade grounds. The troops stayed on the open field, and the inhabitants of the city became frightened because of them. They remained on the parade grounds until midday, at which time a servant came out of the palace. Standing at the palace gate, he called: "The Ruler wishes to know whether you are obedient to him or not?"

They immediately cried back: "We are his obedient servants! But we have committed an offense."

The servant replied: "The Ruler orders you to go back to your places!"

That murdered Jew was named Abū Sa^c^īd (Abū Sa^c^d).[1] He left behind a son and a brother. It is said that his wealth was so great that only the Lord Exalted knew its full extent. They say that on the terrace of his mansion were three hundred silver vases in each of which was set a tree. There were so many that it looked like a garden. And all of the trees bore fruit.

His brother (Abū Naṣr) wrote a letter which he sent to be presented to the Ruler. In it, he offered to make an immediate gift of 200,000 Maghrebi dinars to the treasury, for he was very much afraid. The Ruler sent back the letter and had it publicly torn up, saying: "You may consider yourself safe. Go back to your home, for no one has anything against you. As for myself, I have no need of anyone else's money." Then he offered them (Abū Naṣr and his nephew) his condolences.

Nāṣir-i Khosraw, *Sefer Nameh*,
ed. Charles Schefer
(Paris, 1881), pp. 55–56 of Persian text.

[1] Concerning Abu Sa^c^d, see Part One above, pp. 51–52.

A REPORT ON A COMPOUND OF BUILDINGS DEDICATED AS A CHARITABLE TRUST OF THE JEWISH COMMUNITY (EGYPT, TWELFTH CENTURY)

. . . .

the poor of the two aforesaid denominations (i.e., the Rabbanites and the Karaites) with regard to what has been previously mentioned, is under the supervision of the Jewish Court or of such person as it sees fit to delegate. It is an everlasting pious foundation and an eternal mortmain for the benefit of said poor.[1] It is an inalienable charitable trust which may not be terminated ever.

The witnesses of the will (which left funds for the establishment of the pious foundation) were Tiqva ha-Kōhēn b. R. Nathan (may he rest in Eden), Isaac b. R. Samuel the Spaniard (may his memory be blessed), Samuel b. R. Isaac (may he rest in Eden), and Elijah b. R. Eli the Ḥāvēr (may his memory be blessed). I read the will in the home of the Elder Abū Saᶜīd, the Muqaddam of the Karaites.[2]

With regard to the compound known as Dār al-Nāqa,[3] one half of it is to be dedicated to the Communal Trust.[4] One quarter is already a pious foundation for Sitt al-Ahl, the daughter of Faḍl al-Kōhēn b. al-Shaykh Abu 'l-Karam b. Saᶜdān, from her father's mother, by a will which stipulated that if anything was left from the rent after repairs, two dirhams from this would be paid to her sister Sutayt, the wife of Hiba b. Abī Ghālib al-Ṣā'igh, every month for as long as she lives. Any money remaining beyond this was to be spent either on medicines for the sick, or on shrouds for the dead, or on the poll tax of a scholar with no outside income, but on nothing else.

[1] Since the document uses the synonyms *waqf* and *ḥabs* in Arabic, I have translated them by various English synonyms, such as pious foundation, mortmain, and charitable trust.

[2] *Muqaddam* was the title of a Jewish communal leader. Here it seems to be used for the Head of the Karaites. See S. D. Goitein, *Mediterranean Society,* vol. 2, pp. 68–77.

[3] The name of this compound in Arabic means "The House of the She-Camel." Compounds such at this are very frequently mentioned in the Geniza. See Goitein, "Geniza Documents on the Transfer and Inspection of Houses," *Revue de l'Occident Musulman et de la Méditerranée,* nos. 13–14 (1973) *[Mélanges Le Tourneau],* pp. 406–10.

[4] Ar.–Heb., *lil-heqdēsh.*

This then is the text of the will word for word, with the names of those who appear on it as witnesses, and the names of the two judges who presided over them at the validation. They were known as people who fear God—may He be exalted.

Therefore, after having read this will which was made by the owner of the property himself, in accordance with the laws of Israel, we adhered to it and made the compound a regular charitable trust for the benefit of the poor, for as our Sages—peace be upon them—have said: "It is a religious obligation to fulfill the words of the deceased."[5] Thus, it was not a whim on the part of the Elder Abu 'l-Faraj b. Qusāsā to write as he did in the document of declaration since he was—may God have mercy upon him—a God-fearing man, who performed charitable deeds, and who was philanthropic to the poor and the students of the Torah. It only appears from the case that this money was deposited with him by our Master the Meᶜullēh[6] (may his memory be blessed) until some property would become available to be purchased as a charitable trust with it. Then the Monk came into office—may his bones be ground to dust![7] Now since the date of the written declaration is A.H. 521 (1127), the very year they were confiscating people's property, he (Abu 'l-Faraj) deemed it proper that this money should be spent in acquiring that half (of the Dār al-Nāqa) for the benefit of the poor. No doubt he came to this decision after consulting with our Master the Meᶜullēh (may his memory be blessed). Then he went to a scribe and insisted that he should insert into the written declaration that this money had been received by him from Ibn . . . , and that he directed him to spend it on behalf of the Jewish poor. The scribe wrote as he was requested, although he was not very attentive to the phrasing as he wrote since the desired intent, namely that it was to be acquired for the poor, had already been achieved.

This was a most sensible decision because this way he was safe from the Monk hearing that he had money deposited with him for the Jewish poor with which to purchase property on their behalf, for he would surely send someone to seize it from him, just as he seized the 300 dinars that

[5] Taᶜanīt 21a.

[6] According to Moshe Gil, *Documents of the Jewish Pious Foundations from the Cairo Geniza* (Leiden, 1974), p. 250, n. 13; this title, which means "the Excellent," probably refers to the judge, Nathan b. Solomon ha-Kōhēn.

[7] The Monk was the hated Coptic minister of the Fatimid Caliph al-Āmir, Abū Najāḥ al-Rāhib. In 1126, he began a series of confiscations referred to here. Three years later he was executed. For the literature dealing with this figure, see Gil, *Jewish Pious Foundations,* pp. 250–51.

were deposited with the Meᶜullēh (may his memory be blessed) for Ibn Shuwayᶜ.[8]

Geniza Document
Bodl. MS Heb. f 56 f. 129–30, in Moshe Gil,
Documents of the Jewish Pious Foundations from the Cairo Geniza
(Leiden, 1976), pp. 246–48.

HASDAY B. SHAPRUT MAKES SPANISH JEWRY INDEPENDENT FROM THE AUTHORITY OF BAGHDAD

There were a number of Jewish men of science in Spain. Among those who took an interest in medicine was Ḥasday b. Isaac (Ibn Shapruṭ), who was in the service of al-Ḥakam b. ᶜAbd al-Raḥmān al-Nāṣir li-Dīn Allāh.[1] He specialized in the art of medicine and had an exemplary knowledge of the science of Jewish law. He was the first to open for Andalusian Jewry the gates of their science of jurisprudence, chronology, and other subjects. Previously, they had recourse to the Jews of Baghdad in order to learn the law of their faith and in order to adjust the calendar and determine the dates of their holidays. They used to bring from them (the Jews of Baghdad) a calculation for a span of a number of years, and from it, they were able to know when their seasons began and when their year commenced.

When Ḥasday became attached to al-Ḥakam II, gaining his highest regard for his professional ability, his great talent, and his culture, he was able to procure through him the works of the Jews in the East which he desired. Then he taught the Jews of Spain that of which they had previously been ignorant. They were able as a result of this to dispense with the inconvenience which had burdened them.

Ṣāᶜid al-Andalusī, *Ṭabaqāt al-Umam,* ed.
L. Cheikho (Beirut, 1912), pp. 88–89.

[8] In order to protect the 300 dinars deposited with him from confiscation, Abu 'l-Faraj had a document altered to show that the money had been spent to purchase half of a compound as an inalienable pious foundation. The compound, in reality, already belonged to the communal trust. The report translated here was probably made for the community's private records to keep matters straight.

[1] Ruled 961–76.

SAMUEL AND JOSEPH IBN NAGHRELA
(ELEVENTH-CENTURY SPAIN)

One of his (Rabbi Ḥanokh b. Moses)[1] outstanding disciples was R. Samuel ha-Levi the Nagid b. R. Joseph, surnamed Ibn Naghrēla,[2] of the community of Cordova. Besides being a great scholar and highly cultured person, R. Samuel was highly versed in Arabic literature and style and was, indeed, competent to serve in the king's palace. Nevertheless, he maintained himself in very modest circumstances as a spice-merchant until the time when war broke out in Spain. With the termination of the rule of the house of Ibn Abī ᶜĀmir[3] and the seizure of power by the Berber chiefs, the city of Cordova dwindled, and its inhabitants were compelled to flee. Some went off to Saragossa, where their descendants have remained down to the present, while others went to Toledo, where their descendants have retained their identity down to the present.

This R. Samuel, however, fled to Malaga, where he occupied a shop as a spice-merchant. Since his shop happened to adjoin the courtyard of Ibn al-ᶜArīf—who was the Kātib[4] of King Ḥabbūs b. Māksan, the Berber king of Granada—the Kātib's maidservant would ask him to write letters for her to her master, the Vizier Abu 'l-Qāsim b. al-ᶜArīf. When the latter received the letters, he was astounded at the learning they reflected. Consequently, when, after a while, this Vizier, Ibn al-ᶜArīf, was given leave by his King Ḥabbūs to return to his home in Malaga, he inquired among the people of his household: "Who wrote the letters which I received from you?" They

[1] He was the son and successor of R. Moses b. Ḥanokh, who became the chief scholar of Spain shortly after his arrival from southern Italy sometime in the 950s. Under the patronage of Ḥasday b. Shaprūṭ, Moses b. Ḥanokh and Ḥanokh b. Moses made Spain into a leading seat of Jewish scholarship, more or less independent of the Yeshivot of Iraq and Palestine. A romantic account of the father and son's arrival in Spain is given by Ibn Daud, *Sefer ha-Qabbalah,* ed. and trans. Gerson D. Cohen (Philadelphia, 1967), pp. 46–48 (Heb. text); pp. 63–66 (Eng. trans.).

[2] For a more detailed biographical sketch, see Jefim Schirmann, "Samuel Ha-Nagid, The Man, The Soldier, The Politician," *Jewish Social Studies* 13 (1951): 99–126.

[3] From 981–1002, the actual chief of state in Islamic Spain was Muḥammad b. Abī ᶜĀmir, the caliph's majordomo. He took on the royal title of al-Manṣūr (Almanzor in the European chronicles). He was succeeded by his sons al-Muẓaffar (1002–1008) and ᶜAbd al-Raḥmān Sanchuelo (1008–9). With the latter's assassination, the caliphate of Spain began to dissolve into the anarchy known as the *fitna.* From this emerged the many principalities of the so-called party kings.

[4] The word *kātib* literally means "secretary," but in Spain at this time it indicated the principal minister of state.

replied: "A certain Jew of the community of Cordova, who lives next door to your courtyard, used to do the writing for us." The Kātib thereupon ordered that R. Samuel ha-Levi be brought to him at once, and said to him: "It does not become you to spend your time in a shop. Henceforth you are to stay at my side." He thus became the scribe and counselor of the counselor of the King. Now the counsel which he gave was as if one consulted the oracle of God, and thanks to his counsel King Ḥabbūs achieved success and became exceedingly great.

Subsequently, when the Kātib Ibn al-ᶜArīf took ill and felt his death approaching, King Ḥabbūs paid him a visit and said to him: "What am I going to do? Who will counsel me in the wars which encompass me on every side?" He replied: "I never counseled you out of my own mind, but out of the mind of this Jew, my scribe. Look after him well, and let him be a father and a priest to you. Do whatever he says, and God will help you."

Accordingly, after the death of the Kātib, King Ḥabbūs brought R. Samuel ha-Levi to his palace and made him Kātib and counselor. Thus, he entered the King's palace in 4780 (1019/20).[5]

Now the King had two sons, Bādīs the elder and Buluggīn the younger. Although the Berber princes supported the election of the younger, Buluggīn, as king, the people at large supported Bādīs. The Jews also took sides, with three of them, R. Joseph b. Migash, R. Isaac b. Leon, and R. Nehemiah surnamed Ishkafa, who were among the leading citizens of Granada, supporting Buluggīn. R. Samuel ha-Levi, on the other hand, supported Bādīs. On the day of King Ḥabbūs's death, the Berber princes and nobles formed a line to proclaim his son Buluggīn as king. Thereupon, Buluggīn went and kissed the hand of his older brother Bādīs, thus acknowledging the latter as king. This happened in the year 4787 (1026/27).[6] Buluggīn's supporters turned livid with embarrassment, but in spite of themselves they acknowledged Bādīs as king. Subsequently, his brother Buluggīn regretted his earlier action and tried to lord it over his brother Bādīs. There was nothing, however trivial, that the King would do that Buluggīn would not frustrate. When, after a while, his brother took ill, the King told the physician to withhold medications from his brother, and the physician did just that. Buluggīn then died, and the kingdom was established in the hand of Bādīs. Thereupon, the three leading Jewish citizens mentioned above fled to the city of Seville.

[5] Jefim Schirmann questions both this date and the story of Ibn Naghrela's sudden rise to power; namely, "It appears more likely that Samuel rose gradually to his high office after overcoming all sorts of obstacles." Schirmann, in *Jewish Social Studies* 13 (1951): 103.

[6] Ḥabbūs died in 1038.

Now R. Samuel was appointed as Nagid[7] in 4787 (1026/7). He achieved great good for Israel in Spain, the Maghreb, Ifrīqiya, Egypt, Sicily, indeed as far as the academy in Babylonia and the Holy City. He provided material benefits out of his own pocket for students of the Torah in all these countries. He also purchased many books—copies of the Holy Scriptures as well as of the Mishna and Talmud, which are also among the holy writings. Throughout Spain and the countries just mentioned, whoever wished to devote full time to the study of the Torah found in him a patron. Moreover, he retained scribes who would make copies of the Mishna and Talmud, which he would present to students who were unable to purchase copies themselves, both in the academies of Spain as well as of the other countries we mentioned. These gifts were coupled with annual contributions of olive oil for the synagogues of Jerusalem, which he would dispatch from his own home. He spread Torah abroad and died at a ripe old age after having earned four crowns: the crown of Torah, the crown of power, the crown of a Levite, and towering over them all, by dint of good deeds in each of these domains, the crown of a good name.[8] He passed away in 4815 (1056).

His son, R. Joseph ha-Levi the Nagid, succeeded to his post. Of all the fine qualities which his father possessed he lacked but one. Having been reared in wealth and never having to bear a burden in his youth, he lacked his father's humility. Indeed, he grew haughty—to his destruction. The Berber princes became so jealous of him that he was killed on the Sabbath day, the ninth of Tevet 4827 (December 31, 1066), along with the [Jewish] community of Granada and all those who had come from distant lands to see his learning and power. He was mourned in every city and in every town. . . . After his death, his books and treasures were scattered all over the world. So, too, the disciples he raised became the rabbis of Spain and the leaders of the following generation.

Abraham Ibn Daud, *Sefer ha-Qabbalah*,
ed. and trans. Gerson D. Cohen
(Philadelphia, 1967), pp. 71–76.

[7] This title, which may be translated as "Prince," was first bestowed on a Jewish communal leader only a few years earlier when in 1015 Hay Gaon conferred the title upon Abraham b. ᶜAṭā' (see above p. 46). Ibn Naghrēla, probably received the title from the same *gaon*.

[8] An allusion to Mishna Avot 4: 13.

A POETICAL ATTACK ON THE JEWS OF GRANADA
(ELEVENTH CENTURY)

Go, tell all the Ṣanhāja[1]
 the full moons of our time, the lions in their lair
The words of one who bears them love, and is concerned
 and counts it a religious duty to give advice.
Your chief has made a mistake
 which delights malicious gloaters
He has chosen an infidel as his secretary
 when he could, had he wished, have chosen a Believer.
Through him, the Jews have become great and proud
 and arrogant—they, who were among the most abject
And have gained their desires and attained the utmost
 and this happened suddenly, before they even realized it.
And how many a worthy Muslim humbly obeys
 the vilest ape[2] among these miscreants.
And this did not happen through their own efforts
 but through one of our own people who rose as their accomplice.
Oh why did he not deal with them, following
 the example set by worthy and pious leaders?
Put them back where they belong
 and reduce them to the lowest of the low,
Roaming among us, with their little bags,
 with contempt, degradation and scorn as their lot,
Scrabbling in the dunghills for colored rags
 to shroud their dead for burial.
They did not make light of our great ones
 or presume against the righteous,
Those low-born people would not be seated in society
 or paraded[3] along with the intimates of the ruler.
Bādīs! You are a clever man
 and your judgment is sure and accurate.
How can their misdeeds be hidden from you
 when they are trumpeted all over the land?
How can you love this bastard brood
 when they have made you hateful to all the world?
How can you complete your ascent to greatness

[1] The poet is addressing the Ṣanhāja, the great Berber confederation to which the Zirids belonged.

[2] A standard epithet applied to Jews, based on a koranic reference to Jewish Sabbath-breakers who were transformed into apes (Sura 2:65/61, 5:60/65, and 7:166). Christians are normally referred to as pigs (see 5:60/65).

[3] Under the provisions of the Pact of ᶜUmar Jews should not be permitted to ride horses or to be shown public honors.

when they destroy as you build?
How have you been lulled to trust a villain
and made him your companion—though he is evil company?
God has vouchsafed in His revelations
a warning against the society of the wicked.[4]
Do not choose a servant from among them
but leave them to the curse of the accurst!
For the earth cries out against their wickedness
and is about to heave and swallow all.
Turn your eyes to other countries
and you will find the Jews are outcast dogs.
Why should you alone be different and bring them near
when in all the land they are kept afar?
—You, who are a well-beloved king,
scion of glorious kings,
And are the first among men
as your forebears were first in their time.
I came to live in Granada
and I saw them frolicking there.
They divided up the city and the provinces
with one of their accursed men everywhere.
They collect all the revenues,
they munch and they crunch.[5]
They dress in the finest clothes
while you wear the meanest.
They are the trustees of your secrets
—yet how can traitors be trusted?
Others eat a dirham's worth, afar,
while they are near, and dine well.
They challenge you to your God
and they are not stopped or reproved.
They envelop you with their prayers[6]
and you neither see nor hear.
They slaughter beasts in our markets
and you eat their *trefa*.[7]
Their chief ape has marbled his house
and led the finest spring water to it.

[4]. A reference to Sura 5:25f. where Moses asks God to separate him from the evildoers among the Israelites.

[5] A reference to an Arabic proverb that approximates our "Give him an inch and he takes a mile."

[6] *Bi-asḥārihim,* that is, with their morning prayers (Heb., *shaḥarīt*). The motif of enveloping recalls the Jewish custom of wrapping themselves in prayer shawls for this service.

[7] This accusation that the Jews sell to the Muslims food unfit to eat was to be raised in different times and places. See for example below, p. 366.

Our affairs are now in his hands
  and we stand at his door.
He laughs at us and at our religion
  and we return to our God.
If I said that his wealth is as great
  as yours, I would speak the truth.
Hasten to slaughter him as an offering,
  sacrifice him, for he is a fat ram
And do not spare his people
  for they have amassed every precious thing.
Break loose their grip and take their money
  for you have a better right to what they collect.[8]
Do not consider it a breach of faith to kill them
  —the breach of faith would be to let them carry on.
They have violated our covenant with them
  so how can you be held guilty against violators?
How can they have any pact
  when we are obscure and they are prominent?
Now we are the humble, beside them,
  as if we had done wrong, and they right!
Do not tolerate their misdeeds against us
  for you are surety for what they do.
God watches His own people
  and the people of God will prevail.

Abū Isḥāq of Elvira,
trans. Bernard Lewis, in *Islam in History*, pp. 159–61.

[8] The poet here is inciting the king to the common practice in medieval Islamic government of shaking down or fleecing public officials, which is called in Arabic *muṣādara*. The motif of slaughtering the wicked infidel like a sacrificial beast is a recurrent one. Ṣalāḥ al-Dīn (Saladin) is reported to have slaughtered in this manner captured Crusaders who had intended to desecrate the tomb of Muḥammad in Medina. See Ibn al-Athīr, *al-Kāmil fi 'l-Ta'rīkh* 11 (Beirut, 1965–67): 490–91; and al-Maqrīzī, *Khiṭaṭ*, vol. 2 (Bulaq, 1853), pp. 85–86. In the popular adventures of Mourad Saber, the Algerian James Bond, the same fate is visited upon Israeli agents. See, for example, Youcef Khader, *Délivrez la Fidayia!* (Algiers, 1970), p. 186.

THE FALL OF THE JEWISH VIZIER OF GRANADA (1066)

The Jewish vizier informed the elders of the Jews that Sayf al-Dawla[1] had turned against him. The shrewdest of them, with the keenest judgment, said to him, "Don't expect to prosper when the Shaykh (Sultan Bādīs)[2] is no more and hope for nothing from Sayf al-Dawla. Consider, rather, whom you will enthrone if your sovereign dies. Have you found him? Contrive to poison Sayf al-Dawla. His brother, Māksan, is now a nonentity. If you kill the one and enthrone the other, you will render him a service which he will not forget."

The vizier let himself be tempted to poison Sayf al-Dawla. He was well able to do so because my father[3] often used to drink with him and was often in his house. One day he drank with him as usual in his house. He had hardly left his house when he vomited up all that was in his stomach and fell on his back on the ground. It was only with a great effort that he was able to walk back to his own house. He lingered for two days and then died. May Allah have mercy upon him.

I heard one of Bādīs's chief eunuchs tell this story: One day Sayf al-Dawla sent for me and said: "Go and find my lady Mothers[4] and tell them that I intend to kill the Jew." I said to him, "I will not take this message, for he would undoubtedly hear of it. If you really intend to kill him, then you should not inform me or anyone else among Allah's creatures." I realized that it was his condition which led him to such actions.

Another thing which had previously helped to make trouble was that my father was on terms which were the very opposite of confidence with the palace ladies who had brought up his son, al-Muᶜizz, my brother. The reason was that they lavished money on his son while he was still a small child and refused it to him, so that he had to have recourse to the Jew to get money. The ladies complained to him and tried to prevent him from associating with the Jew, until the latter became aware of this, and my

[1] Buluggīn Sayf al-Dawla, who died in 1064, was heir apparent to the throne of Granada at the time of his death.

[2] Bādīs b. Ḥabbūs b. Zīrī al-Muẓaffar (d. 1073) was the second Zirid sultan of Granada.

[3] The author of this chronicle was the son of Sayf al-Dawla. He was only eight years old at the time of his father's death. At seventeen, he succeeded his grandfather and became the last of his dynasty. In 1090, Granada fell to the Almoravids, and ᶜAbd Allāh spent the rest of his life imprisoned in Aghmat, Morocco, where these memoirs were written.

[4] Each woman of the harem who gave birth to a prince gained the title of *umm al-walad,* or lady mother (literally, "mother of a boy").

father and he agreed to charge the women before the sovereign and accuse them of having stolen the money and sent it out of the country. When my grandfather became aware of the matter and of the quarrel which had arisen between the palace ladies and their son, Sayf al-Dawla, the latter was at the same time blamed by both his father and the women, while the women contrived to exculpate themselves from the slanderous accusation which had been made against them. With his father on the side of the women, Sayf al-Dawla was obliged to make peace with them, and, in the end, the whole story rebounded on the head of the Jew. All this increased the Jew's hatred and vindictiveness, until, at the appointed time, Allah's decree made him the instrument of the death of Sayf al-Dawla.

When the quarrel was just beginning, the Jew had retained for himself a large part of the tax revenue from Guadix. Sayf al-Dawla complained of this to his father. The swine, therefore, contrived to invite my father to his house to drink until he was drunk, whereupon he gave orders to bring out his sons and his women dressed in mourning. My father was shocked by their condition and by their weeping and asked the vizier, "Has someone died in your house?"

"A large sum of money has died in my house," he replied. "It is withheld from you only because of the slowness of the subjects in paying their taxes. But today is a good day. Comfort my family, therefore, by writing a quittance in which you hold me innocent of this sum until your money reaches you. My family are in fear and terror. Complete your benevolence by writing this quittance."

Thus he seized his opportunity and my father wrote him this quittance. Then the Jew took this quittance to his father (Bādīs) and said to him, "He spends his money for the viziers and on constant drinking. Here is a document in which he gives me a quittance. Of what, then, does he complain?"

Sayf al-Dawla again fell into even greater disfavor with his father and lost the day against both the vizier and the women, since it was Allah's will to put a term to his existence. May Allah reward him in the world to come for his good intentions and his sincere behavior toward both the nobles and the common people.

When my father died it was a great calamity for the people, who had hoped that he would make justice prevail. The people were in turmoil and wanted to kill the Jew.[5] These were the first signs of his downfall, but they expected my grandfather, the sovereign, to punish him. The Jew continued his campaign against the Qarawī and alleged to al-Muẓaffar (Bādīs) that members of this family had so extolled wine-imbibing to his son that he had

[5] See the rabble-rousing poem of Abū Isḥāq of Elvira, above, pp. 214–16.

died of it. Because of this the Qarawī family suffered great misfortunes. They were expelled from their lands, their property was seized, and some of them, viziers attached to the person of my father, were put to death because of accusations brought against them, and the real culprit remained undetected.

After the death of Sayf al-Dawla the Jew acted as if he were a Barmecide[6] and tried to install my uncle, Māksan, as heir to the succession. At this time my grandfather was very old. He was inclined to repose, and, because of his age and the death of his son, he undertook no further conquests, leaving the reins of government to the Jew to serve in his place. He was thus able to command and forbid as he pleased.

For a time, there was peace and well-being. The treasury was filled, and for several years no dissension was heard and no disorder seen. Then things went wrong. The Jew—may Allah curse him—played false, and Guadix and all its territory passed into the power of Ibn Ṣumādiḥ.[7] The other princes pounced on our lands until nothing was left to us but Granada, Almuñecar, Priego, and Cabra. The rumor spread among the subjects that the great sovereign was dead. He had, indeed, disappeared from sight. The castles were evacuated by their garrisons, and the populace took the opportunity to move into them, in circumstances which I shall describe later, please God.

It was at the peak of Bādīs's power and glory that al-Nāya came to seek him. He had been a slave of al-Muᶜtaḍid b. ᶜAbbād[8]—may Allah have mercy upon him—and was one of the group who had plotted treason against him, in collusion with his son, whose story is well known. Al-Nāya came to Granada, driven by his inescapable destiny, and a group of the chiefs of the Black slaves befriended him and asked the Sultan to bestow gifts on him. The Sultan granted their request, desiring to please them and thus increase their zeal and loyalty in his service. "This man," they said, "has come to seek you, breaking with another and counting on you. He has placed his hopes in you. Whatever you do for him, you do for us."

He entered Granada at a time most fortunate for him and most troublous for the state. At first he behaved excellently and with modesty in his dealings with officials, so that they praised his conduct and helped him by commending him to the Sultan, who took him into his service and

[6] The Barmecides were the famous family of viziers who rose to the pinnacle of power under Hārūn al-Rashīd. Their wealth and their power became legendary. Like Ibn Naghrēla and his family, they met with a violent end.

[7] Al-Muᶜtaṣim b. Ṣumādiḥ was the ruler of Almería and a rival of the Sultan of Granada.

[8] He was king of Seville from 1042–69. He was Bādīs's most powerful rival among the party kings of Spain.

gave him a military appointment. Because of his desire for vengeance on the ᶜAbbadids, he acquitted himself well in the struggle for Malaga and won over some units of the army in the town where he held a command, which was under Muqātil b. Yaḥyā, the commanding general. This Muqātil, whenever a raiding party went out against the territory of Ibn ᶜAbbād, did not fail to report favorably to al-Muẓaffar [Bādīs] on al-Nāya's role in it, almost to the point of giving him the whole credit, so much so that he received a letter from the Sultan, making them associates. Al-Nāya thus became *qāᶜid*[9] in Malaga with Muqātil. His activity increased and his reputation grew. The Sultan redoubled his favors toward him, and when he went to Malaga he stayed at al-Nāya's house and drank in his company. As time passed, he favored and advanced him still further. Thanks to his intimacy with the Sultan, he would turn his mind against the Jew when he was alone with him or could take advantage of his drunkenness and say to him, "He has eaten your money, he has possessed himself of the greater part of your fortune, and he has built a finer palace than yours.[10] By Allah! You must get rid of him and earn the love of the Muslims by his removal." Al-Muẓaffar then made promises to him and said, "I must, indeed, do this, and I will give you the job of killing him." No doubt he uttered this in the hearing of some of his slaves or palace staff, to whom he paid no attention, and who, at once, went, to report it to the Jew.

That swine's rage and hatred only increased all the more, and he was almost dying with worry and anger, as well as his envy of al-Nāya for the high rank which he had attained to his own disadvantage. What he desired, above all, was to call him to account before the Sultan, but the Sultan was not willing. Seeing that al-Nāya's position became ever stronger and fearing that he would induce the Sultan to kill him, he lost all hope and said to himself, "It is only for the glory of the Sultan that I have treated the people with scorn, counting for my safety on his protection and care. But now, all hope is lost, and I cannot turn to the Sultan for protection. An evil companion incites him against me, the common people desire my death, and we (Jews) are few and feeble in the land."

He had already, before this time, tried to gain a hold over my uncle Māksan, in hope of being able to lean on him. But Māksan responded with the greatest hostility, having no one at his side to guide and instruct him in discretion. He even said to him, face to face, "Do you want to kill me as you killed my brother?" These words worked on the Jew's mind. In addi-

[9] That is, the military governor.

[10] In a fascinating, though somewhat controversial, book, Frederick Bargebuhr has argued that this fine palace was none other than the Alhambra. See Frederick P. Bargebuhr, *The Alhambra: A Cycle of Studies on the Eleventh Century in Moorish Spain* (Berlin, 1968).

tion to all this, Māksan displayed abominable conduct, little charity, and foul language. He uttered so many threats that the people of his father's court loathed and detested him, and there were many complaints about him to his father. His mother ceased to have dealings with the vizier who had tried to gain a hold over her son; instead, she preferred his maternal uncle, another Jew called Abu 'l-Rabīc b. al-Māṭūnī, the collector of revenue. She wrote to him all the time asking for advances of money without interest. The vizier became jealous and decided to take action against him, which would also be against Māksan's mother and entourage. He, therefore, brought a false accusation against them to the Sultan, and it was attested by a group of courtiers who were already hostile to Māksan, as I said above. The Sultan was incited against him to such effect that, revolted by what had been reported to him, he ordered the execution of Māksan's mother, his nurses, and some others connected with them. The vizier had his uncle killed by treachery, in his own house and while drinking, for having opposed him in this and other matters and for fear that he would advise the Sultan. He gave the Sultan a very large sum of money so that he should not condemn him for this murder. The Sultan accepted it from him and would have been glad for him to murder another Jew every day and pay him money for it.

Some time later al-Muẓaffar ordered his son's banishment. One of the chief causes of this banishment was the following incident: One day the Sultan went out to review the troops at the time of the conflict with Ibn Ṣumādiḥ. One of the shaykhs of the army went up to him and said, "It is not fitting for you to place Black slaves or other such at our head and to set aside your own son. Send him with us, and we shall follow him through every calamity." He was speaking of Māksan. This was too much for the father, already angry with him because of what he had seen and of what was reported to him about his son. He feared that behind these words there was a plan to put him aside and transfer power to his son. The Jew was also very alarmed at this and remarked later, "On that day I was sure that I would be put to death." He put the matter to the Sultan, who at once ordered his son's banishment from the country. He sent one of his slaves with him to escort him outside his territory. The Jew—whom Allah curse—advised this slave to take him to a certain place which he named and there, in secret, cut off his head. My brother al-Mucizz had been brought up by our grandfather and had been well treated by him, and the people of his father's household loved him. They all agreed with the Jew to kill Māksan and appoint al-Mucizz as heir, fearing for themselves, lest Māksan turn on them and punish them for loving his nephew and bringing him up. His banishment was, therefore, what they had hoped. My uncle thus left Granada in the worst circumstances, in fear and trembling. Some advised that he be put to death and others objected, demanding only that he be forbidden to remain in any part of the realm. In the end, he went by a certain route and was delivered from his troubles by the death of the Jew, which I shall relate in due course.

When this swine—whom Allah curse—saw the turbulence of the palace women, each group desiring the appointment as heir of whichever of the princes she had brought up, and seeing the change in his master's attitude toward him, the growing strength of al-Nāya, and his determination to destroy him, he could no longer find any escape in the world nor any way to save himself. He consulted the wise elders of his people and one of them said, "Save yourself and send ahead of you the greater part of your fortune to whatever part of the country you choose. You can then go to live there, rich and safe."

"That would be possible," he replied, "except that my exalted sovereign would send a message about me to the ruler of the country in which I had taken refuge, saying to him, 'My vizier has run away with my money. Either you return him or I make war against you.' Do you really think that he would then prefer me to the Sultan? It would only work if I could give him territory so that war would break out between the two of them. This would secure my safety with the ruler to whom I go. He would not be able to hand me over when I have brought him new territory and great glory."

They therefore agreed to approach Ibn Ṣumādiḥ, since he was the most suitable, being a neighbor and close at hand in case of need.

Ibn Ṣumādiḥ's envoy, Ibn Arqam, whom they had chosen for this mission, said: I was received one day by al-Muẓaffar—may Allah have mercy on him—in one of his pleasure palaces to which he had gone. Al-Nāya was with him, and the Jew was behind him. Al-Nāya noticed a Jewish doctor of the vizier. He gave orders that he should be insulted and forced to dismount in the presence of the sovereign. He behaved very insolently and subjected the Jew to violent abuse. The Jew was outraged and said to Ibn Arqam, "What do you think of this intolerable insult? If you can't help me, I shall have to look elsewhere." Ibn Arqam then said to him, "You are well able to stand firm in this affair. What need have you to turn to us when you control the population and the collection of taxes? The Sultan has changed nothing in your situation; these are no more than pinpricks from this slanderer. Contrive to be patient until the shaykh al-Muẓaffar dies, the more so since he is already old. Then you will get a hold over his grandson, al-Muᶜizz, and have the same position with him as you had with his grandfather. That is the best way to save yourself."

To this the Jew replied, "I would do what you say, but al-Muᶜizz is still very young. He is under the influence of the palace ladies, as well as of a large number of palace women of various kinds and their retinues. How can I hope to prevail against them? My situation in that case would be even worse because of their conflicting desires. What is more, I have sure knowledge that the young man hates me because of what people say about my having poisoned his father. I have already pondered on all these aspects of the matter, and I can see no better course before me than to offer myself to al-Muᶜtaṣim [Ibn Ṣumādiḥ]."

Ibn Arqam said: I went to see al-Muẓaffar, gave him some hint of this conversation, and said to him, "Allah help you—be on your guard! You are not all that old, and you have not yet reached an age which obliges you to neglect your affairs of state." I hoped by this to induce him to question me further about the conversation, so that I could tell him more of it. But he sent for the Jew and said to him, "Go find Ibn Arqam and ask him why he has just told me to be on my guard. Get him to explain it to you."

Ibn Arqam continued: The Jew came to me and informed me of the matter. I was appalled and could have dropped dead; I did not know what answer to give. The swine then suspected me, wrote to al-Muᶜtaṣim about me, and advised him to relieve me of my mission and send someone else whom he could trust. Al-Muᶜtaṣim chose his milk-brother and ordered him to concert with the Jew in devising a scheme to get the government of Granada into his hands, in spite of the fact that the city was a mine of troops and Ṣanhāja Berbers,[11] who would never acquiesce in this. The envoy said to the Jew, "Do not involve yourself and al-Muᶜtaṣim in something which cannot be carried through to the end and discredit yourself in the eyes of al-Muzaffar, who is rich and able to wage war. You would be the cause of your own destruction and al-Muᶜtaṣim's ruin." The swine, on this advice, decided to expel from Granada all those whose resistance he feared.

He therefore chose certain prominent persons among the Ṣanhāja and certain slaves from whom he expected trouble and advised the Sultan to send them to the principal castles with letters of appointment to them. He said to them in secret, "You are my brothers, for you have been thrust aside as I have; you have seen it yourselves. I see in the rule of this Sultan things which you are right to disapprove. He puts at your head men who are not of your kind or of your station. His rule will continue to bring you shame and dishonor for as long as it lasts. I have given the Sultan good advice on his affairs, but he has not accepted my advice, though he cannot refute it. Now danger threatens this noble land and he will hand over these fine castles to al-Nāya's men. We would all suffer by this, and we would not be able to prevail against them for the control of the state. They would have dominion over us, and we would have no recourse, except to al-Nāya himself. But if we hold firm in the castles while your kinsmen are at court, he will not dare to scatter you and he will soon lose all power. If he tries to change things, we shall kill him. If the Sultan be-

[11] The great Berber confederation from which the Zirids sprang.

comes angry with one of us and orders his banishment, he can come to a friend's castle."

They approved his words, the more readily because of their greed for governorships, and they hurried off to their posts. He sent Yaḥyā b. Ifrān to Almuñecar, Musakkan b. Ḥabbūs al-Maghralī to Jaen, and the rest to other provincial centers. The Jew persuaded the Sultan that this was to his advantage, that only leading men could defend important centers, and that the negligence and incompetence of the dismissed governors had been proved to him, for so great was his confidence in the Jew that he listened to no one but him on such matters.

The Jew then wrote to Ibn Ṣumādiḥ, to inform him that he had removed the troublemakers from the city, that no one was left there but people without importance whom his sword would mow down as when he entered, and that he was ready to open the gates of Granada to him as soon as he would venture his way. He deliberately neglected all the castles other than the provincial centers, and he omitted, as if by oversight, to send them the supplies and reinforcements which they needed, so that they were evacuated.

Meanwhile, al-Muẓaffar knew nothing of this and devoted himself to drink and idleness. Then the garrisons evacuated the castles, seeing that no one cared for them and that the Sultan no longer showed himself to them, accepting as truth the rumor that he was dead. Calling out to one another, they abandoned the castles and regions which they controlled. Ibn Ṣumādiḥ's troops seized the opportunity and occupied them, until the only castle which remained was that of Cabrera, near Granada, on the road to Guadix. The Jew at once sent a message to Ibn Ṣumādiḥ, urging him to march against the city, since there was no one to prevent him from doing so. But Ibn Ṣumādiḥ backed out of the enterprise, not daring to attack a city like Granada. Meanwhile, the breech grew wider and the upheavals increased. The Jew moved from his house to the casbah[12] to protect himself from the common people until his hopes were fulfilled. People held this against him as also his building the Alhambra with the intention of going there with his family when Ibn Ṣumādiḥ entered the city, and staying until order was restored.[13] Both the common people and the nobles were disgusted by the cunning of the Jews, the notorious changes which they had brought about in the order of things, and the positions which they occupied in violation of their pact. Allah decreed their destruction on Saturday, 10 Ṣafar 459 (December 31, 1066). The previous night the Jew had been

[12] The casbah (Ar., *qaṣaba*) was a fortified government administrative quarter.

[13] See above, n. 10.

drinking with some of al-Muẓaffar's slaves,[14] some who were his allies and confederates and some who secretly hated him. He told them about Ibn Ṣumādiḥ, who, he said, was coming and who would assign them such and such villages in the plain of Granada. One of those slaves who had concealed his enmity went up to him and said, "We know all that! Instead of assigning us estates, tell us if our master is alive or dead." Some of the Jew's followers restrained him and rebuked him for having spoken thus. The slave went out in disgust and ran away, drunken and shouting to the people, "All you who are loyal to al-Muẓaffar! The Jew has betrayed him and this Ibn Ṣumādiḥ is entering the city!" Everybody, the common people and the nobles alike, listened to these words, and they came determined to kill the Jew. He contrived to get al-Muẓaffar to appear before them and said to them "Here is your Sultan, alive!" The sovereign tried to calm them, but could not, and the situation got out of hand. The Jew fled into the interior of the palace, but the mob pursued him there, seized him, and killed him. They then put every Jew in the city to the sword and took vast quantities of their property.

After this, the Ṣanhāja became bold and insolent toward their sovereign, who was faced with rebellion on every side. They became viziers and the real rulers of the state. As a result of all this, al-Muẓaffar was full of fear and ignominy. He hated them for what they had done to his vizier, knowing nothing of his misdeeds and not believing what they said about him. He put up with them as best he could, with fair words and with patience, until his lands were conquered and his authority restored, as I shall relate later, please God.

Sultan ᶜAbd Allāh of Granada,
Kitāb al-Tibyān, trans. Bernard Lewis, in *Islam,* vol. 1, 265–74.

[14] This scene is recounted in colorful detail in Eliyahu Ashtor, *The Jews of Moslem Spain,* vol. 2 (Jerusalem, 1966), pp. 116–17 [Heb.], where the main source is our narrative here. For a slightly different version of the events surrounding Ibn Naghrēla's assassination, see Ibn ᶜIdhārī, *al-Bayān al-Mughrib,* vol. 3, ed. E. Lévi-Provençal (Paris, 1930), pp. 265–66.

A MEDIEVAL CURRICULUM OF ADVANCED JEWISH AND SECULAR STUDIES
(LATE TWELFTH CENTURY)

Reading and Writing: The method of instruction must be so arranged that the teacher will begin first with the script, in order that the children may learn their letters, and this is to be kept up until there is no longer any uncertainty among them. This script is, of course, the "Assyrian,"[1] the use of which has been agreed upon by our ancestors. Then he is to teach them to write until their script is clear and can be read easily. He should not however keep them too long at work striving for beauty, decorativeness, and special elegance of penmanship. On the contrary, that which we have already mentioned will be sufficient.

Torah, Mishnah, and Hebrew Grammar: Then he is to teach them the Pentateuch, Prophets, and Hagiographa, that is the Bible, with an eye to the vocalization and modulation in order that they may be able to pronounce the accents correctly. Then he is to have them learn the Mishna until they have acquired a fluency in it. "Teach thou it to the children of Israel; put it in their mouths" (Deut. 31:19). The teacher is to continue this until they are ten years of age, for the sages said, "At five years the age is reached for the study of the Scriptures, at ten for the study of the Mishna" (Avot. 5:21). The children are then taught the inflections, declensions, and conjugations, the regular verbs . . . and other rules of grammar.

Poetry: Then the teacher is to instruct his pupils in poetry. He should, for the most part, have them recite religious poems and whatever else of beauty is found in the different types of poetry, and is fit to develop in them all good qualities.

Talmud: Then say the wise: "At fifteen the age is reached for the study of Talmud" (Avot 5:21). Accordingly when the pupils are fifteen years of age the teacher should give them much practice in Talmud reading until they have acquired fluency in it. Later, when they are eighteen years of age, he should give them that type of instruction in it which lays emphasis on deeper understanding, independent thinking, and investigation.

Philosophic Observations on Religion: When the students have spent considerable time in study which is directed toward deeper comprehension and thoroughness, so that their mental powers have been strengthened; when the Talmud has become so much a part of them that there is hardly any chance of its being lost, and they are firmly entrenched in the Torah

[1] What is meant is the Aramaic square script that has been standard for Hebrew for the past two millennia.

and the practice of its commands; then the teacher is to impart to them the third necessary subject. This is the refutation of the errors of apostates and heretics and the justification of those views and practices which the religion prescribes.

Philosophic Studies: These studies are divided into three groups. The first group is normally dependent on matter, but can, however, be separated from matter through concept and imagination. This class comprises the mathematical sciences. In the second group speculation cannot be conceived of apart from the material, either through imagination or conception. To this section belong the natural sciences. The third group has nothing to do with matter and has no material attributes; this group includes in itself metaphysics as such.

Logic: But these sciences are preceded by logic which serves as a help and instrument. It is through logic that the speculative activities, which the three groups above mentioned include, are made clear. Logic presents the rules which keep the mental powers in order, and lead man on the path of clarity and truth in all things wherein he may err.

Mathematics, Arithmetic: The teacher will then lecture to his students on mathematics, beginning with arithmetic or geometry, or instruct them in both sciences at the same time.

Optics: Then the students are introduced into the third of the mathematical sciences, namely optics.

Astronomy: Then they pass on to astronomy. This includes two sciences. First, astrology, that is, the science wherein the stars point to future events as well as to many things that once were or now are existent. Astrology is no longer numbered among the real sciences. It belongs only to the forces and secret arts by means of which man can prophesy what will come to pass, like the interpretation of dreams, fortune-telling, auguries, and similar arts. This science, however, is forbidden by God. . . . The second field of astronomy is mathematical. This field is to be included among mathematics and the real sciences. This science concerns itself with the heavenly bodies and the earth.

Music: After studying the science of astronomy the teacher will lecture on music to his students. Music embraces instruction in the elements of the melodies and that which is connected with them, how melodies are linked together, and what condition is required to make the influence of music most pervasive and effective.

Mechanics: This includes two different things. For one thing it aims at the consideration of heavy bodies insofar as they are used for measurements. . . . The second part includes the consideration of heavy bodies insofar as they may be moved or insofar as they are used for moving. It treats, therefore, of the principles concerning instruments whereby heavy objects are raised and whereby they are moved from one place to another.

Natural Sciences, Medicine: Let us now speak of the second section of the philosophic disciplines, that is, the natural sciences. After the students have assimilated the sciences already mentioned the teachers should instruct them in the natural sciences. The first of this group that one ought to learn is medicine, that is, the art which keeps the human constitution in its normal condition, and which brings back to its proper condition the constitution which has departed from the normal. This latter type of activity is called the healing and cure of sickness, while the former is called the care of the healthy. This art falls into two parts, science and practice.

After the students have learned this art the teacher should lecture to them on the natural sciences as such. This discipline investigates natural bodies and all things whose existence is incidentally dependent on these bodies. This science also makes known those things out of which, by which, and because of which these bodies and their attendant phenomena come into being.

Metaphysics: After this one should concern oneself with the study of metaphysics, that which Aristotle has laid down in his work, *Metaphysics.* This science is divided into three parts. The first part investigates "being" and whatever happens to it insofar as it is "being." The second part investigates the principles with respect to proofs which are applied to the special speculative sciences. These are those sciences, each one of which elucidates, along speculative lines, a definite discipline, as for instance, logic, geometry, arithmetic, and the other special sciences which are similar to those just mentioned.

Furthermore, this part investigates the principles of logic, of the mathematical sciences, and of natural science, and seeks to make them clear, to state their peculiarites, and to enumerate the false views which have existed with respect to the principles of these sciences. In the third part there is an investigation of those entities which are not bodies nor a force in bodies.

This is the first among sciences. All the other sciences, which are but the groundwork of philosophy, have this discipline in mind.

Joseph b. Judah Ibn ᶜAqnīn, *Ṭibb al-Nufūs,*
trans. Jacob R. Marcus, in
The Jew in the Medieval World (New York, 1974), pp. 374–77.

FROM THE AUTOBIOGRAPHY OF A JEWISH APOSTATE
(TWELFTH CENTURY)

I should like to recount how Allah granted me Guidance,[1] and how circumstances were leading me ever since I was born to leave the way of the Jews, that this should be an example and an exhortation to whomever it reaches.

My father was called Rav Judah b. Abūn. He was from the city of Fez in Morocco. . . . He was one of the most learned people of his time in the sciences of the Torah, and he was a great master, prolific in composition, and an unmatched extemporizer in Hebrew poetry and prose. The name by which he was addressed in Arabic-speaking society was Abu 'l-Baqā' Yaḥyā b. ᶜAbbās al-Maghribī. . . . He married my mother in Baghdad. She was originally from Basra and was one of three sisters who were distinguished in the study of Torah and Hebrew calligraphy.[2] They were the daughters of Isaac b. Abraham ha-Levi of Basra. . . . This Isaac was a man of learning who taught in Baghdad. Their mother was Nafīsa b. Abī Naṣr al-Dāwūdī,[3] of the line of one of the famous leaders, whose descendants are still living in Egypt.

. . . .

My father had me learn Hebrew calligraphy, then the sciences of the Torah and its exegesis until I had mastered this by the age of thirteen. He next set me to study Indian arithmetic and the solution of astronomical calculations with the Shaykh and Master Abu 'l-Ḥasan b. al-Daskarī, to read medical works with the philosopher Abu 'l-Barakāt Hibat Allāh b. ᶜAlī, and to observe the treatment of diseases and up-to-date surgical techniques as practiced by my maternal uncle Abu 'l-Fatḥ b. al-Baṣrī. I mastered the study of Indian arithmetic and astronomical calculations in less than a year at the age of fourteen, but I continued reading medical texts and observing the treatment of diseases. Then I studied administrative accounting and surveying with the Shaykh Abu 'l-Muẓaffar al-Shahrazūrī. I also studied algebra and equations with him and with the Secretary Ibn Abī

[1] Ar., *al-hudā* is an Islamic technical term.

[2] Although it was unusual for daughters to be given such an education, it was by no means unheard of. The daughter of Gaon Samuel b. Eli (1164–93) taught her father's students both Bible and Talmud. Concerning the education of girls in medieval Jewish society, see S. D. Goitein, *Mediterranean Society*, vol. 2, pp. 183–85.

[3] That is, his maternal grandmother came from a house claiming Davidic origin.

Turāb. I frequented the Master Abu 'l-Ḥasan b. al-Daskarī and Abu 'l-Ḥasan b. al-Naqqāsh to study geometry, until I was able to solve the problems from Euclid that they could solve. And all the while I continued to devote myself to medicine. . . . There remained parts of the Book of Euclid, the Book of al-Wāsiṭī on arithmetic, and al-Karkhī's book on algebra, *al-Badī*ᶜ, for which I could find no one who knew anything, nor who knew anything in the mathematical sciences beyond these—as for example, Shujaᶜ b. Aslam's book on algebra and equations, etc.

I had such a deep passion for these sciences that while engrossed in them I was diverted from any thought of food or drink. I remained secluded in my room for a period of time trying to solve the problems in all of these books and analyzing them. I even refuted errors made by their authors, demonstrated mistakes by the redactors, and resolved to verify and correct their works. . . . I was even able to put Euclid to shame for his arrangement of forms in his book. For when I rearranged the order of his forms, I was able to dispense with a number of them which had become superfluous. . . . All this I achieved by the age of eighteen.

During this time my only income came from the art of medicine, and I prospered greatly from it.

Before becoming occupied with these sciences, I was fascinated by histories and narratives. This was during my twelfth and thirteenth years. I avidly sought to learn about what had happened in ancient times and to gain knowledge of what had occurred in bygone ages. So I studied collected works of tales and anecdotes of all sorts. Then I passed from this to a love for books of bedtime stories and tall tales. Then I went over to large collections such as the *Tales of ᶜAntar, Dhu 'l-Himma, al-Baṭṭāl, Alexander Dhu 'l-Qarnayn, al-Anqā', Ṭaraf b. Lūdhān,*[4] and others. It became clear to me after reading these that most of them were based on the works of historians. I therefore sought the authentic historical narratives. I turned my attention to the histories and read Miskawayh's *The Experiences of the Nations, The Annals* of Ṭabarī and other histories.

There would pass before me in these historical works accounts of the Prophet—may Allah bless him and grant him peace—his razzias, the miracles Allah revealed to him, the wondrous deeds with which He endowed him, the victory and support which He granted him at Badr and Khaybar and elsewhere. I read the account of his origins as a poor orphan, the enmity of his own people for him, and how for many years he would in the midst of his adversaries openly declare his rejection of the religion they then held and summoned them to his faith, until finally Allah allowed

[4] Along with the *Thousand and One Nights* these tales were the popular romances in the Islamic world from the Middle Ages to modern times.

him to emigrate to another home. I saw what disasters befell those enemies who had striven against him, how they were struck down before him by the swords of his friends at Badr and other battles. I saw the revelation of the marvelous verse which foretold the defeat of the Persians and mighty Rustum with them at the head of many thousands. Though they constituted an enormous mass of forces, they were routed by Saᶜd b. Abī Waqqāṣ and his small band of companions. I read about the dream of Chosroes Anushirvan, the collapse of the Byzantines and the destruction of their armies at the hands of Abū ᶜUbayda b. al-Jarrāḥ—Allah's mercy be upon him. Then I read about the leadership of Abū Bakr and ᶜUmar—may Allah be pleased with them—and about their justice and their asceticism.

I came to see the inimitability of the Koran with which human eloquence cannot even compete. I knew the truth of its inimitable nature. Then, when I had improved my mind by the study of the mathematical sciences, in particular geometry and its proofs, I began to reconsider the differences among men in religions and rites. . . . I perceived that reason is the sole arbiter which should be permitted to rule in earthly affairs. Were it not for reason having guided us to follow the prophets and apostles and to believe elders and ancestors, we would certainly not accept the truth of that which has come down to us from them. I further perceived that if the dictates of reason are the basis for adhering to the religions inherited from our forefathers and for following the prophets, then the rule of reason must be granted in all that pertains to that. However, if we apply reason as the main criterion of tradition which has been transmitted to us from our forefathers, we realize that reason does not require us to accept the transmission from our forebears without testing its soundness. . . . It is no proof simply to invoke the forefathers and ancestors. Since if this were a proof, it would also be a proof for all the nonbelieving opponents as well—as the Christians, for example. . . . Thus, if blind imitation of ancestors were an indicator of the correctness of what has been transmitted on their authority, then that would require the acceptance of Christian and Zoroastrian doctrines as well.

Let us suppose that it could be argued that Jewish adherence to their ancestral tradition is a special case different from that of other nations. This could not be accepted unless they brought forth some proof that their ancestors were more intelligent than the forebears of other peoples. Indeed, the Jews do claim that with regard to their ancestors; however, all the historical accounts concerning their forefathers belie them in this claim. Thus, if we put aside any partisanship for them, we find ourselves putting their ancestors on a par with forebears of all other nations.

When it became obvious to me that the Jews were the same as others with regard to what had been transmitted to them from their ancestors, I realized that they possessed no actual proof for the prophethood of Moses except the chain of transmission. But such a chain of transmission exists for Jesus and Muḥammad, just as it does for Moses—peace be upon them all. And if a chain of transmission can serve as confirmation, then all three are true and the prophethood of each is authentic. . . . Neither reason nor wisdom permit us to believe one of them and reject the others. Rather, reason dictates that all must be accepted as true or rejected as false. As to rejecting all as false, reason does not dictate that either.

Thus I was convinced by incontrovertible proof of the prophethood of Jesus and of Muḥammad—may Allah bless and protect them—and I came to believe in them. Although I was convinced of this, I held back for some time from undertaking the religious duties of Islam out of respect for my father. That is because he loved me dearly, could hardly bear to be without me, and was extremely devoted to me. So I remained for a long time without Divine Guidance being revealed to me. This confusion caused by respect for my father did not leave me until my travels separated me from him and my place of residence became far from his. I still persisted in my respect for him and tried to avoid distressing him on my account.

But the time for Guidance arrived. The Divine exhortation came to me in a vision of the Prophet—may Allah bless and protect him—which appeared in a dream on Friday night, the ninth of Dhu 'l-Ḥijja 558 (8 November 1163). This occurred in Marāgha in Azerbayjan.

al-Samaw'al al-Maghribī, "Islām al-Samaw'al al-Maghribī," *Ifḥām al-Yahūd*. Ar. text ed. Moshe Perlmann, in *PAAJR* 32 (1964): 94–106.

MAIMONIDES' EPISTLE TO THE JEWS OF YEMEN
(1172)

(Hebrew Introduction:)

To his honor, our great and holy master and teacher, the wise, discerning, and dearly beloved Jacob, the son of our great and holy master and teacher, Nathaniel Fayyūmī, the distinguished Nagid of Yemen, Head of the Congregations, and Patrician of the Communities. May the Spirit of the Lord rest upon him, encompassing all who are associated with him and all the scholars of the communities of Yemen. May their Rock protect and shield them. From one who loves him, having heard his reputation, though never having seen him, Moses b. Maimon.

Just as the stock bears witness to the true quality of the roots, and just as the flowing waters testify to the goodness of the springs, so has a faithful shoot flowered from the roots of truth and righteousness, and a great river has flowed forth from the spring of lovingkindness in the land of Yemen, watering all gardens and causing buds to flourish. . . . Merchants and traders unanimously tell all who ask that they have found among the inhabitants of Yemen a lovely and pleasing plantation, a good pasture in which the emaciated are fattened and in which their shepherds are faithful. Indeed, they are a source of strength for the poor, giving them bread, and they generously provide hospitality for the wealthy. The caravans of Saba'[1] look toward them in anticipation. Their hands are extended to every wayfarer, and their homes are open wide. Everyone finds respite amongst them. They dispel sorrow and sighs. They study the Torah of Moses daily. They walk upon the path which Rav Ashi has taught. They pursue justice, repair the breaches, and uphold the principles of the Torah in their place. They gather the dispersed of the Lord's people with their encouragement. They meticulously observe all the commandments in their communities. "There is no breach, and no going forth, and no outcry in their broad places" (Ps. 114:14)[2].

Praised be the Lord who has not allowed the extermination of those who uphold the Torah and keep its laws even in the farthest land masses as we are promised in His goodness and mercy by Isaiah, His servant: "From the uttermost part of the earth have we heard songs." (Isaiah 24:16).

You stated in your letter, dear friend, that you have heard some of our brethren—may their Rock preserve them—praise me profusely again and again, comparing me to the illustrious Geonim. It is only out of affection that they have spoken, and merely in their kindness and graciousness that

[1] One of the provinces of Yemen, and the biblical Sheba.
[2] Slightly paraphrased by Maimonides to refer to the Yemenites.

they have written such things. Listen to "a word fitly spoken"[3] by me, and pay no attention to anyone else. I am the least of the least of the scholars of Spain whose splendor has been brought low by exile. And though I am always persevering in my duties, nevertheless, I have not achieved the learning of my forefathers.

With regard to the matters in your letter for which you requested an answer, I deemed it best to respond in Arabic so that everyone—men, women, and children—may read it with ease. It is important that the contents of my reply be thoroughly understood in each and every one of your congregations.

(Arabic Reply:)

You have mentioned the affair of this rebel[4] who has arisen in the land of Yemen and who has decreed forced apostasy upon Israel, compelling people in all the places that have come under his sway to abandon the Faith, just as the Berbers in the Maghreb. This news has broken our backs and has stunned and bewildered all of our community. Rightly so! since this is evil news "the ears of all who hear it shall tingle" (1 Sam. 3:11). Our hearts have been weakened, our thoughts confused, and our strength sapped on account of these terrible calamities which have brought forced apostasy upon us at two ends of the earth, the East and the West, "so that the enemies were in the midst of Israel, some on this side and some on that" (Josh. 8:22). It was concerning such terrible times as these that the Prophet prayed and interceded for us saying, "Lord God, cease I beseech Thee: How shall Jacob stand? for he is small" (Amos 7:5). This is a matter which no religious man may take lightly, nor anyone who has faith in Moses brush aside. There can be no doubt that these are the Birth Pangs of the Messiah which the sages—peace be upon them—prayed God that they should be spared from seeing or experiencing.[5] The prophets would tremble when they envisioned them, as for example, Isaiah, who said when he described them: "My heart is bewildered, terror has overwhelmed me; the twilight that I longed for has been turned for me into trembling" (Isa. 21:4). Furthermore, God in His scripture has proclaimed woe unto him who witnesses it: "Alas, who shall live after God has appointed him?" (Num. 24:23).[6]

[3] Prov. 25:11.

[4] Al-Malik al-Muᶜizz Ismāᶜīl. Until recently, most scholars have identified this unnamed *al-qā'im* (literally, "one who has arisen") with ᶜAbd al-Nabi' b. Mahdī (d. 1175) of the Mahdid dynasty of Zabid. This identification was based on a reference to an Ibn Mahdī below (see n. 19). From the two Geniza letters translated below, pp. 247–50; however, it appears that the forced conversion took place later.

[5] See the rabbinic discussion of the Pangs of the Messiah in Sandhedrin 98b.

[6] In the Yemenite midrashim *Or ha-afēla* and *Midrash Ḥēfeṣ,* this passage

You have mentioned the fact that some people's hearts have been turned aside, that doubt has befallen them, and their belief has been shaken, while others continue to believe and are not shaken. Concerning this matter, we already have the clear warning of our lord Daniel to whom God revealed that if we were to remain for a long time in the Diaspora and be exposed to successive persecutions, then many would abandon the Faith, fall into doubt, and go astray. That is because they have seen our weakness and the triumph of our adversaries and their dominion over us. Others, however, have not fallen into doubt nor have betrayed their belief. This is as Daniel has said, "Many shall purify themselves, and make themselves white, and be refined; but the wicked shall do wickedly; and none of the wicked shall understand; but they that are wise shall understand" (Dan. 12:10).

And now, my brethren, you must all hearken to what I am about to say to you and carefully reflect upon it. You should inculcate your women and children with it so that any weakness or defect in their belief will be made firm, and a sure faith which cannot be moved will be established in their hearts.

What I have to say (may God deliver us and you) is this: Verily, this is the authentic religion of truth. It was revealed to us by the master of all the prophets, early and late. Through it, God has distinguished us from all the rest of mankind, as He has said: "Only the Lord had a delight in your fathers to love them, and He chose their seed after them, even you above all peoples" (Deut. 10:15). This was not because of any worthiness on our part, but rather, it was due to divine favor upon us because our forefathers had first come to recognize Him and obey Him, as He has said: "It is not because you are the most numerous of peoples that the Lord set his heart on you" (Deut. 7:7). Because He has singled us out by His laws and precepts, and because our preeminence has been established over all others by His statutes and ordinances, all the nations have risen up against us out of envy for our religion and a desire to suppress it. For this reason, the kings of the earth have devoted themselves to tyrannically and malevolently pursuing us. They seek to oppose God, but He cannot be opposed! From that time (of the Revelation) until now, every obstinate, tyrant king or mighty conqueror has made his first goal and primary concern the destruction of our religious law, and the abolition of our faith by coercion and force of arms, as did Amalek, Sisera, Sennacherib, Nebuchadnezzar, Titus, Hadrian, and others like them. These men represent one of the two classes which strive to overcome the Divine Will.

The second class consists of the cleverest and most educated nations,

---

is understood as referring to the Pangs of the Messiah. See Maimonides, *Iggeret Tēmān,* ed. Halkin, p. 5, no. 5.

such as the Syrians, Persians, and the Greeks. They too sought to destroy the religious law and to eradicate it through arguments they concocted and by polemics which they composed. They strove to abolish the religious law by their polemical compositions, just as conquerors have tried to do by their swords. But neither the one nor the other shall succeed![7]

Later, there arose another faction which combined both approaches, namely physical subjection, as well as argumentation and debate. It seemed that this was more effective for eradicating any trace of our people. This group contrived to lay claim to prophecy and to bring forth a religious law contrary to the law of God, while asserting that it too was from God just like the true Word. This would create doubt and cause confusion since one contradicted the other, while at the same time both were supposed to be derived from a single Deity.

The first to take up this course was Jesus the Nazarene—may his bones be ground to dust. He was of Israel.

Later, there arose a madman[8] who followed his example since he had paved the way for him. However, he added a further object, namely to seek dominion and complete submission to himself; and what he has established is well known.

All of these men have sought to make religions comparable to the Religion of God—praised be He. But Divine handiwork would resemble human handiwork only for a gullible person who has no knowledge of either. Furthermore, the difference between our religion and the others which resemble it is like the difference between living rational beings and a graven image so expertly fashioned of marble, wood, silver, or gold that it almost resembles a man. Thus when a person who is ignorant of heavenly wisdom or divine work sees a statue which by its outward appearance closely resembles a man in its shape, its features, its proportions, and its coloring, he may think that this workmanship is just like the divine crafting of the human form because of his ignorance of the internal nature of each. As for the wise man who knows what is inside each of them, he perceives that the interior of this graven image possesses no masterly craftsmanship whatsoever, whereas inside the man are true wonders and things which indicate the wisdom of the Creator, such as the extension of the nerves into

[7] Heb., *ve-lo' zeh yiṣlaḥ ve-lo' zeh yiṣlaḥ.*

[8] Medieval Jewish writers commonly referred to Muḥammad as *ha-meshuggac*. The term was pregnant with connotations. In the Bible, it was used contemptuously for those who think themselves prophets (Jer. 29:26; Hos. 9:7). Furthermore, because the pagans of Mecca believed Muḥammad to be just another poet or soothsayer "possessed" by a spirit, the Koran states in several places that Muḥammad is not *majnūn* (mad, or possessed). See, for example, Sura 81:22.

the muscles and their branching out, the twisting of the sinews, their points of connection, the intertwining of the ligaments, and the way they grow, the articulation of the bones and limbs, the network of pulsating and nonpulsating blood vessels and their divisions, the placement of the organs, some with others, internally and externally, every aspect of these in its proportion, form, and proper place.

Likewise, when a person ignorant of the secrets of the inspired Scripture and the inner meanings of our religious law compares this religious law to the one which was fabricated, he might imagine that there is a similarity between them since he will find in both prohibited and permissible things, acts of worship, negative and positive commandments, promises of reward and admonitions of punishment. If only he understood the inner secrets, then he would realize that all the wisdom of the true divine Law is in its esoteric meaning, and that there are no mere positive and negative commandments, but rather matters which are beneficial for human perfection, which remove any impediment to the achievement of such perfection, and which produce moral and rational qualities in the masses to the full measure of their potential and in the elite in accordance with their attainments.[9] Through these, the godly community becomes preeminent in two sorts of perfection at once. The first sort of perfection to which I am referring is for a man to achieve an uninterrupted state of existence in this world under the best and most suitable conditions for a human being. The second sort of perfection is the comprehension of the intelligible to the full measure of human capacity.

As for the religious systems which resemble the true one—they have no inner contents, only mere imitations, pale resemblances, and vague similarities.

We have already received a warning concerning the present danger from God Exalted through Daniel that at some future time there would arise a man who would bring a religion resembling the true faith. He would come with a scripture and an oral tradition. He would make grandiose claims, namely, that his scripture was revealed to him from heaven, and that he conversed with God, as well as many other statements. In his description of the rise of the Arab dominion in the latter days of the Byzantine Empire, Daniel referred to the rise of the Madman and his conquest of Rome, Persia, and Greece in the parable of a horn which grew, became long and powerful. This is clearly indicated in the scriptural text for both the masses and the elite because its meaning has been revealed by actual events and cannot sustain any other interpretation: "I considered the horns, and, behold, there came up among them another horn, a little

[9] This theme is developed by Maimonides throughout his *Guide of the Perplexed,* Eng. trans. Shlomo Pines (Chicago, 1963).

one, before which three of the first horns were plucked up by the roots; and, behold, in this horn were the eyes of a man, and a mouth speaking great things" (Dan. 7:8).

The Exalted One, Whose Name is Glorious, revealed to Daniel that He would destroy that man (Muḥammad, and by extension Islam) after he had attained greatness and longstanding power, and with him those followers of his predecessor [Jesus] who still remained.

God Exalted promised the Patriarch Jacob that even if his descendants were humiliated and subjected by the nations, they would live on after them and survive them.

God Exalted has assured us via the prophets that we shall not perish, we shall not be annihilated, nor shall we cease to be preeminent as a religious community. Just as God's existence cannot be negated, so we cannot be destroyed or made to disappear from the world, as He has said, "For I the Lord change not, and you, o sons of Jacob, will not be consumed" (Mal. 3:6).

Therefore, put your trust in these verses which speak truly, o my brethren. Do not let any series of persecutions, or the victory of enemies over us, or the weakness of our prestige, dismay you. For all this is to test and to purify us so that only the saints and the pious of the pure, unsullied seed of Jacob will steadfastly adhere to the Faith, as it is written, "And among the remnant are those whom the Lord shall call" (Joel 3:5).

Therefore, all of you our brethren of Israel scattered in the Diaspora must encourage one another. The elder should guide the younger, and the elite the masses. You should join together in acknowledging the truth which is unchanging and immutable. . . . Keep in mind the theophany at Mount Sinai, which God commanded us to remember always and warned us never to forget. Furthermore, He enjoined us to teach our children about it so that they grow up with a knowledge of it. . . . It behooves you, my brethren, to enhance your children's imagination of that great spectacle and to discuss its significance and its miraculous nature at every gathering. For this is the very pivot of our religion and the proof which leads one to certainty.

You mentioned the affair of the renegade[10] who has deluded people into believing that the biblical verses Genesis 17:20,[11] Deuteronomy 33:1,[12]

[10] Jud.–Ar., *al-pōshēa*[c]. This was the standard term for an apostate or renegade in medieval Jewish usage, although it is not found in this sense in any Hebrew dictionary. See S. D. Goitein's remarks in *Mediterranean Society*, vol. 2, pp. 300 and 591, n. 4.

[11] "And as for Ishmael, I have heeded you. I hereby bless him. I will make him fruitful and exceedingly numerous. He shall be the father of twelve chieftains, and I will make of him a great nation."

[12] "He appeared from Mount Paran."

and Deuteronomy 18:15,[13] all refer to the Madman. These are tired arguments which have been repeated again and again. . . . Nay, even to cite them as proofs is laughable and totally absurd.

These arguments need not cause any confusion at all even in the minds of the gullible masses. Even the renegades themselves who dupe others with them are not deluded or deceived by them. Their only intent in citing these passages is to gain honor among the Gentiles and to show them that they believe in the statement in the Koran that the Madman is mentioned in the Torah.[14] However, the Muslims themselves do not believe these proofs. They neither accept them nor cite them, because they are so obviously unsound. Since they could not find any proof whatsoever in all of the Torah, nor any verse or allusion which they might latch on to, their only recourse was to say that we had changed and altered the text of the Torah and deleted that man's name (Muḥammad) from it.

(Maimonides proceeds at length to rebut the interpretations of the biblical texts cited by renegades.)

Now you mentioned various attempts at reckoning the End of Days and what our master Saadya[15] (of blessed memory) had to say about it. The first thing you should know is that it is not possible for any human to ever come to know it exactly, as Daniel has clearly pointed out, "For the words are shut up and sealed" (Dan. 12:9). Some scholars have brought forth a wealth of notions about this, and have even imagined that they had come up with the precise answer. . . . God has revealed through His prophets that many would arise who would reckon the End of Days when the Messiah will come, but they would be frustrated and fail. However, He warned against falling into doubt on account of this.

I see that you are inclined to accept astrology and the belief in the influence of planetary conjunctions, past and future. You should remove any thought of this from your mind, and cleanse your imagination as you would wash clothes stained with filth. For these are matters which are not accepted as true by genuine scholars, including those who are not religious, much less those who are.

I have also noted your remark that scholarship is scarce in your country and that you are cut off from wisdom. You placed the blame for this upon a

[13] "The Lord your God will raise up for you a prophet from among your own people."

[14] Sura 7:157/156. See also above, p. 131. For the best summary in English of the arguments employed in these polemics, see Moshe Perlmann, "The Medieval Polemics between Islam and Judaism," in *Religion in a Religious Age* (Cambridge, Mass., 1974), pp. 103–38.

[15] For Saadya's calculations of the End of Days, see Samuel Poznanski, "Die Berechnung des Erlösungsjahres bei Saadja," *MGWJ* 44 (1900): 400–16 and 508–29.

conjunction in the earthly trigon.[16] However, you should know that this state of affairs is not exclusive to your country, but rather is found throughout all Israel today.

(Maimonides goes on at length to refute the validity of astrology for determining the arrival of the Messianic Age.)

One of our well-versed scholars in Spain once reckoned the End of Days by means of astrology. He determined that the Messiah would appear in a specific year. There was not a single one of our scholars and men of distinction who did not brand his view as foolish, point out that he was incapable of doing such a thing, and censure him severely. But reality dealt with him much more harshly than we did, because at the time he had predicted that the Messiah would appear, there appeared instead a rebel in the Maghreb who instituted the forced conversion about which you know only too well.[17] This was the ultimate disgrace for the adherents of this view. It is the hardship of exile which has caused us to resort to all these things, just as a drowning man grasps at straws.[18]

However, my brethren, stand firm! "Be strong and let your heart take courage, all you that wait for the Lord" (Ps. 31:25). Strengthen one another, and establish the belief in the Awaited One—may he appear speedily—firmly in your hearts.

You made mention of a man who has been claiming that he is the Messiah throughout the Yemenite countryside. Upon my life, I am not surprised by this or by the fact that he has followers. He is without a doubt insane, and a sick man can neither be blamed nor censured for his illness, since it is due to no fault of his own. That he has followers is due to their distress and to their ignorance of the Messiah's true rank and exalted status. They think his rise is comparable to that of Ibn Mahdī[19] which they have just witnessed. However, I am amazed at your saying that perhaps he is genuine—you, who are a scholar and who have studied the teachings of the sages! Do you not know, my brother, that the Messiah is an august prophet, greater than all the prophets after Moses our master? . . . How astounding for you to say that he is renowned for his

[16] The twelve signs of the zodiac were divided into four groups of three, each group called a trigon (Ar., *muthallatha*). Each trigon was associated with one of the four elements: earth, fire, water, air.

[17] Maimonides is referring to the forced conversions under the early Almohad rulers ᶜAbd al-Mu'min (d. 1165), Abū Yaᶜqūb (d. 1184), and al-Manṣūr (d. 1199).

[18] Ar., *wa 'l-ghāriq bi-kull ḥabl yataᶜallaq* (literally, "a drowning man will hang on to any cord").

[19] This is either a reference to a Mahdid pretender who had recently arisen (ᶜAbd al-Nabi' and his two brothers had been executed by Saladin's brother, Tūrānshāh, early in 1175), or perhaps to al-Malik al-Muᶜizz.

modesty and his limited education! Are these the attributes of a Messiah? You were forced into this conclusion because you did not give proper consideration to the question of the Messiah's rank, how and where he is to arise, and what are his distinguishing signs.

(Maimonides goes on to describe the qualities of the true Messiah and the signs by which he may be recognized.)

Everything considered, I would say that had this man made his messianic claims out of wickedness and contumely, I would be compelled to judge him worthy of death. But it seems more likely to me—indeed it is surely the case—that he has become unbalanced and lost his mind. I would advise you that in my opinion the best thing, for your sakes as well as for his, would be to chain him for a period of time until it becomes known to all the Gentiles that he has lost his mind. You yourselves should spread this about and let it become known among the people. Then you may let him go. You will, first of all, save his life by this, because when the Gentiles hear his claims after this, they will simply laugh at him and consider him mad—which he is. You will also save yourselves from being harmed by the Gentiles. But if you leave this matter until the Gentiles learn of it, you will be causing his death, and perhaps be inundated yourselves by their wrath.

You know, my brethren, that on account of our sins God has cast us into the midst of this people, the nation of Ishmael, who persecute us severely, and who devise ways to harm us and to debase us.[20] This is as the Exalted had warned us: "Even our enemies themselves being judges" (Deut. 32:31). No nation has ever done more harm to Israel. None has matched it in debasing and humiliating us. None has been able to reduce us as they have. Thus, when David King of Israel was inspired by the Divine Spirit to envision all these persecutions which would be visited upon Israel, he cried out, wailed, and appealed for deliverance specifically from the Dominion of Ishmael, saying, "Woe is me, that I sojourn in Meshech, that I dwell beside the tents of Kedar!" (Ps. 120:5). Note that he specifies Kedar, rather than the Ishmaelites generally. This is because the Madman was from the tribe of Kedar[21] as is well known from his genealogy. Daniel, too, has depicted our humiliation and debasement till we would become

[20] Maimonides is referring to the restrictions imposed on *dhimmīs* by the Pact of ᶜUmar. See above, pp. 157–58.

[21] Maimonides is equating Kedar (Heb., *qedar*) with the tribe of Quraysh. The medieval exegete and grammarian David Qimḥī (d. ca. 1235), in his commentary on Psalms interprets this verse as referring to the Diaspora in Islamic lands (*ha-gālūt asher be-Yishmāᶜēl*). He goes on to explain that Kedar is specifically mentioned because it is the tribe of the most important families and the rulers. See David Qimḥī, *Pērūsh Sēfer Tehillīm* (Tel Aviv, 1945), p. 264.

"like the dust in the threshing."[22] He was describing none other than our condition under the rule of Ishmael—may it speedily be vanquished—when he said, "And some of the host and of the stars it cast down to the ground, and trampled upon them" (Dan. 8:10). We have borne their imposed degradation, their lies, and absurdities, which are beyond human power to bear. We have become as in the words of the psalmist, "But I am as a deaf man, I hear not, and I am as a dumb man that opens not his mouth" (Ps. 38:14). We have done as our sages of blessed memory have instructed us, bearing the lies and absurdities of Ishmael. We listen, but remain silent. . . . In spite of all this, we are not spared from the ferocity of their wickedness and their outbursts at any time. On the contrary, the more we suffer and choose to conciliate them, the more they choose to act belligerently toward us. Thus David has depicted our plight: "I am at peace, but when I speak, they are for war!" (Ps. 120:7). How much worse it would be if we were to stir up a commotion and announce to them with ranting and raving that our dominion is at hand! Then indeed, we would be plunging ourselves into destruction.

I should like to recount to you briefly several incidents which took place after the establishment of the Ishmaelite Empire. These should serve as a lesson to you.

The first of these stories tells of the migration of a great number of Jews—perhaps hundreds of thousands[23]—from the East beyond Isfahan. With them was a man who claimed to be the Messiah.[24] They went armed and with swords unsheathed, killing whoever encountered them. According to the account I heard, they reached the vicinity of Baghdad in the early days of the Umayyad Caliphate.[25] The caliph told all the Jews in his empire, "Send out you scholars to these people. If (they find that) their

[22] 2 Kings 13:7.

[23] The medieval Hebrew translations and the epitomized Arabic version on which they are based all give the figure of 10,000. This number could easily be divided by ten again in order to come up with a plausible number. This type of inflation was absolutely standard for medieval writers, even when dealing with material in less legendary form.

[24] This is apparently a somewhat confused reference to Abū ᶜIsā of Isfahan, who claimed to be a prophet and the precursor of the Messiah, although not the Messiah himself. See the Karaite encyclopedist and historian of Jewish sects, Jacob al-Qirqisānī, (fl. tenth century), *Kitāb al-Anwār,* vol. 1, ed. L. Nemoy, (New York, 1939), p. 10. This passage is translated in L. Nemoy, *Karaite Anthology,* Yale Judaica Series, vol. 7 (New Haven, 1952), p. 51.

[25] Qirqisānī, *Anwār,* vol. 1, p. 10 (Eng. tr., p. 51), dates Abū ᶜIsā to the reign of the Umayyad Caliph ᶜAbd al-Malik (685–705). The Muslim heresiographer al-Shāhrāstāni, *Kitāb al-Milal wa 'l-Niḥal,* ed. W. Cureton (London, 1846), p. 168, places him during the reigns of the last Umayyad Marwan II (744–50) and the second Abbasid al-Manṣūr (754–75). Both periods were marked by messianic fervor and the rise of militant, apocalyptic sects.

claim is true, and that this man is clearly your Awaited One, then we shall conclude a truce with you on your terms. If, on the other hand, their claim be false, then we shall fight them."

So a group of scholars went out to meet them. They were told, "We are from the people of Transoxania."

"Who incited you to undertake this migration?" they asked.

"This man," they replied. "We know him to be pious and virtuous. He is of the House of David. We know for a fact that one night he went to bed a leper and awoke in the morning sound and healthy. And this is one of the signs of the Messiah!"

They maintained that the verse "stricken, smitten of God, and afflicted" (Isa. 53:4) should be interpreted to mean that the Messiah would be a leper. The scholars clearly demonstrated to them that this was not correct and that this man did not possess even some of the signs of the Messiah, much less all of them. Then they implored them, "O our brethren, you are still close to your own land and are able to return. If you stay in this country, you will be destroyed. What is more, you will be undercutting the Word of Moses since people will be misled into thinking that the Messiah has come and has been vanquished. You have no prophet with you, nor any miraculous sign."

They heeded the warning. Then the Sultan[26] sent them so many thousand dinars as a hospitable gesture so that they would leave the country. But when they had departed and returned to their home, he turned against the Jews and imposed a fine upon them for everything he had had to pay. He also prescribed distinguishing badges for their clothes, on which were to be written "accursed." The badge was to be fastened with a metal bar in front and in back.[27] The Jewish communities of Khorasan and Isfahan have felt the severity of the Diaspora ever since. This, in any case, is the oral account[28] which reached me.

The next account, however, we have verified and know to be true as it occurred relatively recently. About fifty years ago, or even less, a pious and virtuous man appeared. He ranked as a scholar among the scholars of Israel. He was known as Moses al-Darᶜī. He came from the Draᶜ Valley[29] to Spain to study with Rabbi Joseph ha-Levi Ibn Megash[30] (of blessed memory) about whom you have heard. Later, he went to the capital of Morocco, Fez. People gathered about him because of his religiosity, his

26 Maimonides is using this term anachronistically.

27 For similar legislation, see above p. 167.

28 Maimonides is careful to emphasize again that this story had only been told to him and that he could not vouch for its veracity.

29 In southern Morocco, on the rim of the Sahara.

30 Great Spanish talmudist who succeeded his teacher Isaac al-Fāsī as head of the famous *yeshiva* of Lucena (1077–1141).

virtue, and his learning. He informed them, "The Messiah is at hand! God has revealed this to me in a dream."

He did not claim, however, as did this madman, that God had told him that he himself was the Messiah, but only that the Messiah had appeared. People followed him and believed his declaration. My father and master (of blessed memory) tried to dissuade people and even forbade them from following him. But only a few obeyed my father. The majority—indeed, almost all—followed R. Moses (may he rest in paradise).[31] Then, in the end, he began to foretell things which proved true no matter what happened. For example, he would say, "Yesterday, it was revealed to me that such and such would occur." And so it did. Finally, he declared that a terrible rain with drops of blood would fall. This would be one of the signs foretold in the verse, "And I will show wonders in the heavens and on the earth, blood, and fire, and pillars of smoke" (Joel 3:3). This took place in the month of Marḥeshvan.[32] Then a very heavy rain did come on that Friday. The rain drops were red and thick, as if mixed with clay. This was the sign that convinced all the people that he was without a doubt a prophet. This, by the way, is not at all forbidden under Jewish Law. As I have told you, prophecy will return prior to the coming of the Messiah. Now that his message had been accepted by virtually all the people, he told them that the Messiah would come that very year on the eve of the Passover. He ordered people to sell their possessions and to take loans from the Muslims with a promise to repay ten dinars for every one, thereby re-enacting the events of the Passover Festival in the Torah,[33] for they would never see them again. And they did as he commanded. When Passover came and nothing happened, the people were ruined since most of them had disposed of their property for a mere pittance and were now beset with debts. The affair became known to their Gentile neighbors and servants who would have killed him had they been able to find him. No Muslim country was safe from him after that. So he emigrated to the Land of Israel,[34] where he died—may his memory be blessed.

According to what I was told by many eyewitnesses, he prophesied at the time of his departure all that was about to happen in the Maghreb, both major and minor events.

My father (of blessed memory) told me that approximately fifteen or twenty years before this incident, there was a group of learned and respect-

[31] Maimonides always speaks of Moses al-Darʿī with respect since he was a scholar—despite his delusions and the trouble he caused.

[32] October 4–November 4, 1130. See Eduard Mahler, *Handbuch der jüdischen Chronologie* (Leipzig, 1916), p. 588.

[33] Exod. 11:2–3, 35–36.

[34] It was under Crusader control at the time.

able people in Cordova, the capital of Spain, a large number of whom were devotees of astrology. They all agreed that the Messiah would come that very year. Night after night they sought revelations in dreams. They determined that the Messiah was a man from the people of their city. They singled out a pious and respectable individual named Ibn Arieh. He was a teacher of the people. They performed miraculous signs and made predictions, just like al-Darʿī, until finally the hearts of all the common folk were won over. When the notables and wisemen of our community heard of this, they gathered in the synagogue and had this Ibn Arieh brought forth and publicly flogged. They imposed a fine upon him and placed him under a ban of excommunication because he had acknowledged by his silence the claims made on his behalf, rather than disavowing them and informing people that this was a violation of the religious law. They did the same to all those who had gathered about him. They were only able to save themselves from the Gentiles with the greatest of difficulty.[35]

(Maimonides cites one more example of a false Messiah who appeared in the land of the Franks.)

These are the kinds of incidents about which the prophets warned us. They have informed us, as I have told you, that when the coming of the true Messiah is near, many pretenders and deluded individuals will appear. Their claims will prove untrue. They will perish, and many will be destroyed with them.

When it was revealed to Solomon (peace be upon him) by the Divine Spirit that during our people's sojourn in the Diaspora they might seek to bestir themselves before the proper time and thereby court destruction and be overwhelmed by calamity, he forewarned us. He entreated us metaphorically, saying, "I adjure you, o daughters of Jerusalem, by the gazelles, and by the hinds of the field, that you awaken not, nor stir up love, until it please" (Song of Songs 2:7). My beloved brethren, abide by his oath, and do not "stir up love, until it please."[36]

(Closing prayer in Hebrew:)

May the Creator of the world remember us and you in accordance with His attribute of mercy. May He gather the exiles who are His special portion so that they might "behold the graciousness of the Lord and visit early in His temple" (Ps. 27:4). May He lead us out of the Valley of the Shadows into which He has relegated us. May He dispell the darkness before our eyes and the gloom in our hearts. May He fulfill the prophecy "The people who walked in darkness have seen a great light" (Isa. 9:1).

[35] We have no other sources for Ibn Arieh and the movement that surrounded him.

[36] Maimonides is following the midrashic interpretation of this verse. See *Ketubōt,* 111a; also *Shīr ha-Shīrīm Rabba.*

May He in His wrath and anger cast into darkness all those who have risen up against us. May He enlighten our benightedness as He has promised us: "For behold, darkness shall cover the earth, and a dense cloud the peoples, but upon you the Lord will shine" (Isa. 60:2).

Peace be upon you, our dearly beloved master of all branches of learning. And upon our fellow scholars and all the common people, peace—peace like a shining light. "An abundance of peace until the moon is no more!" (Ps. 72:7). Amen. Selah.

(Arabic postscript:)

What I would like to request from you is that you send a copy of this epistle to every single community, both rural and urban, so that it may strengthen their faith and cause them to stand firm. Read it communally and individually. In so doing, you will be one of those "that turn the many to righteousness" (Dan. 12:3).[37] Take the utmost precaution against any wicked informer who might reveal its contents to the Gentiles. God preserve us from what might happen then! I was terribly frightened by this when I wrote the epistle. However, I considered it worth the risk to "turn the many to righteousness." And in addition, I was sending it to one such as yourself, and "the secret of the Lord is (safe) with them that fear Him" (Ps. 25:14). The successors of the prophets have promised us that "those sent on a pious mission will not meet harm" (Pesaḥim 8a). And there is certainly no pious mission greater than this.

Peace upon all Israel.

Translated from the Arabic text.
Moses b. Maimon, *Iggeret Tēmān,*
text ed. A. Halkin (New York, 1952), pp. 1–106.

[37] In the Talmud, this phrase from Daniel is used for communal leaders who educate the public and guide them on the right path. See *Bava Batra,* 8b.

. . . .

to Aden. Immediately after his arrival he was brought before the self-styled caliph, who said to him: "Become a Muslim, or you will cause the death of your brethren." He cried bitterly, but there was no other way for him . . . except to embrace Islam. Before his arrival in Aden, all those who were with him on the mountains had apostatized;[1] the physician known as the Efficient, and everyone on the mountains apostatized; only the Jews of Aden remained. But the elder Maḍmūn[2] accepted Islam on Wednesday, the first of Dhu 'l-Qaᶜda (25 August 1198). On Friday, the third, the bell (of the market-crier) was rung: "Community of Jews, all of you, anyone who will be late in appearing in the audience hall after noon, will be killed." Moreover, he (the caliph) ordered that anyone returning to the Jewish faith would be killed. Thus all apostatized. Some of the very religious, who defected from Islam, were beheaded.

As to us (the foreign Jewish merchants), do not ask what we felt, witnessing horrors the like of which we had never seen.

But with us God wrought a miracle and saved us, not through our might and power, but through His Grace and favor. For when we went up with them to the audience hall, the foreigners assembled separately, and the caliph was consulted about them. God put these words into his mouth: "No foreigner should be molested."[3] He ordered that everyone should pay a third of the poll tax.[4] We disbursed this and he dismissed us graciously, thank God. This is the upshot of what happened. But, by the great God, I am really not able to convey to you even part of what happened, for witnessing an event is one thing and hearing about it—quite another.

The merchants were outraged by the new impositions promulgated. Finally, however, God, the Exalted, helped. The caliph had ordered that

[1] Heb., *pāshaᶜ*, literally, "to renounce one's allegiance," was the common word used to express this idea in the Geniza documents. See S. D. Goitein, *Mediterranean Society*, vol. 2, p. 300.

[2] Maḍmūn b. David, head of the Jewish community of Aden. He is the author of the following letter.

[3] S. D. Goitein, *Medieval Jewish Traders* (Princeton, 1973), p. 214, n. 7, observes here: "This shows that, at that time, the Jewish India traders must have been still of considerable importance for the economy of Aden.

[4] Goitein, *Medieval Jewish Traders,* p. 214, n. 8: "The poll tax of non-Muslims was to be paid at their permanent residence. Thus, this imposition was illegal. But the travelers were content to buy their religious freedom with this price."

15 out of 100 dinars should be taken from everyone both at arrival and departure, but God helped, and he ordered that this Kārim[5] should remain unchanged with no rise in tariff. But everyone coming later would have to pay 15 out of 100 dinars from all goods, and also from gold and silver, from wheat and flour, in short, from everything.[6] Such will be the earnings of anyone coming here next year.

(A list of prices for various commodities follows.)

I asked God for guidance and am traveling home in the boat of Ibn Salmūn, the same in which I made the passage out. May God bestow safety upon it. My brother Abū Naṣr will be traveling with me. I am kissing your hands and feet.[7]

Geniza Document,
trans. S. D. Goitein, in *Mosseri Collection,* L–12,
Letters of Medieval Jewish Traders (Princeton, 1973), pp. 213–15.

[5] The Kārim was an organization or league of India merchants. Here, however, the word seems to be used for "the totality of India travelers operating during one year," which Goitein, *Medieval Jewish Traders,* p. 214, n. 9, points out "is very remarkable." See his essay, "The Beginnings of the Kārim Merchants and the Character of their Organization," in Goitein, *Studies,* pp. 351–60.

[6] Goitein, *Medieval Jewish Traders,* p. 214, n. 10: "Meaning that even from the provisions of the travelers 15 percent had to be turned over to the ruler of Aden."

[7] Goitein, *Medieval Jewish Traders,* pp. 215–16, n. 20: "One kisses the hands of a senior relative and the feet of a judge. The writer might have been a relative of the judge Isaac b. Sāsōn, who was the Jewish chief judge of Cairo and a close associate of Maimonides, but also very active in the economic field."

THE SELF-STYLED CALIPH IS ASSASSINATED AND THE FORCED CONVERTS OF ADEN RETURN TO JUDAISM

In the name of the Merciful

Your servant Maḍmūn, son of David, may the spirit of God grant him rest, sends regards to his high and lofty excellency . . .

I received your distinguished letter in which you report about the trouble you had with the pepper carried with you. God knows that my intention in this matter was only to be useful to you. God, the Exalted, will support you and grant you success. Amen, Amen.

I should like you to share this with your servant: the troops killed al-Malik al-Muᶜizz, who claimed to be caliph. He is succeeded by al-Malik al-Nāṣir Ayyūb,[1] the son of the Sultan Sayf al-Islām,[2] who is still a boy, and his Atabeg (guardian and regent) is the Sultan Sayf al-Dīn Sunqur.

After his government had become settled, your servants submitted your case to him. He referred it to the administrative court. But your servants declared that this was a case belonging to the religious court. We obfuscated the matter before the divines and paid the poll tax.[3]

All this happened in the month of Sivan, one day before the eve of Pentecost.[4] We celebrated the feast in the proper way, in happiness and joy. Some Jewbaiters formed menacing groups, but could not do a thing, thank God, the Exalted. All that happened to us has come through the blessings of our lord, the Rayyis Moses (Maimonides)—may the memory of the righteous be blessed[5]—and the blessings of our lord, the pious man, our Master Isaac,[6] and through your blessings, may God, the exalted, grant you good reward for your liberality.[7]

[1] He was al-Malik al-Muᶜizz's younger brother.

[2] Saladin's brother.

[3] S. D. Goitein, *Medieval Jewish Traders* (Princeton, 1973), p. 218, n. 9: "The Muslim divines, like their Jewish colleagues, were local and merchants. The administrative court was in the hand of officers from the foreign mercenary troops, with whom little contact existed. Matters affecting non-Muslims were indeed the domain of the religious court."

[4] May 27, 1202.

[5] Goitein, *Medieval Jewish Traders,* p. 218, n. 11: "Moses Maimonides the Rayyis, or head of the Jewish community in Egypt. The blessing following his name was normally said over a dead person, but in Yemen occasionally also over one alive, especially an eminent divine."

[6] Isaac b. Sāsōn, Jewish chief judge in Cairo. See above, p. 248, n. 7.

[7] Goitein, *Medieval Jewish Traders,* p. 219, n. 16: "The allusion to his liberality means that the arguments based on Islamic law had to be fortified by 'presents' to the proper persons."

Your distinguished letter, containing several orders, has arrived. Your servant hopes to be able to carry them out. I do not doubt that you—may God make your honored position eternal—love me and are concerned with my well-being. May God, the Exalted, help me to satisfy your wishes, as is my duty, if God wills.

I renew my reliance on you for having the two pieces sent with you collated and a third copy made in good script and on fine paper.[8] And have the medical writings of my lord the Rayyis copied for me. And please buy for me any fine copies of useful books you can lay hands on and kindly send them to me—may I never be deprived of you and never miss you. (Postscript by a bystander:) Your servant Maḍmūn b. Jacob, . . . present at the writing of this letter, sends his best regards to his excellency, my master. Thanks to (God?) . . . , the affair with all those Arabs, ended happily in this salvation. We were not worthy of this, but the Holy One Blessed be He did what He is worthy of, for the sake of His great Name, and brought relief to the Jews in the entire country of Yemen. Relief was brought first, slightly before us, to the people of the mountains. Finally the Sultan came to us, and the relief became complete, by the help of God and your success.[9] "They thanked God for His lovingkindness" (Ps. 107:8).[10]

Kind regards to his excellency my lord and to all under his care, and to all connected with him and subordinated to him a million greetings of peace.

Written on 17 Tammuz 1513 of the Documents (9 July 1202).[11] Salvation is near.

Two copies were made and sent by way of the Hijaz.[12]

Geniza Document
TS 28.11, trans. S. D. Goitein, in
Letters of Medieval Jewish Traders
(Princeton, 1973), pp. 217–20.

[8] Goitein, *Medieval Jewish Traders,* p. 219, n. 14: "Most probably a reference to parts of Maimonides' legal code. The writer, like some other readers, had doubts with regard to many passages and wished his copies to be collated with a reliable text. The other members of the rabbinical court needed a copy as well."

[9] Again referring to the addressee's intervention with the authorities.

[10] This verse is cited when one is rescued from danger.

[11] Goitein, *Medieval Jewish Traders,* p. 220, n. 18: "A day on which fasting is obligatory. I have found many letters written on that fast in July; perhaps the merchants were too exhausted to do much business and passed the time in letter-writing."

[12] Goitein, *Medieval Jewish Traders,* p. 220, n. 19: "Overland, and not, as usual, by sea, probably because all the ships of the season had already sailed."

OBADIAH THE PROSELYTE ON THE TREATMENT OF THE JEWS OF BAGHDAD UNDER AL-MUQTADI
(IRAQ, ELEVENTH CENTURY)

Prior to this, the ruler of Baghdad, whose name was al-Muqtadī,[1] had given full authority to his vizier, Abū Shujāᶜ, to make a change in policy regarding the Jews living in Baghdad. Now he (Abū Shujāᶜ) had already sought on many occasions to destroy them, but the God of Israel had thwarted his intention, and on this occasion, too, He protected them from his fury.

He (Abū Shujāᶜ) directed that yellow badges should be affixed to the headgear of every Jewish male. In addition to the badge on the head, another of lead, the weight of a silver coin, was to hang round the neck of every Jew. The lead pendant was to be inscribed with the word "*dhimmī*" indicating that the Jews were tribute bearers. He also imposed that every Jew should wear a distinguishing belt around the waist. Abū Shujāᶜ imposed two distinguishing signs upon Jewish women. Each woman had to wear one red shoe and one black shoe. Furthermore, each woman had to have a small copper bell on her neck or on her shoe which would tinkle so that all would know and differentiate between the women of the Jews and of the Muslims. He assigned cruel Muslim men to watch over the Jewish men and cruel Muslim women to oversee the Jewish women, in order to oppress them with every sort of insult, humiliation, and contempt. The Muslims would mock them, and the common rabble, together with their children, would beat Jews throughout all the streets of Baghdad.

The law regarding the tribute which was collected annually by the servants of the ruler of Baghdad is as follows: From every wealthy Jew, they would collect four and a half dinars; from every Jew of the middle class, two and a half; and from the poorest Jews, one and a half. If a Jew died, not having paid the tribute in full, the Muslims would not let him be buried until the remainder is paid, be the amount large or small. If the deceased left nothing of value, the Muslims demanded it from the Jewish community, and they must redeem their dead by paying the outstanding tribute money out of their own funds. If not, the Muslims would seek to burn the body.

Geniza Document
Kaufmann XV, in Alexander Scheiber,
"Fragment from the Chronicle of
ᶜObadiah, the Norman Proselyte,"
Acta Orientalia Hungarica, vol. 4 (1954), pp. 278–79.

[1] Ruled 1075–94. The writer, Obadiah, came to Baghdad in the early twelfth century, about thirty years after the persecution described here.

BENJAMIN OF TUDELA'S DESCRIPTION OF BAGHDADI JEWRY

(SECOND HALF OF THE TWELFTH CENTURY)

There are in Baghdad some 40,000 Jews of the People of Israel.[1] They live in peace, tranquility, and honor under the great Caliph. Among them are great scholars and heads of Yeshivot who are engaged in the study of Torah. There are ten yeshivot in the city. The head of the largest yeshiva is Rabbi Samuel b. Eli, the Gaon (the Head of the Academy of the Pride of Jacob). He is a Levite and traces his ancestry back to our Teacher Moses—peace be upon him. His brother, Rabbi Hananiah, the Provost of the Levites,[2] is head of the second yeshiva. Rabbi Daniel, who bears the title "Foundation of the Yeshiva," is head of the third yeshiva. Rabbi Elazar the Ḥāvēr[3] is head of the fourth yeshiva. Rabbi Elazar b. Ṣemaḥ the Rōsh Sēder[4] is head of the fifth yeshiva. He traces his lineage back to the Prophet Samuel the Korahite. He and his brethren know how to chant hymns as did the singers at the time when the Temple was standing. Rabbi Ḥasday, who bears the title "Glory of the Scholars,"[5] is head of the sixth yeshiva. Rabbi Haggai the Nasi[6] is head of the seventh yeshiva. Rabbi Ezra, who is called the "Counsel of the Yeshiva," is head of the eighth. Rabbi Abraham, who is called Abū Ṭāhir, is head of the ninth. And Rabbi Zakkay b. Bustanay the Nasi is head of the last.

They are known as the ten *Baṭlānīm*[7] for they occupy themselves with nothing other than the needs of the community. On every day of the week they judge all their Jewish countrymen, except on Monday when everyone comes before Rabbi Samuel Gaon. He sits in judgment with the other nine *Baṭlānīm* for all who come before them. Over all of them is Daniel b. Ḥasday, who is called the "Exilarch of All Israel."[8] He has a written pedi-

[1] This figure is terribly exaggerated. 4,000 would be a more likely number.

[2] *Segen ha-Leviyyīm.*

[3] *Ḥāvēr* was the normal title for members of the Palestinian Academy, but it was also a general term for "scholar."

[4] The *rōsh sēder* (head of a row) was originally the title of seven officers of the Academy, each of whom sat at the head of a row of students. See S. D. Goitein, *Mediterranean Society,* vol. 2, pp. 198–99.

[5] *Pe'ēr ha-Ḥavērīm.*

[6] The title *nāsī* indicates that he was of Davidic descent. Concerning the *nāsīs* in the Middle East, see Goitein, *Mediterranean Society,* vol. 2, p. 19 passim.

[7] The word *baṭlānīm* literally means "men of leisure." It was applied to men who had the leisure to devote themselves to communal service. See Z. Kaplan, "Batlanim," *EJ* 4: 325.

[8] Heb., *Rōsh Galūyōt kol Yisrā'ēl,* literally, "the exilarch of the Diasporas of all Israel." Ben Ḥasday died in 1174.

gree going back to David King of Israel. The Jews address him as Our Lord the Exilarch, and the Muslims[9] as *Sayyidnā Ibn Dā'ūd* (our Master, the son of David). He has been invested with supreme authority over all the congregations of Israel by the *Amīr al-Mu'minīn,*[10] the lord of the Muslims. For thus Muḥammad commanded concerning the Exilarch and his descendants, and he issued him a seal of authority over all the sacred congregations living under his rule. Likewise, he ordered that every individual, be he Muslim or Jew, or member of any other people within his kingdom, should rise up before him and salute him, and that whoever does not rise up before him should receive one hundred stripes.

Every Thursday, when he goes to behold the countenance of the great Caliph, he is accompanied by Gentile and Jewish horsemen, and heralds cry out before him: "Make way for our Lord, the scion of David, as is due him!" In their language they say: *"Iᶜmalū ṭarīq li-Sayyidnā Ibn Dā'ūd."* He rides on horseback wearing garments of embroidered silk with a large turban on his head. Over the turban is a large white shawl upon which is a chain. And on it is the seal of Muḥammad. When he comes before the Caliph, he kisses his hand. Then the Caliph rises before him, seats him upon a throne which Muḥammad had ordered to be made in his honor. And all of the Muslim princes who have come to behold the countenance of the Caliph rise altogether before him. The Exilarch then sits upon his throne facing the Caliph, for thus did Muḥammad command in order to fulfill the scriptural verse:

The scepter shall not pass from Judah,
Nor the ruler's staff from between his feet;
Until he comes to Shiloh,
and the homage of peoples be his. (Gen. 49:10)

The Exilarch grants all communities the right to appoint rabbis and *ḥazzānīm* for each and every congregation from Iraq to Persia and Khorasan, and Sheba, which is Yemen, to Diyar Bakr and Mesopotamia; from Armenia to the land of the Alans (Georgia) which is surrounded by mountains and has no outlet other than the Iron Gates that Alexander built, but which were broken; and from Siberia and the land of the Turks to the mountains of Asveh and the land of Gurgan, whose inhabitants, the Gurganites, dwell by the Gihon River (the Oxus)—these are the Girgashites who practice the religion of the Christians; and as far as the Gates of Samarqand, to Tibet and India. These men come to him to be

[9] Since the exilarch was a descendant of David, whom the Muslims considered a prophet, he was given this title of respect.

[10] Ar., for "commander of the faithful," the caliphal title.

ordained and to receive authority from him. They bring him offerings and gifts from the ends of the earth.

He owns hospices, gardens, and orchards in Baghdad, as well as many plots of land inherited from his forefathers. No man can take anything from him by force. He receives a fixed revenue every week from the Jewish hospices, markets, and local merchants, exclusive of that which is brought to him from distant lands. He is an extremely wealthy man and is learned in both Scripture and Talmud. Many Jews eat at his table each day.

Whenever a new Exilarch is appointed, he must expend a great deal of wealth upon the Caliph, the ministers, and the officials. On the day when the Caliph bestows the writ of authority upon him, he rides in the litter of a viceroy. He is conducted from the Caliph's palace to his home to the accompaniment of tambourines and dancing.

He (the Exilarch) performs the ordination of the Head of the Yeshiva.

The Jews in this city are very learned and wealthy. There are in Baghdad twenty-eight synagogues. These are divided between Baghdad proper and the suburb of al-Karkh which is on the other side of the Tigris—for the river divides the city in two.

M. N. Adler, ed., *The Itinerary of Benjamin of Tudela* (London, 1907), pp. 38–42.

THE MURDERER OF A JEW AND HIS WIFE IS PUNISHED
(THIRTEENTH-CENTURY BAGHDAD)

In that year (649/1251–52), ᶜAli b. Abī 'l-Fatḥ, the son of the vizier Abu 'l-Faraj b. Ra'īs al-Ru'asā', fell upon a Jewish money assayer who was wealthy. When he entered his house, he assaulted and killed him and took his money. The Jew's wife begged for mercy, but he killed her too. He then went out. However, the neighbors caught up with him and seized him. They brought him to the Bāb al-Nūbī where he was executed by being cut in half. He was already notorious for his corruption on account of the reprehensible things he had done prior to this.

Ibn al-Fuwaṭī, *al-Ḥawādith al-Jāmiᶜa*, ed. Muṣṭafā Jawād (Baghdad, 1932), p. 255.

4

THE LONG TWILIGHT

The Jews of Arab Lands in the Later Middle Ages

A DOCUMENT OF PROTECTION (DHIMMA) ATTRIBUTED BY THE JEWS TO MUHAMMAD
(YEMEN, LATER MIDDLE AGES?)

This is the writ of protection which was extended to the Children of Israel by the Prophet Muḥammad—peace be upon him, and Allah's mercy and blessing.

Long ago, the heathens revolted against the Prophet Muḥammad—peace be upon him. But Allah granted him victory over them. He killed their leading men, and he took prisoner Ṣafiyya b. Ḥuyayy b. Akhṭab.[1] Then the Children of Israel came to him saying: "O Prophet of Allah, o distinguished Prophet, who commands all good and forbids all evil, we are with you and for you; we shall fight to the death against the heathens who oppose you." Then the Prophet rose up and fought the unbelievers, causing a great upheaval among them. He destroyed their city, killed their leading men, and took Ṣafiyya b. Ḥuyayy b. Akhṭab prisoner. Then the Children of Israel came to him and said: "O Prophet of Allah, behold we are obedient and not rebellious, and we shall fight on your side in a renewed, fierce holy war." The Prophet replied: "Allah has revealed to me that I shall marry Ṣafiyya b. Ḥuyayy b. Akhṭab. Her freedom will be her dowry." Those who were present, that is, the Muslims, the Believers, the elders, and the scribes, replied: "O Prophet of Allah, yours is the command, yours is the prophecy, and yours is the knowledge."

The Children of Israel fought in his vanguard until Friday noon. The

[1] In the text, Ṣafiyya's father's name is distorted to al-Ḥāwī b. al-Khaṭṭāb.

Prophet had extended his protection to them. He waged a fierce battle, but said to them: "Go and keep your Sabbath, o Children of Israel. As for us, we shall overcome the enemy with Allah's help." The Children of Israel gathered together and went to keep their Sabbath. Meanwhile the foes tried to overwhelm the Prophet Muḥammad—peace be upon him. The Children of Israel and their elders gathered together and fought in the Prophet Muḥammad's vanguard. They said, "O Prophet of Allah, we shall redeem you with our lives and possessions. We have no Sabbath except with your help!" The Prophet replied: "Do not worry.[2] Go and keep your Sabbath. As for us, we shall overcome them with Allah's help." Now this occurred as the sun was setting on the eve of the Sabbath. The Children of Israel desecrated their Sabbath and raided the territory of the unbelievers killing 7000 knights, 7000 riders, and 7000 infantrymen. The Prophet Muḥammad—peace be upon him—was overjoyed when he learned of this, and he said: "O men of the Children of Israel, by Allah, I shall reward you for this—if Allah is willing and with His help. I shall grant you my protection, my covenant, my oath, and my witness for as long as I live and as long as my community shall live after me, until they see my face on the Day of Resurrection."

Then he called on the chiefs,[3] the scribes, the elders, and ᶜAbd Allāh b. Salām.[4] ᶜAlī b. Abī Ṭālib took pen and scroll, and they wrote: "This is my writ of protection, my covenant, my oath, and my witness to those who come after me." The Prophet said: "Write the following"—

In the name of Allah, the Merciful, the Compassionate; by Allah's mercy and His blessing. O people of the tribes of Israel and Muslims and Believers, this is to attest to the fact that Allah gave me, revealed unto me, and sent me as a guidance to the ignorant and as a mercy to the Believers. Listen and pay heed, all of you who are present, as well as those who are absent. The Children of Israel are returning to their villages and their strongholds in which they and their generations to come shall dwell. They will be safe under Allah's security—praised be He—and under the security of the Muslims and the Believers. This is what has been revealed to me, and it includes all of the Children of Israel. For I have taken them as my clients and extended protection to them. I have removed from them all shame, insult, abuse, accusation of wrong-doing, and any disgrace. I have extended security to them in every village, in every market, and in all the land of the Muslims and the Believers. No wrong, no harm, and no crime

[2] Ar., *lā ba's ᶜalaykum* (literally, "may no evil befall you").

[3] Following S. D. Goitein's suggestion of reading *bi-nuẓẓār* for *b-n-ṣ-r* in the text.

[4] He was Muḥammad's first Jewish convert in Medina. See above, pp. 113–14.

should befall them. There shall be no legal claims against them, no usurpation of what is theirs, no tithing of their property, no special levies on their properties, nor on the fruits they bear, namely in their grain fields, their vineyards, and their palmeries. Allah shall not bless anyone who oppresses the Children of Israel even the weight of an atom.[5] I shall testify against him on the Day of Resurrection.

They shall not be prevented from entering mosques, saints' tombs, or schools. They have only to pay the *jizya*: 3 silver mithqāls from those who ride horses,[6] and from the poor among them who have provisions for thirty days and clothing for twelve months, each man should give according to his ability. The righteous among them shall collect it.

Security was extended to them for a distance of three days' travel in the four cardinal directions.

O ᶜAlī b. Abī Ṭālib, Allah has revealed His word unto me. The Children of Israel are to tie the *zunnār* around their turbans[7] so that they will be identified as *ahl al-dhimma,* and no one will lay a hand upon them or oppress them. Furthermore, they are not to forsake their religion for another. They are not to desecrate their Sabbath or do any work on it. They are not to cease reading the Torah which was revealed through Moses b. Amram—peace be upon him—who spoke with the All-merciful on Mount Sinai. They are not to be prevented from praying in their synagogues or from drinking intoxicating beverages in their homes. They are not to be prevented from attending schools or ritual baths.[8]

Allah will afflict whosoever does harm to the Children of Israel with misfortune on himself and upon his household, upon his offspring, his beasts and his fields, from that day forth until the Day of Judgment. He will condemn him to Hell for having acted against my covenant, my seal, my protection, my oath, and my witness. This is the reward of the Children of Israel, who fought for me and desecrated their Sabbath. The Sons of Jacob fought bravely for me, o Quraysh and o my allies. The Children of Israel rallied around me, and we were victorious over the enemy. We routed them, pursued them, and killed 7000 knights, 7000 riders, and 7000 infantrymen with the help of Allah and Children of Israel.

By Allah, by Allah, o Muslims and Believers, may you keep and honor this writ of protection upon which I have placed my seal. Witnessed on

[5] Cf. Sura 99:7–8.

[6] Of course, Jews were forbidden to ride horses in Yemen or anywhere else in the Dār al-Islām.

[7] This is a strange statement since the *zunnār* was a belt worn around the waist.

[8] Ar., *manāhil,* following Goitein's translation of *miqvā'ōt* in *Kirjath Sepher,* vol. 9, p. 512.

20 Ramaḍān, A.H. 9[9] Peace and Allah's mercy upon the Believers. Witnessed by: (ten names follow). Written by ᶜAli b. Abī Ṭālib in his own hand, word for word and letter for letter from the mouth of the Prophet, in the presence of the Emigrants[10] and the Helpers. Signed by the Prophet Muḥammad b. ᶜAbd Allāh.

Trans. from Arabic text, ed. S. D. Goitein, in *Kirjath Sepher,* vol. 9, (1932–33), pp. 508–10.

[9] The date in the Yemenite text published by Goitein reads A.H. 17, which is after Muḥammad's death. Other versions in the Geniza have 5 and 9. The latter is the most fitting. See Goitein's discussion of the dating in *Kirjath Sepher,* vol. 9, p. 521.

[10] The text reads "fighters" (Ar., *mujāhidīn*), but this is certainly a scribal error for *muhājirīn.*

A RETORT TO MUSLIM TRADITIONS CONCERNING JEWS AND THE BIBLE

In the books of the Muslim theologians it is asserted that the Jews and Christians do not object at all to the Prophet's[1] stories of antiquity. But we find that Jews and Christians do contest many of them, such as the story of Solomon, the son of David, and how he subdued the wind and the *jinn*; how he knew the language of the birds, conversed with the hoopoe, and sent it to the queen of Sheba, whose throne was brought to him; about his death, how the beast of the earth gnawed his staff, and the people learned that the *jinn* had not known of Solomon's death until he collapsed or else they would not have persevered in their humiliating punishment.[2]

The same is true of the story of Jesus: that the Jews had not crucified him but had been made to think they had; that his mother was the daughter of ᶜImrān and the sister of Aaron.[3]

The same is true of the story of ᶜUzayr, that the Jews declared him the son of God; also of their statement that God's hand is fettered.[4]

All this is the opposite of what is transmitted by Jews and Christians.

The most repugnant story to them is that of Solomon, for the Jews carry a detailed tradition of his food, wealth, number of wives, stables of horses, years of kingship, length of his life, many of the parables and proverbs that he uttered, his constructive activity in the land, etc. But they doubt not that this particular story is without foundation. Were there any truth in it, it would be more proper for the Jews to carry the tradition than to leave it to somebody else's version. After all, the Jews wish to glorify Solomon, who was one of their kings and of their faith.

Neither the Jews nor the Christians doubt that Jesus, the son of Mary, was crucified, and they transmit the story of his crucifixion with the same certainty as that of his existence. The name of the father of Mary, the

[1] In fact, already in Medina, the Jews objected to Muḥammad's versions of biblical narratives. See Part One above, pp. 11–13.

[2] See Sura 27:16–44; 34:14/13; 38:37/36.

[3] The Koran follows the Docetist heresy in teaching that Jesus was not crucified, but rather, it was only an image that appeared to be Jesus. See Sura 4:157–58/156–57. The Koran also confuses Mary (Ar., Maryam), the mother of Jesus, with Miriam (Maryam), the sister of Moses, and calls her *bint ᶜImrān,* daughter of Amram. She is also called sister of Aaron. See Suras 3:35/31 and 19:28/29.

[4] The passage mentioning ᶜUzayr (usually identified as Ezra) is translated above, p. 151. The passage accusing the Jews of saying God's hand is fettered is translated above, p. 151.

mother of Jesus was, according to the Christians, Joakhin.[5] Mary had no brother.

There is no tradition by the authority of any Jew that ᶜUzayr was the son of God, or that God's hand is fettered, either in the literal sense or in reference to avarice. If any of them said that, he would be considered among them an unbeliever and outside their community.

The stories mentioned in the Koran and in tradition that are contested by Jews and Christians are too numerous for close examination.

Perhaps the scholastics were alluding to the fact that among the Prophet's contemporaries those Jews and Christians of Arab descent were the ones who were not contesting the Koran stories; they did not contest these stories either because the Koran stories had not all reached them, or because these Jews and Christians were ignorant, even as many of the nomadic Arabs are in our time. Perhaps, also, they were afraid to declare their denial and refutation, and kept silent.

Ibn Kammūna, *Examination of the Three Faiths,*
trans. Moshe Perlmann
(Berkeley and Los Angeles, 1971), pp. 131–33.

[5] Moshe Perlmann, trans., *Ibn Kammūna's Examination of the Three Faiths* (Berkeley and Los Angeles, 1971), p. 132, n. 98: "A traditional name, not occurring in the canonical scriptures."

A JEWISH PHILOSOPHER ON ISLAM AND WHY SOME DHIMMIS CONVERT TO IT

Further, how can Muḥammad be called the most perfect man in practical wisdom when Muslim kings, in carrying out government and maintaining law and order in the polity, are compelled to violate the religious law in stipulations on punishment and retaliation, and so on?[1] If the law of Islam were acted upon without any alteration, the regime would be upset, and people's blood and wealth would be forfeited unjustly. This is no secret to anyone acquainted with Muslim jurisprudence and with the evil and corruption the people sink into.

Thus it becomes clear that there is no proof that Muḥammad attained perfection and the ability to perfect others as claimed, nor that anything mentioned on this point has been proved at all—for example, the allegation that the world turned from falsehood to truth, from lie to veracity, from darkness to light, and so on.

That is why, to this day we never see anyone converting to Islam unless in terror, or in quest of power, or to avoid heavy taxation, or to escape humiliation, or if taken prisoner, or because of infatuation with a Muslim woman, or for some similar reason. Nor do we see a respected, wealthy, and pious non-Muslim well versed in both his faith and that of Islam, going over to the Islamic faith without some of the aforementioned or similar motives.

Ibn Kammūna, *Examination of the Three Faiths,*
trans. Moshe Perlmann
(Berkeley and Los Angeles, 1971), pp. 148–49.

[1] For a succinct description of the dichotomy between Islamic law and the actual administrative law in the medieval Muslim world, see Gustave E. von Grunebaum, *Medieval Islam: A Study in Cultural Orientation,* 2d ed. (Chicago, 1962), pp. 163–69, especially 163–65.

THE FALL OF THE ILKHANID'S JEWISH VIZIER
(IRAQ–IRAN, 1291)

The behavior of the Arabs has long been made manifest in the world, and up to the present day no Jew has ever been raised to a position of exalted honor among them; and except as a tanner, or a dyer, or a tailor, the Arab does not even appear among the Jews. But truly the honorable ones and the fortunate among them practice the art of healing and the art of the scribe; but in situations in which others will not demean themselves to work, they will work. And at this time when the Mongols were ruling over these western countries, they did not honor every one who was worthy of honor, and they did not make those who had descended from the loins of kings to rule over the cities and villages which were in subjection to them. With the Mongols there is neither slave nor free man; neither believer nor pagan; neither Christian nor Jew; but they regard all men as belonging to one and the same stock. And every one who approaches them and offers to them any of the mammon of the world, they accept it from him, and they entrust to him whatsoever office he seeks, whether it be great or whether it be little, whether he knows how to administer it, or whether he does not. All they demand is strenuous service and submission which is beyond the power of man to render.

Therefore this Jew (Saᶜd al-Dawla)[1] triumphed in every way, and attained the greatest glory and honor possible in the time of Arghūn, the King of Kings, and he alone brought all political matters to a successful issue, and much else besides. To the nobles of the Camp[2] he paid no heed, and he reduced the taking and giving into their hands, and he treated with contempt the principal Amīrs and the directors of general affairs. The man who could confer a favor, or who could do harm, was never seen at the Gate of Kingdom, unless by chance he was a Jew. And through this state of affairs many Jews who were on the fringes of the world gathered together to him, and they all with one mouth said, "Verily, by means of this man the Lord has raised on high the horn of redemption, and the hope of glory for the sons of the Hebrews in their last days!"

However, when they were boasting proudly of their exaltation, and occupied with their power, suddenly Arghūn, the King of Kings, was attacked by paralysis, and he was grievously afflicted with the disease for a month. The wretched Jew was perplexed by his illness, and with great care

[1] Concerning Saᶜd al-Dawla and his brief career, see Part One above, pp. 65–67, and the sources cited in the notes.

[2] The ruler and his army lived in tent camp and did not settle in the towns of Iraq and Iran.

he endeavored in every way possible to heal him. Then the Amīrs and the nobles of the Camp who despised the Jew utterly, having lost all hope of saving the life of Arghūn, acted as if the Jews himself, through the evil of his machination, was the cause of Arghūn's sickness. They began to roar at the wretched man like lions, until Arghūn ended his life on the fourth day of the week, at the end of January of that year (1291). Then God stirred up His wrath against the Jews who were in every place. This Saᶜd al-Dawla, the Ṣāhib al-Dīwān,[3] they killed there. And with great care they sent ambassadors into all the countries which were under the dominion of the Mongols and they seized his brethren and his kinsfolk, and they bound them with chains, and they plundered their stores of food, and they took their sons, and their daughters, and their slaves, and their handmaidens, and their flocks and herds, and all their possessions. And he who was killed by them was killed, and those who were left alive returned to their original stations. The man who yesterday was an officer, and could bind and set free, and was arrayed in royal apparel, was today swathed in sackcloth, and had dirty discolored hands as if he was a dyer and not a scribe, and a beggar going round from door to door and not an officer. The trials and wrath which were stirred up against the Jews at this time neither tongue can utter nor the pen write down.

Then in Baghdad, when the report of the murder of this Jew was heard, the Arabs armed themselves and went to the quarter of the Jews, because the Jews were all living together in one quarter in Baghdad. And when they wanted to go in and plunder them, the Jews rose up against them in great strength, and they fought against the Arabs, and killed and were killed; and they did not leave alive any Jews to rule over them.[4]

. . . .

Now the whole period during which the Jew was Director and Governor was two years, more or less. And he was killed and his name perished, and because of him the Jews throughout the world were hated and ill treated.

Bar Hebraeus, *The Chronography,* vol. 1,
trans. E. A. Wallis Budge (London, 1932), pp. 490–91.

[3] This was Saᶜd al-Dawla's title as chief of the administrative bureaucracy.

[4] This was by no means the only instance where Jews in the Middle Ages tried to defend themselves against attack either in the Muslim or the Christian world. However, like the Jews of Mainz who tried to fight back against Emicho's Crusaders in 1096, the Jews of Baghad were eventually overwhelmed by superior numbers.

AN ITALIAN JEW'S IMPRESSION OF CAIRO IN THE LATE FIFTEENTH CENTURY

On Wednesday, the 13th of that month (June 1481), we reached Rosetta, a lovely town. We left the donkeys we had ridden outside the city at the main crossroad as is customary, since the Muslims will not issue a permit allowing the donkeys and mules to be led into the city for anyone. Rather, when you arrive in some place, you must leave them. Some people immediately come and take charge of them, for they are appointed for this purpose.

So we dismounted from our donkeys outside the city, because no Jew or Christian is permitted to ride in any city even on donkeys.[1] The Jews wear yellow turbans on their heads in all the provinces of the Sultan's domain.

We arrived in Cairo on Sunday June 17, 1481. I had come to see the Cairenes and their deeds. However, if I were to write about its wealth and its people, all of this book would not be sufficient. I swear that if it were possible to put Rome, Venice, Milan, Padua, Florence, and four more cities together, they would not equal in wealth and population half that of Cairo!

Cairo is more than eighty miles in circumference. If one were to ask, "Did you visit all of Cairo or count all the households and all the people?" I would look like a fool. But I could answer, by God, that the Chief Dragoman of the Sultan, whose name is Taghrī Birdī,[2] told me all this himself. He said that every night officials bring him a written report of all the daily births and deaths in the city. . . . I had gone to see him on the orders of the Nagid, because he is of Jewish descent. He is a Spaniard who came to Egypt to convert to Judaism. But his ship ran aground and all aboard were captured. In order to gain his freedom he turned Moor. He speaks seven languages: Hebrew, Italian, Turkish, Greek, Arabic, German, and French. All of the Sultan's court speak Turkish. He gave me many gifts and privileges so that I did not have to pay any duty on the gems I bought in Cairo which are normally taxed at 10 percent.[3] He also wrote to the Dragoman in Jerusalem ordering that he should not charge me anything, because there Jews pay three ducats a head.

[1] Meshullam had mentioned earlier that only Mamluks could ride horses (*Massāᶜ*, ed. A Yaᶜari [Jerusalem, 1948], p. 46).

[2] He is mentioned several times in Muslim sources. He was still serving in this office under the Sultan al-Ashraf Qānṣūh al-Ghūrī (reigned 1501–16). See A. N. Poliak, "The Jews of the Middle East at the end of the Middle Ages (according to Arabic sources)," *Zion* 2 (1937): 265 (in Hebrew).

[3] This was the canonical customs rate for *Ḥarbīs*. The relevant text is in Abū Yūsuf, above, p. 162.

There are in Cairo approximately 800 Jewish households, 150 Karaite households, and 50 Samaritan. You already know that the Karaites observe the Written Law, while the Samaritans observe some of the Written Law, but they worship the things of this world. . . . The Samaritans live by themselves and have their own synagogue. . . . The Karaites too have their own synagogues. The good Jews who keep both the Written and the Oral Laws as we do, also live by themselves and have six synagogues.

The Sultan has placed over the Jews, Karaites, and Samaritans a Jewish Nagid. He is an honored person, good and learned. His name is R. Solomon b. Joseph. He is very rich and respected. He is a native of these parts, and his father was Nagid before him, as well as the sultan's physician. The Nagid's authority over the Jews extends throughout all the provinces of the Sultan and all his lands, in criminal and civil law. There is no appeal from his decisions. He has under him four judges: R. Jacob b. Samuel, R. Jacob al-Ṭābawiyya, R. Samuel b. ᶜAṭīl, and R. Aaron Maᶜafī; and two secretaries: R. Judah b. Arikha and R. David al-Ḥamr. He has his own prison which is called *Fārīshala Rushīṭī* (?).[4]

The noble Nagid sent for me on the second day of my stay in Cairo and treated me with the greatest respect. This was due to a Jew, R. Moses Marin de Villa Reale, a leading dealer in gems. He spoke well of me to him because twenty-two years ago, he was in our house in Florence, and my father—may he rest in peace—received him very well at our estate Polveroso. He remembered the kindness our father showed him and told the Nagid about my father and myself, saying that we were rich, worth more than 100,000 ducats in those days. He also praised us highly. As a result, from that day forth I had to sit between the Nagid and the judges in the synagogue. I also had to eat with him time and time again. And because his Excellency treated me with such respect in front of the entire congregation, they all honored me, and many of the notables called upon me, in particular, R. Jacob Rakakh, the richest and most honored man in the community, and his father. They looked upon me as though I were royalty and invited me to eat and drink with them with the Nagid's permission. This is because no one would dare serve food or drink to any Jew whom the Nagid had already received as his guest, lest it should seem as if he wanted to be as great as the Nagid.

The Muslims are wicked and sin before God. One cannot place any trust in their word. They would be even worse were it not for fear of the

[4] We cannot make any sense of this name. R. Obadiah of Bertinoro also states that the Nagid had the power to arrest and to inflict punishments; however, this prison is not mentioned in any other source. See Strauss (Ashtor), *Mamluks*, vol. 2, p. 246.

Government. It is forbidden for any Jew or Christian to raise his second finger at a Muslim,[5] because they can force him—God forbid—to become a Muslim or be killed. It is also forbidden for them to go up into their mosques.

Meshullam of Volterra, *Massā*ᶜ, ed. Avraham Yaᶜari (Jerusalem, 1948), pp. 50 and 53–58.

[5] Either in a well-known obscene gesture or pointing the finger of scorn.

THE JEWS' OATH IN MAMLUK EGYPT
(THIRTEENTH–FOURTEENTH CENTURIES)

I swear by God, by God, by God, the Almighty, Everlasting, Unique, Lord as of Old, the One, the Only, the All-reaching,[1] the Damner, Who sent Moses in truth, and Who aided and supported him with his brother Aaron. I swear by the truth of the honored Torah and its contents, and by the Ten Commandments which were revealed to Moses on tablets of precious stone, and by the Tent of Meeting[2] which contained them.

If not (that is, if what I say is not true), then may I be enslaved to Pharaoh and Haman.[3] May I be detached from Israel and brought into the religion of Christianity, that I may declare the truth of Mary in her claim and acknowledge that Joseph the carpenter was innocent. May I deny the Divine Message.[4] May I approach Mt. Sinai with foul deeds. May I charge the Rock (of the Temple Mount) with impurity. May I join Nebuchadnezzar in the destruction of Jerusalem and the slaughter of the Israelites. May I throw excrement on the places where the sacred scrolls are kept. May I be one of those who drank from the river and inclined to Goliath, abandoning the party of Saul.[5] May I deny the Prophets. May I be the one who pointed out Daniel and who informed the tyrant of Egypt as to the location of Jeremiah. May I be with the whores and harlots on the day of John the Baptist's martyrdom.[6] May I say that the fire kindled from the burning bush was the fire of falsehood. May I be one of those who barred the roads to Midian,[7] and may I be the one who said terrible things to Jethro's daughters.[8] May I assist the magicians against Moses.[9] Then

[1] Ar. *al-mudrik,* that is, from whom the sinner cannot escape.

[2] Ar., *qubbat al-zamān,* translating Heb., *ohel ha-mōᶜēd.* The Arabic is a translation of the word *mōᶜēd* in its meaning as "appointed time."

[3] In Islamic tradition Haman is vizier of the pharaoh (see Sura 26:6, 8, and 38).

[4] Ar., *al-khiṭāb,* that is, God's word to the Israelites.

[5] According to Islamic tradition it is Saul who proves his soldiers by having them drink from a stream, rather than Gideon (see Sura 2:249/248).

[6] These women are the wife and the mother of Herod who caused his death. For the Islamic accounts of this story, see M. Grünbaum, *Neue Beiträge zur semitischen Sagenkunde* (Leiden, 1893), p. 239.

[7] According to Islamic legend Moses' pursuers lay in wait for him upon the road to Midian. He, however, was saved by Ḥizqīl, "the believer in Pharaoh's family," who showed him another route—see al-Thaᶜālabī, *ᶜArā'is al-Majālis* (Cairo, 1312), p. 103.

[8] Ignaz Goldziher has suggested that this may be a confused reference to the incident in Numbers 12:1–15, where Aaron and Miriam are stricken with leprosy for speaking against Moses' wife. See I. Goldziher, "Mélanges judéo-arabes XIII," *REJ* 45 (1902): 3, n. 7.

[9] Reading *wa-ajlabtu* for *ajlaytu,* in accordance with Goldziher's suggested emendation—see Goldziher, in *REJ* 45 (1902): 4, n. 1.

may I be separated from those who believe in him. May I be with him who called for pursuit "that we might overtake those who fled."[10] May I be the one who advised leaving Joseph's coffin in Egypt.[11] May I greet al-Sāmirī,[12] and may I settle in Jericho, the city of giants. May I approve of the act of the inhabitants of Sodom. May I transgress the injunctions of the Torah. May I consider the Sabbath profane and desecrate it.[13] May I declare that the Feast of Booths is an error[14] and that Hanukka is an absurdity. May I say that God is indifferent about the laws. May I profess that Jesus son of Mary is the Messiah promised by Moses son of Amram. May I abandon Judaism for another faith.[15] May I consider camel's flesh, fat, intestines, and that which is mixed with bone as permissible.[16] May I interpret that someone who enjoys the usufruct of something forbidden is not considered as someone who enjoys the forbidden thing itself.[17] May I say what the people of Babylon said about Abraham.

If not (that is, if what I say is not true), then may I be excommunicated by a ban in which all the rabbis join together and for which they turn over the mats in the synagogue.[18] May I be returned to the Wilderness, and may the manna and quails be denied me. May I be excluded from all Twelve Tribes, and may I be like those who were kept out of the war with the giants (of Canaan) despite their strength and vigor.

al-ᶜUmarī, *al-Taᶜrīf bil-Muṣṭalaḥ al-Sharīf*
(Cairo, 1312), p. 151.

[10] That is, the one who suggested pursuing the Israelites.

[11] For this legend, see Goldziher in *REJ* 45 (1902): 4, n. 2 and the sources cited there.

[12] The Israelite, who according to Muslim tradition, led the Israelites astray and fashioned the golden calf (see Sura 20:85–97). Abraham Geiger suggested that the name may have been derived from the demon Sammael; see A. Geiger, *Judaism and Islam,* trans. F. M. Young, reprint ed. (New York, 1970), p. 131. Goldziher has shown, however, that al-Sāmirī is representative of the Samaritans and Samaritan secession; see I. Goldziher, "Lā misāsa," *Revue Africaine* 52 (1908): 23–25; see also B. Heller, "al-Sāmirī," *EI*[1] 4: 135–36.

[13] *Wa 'stâbḥtu 'l-sabt wa-ᶜadawtu fīh.* Goldziher has shown the *ᶜadā* (= *iᶜtadā*) is an ancient expression for "to break the Sabbath"—see Goldziher, *REJ* 45 (1902): 4, n. 3.

[14] In Arabic this is a pun based on the confusion between the letter *ḍād* and *ẓā'* in common speech; thus, *inna 'l-maḍalla* (= *maẓalla*) *ḍalāl.*

[15] Goldziher, (*REJ* 45, p. 4, n. 5) suggests that this refers to Islam in light of the foods mentioned in the next sentence.

[16] According to the Koran (Sura 6:147), Jews were forbidden from eating the fat of sheep and oxen, "except that upon the back or entrails." According to this same verse they are also forbidden "that which is mixed with bone."

[17] For references to this legal debate in Islam and Judaism, see Goldziher, in *REJ* 45: 5, n. 2 and the sources cited there.

[18] This was apparently a local Jewish custom.

THE CHARGE OF APPOINTMENT FOR A NAGID IN MAMLUK EGYPT

This is the charge of office to the *Raʾīs al-Yahūd* (the Nagid) which is cited in the *Taʿrīf*:[1]

It is incumbent upon him to unite his community and to gather their various elements in obedience to him. He is to judge them in accordance with the principals of his religion and the customary usages of its religious leaders wherever there are clear indications for him. He is responsible for contracting marriages and for all particulars involved which they consider generally important. He should do whatever is necessary to satisfy the two parties in a marriage or a divorce.

He must abide by the law of his religion in excommunicating anyone, and the person excommunicated must submit to his judgment.

He must act in accordance with what is in the Rabbinic Tradition, and he is also to carry out any action for which there is no specific scriptural evidence, but for which there is a consensus of the Rabbis.

He must pray toward Jerusalem which is the direction of their *qibla*[2] and the holy place of their faith. He is to do everything according to the Law of Moses, the Interlocutor of God, and to follow his example whenever it is certain that this was the action of that noble prophet. He should uphold the restrictions of the Torah as God has revealed them without any falsification, and without any change of wording by allegory or by substitution.[3]

He is to follow what is made incumbent upon them in the Covenant and in all that it requires of him. He should adhere to whatever sustains their remnant and thereby prevents the shedding of their blood. He is to follow whatever the Prophets and Rabbis have decreed, and whatever the Muslims have agreed to from these, and whatever the Hebrews expressed concerning it.

In addition to all this, he must make them fulfill what is required of them and their likes among the *ahl al-dhimma* who inhabit this

[1] The book referred to is al-ʿUmarī's (d. 1349) *al-Taʿrīf bi 'l-Muṣṭalaḥ al-Sharīf*, which like al-Qalqashandī's work was a manual for administration. For the parallel passage in the *Taʿrīf*, see the Cairo edition (A.H. 1312), pp. 142–43.

[2] The *qibla* is the direction a worshiper faces during prayer (that is, for the Jew towards Jerusalem, for the Muslim towards Mecca).

[3] The charge that the Jews (and Christians) have falsified their scriptures goes back to the time of Muḥammad's struggle with the Jews of Medina. It remained a standard accusation in Muslim polemical literature. See above, pp. 12–13 and 165–66.

country. He must also see to it that their persons are protected by their being humble and lowly and by their bowing their heads in submissiveness to the followers of the faith of Islam, by their giving way to Muslims in the streets[4] and when they are intermingled with them in the Bath House. He must also see to it that they bear the *Dhimmī* badge which has been ordained for them as an ornament for their turbans. It is to be fastened upon their heads to preserve them just as amulets are fastened.[5] He should know that their yellow badge is required so their red blood will not be spilled; that they are safe as long as they are under this sign; and that they may live peacefully as long as it is firmly attached. He is to urge them to continually renew the color of the badge. He is to order them that they are continually required to wear such badges clearly visible upon their heads.

They are not to show any contradiction in what he decides, nor let any opposition be understood from it. Anyone who speaks out strongly in opposition to him will meet some punishment short of death.

He is responsible for appointing the various offices of rank among his coreligionists from the rabbis on down according to their degree of merit and in accordance with their agreement. He has the final say in matters pertaining to all of their synagogues which have stood since the establishment of the *Dhimma* Covenant until now and which has been confirmed by the passage of time. There is to be no building of any new synagogues, nor any new additions made to the existing ones. Nothing is to be done which is not included in the *Dhimma* Contract or accorded their ancestors by the founding fathers of this *Umma* (the Muslim Community).

This should suffice. However, the most important of all these things is fear of God and terror of our strength.

al-Qalqashandī, *Ṣubḥ al-Aᶜshā,* vol. 11
(Cairo, 1913–19), pp. 390–91.

[4] Ar., *wa-ᶜadam muḍāyaqatihim fi 'l-ṭuruq*. Literally, "there should be no impeding them (that is, the Muslims) in the streets." *Dhimmīs* were expected to give way and to move to the inauspicious left side.

[5] That is, just as amulets are tightly fastened to protect the wearer from harm, so the badge of differentiation should be worn with the same care.

INSTRUCTIONS TO A MARKET INSPECTOR ON THE SUPERVISION OF DHIMMIS
(EGYPT, CA. 1300)

Know that any show of leniency towards the *Ahl al-Dhimma* in matters of religion is extremely dangerous. The Exalted One has said in His scripture: "O you who believe, do not take My enemy and your enemy as friends, showing them affection . . ."[1] A tradition has come down from the Prophet—may Allah bless him and grant him peace—in which he said: "I shall surely expel the Jews and Christians from the Arabian Peninsula so that I shall leave there only Muslims."[2] He also said: "The Jews and Christians may not live as fellow inhabitants in your capitals unless they have converted to Islam; if anyone apostatizes after his conversion, cut off his head."[3]

It is the duty of the *muḥtasib* to supervise the *ahl al-dhimma.* He should compel them to do what has been stipulated for them and required of them since the early days of Islam. He may not authorize them to neglect anything of this by word or action. He should compel them to fulfill all those things to which they had agreed in writing with the Commander of the Faithful ᶜUmar b. al-Khaṭṭāb—may Allah be pleased with him:—

. . . .[4]

The purpose of differentiating between them and Muslims is so that they shall not be shown any dignity. If any of them were the owners of high houses, they may be confirmed in their ownership of them, because they possessed it in accordance with these qualifications. However, if the building was in ruins, they may not restore it as it was.

If only ᶜUmar b. al-Khaṭṭāb—may Allah be pleased with him—could see the Jews and Christians nowadays! Their buildings rise over Muslim buildings and mosques. They are called by appellations which had been used for caliphs, and they even adopt their *kunyas.*[5] Among their appellations is "al-Rashīd" who was the father of the caliphs. They have such

[1] Sura 60:1.
[2] This is not a canonical *ḥādīth.*
[3] See the preceding note.
[4] An elaboration of the Pact of ᶜUmar follows at this point in the Arabic text. For one version of the Pact, see pp. 157–58.
[5] The *kunya* is the Arabic honorific name composed of *abū,* "father of," or "possessor of," plus the name of one's son or some special quality. According to the pact, it is forbidden for non-Muslims to adopt *kunyas.* This seems to have been almost totally ignored, however, throughout much of the Middle Ages.

kunyas as "Abu 'l-Ḥasan" which was that of ᶜAlī b. Abī Ṭālib—may Allah be pleased with him—and "Abu 'l-Faḍl" which had been the *kunya* of al-ᶜAbbās, the uncle of the Apostle of Allah. They have gone beyond the bounds of their station and have made a show of themselves in their words and deeds. Time has revealed their devilish nature, and yet the hand of the civil authorities has made this possible for them and has aided them. As a result, they ride mounts permitted only to Muslims, wear the finest clothes like theirs, and even employ them as servants. I myself have seen a Jew or a Christian riding, urging on his mount while a Muslim runs alongside his stirrup. Frequently, Muslims will humble themselves before such a one and obsequiously beseech him to remove the burden he has placed upon them.

As for their women—why when they go out of doors and walk in the streets, they are almost unrecognized. The same is true in the bathhouses. Many a time, a Christian woman will sit in the highest place in the bath while Muslim women sit below her. They go out into the market places, sit in the merchants' shops, and are treated with honor on account of their fine clothes. The merchants do not even know that these are *ahl al-dhimma.*

Therefore, it is the duty of the *muḥtasib* to be on the lookout for such things. He must censure this kind of behavior, and chastize whomever of these people openly act this way.

Ibn al-Ukhuwwa, *Maᶜālim al-Qurba,*
ed. Reuben Levy (London, 1938), pp. 38–43.

AL-MALIK AL-SALIH'S DECREE AGAINST THE DHIMMIS

(EGYPT, 1354)

Then they (the *dhimmīs*) returned to civil service posts sometime later.[1] However, the Sultan al-Malik al-Ṣāliḥ, the son of al-Malik al-Nāṣir, took measures to prevent them from this, and he reimposed the Stipulations of ᶜUmar upon them. To this effect, he had a Noble Rescript written. Copies of it were sent to the provincial governors, and it was read out from the pulpits of the mosques. It read as follows:

> A Noble Rescript to the effect that all the Jewish, Christian, and Samaritan communities in the land of Egypt, the divinely protected territories of Islam, and their provinces, are to conform to the authority of the Pact of the Commander of the Faithful ᶜUmar b. al-Khaṭṭāb—may Allah be pleased with him—which he accorded to their forebears. Namely, they are not to build in the Islamic lands any new monasteries, churches, or hermitages, neither are they to rebuild any such buildings which have fallen into ruin. Furthermore, they are not to harbor any spy, nor anyone suspected by the Muslims. They are not to conceal any treachery from the Muslims. They may not teach their children the Koran. They may not make any public show of polytheism. They may not try to prevent any of their kin who wish to embrace Islam from doing so. They may not resemble the Muslims in their dress. They must wear blue and yellow distinguishing costumes. Their women are likewise forbidden from resembling Muslim women. They may not ride on saddles. They are not to wear swords. They are not to ride horses or mules, but only on donkeys, seated sidesaddle on litters. They are not to sell wines.
>
> Furthermore, they are required to wear their special dress wherever they are. They shall bind the *zunnār* which may not be of silk around their waists. Christian women who appear in public are to wear a linen *izār* dyed blue, and Jewish women a yellow *izār*.[2] None of them is to enter a public bath unless he is wearing a sign around his neck which distinguishes him from a Muslim, such as a ring of iron, lead, or the like. They are not to build homes higher than Muslim homes. They may not even be the same height, but only lower. They may only beat the clapper softly and are not to raise their voices in their churches. They may not be employed in the service of our noble state—may Allah make its foundations firm. They may not

[1] That is after the purges under al-Malik al-Nāṣir, which were instituted in Rajab 700 (March–April 1301).

[2] The *izār* is a large, enveloping outer wrap. See above, p. 167.

serve in the employ of any of its amīrs—may Exalted Allah strengthen them. None of them may occupy any position which would give him authority over a single Muslim. The jurisdiction over the estates of their deceased shall be according to the noble Muḥammadan Religious Law. The administrative regulations regarding confiscation apply to them just as they do to the estates of deceased Muslims. *Dhimmī* women may not enter baths with Muslim women. Separate bathhouses shall be made for them, and only these may they enter.

This is in accordance with the rulings of the scholars of the noble Religious Law as it has been interpreted.

al-Qalqashandī, *Ṣubḥ al-Aᶜshā*, vol. 13
(Cairo, 1293/1918), pp. 378–79.

SOME JEWISH ANECDOTES FROM AN ANTI-DHIMMI TREATISE
(EGYPT, LATE THIRTEENTH–EARLY FOURTEENTH CENTURY)

In the days of the Abbasid al-Ma'mūn,[1] some Jew advanced to such a position that he would sit in a higher place than the nobles. So a distinguished Muslim devised a strategem and wrote a note to al-Ma'mūn with the following verse:

> O son of him[2] to whom all men were obedient,
> Whose law was a binding duty,
> Lo, the man whom you honor
> Is—this writer claims—a liar!

Al-Ma'mūn replied: "You have spoken truly and have proven your devotion!" The Jew was immediately drowned.

Al-Ma'mūn then related to those present a story about al-Miqdād b. al-Aswad al-Kindī,[3] a companion of the Apostle of Allah—may Allah bless him and grant him peace. While on one of his journeys, he was accompanied by some Jew for the entire day. On the dawn of the next day, al-Miqdād—may Allah be pleased with him—suddenly remembered the words of the Apostle—may Allah bless him and grant him peace: "No Jew can be alone with a Muslim without plotting to harm him." So al-Miqdād said to the Jew: "I swear by Allah, you shall not part company with me without telling what kind of harm you were planning to do me. If you do not, I shall kill you!" The Jew replied: "Do I have your assurance that no harm will come to me if I tell?" "Yes," he said, and bound himself with a solemn oath.

Then the Jew admitted: "Ever since I have been traveling with you, I have been planning for you to lose your head so I might trample it beneath my shoe." At this al-Miqdād—may Allah be pleased with him—exclaimed: "The Apostle of Allah was right—may Allah bless him and grant him peace!"

It is told that in the time of some king there lived a Jew named al-Hārūnī, who held a high position in his household. Once he played a game of chess with him in his drinking-hall on the promise that he might

[1] He was caliph from 813–33.

[2] The reference is to al-Ma'mūn's father Hārūn al-Rashīd.

[3] He appears several times in the *Sīra*, where he is usually referred to as al-Miqdād b. ᶜAmr.

request whatever he desired for himself should he win. When he did in fact win, he asked the king to fulfill his promise. "Ask what you wish," the king told him. So he replied: "Let the king command that there be stricken from the Koran the verse that reads: "Verily, the true religion in the sight of Allah is Islam."[4]

The king immediately had his head cut off.

I have been informed by the most unimpeachable sources that the physician Moses (Maimonides) was ill, and the Qāḍī al-Fāḍil payed him a visit. The Jew was a scholar and a gentleman. So he said to al-Fāḍil: "Your sense of decency has made you come and visit me. Let me advise you not to receive any medical treatment from a Jew, because with us, whoever desecrates the Sabbath—his blood is licit for us." The Qāḍī thereupon banned Jews from practicing medicine or being employed in that capacity.

al-Wāsiṭī, *Kitāb Radd ᶜalā Ahl al-Dhimma,*
ed. R. Gottheil, *JAOS* 41, no. 5 (1921): 396–97.

[4] Sura 3:19/18.

TRAVELING INCOGNITO WITH A MAMLUK CARAVAN

We left Bilbays[1] on Sunday 13 July (1481)[2] with the two caravans (one of travelers, the other a Mamluk military escort). That same day, we reached a small place called al-Khaṭāra. No Jews were living there. We went continually through the desert, and all the way we wore the white turban like the Arabs and Turks with the permission of the caravan master even though they knew we were Jews, because Jews and Christians have to pay a lot of protection money. Despite the fact that when the natives of the place spoke to me, I could not understand their language, they still believed them (that we were Muslims), because I would sit and eat on the ground and do all that they did. For although the Turks and Arabs have the same faith, they do not understand one another's language. We left al-Khaṭāra on Monday 14 July 1481, and came to al-Ṣāliḥiyya. It is a small place like al-Khaṭāra. There we paid the protection money as though we were Turks. These people are appointed by the Sultan to guard the desert route. They have the permission of the monarch to charge for each horse a half *mu'ayyadī*,[3] which is called *b-r-y-f-m*,[4] which is equivalent to one of our dinars. However, from Jews and Christians they take more than they ought because they are bandits.

It so happened that after we had paid the protection money that a Muslim informed on our translator, saying that he was Jewish. All the natives of the place rose up against us and demanded two ducats[5] for us. The Turkish caravan master came forward brimming with rage and said that the truth of the matter was that he is indeed a Jew, but that I had purchased him as a slave and that he was my bondsman. He extricated us from their grasp by force, even though they were screaming among themselves. So we were freed—praise be to the Living God!

Meshullam of Volterra, *Massāᶜ*,
ed. Avraham Yaᶜari (Jerusalem, 1948), p. 61.

[1] Bilbays was the first stop for caravans and troops going from Cairo to Palestine and Syria. See G. Wiet, "Bilbays," *EI*[2] 1: 1218a.

[2] Actually, Sunday fell upon the fifteenth that year.

[3] This half dirham silver coin was named after the sultan who first issued it, al-Malik al-Mu'ayyad, in 1415. It was called by the European merchants "*maydin*." See E. Ashtor, *Histoire des prix et des salaires dans l'Orient médiéval* (Paris, 1969), p. 279.

[4] I do not know what he intends to signify. The text here is corrupt.

[5] On the importance of the Florentine ducat in Mamluk Egypt, see Jere L. Bacharach, "The Dinar Versus the Ducat," *IJMES* 4 (1973): 77–96.

THE CONDITION OF THE JEWS IN JERUSALEM IN THE EARLY SIXTEENTH CENTURY

Brother. I wish you to know how these dogs of Jews are trampled upon, beaten and ill-treated, as they deserve, by every infidel nation, and this is the just decree of God. They live in this country in such subjection that words cannot describe it. And it is a most extraordinary thing that there in Jerusalem, where they committed the sin for which they are dispersed throughout the world, they are by God more punished and afflicted than in any other part of the world. And over a long time I have witnessed that. Among themselves they are likewise divided, and one hates and persecutes the other in such a way that the Saracens worry them like dogs. No infidel would touch with his hand a Jew lest he be contaminated, but when they wish to beat them, they take off their shoes with which they strike them on the moustaches; the greatest wrong and insult to a man is to call him a Jew. And it is a right notable thing that the Moslems do not accept a Jew into their creed unless he first becomes a Christian.[1] And in point of fact I saw two Jews in Jerusalem, men of reputation and among them not of the lowest condition, who wished to abandon the Mosaic law and become Saracens to be in a position to take revenge of other Jews their enemies, so first they had themselves baptised by the Greeks, seeing that otherwise the Saracens would not accept them.

And if they were not subsidized by the Jews of Christendom the Jews who live in Judea would die like dogs of hunger.[2] Now putting aside everything else, I shall return to the indulgences that are in the city of Jerusalem.

Fra Francesco Suriano, *Treatise on the Holy Land,*
trans. T. Bellorini and E. Hoade
(Jerusalem, 1949), pp. 101–2.

[1] This is absolute fantasy. Under strict Islamic law, conversions may only be made to Islam within the Muslim world, although this was frequently ignored in the cases of Christians converting to Judaism and vice versa. However, that Muslims should have required Jews to convert first to Christianity before accepting Islam is incredible.

[2] The Jewish community in Jerusalem has been heavily dependent upon charitable support throughout much of the Middle Ages and up to early modern times.

THE RISE AND FALL OF A FAMILY OF COURT JEWS
(MOROCCO, BEGINNING OF THE FOURTEENTH CENTURY)

The Sultan Abū Yaᶜqūb (Yūsuf) had a predilection for his pleasures during his youth, which however, he concealed from his father Yaᶜqūb b. ᶜAbd al-Ḥaqq, who was a man of religion and dignity. He would drink wine and was addicted to carousing. A certain Khalīfa b. Waqqāṣa, one of the protégé Jews of Fez, was his majordomo. Having such retainers from among the people of the Pact was customary among the amirs.[1] He ingratiated himself to Abū Yaᶜqūb by performing a variety of services for him. The prince employed him in the pressing of wine and its production. He (Khalīfa) became because of this the prince's intimate confidant, and he became wealthy in his service.

This continued until the death of Yaᶜqūb b. ᶜAbd al-Ḥaqq, when his son Yūsuf took up the burden of his rule. He still spent his private hours in carousing. Ibn Waqqāṣa had the singular distinction of privately attending him as his mayor of the palace. His authority waxed great and his rank in the state rose. The courtiers took orders from him, and he became the leading personality among them. His power seemed to become ever greater as the dynasty grew in strength.

My teacher al-Ābilī informed me that this Khalīfa had a brother named Ibrāhīm and a paternal cousin also named Khalīfa, who was nicknamed "the Younger." His in-laws were the Banū Sabtī[2] family, whose patriarch, a man named Mūsā, was his chief lieutenant in the stewardship of the palace.

The sultan did not awaken from the intoxication and distraction of his youth until he suddenly found them enjoying such a position that the leading chiefs of the tribe,[3] the viziers, the sharīfs,[4] and even the *ᶜulamā'*, courted their favor. This troubled him, and he kept a close watch upon them.[5]

One of his loyal adherents, ᶜAbd Allāh b. Abī Madyan, understood the sultan's attitude toward them, and he took the opportunity to discredit them before him. He devised a way for the sultan to rid himself of them.

[1] That is, the Merinid aristocracy.

[2] The family name indicates that they hailed from Ceuta (Ar., *Sabta*).

[3] That is, the Banū Marīn.

[4] The descendants of the Prophet, who were held in particular veneration in Morocco.

[5] *Wa-taraṣṣada bihim.* The verb in Arabic also has the meaning of "to lie in wait" (in ambush), and this also seems to be the implication here. In other words: "he kept a close watch upon them and waited for his chance to overthrow them."

So the sultan pounced upon them in one fell swoop. They were arrested in Shaᶜbān 701 (April 1302) in his camp at the siege of Tlemcen. He executed Khalīfa the Elder, his brother Ibrāhīm, and Mūsā b. al-Sabtī and his brethren, after they had been examined (under torture). He ordered them mutilated. The catastrophe was visited upon their retainers, their families and relations. No remnant of them was left, with the exception of Khalīfa the Younger, who was the sole survivor because his importance was held in contempt. However, he was killed later, as we shall recount, and he joined the rest of them.

All matters are in Allah's hand—may He be exalted!

Ibn Khaldūn, *Kitāb al-ᶜIbar,* vol. 7
(Bulaq, 1284/1867–68), pp. 232–33.

THE FALL OF IBN BATASH SPELLS CATASTROPHE FOR MOROCCAN JEWRY

On the first of Rabīᶜ I 869 (1 November 1464), while we were in Tlemcen, news kept arriving from Fez of the aggrandizement of the Jews there in authority and importance through the Jewish vizier whom the ruler of Fez, ᶜAbd al-Ḥaqq the Merīnid, had appointed. He did this after having killed a number of viziers of the Waṭṭāsid clan, having expelled a group of them, and after their having rebelled against him outside Fez. The Jews in Fez came to dominate the Muslims, to oppress them, and to cause them harm. They waxed in importance, and their power increased, until there befell the Sultan, the above-mentioned vizier, and the Jews what we shall relate below—if Allah Exalted wills it.

. . . .

On the eleventh of Shawwāl 869 (7 June 1465), the news arrived in Tlemcen from Fez that the great mass of the people of Fez had risen up against the Jews there and had killed them to almost the last man. Only five men and six women—or even less than that—survived. These managed to hide themselves and remain undetected. This was a tremendous event and a great massacre which ended with the slaughtering of ᶜAbd al-Ḥaqq the Merīnid, Sultan of Fez and Ruler of the Further Maghreb, despite the majesty of his rank, the greatness of his position and his kingdom. The rulership was given over after him to one of the Sharīfs of Fez, a man called al-Sharīf Muḥammad b. ᶜImrān.

Regarding this affair, it is reported that ᶜAbd al-Ḥaqq ruled over Fez for more than thirty years, but he was dominated by the Waṭṭāsid viziers. That was the practice in the Maghreb at Fez. It was customary that the supreme authority belong to the viziers who were the real rulers of the people and country. They had the power to command and to forbid, and nothing could be done in that kingdom without their counsel. The Merīnid Sultan was but a tool for them just as the caliphs are in Egypt now with the Turkish sultans (that is, the Mamluks). Of course, the Merīnids were more powerful than the caliphs there. This ᶜAbd al-Ḥaqq continually employed every trick and every device until at last he was able to cause the death of a great number of them and executed the vizier Yaḥyā b. Yaḥyā. . . . The Waṭṭāsid faction was scattered on account of this, and ᶜAbd al-Ḥaqq took control and personally exercised power. He appointed a vizier from the Waṭṭāsid family who agreed with his wishes and who had no real say. Moreover, his position in the vizierate was similar to ᶜAbd al-

Ḥaqq's position in the sultanate previously. He had no importance, no prestige, indeed, no name at all!

He (ᶜAbd al-Ḥaqq) appointed a Jew from Fez by the name of Aaron b. Baṭash, who was a moneychanger or some sort of banker for the viziers, and made him a deputy vizier. And the authority of the vizier was further restricted. He sought by this to spite the Waṭṭāsids—after having already caused the death of some of them, having imprisoned others in Meknes, and having appointed that insignificant vizier from amongst them.

He raised the Jew to an exalted position, although he pretended to be disturbed at having need of him. This Jew remained the de facto vizier, for there was no vizier other than he, and he had the final say in the vizierate—all while remaining in his religion! ᶜAbd al-Ḥaqq was pleased by this because he had achieved through this the utmost vexation and humiliation of the Waṭṭāsids. ᶜAbd al-Ḥaqq made this Jew his intimate confidant—so much so, that the kingdom passed over into his hands. ᶜAbd al-Ḥaqq felt secure with him, since the Jew could not possibly transgress his boundaries or exceed his limitations—or so he thought. The Jew obtained the power to command and to prohibit within the kingdom of Fez, despite his continued adherence to Judaism. He even began to be addressed as vizier sometimes. The Jews in Fez became arrogant during his tenure—even in the provinces. They came to have authority, influence, prestige, and the power to command and be obeyed. Meanwhile, ᶜAbd al-Ḥaqq was pleased with this. Indeed, he was delighted.

Now that vizier wore a sword on an iron belt on which was engraved the "Throne Verse" (Sura 2:256), and perhaps also "There is no God but Allah and Muḥammad is the Apostle of Allah."[1] He would ride horses marked with the vizieral insignia in his master's presence. And the ignorant would salute him with the title of vizier. He would accompany the Sultan to the mosque on Friday, help him dismount, and then stand by the gate of the mosque until the Sultan went in. Then he would sit down at the mosque gate till the Friday prayers were over, at which time he would remount and return with the Sultan.

Many ugly deeds, foul acts, and injustices were clearly attributed to this accursed one. And the domination of the Jews over the Muslims of Fez increased through him. The common people could not bear them. They came to detest ᶜAbd al-Ḥaqq for this, and they sought his downfall, even though the Waṭṭāsids had also committed a great many injustices against the people. But they had been Muslim viziers, as opposed to this accursed one who was not of the Faith.

Sometime later that year, it happened that ᶜAbd al-Ḥaqq left Fez on

[1] The Muslim profession of faith (*shahāda*).

some business, accompanied by his Jewish vizier. This Jew left as his spokesman in Fez another Jew, some relation of his, named Saul b. Baṭash, who was attached to the Royal Palace in Fez Jdīd.[2] This Jew, it seems, summoned a woman of the Sharīfs of Fez for some matter and spoke to her in an offensive manner. It is even said that he actually struck her, or something of the like. News of this incident reached the Preacher of Fez, Sīdī Abū ᶜAbd Allāh Muḥammad. He and the Muslims were furious on account of the situation of the Jews, their ostentation, and their lording over the Muslims. He would always allude to matters concerning the Jews in his Friday sermon at the Great Mosque of Fez, which is called the Qarawiyyīn.[3] He now tried to urge and encourage the common people that perhaps they would rise up for the sake of Exalted Allah after this affair and revolt. His fame spread because of this. When this incident in which the Sharīfa was mistreated occurred, he dedicated himself to Allah, left his home crying out at the top of his voice throughout the streets and byways of Fez with these words: "Whoever does not rise up for Allah's sake has neither Chivalry[4] nor Religion!" He followed this with shouts of "Holy War! Holy War!"

He ordered others also to make this summons to a holy war throughout the streets of Fez. The masses responded to it and joined him in revolt on the spot. A great mass gathered around him from every corner of Fez.[5] They conducted him to the home of the Sharīf Muḥammad b. ᶜImrān, who is the *Mezwār*[6] of the Sharīfs of Fez, which is comparable to the *Naqīb al-Ashrāf* in this country (Egypt). However, notwithstanding his venerability, his authoritative word, and his manifest wisdom, he did not respond when the Preacher entered and called him to revolt with him. He excused himself to him, explaining that he did not deem it proper to revolt himself, and that he could not take the lead in this affair when there were the

[2] New Fez, the quarter founded by the Merinids. See above, Part One, p. 78.

[3] The Qarawiyyīn, which takes its name from the Qarawanese quarter in Old Fez (Fās al-Bālī), remains to this day the leading mosque and institution of higher education in the city. See Henri Terrasse, *La mosquée al-Qaraouiyin à Fès* (Paris, 1968).

[4] Ar., *muruwwa,* Arab manly virtues. See Ignaz Goldziher's classic study "Muruwwa and Dīn" in his *Muslim Studies,* vol. 1, trans. C. R. Barber and S. M. Stern (London, 1967), pp. 11–44; see also S. D. Goitein, *Religion in a Religious Age* (Cambridge, Mass., 1974), p. 10.

[5] Ar., *min kull fajj ᶜamīq,* a koranic expression which literally means "from every deep ravine" (Sura 22:27/28).

[6] The *Mezwār* is the chief officer of the Sharifs (*Shorfa*) in any Moroccan city. The word is from Berber *amzuaru* (first). See Edmond Destaing, *Vocabulaire Français-Berbère* (Paris, 1920), p. 230; and Ernest T. Abdel-Massih, *A Computerized Lexicon of Tamazight* (Ann Arbor, 1971), p. 12.

ᶜ*Ulamā'*[7] in Fez who had not yet been consulted for a legal opinion in the matter.

They immediately hastened to find the ᶜ*Ulamā'* and gathered them together. Among these was the most illustrious of them at that time, the ᶜĀlim and the Muftī of Fez, al-Shaykh al-Imām al-Sharīf, the Scholar of Scholars, Sīdī Abū ᶜAbd Allāh Muḥammad al-Qawrī. They brought him and those whom they had gathered to the home of the Sayyid al-Sharīf. The preacher immediately said to them: "Join us in a holy war, come fight, and bring glory to Islam!" The common people repeated his words and then said: "If you will not fight with us, then we shall do battle with you first. For you are Sharīfs and ᶜ*Ulamā'*, and yet you are content that the Jews rule over you." Then they called out again: "Holy War! Holy War!" and made every effort to incite them by this. They demanded that al-Qawrī issue a *fatwā* (legal opinion) for them, but he refused to do this, and tried to excuse himself, saying he was afraid of the authorities. They continued to press him, and afterwards drafted a written query concerning the incident at hand and concerning what had been done by the Jew and his coreligionists, maintaining that this was a clear violation of the Pact (of ᶜUmar), or even worse. They unsheathed their swords and said to al-Qawrī, "We too have authority and power! We have risen up for Allah's sake and have consecrated ourselves. This is the question for which we have sought a *fatwā* from you conforming to the law of Allah Exalted. If you will not do this, then we shall rid the world of you, for you would be a scholar who did not act in accordance with your own legal practice." They went on to say other things of this sort. There was nothing he could do to extricate himself except writing in his own hand that it was lawful to kill the Jews, to revolt against them, and that it was even lawful to revolt against the Sultan.

When he had finished writing, they rushed to the Jewish Quarter and put them to the sword. They killed as many of them as Allah wished them to kill, not sparing anyone until they had annihilated them, and thus cleared the quarter of them. It was a day to be remembered in Fez and a great slaughter in which a group of Jews of considerable number were killed. Then they set out for the Royal Palace, stormed it, and killed the Jewish deputy vizier who was inside.

The crowd then acclaimed the Sayyid al-Sharīf Muḥammad b. ᶜImrān, who was mentioned above, installed him in the Palace and sought to pay him their formal allegiance. However, some experienced and sensible men, people of intellect and foresight, pointed out that they ought not to do that until they had defeated the Sultan ᶜAbd al-Ḥaqq. Otherwise, he might prove quite harmful to them.

[7] The religious scholars.

They then came up with a plan whereby the notables of Fez and the Sharīf would write to ᶜAbd al-Ḥaqq, who was away from the city, telling him of the incident and of the uprising of the mob and of their rebellion. They would inform him that "the Royal Palace would have been reduced to a plundered ruin if the mood of the crowd had not been calmed by placing the Sayyid al-Sharīf into it, and he is acting as your deputy until the time of your return when measures can be taken for the good of the Muslims and the common people. Nothing will be removed from your authority." They sent him a letter with this and other words to this effect.

When the letter reached him, he immediately made preparations to return to Fez. But the Jew hastened to him and said: "It is not in your best interest to go back. What they have written is to trick my Lord. If my Lord sees fit—may Allah grant him victory—he should flee to Taza[8] or some other city until this flare-up is extinguished and my Lord's position is strengthened. Then he may go to Fez. This is best."

The Jew was right, but when a man's fate has been sealed his insight is blind. So ᶜAbd al-Ḥaqq berated him and said: "It is your advice that is deceitful from beginning to end! All this is because of you!" Nothing good comes from you."

One of the Merinids was present at this session, and when he saw that the Sultan had become enraged with the Jew, he rushed over to him and pierced him with his lance before the very eyes of the Sultan. The Jew immediately fell dead in front of ᶜAbd al-Ḥaqq. He hoped by this that the people of Fez would be appeased when the news reached them. The killer advised ᶜAbd al-Ḥaqq to settle this affair quickly by returning to Fez. Others of ᶜAbd al-Ḥaqq's close companions agreed with him in this. It was poor advice because of inexorable Fate, because of Destiny. ᶜAbd al-Ḥaqq's time had come. His end was at hand.

The sultan made his way back so quickly that he reached Fez ahead of his troops accompanied only by a few soldiers. Most of the troops sensed that Fortune was not with him and that disaster was imminent. So they lagged behind fearing for their lives at the hands of the mob. They were far behind ᶜAbd al-Ḥaqq when he entered Fez with only three men from his entourage.

When news of his arrival reached the people of Fez, the mob went out to meet him, appearing as if they were coming out to welcome him. There went out with them the group known as the *Wakkāra* (whoremongers), who are somewhat like the *Zuᶜar* (debauchees) in this country.[9] The

[8] A town 116 kilometers east of Fez.

[9] By "this country," ᶜAbd al-Bāsiṭ means his native Egypt. These are apparently demimonde types. The *zuᶜar* of Cairo consisted "almost wholly of criminals and thieves recruited among slaves and servants, some of whom were

moment they layed eyes on ᶜAbd al-Ḥaqq, they revolted and shouted to one another, "Holy War! Holy War!" When the soldiers accompanying ᶜAbd al-Ḥaqq heard this, they deserted him and fled. He was seized by the arm and pulled off his horse. It so happened that this took place near the abbatoirs of Fez. He was brought into an abbatoir as is done with a sheep and was immediately bound and slaughtered.[10] This took place on 22 Ramaḍān of that year (18 May 1465).

The crowd then returned to Fez and acclaimed the Sayyid al-Sharīf Muḥammad b. ᶜImrān, acknowledging him as their ruler and pledging their allegiance to him.

When the people in the cities farther away from Fez heard of this event, they revolted against the Jews of those regions and did to them what the people of Fez had done to their Jews. This was a great catastrophe for the Jews, the like of which had perhaps never previously befallen them. There perished as many of them as Allah Exalted willed.

ᶜAbd al-Bāsiṭ b. Khalīl, *al-Rawḍ al-Bāsim*,
ed. Robert Brunschvig, in *Deux récits* . . . (Paris, 1936),
pp. 49–55 (Ar. text), pp. 113–21 (Fr. trans.).

---

free men and others not. . . . The *zuᶜar* were organized into gangs of thugs who sometimes fought each other in broad daylight . . . " (Ira M. Lapidus, *Muslim Cities in the Later Middle Ages* [Cambridge, Mass., 1967], p. 173.) Unfortunately, nothing is known about the Moroccan counterparts of the *zuᶜar* outside of this passage in ᶜAbd al-Bāsiṭ.

[10] On this type of ritual slaughter for villains, see above, p. 216, n. 8.

A FLEMISH SCHOLAR'S OBSERVATIONS ON THE JEWS OF MERINID FEZ
(MID-FIFTEENTH CENTURY)

Fez is divided into two parts. The Old City is quite populous with some 50,000 families. It extends for a distance of approximately half a league from its center to the New City, which is situated outside of it, and is likewise enclosed by its own walls. It is in the New City that the ruler and some of his entourage live, as well as people of a lesser condition, numerous enough to justify calling the place a city. Adjacent to this is the Jewish Quarter, which is likewise surrounded by its own walls. Approximately 4000 Jews dwell there. I reside among them because neither in the Old City nor in the New, would I dare maintain my household. To be sure, the Jews do not hate the Christians any less than do the Muslims, but they are less audacious because they have to pay such a heavy tribute here each month that I too would grieve continually were I in their place. The more the sultan needs money, the more they have to pay. It is for this reason that they—broken by adversity—have become ingenious at providing the money due to the sultan. Thus, neither Christians nor Moor can do anything against Jewish intrigues. These, however, I can easily overlook. How else can these miserable creatures pay such a heavy tribute except by actively stealing? They would prefer to do that than die in prison.

As for me—by the grace of God—I conduct myself in such a way that I fear neither Jews nor Muslims.

Nicholas Clenardus in a letter to Arnold Streyters (April 12, 1451), in Alphonse Roersch, ed. and trans., *Correspondance de Nicolas Clénard* (Brussels, 1940–41), Latin text in vol. 1, p. 186; French trans. in vol. 3, pp. 137–38.

PORTRAIT OF A JEWISH PHYSICIAN BY HIS MUSLIM PUPIL

I pursued the study of medicine with the foremost master, a learned, skillful, and well-read man, Moses b. Samuel b. Judah al-Isrāʾīlī al-Mālaqī al-Andalusī. This Jewish practitioner of the art of medicine was commonly known by his patrynomic (Ibn Samuel) and by the familial name of Ibn Ashqar.[1] May God Exalted guide him to Islam. Never have I heard of or seen any *dhimmī* as skilled as he in this science, as well as in the science of preparing magic squares and calendars[2] and in certain ancient sciences. Despite this, he is extremely pious in his religion, as he himself declares. And he firmly believes in it! He is of Spanish Jewish origin, but was born on Malaga sometime before 820 (1417). He learned from his father and others and excelled in the art of medicine. He moved to Tlemcen and made it his residence. Many distinguished men have sought him out in order to study with him. I attached myself to him for a period of time. I learned many useful things from him in medicine and other subjects. He bestowed his diploma on me.[3]

I have heard recently that he has finally attained the chief medical post in Tlemcen. He is an intimate member of the entourage of the ruler of that city.[4] However due to his intelligence and good sense he does not get involved in anything that has to do with government.

I ask Allah Exalted to let him die in the faith of the Prophet Muḥammad—may Allah bless him and grant him peace.

ᶜAbd al-Bāsiṭ b. Khalīl, *al-Rawḍ al-Bāsim,*
ed. Robert Brunschvig, in *Deux récits* . . . (Paris, 1936),
pp. 44–45 (Ar. text), pp. 107–8 (Fr. trans.).

[1] The names Ibn Ashqar and al-Ashqar were common among Spanish refugees to North Africa. The name in Arabic indicates "reddish-blonde hair" and "fair complexion." For others of this name, see the various articles "Alashkar" in *EJ* 2: 511–13.

[2] The division between science and pseudo-science was hazy during this period.

[3] Ar., *ijāza* (literally, "permission") was the document from a master entitling his pupil to teach and practice what he had taught him.

[4] The ruler was the Zayyanid Abū ᶜAbd Allāh Muḥammad III (ruled 1461–68).

DAMASCENE JEWRY IN 1522

The Jews there (Damascus) number about 500 households. They have three synagogues which are beautifully built and adorned—one for the Sefardim, one for the native Jews,[1] and one for the Sicilians. In each there is a Ḥākhām, who reads a little Maimonides with them every morning after prayers. Rabbi Isaac Ḥāvēr is the Ḥākhām of the Sicilians. He is also an outstanding physician. Rabbi Isaac Masᶜūd is the Ḥākhām of the Sefardim, and Rabbi Shem-Tov al-Furanī of the native Jews. There is no yeshiva there for advanced talmudic studies. There is only primary instruction, each teacher taking thirty or forty pupils.

There is also another synagogue at the end of the town called ᶜUnb.[2] A mile outside of Damascus there is a place called Jawbar,[3] where there is a community of Arabic-speaking Jews numbering about sixty households. There is a very handsome synagogue there, the like of which I have never seen. It is built in colonnades, with six columns on the right and seven on the left. Above the synagogue there is a beautiful cave in which, it is said, Elijah the Prophet—may his memory be blessed—hid. The synagogue is said to date from the time of Elisha. There is a stone upon which they say he annointed Hazael.[4] At a later period, R. Eliezer b. ᶜArakh renovated it.[5] It is indeed an awesome place. According to what many people told me, no enemy has ever dominated it, and many miracles have been performed there. In times of distress, Jews always gather in it, and nobody harms them.

R. Moses Bassola d'Ancona,
Massāᶜōt Ereṣ Yisrā'ēl, ed. Itzhak Ben-Zvi
(Jerusalem, 1938), pp. 67–68.

[1] Like many of the Italian Jewish writers of the period, R. Moses calls the native Jews *Moreschi* (Moors).

[2] This synagogue was located on a tract of land known as Ḥawsh al-Bāshā.

[3] This synagogue is indeed very ancient and is already mentioned in the Talmud (ᶜErūvīn 61b).

[4] 2 Kings 8:7–15; also 1 Kings 19:15–16.

[5] He was a disciple of R. Yoḥannan b. Zakkay (first century).

AN ITALIAN JEW DESCRIBES THE REVIVAL OF SAFED UNDER THE OTTOMANS

(SIXTEENTH CENTURY)

Blessed are you unto the Lord

My brethren,

Be not angry that I do not write you at such length as I had intended to do.

What shall I tell you about this country, as so many people before me have reported its character and greatness in writing and orally? In general, I should like to tell you that, just as in Italy, improvements are being made and new settlements founded, while the population is increasing daily. Such is the case here too. He who saw Safed ten years ago, and observes it now, has the impression of a miracle. For more Jews are arriving here continually, and the tailoring trade grows daily. I have been told that more than 15,000 suits have been manufactured in Safed during this year, besides fancy suits. Every man and every woman who works woolen fabric earns an abundant living.[1]

I have already made inquiries after the Ten Tribes. This matter is a miraculous thing in our eyes, and beyond the reach of all people who travel in distant countries, even more than a whole year's journey through a desert. Many people, and particularly travelers, told me for certain that on the road to Mecca many Jewish tent-dwellers live in the desert in the neighborhood of many Arabs who rob everybody who passes by. The Jews and the Arabs have an equal share in the booty. But when a Jew comes across, they offer him gifts and bring him to a safe place.[2] I heard many stories of this kind. When I was in Tripoli, a Jewish merchant came from Egypt who had 85 servants and handmaids, all Ethiopians. He carried with him a great deal of sugar, rice, paper and other articles; he sold and exchanged them and continued his voyage. Another Jew, a merchant from Tripoli, who carried precious stones and spices with him, came and told me that he had traveled by boat as far as Ethiopia. He saw many miraculous things during a storm on the sea. He traveled on a ship put together without iron nails.[3] When he was there he saw people walking about naked,

[1] On the textile industry in Safed, see also below, p. 296, n. 6, and also Part One above, p. 89.

[2] These legends persisted into modern times. The Jews were usually associated with the people of Khaybar.

[3] The boats that plied the Indian Ocean had an outer netting that held the hull together. See, for example, the thirteenth-century illustration of such a vessel in Richard Ettinghausen, *Arab Painting* (Geneva, 1962), p. 108.

without any clothes because of the great heat. He himself wore nothing else than a shirt of linen, and even this was too heavy for him. He also told me that he had come as far as Sinyēl.[4] This is a big town exclusively inhabited by Jews. They sold to the king of Portugal 40,000 loads of pepper a year. The money they received was used by them in commercial enterprises. They only recognize the Code of Maimonides and possess no other authorities or traditional law.[5]

I have no special news from the country, except that our gracious lord and king (Sultan Sulaymān) has marched from Constantinople into the territories of (Shah Ṭahmāsp) al-Ṣūfī,[6] that is, into the Persian Empire. He has taken his land from him without a fight or a battle as far as Baghdad.

There is nothing new in all the Galilee. There is no particular news in Jerusalem (may it be rebuilt and reestablished speedily and in our days. Amen.), except they have brought water from a well which is on the road to Hebron into the fortress which has been built on Mount Zion. Powder and cannon have also been brought there to strengthen it. I have not been to Jerusalem so far, myself, because of my misfortunes. For on the 5th of Adar (February 10), I entered Safed, and a month later, my son Elijah's servant came, and there occurred that which occurred.[7]

Our sister was in Jerusalem and in Hebron for more than two months. You will hear from her own lips about whatever her eyes have seen. She brings with her also a list of the tombs of all the Saints buried in the Holy Land. It has been handwritten for her by the scribes in Jerusalem.

The ship arriving from Ragusa[8] brought news of the death of Pope Clement VII[9] and of the election of Cardinal Alexander Farnese[10]—may the Lord protect and keep him. I think he, too, will be favorably disposed towards the Jews. Because misfortunes overtook me as soon as I arrived. I have not done any work.

The Exile here is not like in our homeland.[11] The Turks hold re-

[4] Probably Shinkali on the Malabar coast of India. This town had a Jewish community until it was destroyed by the Portuguese about ten years before this letter was written. See Walter J. Fischel, "Cochin," *EJ* 5: 622–23.

[5] The importance of Maimonides' Code was probably due to the close ties with Yemenite Jewry.

[6] He was the second ruler of the Safavid dynasty and reigned from 1524–76.

[7] Dei Rossi's son had been captured by pirates and was being held for ransom.

[8] The Italian name of Dubrovnik.

[9] He was pope from 1523–34 and was favorably disposed towards the Jews.

[10] He became Pope Paul III (1534–49). Dei Rossi's judgment about him was correct.

[11] He means to say that there is no anti-Semitism here as in Italy.

spectable Jews in esteem. Here and in Alexandria, Egypt, Jews are the chief officers and administrators of the customs, and of the king's revenues. No injuries are perpetrated against them in all the empire. Only this year, in consequence of the extraordinary expenditure caused by the war against Shah Ṭahmāsp al-Ṣūfī, were the Jews required to make advances of loans to the princes. Part of the money came from the taxes on the Jewish quarters and part came from town revenues which the Jews tax-farm. Scholars, however, did not have to pay a penny except for the poll tax.

All articles of commerce are available in these regions. Fibers, spun and unspun, are exported from Safed in great quantities, also gallnuts, scammony, oil, honey, and silk in smaller quantities. From the adjoining regions come crimson silk, Cordovan carpets, and all kinds of spices, including pepper, cloves, ginger, and cane-spices. Many people including Jews buy these goods as merchandise.

My daughter-in-law and my grandson Moses are here with me, and tomorrow we shall walk around Safed—God willing. My wife Sarah, since she has come to Safed has recovered with God's help. For the water and the air are unusually good. For this reason illnesses are few here, and therefore, the art of medicine does not flourish here, and physicians do not earn much of a livelihood. Sick people eat cucumbers, both of the large and small variety, squash, and many kinds of fruit.

Now I bless you as long as I live, I talk about you evening and morning, and I pray for you and for all the inhabitants of Italy. . . . Remember me to all our friends and acquaintances. And may the Lord grant that we see each other in the joy of Judea and Jerusalem together with all of Israel our brethren in our lifetime, speedily, and in our days. Amen.

In great, great haste, your brother David dei Rossi, who writes late on Saturday night, shortly before dawn, on the 9th of Nisan 5295 (14 March, 1535). Love and abundant greetings.

Letter of David dei Rossi from the abridged English translation in F. Kobler, *A Treasury of Jewish Letters*, vol. 2 (Philadelphia, 1953), pp. 337–40, revised according to the Hebrew text in Yaari, *Letters from the Land of Israel*, pp. 183–87.

DON JOSEPH ATTEMPTS TO REBUILD TIBERIAS AS A JEWISH CITY

(SECOND HALF OF THE SIXTEENTH CENTURY)

Then Don Joseph Nasi came to Ferrara, among those who escaped from the iron cauldron, Portugal, and lived there for some time. Thence he went to Turkey, where he found grace in the eyes of the King Sulayman, who loved him greatly. And the king gave him the ruins of Tiberias and of seven country villages around it, and made him lord and prince over them at that time.

Don Joseph sent there R. Joseph Adret (Ibn Ardut), his attendant, to rebuild the walls of the city, and he went and he too found favor in the king's eyes, and he gave him sixty aspers[1] each day. The king sent with him eight men born in his house, and gave him the order written and sealed with the imperial seal, and recommended him to the pasha of Damascus and the pasha of Safed, saying: "All that this man desires of you, you shall do."

The law was given in the king's name, saying: "All builders and porters who are in those cities shall go to build Tiberias; and he who does not go shall bear his sin." There was there much stone, for Tiberias had been a great city before the Lord, before the hewer[2] went up against them, and there were twelve synagogues there in the days of R. Ammi and R. Asi.[3] He commanded the inhabitants of those seven country villages to make mortar to do the work, and more also; and there was there moreover much sand, for the Lake of Tiberias was near to them. But Arabs were jealous of them; and a certain *sharīf* who was advanced in years arose and called in the ears of the inhabitants of that land, saying: "Do not permit this city to be built, for it will be bitter for you in the end; for I have assuredly found it written in an ancient book, that when the city that is called Tiberias is built, our faith will be lost, and we will be found wanting." They harkened to his voice, and they were unwilling to go to rebuild the walls. "At that time, an end was made to the building of the walls of Tiberias, and R. Joseph b. Adret was very sad. He went to the pasha of Damascus and called before him: "O my Lord, for the inhabitants of the villages refuse to do the king's bidding." Then the pasha was afraid, and he hastened to send thither, and they took two of the heads of those people, and brought them down in blood to Sheol, so that those who remained might see and not

[1] The asper (Turk., *akça*) was an Ottoman silver coin.

[2] Reference to the Arabs, who are here taken as descendants of Ham-Canaan, and thus are "hewer's of wood and drawers of water."

[3] Rabbis of the Talmudic period.

act presumptuously any more. So they returned and hastened to make the walls of the city. They found there a great stone, and under it was a ladder going down into the earth, and there was a great High Place filled with marble images and altars like in the High Places of the uncircumcised; and the four servants of Don Joseph, which the king's son had given him, of those who had been captured in the Gelibite wars, broke them, and filled that place with dust. They also found three bells at that time, which the uncircumcised had hidden away at the time of Guido, the last Christian king who reigned in that land, at the time when the hewer came up against them; and they made battering-rams of them.[4]

Now the city of Tiberias which they built was one thousand and five hundred cubits in compass. The work ended in the month of Kislev 5325 (November–December 1564). Don Joseph greatly rejoiced and gave thanks unto God.

Then Don Joseph gave orders that many mulberry trees be planted to feed the silk-worms; and he ordered wool to be brought from Spain to make cloth, like the cloth which they make in Venice; for the man Joseph was very great, and his fame was in all the earth.

Joseph ha-Kohen, *ᶜEmeq ha-Bākhā,*
in Cecil Roth, trans., *The House of Nasi: The Duke of Naxos*
(Philadelphia, 1948), pp. 136–37 (slightly revised).

[4] They apparently found the ruins of a Crusader church.

AN ORDER FOR THE DEPORTATION OF THE JEWS OF SAFED TO CYPRUS

15 Rajab 984
(8 October 1576)

Order to the Sanjaq-Beg and the Qāḍī of Safed:

At present I have ordered that a thousand Jews be registered from the town of Safed and its districts and sent to the city of Famagusta in Cyprus. I command that as soon as this order arrives, without delay and in accordance with my noble firman, you register one thousand rich and prosperous Jews, and send them, with their property and effects and with their families, under appropriate escort, to the said city. Once the Jews have been inscribed in the register, do not afterwards, by practicing extortion, remove them from it. Send a sealed copy of the register to my Felicitous Threshold. Thus, in the course of conscribing and registering of the prescribed number of Jews, if anyone receives protection, or any are removed from the register and instead of them others taken, so that in their place not rich but poor Jews are conscribed, your excuses will by no means be acceptable. It will be secretly investigated and dealt with. It is proper that, if it becomes known to us that the matter has been handled in a manner contrary to our noble command, then assuredly it will not end with your deposition, but you will be most severely punished. Accordingly be diligent, and avoid anything contrary to our noble command.

Bernard Lewis, ed. and trans.,
Notes and Documents from the Turkish Archives: A Contribution to the History of the Jews in the Ottoman Empire. Oriental Notes and Studies of the Israel Oriental Society, no. 3 (Jerusalem, 1952), p. 33, no. 1 (Turkish text, p. 31) (slightly revised).

THE SULTAN RESCINDS THE ORDER OF DEPORTATION

16 Rabīʿ I 986
(23 May 1578)

Order to the Sanjaq Beg and the Qāḍī of Safed:

You have sent a letter and have reported that representatives of the Jews residing in the town of Safed have come to the law court complaining that orders have been given to deport them from this holy land to Cyprus. From the time this news spread, those who are traders have not attended to trade or other business, but have abstained from it completely. Until now, whenever their poll tax amounting to a fixed sum of 1500 floris[1] and the extraordinary levies fell due, they were paid in full to the imperial treasury. Moreover, they actually live in a *khān*[2] which is a *waqf* for the mosque of the Friend of the All-Merciful, our Master Abraham the Prophet[3]—blessings upon him and upon our Prophet (Muḥammad)—and for the venerable Dome of the Rock, and pay every year 400 floris rent. The town customs have . . . (?) an income of more than 10,000 floris from them. If it is decided to deport them to Cyprus, the Public Revenue will lose the above-mentioned amount of money and the town of Safed will be on the verge of ruin. The Treasury of Damascus will suffer a great loss since the collection of their poll tax, the impositions on their houses liable to pay extraordinary levies, custom duties, stamp duty on broadcloth,[4] customs on felt,[5] and the tax farming of the dye houses[6] will all be discontinued. Their homes will also remain deserted; no buyer will be found for them. Their landed property will go for nothing. In short, considerable loss and damage will result. If, on the other hand, they stay, the Treasury

[1] Flori (florin) was the Ottoman name for various gold pieces, "especially the Venetian sequin and Ottoman gold pieces of the same, or slightly different, value." See Heyd, *Ottoman Documents,* p. 120, n. 2.

[2] According to Heyd, *Ottoman Documents,* p. 168, n. 3: Here meaning not a caravanserai but a kind of walled enclosure with dwelling-houses, shops, and warehouses.

[3] That is, the revenues of the *khān* are dedicated to the mosque of Abraham in Hebron.

[4] Turk., *çoka damġası.* Concerning this tax, see Bernard Lewis, *Notes and Documents,* p. 14.

[5] Turk., *keçe.* According to Heyd, *Ottoman Documents,* p. 168, n. 6: "The *keçe* manufactured by the Jews of Safed was renowned in many countries."

[6] Turk., *boya-hāne.* The closely related industries of weaving and dyeing flourished among the Jews of Safed in the mid-sixteenth century. See Lewis, *Notes and Documents,* pp. 13–15.

will derive very great benefit in every respect.[7] Hence you have suggested that they shall be excused from being deported to Cyprus.

I have therefore commanded that when this firman arrives you shall desist from deporting the Jews to Cyprus. They shall live at their present places and attend to their businesses. You shall not let the aforesaid be troubled in the said matter.

Uriel Heyd, trans., *Ottoman Documents on Palestine* (London, 1960), pp. 167–68, no. 111.

[7] Heyd, *Ottoman Documents,* p. 168, n. 8, notes at this point: "The *narratio* up to here, or part of it, may be a summary of the statement of the Jewish representatives in the law-court."

THE JEWS OF SAFED SEEK REDRESS FROM THE OTTOMAN SULTAN FOR PERSECUTION BY LOCAL OFFICIALS

30 Dhu 'l-Qaᶜda 984
(18 February 1577)

Given on 26 Dhu 'l-Qaᶜda 984
to the Jew who had presented the petition

Order to the Beglerbeg of Damascus and the Qāḍī of Safed:

The Jews of Safed have now presented a petition to My Imperial Stirrup[1] and have complained of wrong done to them. They have stated: Although according to their customs Jews do not do any work on Saturdays, the Sanjaq-Beg troubles us at present saying, "Most certainly you shall work." He also demands excessive amounts of money. As we are not in a position to pay the money he makes us transport dung on that day. Moreover, robbers raid the house of a Jew. In the ensuing fight the Jew is wounded and after two or three days he dies. Alleging that we have killed him, he (the Beg) detains us three days in . . . (?). When we want to come before the Qāḍī and complain, he gives us permission, but says, "Be careful (in what you are going to state)." The next day, the Sanjaq-Beg imprisons the Jews, gives each of them one hundred strokes with the *çapraz,*[2] and demands five hundred gold pieces. Moreover, the Beg's soldiers break into houses at night. The next day he imprisons some Jews saying, "In the Jewish quarter houses were broken into. Find the thief!" He gives them seventy or eighty strokes with the *kirbac*[3] and extracts from them as high a fine as he wants. And when our merchants who carry on trade with Damascus set out, the night-watchmen come into our path and levy one pāra[4] on every saddle-beast.

I have therefore commanded that . . . you shall investigate . . . and let the Jews take back what is due them according to the law.

After that you shall duly issue strict orders that henceforth neither the

[1] Such petitions were originally presented to the Sultan as he rode out into public. See Uriel Heyd, *Ottoman Documents,* p. 122, n. 4, Doc. 72.

[2] The *çapraz* was a thick band of very springy metal which was used as a whip. See Heyd, *Ottoman Documents,* p. 166, n. 3.

[3] The *kirbac* was a leather whip. See Heyd, *Ottoman Documents,* p. 167.

[4] The pāra was originally the Turkish name given to the half dirham silver coin of the Mamluks which was called in Arabic *mu'ayyadī.* As of the seventeenth century it was struck as a Turkish coin. See Itzhak Ben-Zvi, *Eretz-Israel under Ottoman Rule: Four Centuries of History,* 2nd ed. (Jerusalem, 1966), p. 458; also reprint ed., E. W. Lane, *The Manners and Customs of the Modern Egyptians* (London, 1908), p. 579.

su-başıs and men of the Sanjaq-Beg nor the night-watchmen shall molest them in contravention of the right law and contrary to the ancient regulations. You shall prevent and avert this. If they are not restrained, you shall write and report the actual facts.

Uriel Heyd, trans., *Ottoman Documents on Palestine* (London, 1960), pp. 166–67, no. 110 (slightly revised).

THE OTTOMAN SULTAN ORDERS A NEW CENSUS OF THE JEWS OF SAFED FOR TAX PURPOSES

15 Rajab 985
(28 September 1577)

Order to the Beglerbeg and the Defterdar of Damascus:

It has been reported that the Jews who reside in the sanjaq of Safed do not pay their poll tax according to their obligations in full, but rather, have an insignificant amount registered as a fixed, lump sum. Since their additional population comprises a considerable number of people, it is necessary to cancel their fixed sum and register their names and those of their additional population anew.

A new census of the Jews is to be carried out and the poll tax henceforth to be collected accordingly.

Uriel Heyd, trans., *Ottoman Documents on Palestine* (London, 1960), pp. 121–22, no. 71 (slightly revised).

AN ORDER FROM THE SULTAN TO INVESTIGATE REPORTS OF ILLEGALLY BUILT SYNAGOGUES IN SAFED

20 Dhu 'l-Qaᶜda 992
(23 November 1584)

Order to the Beglerbeg and the Qāḍī of Damascus:

The Qāḍī of Safed has sent a letter to My Threshold of Felicity and has reported that in the town of Safed there are only seven sacred mosques. But the Jews who in olden times had three synagogues have now thirty-two synagogues, and they have made their buildings very high. Furthermore, they have bought much real estate and constituted it as pious foundations for their synagogues. Thus, they have given much annoyance to the Muslims.

I have therefore ordered that you shall personally investigate the said matter and report. . . . Are the above-mentioned synagogues ancient ones, which have remained in existence since the imperial (Ottoman) conquest, or newly established ones? If they are new, how and when were they established?

Uriel Heyd, trans., *Ottoman Documents on Palestine* (London, 1960), p. 169, no. 112 (slightly revised).

FIRMAN CONFIRMING THE CONFISCATION OF THE NAHMANIDES SYNAGOGUE IN JERUSALEM

According to the draft of that Efendi[1]
Sent to Muḥammad Agha[2]
on 15 Ṣafar 997 (3 January 1598)

Order to the Qāḍī of Jerusalem:

Ömer, former Qāḍī of Jerusalem, has sent a letter to My exalted Court. The matter concerns the place which God regards with favour, where the most truthful Apostle (Muḥammad) ascended to heaven and towards which all prophets turn, that is, Jerusalem and the Farther (Aqṣā) Mosque. When our Master ᶜUmar—may Allah Exalted be pleased with him—by the grace of Allah the Conqueror, took that sacred place and eminent and beautiful sanctuary by peaceful agreement in the month of Rabīᶜ I, A.H. 16 (April–May 637), and when afterwards King Ṣalāḥ al-Dīn (Saladin) conquered it by force of arms in the month of Rajab 597 (April–May 1201),[3] then the Christians agreed to the Muslim conditions and the poll tax. Therefore, the churches which were in their possession were left in existence and charters were given to them. As for the Jews, however, it is well known and recorded that they did in fact not take possession of a place of worship in Jerusalem either before or after the conquest. But it is now a few years since that community (the Jews) in that holy territory have appropriated as their place of worship a place which is contiguous to the wall of the sacred mosque of our Master ᶜUmar[4]—may Allah be pleased with him—and it is both joined with and similar to the building of the mosque. In the time of former qāḍīs that synagogue was investigated again and again, and noble firmans to prohibit it by law arrived in Jerusalem.[5] Muslim residents of the quarter have now come to

[1] Uriel Heyd, *Ottoman Documents,* p. 169, no. 113, n. 1, identifies this individual as the *Defterdār Efendi* (head of the treasury).

[2] Heyd, *Ottoman Documents,* p. 169, no. 113, n. 2: "Most probably Ḥabeşī Meḥemmed Agha, the powerful chief of the black eunuchs of the Sultan's harem (*dāru 's-seᶜādet agası,* or *kızlar agası*), who was also inspector of many imperial *waqfs* (*evkaf nazırı*)."

[3] Heyd, *Ottoman Documents,* p. 170, n. 6: "In fact the city surrendered to Saladin on 27 Receb [Rajab] 583 (2 Oct. 1187)."

[4] This is the mosque called Sīdnā ᶜUmar in the Jewish quarter of Old Jerusalem.

[5] Heyd, *Ottoman Documents,* p. 171, n. 8: "A firman (vol. xlviii, no. 1026) issued in 991 (1583) refers to the refusal of the Jews to remove an *āb hāne* (ritual bath for women, toilet?) that they had built close to the prayer-niche (*miḥrāb*) of the mosque which adjoined their synagogue (*bīᶜa*).

lodge a complaint and bring a charge stating: "The noisy ceremonies of the Jews in accordance with their false rites hinder our pious devotion and divine worship." Therefore the door of the synagogue has been locked and sealed.

You have reported that for the sake of Religion and State it would be proper that members of that religious community should henceforth not come to that place and that it be left standing with its entrance barred, or that it should be annexed to the mosque, or that it should become a place yielding revenue for the expenses of the sacred mosque and be annexed as such to the sacred mosque.

Now I have ordered that the great *ulema* and the venerable shaykhs sign the noble *fatwā* (legal opinion) given in that matter, that action be taken in accordance with its purport and that that place be annexed to the sacred mosque.

I have commanded that when this firman arrives you shall duly and diligently attend to this matter. You shall, as required by the sacred law, prevent the above-mentioned community from appropriating the said place as their place of worship and annex it to the said mosque. You shall not let anyone dispute this contrary to the law. And you shall write and report in what manner the law has been enforced and My order carried out.[6]

Uriel Heyd, trans., *Ottoman Documents on Palestine* (London, 1960), pp. 169–71, no. 113 (revised).

[6] For an earlier firman in what must have been a lengthy correspondence regarding this synagogue, see Amnon Cohen, *Ottoman Documents on the Jewish Community of Jerusalem in the Sixteenth Century* (Jerusalem, 1976), Doc. 23, Turkish text, p. 96; Hebrew trans., pp. 63–64.

"THE MURDER IS TO OUR DETRIMENT, YET WE HAVE TO PAY THE BLOOD PRICE"
(LATE SIXTEENTH-CENTURY MOROCCO)

Here is what happened to a Jew named Saᶜīd b. ᶜAwād in the year 5355 (1595).

While walking in the gardens of the Sultan Mawlāy al-Shaykh, he became involved in a quarrel with a Muslim and struck him with a bone. The victim went to find the Governor Shaykh Yaḥyā, who had the Jew conducted to the Casbah.[1] He inflicted various cruelties upon him from the 25th of Nisan (4 April) until the Muslim was fully recovered.

The governor wore himself out with threats of death in the hope of getting something out of him, but he would not give in. Finally, during the week when one reads the Torah portion which mentions the punishment for the blasphemer (Lev. 24:10–23),[2] he was stoned, then burned while still alive—all for a futile cause. He died a martyr, steadfast in his faith—so much so, that we have even heard Muslims praise him, saying, "How firm he is in his religion!"

After that, the Jews gave the governor 17 mithqāls[3] and gathered the remains for burial. Those who saw him say that nothing remained of him except his spinal column which was all shriveled up.

On that same day, the Sultan imposed a levy of 2000 ūqiyyas[4] and thereby fulfilled upon us the proverb: "The murder is committed to our detriment, yet we have to pay the blood price."

Solomon b. Danān, from the unedited chronicle of the Ibn Danān family, *al-Tawārīkh,* in *Un recueil de textes historiques judéo-marocains,* ed. and trans. Georges Vajda (Paris, 1951), pp. 19–20.

[1] The administrative center of the city.

[2] This portion is read during the week of Sivan 20–27 (May 28–June 4). Thus, the Jew was held for two months before being executed.

[3] The number is not clear in the manuscript. Vajda believes that it is perhaps 17. See Vajda, *Receuil,* p. 20, n. 2.

[4] The manuscript only gives the number 2,000 and not the denomination.

THE LOT OF THE JEWS IN EARLY ᶜALAWID MOROCCO

(LATE SEVENTEENTH CENTURY)

The Jews are very numerous in Barbary, and they are held in no more estimation than elsewhere; on the contrary, if there is any refuse to be thrown out, they are the first employed. They are obliged to work at their crafts for the king, when they are called, for their food alone. They are subject to suffering the blows and injuries of everyone, without daring to say a word even to a child of six who throws stones at them. If they pass before a mosque, no matter what the weather or season might be, they must remove their shoes, not even daring in the royal cities, such as Fez and Marrakesh, to wear them at all, under pain of five hundred lashes and being put into prison, from which they would be released only upon payment of a heavy fine.

They dress in the Arab fashion, but their cloaks and caps are black in order to be distinguishable. In Fez and Marrakesh, they are separated from the inhabitants, having their quarters apart, surrounded by walls, the gates of which are guarded by men set by the king so that they can conduct their business in peace and sanctify their sabbath and their other holidays. In the other cities, they are mixed with the Moors. They traffic in nothing other than merchandising and their trades. There are several of them who are quite rich, who do not bear themselves any higher than the least of them. They are in correspondence with Jews who live in Europe and who send them with the consent of the consuls arms and munitions.

They have in each of the cities a shaykh[1] and chief whom they elect, or whom the king gives them from amongst them. This shaykh is the one who levies the taxes[2] on each household to be paid to the king. They rarely go alone into the countryside because the Arabs and Berbers slaughter them for the most part.

There is practically never justice for them in these lands. If they speak too much before a governor in defense of their rights (for in Barbary, one uses neither advocate nor prosecutor, each pleads his own case), he has them given some slaps in the face by the guards. When they inter one of their own, the children harass them with blows, spit in their face, and curse them with a thousand maledictions.[3]

[1] That is, the Shaykh al-Yahūd, or *nāgīd*.

[2] The word translated here as "taxes" is *garammes*. The Arabic *gharām,* or *gharāma,* usually means "penalty," or "fine." In the Maghreb, however, the word also indicated "tax," or "tribute." See Reinhart Dozy, *Supplément,* vol. 2, pp. 209b–10a.

[3] Since *dhimmī* funeral processions were considered a violation of the Pact

For the rest, they have an admirable sense of charity towards their poor. In order that they should never be allowed to beg, their shaykh taxes them, each according to his means, in order to provide for their necessities.

There, in a few words, are the miseries which this people, formerly so dear to God, suffer, and who are today the laughingstock and scum of all nations in accordance with the words of the 26th chapter of Leviticus.

Germaine Mouette, *Histoire des conquestes de Mouley Archy,* (Paris, 1683). Reprinted in *Les sources inédites de l'histoire du Maroc: Archives de France,* sér. 2, vol. 2 (Paris, 1924), pp. 176–77.

VIGILANTE JUSTICE FOR A JEW IN EIGHTEENTH-CENTURY ALGIERS

On the opposite side we saw the Jews' burying-place, where we were shewed the spot whereon, five or six days before, they had burned a Jew, who, in the opinion of sensible people, was quite innocent. A certain Turk, agitated by a strange fury (whether proceeding from the excessive heat of choler or from sudden fit of frenzy) having killed with his knife five or six Jews, and wounded several others (whom he accidentally met with in his way) was soon after seen at home without his tongue. Being found in this condition, wholly unable to discover how he came so, people grew inquisitive, who could be the author of his misfortune: When another Turk said, "They ought not to seek any other author than himself, since, in that height of fury he then was, he might well have turned his rage against himself, and have bit off his own tongue." He was believed. But two Turks, next day, having charged that Jew with being the author of his mutilation, he was seized and burned immediately, without further trial or ceremony. On the place we saw heaps of stones, thrown at him by the children and populace during his execution. Such accidents happen frequently to the Jews, who, by a terrible judgment of the Almighty, are become the objects of universal hatred.

Jean Baptiste La Faye, *Several Voyages to Barbary,* trans. John Morgan (London, 1736).

---

of ᶜUmar's restriction of public ceremonies, harassments of this sort were common in every period. For examples of incidents caused by funeral processions in the Middle Ages, see S. D. Goitein, *Mediterranean Society,* vol. 2, p. 285; and also the passage translated above, pp. 201–3.

A JEW IS APPOINTED MOROCCAN PUBLIC MINISTER TO THE ENGLISH COURT
(EIGHTEENTH CENTURY)

My Lord,

I beg leave to embrace the earliest opportunity to acquaint Your Lordship that I have the honor of being appointed by His Imperial Majesty the Emperor of Morocco his public minister at this Court, and am charged to deliver in His Britannic Majesty's Hands a letter from His Imperial Majesty containing my ample credentials, being entrusted with many important matters, both of a public and private nature.

His Excellency General Cornwallis, in consequence of a strong recommendation from the Imperial Court to expedite my departure from Gibraltar, disposed of my passage to Lisbon on board the Raver Sloop of War, the commander thereof being directed to acquaint the English Minister at Lisbon with the urgency of my expedition, he immediately procured my passage by the first Packet to Falmouth, from whence I am but just arrived.

Your Lordship, I doubt not, will be pleased to direct what on similar occasions has been usually granted.

I should deem it a special favor to be honored with Your Lordship's answer as soon as convenient, that I may be apprised when and in what manner I may proceed in the discharge of my Commission.

I have the honor to remain with great respect.

My Lord
Your Lordship's
most devoted humble servant

Suffolk Street 7th August 1772. (signed) Jacob Benider

To the Right Hon.[ble] The Earl of Rochford one of His Majesty's Principal Secretaries of State Etc. Etc. Etc.

Public Records Office (London)
SP 71/21.

A JEWISH EMISSARY FROM MOROCCO ASKS TO PRESENT HIS CREDENTIALS TO THE BRITISH SECRETARY OF STATE
(EIGHTEENTH CENTURY)

My Lord,

Having received a letter for your Lordship from his Excellency Ahmed El Gazal,[1] Prime Minister of the Emperor of Morocco, wrote by his command, I humbly desire your Lordship's directions appointing the time and place for my having the honor of waiting on your Lordship for the Delivery of the original with a translation thereof, and as the subject matter is on his said Imperial Majesty's service, containing also a recommendation in my behalf, my personal attendance on your Lordship will be requisite to explain the services with which I am entrusted by the Emperor my Master.

I have the honor to be with the greatest respect—

My Lord
Your Lordship's
most devoted & obedient
humble servant
Jaime Toledano

London the 22nd Septemr. 1772

To the Right Hon.[ble] the Earl of Rochford.
one of his Majesty's Principal Secretaries of State etc. etc. etc.—

Public Records Office (London)
SP 71/21.

[1] Aḥmad al-Ghazzāl was an important Moroccan civil servant under Sīdī Muḥammad. On several occasions, he acted as special ambassador to Spain and elsewhere. Nowhere, to our knowledge, is he mentioned as ever being first minister. Concerning this figure, see Ramón Lourido Díaz, *El Sultanato de Sīdī Muḥammad b. ᶜAbd Allāh* (Granada, 1970), pp. 86, 103, 105, 131, 132.

THE TETOUAN POGROM OF 1790

On the 17th of the past month (April 1790), as the new ruler (Mawlāy Yazīd) entered the city of Tetouan, he commanded that all the Jews should be gathered and imprisoned in a house, meanwhile permitting the Moors to rob all their homes and cellars, which they obeyed with their own particular ferocity. Thus, they stripped all the Jews and their wives of all the clothes which they had on their body with the greatest violence, so that these unfortunates not only had to watch all their belongings being stolen, but also had to bear the greatest injury to their honor. During all this, six or eight Jews lost their lives, not counting the large number of children who met a similar fate in such general disorder. For three full days most of the Jews remained naked in the prison. A few in order to escape from their personal misfortunes, fled to the graves of the Moorish saints where they were hardly certain of their lives.

At this point Mawlāy Yazīd ordered that the head of a Jew who had served his father, the late king, be cut off, and stuck it for display on the ramparts of the city. Another Jew, who for many years had overseen the Spanish ships in the Tetouan harbor at the order and petition of the consul—since at that time no Christian could remain there[1]—was hung by his feet for thirty-six hours on account of sundry accusations of the Moroccans, until finally his head was cut off and his body burned.

He gave complete license to more than 2000 Blacks[2] to plunder the houses of the Jews, which the above-mentioned hordes obeyed to the letter. But on top of this, their bestiality showed itself to such an extent that they stripped the Jewesses of their clothes, forthwith satisfied their desires with them, and then threw them naked into the streets. Some of these unfortunates fled that very same night to the tomb of a Moorish saint, others to the mosque where they met the king. As he walked past them the following day, they cried to him, "Long live Mawlāy Yazīd!" This appeared to touch the almost impervious heart of the tyrant a little, since he immeditely ordered it proclaimed by four heralds that those who in the future

[1] In 1770, Sīdī Muḥammad, Mawlāy Yazīd's father, banned all further European residence in Tetouan after a Muslim woman was accidently wounded by a European while hunting. See William Lempriere, *A Tour from Gibraltar to Tangier, Sallee, Mogodore, Santa Cruz, Tarudant . . .* (London, 1791), p. 7; and Louis de Chénier, *The Present State of the Empire of Morocco,* vol. 1 (London, 1788), p. 19.

[2] These were the Negro slave-soldiers known as the *ᶜabīd al-Bukhārī.* Concerning them, see Allan Richard Meyers, "The ᶜAbid 'l-Buhārī: Slave Soldiers and Statecraft in Morocco, 1762–1790" (Ph.D. diss., Cornell University, 1974).

did any harm to a Jew or Jewess would be punished in the most severe fashion. But this order was all too late because all these families had already been ruined in reality.

Report of Franz von Dombay to the Hapsburg Chancellery (May 17, 1790), Marokko Karton 3, No. 17 in Haus-, Hof- und Staatsarchiv, Vienna, ed. and trans. N. A. Stillman, "Two Accounts of the Persecution of the Jews of Tetouan in 1790," *Michael*, vol. 5 (Tel Aviv, 1978), pp. 133–41.

A MOROCCAN ACCOUNT OF THE SAME INCIDENT

On Saturday, the second of the above-mentioned month of Shaᶜbān, our Master al-Yazīd—may God grant him victory—ordered the pillaging of the Mellāḥ of Tetouan. They found in it a great deal of valuable property—approximately 100 cwts. of goods which included *s-l-m* (apparently a textile), linen, and woolen cloth. Among the items of jewelry belonging to the Jews were gold, silver, gems, etc.

They fell upon the Jews' women and took their virginity, and they did not leave a single one of them. They plundered whatever was on them, and left their naked corpses as a lesson to those who take warning. They destroyed the roofs of the houses, excavated them, and went down into their wells. They mistakenly did this to some houses belonging to neighboring Muslims. It was a tremendous event! Until, it was related that one of the looters seized a Jewish virgin. She, however, grasped the parapet railing on top of the house. It came down upon her. Thus, she fell along with the one who had seized her, and they both perished together.

Many people profited from them (that is, the Jews).

Muḥammad al-Ḍuᶜayyif al-Ribāṭī, *Ta'rīkh al-Ḍuᶜayyif* (MS 277, Bibliothèque Royale, Rabat), ed. and trans. N. A. Stillman, "Two Accounts of the Persecution of the Jews of Tetouan in 1790," *Michael*, vol. 5 (Tel Aviv, 1978), pp. 141–42.

THE WIDOW OF A MOROCCAN JEWISH DRAGOMAN PETITIONS THE KING OF ENGLAND
(1772)

TO the King's Most Excellent Majesty
The humble Petition of Rachael Namias
Widow of Salom Namias
Thewith [*sic*]

That your petitioner's said late husband for several years resided in London and acted in the capacity of merchant, and the better to carry on his business about six years ago went over to Sale in the Kingdom of Barbary carrying with him not only all his own effects but also the effects of several merchants of this nation to dispose thereof to their best advantage.[1]

That your petitioner's said husband following his business in the said city at the time when the Moors made a prize of an English vessel and brought her into the said port of Sale; whereupon John Leonard Solicofre Esq., Your Majesty's consul then residing in the said city, applied to your petitioner's said husband and desired that in regard that your petitioner's said husband understood the English and Arabic languages, he would serve as his interpreter and thereby assist him in claiming and procuring the said ship's release.

That your petitioner's said husband being always ready to do the British Nation all the services in his power did in pursuance to the said consul's request attend him to the Emperor of Morocco and according to the custom of the said country acquainted him with the said consul's business and desired to have restitution of the said pretended prize, which so exasperated the said Emperor that without any other cause he ordered your petitioner's said husband to be burnt alive and all his effects should be confiscated to the said Emperor's use, which dreadful command was immediately put in execution, and thereby your petitioner was deprived of the best of husbands and the common necessaries of life.

That your petitioner has an old infirm mother and two small children

[1] The other merchants submitted a petition to the Duke of Newcastle to try and recoup the loss of £3,500 in goods confiscated when Namias was executed. From their names, they were apparently all Jews—Abraham and Jacob Franco, the Widow Portello de Quiras, Michael Pacheco da Silva, Jacob Abenetar Pimentel, and Joseph and David Franco (Public Records Office [London] SP 71/21, f. 24).

wholly unprovided for, and as your petitioner's said husband lost his life and fortune for the benefit of Your Majesty's subjects in assisting the said consul in manner aforesaid,

Your petitioner most humbly prays Your Majesty to take this her deplorable case into consideration and to grant her such relief as Your majesty in Your great wisdom shall seem meet.

And your petitioner shall ever pray etc.—

Public Records Office (London)
SP 71/21, f. 19.

THE MANNERS AND CUSTOMS OF MOROCCAN JEWRY (LATE EIGHTEENTH CENTURY)

The Jews in most parts of this empire live entirely separate from the Moors; and though in other respects oppressed, are allowed the free exercise of their religion. Many of them, however, to avoid the arbitrary treatment which they constantly experience, have become converts to the Mahometan faith; upon which they are admitted to all the privileges of Moors, though they lose their real estimation in the opinion of both sects.

In most of the sea-port towns, and particularly at Tetuan and Tangier, the Jews have a tolerable smattering of Spanish; but at Morocco (Marrakesh), Tarudant, and all the inland towns, they can only speak Arabic and a little Hebrew. They nearly follow the customs of the Moors, except in their religious ceremonies; and in that particular they are by far more superstitious than the European Jews.

The Jews of Barbary shave their heads close, and wear their beards long; their dress indeed, altogether, differs very little from that of the Moors (which I shall hereafter describe) except in being obliged to appear externally in black. For which purpose they wear a black cap, black slippers, and instead of the *Haick*[1] worn by the Moors, substitute the *Alberoce*,[2] a cloak made of black wool, which covers the whole of the under dress. The Jews are not permitted to go out of the country, but by an express order from the emperor; nor are they allowed to wear a sword, or ride a horse, though they are indulged in the use of mules. This arises from an opinion prevalent among the Moors that a horse is too noble an animal to be employed in the service of such infidels as Jews.

The dress of the Jewish women[3] consists of a fine linen shirt, with large and loose sleeves, which hang almost to the ground; over the shirt is worn a *Caftan*,[4] a loose dress made of woollen cloth, or velvet, of any colour, reaching as low as the hips, and covering the whole of the body, except the neck and breast, which are left open, and the edges of the *Caftan*, as worn

[1] Ar., *ḥā'ik* (a large, enveloping outer wrap somewhat resembling a bed sheet). See Reinhart Dozy, *Dictionnaire détaillé des noms des vêtements chez les arabes* (Amsterdam, 1845), pp. 147–53.

[2] Ar., *al-burnus* (a cark, or hooded cloak). See Dozy, *Vêtements*, pp. 73–80.

[3] For an illustrated survey of Moroccan female attire, see Yedida K. Stillman, "The Costume of the Jewish Woman in Morocco," in D. Noy, ed., *Aspects of Jewish Folklore* (forthcoming, the Association for Jewish Studies, Cambridge, Mass., 1979).

[4] Ar., *qafṭān*. See Dozy, *Vêtements*, pp. 162–68, *s.v. khaftān*.

by the Jewesses of Morocco, are embroidered with gold. In addition to these is the *Geraldito,*[5] or petticoats, made of fine green woollen cloth, the edges and corners of which are sometimes embroidered with gold. They are fastened by a broad sash of silk and gold, which surrounds the waist, and the ends of it are suffered to hang down behind in an easy manner. This is the dress they wear in the house, but when they go abroad, they throw over it the Haick. The unmarried women wear their hair plaited in different folds, and hanging down behind. They have a very graceful and becoming method of putting a wreath of wrought silk round the head, and tying it behind in a bow. This dress sets off their features to great advantage, and distinguishes them from the married women, who cover their heads with a red silk handkerchief, which they tie behind, and over it put a silk sash, leaving the ends to hang loose on their backs. None of the Jewish women use stockings, but wear red slippers, curiously embroidered with gold. They wear very large gold ear-rings at the lower part of the ears, and at the upper three small ones set with pearls or precious stones. Their necks are loaded with beads, and their fingers with small gold or silver rings. Round each wrist and ankle they wear large solid silver bracelets; and the rich have gold and silver chains suspended from the sash behind.

Their marriages are celebrated with much festivity for sometime previous to the ceremony, and the intended bride, with all her female relations, go through the form of having their faces painted red and white, and their hands and feet stained yellow, with an herb named *Henna.* A variety of figures are marked out on them with a needle, and then this herb, which is powdered and mixed with water into a paste, is worked into the holes made by the needle, and these marks continue on the hands and feet for a long space of time.[6] Upon the death of a Jew (before and after burial) all the female relations, with other women hired for the purpose, assemble in the room of the deceased, and for several days lament his loss by most dreadful shrieks and howlings, and tearing their cheeks and hair.

The Jewesses of this empire in general are very beautiful and remarkably fair. They marry very young, and when married, though they are not obliged to hide their faces in the street, yet at home they are frequently treated with the same severity as the Moorish women. Like the Moors, the Jewish men and women at Morocco eat separate; and the unmarried women

[5] This garment is called by a variety of names in the Judeo-Arabic and Ladino vernaculars of Morocco, all from the same Spanish origin and indicating a turning or whirling skirt. See Yedida K. Stillman, "The Costume of the Jewish Woman in Morocco," n. 30.

[6] The most recent survey of the Moroccan Jewish wedding is I. Ben-Ami, "Le mariage traditional chez les Juifs marocains," in his collection of studies *Le Judaïsme marocain: Etudes ethnoculturelles* (Jerusalem, 1975), pp. 9–103.

are not permitted to go out, except upon particular occasions, and then always with their faces covered.

A disposition for intrigue in the female sex is always found to accompany tyrannical conduct and undue restraint on the part of ours; and this disposition is again made the excuse for the continuance of these restraints. Thus the effect becomes a cause, and when women cease to be the guardians of their own honor, they derive no credit from the preservation of it, and incur in their own estimation but little disgrace by its loss. The Jews allege, in extenuation of their severity, the licentious inclinations and artful dispositions of their women, and that a single act of criminality in a daughter would be an effectual bar to her ever forming a legal connection. The same objection not being so applicable to their married women, they are permitted to go out without restraint. Indeed many of their husbands, from interested motives, are too apt to connive at a conduct, which, in other countries, would infallibly bring down upon them well-merited contempt.[7]

William Lempriere, *A Tour* . . . (London, 1791), pp. 192–98.

[7] This final paragraph reveals almost as much about Lempriere's views of women as it does that of Moroccan Jews.

THE JEWS OF MARRAKESH
(LATE EIGHTEENTH CENTURY)

The Jews, who are at this place [Marrakesh] pretty numerous, have a separate town to themselves, walled in, and under the charge of an *Alcaide,*[1] appointed by the emperor. It has two large gates, which are regularly shut every evening about nine o'clock, after which time no person whatever is permitted to enter or go out of the Jewdry, till they are opened again the following morning. The Jews have a market of their own, and, as at Tarudant,[2] when they enter the Moorish town, castle, or palace, they are always compelled to be barefooted.

The Jews in general are obliged to pay to the emperor a certain annual sum, in proportion to their numbers, which is a considerable income, independent of his arbitrary exactions. Those of Morocco (Marrakesh) were exempted by the late emperor from this tax, and in its room he compelled them to take goods of him, of which they were to dispose in the best manner they could, and pay him five times their value; by which means they were far greater sufferers than if they paid the annual tax.

Every part of the empire more or less abounds with Jews, who originally were expelled from Spain and Portugal, and who fled into Barbary as a place of refuge. These people are not confined to towns, but are spread over the whole face of the country, Mount Atlas itself, not excepted.

In every country where they reside, these unfortunate people are treated as another class of beings; but in no part of the world are they so severely and undeservedly oppressed as in Barbary, where the whole country depends upon their industry and ingenuity, and could scarcely subsist as a nation without their assistance. They are the only mechanics in this part of the world, and have the whole management of all pecuniary and commercial matters;[3] except in the collecting of the customs. They are, however, entrusted in the coinage of money, as I myself have witnessed.

[1] Ar., *al-qā'id,* in Morocco, a military officer and governor.

[2] The capital of the province of Sūs in southwestern Morocco. William Lempriere stopped over in Tarudant on his way to Marrakesh. While in Tarudant, he was lodged by the governor in the Jewish quarter, in the home of the leading Jewish protégé. Lempriere was so taken aback by the wretchedness and filth of the place that he was about to ask for other quarters until he was told that it was in fact the best in Tarudant. See Lempriere, *A Tour,* pp. 118–21.

[3] This is somewhat of an overstatement. There were some Muslims involved in trade with foreigners as well. Jews, however, did predominate in international trade because of their knowledge of Spanish and other European

The Moors display more humanity to their beasts than to the Jews. I have seen frequent instances where individuals of this unhappy people were beaten so severely, as to be left almost lifeless on the ground, and that without being able to obtain the least redress whatever, as the magistrates always act with the most culpable partiality when a Moor and a Jew are the parties in a suit. What they lose by oppression, however, they in a great measure make up by their superior address and sagacity, which frequently enables them to overreach the Moors—as I cannot compliment the Jews of Barbary in general upon their probity and principle.

Jacob Attal, the late emperor's[4] Jewish and favorite secretary, had more influence with his royal master, and did more mischief by his intrigues and address, than all the other ministers put together. This young man, who was a native of Tunis, and who was tolerably well acquainted with the English, Spanish, Italian, French, and Arabic languages, was of an active and enterprizing mind, and had so well informed himself of the natural disposition of the Moors, and particularly of that of Sidi Mahomet, that he had gained an entire ascendency over the emperor. As he knew that an unbounded love of money was the ruling passion of his royal master,[5] he not only surrendered to him half of his own gains, but also furnished the emperor with the earliest and best information concerning those who were in possession of wealth, as well as with a project for extracting it from them. By thus attacking the emperor on the weakest side, he secured his friendship; but he secured it by means which exposed him to the resentment and revenge of thousands as soon as the emperor died, which has been since too fatally proved. I must, however, do this young man the justice to add, that throughout the whole of his administration, though in some instances perhaps contrary to his own interest, he shewed an exclusive preference to the English; and of this the Moors in general were so sensible, that they gave him the appellation of the English ambassador.

William Lempriere, *A Tour* . . . (London, 1791), pp. 188–92.

---

languages and because of their contacts and relatives abroad. Needless to say, such Jews were only a minute fraction of the Moroccan Jewish population and resided mainly in the ports.

[4] The sultan referred to is Sīdī Muḥammad b. ᶜAbd Allāh (1757–90).

[5] This seems to have been the prevailing assessment of other European observers, such as Höst, de Chénier, and Dombay. De Chénier's view is more tempered. See Louis S. de Chénier, *The Present State of the Empire of Morocco,* vol. 2, (London, 1788), pp. 344–46.

17. Jazzār Pasha passes judgment on a criminal while his Jewish adviser, Ḥayyīm Farḥī (with patched eye and amputated nose) stands nearby holding a list of accusations. Early nineteenth century

F. B. Spilsbury, *Picturesque Scenery in the Holy Land and Syria delineated during the Campaigns of 1799 and 1800* (London: G. S. Tregear, 1823)

LEFT:

18. A street in the Jewish quarter of Old Jerusalem

Izhak Ben-Zvi, *Eretz-Israel under Ottoman Rule* (Jerusalem: Ben-Zvi Institute, 1966)

19. A well-to-do Jewish family at home on Mount Zion, ca. 1840

W. H. Bartlett, *Walks about the City and Environs of Jerusalem*, 2d ed. (London, 184?)

20. Scene in the Elijah the Prophet Synagogue, Jerusalem, nineteenth century

Syria, The Holy Land, Asia Minor, etc. Illustrated. in a series of views drawn from nature by W. H. Bartlett, William Purser, etc. (London & Paris, 1838)

21. A Jewish moneylender in Jerusalem, nineteenth century
P. Lortet, *La Syrie d'aujourd'hui* (Paris, 1884)

22. *A Jewish couple in Jerusalem, 1873*

Hamdy Bey, *Les costumes populaires de la Turquie en 1873* (Constantinople, 1873), Fig. XXXVI. Courtesy of the Philadelphia Museum of Art, The Marian Angell Boyer and Francis Boyer Library

23. *A Jewish woman in Tiberias, nineteenth century*

Lortet, *La Syrie d'aujourd'hui*

24. *Beiruti Jews, nineteenth century*
Lortet, *La Syrie d'aujourd'hui*

25. *Courtyard of a wealthy Jewish household in Damascus, nineteenth century*
Lortet, *La Syrie d'aujourd'hui*

26. A Jewish woman of Aleppo wearing the headdress and false tresses of a married woman, nineteenth century

Hamdy Bey, *Les costumes de la Turquie en 1873.* (Constantinople, 1873), Fig. XXV (detail). Courtesy of the Philadelphia Museum of Art, The Marian Angell Boyer and Francis Boyer Library

THE RECRUITMENT OF A JEWISH INTERPRETER IN TANGIER
(1789)

The governor of the town had orders to supply me with a tent, mules, and an interpreter. But it was not without much difficulty that a person could be found in Tangier who could speak the English and Arabic languages sufficiently well to perform that office; and it was owing to an accident that I at length was enabled to obtain one.

After searching the whole town in vain, the governor ordered, during the Jewish hour of prayer, that enquiries should be made among all the synagogues for a person who understood both languages. An unfortunate Jew, whose occupation was that of selling fruit about the streets of Gibraltar, and who had come to Tangier merely to spend a few days with his wife and family during a Jewish festival, being unacquainted with the intent of the enquiry, unguardedly answered in the affirmative. Without further ceremony the poor man was dragged away from his friends and home, and constrained by force to accompany me.

Of the mode in this despotic government of seizing persons at the arbitrary pleasure of a governor, an Englishman can scarcely form an idea. Three or four lusty Moors, with large clubs in their hands, grasp the wretched and defenceless victim with as much energy as if he was an Hercules, from whom they expected the most formidable resistance, and half shake him to death before they deliver him up to the superior power.—Such was exactly the situation of my unfortunate interpreter.

From the sudden and abrupt manner in which he was hurried away, in the midst of his devotions, the women immediately took the alarm, flew in a body to the house of the consul, and with shrieks and lamentations endeavoured to prevail on him to get the man excused from his journey. The immense distance, and the ill treatment which they knew was offered to Jews by the Moors, when not under some civilized controul, were certainly sufficient motives for this alarm on the part of the women. Upon the consul's assuring them, however, that the wife should be taken care of, and the husband sent back without any expence to him on our arrival at Mogodore, where I was to be furnished with another interpreter, and upon my promising to protect the Jew from insult, and, if he behaved well, to reward him for his trouble, the women immediately dispersed, and returned home apparently satisfied.

William Lempriere, *A Tour* . . . (London, 1791), pp. 12–14.

The computed number of Jews at Aleppo, is about five thousand. They dwell within the walls, in those parts of the city contiguous to the ramparts, between the Dark Gate and St. George's; in the quarter bounded by Bahsyta (*Baḥsīta*),[1] and the street leading westward from the Mahkamy (*Maḥkama*).[2] Their houses, which have already been described, lie near each other, but some Turkish houses are interspersed. They have one synagogue, situated in what is called the Jew's street, where a manuscript of the Old Testament is preserved, which, as they pretend, is of very high antiquity. The synagogue has been very well described by Pietro della Valle.[3]

The Jews are easily distinguished by their violet colored babooge (*bābūj*),[4] and their turban: not to mention the peculiar cast of countenance so universally remarkable in that nation. Their turban is somewhat lower than that of the Christians, though the striped shash (*shāsh*)[5] be much the same. They wear also shashes of other colors, and tie them in a most slovenly manner. "Before the year 1600 (according to Biddulph) the Jews wore red hats without brims, but about that time a Grand Vizier, offended at the red color obliged them to wear blue hats."[6] By hats he means turbans; and the shashes of some of their turbans are still red. They all wear the beard; and even the Frank Jews[7] are obliged by the Khakhan (*Ḥākhām*) to comply with the custom.

It is observed of them that they speak a more corrupt Arabic than the

[1] A quarter of the city. See Jean Sauvaget, *Alep: Essai sur le développement d'une grande ville syrienne, des origines au milieu du XIXe siécle* (Paris, 1941), p. 61.

[2] The Muslim court. See Sauvaget, *Alep*, p. 182.

[3] *Viaggi di Pietro della Valle* (Rome, 1650), Parte terza. p. 424. Della Valle (1586–1652) was an Italian nobleman who traveled to the Near East and India.

[4] Oriental slippers. See Reinhart Dozy, *Dictionnaire des vêtements,* pp. 50–53.

[5] The *shāsh* was the piece of cloth wound around a cap to form the turban. See Dozy, *Dictionnaire des vêtements*, pp. 235–40.

[6] "Part of a Letter of Master William Biddulph from Aleppo," in Samuel Purchas, *Hakluytus Posthumus or Purchas His Pilgrimes*, vol. 8, reprint ed. (New York, 1965), p. 271 (= p. 1342).

[7] That is, Jews from Europe, who were called in Ladino *Francos* and in Arabic *Franj*. A considerable number of Francos from Italy and France settled in Aleppo in the latter part of the seventeenth century. Concerning them, see Alexander Lutzky, "The 'Francos' and the Effect of the Capitulations on the Jews in Aleppo (from 1673 till the time of the French Revolution)," *Zion* 6 (1940): 46–79 [Heb.].

Christians. In their morning salutation on the Sabbath day, they frequently use the Hebrew; but it goes no further than a few words; none of them speaking that language familiarly, though many read it. In writing the Arabic, they very often make use of Hebrew characters, in which their letters are usually composed, thus a stranger may be led into the mistake of supposing them to correspond in the ancient language. . . . Their children are universally sent to the reading school, but their learning seldom extends beyond the Psalms of David. Most of their printed books and almanacks are brought from Venice.

Few of the Jews apply either to manufactures, or to manual trades. The principal persons are bankers, or merchants; the others are brokers, grocers, or pedlars. The established banker of the Seraglio is a Jew,[8] and the private bankers of most of the Grandees are likewise Jews; whence it probably happens, that their nation possesses such extensive influence among a haughty people, by whom, in a religious light, they are held in still greater contempt than the Christians.

In general, the Jews are a more sober people than the Christians. Many of them are secured from intemperance by poverty, besides which, their attendance twice a day at the synagogue on all festivals, and their living so much under the eye of their Khakhans, render it more difficult to conceal debauchery, than it would among a more numerous nation. The lower people live chiefly on bread, pulse, herbs, and roots, dressed with the expressed oil of sesamum, which is seldom eaten by the other inhabitants. They consume more poultry than any other animal food, their market being often ill supplied with mutton; and, as their meat must be killed in a particular manner, by a Jewish butcher, they cannot provide themselves from the Turkish markets. Their meat is sold to their poor at an under price, the difference being made up to the seller out of the national chest. But the avarice of the managers of this well intended charity, often starves the market, so that even the opulent Jews are obliged, like the others, to have recourse to poultry, which can be easily killed at home.

The lower class of Jews are of all people the most slovenly and dirty. No positive institution could have been more wisely devised, than one by which they are laid under an obligation of cleaning their houses, as well as their persons, at least once a week; and, in this respect, their Sabbath is strictly observed. It commences on the Friday night at sun set, and ends about the same time next day; but the preparation begins on the Friday forenoon, and the women, after cleaning their house, and cooking the

[8] He is perhaps referring to a member of the Farḥī family, who by the end of the eighteenth century became the leading court bankers in Syria. Concerning this family, see Hayyim J. Cohen, "Farḥi," *EJ* 6: 1181–83.

victuals intended for the Sabbath, go themselves to the Bagnio, and dress there.

Of the women, some may be reckoned extremely handsome, but the proportion is less than in the other nations. Their head dress differs considerably in its fashion from that of the Turkish and Christian ladies, and is for the most part richy decked with pearls. In the other parts of their dress, and in their jewels after the Eastern mode, there is nothing remarkable: only that their thin boots and slippers are of a violet color. Their veil is white, but they wear it in such a manner as to leave one arm at liberty. They have a singular mode of salutation which is imitated by the children, but not commonly practiced by the men, except in their houses. Instead of laying the hand upon the left breast, the person saluting presents both hands joined at the point of the fingers, which the other touches gently, sliding her fingers over them, and then each, by an easy motion, carries her hands, joined at the finger points, to her own lips. They have also a peculiar way of expressing an absolute negative, by biting the thumb nail of the right hand, and then quickly thrusting the hand forward.

The Jewesses, in common discourse, employ several phrases and terms not in use among the other natives, and they speak the Arabic with a remarkable and peculiar accent.[9]

The women, in the presence of strangers, are always veiled; and, in common, they do not eat at the same table with the men: though on holydays, when there are no strangers, they often dine together. On their Sabbaths, they remain a considerable time at table, drinking wine made according to their law; and, on those occasions, they may sometimes be heard singing in chorus; but their songs have nothing gay, or festive, they are more like Psalms chanted in what is meant for a tune, but happens unfortunately to be the opposite to all melody. Sandys appears to have entertained a notion of their vocal music equally unfavorable. Speaking of their singing the liturgy in the synagogue, he observes "they sing in tunes that have no affinity with music."[10]

. . . .

From the common circumstance of several families living in the same house, and of intermarriages among kindred, it naturally happens that the Jews live rather more familiarly with the women, than either the Turks or

[9] Throughout the Arabic-speaking world, women have their own distinct speech which frequently constitutes a subdialect. One reason for this is their lack of formal education.

[10] "A Relation of a Journey begun, Anno Dom. 1610, written by Master George Sandys," in Purchas, *Purchas His Pilgrimes*, vol. 7, p. 172 (= 1306).

Christians, and the women appear more negligent in veiling before persons of their own nation.

The chief priest is by way of eminence called the Khakhan or great Khakhan,[11] but the title is given also to all the priests in general. They are distinguished from the other Jews by the size and color of the turban, and by the long wide sleeves of their outer garment.

The Khakhan exercises temporal as well as spiritual authority, and his decisions are for the most part more respected, than those of the Bishop are by the Christians. His civil jurisdiction however is very limited, and the parties may always appeal to the Mahkamy.

. . . .

From the extensive connection of the Jews with the commercial world, their fasts and festivals occasion an almost universal stagnation of trade. They not only prove an impediment to the departure of the great caravans, but retard their march when actually upon the road; and even the Bashaws, and other Grandees, are sometimes obliged to postpone the dispatch of their own affairs, when it happens to interfere with the Jewish holydays.

In the Bassora caravans, it is usual for the Jews, when in the desert, to procure an escort from the caravan-bashi, and make a forced march on the Friday, in order to rest on their Sabbath. The caravan marches as usual, and either takes them up on the road, or they overtake it on the Saturday night.[12] When their holydays happen about the time of a caravan's departure from the city, they generally find means of prevailing on the caravan-bashi to delay setting out till after the feast.

That a people so despised should be able, amid so many obstacles, to maintain such a strict observance of ancient institutions, is at once a proof of the power of determined pertinacity, and of the tolerant spirit of the Turks.

Alexander Russell, *The Natural History of Aleppo*,
2d ed., vol. 2 (London, 1756), pp. 58–64 and 78–79.

[11] That is, *ḥākhām-bāshī.*

[12] Such special arrangements for Jews who traveled by caravan but wished to observe their Sabbath have a long history. See S. D. Goitein, *Mediterranean Society,* vol. 1, pp. 280–81.

THE JEWISH COMMUNITY OF SAN^c^A IN THE LATE EIGHTEENTH CENTURY

Jews are not permitted to live in the city of Sana. They live by themselves in a village, named Kaa el Ihud (*Qāᶜat al-Yahūd*), situated near Bir el Assab (*Bi'r al-ᶜAzab*).[1] Their number amounts to two thousand. But, in Yemen, they are treated even more contemptuously than in Turkey. Yet, the best artisans in Arabia are Jews; especially potters and goldsmiths, who come to the city, to work in their little shops by day, and in the evening retire to their village.

Those Jews carry on a considerable trade. One of the most eminent merchants among them, named Oroeki (ᶜArāgī),[2] gained the favor of two successive Imams, and was for thirteen years, in the reign of El Mansor,[3] and for fifteen years under the present Imam (al-Mahdī al-ᶜAbbās),[4] comptroller of the customs and of the royal buildings and gardens; one of the most honorable offices at the court of Sana. Two years before our arrival here,[5] he had fallen into disgrace, and was not only imprisoned, but obliged to pay a fine of 50,000 crowns. Fifteen days before we arrived at Sana, the Imam had let him at liberty. He was a venerable old man, of great knowledge; and although he had received the Imam's permission, had never chosen to assume any other dress than that commonly worn among his countrymen. The young Jew, who had been our servant, was one of his relations, and had mentioned us so favorably to him, that he conceived a

[1] This Jewish suburb was located nearby two kilometers outside the walls of Ṣanᶜa and was separated from it by several garden quarters, one of which was the Bi'r al-ᶜAzab. Until 1679, the Jews lived in their own quarter within the city walls. They were forced into exile at Mawzaᶜ near Mokha. When they were permitted to return a short time later, they were required to settle in the Qāᶜat al-Yahūd. In the early nineteenth century, the Jewish quarter was connected, along with the gardens in between, to the city itself. See Carl Rathjens, "Jewish Domestic Architecture in Sanᶜa, Yemen," *Oriental Notes and Studies* 7 (Jerusalem, The Israel Oriental Society, 1957), p. 12. See Illus. 12 and 13.

[2] Concerning this important family that was apparently not of Yemenite origin, cf. Erich Brauer, *Ethnologie der Jemenitischen Juden* (Heidelberg, 1934), pp. 39–41.

[3] The Imām Ḥusayn b. Qāsim al-Manṣūr reigned 1719–40. See R. L. Playfair, *A History of Arabia Felix or Yemen* (Bombay, 1859; reprint ed., 1970), p. 115.

[4] He ruled in fact from 1740–74, although his reign officially began in 1759 with the death of his brother the legitimate heir, whom he had kept imprisoned for nineteen years. See Playfair, *Arabia Felix,* p. 116.

[5] Niebuhr visited Sanᶜa in 1763. Thus, ᶜArāgī's disgrace must have occurred around 1761.

desire to see us. But we durst not hold frequent intercourse with a man so newly released out of prison.

The disgrace of Oroeki had drawn a degree of persecution upon the rest of the Jews. At that period, the government ordered fourteen synagogues, which the Jews had at Sana, to be demolished. In their village are as handsome houses as the best in Sana. Of those houses likewise all above the height of fourteen fathoms (84 feet) was demolished, and the Jews were forbidden to raise any of their buildings above this height in future. All the stone pitchers in which the inhabitants of the village had used to keep their wines were broken. In short, the poor Jews suffered mortifications of all sorts.

Carsten Niebuhr, *Travels in Arabia,*
in J. Pinkerton, abr. and trans.,
A General Collection of the Best and Most Interesting Voyages and Travels in All Parts of the World,
vol. 10 (London, 1811), p. 69.

5

THE DAWN OF MODERN TIMES
The Jews of Arab Lands in the Nineteenth Century

CAIRENE JEWRY IN THE FIRST HALF OF THE NINETEENTH CENTURY

There are in this country about five thousand Jews, most of whom reside in the metropolis, in a miserable, close, and dirty quarter, intersected by lanes, many of which are so narrow as hardly to admit of two persons passing each other in them.

In features, and in the general expression of countenance, the Oriental Jews differ less from other nations of South-western Asia than do those in European countries from the people among whom they live; but we often find them to be distinguished by a very fair skin, light-reddish hair, and very light eyes, either hazel or blue or gray. Many of the Egyptian Jews have sore eyes and a bloated complexion; the result, it is supposed, of their making an immoderate use of the oil of sesame in their food. In their dress, as well as in their persons, they are generally slovenly and dirty. The colors of their turbans are the same as those of the Christian subjects. Their women veil themselves, and dress in every respect, in public, like the other women of Egypt.

The Jews have eight synagogues in their quarter in Cairo; and not only enjoy religious toleration, but are under a less oppressive government in Egypt than in any other country of the Turkish empire. In Cairo, they pay for the exemption of their quarter from the visits of the Moḥtesib;[1] and they

[1] The *muḥtasib* was the inspector of the markets in Muslim countries and a sort of censor of public morals. Lane describes his functions in Cairo at this time in his *Modern Egyptians,* pp. 125–28. In the Middle Ages, the *muḥtasib* was also responsible for seeing that the laws of differentiation for *dhimmīs*

did the same also with respect to the Walee,[2] as long as his office existed. Being consequently privileged to sell articles of provision at higher prices than the other inhabitants of the metropolis, they can afford to purchase such things at higher rates, and therefore stock their shops with provisions, and especially fruits, of better qualities than are to be found in other parts of the town. Like the Copts, and for a like reason, the Jews pay tribute, and are exempted from military service.

They are held in the utmost contempt and abhorrence by the Muslims in general, and are said to bear a more inveterate hatred than any other people to the Muslims and the Muslim religion. It is said, in the Koran, "Thou shalt surely find the most violent of all men in enmity to those who have believed to be the Jews. . . ."[3] On my mentioning to a Muslim friend this trait in the character of the Jews, he related to me, in proof of what I remarked, an event which had occurred a few days before.—"A Jew," said he, "early one morning last week, was passing by a coffee-shop kept by a Muslim with whom he was acquainted, named Muḥammad. Seeing a person standing there, and supposing that it was the master of the shop (for it was yet dusk), he said, 'Good morning, shaykh Muḥammad'; but the only answer he received to his salutation was a furious rebuke for thus addressing a *Jew*, by a name the most odious, to a person of his religion, of any that could be uttered. He (the offender) was dragged before his high-priest, who caused him to receive a severe bastinading for the alleged offence, in spite of his protesting that it was unintentional." —It is a common saying among the Muslims in this country, "Such a one hates me with the hate of the Jews." We cannot wonder, then, that the Jews are detested by the Muslims far more than are the Christians. Not long ago, they used often to be jostled in the streets of Cairo, and sometimes beaten for merely passing on the right hand of a Muslim. At present, they are less oppressed; but still they scarcely ever dare to utter a word of abuse when reviled or beaten unjustly by the meanest Arab or Turk; for many a Jew has been put to death upon a false and malicious accusation of uttering disrespectful words against the Koran or the Prophet. It is common to hear an Arab abuse his jaded ass, and, after applying to him various opprobrious epithets, end by calling the beast a Jew.

A Jew has often been sacrificed to save a Muslim, as happened in the following case. —A Turkish soldier, having occasion to change some money,

---

were observed. See the passage translated from a *muḥtasib*'s handbook which is translated above, pp. 271–72.

[2] The *wālī* was the police chief of Cairo from the later Middle Ages until the early nineteenth century. See Lane, *Modern Egyptians,* p. 122.

[3] Sura 5:82/85.

received from the ṣeyrefee (or money-changer),[4] who was a Muslim, some Turkish coins called ᶜadleeyehs, reckoned at sixteen piasters each. These he offered to a shopkeeper, in payment for some goods; but the latter refused to allow him more than fifteen piasters to the ᶜadleeyeh, telling him that the Bāshā had given orders, many days before, that this coin should no longer pass for sixteen. The soldier took back the ᶜadleeyehs to the ṣeyrefee, and demanded an additional piaster to each; which was refused: he therefore complained to the Bāshā himself, who, enraged that his orders had been disregarded, sent for the ṣeyrefee. This man confessed that he had been guilty of an offence, but endeavored to palliate it by asserting that almost every moneychanger in the city had done the same, and that he received ᶜadleeyehs at the same rate. The Bāshā, however, disbelieving him, or thinking it necessary to make a public example, gave a signal with his hand, intimating that the delinquent should be beheaded. The interpreter[5] of the court, moved with compassion for the unfortunate man, begged the Bāshā to spare his life. "This man," said he, "has done no more than all the money-changers of the city: I, myself, no longer ago than yesterday, received ᶜadleeyehs at the same rate." "From whom?" exclaimed the Bāshā. "From a Jew," answered the interpreter, "with whom I have transacted business for many years." The Jew was brought, and sentenced to be hanged; while the Muslim was pardoned. The interpreter, in the greatest distress of mind, pleaded earnestly for the life of the poor Jew; but the Bāshā was inexorable: it was necessary that an example should be made, and it was deemed better to take the life of a Jew than that of a more guilty Muslim. I saw the wretched man hanging at a window of a public fountain which forms part of a mosque in the main street of the city.[6] One end of the rope being passed over one of the upper bars of the grated window, he was hauled up; and as he hung close against the window, he was enabled, in some slight degree, to support himself by his feet against the lower bars; by which his suffering was dreadfully protracted. His relations offered large sums of money for his pardon; but the only favor they could purchase was that of having his face turned towards the window, so as not to be seen by the passengers. He was a man much respected by all who knew him (Muslims, of course, excepted); and he left a family in a very destitute state; but the interpreter who was the unintending cause of his death contributed to their support.

[4] Ar., *ṣayrafī.*

[5] The pasha, who was Turkish, did not speak Arabic.

[6] Lane has a footnote here that says: "It is surprising that Muslims should hang a *Jew* against a window of a *mosque,* when they consider him so unclean a creature that his blood would defile the sword. For this reason a Jew, in Egypt, is never beheaded.

The Jews in Egypt generally lead a very quiet life: indeed, they find few but persons of their own religion who will associate with them. Their diet is extremely gross; but they are commonly regarded as a sober people. The more wealthy among them dress handsomely at home; but put on a plain or even shabby dress before they go out: and though their houses have a mean and dirty appearance from without, many of them contain fine and well-furnished rooms. In the house, they are not so strict as most other Orientals in concealing their women from strange men, or, at least, from persons of their own nation, and from Franks; it often happens that a European visitor is introduced into an apartment where the women of the Jew's family are sitting unveiled, and is waited upon by these women. The same custom also prevails among many of the Syrian Christians residing in Cairo. Intrigues are said to be common with the Jewesses; but there are no avowed courtesans among them. The condition of the lower orders is very wretched; many of them having no other means of subsistence than alms bestowed upon them by their superiors of the same religion.

Avarice is more particularly a characteristic of the Jews in Egypt than those in other countries where they are less oppressed. They are careful, by every means in their power, to avoid the suspicion of being possessed of much wealth. It is for this reason that they make so shabby a figure in public, and neglect the exterior appearance of their houses. They are generally strict in the performance of their religious ordinances; and, though overreaching in commercial transactions, are honest in the fulfillment of their contracts.

Many of the Egyptian Jews are "ṣarrāfs" (or bankers and money-lenders): others are ṣeyrefees, and are esteemed men of strict probity. Some are goldsmiths or silversmiths; and others pursue the trades of retail grocers or fruiterers, etc. A few of the more wealthy are general merchants.

Edward William Lane, *The Modern Egyptians* (London, 1908), pp. 558–62.

THE JEWISH QUARTER OF JERUSALEM
(EARLY NINETEENTH CENTURY)

The Jews have many synagogues, but very small, and more filthy than those I have seen in other parts of the East. Although they are oppressed and treated with more contempt at Jerusalem than elsewhere, they still flock to it. To sleep in Abraham's bosom is the wish of the old; the young visit it in the hopes of the coming of the Messiah; some are content to remain, for the commerce they carry on.

They pay a heavy tax to the Turkish governor at Jerusalem. The sums to the aga of Jaffa when they land, and to the chief of St. Jeremiah[1] for safe conduct, produce a large revenue to both. The Jewish quarter, as in all Eastern towns, is separate from the rest. I found men from all nations, except England.

Henry Light, *Travels in Egypt, Nubia, Holy Land, Mount Libanon, and Cyprus, in the Year 1814* (London, 1818), p. 184.

[1] The writer is referring to the village of Abu Ghosh which lies eight miles west of Jerusalem. The village chiefs imposed a toll on all travelers entering and leaving Jerusalem until around 1835.

THE SYNAGOGUES AND SCHOOLS OF JERUSALEM IN THE 1830s

There are five large synagogues in Jerusalem which have existed already for several centuries. Four belong to the Sephardim congregation, and one to the Ashkenazim, or rather to the Germans, since when it was founded, the name of the Polish, Russian, or Galician Jews was not known. I shall, however, speak more in detail of the last mentioned in the sequel.

Among the first four is the so-called Zion Synagogue. It is the oldest and largest; and if a common tradition is to be believed, for which, however, I know of no proof, it was the former college (Midrash) of Rabbi Yochanan Ben Zakkai. . . . The other three were built at a much later period.

All these four synagogues form, properly speaking, but a very large single building, since they stand near one another, so that one can walk from one into the other, and the centre one, the smallest of all, has no entrance from the street, and you have to reach it through either of the three others. On my arrival, in the year 5593 (1833), I found them in a most miserable and lamentable condition, since they were at the time greatly out of repair, and almost threatened to tumble in, and were useless in rainy weather, inasmuch as they were roofed in with nothing but old rotten boards, and our brothers could not obtain the permission from "the pious faithful"[1] to drive as much as a single nail to fasten anything in the building without being first authorized by the *most worthy* persons in authority, and such a favor, not to mention to permit the making of repairs, and much less to rebuild the synagogues, could not be granted in order not to commit a terrible sin against Allah and his Nebbi (prophet); independently of which, the *silver* to procure the consent was not easily obtainable in Jerusalem.

But in the year 5595 (1834/1835), Abraim Pacha[2] of Egypt, who understood and was able to instruct and convince his people "that even the Nebbi had grown more tolerant in modern times," gave the permission to rebuild anew from the foundation all these four synagogues, and they are accordingly at present four fine buildings. Their situation is opposite to the south-southwest corner of the temple mount, on the declivity of the former Tyropoeon.[3]

[1] A sarcastic reference to the Muslims who refer to themselves as *al-mu'minūn* (the Faithful, or the Believers).

[2] That is, Ibrāhīm Pasha, the son of Muḥammad ᶜAlī, the viceroy of Egypt, who was his father's governor in Syria and Palestine between 1833 and 1840.

[3] The four attached synagogues were renovated after the reunification of

Besides the above five synagogues,[4] there are a great many smaller and private ones, which have been founded quite recently, and public and private schools (yeshiboth) and colleges (midrashim) by which are understood public libraries, large collections of nearly all the accessible Hebrew books of modern and (more especially) of more ancient times, and manuscripts likewise, where everyone is permitted to enter and make use of the literary treasures.

For the most part there meet, in each Yeshibah or Beth Hammidrash, societies who study and discuss together a particular subject, for instance, a masekhta or treatise of the Talmud; and they have usually one person, and this the most capable and learned, as teacher or chief, called Rosh Hayeshibah.[5]

These Yeshiboth are foundations instituted by our worthy brothers in Babel, Asia Minor, Turkey, Italy, Barbary, Holland, Germany, England, and Poland (and why should not America follow the example?). They devoted a sufficient capital, the proceeds of which will be enough to support a Yeshibah, together with the society meeting therein.

It is but lately that I obtained from the respectable firm of the Messrs. Landauer, of Hürben near Augsburg in Bavaria, a permanent capital, which will always procure me the rent for my own residence and Yeshibah.

Several Yeshiboth have at the same time a synagogue, which is also the case with mine.[6]

In the principal Yeshibah there is also the seat of the high court (Beth Din Haggadol), which has to decide on the gravest and most important proceedings.

The following are the principal Yeshiboth and Bathé Hammidrash in Jerusalem; beside which there are several unnamed smaller ones. The name given to them bears generally an allusion to that of the founders; and as female names are also met with, it proves that worthy ladies were likewise founders of these institutions:

1. Beth-El; 2. Beth Jaacob; 3. Chesed Leäbraham; 4. Nevéh Shalom; 5. Berith Abraham; 6. Kissay Eliyahu; 7. Keneseth Yisrael; 8. Kedushath Yome Tobe; 9. Orach Chayim; 10. Damesek Eleazer; 11. Ruach Eliyahu;

Jerusalem resulting from the June 1967 Arab-Israeli war. See Elchanan Reiner, *The Yochanan Ben Zakkai Four Sephardi Synagogues* (Jerusalem, 1973).

[4] That is, the four Sephardi plus the Ashkenazi synagogue.

[5] In Leeser's edition, the words *rōsh ha-yeshīva* are given in Hebrew characters, but the transliteration next to them reads *rashe hayeshibah,* which is plural. I have followed Leeser's system of transliteration throughout this passage, even where he gives only the Hebrew characters, for the sake of consistency.

[6] Schwarz first directed an elementary *yeshiva* (Heb., *yeshīva qeṭāna*) and later a *yeshiva* of higher learning.

12. Bné Yitzchak; 13. Toledoth Yitzchak; 14. Bné Moshéh; 15. Aholé Zadikim; 16. Chayim Vachesed; 17. Kinnor Naim; 18. Pirché Kehunnah; 19. Kehunnath 'Olam; 20. Emeth Leyaakob; 21. Magen David; 22. Beth Aharon; 23. Dath Yehudith; 24. Ohel Rachel Ubeth Yehudah; 25. Sukkath Shalom; 26. Eduth Bihoseph (my own); and 27. Or Hachayim.

These colleges and schools are all in Jerusalem; but there are several, although as might be expected in less numbers, in Hebron, Zafed, and Tiberias.

. . . . (a long historical excursus on the Ashkenazi Synagogue compound follows).

. . . .

In these synagogues is also bestowed a Jewish elementary education. It is indeed very simple, still very correct and good, and considerably better than with the Ashkenazim. But the higher school, where the child obtains instruction in the Talmud, holds a higher rank among the German than the Portuguese: and we can soon distinguish whether a child has been educated in one or the other talmudic school; since the Ashkenazim endeavor to improve the child more than the others in sharp and deep thought and wit.

Rabbi Joseph Schwarz,
Descriptive Geography and Brief Historical Sketch of Palestine,
trans. Isaac Leeser (Philadelphia, 1850), pp. 274–83.

A GLIMPSE OF A WEALTHY JERUSALEM JEWISH FAMILY

(FIRST HALF OF THE NINETEENTH CENTURY)

On the level brow of Zion, exactly opposite to the Tower of Hippicus, is the residence of the wealthiest Jew in Jerusalem. On passing through the outer door of his dwelling, we entered a small court, overshadowed by a vine-covered trellis, on one side of which are the principal apartments, which we found comfortable and in good order. This personage is mentioned by many travelers, and he presents a remarkable instance of the two motives which popular prejudice generally supposes to actuate the Jew—intense love of money, and an equally tenacious adherence to the traditions of his people. His career is remarkable; in his youth he had been a wanderer under the burning tropics, as well as in England and in Spain, and by various means having accumulated a sum sufficient to render him the envy of his poor abject brethren, he repaired to the city of his fathers, to die there and to be buried in the Valley of Jehoshaphat.

On entering his dwelling, we found him seated on the low divan, fondling his youngest child; and on our expressing a wish to draw the costume of the female members of his family, he commanded their attendance; but it was some time before they would come forward; when, however, they did present themselves, it was with no sort of reserve whatever. Their costume (see illustration 19) was chastely elegant. The prominent figure in the sketch is the married daughter, whose little husband, a boy of fourteen or fifteen, as he seemed,[1] was wanted nearly a head of the stature of his wife, but was already chargeable with the onerous duties of a father. An oval head-dress of peculiar shape, from which is slung a long veil of embroidered muslin, shown as hanging in the sketch from the back of another figure, admirably sets off the brow and eyes; the neck is ornamented with bracelets, and the bosom with a profusion of gold coins, partly concealed by folds of muslin; a graceful robe of striped silk with long open sleeves, half-laced under the bosom, invests the whole person, over which is worn a jacket of green silk with short sleeves, leaving the white arm and braceleted hand at liberty. The elder person on the sofa is the mother, whose dress was more grave, her turban less oval, and of blue shawl, and the breast covered entirely to the neck with a kind of ornamented gold tissue, above which is seen a jacket of fur. She was engaged in knitting, while her younger daughter bent over her in conversation. Her dress is

[1] The Mishna (*Avot* V, para. 24) recommends eighteen as the normal age for a man to marry. However, marriages in early adolescence were not uncommon amongst Middle Eastern Jews even into the present century.

similar to that of her sister, but with no gold coins or tight muslin folds; and instead of large earrings,[2] the vermilion blossom of the pomegranate formed an exquisite pendant, reflecting its glow upon the dazzling whiteness of her skin.

We were surprised at the fairness and delicacy of their complexions and the vivacity of their manner. Unlike the wives of oriental Christians, who respectfully attend at a distance till invited to approach, these pretty Jewesses seemed on a perfect footing of equality, and chatted and laughed away without intermission.

W. H. Bartlett,
Walks about the City and Environs of Jerusalem,
2d ed. (London, 184?), pp. 191–93.

[2] This was because she was still unmarried. Most of a woman's jewelry came as part of her trousseau.

A VISIT WITH THE CHIEF RABBI OF JERUSALEM
(MID-NINETEENTH CENTURY)

I betook myself to the Chief Rabbi of Jerusalem Hayyim Nissim Abulafia.

Some years ago, the Turkish government which honors the Hakham Bashi among its acknowledged dignitaries, placed a double honor guard at his house. He would thankfully have excused it for one-tenth the cost. I climbed up a narrow stone stairway, walked across an open terrace where two women quickly covered their faces, and conducted me to a large hall furnished with low divans in oriental fashion. On one of these, an elderly gentleman of more than eighty years was seated. His head was wound with a blue-gray turban which concealed the hair, and a long white beard fell upon his white robe. He had himself lifted up by two servants so that he could greet me. His was an estimable patriarchal figure. He laid his hand upon his breast and forehead and motioned to me to sit beside him.

"Our apologies," he began in Spanish, "for not having met you before the gate of the city."

"It would have been embarrassing if you, a distinguished elderly gentleman, had come to meet me, a younger man."

"When sacrifices were brought to Jerusalem, the High Priest always went forth to meet them. And you are bringing an offering.[1] Have you not traveled a great distance?"

"A lifetime desire of mine has been fulfilled—to see Jerusalem. Look at my signet ring. It has next to the shield of David the words pronounced at the Passover supper: *Le-shānā ha-bā'ā bīrūshālayīm.*"[2]

"You have reason to rejoice! You have obtained greater salvation than Moses, our teacher. He could only see the Promised Land from afar off. You have set foot on it. We, however, who were born here, wait expectantly and sorrowfully for the Messiah."

"With the gesture of greeting, his hand on breast and forehead, he reached for my letters of introduction. Meanwhile, some rabbis in oriental dress, who had come to assist the master of the house in honoring the guest, assembled and took their places. Two servants brought *tschibuk*[3] and coffee and cups of sweet fruit and lemonade. But before anyone ate or drank, a short blessing was recited according to custom. The master of the house leaned toward me, having made the gesture of placing the hand on breast and forehead, and I enjoyed the things which were brought in.

[1] A reference to the purpose of Frankl's visit to Jerusalem.
[2] "Next Year in Jerusalem."
[3] Turk. for "pipe."

The Hakham Bashi chose from among these to smoke the *tchibuk*. He read the letters attentively, and then addressed me:

"These letters gratify me; they are, however, unnecessary. Whoever does good work has sufficient recommendation."

"God, perhaps. But not man. You do not know me, so these letters seemed necessary to me."

"You are an excellent man. Has anyone yet chosen you directly? We are all the servants of God."

"Give me your advice. I would not want to venture into the Holy City without it. Perhaps there are many things, acceptable elsewhere, but which are not customary in this land.

"Very good; I have heard this before! I am an old man, but I will do what I can to help you."

"Your appearance is old and venerable, but your spirit is young."

"That is by the grace of God."

"I am happy to have come to see you. Your name is known in the West as it is in the East."

"Music is played everywhere."

"Allow me to visit you again."

"If you come to me, I will assist you. I can," he said, hinting to the rabbi who was nearby, "inasmuch as the race of the Tannaim and Amoraim[4] has not yet died out."

I departed, though not before placing my hand on the mezuzah on the doorpost and on my lips, as I had done when I arrived, for this pious custom is always observed in Jerusalem.

Two days later, the Hakham Bashi returned to me surrounded by his venerable rabbinical staff, and solemnly preceded by his servants. I noticed that all of them, even though it was the Sabbath—the so-called Spanish Sabbath—carried silver-tipped sticks with them, for the German Jews consider it a sin to use a walking stick on the Sabbath. Prior to his visit the Hakham Bashi had sent sweet cakes to me "so that my visit to the Holy City would be a savory one."

Ludwig August Frankl,
Nach Jerusalem (Berlin, 1935), pp. 28–29.

[4] The sages whose discussions comprise the Mishna and Gemara, respectively.

THE JEWISH COMMUNITY OF TIBERIAS IN THE EARLY NINETEENTH CENTURY

Tabaria, the ancient Tiberias, stands close to the lake, upon a small plain, surrounded by mountains. Its situation is extremely hot and unhealthy, as the mountain impedes the free course of the westerly winds which prevail throughout Syria during the summer. Hence intermittent fevers, especially those of the quartan form,[1] are very common in the town in that season. . . . The town is surrounded towards the land by a thick and well built wall, about twenty feet in height, with a high parapet and loop-holes.

Tabaria, with its district of ten or twelve villages, forms a part of the Pashalik of Akka (Acre). Being considered one of the principal points of defence of the Pashalik, a garrison of two or three hundred men is constantly kept here, the greater part of whom are married and settled.

There are about four thousand inhabitants in Tabaria, one-fourth of whom are Jews. The Christian community consists only of a few families, but they enjoy great liberty, and are on a footing of equality with the Turks. The difference of treatment which the Christians experience from the Turks in different parts of Syria is very remarkable.

The Jews of Tiberias occupy a quarter on the shore of the lake in the middle of the town, which has lately been considerably enlarged by the purchase of several streets. It is separated from the rest of the town by a high wall, and has only one gate of entrance, which is regularly shut at sunset, after which no person is allowed to pass. There are one hundred and sixty, or two hundred families, of which forty or fifty are of Polish origin, the rest are Jews from Spain, Barbary, and different parts of Syria. Tiberias is one of the four holy cities of the Talmud; the other three being Szaffad (Safed), Jerusalem, and Hebron. It is esteemed holy ground, because Jacob is supposed to have resided here, and because it is situated on the lake Genasereth, from which, according to the most generally received opinion of the Talmud, the Messiah is to rise. The greater part of the Jews who reside in these holy places do not engage in mercantile pursuits; but are a society of religious persons occupied solely with their sacred duties. There are among them only two who are merchants, and men of property, and these are styled Kafers[2] or unbelievers by the others, who do nothing but read and pray. Jewish devotees from all parts of the globe flock to the four holy cities, in order to pass their days in praying for their own salva-

[1] That is, a fever that recurs approximately every four days. The writer is probably referring to malaria.

[2] Ar., *kāfir*.

tion, and that of their brethren, who remain occupied in worldly pursuits. But the offering up of prayers by these devotees is rendered still more indispensible by a dogma contained in the Talmud, that the world will return to its primitive chaos, if prayers are not addressed to the God of Israel at least twice a week in these four cities; this belief produces considerable pecuniary advantage to the supplicants, as the missionaries sent abroad to collect alms for the support of these religious fraternities plead the danger of the threatened chaos, to induce the rich Jews to send supplies of money in order that the prayers may be constantly offered up. Three or four missionaries are sent out every year; one to the coasts of Africa from Damietta to Mogadore, another to the coasts of Europe from Venice to Gibraltar, a third to the Archipelago, Constantinople, and Anatolia, and a fourth through Syria. The charity of the Jews of London is appealed to from time to time; but the Jews of Gibraltar have the reputation of being more liberal than any others, and from four to five thousand Spanish dollars are received annually from them. . . . Great jealousy seems to prevail between the Syrian and Polish Jews. The former being in possession of the place, oblige the foreigners to pay excessively high for their lodgings; and compel them also to contribute considerable sums towards the relief of the indigent Syrians, while they themselves never give the smallest trifle to the poor from Poland.[3]

The pilgrim Jews who repair to Tiberias are of all ages from twelve to sixty. If they bring a little money with them the cunning of their brethren here soon deprives them of it; for as they arrive with the most extravagant ideas of the holy cities, they are easily imposed upon before their enthusiasm begins to cool. To rent a house in which some learned Rabbin or saint died, to visit the tombs of the most renowned devotees, to have the sacred books opened in their presence, and public prayers read for the salvation of the new-comers, all these inestimable advantages, together with various other minor religious tricks, soon strip the stranger of his last farthing. He then becomes dependent upon the charity of his nation, upon foreign subsidies, or upon the fervor of some inexperienced pilgrim. Those who go abroad as missionaries generally realize some property, as they are allowed ten percent upon all alms collected, besides their traveling expenses. The Jewish devotees pass the whole day in the schools or the synagogue, reciting the Old Testament and the Talmud, both of which many of them know entirely by heart. They all write Hebrew, but I did not see any fine handwriting amongst them. Their learning seems to be on the same level as that of the Turks, among whom an Olema[4] thinks he has

[3] For another example of the tension between the Ashkenazim and Sefardim, see below, pp. 365–66.

[4] A Muslim scholar (from Ar., *ᶜālim;* pl., *ᶜulamā'*).

attained the pinnacle of knowledge if he can recite all the Koran together with some thousand of Hadeath (*ḥadīth*), or sentences of the Prophet, and traditions concerning him, but neither Jews, nor Turks, nor Christians, in these countries have the slightest idea of that criticism which might guide them to a rational explanation or emendation of their sacred books.

There are some beautiful copies of the books of Moses in the Syrian synagogue, written upon a long roll of leather, not parchment, but no one could tell me when or where they were made. I suspect, however, that they came from Baghdad, where the best Hebrew scribes live, and of whose writings I had seen many fine specimens at Aleppo and Damascus. The libraries of the two schools at Tiberias are moderately stocked with Hebrew books, most of which have been printed at Vienna and Venice. Except some copies of the Old Testament and the Talmud, they have no manuscripts.

They observe a singular custom here in praying. While the Rabbin recites the Psalms of David or the prayers extracted from them, the congregation frequently imitate by their voice or gestures the meaning of some remarkable passages. For example, when the Rabbin pronounces the words "praise the Lord with the sound of the trumpet"[5] they imitate the sound of the trumpet through their closed fists. When "a horrible tempest"[6] occurs, they puff and blow to represent a storm; or should he mention "the cries of the righteous in distress",[7] they all set up a loud screaming; and it not infrequently happens that while some are still blowing the storm, others have already begun the cries of the righteous, thus forming a concert which it is difficult for any but a zealous Hebrew to hear with gravity.

The Jews enjoy here perfect religious freedom, more particularly since Soleiman,[8] whose principal minister Haym Farkhy[9] is a Jew, has succeeded to the Pashalik of Akka. During the life of Djezzar Pasha they were often

[5] Ps. 150:3.

[6] Jon. 1:4.

[7] Ps. 9:13.

[8] Sulaymān Pasha succeeded the notorious Aḥmad Jazzār Pasha as governor of Acre in 1804. He ruled until his death in 1818 or 1819.

[9] Ḥayyīm Farḥī was a member of the important Jewish banking family of Syria founded by his father Saul in the late eighteenth century. He was the adviser and financial agent (Ar., *ṣarrāf*) of three successive Turkish governors. His first patron, Aḥmad Jazzār Pasha, in a fit of rage, ordered that his right eye be gouged out and his nose cut off (see illus. 17), but later reinstated him. His third master, ᶜAbd Allāh Pasha, had him executed in 1820 and his body tossed into the sea. See Itzhak Ben-Zvi, *Eretz-Israel under Ottoman Rule,* 2d ed. (Jerusalem, 1966), pp. 319–22 and 339–43 [Heb.]; also Aryeh Shmuelevitz, "Farḥi," *EJ* 6: 1,181–83.

obliged to pay heavy fines; at present they merely pay the Kharadj. Their conduct, however, is not so prudent as it ought to be in a country where the Turks are always watching for a pretext to extort money. They sell wine and brandy to the soldiers of the town, almost publicly, and at their weddings they make a dangerous display of their wealth. On these occasions they traverse the city in pompous procession, carrying before the bride the plate of almost the whole community, consisting of large dishes, coffee pots, coffee cups, etc., and they feast in the house of the bridegroom for seven successive days and nights. The wedding feast of a man who has about fifty pounds a year, and no Jew can live with his family on less, will often cost more than sixty pounds. They marry at a very early age, it being not uncommon to see mothers of eleven and fathers of thirteen years. The Rabbin of Tiberias is under the great Rabbin of Szaffad, who pronounces final judgment on all contested points of law and religion. I found amongst the Polish Jews, one from Bohemia, an honest German, who was overjoyed on hearing me speak his own language, and who carried me through the quarter introducing me to all his acquaintance. In every house I was offered brandy, and the women appeared to be much less shy than they are in other parts of Syria. It may easily be supposed that many of these Jews are discontented with their lot. Led by the stories of the missionaries to conceive the most exalted ideas of the land of promise, as they still call it, several of them have absconded from their parents to beg their way to Palestine, but no sooner do they arrive in one or other of the four holy cities, than they find by the aspect of all around them that they have been deceived. A few find their way back to their native country, but the greater number remain, and look forward to the inestimable advantage of having their bones laid in the holy land. The cemetery of the Jews of Tiberias is on the declivity of the mountain, about half an hour from the town, where the tombs of their most renowned persons are visited much in the same manner as are the sepulchres of Musulman saints.

John Lewis Burckhardt,
Travels in Syria and the Holy Land
(London, 1822), pp. 320–28.

AGITATION AGAINST THE JEWS OF SAFED (1834)

It is one of the holy cities of the Talmud; and according to this authority, the Messiah will reign there for forty years before he takes possession of Sion. The sanctity and historical importance thus attributed to the city by anticipation render it a favourite place of retirement for Israelites; of these it contains, they say, about four thousand, a number nearly balancing that of the Mahometan inhabitants. I knew by my experience of Tabarieh that a "holy city" was sure to have a population of vermin somewhat proportionate to the number of Israelites, and I therefore caused my tent to be pitched upon a green spot of ground at a respectful distance from the walls of the town.

The Jews of the place, though exceedingly wealthy, had lived peaceably and undisturbed in their retirement until the insurrection of 1834; but about the beginning of that year a highly religious Mussulman, called Mohammed Damoor, went forth into the market-place, crying with a loud voice, and prophesying that on the fifteenth of the following June the true believers would rise up in just wrath against the Jews, and despoil them of their gold, and their silver, and their jewels. The earnestness of the prophet produced some impression at the time; but all went on as usual, until at last the fifteenth of June arrived. When that day dawned, the whole Mussulman population of the place assembled in the streets, that they might see the result of the prophecy. Suddenly Mohammed Damoor rushed furious into the crowd, and the fierce shout of the prophet soon insured the fulfilment of his prophecy. Some of the Jews fled and some remained, but they who fled and they remained alike and unresistingly left their property to the hands of the spoilers. The most odious of all outrages, that of searching the women for the base purpose of discovering such things as gold and silver concealed about their persons, was perpetrated without shame. The poor Jews were so stricken with terror, that they submitted to their fate, even where resistance would have been easy. In several instances a young Mussulman boy, not more than ten or twelve years of age, walked straight into the house of a Jew, and stripped him of his property before his face, and in the presence of his whole family. When the insurrection was put down, some of the Mussulmans (most probably those who had got no spoil wherewith they might buy immunity), were punished, but the greater part of them escaped; none of the booty was restored, and the pecuniary redress which the Pasha had undertaken to enforce for them had been hitherto so carefully delayed that the hope of ever obtaining it had grown very faint. A new governor had been appointed to the command of the place with stringent orders to ascertain the real extent of the losses, to discover the spoilers, and to compel immediate restitution. It was found, notwithstanding the urgency of his instructions, the governor did not push on the affair with any perceptible vigour; the Jews complained; and either by the protection of the British consul at Damascus, or by some other means, had influence enough to induce the appointment of a special commissioner—they call him "the Modeer"—whose duty it was to watch for and prevent anything like connivance on the part of the governor, and to push on the investigation with vigour and impartiality.

Such were the instructions with which some few weeks since the Modeer came charged; the result was that the investigation had made no practical advance, and that the Modeer, as well as the governor, was living upon terms of affectionate friendship with Mohammed Damoor, and the rest of the principal spoilers.

Thus stood the chance of redress for the past. But the cause of the agonising excitement under which the Jews of the place now laboured was recent and justly alarming: Mohammed Damoor had again gone forth into the market-place, and lifted up his voice, and prophesied a second spoilation of the Israelites. This was grave matter; the words of such a practical and clear-sighted prophet as Mohammed Damoor were not to be despised.

. . . .

The course of my travels soon drew me so far from Safet that I never heard how the dreadful day passed off which had been fixed for the accomplishment of the second prophecy.

Alexander William Kinglake, *Eothen* (London, 1911) pp. 216–20.

A GERMAN ORIENTALIST IS CAUGHT IN AN ATTACK UPON THE JEWS OF SAFED (1838)

I went from there (the holy sites around Safed) and came to Ra's al-Aḥmar.[1] After sunset I rested in Dallata.[2] There I found Ḥākhām Shushan, who had visited me in Safed. He begged me to wait with him until it was known whether the tempest had passed. While coming from Safed, he himself had seen a badly wounded man from the village of Jisr Yaᶜqūb[3] who told him that the Druze had attacked the soldiers of Ibrahim Pasha who were stationed there. They captured 300 camels loaded with gunpowder. From there the rebels turned toward Safed. This news shook me greatly. I was worried about my belongings and my notebooks which I had left in Safed. So I hurried to return.[4]

As I got there, the brother of the Governor of Acre, ᶜAbd al-Hādī, arrived also at the head of several hundred soldiers in formation. He was prepared to attack the Druze and asked the Jews to pray for him. Then all the synagogues were opened. The people called upon God with all their strength. I transcribed their prayer into Arabic and brought it to him along with a petition on behalf of the entire community humbly beseeching him not to let them down. He answered me that they could rest easy and remain in the city without fear because he had strict orders from the Musellim (the governor of the city) to protect the town with all his vigor, and he had enough weapons to carry out that assignment. I had in mind leaving the city as I had heard the Muslims daring to talk openly that in a few days they would have everything belonging to the Jews. But I had no horse, no donkey, not even a valet. Those inhabitants of the city who knew the extent of the Arabs' ferocity were frightened when they heard them say these things. The Jews gathered together and decided to guard the city streets at night with 30 Jewish watchmen. On that Sabbath eve, the Arabs committed their first act of despoilation, robbing a horse from a Jew on the road. The rumor was spreading and getting stronger among the Muslims that the time for the Jews was drawing near. As a result of this they were afraid to go to sleep in their own beds and stayed in the streets all night—

[1] About eight kilometers northwest of Safed.

[2] About five kilometers north of Safed.

[3] This is probably Jisr Banāt Yaᶜqūb, which is approximately eleven kilometers northeast of Safed on the Jordan River.

[4] This Ḥākhām Shushan depended apparently upon his villagers in time of trouble, for indeed, he owned nearly all the chattels in the village of Dallata, and everyone loved him. Only Sefardic Jews are considered citizens of the land with permission to buy property (Loewe's note).

they, their wives, and their children—with broken spirits and sullen faces. I alone took courage and put on a smiling face for them so that they too might gather some courage. Just before the dawn of the 12th of Tammuz (July 5, 1838), while it was still night, the entire city was suddenly terrified because unknown men were seen walking around the streets, and there were signs of malice on their face. I was hurriedly called to come to Rabbi Abraham Dov.[5] I went to him amidst a throng of wailing women and weeping children. The Rabbi asked me to write a petition to the Musellim not to forsake them in this hour of trouble, but to be their protector as ᶜAbd al-Hādī had directed him.

I did as the Rabbi wished. The Governor replied in Arab fashion that he swears by his head and his eyes that he would not move from the city. Despite this, we all knew that there was no substance in his oath. The suffering which encompassed the Jews here only a few years ago were reminiscent of the description of the Destruction of the Judaean Commonwealth in the talmudic tractate *Giṭṭīn*.[6] And now, here I had come from a peaceful and quiet land to drink the cup of wrath with them, I who could not imagine the tyranny of the inhabitants of Asia. Around me on all side were women with their young children sleeping on the ground. At times even this sort of sleep was denied them by terrifying dreams. I alone was awake among them, calculating the evil that was bound to come. Silence fell around us and only at a distance was some shooting heard. As I was sitting there disconsolately, my landlord came to me and begged me to get some sleep myself. I had almost dozed off when I was called again to come to the Rabbi by a howling voice that said, "The Druze are coming!" At hearing that, I quickly tucked my cash into my bosom. I had intended to bury it in the ground. I left my belongings and my notebooks in my room because I was afraid to draw any attention to them. At that very moment I saw one of the Druze aiming his weapon at an old woman. I entered the Rabbi's chamber, and there were men, women, and children falling upon each other's neck, hugging each other, and weeping profusely. The honorable Rabbi, his face white as a deadman's, was among them. He said to me, "Let's go to the enemies' commander and ask him what he wants from us. But you, dear friend, go at our head, because you speak their language and you are under protection of the foreign consuls. Maybe

[5] Rabbi Abraham Dov Baer of Ovruch was the leader of the Hasidim in Safed from 1831 until his death in the plague of 1840. He headed relief efforts after the various disasters that struck the Jewish community and, as can be seen from this letter, encouraged people not to abandon this ancient Jewish community. For more biographical information, see Abraham Yaari, *Iggerōt Ereṣ Yisrāʾēl* (Letters from the Land of Israel) (Ramat Gan, 1971), pp. 380ff.; also *EJ* 2: 157.

[6] 57a–b.

they will treat you favorably." As I was about to go, one of the Druze came to us. I went forward to him and said, "If things be in earnest, then you are coming here in truth, religion, and justice." (Normally, the first things the Druze say is, "In truth, religion, and justice, we have come. Do not be afraid. Do not be afraid.") "Would you please tell us what you are seeking, because we are prepared to give you everything which may be found in our possession, only do not touch anyone's person." But he answered me with a malicious tone, "I know for myself what I wish to do, but first hand over your money." The words were still on his lips while his hands were hastening to do evil. He stripped my clothing off me and took my money. While this oppressor was maltreating me, his friends rushed in after him like a flood of stormy water.

The Governor did not stand by his promise, but fled for his life. We abandoned our houses and sought refuge in the cemetery. Meanwhile, the Druze ran after us shouting, "*Lā takhāf! Lā takhāf!* (Have no fear! Have no fear!)." They tried to bring us back with kind words because they imagined to find more valuables concealed on our persons. However, when none of us listened to their soft words, they became enraged and broke through upon us from every side. As for the Muslim inhabitants of the city, they were with them, acting in concert. Thus, we lost all hope. Nevertheless, I stood up and looked calmly behind me, for now I had nothing to worry about except my life. And what value is one's life after seeing the destruction of several thousand innocent souls of my people. That is why I did not care to escape, and what is more, I knew no place of refuge for me anyway. My feet naively carried me to one of the nearby villages, called ᶜAyn Zaytūn,[7] so at least I should not see the misery befalling thousands of my people. The enemy showered me with a rain of stones and bullets. There too, I was encircled by old men, women, and children, all bemoaning their calamity. The local people of this village, who are also Druze, hurried us into one place and locked us in a small synagogue.

In order to fill their measure of cruelty and savagery, they started mocking us with a frightfully cruel laughter. Five Druze approached us armed with rifles, knives, axes, and clubs. They beat us on the most delicate parts of our body. They wounded us till blood flowed. Afterwards, they chased us outside. A thousand times they pointed their swords at our hearts to force us to reveal the place where our treasures were buried, until most of us fell to the ground and fainted. Then they fell upon us, stripped off our clothes, and left us lying naked in the field. But even as these men went away, others came to renew their cruelty. With an eye

[7] About three kilometers northwest of Safed.

full of detachment I looked at the death which was hovering about my face. How many times did I incline my head toward the sword, asking them to cut it off once and for all. Those cruel men did not want to fulfill my wish, but continued molesting us with endless torments, until the night ended our misery. The next morning, we felt relieved, and whoever had any strength left in him lifted his feet and returned to Safed because the ferocious Druze had left the city at the seventh hour of the morning. When I got back to the city, I immediately went to my room to see if the looters had left anything. None of my clothes or belongings remained. I was not concerned about them, but about my notebooks which I had put together and into which I had copied so much. They had been ready to go to the publisher, and now some of them were burnt, some torn to such small pieces that I could not possibly put them back together. My landlord was among those who had fled. In his house I found nothing but broken vessels, torn clothes, scattered feathers, and ripped books. From here, I went to the Rabbi's house. I found him crying his heart out before God in the company of his wife and some of his household. We cried a great deal together because of our distress, until finally, I took heart and put on a better face. With a smile, I blessed God for having saved our lives from the swords of these savage men.

Then Rabbi Dov told me that when I became separated from him the Druze surroundered them too. They tortured and tormented them without pity. Whatever they found they pillaged. Even after they gave them all the money they had, totalling 150 purses (a purse is equal to the sum of £5 sterling), they obstinately asked for 1000 purses more. They took the honorable Rabbi Abraham Dov prisoner, and he prepared himself to die a cruel death. He calmly stood there and asked for a little water to wash his hands and fulfill the law in these things. . . . Finally, after inflicting him with numerous torments, they let the Rabbi go. And here he was alive and standing in front of me as if nothing had happened.

The Druze left the city and the Muslims returned to it. The first thing they did upon returning was to force the Jews to give them a document testifying that they the Muslims had protected them faithfully with all their might from the wrath of the Druze. They threatened the Jews that if they should refuse to give them this false document, they would stir up the Arabs living around the city against them. Their threats were by no means empty talk since already the traces of the new destroyers were to be seen in known places. Thus, they were obliged to give them in writing the document they demanded.

The question now arose, what to do now? The congregation loudly implored me to induce the Rabbi to accompany me to Acre, and from there to Haifa where many of the European consuls maintain their residence because it is secure from the fear of the enemy and is easy to escape from in time of danger. The Rabbi rightly replied that if the majority of the people were in agreement on this course of action, it was incumbent upon him to follow the majority and accede to the will of the congregation. However, it was his opinion that they should sit still in this place of theirs whatever happens, so that they would maintain the settlement of this ancient community and safeguard the synagogues on their foundations which would surely turn to ruins should they move out of the city. With these words, the Rabbi countered their opinion that this was the time described in the Talmud with the statement "And the Galilee will be in ruin."[8] He thus inclined the hearts of the congregants to stay where they were. I alone did not heed the Rabbi's advice. He kindly suggested that I remain with him until I receive help from abroad so that I could have new clothes made to cover my nakedness. However, I took from them enough bread for two days, which they tearfully gave me, and I departed from the city that very day.

As I was still talking, an Arab by the name of Muṣṭafā Muḥammad, who lived in Safed, came and brought to the Rabbi all of the money he had on his person as a sacrificial offering for the good of the community. Now this man had always shown kindness toward the Jews. In fact, he had tried this time, too, to appease the Druze with several thousand *qurūsh*[9] so that they would keep their hands off the Rabbi, but he had been unsuccessful. Their not listening to him was only the least of it, for they sought to kill him also because he spoke on behalf of the Jews. When this man saw me covered with a torn garment, he gave me decent clothes and 12 *qurūsh* in coin. There I was at that moment still wounded from head to toe. But thank God in His mercy I was still alive. My notes had been lost, but the main body of my writings had been deposited with the Prussian Consul General in Alexandria. Nevertheless, several years of work would pass before I would repair the damage entirely. But I shall not hold back my work, nor spare myself any labor. In general, my spirit had not been weakened, and I am hoping to make my way to Jerusalem.

Louis Loewe, A Letter from Safed to the *Allgemeine Zeitung des Judenthums,* in A. Yaari, ed., *Iggerōt Ereṣ Yisrāʾēl* (Letters from the Land of Israel) (Ramat Gan, 1971), pp. 387–92.

[8] According to R. Eliezer the Great this is one of the signs of the coming of the Messiah. See Mishna *Soṭa* 9:15.

[9] Plural of *qirsh,* the Turkish piaster.

THE JEWISH SETTLERS IN MASQAT
(FIRST HALF OF THE NINETEENTH CENTURY)

The greater portion of the inhabitants of Maskat are of a mixed race, the descendants of Arabs, Persians, Indians, Syrians, by way of Baghdad, Kurds, Afghans, Beluches, etc., who, attracted by the mildness of the government, have settled here, either for the purposes of commerce, or to avoid the despotism of the surrounding governments. This we discover has been the case from a very early period; two centuries before the birth of Mohammed, a powerful tribe, then residing on the shores of the Persian Gulf, sought refuge here against the oppression of the Persians, and, as late as 1828, a party of Jews, unable any longer to endure the exactions and tyranny of Daud Pacha, were received by the Imām with much kindness.[1]

. . . .

There are a few Jews in Maskat, who mostly arrived there in 1828, being driven from Baghdad, as we have before stated, by the cruelties and extortions of the Pacha Daud. Nearly the whole of this race were compelled to fly. Some took refuge in Persia, while others, in their passage towards India, remained here. The same toleration exercized towards all other persuasions is extended to the Beni Israel, no badge or mark as in Egypt or Syria, being insisted on. They are not, as in the town of Yemen,[2] compelled to occupy a distant and separate part of the town, nor is the observance, so strictly adhered to in Persia, of compelling them to pass to the left of Mussulmans when meeting in the streets, here insisted on. Their avocations in Maskat are various, many being employed in the fabrication of silver ornaments, others in shroffing money, and some few retail in intoxicating liquors.

[1] Dā'ūd Pasha (1816–31) was the last of the Mamluk governors (*kölemen*) of Baghdad. Although he began his career there with the help of some wealthy Baghdadi Jews, the most important of whom were Ezra b. Yūsuf Nissīm Gabbay, the *nāsī* of the Jewish community, and his brother Ezekiel, Dā'ūd Pasha later turned on them and instituted a persecution which resulted in the flight of many to Syria, Egypt, Persia, India, and even Australia and China. See A. Ben Ya^caqov, *A History of the Jews in Iraq* (Jerusalem, 1975), pp. 103–5 [Heb.]. The earlier Danish traveler, Carsten Niebuhr, also testifies to the fact that the Jews were treated better in Oman than elsewhere in Arabia. See Carsten Niebuhr, *Travels in Arabia*, in *A General Collection of the Best and Most Interesting Voyages and Travels in All Parts of the World*, vol. 10, ed. John Pinkerton (London, 1811), p. 142.

[2] The writer is referring to Ṣan^ca'. On the enforced isolation of this community, see above, pp. 322–23.

I should fix the population of Maskat and Muttrah[3] at sixty thousand souls.

This town is entitled to a high rank among Oriental cities, not only as the emporium of a very considerable trade between Arabia, India, and Persia, but also, in reference to its extensive imports, of some note as the seaport of Oman.

Lieut. J. R. Wellsted, F.R.S.,
Travels in Arabia, vol. 1 (London, 1838), pp. 14–22.

[3] Masqat and Muttrah (Maṭraḥ) are the two principal towns of Oman.

A FAMOUS JEWISH TRAVELER VISITS HIS BRETHREN IN ADEN

(MID-NINETEENTH CENTURY)

This is Aden in the land of Yemen, east of the Red Sea and west of the Persian Gulf, near the Bab al-Mandab. It was a barren desert in the days of the savage Arab rulers, but has become a paradise in the hands of the benevolent Government of England. . . . It is said about this town of Aden, that its Jewish inhabitants have lived here since the time that it was biblical Ezion-Geber.[1]

There is no end to all the improvements, benevolent institutions, opportunities for employment, and the myriad of expenditures (above and beyond the revenue collected) which the government of blessed England made in the place. The writer's pen cannot describe it! For this reason, the population of the town has swelled. People of all nations and languages have flocked here from surrounding Yemen, from Ethiopia, India, Persia, Masqat, and Egypt. They are actively engaged in commerce, dealing in the products of the land, such as oil, butter, honey, wax (which is brought from the coastal towns of Abyssinia . . .), coffee (more than any other product), all sorts of aromatics, precious stones, and handcrafted wares. Indeed, even most of the Arab inhabitants enjoy the freedom, liberty, justice, and increased commerce and wages, which have come in the wake of these benevolent rulers, and they do not long for their former savage kings.

So too, our poor Jewish brethren who dwell here also shook themselves from the dust of their humiliation and misery, raised their head, and became free men. Some are merchants who buy and sell. They own carts and carriages. Others maintain the crafts they practiced previously, namely, goldsmithing, weaving, and artisanry, etc., etc.[2] Their property consists of two streets (specifically for Jews) inside the built city which they had before the conquest. They also live throughout the city when they can, and no one bothers them.

The Jews here still remember the Holy Sabbath of the Portion *Beshallaḥ* (Exod. 13:17–14:16), 5608, the day on which the British

[1] The biblical port of Ezion-Geber (cf. 1 Kings 9:26 and elsewhere) was located somewhere between present-day Eilat and Aqaba, far to the north of Aden.

[2] Most of the Jews in Aden were engaged in manual occupations at this time. Most of the skills and handicrafts in which the Jews excelled soon became economically marginal as Aden developed into a modern port under British rule. Those Jews who served in the British administration were mainly from India. See S. D. Goitein, "Aden: Modern Period," *EJ* 2: 262f.

entered this city.[3] Early on the morning of the day before, the ministers and soldiers of the Arab king worked them hard and made them stand with them on the battlefield on top of the mountains overlooking the sea. They forced them to haul up the cannons and shells to them. The Jews gathered at dawn (the next day) at the synagogue in accordance with their custom and said: "Whatever may happen to us, we shall not go out on the sabbath to work and carry!"[4] In any event, before noon the streets of the city were full of English soldiers. It was not by their hosts, nor by force, nor by battle, nor by cannon or fire. Buildings did not fall. There were no voices screaming, and not a garment was soiled with blood. . . . They had orders not to spill innocent blood, and these were obeyed. When the king realized what trouble had overtaken him and that he could not withstand them, he escaped at dawn to Laḥj,[5] a town one day's journey from here.

The first thing the English did was to look after the welfare of the Jews. They put guards at their synagogues, homes, and streets so that no ill befell them. That is why the Jews remember them well.

Now there are to be found about 250 households of our brethren, the Children of Israel. Most of them come from the other cities of Yemen and from the ruined Mokha, and have thus filled Aden. This does not even include those who fall into their midst every day as refugees from war and hunger in the Yemenite interior and those fleeing religious persecution.[6] The refugees are a burden upon the inhabitants of the city because they come poor, hungry, and naked. They go around town for a crust of bread, and the receivers are twice as many as the givers.

Recently, a large, new synagogue was built in the Street of the Jews. It is a beautiful building which holds 2000 men. The women do not come to the synagogue anywhere in Yemen because they cannot pray from the prayerbook. That is why no women's gallery was built there. Some women come and stand at the door of the synagogue to prostrate themselves in front of the Torah when it is taken from the ark to the reader's platform, and from this distance they raise their palms facing the Torah and kiss them. . . . The men sit on straw mats and hides spread on the floor of the

[3] Sapir's date is incorrect. Aden was taken by the British in January 1839, which corresponds to 5599 on the Jewish calendar.

[4] The Jews of Aden were very strict Sabbath observers, which together with their lack of knowledge of English was one of the principal reasons that they were not employed in government service under the British. See Goitein, "Aden," *EJ* 2: 262.

[5] This town was the ancestral home of the ᶜAbdalī sultans, who had ruled Aden since 1735. See O. Löfgren, "ᶜAdan," *EI*² 1: 181.

[6] The Hebrew text reads: *ve-ha-nimlaṭīm mē-ᶜōl ha-madhaba,* literally, "those fleeing from the yoke of the Islamic sect" (that is, the Zaydī Shiᶜites of Yemen).

synagogue. They remove their shoes outside as is customary from days of old throughout Yemen.

About a year ago, there passed through the honorable gentleman and scholar, R. Sason, the son of the pious leader who was known as R. David Sassoon (may his memory be blessed) of Bombay.[7] Work on the synagogue was not fully completed at that time. He donated to them 100£ sterling for chairs to sit on as is customary in other countries. Large chairs were made to be put around the walls and in the center. However, they are still standing outside in the courtyard of the synagogue. They have not been brought inside because these people like their ancestral custom and regard it as sacred to sit on floor mats. Furthermore, the synagogue holds more men when they sit on the ground one next to the other.

They have not changed their attire or their ways of doing things. They will not forsake their customs. Whatever they used to do, they still do. And thus it pleases them.

Their customs in regard to Torah, prayer, the religious duties and other Jewish practices are the same as in the Yemenite interior. They speak Arabic. Their accent in the Holy Language and their manner of reading the Torah is like the rest of the Yemenites, although not as clear as in Ṣanᶜa. They have dispensed with the translation of the Torah reading in the synagogue here.[8]

They have a single leader, the venerable rabbi and honored gentleman Mōrī[9] Menahem Moses—may his light shine. He is learned, pious, and very rich. He is respected even in the eyes of the government, because he made gestures of affection and personally performed good deeds with his strength and wealth for the British army and officials who first came with the conquest of the city. He supplied their needs, and thus they found him more faithful than the other leaders of the peoples who were there. He is a big merchant, dealing with India, Ethiopia, and Egypt. He owns many houses in the city itself and outside, and he has ships at sea. His good reputation has spread through all these countries, namely that he is faithful to God and man. He has four sons who are—praise the Lord—wise and God-fearing.

There is a Bēt Dīn[10] here which is composed of outstanding scholars: the pious, humble elder Mōrī Isaac Cohen (may his light shine); the

[7] Sassoon David Sassoon (1832–67) was one of the eight sons of the great Bombay merchant David S. Sassoon. See Walter J. Fischel, "Sassoon," *EJ* 14, p. 898 (Family Tree).

[8] In Yemen it was customary to read both the Targum and the Arabic translation of Saᶜadya Gaon after reading the Torah portion in Hebrew.

[9] Mōrī (*mārī*, in Sefardic pronunciation) was the Yemenite term for rabbi, and like it means "my master."

[10] Jewish law court.

venerable rabbi Mōrī Menahem Bunino (may his light shine); the venerable rabbi and judge Mōrī Samuel Dayyan (may his light shine).

There is also here a gentleman and merchant, a man of wisdom and discernment, R. Moses Ḥanokh ha-Levi (may his light shine). He was born in Turkey and came in his youth to Ṣanᶜa where he studied Torah and ritual slaughtering. Later, he achieved great success and blessing in India and then settled here in Aden. He has prospered in everything to which he has put his hand. He has extended his protection over the masses, and he supplied all of Yemen with many books, including Pentateuchs with all the commentaries, ᶜEyn Yaᶜaqōv,[11] the *Zohar*,[12] the *Shulḥān ᶜArūkh*,[13] *Menōrat ha-Mē'ōr*,[14] and *Rēshīt ha-Ḥokhma*.[15] These have been brought from Livorno[16] at great expense. He has distributed them throughout all the districts of Yemen which never had them before. He knows how to sustain his deeds, and he has seen in this a sign of blessing.

Jacob Safir, *Iben Sāfīr,* vol. 2
(Mainz, 1874), pp. 1–9.

[11] A popular work by Jacob b. Ḥabīb of Salonika (d. 1515/16) containing talmudic *aggādōt* and commentaries.

[12] The classic work of kabbala mysticism.

[13] The law code of Joseph Karo (d. 1575 in Safed), which by this time had become the principal law code for all of world Jewry.

[14] An ethical work by Israel al-Nakawa of Toledo (d. 1391).

[15] An important work on morals by Elijah de Vidas of Safed (d. late sixteenth century).

[16] This Italian town was a great center for the publication of Hebrew and Judeo-Arabic books in the nineteenth century.

THE HOME OF A WEALTHY DAMASCENE JEW
(MID-NINETEENTH CENTURY)

Externally, all the houses of Damascus are alike, plastered over with a yellowish stucco, or mud, and showing no windows on the street. They present, therefore, only dead yellow walls on both sides of the way as you pass along.

The house of a wealthy Jew is said to be the finest in the city. I was in it one morning. It is built on the general Damascus plan. A cross, the four arms of which are of equal length, is the ground plan of the court. The arms of the cross are raised a foot or two from the level of the court, and arched over, making four alcoves, fronting on the central fountain. The corners are then built up with lofty and gorgeously adorned rooms. This house was built of the finest Italian marble, brought on mules from the sea coast.

It was carved in all manner of quaint arabesque patterns. Clusters of golden fruits and flowers hung from the sides of the rooms and the ceilings. The doors were finely carved and gilded. The furniture was superb. One of the alcoves was furnished with a single diwan, which cost sixty-five thousand piastres—a New York lady might be contented with a sofa worth three thousand dollars, especially if it were as this was, a mere cushion of silk and gold, without any wood or iron about it. The entire house was furnished with silver articles—bowls, pitchers, narghilehs, perfume-bottles, cups, water-goblets, and every thing that could be made of this metal.

But, by way of illustration of oriental manners and customs, I may add that the lady who presided in this palace, and who, being a Jewess, had no scruples about being seen by strangers, received us in a dress of calico, outrageously dirty, while her trowsers, once clean, looked as if she had dragged them through all the mud of Damascus, and her hair had been destitute of a combing for a month. Notwithstanding this, a diamond, worth the price of a German principality, shone in the center of her forehead, and another, on her finger, would have bought a New York up-town establishment, ladies, dresses, and all.

The cost of building this house in Damascus had been fifteen hundred thousand piastres (about seventy thousand dollars) at the time of our visit, and was yet to be much more before it should be completed.

William C. Prime, *Tent Life in the Holy Land*
(New York, 1857), pp. 434–35.

A BRITISH CONSUL ASSESSES THE GENERAL FEELING TOWARD JEWS AND CHRISTIANS IN THE LEVANT

(MID-NINETEENTH CENTURY)

Copy/

Jerusalem, 24th May 1841

Sir,

I do myself the honor of addressing you a public letter as the Officer in Command of the British Detachments in Syria, with a view of bringing under your consideration the state of feeling continually manifested in this district by the Musulman population towards the Christians and Jews, and to beg the aid of your influence with the Supreme Authority of this country, to check an evil which if allowed to continue will be productive of serious consequences.

I regret to inform you that during the past month I have received reports from the several Consular Agents under my jurisdiction, residing in Sidon, Tyre, Acre, and Caiffa, complaining of the bigotry, and, in some instances, outrageous conduct of the Musulmans towards Christians, and of the inability, or indisposition of the Local Authorities to maintain order, and a good understanding between the parties referred to.

These reports are in a measure confirmed by what I have also observed of the spirit and disposition of the Musulman population to tyrannize over and insult the Christian and Jew in this city. And I regret to say for the most part with impunity. I believe the Executive here is altogether feeble—this, added to the natural indisposition to punish their coreligionists tends to augment the evil. I would not wish to convey the idea, that I believe the Christian and Jew to be always free from blame. But you are probably aware, Sir, that the sheiks in this neighborhood, as well as some of the leading inhabitants of the city are considered among the most bigoted and troublesome of any in Syria, and I would beg leave to take the present occasion to observe, as a suggestion to the Turkish Authorities to whom the administration of affairs in Syria is committed that without a very active, firm, and decided system of government in this part of the country, it is in vain to expect permanent good order and tranquility in this district. In respect to the Judicial Authority here, I believe I am justified in stating that nothing can exceed its venality, and it is chiefly under this influence that the Executive is conducted.

Last week a case occurred which will no doubt be reported to you. Major Haney's servant was outrageously assaulted, and apparently for no just cause.[1] One of the offenders was arrested and immediately imprisoned,

[1] The victim in question was undoubtedly a Christian. Incidents such as

but as he was of a chief family, adequate satisfaction could not be obtained. After much vacilation and attempting to justify the case, the Local Authorities confessed that they dared not render the justice which the nature of the outrage demanded. On Major Haney's appealing to me, I gave it as my humble opinion, that in the present inefficient state of the Local Administration, it seemed expedient to appear satisfied with such justice as could be obtained, without compromising his position, rather than run the risk of exasperating the Musulman population to commit greater outrages against their comparatively defenceless fellow subjects.

In conclusion I may add, that the Turkish troops, both officers and men, are much more orderly and better conducted in their intercourse with the people than the Egyptians[2] were.

I have the honor to be
Sir,
Your obedient
humble servant
signed / W. L. Young

Public Records Office (London)
FO 195/170.

---

this aimed against non-Muslims in the service of foreigners or under foreign protection are frequently reported in British consular correspondence from all over the Middle East throughout the nineteenth century.

[2] The reference here is to the Egyptian troops under Ibrāhīm Pasha, the son of Muḥammad ᶜAlī, who occupied Greater Syria from 1831–40.

A BRITISH CONSUL'S GENERAL OBSERVATIONS ON THE JEWS OF PALESTINE

(MID-NINETEENTH CENTURY)

An important element in the present condition of Palestine has been the transfer of Russian Jews to British protection. These persons form a considerable portion of the population of Jerusalem, Safed, and Tiberias and enjoy a protection far more efficient than that enjoyed by the Jews of other European protection, and are visited by the Consul or Chancelliere, once or sometimes twice a year.

But of Jews in general it is to be remarked that in Safed and Tiberias, if not in Jerusalem, they form the majority of the inhabitants, and very few of them are Turkish subjects. They present the curious anomaly of so considerable a population living exempt from Turkish rule. It is true they are not so efficiently attended to as might be desired, but in them lies a germ of development for future time and a character different from that of the ordinary population of Palestine.

The Jews are almost the only artisans—for it is remarkable that the glaziers, shoemakers, bookbinders etc., are almost exclusively Jews.

In these as well as in the Christian elements cooperating in Palestine, it is Europeanism alone which keeps the province from sinking, and which gives a tone to affairs and polities unknown in other Turkish provinces.

These elements are not likely to sleep again, being sustained by deep religious feeling of the people, and the support of European powers.

Moslem veneration for the Holy City is a non-entity except within the precincts of the great mosque.

Among the European powers, I need scarcely say that the British name, however used with propriety, has immense weight.

All these considerations, however encouraging, are nevertheless accompanied by gross venality and oppression exercised by Turkish officials on the unfortunate subjects of their authority. Wherever this has full play, the misgovernment is as palpable as ever it was.

Report from James Finn to Sir Stratford Canning,
dated Jerusalem, 7 November 1851 (No. 20),
in Public Records Office, (London), FO 195/369, ff. 82–83.

THE KHATT-I HUMAYUN
(FEBRUARY 18, 1856)

May this be carried out in conformity with its contents. To you my Grand Vizier, Muḥammad Amīn ᶜAlī Pasha, who have been decorated with my Imperial Order of the Majidiyya First Class and with the Order of Individual Merit—may Allah accord you grandeur and double your power.

My fondest desire has always been to insure the happiness of all classes of the subjects whom Divine Providence has placed under my imperial scepter; and ever since my coming to the throne, I have not ceased to expand all my efforts in behalf of this goal. Praised be the Almighty—these unceasing efforts have already borne useful and numerous fruits. The happiness and prosperity of my territories grow from day to day.

It is Our desire today to renew and expand still further the newly instituted regulations with the aim of arriving at a state of affairs conforming to the dignity of my Empire and the position which it occupies among the civilized nations. We have today, through the fidelity and the praiseworthy efforts of all my subjects and with the benevolent and friendly concurrence of my noble allies, the Great Powers, received a ratification of what ought to be the beginning of a new era. I wish to augment by this the well-being and internal prosperity, the happiness of my subjects, who are all equal in my sight and are equally dear to me, and who are united by the cordial ties of patriotism, and to assure the means of making my Empire's prosperity grow from day to day.

I have therefore resolved and I order the execution of the following measures:

1. The guarantees promised by us to all the subjects of my Empire by the Imperial Rescript of the Rose Garden[1] and the laws of the Tanzimat, without distinction of class or religion, for the security of their persons, their possessions, and the preservation of their honor, are today confirmed and consolidated. Effective measures will be taken so that they will be fully and completely implemented.

2. All of the privileges and spiritual immunities accorded from ancient times by my ancestors to all the Christian communities or to other non-Muslim rites established within my Empire, are confirmed and maintained under my protective aegis.

Each Christian community and other non-Muslim rite will, within a fixed period and with the concurrence of a commission formed ad hoc from within its midst, be obliged to proceed, with my high approbation and under

[1] That is, the Khaṭṭ-i Sherif of Gülhane. See Part One above, pp. 96–99.

the surveillance of my Sublime Porte, with an examination of its present immunities and privileges, and to discuss them and submit to my Sublime Porte those reforms required by the progress of enlightenment and by the times.

The powers conceded to the patriarchs and bishops of the Christian denominations by Sultan Muḥammad II[2] and his successors will be harmonized with the new position which will be assured these communities by my generous and benevolent intentions.

3. The principle of nomination of patriarchs for life, after the revision of the rules of election now in force, will be applied in exact conformity to their *berāt*[3] of investiture. The patriarchs, metropolitans (archbishops), delegates, bishops, as well as chief rabbis, will take an oath upon their entry into office, according to a formula devised jointly by my Sublime Porte and the Spiritual chiefs of the diverse communities.

4. The ecclesiastic dues, of whatever form and whatever nature, will be suppressed and replaced by fixed revenues for the patriarchs and the leaders of the communities, and by the allocation of emoluments and salaries equitably proportionate to the importance, rank, and dignity of various members of the clergy. . . . The temporal administration of the Christian communities or of other non-Muslim rites will be entrusted to a council chosen from within each of the said communities, from among the members of the clergy and the laity.

5. In those cities, towns, and villages where the population belongs entirely to one religion, no obstacles will be raised to the repairing of their houses of worship according to their original plan, as well as schools, hospitals, and cemeteries. In case any new edifices of this kind are to be erected, the plans approved by the patriarchs or communal leaders, should be submitted to my Sublime Porte which will order their execution by my Imperial *irade*[4] or will make known its observations on the subject within a certain period of time.

If a religious community lives alone in a locality where there is no other sect, it will not be put under any sort of restriction in the public exercise of its cult.

In those cities, towns, and villages where different religious communities are intermingled, each community which inhabits a distinct quarter and conforms to the above-mentioned regulations, shall likewise have the right to repair and restore its churches, hospitals, schools, and cemeteries.

[2] Mehmed Fātiḥ, the conqueror of Constantinople (ruled 1451–81).

[3] Ar., *barā'a* (diploma, or patent). The Ottoman *berāt* was a document conferring, among other things, an office or privilege.

[4] Ar., *irāda* (will, or desire). In Ottoman usage, it was an imperial order.

When the construction of new edifices is concerned, the necessary authorization will be requested from my Sublime Porte through the office of the patriarchs or the leaders of the community. The Porte will make a sovereign decision in according the authorization with a minimum of administrative obstacles.

The intervention of the administrative authority in all matters of this nature will be entirely gratis.

6. Energetic measures will be taken by my Sublime Porte to assure each sect, whatever the number of its adherents, complete freedom in the exercise of its religion.

7. Every distinction or appellation tending to render any class whatsoever of the subjects of my Empire inferior to another class because of religion, language, or race, shall be forever erased from administrative protocol. The law will deal severely with the use of any injurious or offensive term either by private individuals or the authorities.

8. Since all religions are and shall be freely practiced in my dominions, no subject of my Empire shall be in any way disturbed in the exercise of the religion he professes nor caused any anxiety on that account. No one shall be compelled to change his religion.

9. The nomination and choice of all functionaries and employees of my Empire, being entirely dependent upon my sovereign will, all subjects of my Empire without distinction of nationality, will be admissible to public employment and be qualified to occupy such posts, according to their capacities and merit, and in conformity with generally applied rules.

All the subjects of my Empire, without distinction, shall be accepted into the government civil and military schools, providing they otherwise satisfy the conditions of age and examination requirements specified in the regulations of said schools.

10. Furthermore, each community is authorized to establish public schools of science, art, and industry. However, the method of instruction and the choice of teachers in the schools of this category shall be under the control of a mixed council of public instruction whose members shall be named by my sovereign command.

11. All commercial, correctional, and criminal affairs between Muslims and Christians or other non-Muslims, or between Christians and others of different non-Muslim faiths, will be referred to mixed tribunals.

12. The sessions of these tribunals will be public; the parties must be present and produce their witnesses whose depositions will be received without distinction, under an oath sworn according to the religious law of each faith.

13–16. (More on the justice system and reform of the police.)

17–24. (Tax and administrative reforms.)

Issued at Constantinople during the first third of Jumāda II, 1272 (18 February 1856).

translated from Edouard Engelhardt,
La Turquie et le tanzimat . . . , vol. 1, pp. 263–70.

A MUSLIM VIEW OF THE KHATT-I HUMAYUN
(FEBRUARY 1856)

In accordance with this firman,[1] Muslim and non-Muslim subjects were to be made equal in all rights. This had a very adverse effect on the Muslims. Previously, one of the four points adopted as the basis for peace agreements[2] had been that certain privileges were accorded to Christians on condition that these did not infringe on the sovereign authority of the government. Now the question of specific privileges lost its significance; in the whole range of government, the non-Muslims were forthwith to be deemed the equals of the Muslims. Many Muslims began to grumble: "Today we have lost our sacred national[3] rights, won by the blood of our fathers and forefathers. At a time when the Islamic *millet* was the ruling *millet,* it was deprived of this sacred right. This is a day of weeping and mourning for the people of Islam."

As for the non-Muslims, this day, when they left the status of *raᶜāya*[4] and gained equality with the ruling *millet,* was a day of rejoicing. But the patriarchs and other spiritual leaders were displeased, because their appointments were incorporated in the firman. Another point was that whereas in former times, in the Ottoman state, the communities were ranked, with the Muslims first, then the Greeks, then the Armenians, then the Jews, now all of them were put on the same level. Some Greeks objected to this, saying: "The government has put us together with the Jews. We were content with the supremacy of Islam."

As a result of all this, just as the weather was overcast when the firman was read in the audience chamber, so the faces of most of those present were grim. Only on the faces of a few of our Frenchified gentry dressed in the garb of Islam could expressions of joy be seen. Some notorious characters of this type were seen and heard to say: "If the non-Muslims are spread among the Muslims, neighborhoods will become mixed, the price of our properties will rise, and civilized amenities will expand." On this account they expressed satisfaction.

Jevdet Pasha, *Tezakir* (Ankara, 1953), pp. 67–68,
trans. Bernard Lewis (unpublished).

[1] That is, the Khaṭṭ-i Humayun.
[2] Ar., *muṣālaḥa.*
[3] Ar.–Turk., *milliyye.*
[4] The Arabic word for "grazing cattle," which was the standard Ottoman epithet for the non-Muslim populace.

A PETITION FOR THE ESTABLISHMENT OF THE FIRST HEBREW JOURNAL IN PALESTINE (1863)

A.

No. 27.

British Consulate
Jerusalem, November 22, 1863

His Excellency
The Right Honorable
Sir H. L. Bulwer G.C.B.
Her Majesty's Ambassador Extraordinary
Etc. Etc. Etc.
Constantinople

Sir,

I have the honor to enclose to Your Excellency a copy of a letter addressed to me by Mr. Jechiel Juda Lip-Bril, a British subject, native of India, applying for a licence from the Porte for opening a printing press and publishing a Hebrew newspaper, called "Halbanon," at Jerusalem. I have also transmitted a copy of Mr. Bril's application to the Pasha of Jerusalem, requesting him to take the necessary steps to procure the licence, which His Excellency has promised to do.

Mr. Bril having opened a printing press and published his newspaper without a licence, in consequence of alleged ignorance of the regulations on this subject, he has been under the necessity of suspending the publication of his journal. An early receipt of the licence would therefore save him much loss and inconvenience.

I have the honor to be Sir,

Your Excellency's
Most obedient humble servant
(signed) Noel Temple Moore

B.

Copy (pencilled note) French translation for the Porte

A Petition

to

Her Britannic Majesty's Consul

Jerusalem, October 27, 1863

The Undersigned wishes to print and publish in Jerusalem a religious newspaper in the Hebrew language, which will also contain the local news, and petitions Her Britannic Majesty's Consul, Jerusalem, to request permission from the Turkish Government that he may be allowed to do so. He binds himself to observe all the laws and regulations of the Government.

With all respect etc.

(signed Jechiel Juda Lip-Bril)

Public Records Office (London)
FO 195/761.

JEWISH MERCHANTS IN HAIFA PETITION TO KEEP THEIR SYNAGOGUE OPEN
(SECOND HALF OF THE NINETEENTH CENTURY)

Caiffa, 2nd June 1864

Thomas B. Sandwith Esq.
British Vice Consul
Caiffa

Sir,

We the undersigned, being Israelites dwelling at Caiffa, have been in the habit, in common with about 16 or 20 others of our coreligionists, of worshipping for nearly two years in a small upper room situated in our quarter.[1] The Turkish Authorities here made no objection to our thus assembling for prayer until quite lately, when they declared that we cannot meet together without being possessed of a Firman from Constantinople. As six of us are British subjects[2] (the rest being natives of Morocco) we beg to petition you to procure for us the requisite Firman, in order that we may not be prevented from worshipping the God of our fathers in peace.

We have the honor to be
Sir,
Your most obedient, humble servants

Deborah O. Cohen
Rabbi Abraham Kalfun
Abraham Cohen
Salomon Naûm
Joseph Benaim
Shalum Benaim

Public Records Office (London)
FO 195/866.

[1] The Jewish quarter of Haifa (Ar., *ḥārat al-yahūd*) was located in "the poor Muslim district in the eastern part of the lower city." In 1864, there were 384 Jews in the city. See Alex Carmel, "Haifa," *EJ* 7: 1,137.

[2] These six British subjects were probably from Gibraltar. Their names indicate that they were of Moroccan extraction.

THE ASHKENAZI JEWS OF PALESTINE ESTABLISH SEPARATE BUTCHERS

No. 4.

Her Majesty's Consulate
Jerusalem, March 19, 1867

His Excellency, The Right Honorable
The Lord Lyons G.C.B.
Her Majesty's Ambassador Extraordinary
Etc. Etc. Etc.
Constantinople

My Lord,

I have the the satisfaction to report to Your Excellency the removal, through the joint intervention of myself and my Prussian and Austrian colleagues, of a long-standing grievance of the Ashkenaz [*sic*] or European Jews of this city, connected with the supply of animal food to that community.

The slaughter and sale of meat to the Israelites has hitherto been monopolized by the Rabbis of the Sephardim, or native Jews, who in various ways abused the privilege to the prejudice of their European brethren. In 1853 and 1862 strenuous attempts were made by the latter to obtain relief, but ineffectually. (Vide Mr. Consul Finn's[1] despatch No. 14 of May 22, 1862.) About a fortnight ago, the Ashkenazim addressed to me and to my Prussian and Austrian colleagues, as their protecting consuls, collective memorials complaining of a heavy over-charge in the price of the meat sold to them by their native coreligionists which put this important article of food beyond the reach of the poor of their community, numbering several thousand souls, of which the great majority come under that category, and praying us to provide a remedy by obtaining for them the power of slaughtering and selling their own meat separately.

Our first step was to hold a meeting at the house of the Prussian Consul, as "Doyen," at which we invited the attendance of delegates on the part of either community with the view of endeavoring to bring about an amicable arrangement of the dispute. This failed through the refusal of the Sephardim delegates to come to terms. The affair was causing much excitement and ill-feeling; on the following morning we had an interview on the subject with Izzet Pasha, the Governor of Jerusalem, and succeeded there

[1] James Finn served as British Consul in Jerusalem between 1845 and 1862. He was a philo-Semite and was in turn greatly liked by the Jerusalem Jewish community. See above, p. 356.

and then in obtaining His Excellency's sanction, and through him that of the requisite Mahommedan spiritual authorities to the establishment of a separate butchery and shop for the sale of meat by the Ashkenazim, the latter readily agreeing to give a guarantee that they would conduct the slaughter of animals according to the mosaic law.

A few words will be necessary to explain why this sanction was needed—as there is no law prohibiting any person or community from killing and selling meat. By the Jewish law, certain parts of the animal killed for food are "Taref" or unlawful, and may not be eaten. These are sold to the Moslems to prevent the serious loss by waste that would otherwise accrue.[2] Among the latter an idea was disseminated—it is understood by the Sephardim—that the Ashkenazim were not true Israelites and therefore their killing was unlawful to the Mahommedans, who consequently would not buy of their meat and might even have made an outcry about their killing at all on the plea that some of them might unwittingly buy and eat unlawful meat. This notion has now been exploded as above related.

Much praise is due to the Pasha for his immediate attention to, and prompt action in, the matter.

The Ashkenazim have addressed me a letter of thanks in German and Hebrew, a translation of which I beg to enclose.

I have the honor to be,
My Lord,
Your Excellency's
most obedient
humble servant,
(signed) Noel Temple Moore

Public Records Office (London)
FO 195/808, ff. 279–82.

[2] This fact was at times twisted and hurled back at the Jews by Jew-baiters. See, for example, the poem by Abū Isḥāq of Elvira, above, p. 215.

JEWISH MERCHANTS OF GIBRALTAR SEEK EXEMPTION FROM THE MOROCCAN DRESS CODE FOR DHIMMIS
(EARLY NINETEENTH CENTURY)

A. Cardozo, Esquire[1] Gibraltar, 13th November 1806

Sir,

We beg leave to state to you, that, in consequence of a memorial made by the undersigned subjects of His Britannic Majesty, and through your medium presented to James Green Esquire, His said Majesty's Consul General in all the dominions of the Emperor of Morocco, praying that he might be pleased to request the Emperor aforesaid, to annul a certain order, said to be by His Imperial Majesty made, prohibiting all persons professing the Hebrew Religion in general from appearing in any of his dominions wearing the European dress. Mr. Green was pleased to say that he would represent the case to His Imperial Majesty on his obtaining an audience.

The undersigned were by you informed that Mr. Green had already obtained such audience from His Imperial Majesty, who was pleased to declare that he annulled that order.

We therefore pray you may have the goodness to request Mr. Green to state whether such declaration of His Imperial Majesty is already published in his dominions, and whether we are now permitted to appear there with our usual dress, it being of much importance to us, who find ourselves occasionally under the necessity of going there on matters of Trade etc.

We remain
Sir
Your most humble servants,
Joseph Benzaquen
S. Sequerry
Aaron Abecasis
Jos. Israel

Hm. Azuelos
Moses Benzaquen
Solomon Benamor
M. I. Taurel
illegible

Public Records Office (London)
FO 174/10.

[1] The addressee is most certainly Aaron Nuñez Cardozo, a leading merchant and public figure in Gibraltar at that time. Cardozo had served as an intermediary between the British government and the rulers of the Barbary States. See Cecil Roth, "Cardozo, Aaron Nuñez," *EJ* 5:163.

THE JEWS OF MOGADORE PAY THEIR POLL TAX
(EARLY NINETEENTH CENTURY)

The Jews, that were overjoyed at the recent change,[1] soon turned their joy into mourning, when they received, a day or two after, an order to pay their *Gazier*,[2] or yearly tribute to the Sultan; the order was for about three thousand five hundred dollars, including expenses, (for the Moor who brought the order must be paid), in a gross sum to be raised directly; the gates of the Jews' town, or Millah,[3] were immediately closed upon them, nor were any suffered to go out until the money was forthcoming.

The whole number of Jews here does not probably exceed six thousand souls, and they are very poor; the priests and rabbies soon convened them in their synagogues, and apportioned the tax according to their law. They were classed thus: the four Jew merchants, Ben Guidallas, Macnin, Abilbol (Abitbol), and Zagury,[4] formed the first class, and I was told their share was two thousand dollars or more; the few petty traders the second, the mechanics[5] the third, and the lowest order of miserable laborers the fourth class. The priests and rabbies (who are a great proportion of their number) were of course exempted, as the other classes support them at all times. Not a Jew, either man, woman, or child, was allowed to go out of their town for three days, except they were wanted by the Moors or Christians to work, and not then without an order from the alcayd.[6]

During this period I visited the Jews' town several times, but never without seeing more or less of these miserable wretches knocked down like bullocks by the gate-keepers, with their large canes, as they attempted to rush past them, when the gates were opened, to procure a little water or food for their hungry and thirsty families. On the fourth day, when the arrangements had been made by the priests and elders, they sent word to the governor, and the three first classes were ordered before him to pay their apportionment. I knew of it because I was informed by Mr. Willshire's interpreter and broker, who was a Jew of considerable understand-

[1] The pasha of Dukkāla Province, whose residence was in Mogadore, had just been thrown into prison.

[2] Ar., *jizya*.

[3] Concerning the Jewish quarters of Morocco called *mellāḥs*, see Part One above, pp. 79–86.

[4] These merchants figure prominently in the British consular correspondence of the period. See, for example, Public Records Office (London) FO 174/13 passim.

[5] That is, artisans.

[6] Ar., *al-qāʾid*, the governor of the city (as opposed to the pasha, or governor of the province).

ing, named Ben Nahory—he was one of the committee of arrangement to wait on the governor. I wished to see the operation, and went near the house of the alcayd for that purpose. The Jews soon appeared by classes; as they approached, they put off their slippers, took their money in both their hands, and holding them alongside each other, as high as the breast, came slowly forward to the talb,[7] or Mohammedan scrivener, appointed to receive it. He took it from them, hitting each one a smart blow with his fist on his bare forehead, by way of receipt for his money, at which the Jews said, *Nahma Sidi* (thank you, my lord),[8] and retired to give place to his companion.

Thus they proceeded through the three first classes without much difficulty, when the fourth class was forced up with big sticks. This class was very numerous, as well as miserable. They approached very unwilling, and were asked one by one if they were ready to pay their *gazier*. When one said yes, he approached as the others had done, paid his money, took a similar receipt, and then went about his business. He that said, no, he could not, or was not ready, was seized instantly by the Moors, who throwing him flat on his face to the ground, gave him about fifty blows with a thick stick upon his back and posteriors, and conducted him away, I was told into a dungeon, under a bomb proof battery, next to the western city wall, facing the ocean. There were many served in this way—the Jews' town was all this time strongly guarded and strictly watched. At the end of three days more, I was informed that those who were confined in the dungeon were brought forth, but I did not see them. The friends of some of these poor creatures had made up the money, and they were dismissed; whilst the others, after receiving more stripes, were remanded and put in irons. Before the next three days had expired, many of them changed their religion, were received by the Moors as brothers, and were taken to the mosque, and highly feasted, but were held responsible for the last tax notwithstanding.[9]

James Riley, *An Authentic Narrative of the Loss of the American Brig Commerce, Wrecked on the Western Coast of Africa, in the Month of August, 1815* (Hartford, 1847), pp. 198–200.

[7] Ar., *ṭālib*. In Morocco, this term is applied to petty-grade scholars.

[8] Ar., *naʿam yā sīdī* (literally, "yes, my lord"). The entire proceedings are conducted in fulfillment of the letter of the koranic verse 9:29. See above, p. 149.

[9] That the convert is still liable for back taxes is in complete accordance with Islamic law. See above, p. 159.

A MOROCCAN JEWISH MERCHANT AIDS IN THE REDEMPTION OF BRITISH CAPTIVES FROM THE CORSAIRS

(EARLY NINETEENTH CENTURY)

London 21 December 1811

To His Britannic Majesty's
British Vice Consul Peter Gwyn Esq.

Honorable Sir,

I take the liberty to acquaint you that some gentlemen of this city, having applied to me requesting me to undertake bringing to England all the British subjects which having been made slave in the Coast of Barbary, Guinea, or at any other part in Barbary, they at the same would engage to furnish me with the necessary means accordingly, in answer to which, I have suggested to them that His Imperial Majesty the Emperor of Morocco, always does what is necessary for the relief of such slaves whenever it is made known to him that there are persons so situated in any part of his dominions. I have also referred them entirely to you on the subject. In the meanwhile they wished me to remit to you one thousand dollars[1] and to solicit your attention to the request in question, which I have no doubt you will attend thereto with your utmost zeal and feeling as a man in your situation. I have on compliance thereto shipped on board the Arrethusa one Box WES containing 1000 dollars to your address which please to retire from said vessel on her arrival, at your place, and favor me with your acknowledgment of having received the same. The Bill of Lading of the same, I herewith have the pleasure to hand you, and remain Honorable Sir with due respect, I have the honor to be

your very obedient humble servant
(signed) M. Abitbol

Public Records Office (London)
FO 174/20.

[1] The Spanish trade dollars were standard currency in Morocco.

A DECREE IN FAVOR OF MOROCCAN JEWRY
(SECOND HALF OF THE NINETEENTH CENTURY)

During that year (1280/1864), a Jew from London came before the Sultan in Marrakesh to seek from him the emancipation of the Jews of Morocco. After the Tetouan incident,[1] people were suddenly taken unawares by the concession of foreign protections, most of which were taken by Jews. But the Jews were not satisfied with that and wished for emancipation similar to that of Egypt and countries like it.[2] So they wrote to a great Jewish merchant in London whose name was Rothchild.[3] This Jew was the *Qārūn*[4] of his time, and he had great influence with the English government because of its need for him, for he would lend it huge sums of money. There are famous stories about him on this account.

Thus, the Jews of Morocco—or some of them, at any rate—wrote him complaining about their debasement and degradation. They requested his intervention on their behalf with the Sultan—may Allah have mercy upon him—so that they would be granted emancipation.

This Jew appointed an in-law of his to head a delegation to the Sultan—may Allah have mercy upon him—for this object and others. He sent along with him fine gifts. He also asked the English government to intercede on his behalf with the Sultan and to write to him to comply with his desired objective—which the government did.

He (Montefiore) came before the Sultan in Marrakesh and presented his gifts. He then requested the fulfillment of his petition. The Sultan—may Allah have mercy upon him—was loathe to send him away a failure and granted him a dahir which the Jew received with his own hands. It contained a clear statement of the Religious Law, namely what Allah has required regarding them—upholding the pact of protection and eschewing oppression and tyranny. However, he did not grant them emancipation comparable to that of the Christians.

The text of the dahir which bore the great seal is as follows:

In the Name of Allah, the Merciful, the Beneficent. There is no Power and no Strength except in Allah, the Exalted, the Mighty.

[1] A reference to the agreement signed between Spain and Morocco on October 30, 1861, at the end of the Spanish-Moroccan War, whereby Spain agreed to give up its occupation of Tetouan upon payment by Morocco of a large indemnity as well as other concessions. See Muḥammad Dāwūd, *Mukhtaṣar Ta'rīkh Tiṭwān*, vol. 1 (Tetouan, 1955), pp. 148–77; and Jamil M. Abun-Nasr, *A History of the Maghrib*, 2d ed. (Cambridge, 1975), p. 292.

[2] The writer is referring to the reforms of the status of Ottoman subjects, which began with Khaṭṭ-i Sherif of Gülhane (see above, pp. 96–99).

[3] The Arabic text has *rūshābīl*.

[4] The equivalent in Islamic tradition of Croesus.

We command all of our servants, governors, and functionaries who read this letter of ours (may Allah exalt it, may He strengthen the command it contains, and may He raise its shining sun and moon into the highest heavens) that they should treat the Jews in all of our provinces in accordance with that which Allah Exalted has required, by setting a scale of justice and equality between them and others in the administration of the law so that none of them will be afflicted by even an atom's weight of injustice, nor be injured. Nothing reprehensible[5] should be done against them, nor any oppression brought to bear upon them.

Neither the officials nor anyone else should commit hostile acts against them, be it against their persons or their possessions. They should not put to work any Jewish artisans unless the latter are willing, and on condition that they be paid in full what is due them for their labor.[6] For injustice means darkness on the Day of Resurrection.[7] As for us, we shall not approve of him (who acts unjustly) with respect to them or with respect to others. We shall not be pleased with him. For all men are equal in our sight so far as justice is concerned. We shall punish by the power of Allah whoever oppresses any of them or commits hostile acts against them.

This matter which we have confirmed, clarified, and elucidated was already well established, well known, and recorded. However, we have added this document as an emphatic confirmation and as a warning to anyone who wishes to oppress them. It also serves to increase the Jews' security and to strike fear into those who would commit aggression against them.

Our order, glorious in Allah, has been promulgated this 26th of Shaᶜbān the Blessed, 1280 (February 5, 1864).

When the Sultan gave them this dahir, they made copies of it, and distributed them among all the Jews of Morocco. But then they became arrogant and reckless, and they wanted to have special rights under the laws among themselves—especially the Jews of the ports.[8] For they entered into alliances and contractual relations on the basis of that. But then Allah frustrated their machinations and caused their efforts to fail, because as soon as the Sultan—may Allah have mercy upon him—realized the Jews' rashness, he followed up this dahir with another letter clarifying its intent. It stated that the dahir had been issued on behalf of the repectable Jews and their poor, who are occupied with that which concerns them.

[5] Ar., *makrūh* means that which is disapproved of by Islamic law.

[6] This was a notable improvement since the Jews of Morocco had long been subject to corvée labor (see above, p. 304).

[7] A play on the Arabic words *ẓulm* (injustice) and *ẓulumāt* (darkness).

[8] These Jews were both the most westernized and the least subject to the Sherifan empire because many possessed either foreign protection or foreign citizenship.

But as for their good-for-nothings, who are notorious for their depravity, for their arrogance toward people, and for plunging into what does not concern them[9]—they shall receive the punishment they deserve.

(The text goes on at great length to say that European-style liberty is really atheism and libertinism. True liberty is to be found in the precepts of the Koran and the Sunna.)

al-Nāṣirī, *Kitāb al-Istiqṣā'*, vol. 9
(Casablanca, 1956), pp. 112–14.

[9] This clarification in effect nullified the concessions of the dahir. The Sultan is saying that Jews who do not act in accordance with their humble *dhimmī* status are not protected. On the importance of conforming to what the Muslim majority perceived as correct behavior, see Norman A. Stillman, "Musims and Jews in Morocco: Perceptions, Images, Stereotypes," *Proceedings of the Seminar on Muslim-Jewish Relations in North Africa* (New York, 1975), pp. 13–27.

IRAQI JEWS IN THE INDIA TRADE
(EARLY NINETEENTH CENTURY)

List of merchants returned from India and agents to the merchants now residing in India recommended by the Indian Government to the care and protection of the Political Agent at Baghdad in the year 1818, and confirmed by a Vezirial letter from Constantinople dated A.H. 1257, Rabeh el avel 28.

Names	Cast	Remarks
Yacoob Sima	Jew	Resided about 30 years in India & on his return was recommended by the Government of Bombay.
Yoosef Bahar	—do—	Ditto. 13 years in Calcutta do-do- & agent to Dawood Bahar of that city.
Hiskiel Rooben	—do—	Ditto 19 -do-do- by Govt. of India
Shaool Liniado	—do—	Originally a European Jew recommended by my predecessor.
Isaac Shukur	—do—	Agent to Ruben Shukur of Calcutta
Yusef Ozer	—do—	D° to Moshi Ezrah of Bombay, recommended by that Government.
Hiskiel Dawood Hayim	—do—	A merchant of Surat and agent to his brother in that city, recommended by the Bombay Government.
Abdolla Faraj Hayim	—do—	An agent of Faraj Hayim of Calcutta, recommended by the Government of India
Avit Markar	Christian	The son of the late Native Agent & a pensioner of Government.
Yoosef Asfar	—do—	The agent of Fathholla Asfar of Calcutta
Fathholla Abood	—do—	Recommended by my predecessor for
Gregor Seth	—do—	Services performed by them.

Public Records Office (London)
FO 195/204, f. 223.

BAGHDADI JEWS IN THE SERVICE OF BRITISH MERCHANTS
(EARLY NINETEENTH CENTURY)

No.	Names	Cast	Remarks
		Servants of the Residency & Consulate	
1	Yoosef Ezrah & Yamin	Jews	Bankers
1	Ibrahim Soomekh	—do—	Simsar[1]
1	Alias Esaw	Christian	Broker
1	Tattos	—do—	Vekil Kharj[2]
8	Persian Armenians	—do—	servants of the Residency
3	—do—do—	—do—	—do—Surgeons
		Messrs. Stephen Lynch & Co.	
1	Saleh Yoosef	Jew	Banker
1	Owannes Abraham	Christian	Clerk
1	Khumais	Mahomedan	Porter
1	Mahmood	—do—	Native Agent
		Personal Servants	
1	Kadem	Mahomedan	Groom
1	Kavork	Christian	Door Keeper
3	Servants	—do—	

[1] Ar., *simsār* (a broker or middleman).
[2] Turk.–Ar., *wakīl kharj* (tax agent).

No.	Names	Cast	Remarks
	Messrs. A. Hector & Co.		
1	Faraj	Christian	Clerk
1	Gorgis Faraj	—do—	—do—
1	Kadem	Mahomedan	Warehouse Keeper
2	Azooree & Yoosef	Jew	Banker
2	Yoosef & Ibrahim Bashee	—do—	—do—
2	Yacoob & Heyoo	—do—	—do—
5	Dawood eben Fooaki Ushur Eliahoo Shamoon & Haron	—do—	—do—

Public Records Office (London)
FO 195/204, f. 223a–b.

THE JEWS OF BAGHDAD MEET ENGLISH MISSIONARIES
(MID-NINETEENTH CENTURY)

A.

Baghdad February 4, 1846

Major H. C. Rawlinson, C. B.
H.B.M.'s Representative

My dear Sir,

In compliance with your request, I beg to hand you a written statement of the object which called me to the Residency on Friday the 30th January last.

As, however, you have kindly promised to send this to His Excellency Sir Stratford Canning, Bart., H.B.M.'s Ambassador to the Turkish Court at Constantinople, it will doubtless be advisable to write in the first instance a short history of some of the proceedings relative to the Church of England Mission to the Jews in Baghdad, of which Mission I have the honor to be a member.

On October 19, 1844, by the good Province of God, I arrived here with Mrs. Vicars, and two other companions, the two latter and myself being ordained by the late Bishop of Jerusalem clergymen of the Church of England. Soon after our arrival and whilst yet in lodgings, we were visited by many Jews. Scarcely, however, had we got into our relative dwellings than the Jews came in flocks, especially on Saturday, the Jewish Sabbath. This continued to go on quietly until two of them stated to us their great desire to be instructed in the Christian Religion. One was moderately acquainted with Hebrew literature, though rather poor. The other was poor and ignorant. They came regularly for about two or three weeks. They attended our morning Hebrew Divine Service which is from a translation of the English Common Prayer Book. The Hachamim, or great men among the Jews, heard of this and endeavored to prevent not only these two, but all the Jews coming to us by pronouncing a curse on all who should in future visit us. This had little or no effect; our houses were still crowded. Again a curse was pronounced and my house watched by several Jews sent for that purpose by the Hachamim. These spies I soon drove away, not considering that it was to be submitted to. Our houses were again filled; but next Saturday, or the Jewish Sabbath, the most frightful curse was pronounced, not only we understood, upon us, but on any who should visit us. As to the curse on ourselves, I could only pity those who were so ignorant as to take the trouble to inflict it. The word of God says, that "The curse causeless shall not come," Proverbs 26:2.

For six or seven months we did not see a Jew in our houses, though some expressed in a most feeling manner their being prevented. One told us that his heart was still with us. We hoped that time might soften matters, and therefore thought it prudent to be still.

About the middle of November last, three or four respectable Jews who had been at Constantinople and had returned to Baghdad with the present Pasha, enjoying somewhat of his protection, visited a few times my companions the Reverends Sternshuss and Stern. The two latter left Baghdad on the 20th of November last for Persia on a mission to the Jews in that country. Soon after their departure, these same Jews came to us and requested to be instructed in the English language. We of course were rejoiced at hearing such a request, and therefore acceeded most cordially. The Scriptures say, "Blessed is he who blessed thee, and cursed is he who curseth thee," Numbers 24:9. This of course is not meant of the common everyday complimentary blessing pronounced with the lip alone, but means real kindness shown towards the Jews. We ought therefore to be kind to the Jews, however ill they may act towards us. I would therefore take this opportunity of saying that in now writing about the Jews, I have not the slightest ill-will towards any one of the Hachamim, nor do I wish to raise any ill feeling in the breast of any against them, quite the contrary, and I hope to prove that my present object is to seek simply the glory of God Almighty, the welfare and prosperity of the country in which I live, to be though on humble means, under Providence, a peacemaker between the Great God and His ancient people the Jews; but at the same time humbly to pray the Ottoman Porte that my rights as an Englishman may not be infringed on. This request I should not have mentioned had I not been informed by most respectable persons that my house was again to be watched.

Lately, I have had as many as nine Jews in our house of an evening, most of them anxious to learn English, and considering the distance of our house from the Jewish Quarter, and the great rains which have lately fallen, they must have an important object in view to bring them so far and cause them to remain almost late at night. On Saturdays we have had lately from twelve to twenty in our house.

. . . .

Several of those Jews who have come to me for instruction in English are most anxious to visit England and there to improve themselves in literature, professions, trades and manufacturers. I encourage them in this desire, tell them they ought to go and then return with their acquired knowledge; for that as they are already acquainted with the languages of their countries, they can much more readily teach their friends and neighbors than one who like myself has previously to learn some of the most difficult languages in the world.

But I am not helped forward in this work by the Hachamim, on the contrary, I am retarded. Almost all who used to come and were making rapid progress in reading and writing English are prevented by fear of course, or intrigues. A few still persevere, and as it were steal in at different times. But whilst with me they are in an almost constant state of agitation and alarm and are afraid if they hear a door shut or open. They therefore are not in a fit state to judge with a clear mind, they cannot learn as they ought.

. . . .

B.

No. 42 of 1846

British Consulate
Baghdad August 3, 1846

His Excellency
The Right Honorable
Sir Stratford Canning G.C.B.
H.M.'s Ambassador,
Constantinople

Sir,

In my despatch No. 5 of February 4, 1846, Your Excellency was informed of the growing discussion between the Jewish Rabbins of this place and the British Missionaries, as well as of the reluctance which I left to solicit the interference of the Government. The Missionaries however have at last by appealing to their privileges as Englishmen obliged me to come officially forward, and the local reference as I expected has terminated unfavorably to their cause.

Some time back, the Reverends Messrs. Vicars, Stern and Sternshuss waited on me and represented that they considered their rights as Englishmen infringed on by a certain curse which had been pronounced in the Jewish Synagogue a few days previously against all parties holding communication with them. They tendered to me at the same time an English translation of the curse, copy of which is annexed for Your Excellency's information, and observed that they required my protection to relieve them from the opprobrious epithets applied to them of "heretics" and "schismatics" as well as to procure for them an unrestricted intercourse with all classes of Turkish subjects at Baghdad. On looking over the paper I frankly told them that I did not think the local Government would interfere further than by countermanding the interdict on commercial transactions, as the Rabbins would maintain on the one hand that

Christians according to the Jewish creed were heretics and schismatics, and as the prohibition against social intercourse would on the other be defended on the ground of the privilege generally accorded to the heads of religious communities in the Turkish Empire to adopt all legitimate precautions for the maintenance and consolidation of their faith. I also particularly warned the Missionaries that by drawing the attention of the local Government to their position, they might cause a question to be raised as to their being permitted to continue their efforts for the conversion of the Jews, Muhammedan functionaires of all classes viewing with extreme jealousy any Christian interference with the religious tenets of the subjects of the Porte, and Nejib Pasha being especially distinguished amongst Turkish governors for his excitable feelings on questions of this nature. The Reverend Gentlemen however decided that a crisis, whatever might be its termination, was preferable to remaining passive under the operation of so violent an anathema. They approved of a prior extra-official communication on my part with the Jewish Priesthood, but in the event of the Rabbins declining to annul the curse, they insisted on an appeal to the Government.

I applied accordingly in the first instance to the Rabbins and was unsuccessful. The latter parties disclaiming the intention of using offensive language. They deprecated the displeasure of the British Consulate, to the protective influence of which the Jewish community of Baghdad had been frequently indebted. They volunteered even to facilitate the distribution of Hebrew Bibles, which the Missionaries had alledged to be their main object in view in courting an intercourse with the Jews, but at the same time they maintained that it was incumbent on them in their capacity of spiritual teachers of their people to counteract all attempts either direct or indirect against the Jewish faith, and they firmly but respectfully declined to annul the anathema which for this purpose they had published in the Synagogue.

In communicating the above declaration to the Rev. Mr. Vicars, I stated that I was prepared to lay his complaint before the Government, and if necessary to forward an appeal to Constantinople, but that it behooved him to reflect again whether by giving prominence to his collision with the Jewish Priesthood, he might not defeat the objects of his Mission, and even endanger its stability. The Rev. gentleman's reply, copy of which is annexed marked No. 2,[1] left me no resource—but to lay the anathema before Nejib Pasha, and to state at the same time that I considered an interdict on buying and selling with British subjects to be an infraction of the privileges secured to us by treaty in the Turkish Empire. After a very protracted argument between the Turkish authorities and the Rabbins consequent on this application, the latter parties being supported by the Jewish merchants, who constitute as I have before mentioned to Your

[1] Not included here.

Excellency, the most wealthy and influential class of the Baghdad community, Nejib Pasha delivered to me his answer, and I at once communicated the same to the members of the Missionary establishment.

Your Excellency will be able to judge from this answer (enclosure No. 3) and from the Rev. Mr. Vicar's rejoinder (No. 4)[2] in what light the affair is likely to be viewed at Constantinople. Nejib Pasha has today informed me that he intends to forward to the Porte the obnoxious Hebrew tract[3] denounced by the Jewish Rabbins, to be examined by competent parties at the Capital, and he has at the same time assured me, that as far as religious interests are concerned, he shall abstain from offering any remarks which may be calculated to prejudice either one cause or the other. Nejib Pasha will, I believe, ground his protest against the continued establishment at this place of a Mission avowedly engaged in proselytizing the subjects of the Porte, on the political danger arising from religious agitation in so exposed and inflammable a quarter as the city of Baghdad.

As the Rev. Mr. Vicars appears to hope that the Society to which he has the honor to belong will endeavor to obtain the official support of H.M.'s Secretary of State,[4] I venture to suggest the expediency of Your Excellency transmitting copies of the present correspondence to the Foreign Office, accompanied with such observations on the question at issue as Your Excellency's experience of the temper of the Turkish Ministry may appear to render necessary.

I have the honor to be
Your Excellency's
Most obedient humble servant,
(signed) H. C. Rawlinson
Consul at Baghdad

C.

Translated copy of the *Harem* (*ḥerem*) or *curse*[5] pronounced in the Jewish Synagogue in Baghdad—Thursday, July 9, 1846.

My Masters, that which the Wise Men have formerly decreed, the Excellency of the Hachamim, and the Chosen of the Congregation—the Lord preserve them—concerning the known heretics[6] which are among

[2] See preceding note.

[3] The tract was part of the missionary literature cited in the Jews' petition to Nejib Pasha, which is translated below, pp. 382–83.

[4] At this time Viscount Palmerston, who was keenly interested in the Mission to the Jews.

[5] Not exactly a curse, but rather a ban.

[6] Translating Heb., *pōqerīm*.

you; that it should not be permitted for any one to go among them, and not to set a foot in their house, and not to buy and sell with them. We cast upon them the greatest anathemas, the greatest excommunications, the greatest execrations and the greatest curses, even upon those that transgress as to any of these things.

And at this very hour we have heard that there are some who go to them. But the Beth Din will summon those individuals and severely judge them.

Now one says, he does not know anything of what is decreed. Another says he does not know what the judges decreed formerly. But now let the decree be remembered by your Excellencies, so that no one may be ignorant and fall into error; God forbid.

And this is the object of the decree and anathema, which we have formerly made. By permission of the Council in Heaven, and by permission of the Council on Earth, we excommunicate, anathematize and execrate everyone who shall go to and enter the house of the heretics and schismatics[7] abovementioned, whether great or little, whether man or woman; cursed be he by day, and cursed be he by night, cursed be he in his lying down, and cursed be he in his rising up, cursed be he in his walking, and cursed be he in his sitting, cursed be he in his going out, and cursed be he in his coming in. God will refuse to forgive him. And the whole curse written in the Book of the Law shall cleave to him. And God shall blot out his name from under Heaven. He is separated and divided from the Congregation of Israel. And all the curses of the Law shall rest upon his head. And everyone who knows of one who went to the house of the heretics abovementioned and transgressed the words of this decree abovementioned, he is in duty bound to come and inform the Beth Din of the same; and whosoever will not thus inform, shall bear his sin. But he who obeys us shall rest in peace, and upon him shall come a good blessing. Amen, so be it.

D.

Translation of a petition addressed by the Jewish community of Baghdad to H. E. Nejib Pasha—

We beg to represent to Your Excellency that a party of Englishmen having come to Baghdad some time ago, have been ever since employed in distributing money and books among the Jewish population, the books in question containing much vain matter written in the Hebrew tongue together with language offensive to the Jewish faith.

[7] Translating Heb., *mīnīm*.

Enjoying as we do in our capacity of Turkish subjects and in common with the subjects of foreign nations perfect liberty and freedom under your exalted Government, our Rabbins, when they found it was the aim of the parties above-mentioned to bring our religion into discredit, issued a decree prohibiting the Jews from intercourse with them. Lately also as it has come to our knowledge that certain ignorant parties have continued to visit them, we have found it necessary to repeat the prohibition, the decree in this instance being delivered in writing in the Hebrew language according to the annexed translation, and being prepared in consonance with the rules of our religion for the mere purpose of shielding the Jewish faith from further injury.

The books above-mentioned alluded to contain not only language offensive to our Jewish feelings, but perhaps they may be considered to offend other religions also. We beg therefore to present Your Excellency with a copy of one of the said books, and we would suggest that Your Excellency should cause it to be translated in order to be certified of its contents.

As we are Turkish subjects and have hitherto enjoyed the shelter of Your Excellency's favor we have been emboldened to lay this matter before you, and treating that you will be pleased to continue as heretofore to defend us from injury agreeably to the ordinances of the exalted Government to which we owe allegiance, we beg to recommend our case to Your Excellency's kind consideration.

Public Records Office (London)
FO 195/237.

JEWISH AND CHRISTIAN INHABITANTS JOIN IN THE DEFENSE OF AL-JAZIRA AGAINST THE KURDS

(MID-NINETEENTH CENTURY)

Moossul
December 5, 1853

His Excellency
The Right Hon. Viscount Stratford de Redcliffe G.C.B.
Etc. Etc. Etc.
Constantinople

My Lord,

I have the honor to acquaint Your Excellency that on the 15th of last month a large body of Kurds from various tribes collected themselves together and marched upon the town of Jezeerah, headed by ten of their chiefs, and clamorously demanded that the person of Hajjy Suliman Agha[1] should be given over to them (this is the same individual whom I had the honor of mentioning to Your Excellency in my Despatch No. 13). Suliman Agha finding his situation so precarious disguised himself and fled into the mountains of Buhtan, and from thence proceeded to Diarbekr. The Kurds seeing that their demand was not complied with, commenced attacking the town on the west side, and as there were no troops in the place, all the inhabitants, Mohammedans, Christians, and Jews under the command of the Mutsellim Hasney Bey[2] carried arms, and made a bold attack upon the Kurds. The enemy seeing that the west side of the town was so well defended retired to the east side, and attacked it with such violence that the inhabitants were defeated and the town thrown into the greatest confusion. Happily however for Jezeerah a Hayta Bashi[3] with about 100 horsemen arrived at this juncture. The natives receiving this timely assistance rallied and made another desparate assault upon the Kurds, in which, according to the report of my correspondent about 267 were killed, 243 made prisoners, and the number of wounded was not known.

. . . .

(signed) C. A. Rassam

Public Records Office (London)
FO 195/394, f. 84.

[1] The local Turkish administrator of the region.
[2] The governor of the town.
[3] The commander of a mounted patrol that escorted caravans.

A RABBI IS ACCUSED OF DISRESPECT TO MUHAMMAD

(IRAQ, MID-NINETEENTH CENTURY)

No. 12.

Moossul
October 24th 1853

The Right Honble Viscount Stratford de Redcliffe G.C.B.
Etc. Etc. Etc.
Constantinople

My Lord,

. . . .

Since the departure of the last post a melancholy occurrence took place in Moossul in which the Ulemas behaved very insolently towards the Cady, and displayed a spirit of fanaticism which has not been demonstrated here for some years back.

A Jewish Rabbin was indicted by two Mohammedans of having used disrespectful epithets against their Prophet some four years ago. The Cady summoned the Jew to the Mahkama,[1] and after a long trial, and a very cautious examination of the witnesses, he decided that the case deserved punishment, but not death, and accordingly committed the offender to prison.

The day following the affair presented a more serious aspect, several Ulemas waited upon the Cady and urged the case very warmly; the Judge informed them that he would not go out of the precincts of the law, and notwithstanding they had produced a number of witnesses, still their testimony was not sufficiently clear to condemn the Jew. This apparently exasperated the Ulema, and two days after they again repaired in a body to the Mahkama with a fanatical Sheikh, named Said (Sayyid) Mohammed, at their head and abused the Cady openly, telling him that he had taken a bribe from the Jewish community, that he was not a true Mussulman, and finally demanded that the Jew should be made over to them that they might dye their hands in his blood, and if he persisted in not drawing up an Elam[2] for his execution they would go to the prison and kill him.

The Cady fearing the rage of such a large body of influential fanatics chose the lesser evil, and with the greatest reluctance drew up and signed a sentence of death against the unfortunate Jew, which leaves by this post for ratification at Constantinople.

[1] Ar., *maḥkama* (court of law).
[2] Ar., *iʿlām* (a decree).

I have the honor to be

with great respect,

My Lord,
Your Excellency's
Most obedient
humble servant,
C. A. Rassam

(Embassy note on the back)
The sentence of death against the Jewish Rabbin referred to in this dispatch has been received at the Porte. After a cautious examination of it by the Supreme Council and a *Fetva*[3] given by the Sheik-ul-Islam,[4] the case appears to deserve no death, but only severe punishment. The Porte, therefore, in order to avoid any misinterpretation of the law, and with a view to save the Jew from a longer confinement and punishment, have decided upon writing to the Governor of Moussool to send the Jew to Constantinople without delay.

Pera,[5] November 28, 1853.

E. A. Pisani

Public Records Office (London)
FO 195/394, ff. 80–81.

No. 13.

Moosul
November 7, 1853

His Excellency
The Right Honorable Viscount Stratford de Redcliffe G.C.B.
Etc. Etc. Etc.
Constantinople

My Lord,

I have the honor to acquaint Your Excellency that since the date of my last Despatch No. 12, I have had an interview with the Cady respecting the Jewish Rabbi. The Cady informed me that he had represented the case to the Sheikh el Islam, giving him a full statement of the unsatisfactory evidences of the witnesses produced, and the violent conduct and threats of the Ulema towards him for keeping within the precincts of the Law, and he was only induced by intimidation and fear lest they should lay violent

[3] Turkish form of Ar., *fatwā* (a legal opinion issued by a *muftī*).

[4] The *Shaykh al-Islām* was the chief *muftī* of the Ottoman Empire and the recognized head of the Islamic legal hierarchy. Concerning this office, see Joseph Schacht, *An Introduction to Islamic Law* (Oxford, 1964), p. 90.

[5] The quarter of Constantinople reserved for foreigners.

hands upon his own person as well as the Jew, to draw up an Elam for his execution. I presume His Excellency Helmy Pasha has likewise written to his Government on the subject; but neither functionaries have the remotest idea of what will be the issue.

This occurence has not only thrown the Jewish community into consternation, but also the Christians.

. . . .

(signed) C. A. Rassam

Public Records Office (London)
FO 195/394, f. 82.

No. 3.

Moosul
February 27, 1854

His Excellency
The Right Honorable Viscount Stratford de Redcliffe G.C.B.
Etc. Etc. Etc.
Constantinople

My Lord, With extreme satisfaction and delight I have the honor to acquaint Your Excellency that the last post from the capital brought an Imperial Firman to His Excellency Helmy Pasha, and a Fetwah (*fatwā*) accompanied by a letter from the Sheikh El-Islam annulling the capital punishment of the Jew whose case I had the honor of representing to Your Excellency in my Despatch Nos. 12–13 of last year. The Sheikh-el-Islam in his last letter severely reprimanded the Ulema and Mullahs for their violent conduct and misconstruction of the Law, and calls upon them to be more careful in future.

The Imperial Firman also orders His Excellency Helmy Pasha to send the Jew to Constantinople; this caution I presume is taken to prevent public discontent. The whole of the Jewish Community are deeply sensible of this renewed insistance of His Majesty's clemency, and openly manifest the gratitude and devotion for the protection and quiet which they enjoy in this part of the Sultan's dominions.

. . . .

(Signed) C. A. Rassam

Public Records Office (London)
FO 195/394, f. 95.

AN ANTI-JEWISH INCIDENT IS PREVENTED BY A ZEALOUS TURKISH OFFICIAL
(BAGHDAD, 1860)

No. 31 of 1860

British Cons^{te} General
Baghdad 10 October 1860

His Excellency
The Right Honorable
Sir H. L. Bulwer G.C.B.
H.B.M.'s Ambassador
Constantinople

Sir,

On the occasion of a panic amongst the Christians and Jewish inhabitants of Baghdad, in the beginning of August, the Reïs Pasha Ahmed Towfik,[1] on hearing of a crowd of evil disposed persons having assembled in the neighborhood of the Jewish quarter, immediately ordered out a strong body of troops with which he and Ibrahim Pasha patrolled the streets during the whole night.

Mustaffah Noori Pasha[2] reproved the Reïs for having acted in this manner and accused him of wishing to provoke a disturbance that he might have the credit of having put it down. The Musheer,[3] however, on hearing that Ahmed Pasha's proceedings had met with general approval and commendation, took the credit to himself and let it be understood that the precautions which had been taken had emanated from himself.

. . . .

(signed) J. M. Hyslop

Public Records Office (London)
FO 195/624.

[1] He became the *wālī* not long afterwards, replacing the much-hated Muṣṭafā Nūrī Pasha. He was considered a just ruler and treated the Jews well; however, he was only in office six months. See Abraham Ben-Jacob, *A History of the Jews in Iraq* (Jerusalem, 1965), pp. 144–45 [Heb.].

[2] He was considered by the Jews to be a *sōnē Yisrā'ēl* (a hater of Jews). For his part in the conflict over Ezekiel's tomb, see the following set of documents, pp. 389–92.

[3] Ar.–Turk., *mushīr*. This was the governor's military rank, more or less equivalent to field marshal.

A DISPUTE OVER THE CUSTODY OF EZEKIEL'S TOMB

(IRAQ, NINETEENTH CENTURY)

A. A Report by the British Consul in Baghdad

No. 15 of 1860

His Excellency
The Right Honb[le]
Sir H. L. Bulwer GCB
HBM's Ambassador
Constantinople

British Cons.[te] General
Baghdad 9th May 1860.

Sir

His Excellency Mustaffah Noorie Pasha (Muṣṭafā Nūrī Pasha)[1] has intimated to the Jewish community of Baghdad that it is his intention to take from them the Tomb of the Prophet Ezekiel which has been in their custody from time immemorial. His alleged reason for this step is that the courtyard of the Tomb belongs to a Mohammedan Mosque which formerly existed there.

The Jews declare that the Tomb has been in their possession for upwards of 2000 years and that their right to it has never before been questioned. As the Pasha however would listen to no arguments on the point, the principal Jewish inhabitants and clergy waited upon me to request that I would submit their case to Your Excellency's consideration.

The enclosed is a copy and translation of a letter which they have written to the Pasha on this subject and which they have also presented to the English and French Consulates at this place.

I have the honor also to enclose for Your Excellency's information a sketch and plan of Kiffle (al-Kifl),[2] which was lately visited by Captain Selby; this plan shows the positions of the Tomb of Ezekiel and the Minaret which is all that now exists of the Mohammedan Mosque. The Mosque was situated directly under the minaret and as the latter is at some distance from the Jewish Tomb, it appears unlikely that it (the Tomb)

[1] He was *wālī* (governor) from 1859–60.

[2] The traditional tomb of Ezekiel is located in the village of al-Kifl twenty miles south of the town of Ḥilla in central Iraq. The name of the town is derived from the Prophet's epithet in Arabic, *Dhu 'l-Kifl* (the Guarantor). Although Ezekiel is not mentioned by name in the Koran, he does have a place in Muslim prophetic tales. See the articles "Ezekiel's Tomb," and "Ezekiel in Islam," in *EJ* 6: 1,096–97; and "Ḥizḳīl," in *EI*[2] 3: 535.

could ever have appertained to the Mosque. Be this however as it may, it is certain that the Jews have long been in undisturbed possession of the place as it now stands and that if they have encroached, it must have been with the permission of their Mohammedan rulers. My own opinion of the case, founded on any knowledge of the locality, is that the properties of the Mosque and Tomb were distinct and that therefore the Pasha has no right to remove the Jews from a place in which they have worshipped for ages.

The Pasha, in proof of his assertion brings forward witnesses who can depose that they have prayed in the courtyard of the Jewish Tomb, but this is not denied by the other party, and proves nothing except that Ezekiel was looked upon as a Prophet by the Mohammedans as well as Israelites. Mustaffah Pasha's proceedings in this case may be prompted partly by his fanatical spirit, but I believe that at first, it was only a threat used for the purpose of extorting money from the Jewish Community. Now that he has met with unexpected opposition from them, he will probably endeavor to establish his case and for this purpose he has sent out to Kiffle a commission to collect evidence, which there is little doubt will be entirely in his favor. Mustaffah Noorie Pasha's want of consideration for the non-Mussulman portion of the population is so well known that the fanatical party is increasing in boldness and a disagreeable feeling has arisen among the different sects in this city. This feeling too has been considerably excited of late by the reception into the Roman Catholic Church, by two Latin Priests, of several converts from Islamism. Christians have been abused and imprisoned by Mohammedans who have brought forward trivial complaints against them and the Jews, who generally meet with worse treatment than Christians, are beginning to be seriously alarmed. Should the Pasha succeed in this case against the Jews, he will be emboldened to act in a similar way towards the Christians, in fact he has already commenced to do so, by claiming as Wakkuf (*waqf*) some property belonging to the Armenian Church.

I have the honor to be,
Sir/
With the Utmost respect,
Your Excellency's
Most obed[t] humble servant,
J. M. Hyslop
HM's Offg. Consul General at Baghdad

Public Records Office (London)
FO 195/624.

B. *Letter Addressed by the Jewish Community of Baghdad to the Wālī Muṣṭafā Nūrī Pasha*

Having been made acquainted with the message conveyed by Your Excellency's order through the Agent of our community for our information, to the effect that you had been informed by some interested parties that our worshiping place situated close to the Tomb of the Prophet Ezekiel had been originally a Mohammedan mosque, we beg to inform you that the place itself shows what it is. And if they say that there is a minaret existing in the neighborhood, we reply it is well known that there is a great distance between the minaret and the worshiping place in question, which it is evident has been in existence for some thousands of years and which has been in the hands of the Jews all that time, handed down from one generation to another, as is well known to all. It has been customary from olden time that in the occasions of pilgrimage an Officer is sent by the Government for the protection of the Jews and strict orders are issued to the Chiefs of the different tribes to the same effect.

All the houses and other buildings erected around the place for its protection and preservation from injury by inundations, and all the repairs which have been made from time to time have been made by contributions (which have amounted to large sums) from the Jews, not only those residing in Baghdad, but those from all parts of the Ottoman dominions as well as from foreign countries; these contributions are still being received up to the present time, and in order to insure ourselves from being blamed by those parties, we beg that your Excellency will allow us time to refer the case to them and to await their answer on the subject, or if Your Excellency will not grant this, we request that you will communicate on the subject with the Agents of the Foreign Power [*sic*]

13 Shawwāl 1276 (4 May 1860)

Seal & Signature of—

Khakham Obediya	Benyamin Sasone	Dawood Sowdai
Khakham Sasone	Shawool Ghalla	Coççio Cohen
Khakham Nessim	Yussif Gourgee	Herman [*sic*]
Shelumo Sofer	Shelumo Murad	I. Lurian[1]
Saleh Youda	Nessim Zelkha	

Public Records Office (London)
FO 195/624.

[1] The last three individuals on this list were foreign Jews residing in Baghdad. Coççio Cohen was a merchant whose name occurs on a number of occasions in the correspondence of the British consul at Baghdad during this period. No initial or forename is given for the individual listed as Herman. I. Lurian is identified as *Horloger* (clockmaker).

C. *The Report of the Commission sent by Muṣṭafā Nūrī Pasha to al-Kifl*

On our arrival at Kiffle according to Your Excellency's orders, a searching and complete enquiry was made regarding the mosque in question from intelligent parties who are well acquainted with the place.

It appears that the said mosque was originally a large and extensive one, in which prayers were said five times a day. Some time ago one side having fallen down, it remained in a ruined state; part of it was repaired by the Jews themselves some years ago; part was turned into new houses and part remained. Some repairs have been made upon it. Three or four years ago the mosque together with the adjoining tomb was painted by the Jews. This community originally had a large worshipping place (Towrat) behind and adjoining the mosque, being a separate place for themselves. The door of this place being shut from behind, it can therefore have no connection with the mosque.

This door may be opened in the old place and the new houses may either be destroyed or subjected to a ground rent,[1] by which arrangement no damage will be done either to the said mosque or to the Jewish Community. Repairs are necessary for building a *miḥrāb* and *maḥifal*[2] as well as for removing the buildings in order to turn into their old state, the twenty-five rooms which formerly existed for the use of strangers and law students, but these are subject to Your Excellency's order.

Yes, we certify by Allah to the truth of what is written in this Muzbetteh,[3] viz., that there was a mosque and that prayers were said in it five times a day, and that on several occasions we have prayed in it and that it had a *miḥrāb,* and that the Jews turned it into a worshipping place, of which we have full cognizance.[4]

(Signed)

Nā'ib Zāde Aḥmad Efendī
ᶜAbd Allāh Aghā Zāde
Ṣalāl al-Ṣabbār

Public Records Office (London)
FO 195/624.

[1] In the Turkish text, *ijāret zamiyya.*
[2] For *maḥfal* (gathering place).
[3] For *maḍbaṭa* (report).
[4] This last paragraph is in Arabic; whereas, the preceding paragraphs are in Turkish.

27. *Sir Moses Montefiore presenting a petition on behalf of Moroccan Jews to Sultan Muḥammad IV in Marrakesh, February 1, 1864*

Thomas Hodgkin, *Narrative of a Journey to Morocco in 1863 and 1864* (London: T. Cautley Newby, 1866)

28. *David Sassoon, founder of the Bombay banking house, in his native Iraqi costume, ca. 1864*

Alfred Rubens, *A History of Jewish Costume* (London: Valentine, Mitchell, & Co., 1967)

29. *Well-to-do Iraqi Jew and his wife, nineteenth century*

D. S. Sassoon, *Massa*[c] *Bavel* (Jerusalem, 5715)

30. *The tomb of the Prophet Ezekiel at al-Kifl, Iraq*
D. S. Sassoon, *A History of the Jews in Baghdad* (Letchworth, 1949)

31. *The rabbis of Baghdad, twentieth century*
D. S. Sassoon, *Massaᶜ Bāvēl* (Jerusalem, 5715)

32. *Jewish woman of Rabat veiled in the traditional* ḥayk, *early twentieth century*
L. Goulven, *Les Mellahs de Rabat-Sale* (Paris: P. Geuthner, 1927)

33. *Moroccan Jewish bride, from a portrait by Delacroix*
Israel Museum Catalogue No. 103

34. The martyrdom of Sol Hatchuel (Lalla Suleika), from a painting by Alfred Dehodencq

Israel Museum Catalogue No. 103

35. R. Moses Serusi, Tripolitanian scholar, author of Va-Yeshev Moshe, *late nineteenth or early twentieth century*

Schwadron Collection, Jewish National University Library, Jerusalem

A PLEA FOR AID IN THE DAMASCUS AFFAIR

To Messrs. Abram Conorte and Aron Coen,

Expressing my best wishes for your health; to my deep regret I address you these few lines to repeat the state of misery in which our brethren, inhabitants of Damascus, now are, as communicated to you in my letter of 17 Adar (February 16) by the Steam Packet. I had hoped to advise in this letter that the circumstance respecting which they were calumniated has been discovered; but in this I have been sadly disappointed. I will therefore now repeat every thing in detail, and it is thus:

On Wednesday the 6th day of the month of Adar (February 5) there disappeared from Damascus a priest who with his servant had dwelt for forty years in this city. He exercised the profession of physician and visited the houses of Catholics, Jews, and Armenians for the purpose of vaccination.

The day following, viz. Thursday, there came people into the Quarter of the Jews to look for him, stating that they had seen both him and his servant on the previous day in that Quarter. In order to put in execution their conspiracy, they seized a Jewish barber, telling him that he must know all about the matter, and thence carried him before the Governor, before whom they accused him, and gave him five hundred stripes inflicting other cruelties. In the intervals between these inflictions they urged the delinquent to accuse all the Jews as accomplices, and he thinking by these means to relieve himself, accused Messrs. David Arari, Isaac Arari, Aron Arari, Joseph Lagnado, Moses Abolafia, Moses Benar Juda, and Joseph Arari, as instigating accomplices who had offered him 300 piasters to murder the abovementioned, inasmuch as the Passover Holidays approaching, they required blood for their cakes, that he did not however give ear to their instigations while at the same time he knew not what might have happened to the Priest and his servant. Upon this, the Pasha caused the aforesaid traduced persons to be arrested as instigators, and punished with blows and other torments of the most cruel nature, but as they were innocent they could not confirm as true what was a calumny, and therefore in contradiction they maintained the truth of their statement, appealing to the sacred writings which strictly prohibit the Jews feeding upon blood, much more that of a fellow creature, a thing totally repugnant to nature. Nevertheless they were imprisoned and daily with chains around their necks inflicted on them the most severe beatings and cruelties, making them stand for fifty hours fasting.

Subsequently to this the Hebrew butchers were cited to appear, and were put in chains together with the Rabbins Messrs. Jacob Autevi, Salomon Arari, and Azaria Jalfon, and caused them to be beaten to such an extreme that their flesh hung in pieces upon them, and this in order that they should confess whether or not they used blood in the Passover cakes to which they replied that if such had been the case, many Jewish proselytes would have published the fact.

This however was not sufficient. Subsequently to this, the same Governor went to the College of the boys, had them carried to prison, loaded with chains, and forbade the mothers to visit their imprisoned children, to whom they only allowed per day ten drachms of bread and a cup of water—the Governor expecting that the fathers, for the sake of liberating their children, would confess the truth of the matter.

After this a Jew who was free, presented himself before the Governor, stating that the calumny that we make use of blood for our Passover cakes, had been discussed before all the Powers, who after consulting their divines, had decreed the inadmissibility of such a calumny, and he added that it could not be other than that Christians had killed them, or that they had clandestinely absented themselves from the country, and that the barber, in order to save himself from persecution, had stated that which was not true.

Upon this the Governor replied that as he had said that the Christians had killed them, he must know who was the murderer, and in order that he should confess he was beaten to such an extreme that he expired under the blows.

After this the Governor with a body of 600 men proceeded to demolish the houses of his Jewish subjects, hoping to find the bodies, but not finding any he returned and again inflicted on them further castigations and torments, the most cruel of which was the tying one end of a cord to the member of virility by the other end of which they were dragged through the Governor's Palace to a water closet into which they were thrown. Incapable of bearing further torments, they preferred to die, and confessed that the calumny was true.

The Governor hearing the confession asked them where they had secreted the blood of the murdered men, to which one of them replied that it had been put into a bottle and delivered to Mr. Moses Abolafia, who declared he knew nothing of it; and in order that he should confess, they inflicted on him a thousand stripes, but not obtaining his confession they inflicted on him other insupportable torments which at length compelled him to declare that it was at home in a chest of drawers.

Upon which the Governor ordered that he should be carried on the shoulders of four men (for he could not walk), in order that he might open the bureau; this was opened, but nothing found in it, except a quantity of money which the Governor seized, asking him at the same time where was the blood, whereupon Abolafia replied that he made that statement in order that the Governor should see the money in the bureau, trusting by these means to save himself from the calumny. Upon this the torments were repeated, and Abolafia to save himself embraced the Turkish Religion.

It is thus that they treated the whole, and they have now been for one month in this misery. In Beirout, and much more in Damascus, the Jews are not at liberty to go out.

After this an individual came forward and stated that by means of astrology he had discovered and ascertained that the seven individuals abovenamed assassinated the priest, and that the servant was killed by Raphael Farhi, Nathan Levi, Aron Levi, Mordohài Farhi, Asser of Lisbon—the two first of these were immediately arrested; the others it appears sought safety in flight.

You will judge from this, dear friends, what sort of justice is administered by means of astrology, and how; and there is no one who is moved to compassion in their favor. Even Mr. Behor Negri, the Governor's banker, unable to bear these afflictions, has embraced Islamism.

Read, dearest friends, this to Messrs. Camondo, Katterm and Carmona,[1] in order that they may cooperate for the safety of our unfortunate and calumniated brethren, with such persons as they may deem most fitting.

Public Records Office (London)
FO 195/162.

[1] Leaders of the Istanbul Jewish Community.

A REPORT ON THE TREATMENT OF JEWISH PRISONERS IN THE DAMASCUS AFFAIR

On the Punishments and Tortures practiced at the Palace and at Sheriff Pasha's private dwelling on the accused and other Jews and the conduct of the Government towards them personally since they have been under arrest and as to their Interests and Property.—

The Barber Solyman Hallak was tortured by the application of a torniquet or common cord round his head temples, on the stick twisting this breaking, a few minutes afterwards a second application of a silken cord was on the point of being made when he consented to make a confession. No traces remain of this torture. He was bastinadoed four times on the soles of his feet. His right foot now bears traces of this punishment, the wound not having healed. His beard stated to have turned white is quite black.

The Servant Murad El-Fattal was bastinadoed once on his feet of which no traces remain.

Rabbi Mousa Aboul'afié was twice bastinadoed, once on the soles of the feet and once on the posteriors. The soles of his feet are still wounded and his walk lame. (He) was prevented taking sleep, at two different times, each three days. (He) was taken by the genitals and pressed with the hand twice. He turned Mohametan and took the name Mohamed Effendi.

Isaac Arrari, states he was beaten a little, was prevented sleeping as the former. He complains of having received several slaps and boxes on the face. His ears were pulled and his beard and nostrils burnt with a candle. He, however, does not wish note to be taken of this because the light approached his nose without burning it. He was plunged in a reservoir of water, where he remained a quarter of an hour. His genitals were also pressed. Of these tortures, the only traces which remain are the scars on the calves of the legs received from the Courbash.[1]

David Arrari states to have been beaten less than the others. (He) was however bastinadoed three or four times. His arms were pinched with the nippers used to place fire on the tobacco bowls, but they were not heated. The genitals were once pressed with the hand. His

[1] Turk., *kıbaç*, a scourge or whip.

ears were pulled. The right ear was torn, is deformed, and the lower smaller outer part has been removed by the surgeon. The calves of the legs are marked with the bastinado or Courbash. His right leg has a deep scar of this kind. He was prevented sleeping as the former.

Aaron Arrari was bastinadoed with the Courbash once.—one or two hundred stripes, he don't [*sic*] recollect, perhaps less. The soles of his feet bear no marks. The upper part of his feet bear circular scars occasioned by the Courbash. (He) was deprived of sleep three different times and had the genitals pressed three times so hard that a wound remained, but on examination nothing can be observed. He complains of a perspiration or extrudation from that part. He complains of having been thrown down and his eye wounded and bled and that his beard was burned with a candle.

Rabbi Mousa Salonickli—he was bastinadoed with the Courbash twice, received two or three hundred blows on the soles of his feet and posteriors. His left sole is scarred an inch long. His ears were pulled. Reeds were pierced between the flesh and the nails of four of his fingers of the right hand and three of the left. The nails of these fingers are still deformed.

Rabbi Yacoub Aintabli was plunged in a reservoir of water like Isaac Arrari.

. . . .

Of the accused Jews, Rabbi Yussuff Lignado aged fifty, he was bastinadoed on his feet and died about ten days after in consequence of the infliction of this violent punishment. He was rather of a delicate constitution and of a timid meagre complexion.

Yussuff Arrari—aged sixty-five. He was twice bastinadoed and died about ten or twelve days after in consequence of this punishment. He was of a feeble and aged constitution. Of the witnesses for the defence—the gate keeper of the Jewish Quarter, aged about sixty years. He was bastinadoed once, but to a violent degree and died in consequence about five days after. A finder of Tumbeck,[2] aged twenty-two years. He was once bastinadoed, but to a violent degree and died forty-eight hours after in consequence.

The interests and property of the accused have not been sequestrated or confiscated by the Government, and persons having interests pend-

[2] Ar., *tunbāk,* Persian tobacco used in narghileh.

ing with them have been permitted access to them, to regulate and settle accounts with them.

The Rabbis Halfon and Raffael Arrari were detained, but subsequently liberated without being beaten or ill treated.

Maalim Raffael Farhi, the father of Aslan Farhi[3] and considered the chief of the Israel nation here, was arrested and closely confined in a room at the Barracks ninety-five days, was attended by his servant and obtained whatever else he required from his house.

. . . .

Public Records Office (London)
FO 78/410, ff. 228–31.

[3] The Farḥīs were a prominent family of court bankers in Syria during the eighteenth and nineteenth centuries. See Hayyim J. Cohen, "Farḥī," *EJ* 6:1, 181–1, 183.

THE BRITISH CONSUL IN EGYPT TRIES TO INTERCEDE FOR THE ACCUSED IN THE DAMASCUS AFFAIR

I waited this evening on the Pasha to urge on his attention anew and verbally the views of Her Majesty's Government respecting the proceedings at Damascus.

The Pasha expressed his determination to do nothing in the matter until the arrival of the report of the French "Elève Consulaire" who has been sent to Damascus by order of the French Administration for the purpose of investigating the recent trials.

It is my duty to remark to Your Lordship that from the measure I have mentioned little advantage is likely to accrue to the cause of the Jews. I say it of my own knowledge that the French Consul General in Egypt, the "Elève Consulaire" already noticed, and the majority of French subjects resident in this place, are strongly impressed with a belief in the culpability of the Jews; and I can by no means anticipate for their cause a cool and impartial consideration before a tribunal so completely biased and prepossessed. I need only add that, in this affair, the Viceroy will certainly be entirely guided by the opinions and wishes of France: neither does it appear to me that the remonstrances of any other Power will have the slightest influence.

I ought not to neglect observing that in the course of the conversation of which I have spoken, Mehemet Ali declared that torture always was and still remains the Law of the Land. The Pasha only noticed the fact; but expressed no opinion as to the merits or disadvantages of that method of procedure. Of course this assertion supposes—what is indeed the fact—that the late reforms in the Turkish Empire[1] have no effect in Egypt and its Dependencies.

I regret to say that the popular odium and exasperation excited against the Jews by the accusations and trials to which they have been exposed, is every day productive of new insults and injuries to that unhappy people. Advices of the 12th Instant from Jaffa, assure me that recently eight Jews, four Mussulmans, and three Christians, journeying between Damascus and Saida (Sidon), were stopped by the Syrian insurgents.[2] The Jews were all

[1] The consul is referring to the reforms of the Khaṭṭ-i Sherif of Gülhane, which was promulgated in 1839. See above, pp. 96–97.

[2] Both the Druze and the Lebanese Maronites were in general revolt at this time.

murdered, in consequence of the late events in Damascus; but the Mussulmans and Christians were liberated.

I have the honor to be with the highest respect,

My Lord, Your Lordship's most obedient
Very humble servant
G. Lloyd Hodges

Public Records Office (London)
FO 78/405, ff. 32–34.

MONTEFIORE AND CREMIEUX APPEAL TO MUHAMMAD ʿALI

No. 73

Alexandria 5th August 1840

My Lord,

I have the honor to acknowledge Your Lordship's despatch Separate of July 27, 1840, instructing me to afford every countenance and protection in my power to Sir Moses Montefiore and the Deputation for the defense of the Jews persecuted at Damascus, as well as to further their objects by the exercise of my influence with H. H. Mehemet Ali.

The gentlemen to whom I have alluded arrived here yesterday, and this morning I present them to H. H. the Viceroy who received them with courtesy, but with a degree of coolness sufficiently obvious.

I have before assured Your Lordship that the affair of the unfortunate Jews will not easily be settled in Alexandria, but must have its solution in Paris. Any efforts here are likely to be unavailing. Such is my own opinion, and I may add that of all my Colleagues. The Pasha, as regards this question, is completely under the influence of France; and as long as the Cabinet of the Tuileries shall think proper to support the French Consul at Damascus, I have little hope that Mehemet Ali will listen to my representations.

Still I shall exert my utmost efforts to carry the instructions of Your Lordship into execution.

I have the honor to be with the highest respect

My Lord, Your Lordship's most obedient
Very humble servant
(signed) G. Lloyd Hodges

Public Records Office (London)
FO 78/405, ff. 201–2b.

THE OTTOMAN SULTAN ISSUES A FIRMAN CONDEMNING THE BLOOD LIBEL (1840)

A Firman addressed to the Chief Judge at Constantinople at the head of which His Imperial Majesty the Sultan has written with his own hands the following words

"Let that be executed which is prescribed in this Firman"—

An ancient prejudice prevailed against the Jews. The ignorant believed that the Jews were accustomed to sacrifice a human being to make use of the blood at their feast of the Passover.

In consequence of this opinion the Jews of Damascus and Rhodes (who are the subjects of our Empire) have been persecuted by other Nations.[1] The calumnies which have been uttered against the Jews and the vexations to which they have been subjected have at last reached our Imperial Throne.

But a short time has elapsed since some Jews dwelling in the Isle of Rhodes have been brought from thence to Constantinople where they have been tried and judged according to the New Regulations, and their innocence of the accusations made against them fully proved. That therefore which justice and equity required has been done in their behalf.

Besides which the Religious Books of the Hebrews have been examined by learned men, well versed in their theological literature, the result of which examination is that it is found that the Jews are strongly prohibited not only from using human blood but even that of animals. It therefore follows that the charges made against them and their religion are nothing but pure calumnies.

For this reason, and for the love that we bear to our subjects, we cannot permit the Jewish Nation (whose innocence of the crime alleged against them is evident) to be vexed and tormented upon accusations which have not the least foundation in truth, but that in conformity to the Hatti Sheriff which has been proclaimed at Gul Hane[2] the Jewish Nation shall possess the same advantages and enjoy the same privileges as are granted to the numerous other nations who submit to our authority.

The Jewish Nation shall be protected and defended.

To accomplish this object We have given the most positive orders

[1] The reference here is to the Christians. The word "nations" is used here in a nineteenth-century sense and most probably translates *millet* or *taifa.*

[2] The Hatti Sherif of Gul Hane, or Khaṭṭ-i Sherif of Gülhane (Noble Rescript of the Rose Chamber), was the first great Ottoman reform edict, issued on November 3, 1839.

that the Jewish Nation dwelling in all parts of our Empire shall be perfectly protected as well as all other subjects of the Sublime Porte, and that no person shall molest them in any manner whatever (except for a just cause) neither in the free exercise of their religion nor in that which concerns their safety and tranquility. In consequence, the present Firman which is ornamented with our "Hoomaioon"[3] (sign manual) and emanates from our Imperial Chancellerie has been delivered to the Israelitish Nation.

Thus you the above mentioned Judge, when you know the contents of this Firman will endeavor to act with great care in the manner therein prescribed. And in order that nothing may be done in opposition to this Firman, at any time hereafter, you will register it in the archives of the Tribunal; you will afterwards deliver it to the Israelitish Nation, and you will take great care to execute our orders and this our sovereign will.

Given at Constantinople the 12th Ramaḍān 1256
(6 November 1840)

Public Records Office (London)
FO 78/416, ff. 163–64.

[3] Humāyūn (royal, or imperial) in Turkish usage.

THE PRUSSIAN CONSUL TRIES TO INTERCEDE FOR THE JEWS OF DAMASCUS
(1860)

Herr Count von der Golz
Constantinople
Damascus, 24 September 1860

Herr Minister,

Whereas owing to the destruction of the Christian Quarter, legal prosecutions of the local Muslims have ensued, and it would appear, in short, that all your aims have been achieved, a storm is gathering over the local Jewish Quarter. In a previous letter I had the honor of reporting to Your Excellency concerning the steps I have already had to take on behalf of the local Jewish community directly with Fu'ād Pasha,[1] as well as with Khurshīd Effendī, the local president of the "Extraordinary Court of Justice."

Those actions were not without success. Since then, however, Fu'ād Pasha has traveled to Beirut, and things have now become more violent. An Israelite, who was blind and crippled, and yet in spite of that charged with murder, is today in danger of death. Others—and I dare say most—are stricken with extreme fear, and no move has been made to settle the accusations raised against them. These accusations are made entirely by the Christians here. The Jews have been accused of having murdered and looted during the catastrophe in the Christian Quarter. Yesterday seventeen Jews were imprisoned, and today a long list of wanted Jews has been published by the Chief of Police. Since the *Tüfenqjī-bāshī*[2] is an old acquaintance of mine, I have seen this list myself. The fear which arose among the Jews has induced me to open up the Consulate Building once again this morning, as I had done at the time of the Christian persecution. Fourteen men have taken refuge there, and I will accord them complete protection until either Fu'ād Pasha directs the local government to put a stop to the violence against the Jews, or an emphatic order to that effect arrives from Constantinople. In the interest of humanity toward the in-

1 The Turkish foreign minister who was sent to Syria as commissioner extraordinary to investigate the massacre of the Christians and to punish the perpetrators.

2 Chief of the police unit known as the "musketeers." See Abdul-Karim Rafeq, *The Province of Damascus (1723–1783)* (Beirut, 1966), p. 169.

jured, I paid a call at noon today to the Governor Huammar Pasha and to Khurshīd Effendī. The former was beside himself over the quantity and urgency of business, and the latter stressed, in his words, that "he had exercised justice in the case of Muslims and must do so in the case of the Jews." This was emphasized so strongly that both meetings could have favorable consequences for the Jews. To this end, I have today also addressed the Royal Consul in Beirut, where Fu'ād Pasha now is, and I have addressed myself concerning these matters through this humble communication to Your Excellency to request that you, Herr Count:

> intercede directly with His Majesty the Sultan on behalf of the local Jewish community and most kindly request that an order be issued for the cessation of the organized persecution of the said community.

The sooner this happens, the more effective it will be, for at a time when the Christians are ruined and the wealthy Muslims have all fled, the market traffic is borne only by the Jews. Should the continuing hostilities result in even their disappearance from the market, then will total ruin be visited upon Damascus.

The causes of the Jewish persecution are as follows: An age-old hatred of the Jews on the part of the local Christians of the Greek rite; further, the fury of the Muslims because so many Believers have been executed, and the desire to hold the Jews responsible for it; and finally, the immoderate fear of the Israelite race. The chief cause, however, is the covetousness, for which the charges raised against the Jews are the vehicle, to make them pay, just as in the year 1839, when there occurred the abominable trial of Jews in the case of the disappearance of Father Thomas, in which a dozen Jews were tortured to death and three times as many were heavily fined.[3]

Already the local Israelites have written to Montefiore and Crémieux[4] and soon the European press will be complaining, not so much about Turkish intolerance as about consular activity. The Russian and French consulates nevertheless seem to be in the process of favoring the Christian accusers of the Jews.[5] The English consul is an old man not concerned about anything, and the Austrian Consulate presently is good for nothing.

[3] Concerning this infamous affair, which actually occurred in 1840, see above pp. 393–402.

[4] That is, Sir Moses Montefiore and Adolphe Crémieux, both of whom had intervened in the Damascus Affair of 1840.

[5] This incident was in fact played up in the anti-Semitic French and Russian press. See Salo W. Baron, "The Jews and the Syrian Massacres of 1860," *PAAJR* 4 (1932–33): 7–8.

What I could do, I have done, but only Fu'ād Pasha or an imperial command can guarantee effective redress.

Respectfully yours, etc.

Wetzstein

Document from the Secret Prussian State Archive (Berlin),
AA Sect. III, Rep. XVI, I, No. 1, vol. 7.
The German text has been published by
Salo W. Baron in *PAAJR* 4 (1932–33): 27–29.

INSTRUCTIONS FROM H. B. M.'S AMBASSADOR TO CONSTANTINOPLE REGARDING JEWS SEEKING BRITISH PROTECTION

Constantinople
June 12, 1863

No. 1.
George J. Eldridge Esq.
(Consul-General, Beirout)

Sir,

With reference to Mr. Wrench's[1] despatch No. 23 of the 16th Ultimo, applying for instructions to know if Jews cannot be granted British protection, I have to observe that such protection cannot be granted to them unless Her Majesty's Consul is fully satisfied that they are bona fide British subjects.

It is difficult to lay down a positive rule as to what evidence suffices, but unless the Consul to whom application is made feels certain in his own mind, that it is a just one, he must not sanction the application.

The declaration of the two unknown Jews before the Lord Mayor is certainly not sufficient proof, but if well known and respectable Jews in London swore to the justice of the claim, the case would be different.

I am, Sir etc.
(signed) H. L. Bulwer

Public Records Office (London)
FO 195/976.

[1] He was acting consul general before the arrival of Eldridge.

A LIBYAN JEW TRIES TO REGAIN LOST BRITISH PROTECTION

A.

No. 9.

Tripoli, Barbary
December 23, 1872

His Excellency
The Right Honorable
Sir H. G. Elliot G.C.B.
Her Majesty's Ambassador Extraordinary
Etc. Etc. Etc.
Constantinople

Sir,

In reply to Your Excellency's Despatch No. 4 of the 15th ultimo transmitting a petition signed by David Buharon, and directing me to acquaint Your Excellency with the circumstances of his case: I have the honor to state that the protection was discontinued in this instance in consequence of my having discovered that David Buharon was an Ottoman subject, a native of Bengasi, whose parents were also Ottoman subjects and natives of this country, and who had no other claim to British protection than the questionable one of a protection given by former Consuls and Vice Consuls on their own responsibility and which, on becoming aware of his nationality, I did not consider myself justified in continuing; especially as such protection was regarded by the Local Government as an unjustifiable interference between Ottoman subjects and their legitimate authorities. My particular attention was called to the case of David Buharon in consequence of his name having been prominently brought under my notice at a moment when the Governor General had made urgent representations to the different foreign consulates here with reference to abuses of this kind.

I subsequently directed Mr. Henderson to discontinue the protection of Nissim Buharon, the father of the petitioner on the same grounds.

I have the honor to be,
Sir,
Your Excellency's
Most obedient
Humble servant.
J. R. Drummond Hay

P.S. The petition of David Buharon is herewith returned.

Public Records Office (London)
FO 195/1010.

B.

To His Excellency,
The Right Honorable
Sir Henry G. Elliot.
Ambassador Extraordinary and Plenipotentiary
of H.B.M. to the Sublime Ottoman Porte
Etc. Etc. Etc.
EXCELLENCY!

The humble petition of David Buharon of Bengazi in Africa showeth

That petitioner's whole family, friends, and relations, namely the Buharon family have for long many years now, enjoyed everywhere the British Protection, and petitioner himself, born under such protection has enjoyed the same for 29 years, that is to say from the time of his birth till 1870.

That petitioner after 1870 has been deprived, by order of the British Consul General of Tripoli, of the British protection, and has been deprived of the same without any plain reason, and unjustly.

That petitioner, whilst at Bengazi when Mr. W. D. Chapman, nephew or relative of the said Consul General, was Vice-Consul there, has signed a petition with other British subjects directed to Her Majesty against the said Consul, and he was in consequence of it, turned out of the situation of Vice Consul (the said Mr. Chapman).

That Petitioner stood as attorney for his father in a case with a certain Tajar,[1] Mr. Chapman's friend, and having lost the case in Bengazi, obtained here, an order for rehearing, which Mr. Chapman did not obey, for which reason petitioner came here in Constantinople. A second time[2] the order was renewed but always in vain, as Mr. Chapman having declared himself an enemy to poor petitioner has acted and has used all his influence till petitioner lost British protection, or rather say his nationality, as such protection became a nationality to the Buharun [*sic*] family.

That petitioner considers himself wrongfully deprived of the British protection, when his father, brother, sisters, uncles, and cousins in Bengazi, Alexandria, and Tripoli enjoy the British protection.

And therefore humbly prays

[1] Ar., *tājir* (big merchant).

[2] There is one long run-on sentence here which I have broken up to make the best sense.

That Your Excellency may kindly in the name of justice, and British generosity and philanthropy, restore your humble Petitioner in his primitive rights of British protected [*sic*]. And may forever the Omnipossent grant glories to British justice and its administration.

Constantinople 6 November 1872.

Your Excellency's
Most humble and obedient servant
(signed in Hebrew) David Buharun

(Note on bottom)

to be returned

Inform him that his protection was withdrawn when it was ascertained to have been improperly given, he and all his family being Ottoman subjects.

January 17. 73

Public Records Office (London)
FO 195/1010.

A RESIDENT JEW IS APPOINTED AUSTRIAN CONSULAR REPRESENTATIVE IN TRIPOLI, LIBYA

(LAST QUARTER OF THE NINETEENTH CENTURY)

His Excellency
The Right Honorable
A. H. Layard
etc. etc. etc.

Tripoli, 3rd September 1877

Sir,

In reply to your Excellency's despatch of the 12th ultimo, requesting information respecting Mr. Saul Labi, a British subject residing here, I have the honor to inform Your Excellency that Mr. Labi is the leading merchant of this place, and is a comparatively wealthy man, disposing, I have reason to believe, of a capital of about twelve thousand pounds. He bears a high character for uprightness and general respectability and is an active and intelligent man. He was educated at Leghorn, has traveled a good deal in Europe, speaks and writes Italian fluently and has a fair knowledge of French and Arabic, and is, I believe, well qualified to fill the office of the Austrian Consular Representative here. Mr. Labi, who is a liberal minded man, is of the Jewish persuasion and has for many years been the president of the Local Committee in connection with the "Alliance Israelite" at Paris. I may mention that he is the person who has been generally selected by me on account of his ability and honesty, to act as arbitrator or assessor in important cases that come before my Consular Court.

I have the honor to be
Sir,
Your Excellency's most obedient humble servant,

J. R. Drummond Hay

Public Records Office (London)
FO 195/1082.

A REPORT TO THE ALLIANCE CONCERNING THE PILLAGE OF THE JEWISH QUARTERS ON THE TUNISIAN ISLAND OF DJERBA (1864)

Another disaster to report! Muslim fanaticism tolerated, if not encouraged by the local authorities, has once more been unleashed against our brethren on the island of Djerba.[1] They are in the greatest misery: a whole people, having undergone all the excess of unspeakable barbarity, is today sunk in despair and the most dreadful destitution.

The Arab tribes of Akara and Ūrghamma[2] invaded the rich and populous island of Djerba. After attempting to lay waste the markets, from which they were repulsed by the resistance of the Muslims, these violent men turned upon the weakest, falling upon the Jewish quarters,[3] which they sacked, destroying everything.

This happened on the tenth of this month (October 10), the day of Yom Kippur; the synagogues were invaded, profaned, and defiled. The Scrolls of the Law torn in pieces and burnt; the men injured and trampled upon, all the women and girls raped, and my pen refuses to set down the terrifying tale of atrocities in all its horror, which these unfortunate people have undergone.

It is worth noting that the Governor of the island refused to intervene to reestablish order; need one say more than that the pillage did not cease for five days and nights, and that the invaders' rapacity was not satiated until the last rags had been stripped from the Jews of Djerba.[4]

From a letter by Solomon Garsin of the Tunis AIU Committee to the president of the Alliance Israélite Universelle in Paris, October 28, 1864.
AIU Tunisie, I.C.3. Translated by David Littman in
The Wiener Library Bulletin 28, n.s., nos. 35/36 (1975): 67.

[1] Djerba (Ar., Jarba) is the largest island off the North African coast and is located just south of Tunisia proper.

[2] That is, the Bedouin tribes of ᶜAkkāra and Urghamma, or Warghamma.

[3] There are two Jewish quarters on the island, called al-Ḥāra al-Kabīra and al-Ḥāra al-Ṣaghīra (the Great Quarter and the Small Quarter, respectively).

[4] The incident described here was typical of the sort of violence to which Jews were subject in nineteenth-century North Africa. It is clear from the report that initial violence was not specifically anti-Jewish. However, as the Jews were the most vulnerable element in the population, they soon became the principal victims of the marauders. Tribal insurrection caused by an increase in taxes had already broken out earlier that same year. See Jamil M. Abun-Nasr, *A History of the Maghrib*, 2d ed. (Cambridge, 1975), pp. 267–68.

TUNISIAN JEWRY COMPLAINS TO THE ALLIANCE ISRAELITE UNIVERSELLE (1869)

Every epistle requires a preamble, but this needs none. The enclosed document in Hebrew signed by rabbis, by prominent merchants, and countersigned by the Chief Rabbi will explain all. It is the cry of an entire nation abandoned to its own devices in the face of Muslim ferocity.[1] Eighteen Jews have already fallen in a few months to the knives of fanatical murderers; and His Highness's[2] Government, far from punishing the guilty, protects and apparently encourages them.

The Government's conduct towards us is machiavellian beyond words. We are not directly persecuted, but such is the scornful treatment we receive when we ask for justice from the Beg or his ministers that open persecution would be a hundred times better. Acknowledged persecution, however, would expose the executioner and his victim to the world, and the Tunisian Government wishes to appear impartial, whilst masking killers surreptitiously; and all these efforts tend to overlook the victim in presenting to us merely an unskilled and powerless judge! ! !

Under such a policy, corpses multiply: impunity encourages the murderers.

The Tunisian Jews, simply as Jews, are constantly exposed to stringent measures on the part of the local authorities; they have no legal rights, and are treated by the population with the utmost hostility.

We cannot refrain from stating that the situation appears to us to be extremely black: our goods, our lives, our honor, today all are in jeopardy.

The enclosed document was composed under the sway of this fear: it is the cry of anguish from an oppressed people seeking help from their European brethren, and especially appealing to you, sir,[3] who have long shown yourself as an indefatigable champion in the crusade of justice against fanaticism, you who have always held high the banner of an unjustly oppressed nation.

Eighteen victims have already fallen, but the sword of justice has not

[1] This is fairly typical of the rhetoric of the period. The hysterical tone of this letter, however, is perhaps even more high pitched than usual.

[2] That is the Beg Muḥammad al-Ṣādiq (ruled 1859–82). In 1864, he rescinded the Covenant of Security, or Fundamental Pact, which brought about an improvement in the legal position of Jews. See Part One above, p. 98.

[3] That is, Adolphe Crémieux, the president of the Alliance at that time and a famous champion of human rights.

been raised to impose a salutary lesson of fear! . . . Eighteen! . . . What then will be our future if the present is so monstrous?[4]

The time for deliberation is past, the future is exemplified by the past; and if you do not come to our aid, the Jewish condition in this area will be so unnatural that there will no longer be time to remedy it. And besides, dead men do not return! Your support can never be more effective for us than at this moment.

With our ever-characteristic mildness, we do not seek an eye for an eye, blood for blood, but that the guilty should be condemned and legally condemned. Then the present state of our despair will cease and, in this country, our nation will once again take its proper rank amongst civilized nations.

Instinctively pacific, we demand peace and justice. Shall they be denied us in a century of progress such as ours?

A letter from the members of the Tunis Alliance Israélite Universelle Committee to Adolphe Crémieux, president of the AIU in Paris, dated February 14, 1869. AIU, Tunisie, I.C.3. Translated by David Littman in *The Wiener Library Bulletin* 28, n.s., nos. 35/36 (1975): 67–68.

[4] Concerning these killings, which took place in 1868, see H. Z. [J. W.] Hirschberg, *The Jews in North Africa,* vol. 2, p. 149 [Heb.].

A DIPLOMATIC INCIDENT OVER THE GERMAN NATURALIZATION OF SOME TUNISIAN JEWS

Tunis 9th November 1874

No. 54
The Right Honorable
The Earl of Derby
Etc. Etc. Etc.
Foreign Office

My Lord,

I have the honor to report an incident which has occurred here and which, having been advisably referred by the Bey to the Ottoman Government, is likely to raise a question between it and the Cabinet of Berlin. It refers to the naturalization of 23 individuals appertaining to the Israelite Community, who were born in Tunis; some of whom held fiscal employments and whose ancestors, it is said, have been here for upwards of two hundred years. With the exception of one or two of these individuals, none of them have ever quitted their native country.

The circumstances connected with this incident are the following:

The chief of the family, Haï Sebagh,[1] was the agent or banker of the ex–Prime Minister. When His Excellency was removed from office, he took refuge in the Italian Consulate under false pretences, but chiefly on the ground that he apprehended danger to himself, notwithstanding the repeated assurances of the Government that, having no cause of complaint against him, he need not fear any molestation on its part. He subsequently quitted the Italian Consulate, and having asked for permission to proceed to Leghorn on his private affairs, leave was granted to him—a proof that the Government had no wish or intention to put any restraint upon his personal liberty.

Haï Sebagh proceeded from Italy to Vienna where he endeavoured, through a certain banker by name Morpourgo,[2] to obtain Austrian protection. Failing in this, he repaired to Berlin with letters of recommendation from the same banker to Messrs. Oppenheim & Co.,[3] where he succeeded to obtain letters of citizenship for himself and for all the members of his family.

[1] The name Sebagh, Sebag, and similar ones from the Ar., *ṣabbāgh* (dyer), is very common among Jews throughout North Africa.

[2] He was probably a member of the well-known Jewish family of Morpurgo. See Emmanuel Beeri, "Morpurgo," *EJ* 12: 348–49.

[3] This was the famous banking house founded by Solomon Oppenheim, Jr. See Hanns G. Reissner, "Oppenheim," *EJ* 12: 1418–19.

It is not known by what representations he induced the German Government to accede to his request; but Prince de Bismark has instructed the Prussian Consul General to protect the Sebaghs as German citizens and to announce it to the Bey.

The Tunisian Government, unable to recognize the right of a Foreign Power to naturalize Tunisians while yet residing in their native country, and unwilling to discuss through the Prussian Agent here a matter involving an important question of international law and comity, has deemed it advisable and prudent to refer it to the Porte, which is in a more favorable position to ask for explanations of the Cabinet of Berlin.

The question is one of very serious importance to the Tunisian Government. If the principle is once admitted and the precedent established that a Foreign Power can issue letters of naturalization to native born Tunisians who have never quitted the country and who still continue to reside in it, there is every reason to fear that the precedent will be speedily availed by such of the Powers as are interested in increasing their colonies in the Regency either for commercial or other purposes.

There are thirty thousand Israelites in the Regency; but the greatest and most serious danger arises from the vicinity of Algiers and from the fact that many of the Arab tribes occupy the country on the borders.

Each tribe is divided into sections, each of which recognizes as its hereditary chief, the head of the family or stock from which it (the section) descends. The members, therefore, who compose a section are related to each other; and were the Tunisian Government to permit the establishment of the precedent alluded to, it would incur the danger of seeing many of the hereditary chiefs naturalized as Algerian subjects and with them the relatives comprised in their several sections. In this manner, the Tunisian tribes on the frontiers would be free to throw off their allegiance to the Bey and to continue to occupy, under French protection, the grounds allotted to them.

Besides this consideration, there are some thousands of Algerians who have expatriated themselves at the time of the conquest of their country, who are at present considered as Tunisians, but who as well as the Israelites and the Arab tribes would seek foreign citizenship to avoid paying taxes and tribute and to enjoy the privileges accorded by treaties to foreigners.

The state of things that would be thus produced would be disastrous to the Regency. The Administration would lose its prestige and authority, and its efforts to uphold its undoubted rights would lead to international questions and to the complications which it eventually apprehends from the establishment of a precedent which would open the door to abuses of every description.

It is difficult to explain the exact reasons which have induced the Cabinet of Berlin to accede to the request of the Sebaghs unless it allowed itself to be influenced by representations with reference to their position here destitute of foundation. And the Bey still hopes that when Prince de Bismark becomes acquainted with the true state of the case, His Excellency will be pleased to relieve His Highness' Government from the inevitable consequences that will accrue from the naturalization of natives residing in Tunisian territory.

I may be permitted to state, in conclusion, that Haï Sebagh, while yet a refugee in the Italian Consulate, had procured British passports for himself and his two brothers as British subjects traveling on the continent, but I declined their application to recognize them on the ground that they must have obtained them surreptitiously.

I have the honor to be,
With the highest respect,
My Lord,
Your Lordship's most obedient
humble servant,

(signed) Richard Wood

Public Records Office (London)
FO 195/1010.

A DESCRIPTION OF THE JEWS OF TUNIS SHORTLY BEFORE THE FRENCH TAKEOVER
(LAST QUARTER OF THE NINETEENTH CENTURY)

Amongst all the countries known to us, Morocco and Tunis are the only ones where the Jewish element has preserved its patriarchal customs of olden times, and where it still occupies the exceptional position imposed upon it by despotism. The greater the liberties which other countries granted them, the more they amalgamated with the people—as, for instance, in France and England—without, however, giving up their religion unconditionally; in Tunis they only obtained this liberty latterly, and then only limited.[1] The curious habits and peculiarities which adhere to them would, considering their wonderful capacity to accommodate themselves to all circumstances, disappear as quickly here as they have done in the neighboring Algiers, but they still live the life of their Fathers. This latter is, in its strange mixture of Arabian, Jewish, and Spanish customs, so interesting that a description will be justified. The importance of the Jewish element increases, moreover, in the towns of Barbary, and also in the districts near the Sahara, more and more; in all the towns on the African coasts it actually forms from a third to a fifth of the whole populace. Since the Jews enjoy the protection of the Consuls and greater rights on the part of the Governments, they supplant the Arabs more and more in trade and industry, so that the time is not far off when they will be the more important element of the districts along the coasts.

It has lasted long enough before the Jews enjoyed in those countries an existence worthy of human dignity. Centuries of the greatest misery and of the most cruel oppression have succeeded in bending them, but with the toughness peculiar to their race, they have revived since they share the rights and liberties of the hereditary people. It is therefore not to be wondered at if the Moors and Bedouins look at them with an evil eye and fear them. This fear and jealousy is added to the hatred of centuries, and the old "Dshifa, ben Dshifa" (carrion, sons of carrion),[2] is still the usual designation when they speak of Jews.

The oppressions to which those latter are exposed, even to this day, are almost incredible. In Algiers the French Government emancipated them some forty years ago,[3] but in Tunis, Morocco, and Tripolis they only got

[1] The writer is referring to the ᶜAhd al-Amān, which was promulgated in 1857. See Part One above, p. 98.

[2] Ar., *jīfa b. jīfa.*

[3] The process of emancipation for Algerian Jewry proceeded in stages during the 1830s and 1840s. It culminated in the Décret Crémieux in 1870, by which the Jews of Algeria were granted French citizenship.

certain liberties during the last few years. Till then they had to live in a certain quarter, and were not allowed to appear in the streets after sunset. If they were compelled to go out at night they had to provide themselves with a sort of cat-o'-nine-tails at the next guard-house of the "Zaptieh,"[4] which served as a kind of passport to the patrols going round at night. If it was a dark night, they were not allowed to carry a lantern like the Moors and Turks, but a candle, which the wind extinguished every minute. They were neither allowed to ride on horseback nor on a mule, and even to ride on a donkey was forbidden them except outside the town; they had then to dismount at the gates, and walk in the middle of the streets, so as not to be in the way of Arabs. If they had to pass the "Kasba," they had first to fall on their knees as a sign of submission, and then to walk on with lowered head; before coming to a mosque they were obliged to take the slippers off their feet, and had to pass the holy edifice without looking at it. As Tunis possesses no less than five hundred mosques, it will be seen that Jews did not wear out many shoes at that time. It was worse even in their intercourse with Mussulmans; if one of these fancied himself insulted by a Jew, he stabbed him at once, and had only to pay a fine to the State, by way of punishment. As late as 1868, seventeen Jews were murdered in Tunis without the offenders having been punished for it:[5] often a Minister or General was in the plot to enrich himself with the money of the murdered ones. Nor was that all. The Jews—probably to show their gratefulness for being allowed to live in the town, or to live at all—had to pay 50,000 piastres monthly to the State as a tax!

And, notwithstanding all these oppressions and humiliations, the Jews continued to assert themselves in the midst of the Moorish populace, and could even boast of greater wealth than their oppressors, over whom they gained an advantage by their superior capacities and greater cunning. The Tunisians were in want of the Jews to get rid of the booty they brought home from their piratical expeditions. How the Jews managed to buy and sell these goods, considering their strict exclusion, is a puzzle. But still, they always possessed the money to buy the stolen wares, to lend money on precious stones, and turn gold and coins into jewels.

Many Jews, especially those whose ancestors were driven from Spain, have by reciprocal services or bribery succeeded in putting themselves under the protection of the European Consulates, and so escaped the power and jurisdiction of the Bey and his Ministers. This is the reason that some of the Consulates in Tunis count their subjects or proteges by hundreds, and even thousands, amongst the Tunisian Jews.

In our days when, through the agency of Consuls, especially the

[4] Turk., *zaptiye* (gendarmerie).

[5] See above, pp. 411–12.

French one, the oppression of the Jews has come to an end, and when they are equal before the law with Moors, Bedouins, and Christians, they have no more cause to hide their wealth. They build new houses in European style, show themselves in smart dresses, and, owing to their intellectual superiority, get business into their own hands with surprising rapidity. The old servants and slaves have become the masters of the Arabs, at least as far as business and finances go. They, once scorned, occupy now honored positions in the Government. The Bey's treasurer is a Jew. There are amongst them many physicians, bankers, merchants, stockbrokers, and lawyers, who do business with the Government, and who, compared with their Arabian colleagues, occupy a better position and have a more lucrative income. But the Arabians still avoid them. The social ban to which they have been subject for centuries past exists still today, though more to the disadvantage of the Arabian than their own. In that same bazaar where once they were debarred from trading otherwise than in the "Suk-el-Zara" (jewel bazaar),[6] they are masters now, and have driven the Moorish dealer from many streets. Thanks to the beneficent activity of the Paris Society "Union Israelite,"[7] poor Jewish children are sent to good schools and taught some trade or a branch of industry gratuitously. Besides Arabic, their own language, they learn French and Italian; and they show so much talent that no doubt before another generation has passed they will, financially, be masters of all the commerce in the whole Regency.

The Jew is known at once by his looks and by his dress. Tall and strongly-built, with fine, noble features and long beards, they show still more to advantage in their peculiar, picturesque costumes. They are not bound to wear a certain dress, as formerly, but they seem desirous of their hereditary appearance. They have only changed their headdress. Formerly they were forbidden to wear the red fez or sheshia[8] of the Arab, but wore the prescribed black turban wound round a white fez—a kind of nightcap. They have now adopted the red fez, but keep to the black turban, while the younger generation has given up the turban altogether. They are allowed to wear the white turban of the Arabs, but they never make use of this permission. Their short jackets are of a light color, richly embroidered with gold and open in front; and while the old orthodox Jews still keep to the black trousers, with many folds tied below the knee, the younger generation has adopted light-colored ones. They all wear snow-

[6] Ar., *sūq al-zahra* (literally, "the bazaar of splendor").

[7] The writer is referring to the Alliance Israélite Universelle. Concerning the Alliance's educational activities in Tunisia at this time, see Narcisse Leven, *Cinquante ans d'histoire: l'Alliance Israélite Universelle (1860–1910),* vol. 2 (Paris, 1920), pp. 106–19.

[8] See Reinhart Dozy, *Dictionnaire des vêtements,* pp. 240–44.

white stockings; and the yellow or red leather slippers of the Arabs have been discarded by the Jewish swell in favor of the patent leather shoes imported from Europe, but which he treads down, so that his heel projects one or two inches beyond the shoe.[9] A broad shawl, generally richly embroidered, is thrown round the loins, and while in winter their costume is completed by a long circular cloak of light blue color, they replace this in summer by a fine cloak of spotless whiteness, called the R'fara.[10]

Neither they nor the Arabs carry arms; and they are scarcely necessary in Tunis, which is safer than European towns. Stately as a Jew's appearance is, and tasteful as is his dress, it is only so long as he keeps his fez on his head. Like the Arabs, they are in the habit of shaving their heads, only leaving a small tuft of hair on the top, which has a most ludicrous effect.

It is not very long ago that the Jews, who number 30,000 here, were allowed to live in a Moorish quarter; and the limits of their own quarter were so strictly fixed and watched, that they scarcely dared to step beyond it, the more so if a mosque was in the neighborhood.

The strange costumes of the Jewish women,[11] the handsome men I met in Tunis, and the many peculiar habits and customs of which I had heard so much before, induced me to devote more attention to the Jewish quarter than other travelers had done until now. During my stay of several months in Tunis, I spent many a day in the midst of this strange people, and was the witness of many a family festivity and public occurrence. They received me everywhere with the greatest readiness and attention; and my experiences did not at all agree with the reports of former travelers, especially Maltzan, who one and all described them, more or less, as depraved.[12]

He who enters the Jews' quarter[13] for the first time is astonished how it is possible for human beings to live here, and to carry on business and have intercourse into the bargain. There is an indescribable entanglement of narrow, angular lanes, twisted and interlaced in all directions, where the rays of the sun never penetrate entirely. There is no passage in this endless labyrinth where you could not touch the walls on both sides if you stretched out your arms. If they are a little broader in some places, this waste of room is compensated for a little lower down, where the lane is so narrow that two people meeting here have to press against the wall if they

[9] I myself have seen this done in Morocco.

[10] Ar., *ghifāra.* Concerning this garment, see Dozy, *Dictionnaire des vêtements,* pp. 312–19; and idem, *Supplément,* vol. 2, p. 218.

[11] The writer devoted an entire chapter to "The Jewish Women of Tunis," in his *Tunis: Land and People,* pp. 129–37.

[12] The writer is referring to Heinrich Freiherr von Maltzan, *Reise in den Regenschaften Tunis und Tripolis,* vol. 1 (Leipzig, 1870), where the Jews of Tunis are discussed on pp. 68–74 passim.

[13] In Arabic it was called *ḥārat al-Yahūd.*

wish to pass each other. The houses are generally dingy, dirty, and dilapidated. Some hang over the street as if they wanted to prop each other up and prevent a possible fall; others are built right across, and form dark, long passages, from which dampness and dirt do not disappear summer or winter, and which remain cool even under a burning sun. On the upper floor there are usually one or two grated windows, just as in Moorish houses, which in their outward appearance they resemble altogether. The pavement is miserable, full of big stones and deep holes covered with puddles and every refuse, which being never removed, putrifies and exhales in summer the most offensive smells. The accumulation of dirt of centuries may be the reason why the streets are all higher than the houses, and that only by going down a few steps the inner yard is reached. This is partly the fault of the owners of these pest-houses, but the greater blame falls on the shoulders of the local authorities. They receive from each family in Tunis six piastres (three shillings) yearly, as a tax for removing all dirt from the streets, whereas the families have done their duty when they have forwarded the filth from their houses and piled it up in the middle of the narrow street. But how is the cleansing of streets possible when scarcely two or three streets are wide enough to admit a small cart or even a beast of burden? So the filth remained; it was partly washed away by the rain, while the rest settled by the constant traffic. Occasionally holes had been filled up with stones, and so the streets are higher now than the houses.

The houses are nearly all alike, and all seem poor and decayed, even desolate. There are good reasons for that. The Tunisian officials and dignitaries, from the Prime Minister down to the common soldier, took every opportunity to oppress and rob the Jews. They need only hear that this one or the other possessed great wealth to be after him at once for the purpose of confiscating his fortune for the paltriest of reasons, or to extort as many thousands of piastres as they thought he was worth. The Jews had therefore to hide their wealth, which, doubtless, was very great, as much as possible, and this reason contributed to their leaving their streets in this dreadful state. There is an end of this today, and the Jews build their houses on the Marina and in the European quarter.

But for all this the Hebrews are very religious here: they keep their festivals conscientiously, and are attached to their religious service. Strange are their pilgrimages to Jerusalem, which seem as holy to them as those of the Moslems to Mecca. Every year a number of pious Jews leave their homes to walk through the deserts of Tripolis and Egypt to Palestine. The difficulties and dangers of this endless journey do not prevent them from wandering to the cradle of their race, there to end their days. Many go forth, but a few only reach the far-off goal, for the journey through the desert is too perilous. Rich Jews travel to Jerusalem by steamer and return the same way to Tunis.

There are a great many synagogues in the Ghetto of Tunis, but most of them are poorly furnished and insignificant, scarcely to be distinguished from the ordinary houses. The entrances are small, half hidden; the place where they worship lies deep under the earth, so that twenty or thirty steps have to be passed before it is reached. On a level with the street is a gallery leading into the synagogue; it is barred, and is intended for the women. These are not allowed to enter the synagogue itself. Many small lamps hang down from the ceiling; along the walls run seats covered with straw, and in the centre is the raised platform for the rabbi, as is to be found in every synagogue. Saturdays bring much of life into these synagogues. Christians are allowed to be present at the service, and are even welcome, though the spectacle offered them here is not very flattering to the Jews. All the worshippers wear round their shoulders a broad white shawl with black stripes at the edges, and round the lower arm a black leather strap is wound.[14] Very few are devout during the time of service; some sing, others talk and laugh, and while the rabbi prays he looks about him in so indifferent a manner that it has always been a puzzle to me how the Tunisian Jews could possibly be called pious. To me the synagogue seemed exchange, dancing-room, and coffeehouse at the same time, and hour of prayer any thing but edifying. Only for one moment, towards the end of the service, did they interrupt the uproar, and also silenced the boys who were running about the whole place. I was told afterwards it was the moment when the rabbi gives absolution to his flock for their sins for a whole month, a custom which probably exists nowhere else amongst Jews.[15] After this solemn moment, during which all those present embraced and kissed each other, they folded their shawls and leather straps and left the place.

Benevolence is one of the greatest virtues of Tunisian Jews. The rabbis, for instance, live exclusively by alms; the sick poor are nursed by the Jewish community, and physician and medicines are sent to their homes, as to this day the Jews possess no hospital in Tunis. Up to recent times everything concerning schools was in a very backward state. Only very lately an excellent school was founded by the munificence of the Jewish Baron Castelnuovo, a noble and high-minded man, who was formerly physician to King Victor Emanuel, and the Austrian Baron Hirsch. The "Union Israelite" supports it, and eight hundred children are instructed there gratuitously. They also begin to dress those children in the European style. There is a second school which was founded by the London Society

[14] The writer confused the weekday morning service, when *tefillīn* (phylacteries) are worn, with the Sabbath morning service, when they are not.

[15] This custom is unknown to me. Perhaps he is referring to the Prayer for Rōsh Ḥoddesh (the new month).

for the conversion of the Jews, and which is very well administered by the English missionary, Frankel; four hundred children are taught there, of whom about one hundred are girls; all of these show great talent for languages and a great wish to learn. They study amongst other things the New Testament and the Christian religion, and the parents have no objection to it.[16] Whether this arises from religious indifference, or the consciousness that the Christian doctrines will not make any deep impression, but that the secular instruction only will be listened to, I cannot tell, but I presume the latter.

Chevalier de Hesse-Wartegg,
Tunis: The Land and the People,
new ed. (London, 1899), pp. 115–28.

[16] This is in marked contrast to the Jewish attitude toward missionary schools elsewhere. See for example, above, pp. 377–83.

A SABBATH AMONG THE JEWS OF PORT SAID (1879)

Port Said is situated at the Mediterranean extremity of the Suez Canal. Regarded as a town, it is a dismal failure. When the canal was inaugurated, crowds of hungry and eager traders flocked thither, expecting it to prove a second Alexandria. But of this there are no present signs, and little future prospect. It contains, however, some 3000 to 4000 Europeans, and more advanced Asiatics and Africans, and some 8000 Arabs. . . . Built upon sand, which produces nothing but opthamalia, and affords pasture-land only for ants and other insects, all that is consumed, in the way of food, in Port Said has to be brought from Alexandria, Damietta, and Jaffa.

Wandering through the streets . . . I chanced to notice an unmistakably Jewish physiognomy at a shop door. Could the owner of that physiognomy tell me if there were Jews in Port Said, and, if so, where a kosher dinner was to be obtained? The owner of the physiognomy replied that there were Jews in Port Said, and that, *moyennant finance,* he would be glad to supply me with the meat after which my soul longed, and more than that, he would be proud (it being Friday) to conduct me to synagogue at half-past four, for, although, perhaps, the poorest and smallest congregation in Egypt, they still had managed to obtain a synagogue, such as it was. A very curious place, too, it proved to be. A mere wooden shanty divided in two by a partition, for all the world like a small booth at a fair. The ceiling of plain wood, with no other decoration but cobwebs; the *Almemar,*[1] a converted stand for distributing boat tickets; the Ark, a cupboard covered with a striped green and yellow curtain with a *Mogen David*[2] braided upon it. A few deal forms or benches, two or three soiled Hebrew prints, a few tin stands for oil-lamps, some parcels of merchandise left for safe custody by Jewish traders going through to Jaffa, completed the contents of this little place of worship. Yet the shabby curtain was reverently kissed by the people who crowded into the small synagogue, and the service, attended on Friday evening by some fifteen, and on Saturday morning by some fifty worshippers was conducted with an amount of fervor, devotion, and earnestness that is frequently lacking in a more pretentious House of God. It seemed as if these poor people had strained every resource to get a place of meeting at

[1] The reader's platform, most commonly called *bīma* by European Jews. The form *almēmar* is derived from Ar., *al-minbar* (the pulpit).

[2] Heb., *māgēn Dāvīd,* (shield of David—the so-called Jewish star, or Star of David).

all. It had cost them £60, and now the landlord was endeavoring to prove that, instead of selling them the wretched shanty and its land outright, he had only let it to them for three years. Hence they are in great tribulation. The service was read by a swarthy Tunisian, who combines the functions of Rabbi, Reader, Shochet,[3] and Mohel,[4] all for the inconsiderable remuneration of twelve shillings per week, plus such chance offerings as might be made on his behalf. The *Mitzvoth*[5] are sold by auction, the bidding being by steps of half-a-franc at a time. On the day of my visit prices seemed to rule high, the *Haphtorah*[6] being knocked down for as much as three francs. There are about twenty Jewish families resident in Port Said, numbering, all told, about seventy souls.

They live by money-changing, tailoring, and retailing small articles, fancy goods and curiosities. All are very poor, but none of them keep their shops open upon the Sabbath, nor do they go on board the vessels to hawk their goods or change moneys upon that day. So that their poor little synagogue, with its *Sefer Torah* ornaments, of unornamented block tin, is the outcome of genuine piety and love of their faith, and is thus invested with no small amount of dignity. There are, however, in Port Said, several Jews and Jewesses (especially the latter) who follow the worst of professions. These form but a small minority, but it is well that the fact should here be made public, for it is better that Jews should themselves expose, and endeavor to correct, any plague-spots in their midst, than that it should be done by prejudiced and superficial observers.

The dinner was served in the bedroom of the family, but both it and all its surroundings were scrupulously clean. Mine hostess, a Smyrniote woman, was tastefully attired in a striped cretonne dressing gown—the remainer of which stuff, as I saw for myself, had formed the mantles of the three *Sephorim*[7] possessed by the synagogue—and she wore the strangest head-dress that can be imagined: a Scotch cap decorated with artificial paper flowers, and a bunch of live ferns stuck behind her hair. The dinner passed off pleasantly enough, save for the storm of questions by which it

[3] Heb., *shōḥēṭ* (ritual slaughterer).

[4] Heb., *mōhēl* (circumciser).

[5] Heb., *miṣvōt* (literally, "commandments," or "good deeds") but here used for the various honors given to participants during the service, such as opening and closing the ark, or reading from the Torah.

[6] Heb., *hafṭāra,* the prophetic portion that follows the Torah section.

[7] Heb., *sefārīm;* sing., *sēfer* (literally, "books"), but used to refer to the Torah scrolls.

was accompanied. Why is it that the ordinary Israelite always thinks it his duty to cross-examine his foreign brother concerning every particular of his public, private, and family history, and why is it that he seems quite hurt if the latter do not lay bare his whole soul before him?[8]

Sydney Montagu Samuel,
Jewish Life in the East
(London, 1881), pp. 12–17.

[8] I can personally corroborate this last observation of Montagu's from my own experience among the Jews of Morocco.

A REPORT ON BLOOD LIBELS IN DAMANHUR, EGYPT (1873–77)

We are taking the liberty of writing you the present report which has no other purpose than to apprise you of a succession of events which have occurred here so that you might see the extent of indignity suffered by your unfortunate brethren in Damanhour (near Alexandria) on account of the barbarities which reign even until now in Egypt.

On the 17th of Heshvan 5634 (November 7, 1873), a child was found cast out into the street with his virile member cut off. The authorities after having made the necessary investigation were able to discover through his father and mother that it had been a dog which had taken off his organ. The child was sent to the local hospital for treatment.

Unfortunately, however, there was present at the Inquiry a native named Bassiouni Bechara,[1] who, together with the local doctor, incited the boy's father to say that it was Rabbi Moses Salomon (the local shohet)[2] who had done this wicked deed in accordance with the custom of the Jews to commit acts of this kind. The father of the boy being in dire poverty and hoping to make a great profit from this consented to their counsel.

As a result, poor Rabbi Moses was summoned before the Moudir (the local magistrate)[3] who wanted to put him in prison before proceeding any further. However, seeing he was depressed by this terrible mishap, he postponed the hearing for three more days, notifying him that he was to present himself together with the rest of the Jews living in Damanhour.

They, therefore, wrote from Damanhour to Baron Jacques Menache Cattaoui of Cairo and to Mr. Ibrahim Piha of Alexandria[4] informing them of this fact. These (two notables) immediately sent dispatches through the Provincial Governor to the Moudir so that he would take no action against the said Rabbi Moses nor threaten him. The Moudir following the dispatches did not prosecute the abovementioned Rabbi, but did demand that he make a deposition in writing to be verified, and the latter complied.

However, Bassiouni Bechara, having exalted himself to the utmost degree, kept seeking to accuse the Jews of some crime, and he indeed succeeded, for on the seventh day of Passover 5637 (April 4, 1877), we

[1] His name indicates that he was a Christian.

[2] Heb., *shōḥēṭ* (ritual slaughter).

[3] Ar., *mudīr* (district administrator). He could, however, act in a judicial capacity.

[4] Concerning these Jewish notables, see Jacob M. Landau, *Jews in Nineteenth-Century Egypt,* Index, *s.v.*

were accused of having killed a little girl and of having cast her body into the latrine of the School.

Then most of the native Turks[5] gathered together and entered the School, beating the Jews who were found there, breaking the ark of the Holy Law, while searching everywhere for the girl. The local Magistrate was present at this incident, but fearing an insurrection dared say nothing. At three in the afternoon the girl was found in the fields. Once again letters were sent to Baron Menache and to Mr. Piha, who pledged themselves to undertake the case without delay; but they have not fulfilled their promises since each one handles it for his own interests and not for the common interest, especially in these cases which concern the honor of all Jews.

In consequence, we are resolved to address this letter to you invoking your assistance, certain that you would wish to grant us that since the local authorities never cease to summon us from time to time for these affairs.[6] We can no longer bear these barbarities in Egypt which is now—one might say—a part of Europe.

Please, sirs, help us and cause this folly to exist no more. God will know how to reward your beneficence.

A letter from Moses Salomon and Moussa Serussi
to the Alliance Israélite Universelle in Paris,
dated September 15, 1879. AIU, Egypte, I.C.1.
The French text is published in Jacob M. Landau,
Jews in Nineteenth-Century Egypt, pp. 199–200.

[5] The writers are using the term "Turks" to refer to the Muslim population.

[6] The Blood Libel was raised against the Jews of Damanhur again in April 1879 and in March 1881. See Landau, *Jews in Nineteenth-Century Egypt*, pp. 200, n. 9, and 203–4.

BIBLIOGRAPHY

ABBREVIATIONS OF JOURNALS AND ENCYCLOPEDIAS

AIEO	*Annales de l'Institut d'Etudes Orientales d'Alger*
BSOAS	*Bulletin of the School of Oriental and African Studies of the University of London*
EI[1]	*Encyclopaedia of Islam,* first edition
EI[2]	*Encyclopaedia of Islam,* new edition
EJ	*Encyclopaedia Judaica,* new English edition
HUCA	*Hebrew Union College Annual*
IJMES	*International Journal of Middle East Studies*
JA	*Journal Asiatique*
JESHO	*Journal of the Economic and Social History of the Orient*
JNES	*Journal of Near Eastern Studies*
JQR	*Jewish Quarterly Review,* old series
JQR n.s.	*Jewish Quarterly Review,* new series
JRAS	*Journal of the Royal Asiatic Society*
Kirjath Sepher	*Kirjath Sepher: Bibliographical Quarterly of the Jewish National and University Library, Jerusalem* [Hebrew]
MGWJ	*Monatsschrift für die Geschichte und Wissenschaft des Judentums*
PAAJR	*Proceedings of the American Academy for Jewish Research*
REI	*Revue des Etudes Islamiques*
REJ	*Revue des Etudes Juives*
Sefunot	*Sefunot. Annual for Research on the Jewish Communities in the East* [Hebrew]
Shalem	*Shalem. Studies in the History of the Jews in Eretz-Israel* [Hebrew]
Tarbiz	*Tarbiz. A Quarterly for Jewish Studies* [Hebrew]
ZDMG	*Zeitschrift des Deutschen Morgenländischen Gesellschaft*
Zion	*Zion: A Quarterly for Research in Jewish History* [Hebrew]
Zion o.s.	*Zion,* old series [Hebrew]

ARCHIVAL AND MANUSCRIPT SOURCES

Geniza Documents

Antonin Collection, Saltykov-Schedrin State Public Library, Leningrad:
Antonin 904

Bodleian Library, Oxford:
Bodl. MS Heb. d 65, f. 9
Bodl. MS Heb. f 56, fs. 129–30

Elkan N. Adler Collection, Jewish Theological Seminary of America, New York:

ENA Unnumbered fragment
Freer Collection, Washington, D.C.:
Gottheil-Worrell XIII
Taylor-Schechter Collection, University Library, Cambridge:
TS 20.180
TS 28.11
TS 13 J 7, f. 29
TS 13 J 11, f. 5
TS Arabic Box 6, f. 1
University Library, Cambridge (Geniza material not in Taylor-Schechter Collection):
ULC Or 1081 J 13

Public Records Office, London

State Papers:
SP 71/21
Foreign Office:
FO 78/405, fs. 32–34 and 201–2b
FO 78/410, fs. 228–31
FO 78/416, fs. 163–64
FO 174/10
FO 174/20
FO 195/162
FO 195/170
FO 195/204, fs. 223 and 223a–b
FO 195/228
FO 195/237
FO 195/369, fs. 82–83
FO 195/394, fs. 80–81, 82, 84, and 95
FO 195/624
FO 195/761
FO 195/808, fs. 279–82
FO 195/866
FO 195/976
FO 195/1010
FO 195/1082

Haus-, Hof- und Staatsarchiv, Vienna

Marokko Karton 3, No. 17

Bibliothèque Royale, Rabat:

MS 277—Muḥammad al-Ḍuᶜayyif al-Ribāṭī, *Ta'rīkh al-Ḍuᶜayyif*

SELECTED PUBLISHED WORKS

(An asterisk indicates that one or more passages from the work cited has been included in Part Two.)

ᶜAbd al-Bāsiṭ b. Khalīl. *al-Rawḍ al-Bāsim.* In *Deux récits de voyage inédits en Afrique du Nord au XVᵉ siecle, ᶜAbdalbasit b. Ḫalil et Adorne.* Edited by Robert Brunschvig. Paris, 1936.*

ᶜAbd al-Wāḥid al-Marrākushī. *Kitāb al-Muᶜjib fī Talkhīṣ Akhbār al-Maghrib* [The History of the Almohades]. Reprint ed., with an English preface by Reinhart P. A. Dozy. Amsterdam, 1968.

ᶜAbd Allāh, Sultan of Granada. *Kitāb al-Tibyān.* In *Islam from the Prophet Muhammad to the Capture of Constantinople* I. Translated by Bernard Lewis. New York, 1974.*

Aboab, Imanuel. *Nomologia o discursos legales compuestos.* Amsterdam, 1629.

Abramson, Shraga. *Ba-Merkāzīm ūva-Tefūṣōt biTqūfat ha-Ge'ōnīm.* Jerusalem, 1965.

Abū Yūsuf, *Kitāb al-Kharāj.* Cairo. 1382/1962–63.*

Abun-Nasr, Jamil M. *A History of the Maghrib.* 2d ed. Cambridge, 1975.

Adler, Cyrus, and Margalith, Aaron M. *American Intercession on Behalf of Jews in the Diplomatic Correspondence of the United States, 1840–1938.* Publications of the American Jewish Historical Society, no. 36. New York, 1943.

Adler, Elkan Nathan, ed. *Jewish Travellers: A Treasury of Travelogues from 9 Centuries.* 2d ed., with a preface by Cecil Roth. New York, 1966.

Altmann, Alexander, and Stern, S. M. *Isaac Israeli: A Neo-Platonic Philosopher of the Early Eleventh Century.* London, 1958.

Amedroz, H. F. "Tales of Official Life from the 'Tadhkira' of Ibn Hamdun, etc." *JRAS,* n.v. (1908).

Andrae, Tor. *Les origines de l'Islam et le Christianisme.* French translation by J. Roche. Paris, 1955.

Andrae, Tor. *Mohammed the Man and his Faith.* Translated by T. Menzel. New York, 1955.

Anon. *Akhbār Majmūᶜa [Crónica Anónima del Siglo XI].* Edited by Emilio Lafuente y Alcántara. Madrid, 1867.*

Anon. *al-Dakhīra al-Saniyya fī Ta'rīkh al-Dawla al-Marīniyya.* Edited by Mohamed Bencheneb. Algiers, 1921.

Arberry, A. J. *Arabic Poetry: A Primer for Students.* Cambridge, 1965.

———, ed. *Religion in the Middle East: Three Religions in Concord and Conflict, I: Judaism and Christianity.* Cambridge, 1969.

Ashtor, Eliyahu. *Histoire des prix et des salaires dans l'Orient médiéval.* Paris, 1969.

———. *The Jews of Moslem Spain.* Vol. 1. Philadelphia, 1973. (Vol. 2 is as yet available only in the Hebrew edition, *Qōrōt ha-Yehūdīm bi-Sfārād ha-Mūslimīt.* Jerusalem, 1966.)

———. "The Number of Jews in Moslem Spain," *Zion* 28 (1963) [Hebrew].

———. "Prolegomena to the Medieval History of Oriental Jewry," *JQR* n.s. 50 (1959–60). 2 pts.

———. "Some Features of the Jewish Communities in Medieval Egypt," *Zion* 30, nos. 1–2 (1965) [Hebrew].

Ashtor-Strauss, Eliyahu. "Saladin and the Jews," *HUCA* 27 (1956). (*See also* under Strauss [-Ashtor].

Assaf, Simha. *Meqōrōt ū-Meḥqārīm be-Tōledōt Yisrā'ēl.* Jerusalem, 1946.*

———. *Teqūfat ha-Ge'ōnīm ve-Sifrūtāh.* Jerusalem, 1955.

———, et al., eds. *J. N. Epstein Jubilee Volume.* Jerusalem, 1950. [Hebrew].

———, Mayer, L. A., et al., eds. *Sēfer ha-Yishūv II: Mi-Yemē Kibbūsh Ereṣ Yisrā'ēl ᶜal Yedē hā-ᶜAravīm ᶜad Masseᶜē ha-Ṣelāv.* Jerusalem, 1944.*

Attal, Robert. *Les Juifs d'Afrique du Nord: Bibliographie.* Jerusalem, 1973.

Avitsur, Shmuel. "Safed—Center of the Manufacture of Woven Woolens in the Fifteenth Century," *Sefunot* 6 (1962) [Hebrew].

Bacharach, Jere L. "The Dinar Versus the Ducat," *IJMES* 4 (1973).

Baer, Yitzhak. *A History of the Jews in Christian Spain.* 2 vols. Philadelphia, 1971.

al-Balādhurī. *Futūḥ al-Buldān.* Edited by Riḍwān Muḥammad Riḍwān. Cairo, 1959.*

Bargebuhr, Frederick P. *The Alhambra: A Cycle of Studies on the Eleventh Century in Moorish Spain.* Berlin, 1968.

Bar Hebraeus, Gregory Abu 'l-Faraj. *The Chronology.* Translated by E. A. Wallis Budge. London, 1932.*

Baron, Salo Wittmayer. *Ancient and Medieval Jewish History.* Edited with a foreword by Leon A. Feldman. New Brunswick, N.J., 1972.

———. *The Jewish Community: Its History and Structure to the American Revolution.* Reprint ed. (in 3 vols.). Westport, Conn., 1972.

———. "The Jews and the Syrian Massacres of 1860," *PAAJR* 4 (1932–33).*

———. *A Social and Religious History of the Jews.* Vols. 3–9. New York and Philadelphia, 1957–65.

———, and Wise, George S., eds. *Violence and Defense in the Jewish Experience.* Philadelphia, 1977.

Bartlett, W. H. *Walks about the City and Environs of Jerusalem.* 2d ed. London, 184?.*

Beaufort, Emily A. *Egyptian Sepulchres and Syrian Shrines, Including a Visit to Palmyra.* London, 1874.

Beinart, Haim. "Fez as Centre of Return to Judaism in the XVI Century," *Sefunot* 8 (1964) [Hebrew].

Beldiceanu, Nicoară. "Une acte sur le statut de la communauté juive de Trikala," *REI* 40 (1972).
Bell, Richard. *The Origin of Islam in its Christian Environment.* London, 1926.
Ben-Arieh, Yehoshua. *The Rediscovery of the Holy Land in the Nineteenth Century.* Jerusalem, 1970 [Hebrew].
Ben-Jacob, Abraham. "Ezekiel's Tomb," *EJ* 6 (1971).
———. *A History of the Jews in Iraq: From the End of the Gaonic Period (1038 C.E.) to the Present Time.* Jerusalem, 1965 [Hebrew].
Ben-Menaḥem, Naphtali. "A Bibliography on Publications on Safed," *Sefunot* 6 (1962).
Ben Ze'ev, Yisra'el. *Ha-Yehūdīm ba-ᶜArāv.* Jerusalem, 1957.
Ben-Zvi, Itzhak. *Eretz-Israel under Ottoman Rule: Four Centuries of History.* 2d ed. Jerusalem, 1966 [Hebrew].
———. *The Exiled and the Redeemed.* Translated by I. Abbady. Philadelphia, 1957.
———. "Two Documents Concerning the Forced Converts of Meshed," *Zion* 4 (1938) [Hebrew].
Benjamin of Tudela. *The Itinerary of Benjamin of Tudela.* Edited and translated by M. N. Adler. London, 1907.*
Bentov, Haim. "Jewish Artisans in Fez during the 17th and 18th Centuries," *Sefunot* 10 (1966) [Hebrew].
Binswanger, Karl. *Untersuchungen zum Status der Nichtmuslime im Osmanischen Reich des 16. Jahrhunderts: mit einer Neudefinition des Begriffes "D̲imma."* Munich, 1977.
Blumenkranz, Bernhard. "Badge, Jewish," *EJ* 4.
Bosworth, C. E. "Buᶜāth," *EI*² 1.
Bowie, Leland. "An Aspect of Muslim-Jewish Relations in Late Nineteenth-Century Morocco: A European Diplomatic View," *IJMES* 7, no. 1 (January, 1976).
Braslavksi, Joseph. "Don Yosef Nasi's Work in Palestine" *Yerushalayim: Journal of the Jewish Palestine Exploration Society* 1 (1928) [Hebrew].
———. "Jewish Settlement in Tiberias from Don Joseph Nasi to Ibn Yaish," *Zion* 5, no. 1 (1940) [Hebrew].
Braudel, Fernand. *The Mediterranean World in the Age of Philip II.* 2 vols. Translated by Siân Reynolds. New York, 1972–73.
Brauer, Erich. *Ethnologie der Jemenitischen Juden.* Heidelberg, 1934.
Brawer, A. I. "Damascus Affair," *EJ* 5.
———. "The Jews of Damascus after the Blood Libel of 1840," *Zion* 11 (1946) [Hebrew].
Brown, Kenneth L., *People of Salé: Tradition and Change in a Moroccan City.* Manchester, 1976.
Browne, Edward G. *A Literary History of Persia III: The Tartar Dominion (1265–1502).* Reprint. Cambridge, 1964.

Brunschvig, Robert. *Deux récits de voyage inédits en Afrique du Nord au XVe siecle, ^cAbdalbasit b. Ḥalil et Adorne.* Paris, 1936.

———. *La Berbérie Orientale sous les Ḥafṣides des origines à la fin du XVe siècle.* 2 vols. Paris, 1940–47.

Buhl, Frants. *Das Leben Muhammeds.* German translation by H. H. Schaeder. Heidelberg, 1930.

al-Bukhārī. *al-Jāmi^c al-Ṣaḥīḥ.* 4 vols. Edited by M. Ludolf Krehl and completed by Th. W. Juynboll. Leiden, 1862–1908.

Burckhardt, John Lewis. *Travels in Syria and the Holy Land.* London, 1822.*

Cahen, Claude. "Dhimma," *EI*² 2.

Canard, Marius. "al-Ḥākim bi-Amr Allāh," *EI*² 3.

"Canonici Hebronensis Tractatus de inventione sanctorum patriarchum Abraham, Ysaac et Jacob" In *Recueil des historiens des croisades: historiens occidentaux.* Vol. 5. Paris, 1895.*

Capsali, R. Eliyahu b. Elqana. *Seder Eliyahu Zuta.* Vol. 1. Edited by Aryeh Shmuelevitz et al. Jerusalem, 1975.

Castries, Henry de, et al., eds. *Les sources inédites de l'histoire du Maroc: Archives et bibliothèques de France.* Second series (7 vols.). Paris, 1922–70.

Cazès, David. *Essai sur l'histoire des Israélites de Tunisie: depuis les temps les plus reculés jusqu'à l'établissement du protectorat de la France en Tunisie.* Paris, 1889.

Cenival, Pierre de; Lopes, David; and Ricard, Robert, eds. *Les sources inédites de l'histoire du Maroc: Archives et bibliothèques du Portugal.* First series (5 vols.). Paris, 1934–51.

Chénier, Louis S. de. *The Present State of the Empire of Morocco.* Vol. 2. London, 1788.

Chouraqui, André N. *Between East and West: A History of the Jews in North Africa.* Translated by Michael M. Bernet. New York, 1973.

———. *Cent ans d'histoire: l'Alliance Israélite Universelle et la renaissance juive contemporaine, 1860–1960.* Paris, 1965.

———. *La condition juridique de l'Israélite marocain.* Paris, 1950.

Clenardus, Nicholas. *Correspondence de Nicolas Clénard.* 3 vols. Edited with a French translation by Alphonse Roersch. Brussels, 1940–41.*

Cohen, A. "Die Wirtschaftliche Stellung der Juden in Bagdad im 10. Jahrhundert," *MGWJ* 79, no. 5 (1935).

Cohen, Amnon. *Ottoman Documents on the Jewish Community of Jerusalem in the Sixteenth Century.* Jerusalem, 1976.

———. *Palestine in the 18th Century: Patterns of Government and Administration.* Jerusalem, 1973.

Cohen, Gerson D. "The Story of the Four Captives," *PAAJR* 29 (1960–61).

Cohen, Hayyim J., and Yehuda, Zvi, eds. *Asian and African Jews in the Middle East, 1860–1971: Annotated Bibliography.* Jerusalem, 1976.

Cohen, Mark Robert. "The Jews under Islam: From the Rise of Islam to

Sabbetai Zevi." In *The Study of Judaism II: Bibliographical Essays in Jewish Medieval Studies.* New York, 1976.
———. *The Origins of the Office of Head of the Jews ("Ra'īs al-Yahūd") in the Fatimid Empire: The Period of the House of Mevorakh b. Saadya, ca. 1064–1126.* Unpublished doctoral dissertation, Jewish Theological Seminary of America, 1976.
Constantelos, Demetrios J. "The Moslem Conquests of the Near East as Revealed in the Greek Sources of the Seventh and the Eighth Centuries," *Byzantion* 42, pt. 2 (1972).
Corcos, David. "The Jews of Morocco under the Marinides," *JQR* n.s. 55, 3 pts. (1964–65).
———. "le-Ofī Yaḥasām shel Shelīṭē hā-al-Muwaḥḥidūn Līhūdīm." *Zion* 32 (1967).
———. "Les Juifs au Maroc et leur mellahs." *Zakhor le-Abraham: Mélanges Abraham Elmaleh.* Edited by H. Z. Hirschberg. Jerusalem, 1972.
———. "Moroccan Jewry in the First Half of the 16th Century," *Sefunot* 10 (1966). [Hebrew].
Creswell, K. A. C. "Architecture," *EI*² 1.
David, Abraham. "Netira," *EJ* 12.
David d'Beth Hillel. *The Travels of Rabbi David D'Beth Hillel from Jerusalem through Arabia, Koordistan, Part of Persia and India to Madras.* Madras, 1832.
Davison, Roderic H. *Reform in the Ottoman Empire, 1856–1876.* New York, 1973.
Dāwūd, Muḥammad. *Mukhtaṣar Ta'rīkh Tiṭwān.* 2 vols. Tetouan, 1955.
Dennet, Daniel C. *Conversion and the Poll Tax in Early Islam.* Harvard Historical Monographs, vol. 22. Cambridge, Mass., 1950.
Dols, Michael W. *The Black Death in the Middle East.* Princeton, 1977.
Dozy, Reinhart. *Dictionnaire détaillé des noms des vêtements chez les arabes.* Amsterdam, 1845.
———. *Die Israeliten zu Mekka von Davids Zeit bis ins fünfte Jahrhundert unserer Zeitrechnung.* Leipzig, 1864.
———. *Supplément aux dictionnaires arabes.* 2 vols. 3rd ed. Paris, 1967.
Eisenberg, J., and Vajda, G. "Ḥizḳīl," *EI*² 3.
Eisenbeth, Maurice. *Les Juifs au Maroc: Essai historique.* Algiers, 1948.
Encyclopaedia of Islam. 1st ed., 4 vols. and *Supplement.* Leiden, 1913–42. New ed., 4 vols., published as of 1978. Leiden, 1960—.
Encyclopaedia Judaica. 16 vols. Jerusalem, 1971.
Engelhardt, Edouard. *La Turquie et le Tanzimat, ou histoire des reformes dans l'Empire Ottoman depuis 1826 jusqu'à nos jours.* 2 vols. Paris, 1882–84.*
Epstein, Isidore. *The Responsa of Rabbi Simon b. Ẓemaḥ Duran as a Source of the History of the Jews in North Africa.* London, 1930.

Fabri, Félix. *Le voyage en Egypte de Félix Fabri, 1483.* 3 vols. French translation by Jacques Masson. Paris, 1975.
Fagnan, E. "Le signe distinctif des Juifs au Maghreb," *REJ* 28 (1894).
Fattal, Antoine. *Le statut légal des non-musulmans en pays d'Islam.* Beirut, 1958.
Finn, James. *Stirring Times, or Records from Jerusalem Consular Chronicles of 1853 to 1856.* 2 vols. Edited by author's widow. London, 1878.
Fischel, Walter J. "Arabische Quellen zur Geschichte der babylonischen Judenheit im 13. Jahrhundert," *MGWJ* 79, no. 4 (1935).
———. "Djahbadh," *EI*² 2.
———. "Ibn Khaldun: On the Bible, Judaism, and Jews." In *Ignace Goldziher Memorial Volume.* Vol. 2. Edited by Samuel Löwinger et al. Jerusalem, 1958.
———. *Jews in the Economic and Political Life of Mediaeval Islam.* With a new introduction by the author on "The Court Jew in the Islamic World." New York, 1969.
———. "Qehillat hā-Anūsīm be-Fāras," *Zion* 1 (1935).
———. "The 'Resh-Galuta' in Arabic Literature." In *Magnes Anniversary Book.* Edited by F. I. Baer et al. Jerusalem, 1938 [Hebrew].
———. "Sassoon," *EJ* 14.
Fraenkel, Siegmund. *Die aramäischen Fremdwörter im Arabischen.* Reprint. Hildesheim, 1962.
Franco, M. *Essai sur l'histoire des Israélites de l'Empire Ottoman depuis les origines jusju'à nos jours.* Paris, 1897.
Frankl, Ludwig August. *Nach Jerusalem.* Reprint. Berlin, 1935.*
Freimann, Aharon, and Hidesheimer, Meir. *Birkat Avraham.* Vol. 1 [= *Berliner Festschrift*]. Reprint. Jerusalem, 1969.
Galanté, Abraham. *Documents officiels turcs concernant les Juifs de Turquie: Recueil de 114 lois, règlements, firmans, bérats, ordres et décisions de tribunaux.* Istanbul, 1931.
García-Gomez, Emilio. "Polémica religiosa entre Ibn Hazm e Ibn al-Nagrila," *al-Andalus* 4 (1936).
Gaudefroy-Demombynes, Maurice. *Mahomet.* Paris, 1956.
———. "Marocain mellāh," *JA* 11, ser. 3 (1914).
Geiger, Abraham. *Judaism and Islam.* Translated by F. M. Young. Reprint. New York, 1970.
Gerber, Jane Satlow. *Jewish Society in Fez: Studies in Communal and Economic Life.* Unpublished doctoral dissertation, Columbia University, 1972.
———. "The Pact of ᶜUmar in Morocco: A Reappraisal of Muslim-Jewish Relations." In *Proceedings of the Seminar on Muslim-Jewish Relations in North Africa.* New York, 1975.
Gil, Moshe. "The Constitution of Medina: A Reconsideration," *Israel Oriental Studies* 4 (1974).

———. *Documents of the Jewish Pious Foundations from the Cairo Geniza.* Leiden, 1976.*
———. The Jewish Quarters of Jerusalem during Early Muslim Rule (634–1099)," *Shalem* 2 (1976) [Hebrew].
———. "The Rādhānite Merchants and the Land of Rādhān," *JESHO* 17, pt. 3 (1974).
Ginzberg, Louis. *Geonica.* Vol. 1. Reprint. New York, 1968.
Goitein, S. D. "Aden: Modern Period," *EJ* 2.
———. "Baᶜayōt Yesōd be-Histōriyya ha-Yehūdīt." *Proceedings of the Fifth World Congress of Jewish Studies.* Vol. 2. Jerusalem, 1972.
———. "The Biography of Rabbi Judah ha-Levi in the Light of the Cairo Geniza Documents," *PAAJR* 28 (1959).
———. "A Caliph's Decree in Favour of the Rabbinite Jews of Palestine," *Journal of Jewish Studies* 5, no. 3 (1954).*
———. "A Deed of Privileges in Favour of the Jews Attributed to Muhammad, of Yemenite Origin," *Kirjath Sepher* 9 (1932–33) [Arabic and Hebrew].*
———. "Elḥanan b. Shemarya as Communal Leader," *Joshua Finkel Jubilee Volume.* New York, 1973.
———. "Geniza Documents from the Mamluk Period," *Tarbiz* 41, no. 1 (October–December 1971).
———. "Geniza Documents on the Transfer and Inspection of Houses," *Revue de l'Occident Musulman et de la Méditerranée,* nos. 13–14 (1973) *[Mélanges Le Tourneau].*
———. *Hā-Islām shel Muḥammad.* Jerusalem, 1956.
———. "Ibn ᶜUbayya's Book Concerning the Destruction of the Synagogue of Jerusalem in 1474," *Zion* 13–14 (1948) [Hebrew].
———. "Jewish Society and Institutions under Islam." In *Jewish Society Through the Ages.* Edited by H. H. Ben Sasson and S. Ettinger. New York, 1971.
———. *Jews and Arabs: Their Contacts Through the Ages.* 3rd ed. New York, 1974.
———. *Letters of Medieval Jewish Traders.* Princeton, 1973.*
———. *A Mediterranean Society: The Jewish Communities of the Arab World as Portrayed in the Documents of the Cairo Geniza.* Vol. 1: *Economic Foundations.* Vol. 2: *The Community.* Berkeley and Los Angeles, 1967–71. Vols. 3 and 4, forthcoming.
———. "New Sources on the Palestinian Gaonate." *Salo Wittmayer Baron Jubilee Volume, on the Occasion of his Eightieth Birthday.* Edited by Saul Lieberman, with Arthur Hyman. Jerusalem, 1975.
———. "The Qayrawan United Appeal for the Babylonian Yeshivoth and the Emergence of the Nagid Abraham Ben-ᶜAta'," *Zion* 27, nos. 2–4 (1962) [Hebrew].
———. "Religion in Everyday Life as Reflected in the Documents of the Cairo Geniza." In *Religion in a Religious Age.* Edited by S. D. Goitein. Cambridge, Mass., 1974.

———. "Shemarya b. Elḥanan: With Two New Autographs," *Tarbiz* 32, no. 3 (1963) [Hebrew].
———. *Studies in Islamic History and Institutions*. Leiden, 1966.
———. "The Time and the Circumstances of the Lamentations of Joseph Ibn Abitur," *Yediot Bahaqirat Eretz Israel Weatjqoteha* 28, nos. 3–4 (1964) [Hebrew].
———. "La Tunisie du XIe siècle à la lumière des documents de la Geniza du Caire," *Etudes d'Orientalisme dédiées à la mémoire de Lévi-Provençal*. Paris. 1962.
Golb, Norman. "Sixty Years of Genizah Research," *Judaism* 6 (1957).
———. "The Topography of the Jews of Medieval Egypt," 2 pts. *JNES* 24 (1965) and *JNES* 33 (1974).
Goldman, Israel M. *The Life and Times of Rabbi David Ibn Abi Zimra: A Social, Economic and Cultural Study of Jewish Life in the Ottoman Empire in the 15th and 16th Centuries as Reflected in the Responsa of RDBZ*. New York, 1970.
Goldziher, Ignaz. "Lā misāsa," *Revue Africaine* 52 (1908).
———. "Mélanges judéo-arabes XIII." *REJ* 45 (1902).
———. *Muslim Studies*. 2 vols. Translated by C. R. Barber and S. M. Stern. London, 1967–71.
———. "Notes et mélanges: renseignements de source musulmane sur la dignité de Resch-Galuta," *REJ* 8 (1884).
Gottheil, Richard. "An Eleventh-Century Document Concerning a Cairo Synagogue," *JQR* 19 (1907).*
———, and Worrell, William, eds. *Fragments from the Cairo Genizah in the Freer Collection*. University of Michigan Studies, Humanistic Series, vol. 13. New York, 1927.*
Graetz, Heinrich. *History of the Jews*. Vol. 3. Philadelphia, 1946.
Grünbaum, M. *Neue Beiträge zur semitischen Sagenkunde*. Leiden, 1893.
Güdemann, Moritz. *Das jüdische Unterrichtswesen während der spanisch-arabischen Periode*. Reprint. Amsterdam, 1968.
Guillaume, Alfred., trans. *The Life of Muhammad: A Translation of Isḥāq's* [*sic*] *Sīrat Rasūl Allāh*. Lahore, 1968.
Halkin, Abraham S. "The Judeo-Islamic Age: The Great Fusion." In *Great Ages and Ideas of the Jewish People*. Edited by Leo W. Schwarz. New York, 1956.
al-Ḥarīzī. *Taḥkemōnī*. Edited by Y. Toporovsky. Tel Aviv, 1952.
Harkavy, Alexander. "Netira und seine Söhne: Eine angesehene jüdische Familie in Bagdad am Anfang des X. Jahrhunderts," *Birkat Avraham*. Vol. 1 [=*Berliner Festschrift*]. Reprint. Jerusalem, 1969 [Hebrew and Arabic].
Heller, Bernard. "al-Sāmirī," *EI*1 4.
Hershman, Abraham M. *Rabbi Isaac ben Sheshet Perfet and His Times*. New York, 1943.
Hesse-Wartegg, Chevallier de. *Tunis: The Land and the People*. 2d ed. London, 1899.*

Heyd, Uriel. *Ottoman Documents on Palestine*. London, 1960.*
———. "Ritual Murder Accusations in 15th and 16th Century Turkey," *Sefunot* 5 (1961) [Hebrew].
———. "Turkish Documents on the Rebuilding of Tiberias in the Sixteenth Century," *Sefunot* 10 (1966) [Hebrew].
Hinz, Walther. *Islamische Masse und Gewichte*. Leiden, 1955.
Hirsch, Daniel, "Rapport sur les écoles et les commaunautés du Maroc," *Bulletin de l'Alliance Israélite Universelle* 1er semestre (1873).
Hirschberg, H. Z. [J. W.]. "Arabic Sources for the History of the Jews in Arabia," *Zion* 10–11 (1945–46) [Hebrew].
———. "Ezekiel in Islam," *EJ* 6.
———. *A History of the Jews in North Africa*. Vol. 1. Leiden, 1974. Vol. 2 is available only in the Hebrew edition, *Tōledōt ha-Yehūdīm be-Afrīqa ha-Ṣefōnīt*. Jerusalem, 1965.
———. "The Jewish Quarter in Muslim and Berber Areas," *Judaism* 17, no. 4 (Fall 1968).
———. *Yisrā'ēl ba-ᶜArāv*. Tel Aviv, 1946.
Horovitz, Josef. "Judeo-Arabic Relations in Pre-Islamic Times," *Islamic Culture* 3 (1929).
Hyamson, Albert M., ed. *The British Consulate in Jerusalem in Relation to the Jews of Palestine, 1838–1914*. 2 vols. London, 1939–41.
———. "The Damascus Affair—1840," *Transactions of the Jewish Historical Society of England* 16 (1952).
Ibn Abī Uṣaybiᶜa. *ᶜUyūn al-Anbā' fī Ṭabaqāt al-Aṭibbā'*. Edited by Nizār Riḍā. Beirut, 1965.
Ibn Abī Zarᶜ. *Rawḍ al-Qirṭās*. French translation by A. Beaumier. Paris, 1860.
Ibn al-Aḥmar. *Rawḍat al-Nisrīn*. Edited and translated into French by C. Bouáli and G. Marçais. Paris, 1917.
Ibn Daud, Abraham. *The Book of Tradition (Sefer ha-Qabbalah)*. Edited with a translation and notes by Gerson D. Cohen. Philadelphia, 1967.*
Ibn Ezra, Moses. *Sēfer Shīrat Yisrā'ēl [Kitāb al-Muḥāḍara wa'l-Mudhākara]*. Hebrew translation by B. Halper. Reprint. Jerusalem, 1966–67.
Ibn al-Fuwaṭī. *al-Ḥawādith al-Jāmiᶜa wa 'l-Tajārib al-Nāfiᶜa*. Edited by Muṣṭafā Jawād. Baghdad, 1932.*
Ibn al-Ḥājj. *al-Madkhal*. Vol. 4. Cairo, 1960.
Ibn Hishām. *al-Sīra al-Nabawiyya*. 2 vols. Cairo, 1375/1955.*
Ibn ᶜIdhārī. *Kitāb al-Bayān al-Mughrib fī Akhbār al-Andalus wa 'l-Maghrib*. Vols. 1–2. Edited by G. S. Colin and E. Lévi-Provençal. Leiden, 1948–51.
Ibn Kammūna. *Examination of the Three Faiths*. Translated by Moshe Perlmann. Berkeley and Los Angeles, 1971.*
———. *Saᶜd B. Manṣūr Ibn Kammūna's Examination of the Inquiries into*

the Three Faiths. Edited by Moshe Perlmann. Berkeley and Los Angeles, 1967.

Ibn Kathīr. *al-Bidāya wa 'l-Nihāya*. Vol. 14. Cairo, 1939.

Ibn Khaldūn. *Kitāb al-ᶜIbar*. Vol. 7. Bulaq, 1284/1867–68.*

Ibn Khurradādhbih. *al-Masālik wa 'l-Mamālik*. Edited by M. J. de Goeje. Leiden, 1889.*

Ibn Muyassar. *Ta'rīkh Miṣr [Annales d'Egypte]*. Edited by Henri Massé. Cairo, 1919.

Ibn Saᶜd. *Kitāb al-Ṭabaqāt al-Kabīr*. Vols. 1–2. Edited by Eduard Sachau et al. Leiden, 1905–17.

Ibn al-Sāᶜī. *al-Jāmiᶜ al-Mukhtaṣar*. Vol. 9. Edited by Muṣṭafā Jawād with Père Anastase Marie. Baghdad, 1934.*

Ibn Shahīn. *The Arabic Original of Ibn Shahin's Book of Comfort*. Edited by Julian Obermann. New Haven, 1933.

———. *An Elegant Composition Concerning Relief after Adversity*. Translated by William M. Brinner. New Haven, 1977.

Ibn Shemuel (Kaufmann), Yehuda, ed. *Midreshē Ge'ulla*. Jerusalem and Tel Aviv, 1953.

Ibn Taghrī Birdī. *History of Egypt, 1382–1469* A.D. Translated by William Popper. University of California Publications in Semitic Philology. Vols. 13, 14, 17, 18, 19, 22, 23, and 24. Berkeley and Los Angeles, 1954–63.

———. *al-Nujūm al-Zāhira*. Vol. 2, pt. 2–Vol. 7. Edited by William Popper. Berkeley, 1909–33.

Ibn al-Ukhuwwa. *Maᶜālim al-Qurba fī Aḥkām al-Ḥisba*. Edited by Reuben Levy. E. J. W. Gibb Memorial Series, n.s., vol. 12. London, 1938.*

Ibn Verga, Shelomo. *Sēfer Shevet Yehūda*. Hanover, 1855.

Idris, Hady Roger. *La Berbérie Orientale sous les Zīrīdes, Xᵉ–XIIᵉ siècles*. 2 vols. Paris, 1962.

———. "Deux maîtres de l'école juridique kairouanaise sous les Zīrīdes (XIᵉ siècle): Abū Bakr b. ᶜAbd al-Raḥmān et Abū ᶜImrān al-Fāsī." *AIEO* 13 (1955).

———. "Les tributaires en Occident Musulman médiéval d'après le ⟨⟨Miᶜyār⟩⟩ d'al-Wanšarīšī." In *Mélanges d'Islamologie: Volume dédié à la mémoire de Armand Abel*. Edited by Pierre Salmon. Leiden, 1974.

Issawi, Charles, ed. *The Economic History of the Middle East, 1800–1914: A Book of Readings*. Chicago, 1966.

al-Jāḥiẓ. *al-Radd ᶜala 'l-Naṣāra*. Edited by Joshua Finkel. Cairo, 1926.*

Jeffery, Arthur. *The Foreign Vocabulary of the Qur'ān*. Baroda, 1938.

Judah ha-Levi. *Judah Hallevi's Kitab al-Khazari*. Translated by Hartwig Hirschfeld. Rev. ed. London, 1931.

Kahana, David. R. *Avraham b. ᶜEzra*. Warsaw, 1894.

Kenaᶜani, Yaᶜaqov. "ha-Ḥayyīm ha-Kalkaliyyīm biṢfāt ūvi-Svivōtēhā be-Mē'a ha-Shesh ᶜEsre ve-Ḥaṣī ha-Mē'a ha-Shevaᶜ ᶜEsre." *Zion* o.s. 6 (1933–34).

Khader, Youcef. *Délivrez la Fidayia!* Algiers, 1970.
Kinglake, Alexander William. *Eothen, or Traces of Travel Brought Home from the East.* Reprint. London, 1911.*
Kobler, Franz, ed. and trans. *A Treasury of Jewish Letters.* 2 vols. Philadelphia, 1953.*
Kraemer, Joel L. "War, Conquest, and the Treatment of Religious Minorities in Medieval Islam." In *Violence and Defense in the Jewish Experience.* Edited by Salo W. Baron and George S. Wise. Philadelphia, 1977.
Kremer, A. von. "Zwei arabische Urkunden," *ZDMG* 7 (1853).
La Faye, Jean Baptiste. *Several Voyages to Barbary.* Translated by John Morgan. London, 1737.*
Landau, Jacob M. *Jews in Nineteenth-Century Egypt.* New York, 1969.*
———. "Ritual Murder Accusations and Persecutions of Jews in 19th Century Egypt," *Sefunot* 5 (1961) [Hebrew].
Lane, Edward William. *The Manners and Customs of the Modern Egyptians.* Reprint. London, 1908.*
Lane-Poole, Stanley. *A History of Egypt in the Middle Ages.* Reprint. London, 1968.
Lempriere, William. *A Tour from Gibraltar to Tangier, Sallee, Mogodore, Santa Cruz, Tarudant, and thence over Mount Atlas, to Morocco: Including a Particular Account of the Royal Harem etc.*, London, 1791.*
Le Tourneau, Roger. *Fez in the Age of the Marinides.* Translated by Besse Alberta Clement. Norman, Oklahoma, 1961.
Leven, Narcisse. *Cinquante ans d'histoire: l'Alliance Israélite Universelle, 1860–1910.* 2 vols. Paris, 1911–20.
Lévi-Provençal, Evariste. *Histoire de l'Espagne Musulmane.* 3 vols. Paris, 1950–67.
Levitats, Isaac. "Oath More Judaico or Juramentum Judaeorum," *EJ* 12.
Lewis, Bernard. "An Apocalyptic Vision of Islamic History," *BSOAS* 13, pt. 2 (1950).
———. *The Arabs in History.* Rev. ed. New York, 1966.
———. "Berātlı," *EI*² 1.
———. *The Middle East and the West.* New York, 1966.
———. *Notes and Documents from the Turkish Archives: A Contribution to the History of the Jews in the Ottoman Empire.* Oriental Notes and Studies of the Israel Oriental Society, no. 3. Jerusalem, 1952.*
———. "On That Day: A Jewish Apocalyptic Poem on the Arab Conquests." In *Mélanges d'Islamologie, Volume dédié à la mémoire de Armand Abel.* Edited by Pierre Salmon. Leiden, 1974.
———, ed. and trans. *Islam from the Prophet Muhammad to the Capture of Constantinople.* 2 vols. New York, 1974.*
Lichtenstadter, Ilse. "Dress of Non-Muslims in Islamic Countries," *Historia Judaica* 5, no. 1 (April 1943).

———. "Some References to Jews in Pre-Islamic Arabic Literature," *PAAJR* 10 (1940).

Light, Henry. *Travels in Egypt, Nubia, Holy Land, Mount Libanon, and Cyprus, in the Year 1814*. London, 1818.*

Littman, David. "Jews under Muslim Rule in the Late Nineteenth Century," *The Wiener Library Bulletin* n.s. 28, nos. 35–36 (1975).*

Löfgren, Oscar, "ᶜAdan," *EI*² 1.

Løkkegaard, Frede. *Islamic Taxation in the Classic Period, With Special Reference to Circumstances in Iraq*. Copenhagen, 1950.

Lourido Díaz, Ramón. *El Sultanato de Sīdī Muḥammad b. ᶜAbd Allāh (1757–1790)*. Cuadernos de Historia del Islam, Serie Monográfica-Islamica Occidentalia, no. 2. Granada, 1970.

Luncz, Abraham Moses, ed. *Jerusalem, Yearbook for the Diffusion of an Accurate Knowledge of Ancient and Modern Palestine*. Vol. 1. Vienna, 1881 [English and Hebrew].

Mahler. Eduard. *Handbuch der jüdischen Chronologie*. Leipzig, 1916.

Maimonides [Moses b. Maimon]. *Epistle to Yemen [Igeret Teman]*. Edited by Abraham S. Halkin, with a translation by Boaz Cohen. New York, 1952.*

———. *Guide of the Perplexed*. Translated by Shlomo Pines. Chicago, 1963.

Mann, Jacob. *The Jews in Egypt and Palestine under the Fāṭimid Caliphs*. 2 vols. in one. Reprinted with preface and reader's guide by S. D. Goitein. New York, 1970.*

———. *Texts and Studies in Jewish Literature*. Vol. 1. Reprinted with an introduction by Gerson D. Cohen. New York, 1972.

Maᶜoz, Moshe. *Ottoman Reform in Syria and Palestine, 1840–1861: The Impact of the Tanzimat on Politics and Society*. Oxford, 1968.

al-Maqrīzī. *Kitāb al-Mawāᶜiẓ wa 'l-Iᶜtibār fī Dhikr al-Khiṭaṭ wa 'l-Āthār*. 2 vols. Bulaq, 1853–54.

———. *Kitāb al-Sulūk li-Maᶜrifat Duwal al-Mulūk*. Vol. 4, pt. 1. Edited by S. ᶜAbd al-Fattāḥ ᶜAshūr. Cairo, 1972.*

Marçais, Georges. *La Berbérie musulmane et l'Orient au moyen âge*. Paris, 1946.

Marcus, Jacob Rader, ed. and trans. *The Jew in the Medieval World: A Source Book: 315–1791*. Reprint. New York, 1974.*

Margoliouth, D. S. *The Relations between Arabs and Israelites Prior to the Rise of Islam*. London, 1924.

al-Marrākushī. *al-Muᶜjib fī Talkhīṣ Akhbār al-Maghrib [The History of the Almohades]*. Edited by Reinhart Dozy. 2d ed. Reprint. Amsterdam, 1968.

Massignon, Louis. "L'influence de l'Islam au moyen âge sur la fondation et l'essor des banques juives." *Bulletin des Etudes Orientales de l'Institut Français de Damas* 1 (1931).

Mayer, L. A. *Mamluk Costume: A Survey*. Geneva, 1952.

———. "The Status of the Jews under the Mamluks." In *Magnes Anniversary Book*. Edited by F. I. Baer et al. Jerusalem, 1938 [Hebrew].
al-Māwardī. *al-Aḥkām al-Sulṭāniyya*. Edited by Maximilian Enger. Bonn. 1853.
Meakin, J. E. Budgett. "The Jews of Morocco," *JQR* 4 (1892).
Menaḥem b. Saruq. *Ha-Maḥberet [Antiquissimum Linguae Hebraicae et Chaldaicae Lexicon a Menahem Ben Saruk]*. Edited by Z. H. Filipowski. London, 1854.
Meshullam b. Menaḥem. *Massāᶜ Meshullām mi-Volterra be-Ereṣ Yisrā'ēl bi-Shnat 5241*. Edited by Abraham Yaᶜari. Jerusalem, 1948.*
Meyers, Allan R. "Patronage and Protection: Notes on the Status of Jews in Precolonial Morocco." Unpublished paper presented at the Association for Jewish Studies Meeting, Boston, Mass., on December 18, 1977.
Mez, Adam. *The Renaissance of Islam*. Translated by Salahuddin Khuda Bakhsh and D. S. Margoliouth. Patna, 1937.
Mingana, A. "A Charter of Protection Granted the Nestorian Church in A.D. 1138, by Muktafi II, Caliph of Baghdad," *Bulletin of the John Rylands Library, Manchester* 10 (1926).
Mirsky, A. "ᶜArkhē ha-Shīra hā-ᶜIvrīt bi-Sfārād." *The Sephardi Heritage* I. Edited by Richard Barnett. New York, 1971.
Mouette, Germain. *Histoire des conquestes de Mouley Archy, connu sous le nom de roy de Tafilet, et de Mouley Ismaël ou Seméin, son frère et son successeur à présent régnant, tous les deux rois de Fez, de Maroc, de Tafilet, de Sus, etc.* Reprinted in *Les sources inédites de l'histoire du Maroc: Archives et bibliothèques de France*. Vol. 2. Second series. Edited by Henry de Castries. Paris, 1924.*
al-Mubarrad. *Kitāb al-Kāmil*. Vol. 1. Edited by W. Wright. Leipzig, 1864.
Müller, Joel. *Teshūvōt Ge'ōnē Mizrāḥ ū-Maᶜarāv*. Reprint. New York, 1958–59.
al-Nāṣirī. *Kitāb al-Istiqṣā' li-Akhbār Duwal al-Maghrib al-Aqṣā*. 9 vols. Casablanca, 1954–56.*
Nedkoff, Boris Christoff. *Die Gizya (Kopfsteuer) im Osmanischen Reich: Mit besonderer Berücksichtigung von Bulgarien*. Leipzig, 1942.
Neubauer, Adolf, ed. *Mediaeval Jewish Chronicles and Chronological Notes*. 2 vols. Oxford, 1887–95 [Hebrew].*
Neusner, Jacob. *A History of the Jews in Babylonia V: Later Sasanian Times*. Leiden, 1970.
Newby, Gordon D. "Observations About an Early Judaeo-Arabic," *JQR* n.s. 61 (1970).
Niebuhr, Carsten. *Travels in Arabia*. Abridged and translated in J. Pinkerton, *A General Collection of the Best and Most Interesting Voyages and Travels in All Parts of the World*. Vol. 10. London, 1811.*
Obadia, Jaré da Bertinoro. "Letter from Jerusalem." In *Letters from the*

Land of Israel. Edited by Avraham Yaari. Ramat Gan, 1971 [Hebrew].*

Obermann, Julian. "Islamic Origins: A Study in Background and Foundation." In *The Arab Heritage*. Edited by Nabih Faris. Princeton, 1944.

Paret, Rudi. *Der Koran: Kommentar und Konkordanz*. Stuttgart, 1971.

———. *Mohammed und der Koran*. Stuttgart, 1957.

———. "Sure 2,256: lā ikrāha fī d-dīni. Toleranz oder Resignation?," *Der Islam* 45 (1969).

Pedersen, Johannes. "Masdjid," *EI*[1] 3.

Pérès, Henri. *La poésie andalouse en arabe classique*. Paris, 1953.

Perlmann, Moshe. "Asnawi's Tract Against Christian Officials." In *Ignace Goldziher Memorial Volume*. Vol. 2. Edited by Samuel Löwinger et al. Jerusalem, 1958.

———. "Eleventh-Century Andalusian Authors on the Jews of Granada," *PAAJR* 18 (1948–49).

———. "The Medieval Polemics between Islam and Judaism," *Religion in a Religious Age*. Edited by S. D. Goitein. Cambridge, Mass., 1974.

———. "Notes on Anti-Christian Propaganda in the Mamlūk Empire," *BSOAS* 10 (1940–42).

———. "Notes on the Position of Jewish Physicians in Medieval Muslim Countries," *Israel Oriental Studies* 2 (1972).

Peters, F. E. *Allah's Commonwealth: A History of Islam in the Near East, 600–1100* A.D. New York, 1973.

Pines, Shlomo. "Un notice sur le Rech Galuta chez un écrivain arabe du IX[e]siècle," *REJ 199–200* (1936).*

Poliak, A. N. "The Influence on Chingiz-Khan's Yāsa upon the General Organization of the Mamlūk State," *BSOAS* 10 (1940–42).

———. "The Jews of the Middle East at the End of the Middle Ages (according to Arabic Sources)," *Zion* 2 (1937) [Hebrew].

———. "Some Notes on the Feudal System of the Mamlūks." *JRAS* n.v. (1937).

Popper, William. *Egypt and Syria under the Circassian Sultans, 1382–1486* A.D.*: Systematic Notes to Ibn Taghrī Birdī's Chronicles of Egypt*. 2 vols. University of California Publications in Semitic Philology (UCPSP). Vols. 15–16. Berkeley and Los Angeles, 1955–57.

Poznanski, Samuel. "Anshē Qayrawān," *Festschrift zu Ehren des Dr. A. Harkavy*. St. Petersburg, 1908.

———. "Die Berechnung des Erlösungsjahres bei Saadja," *MGWJ* 44 (1900).

Prime, William C. *Tent Life in the Holy Land*. New York, 1857.*

al-Qalqashandī. *Ṣubḥ al-Aᶜshā*. 14 vols. Cairo, 1913–19.*

Qimḥī, David. *Pērūsh Sēfer Tehillīm*. Tel Aviv, 1945.

Rafeq, Abdul-Karim. *The Province of Damascus (1723–1783)*. Beirut, 1966.

Raymond, André. "La France, la Grande-Bretagne et le problème de la réforme à Tunis (1855–1857), *Etudes Maghrébines: Mélanges Charles-André Julien*. (Paris, 1964), pp. 137–64.
Reinach, Salomon. "Les Juifs d'Orient d'après les géographes et les voyageurs," *REJ* 18 (1889).
Ricard, Robert. *Les Portugais au Maroc*. Rabat, 1937.
Richardson, Robert. *Travels along the Mediterranean, and Parts Adjacent; in Company with the Earl of Belmore, during the Years 1816–18*. 2 vols. London, 1822.*
Riley, James, *An Authentic Narrative of the Loss of the American Brig Commerce, Wrecked on the Western Coast of Africa, in the Month of August, 1815*. Hartford, 1847.*
Rodinson, Maxime. *Mohammed*. New York, 1974.
Romanelli, Samuel. *Massāᶜ ba-ᶜArāv*. Edited by Jefim [Ḥayyim] Schirmann. In *Ketāvīm Nivḥārīm [Selected Writings of Samuel Romanelli]*. Jerusalem, 1968.
Rosanes, Salomon A. *Histoire des Israélites de Turquie (Turquie, Hongrie, Serbie, Bulgarie, Bosnie, Albanie, et Grèce) et de l'Orient (Syrie, Palestine, Egypte . . .)*. 6 vols.: vol. 1, Tel Aviv, 1930; vol. 2, Sofia, 1937–38; vol. 3, Sofia, 1938; vol. 4, Sofia, 1934–35; vol. 5, Sofia, 1937–38; vol. 6, Jerusalem, 1945 [Hebrew].
Rosen, Lawrence. "Muslim-Jewish Relations in a Moroccan City," *IJMES* 3, no. 4 (October 1972).
Rosenstock, Morton. "Economic and Social Conditions Among the Jews of Algeria: 1790–1848," *Historia Judaica* 18 no. 1 (April 1956).
Rosenthal, Erwin I. J. *Judaism and Islam*. London and New York, 1961.
Roth, Cecil. *The House of Nasi: Doña Gracia*. Philadelphia, 1947.
———. *The House of Nasi: The Duke of Naxos*. Philadelphia, 1948.*
Russell, Alexander. *The Natural History of Aleppo*. Vol. 2. 2d ed. London, 1756.*
Safir, Jacob. *Iben Sāfīr*. 2 vols.: vol. 1, Lyck, 1866; vol. 2, Mainz, 1874 [Hebrew].*
Ṣāᶜid al-Andalusī. *Ṭabaqāt al-Umam*. Edited by L. Cheikho. Beirut, 1912.*
St. John, Bayle. *Two Years' Residence in a Levantine Family*. London, 1850.
al-Samaw'al al-Maghribī. *Ifḥām al-Yahūd*. Edited and translated by Moshe Perlmann. New York, 1964 [= *PAAJR* 32 (1964)].*
al-Samaw'al b. ᶜAdiyā'. *Der Dīwān des as-Samaùal ibn ᶜAdijā'*. Edited by J. W. [H. Z.] Hirschberg. Krakow, 1931.
Samuel ha-Nagid Ibn Naghrēla. *Divan Shmuel Hanagid*. Edited by Dov Jarden. Jerusalem, 1956.
Samuel, Sydney Montagu. *Jewish Life in the East*. London, 1881.*
Sassoon, David Solomon. *A History of the Jews in Baghdad*. Letchworth, 1949.
Schaar, Stuart. "Conflict and Change in Nineteenth-Century Morocco." Unpublished doctoral dissertation, Princeton University, 1965.

Schacht, Joseph. *An Introduction to Islamic Law*. Oxford, 1964.
Schechter, Solomon. "Geniza Specimens: A Letter of Chushiel," *JQR* 11 (1899).
———. *Studies in Judaism*. 2d ser. Philadelphia, 1945.
Scheiber, Alexander. "Fragment from the Chronicle of ᶜObadyah, the Norman Proselyte," *Acta Orientalia Hungarica* 4 (1954).*
Schirmann, Ḥayyim [Jefim]. *ha-Shīra hā-ᶜIvrīt bi-Sfārād ūve-Prōvāns*. 2 vols. (in 4 pts). 2d ed. Jerusalem and Tel Aviv, 1960–61.*
———. "Samuel Han-Nagid, the Man, the Soldier, the Politician," *Jewish Social Studies* 13 (1951).
Scholem, Gershom G. "The Cabbalist Rabbi Abraham Ben Eliezer Halevi," *Kirjath Sepher* 2, nos. 2 and 4 (1925) [Hebrew].
———. *Sabbetai Ṣevi: The Mystical Messiah (1626–1676)*. Princeton, 1973.
———. "Chapters from the History of Cabbalistical Literature, 9: New Researches on R. Abraham b. Eliezer Halevi," *Kirjath Sepher* 7, no. 1 (1930) [Hebrew].
Schreiner, Martin. "Notes sur les Juifs dans l'Islam," *REJ* 29 (1894).
Schwarz, Joseph. *Descriptive Geography and Brief Historical Sketch of Palestine*. Translated by Isaac Leeser. Philadelphia, 1850.*
Semah, Y. D. "Une chronique juive de Fès: Le 'Yahas Fès' de Ribbi Abner Hassarfaty," *Hespéris* 19, fasc. 1–2 (1934).
Serjeant, R. B. "The Constitution of Medina," *The Islamic Quarterly* 8 (1964).
Shaked, Shaul. *A Tentative Bibliography of Geniza Documents*. Prepared under the direction of D. H. Baneth and S. D. Goitein. Paris and the Hague, 1964.
———, ed. *Aspects of Jewish Life under Islam*. Cambridge, Mass.: Association for Jewish Studies, forthcoming.
Shamir, Shimon. "Muslim-Arab Attitudes Toward Jews: The Ottoman and Modern Periods." In *Violence and Defense in the Jewish Experience*. Edited by Salo W. Baron and George S. Wise, Philadelphia, 1977.
Shaw, Stanford J., and Shaw, Ezel Kural. *History of the Ottoman Empire and Modern Turkey*. 2 vols. Cambridge, 1976–77.
Sherira Gaon. *Iggeret [From the Gaonic Period. 2: The Epistle of R. Sherira Gaon, arranged in two versions, originating from Spain and France, with variae lectiones from all the Mss. and Geniza fragments in the world]*. Edited by Benjamin M. Lewin. Haifa, 1921 [Hebrew].
Shorter Encyclopaedia of Islam. Edited by H. A. R. Gibb and J. H. Kramers. Leiden, 1965.
Simon, Marcel. *Verus Israël: Etudes sur les relations entre Chrétiens et Juifs dans l'Empire Romain (135–425)*. Paris, 1964.
Slouschz, Nathan. "La colonie des Maghrabim en Palestine, ses origines et son état actuel," *Archives Marocaines* 2 (1904).

Spiegel, Shalom. "On Medieval Hebrew Poetry." In *The Jews: Their History, Religion, and Culture*. Vol. 2. Edited by Louis Finkelstein. Philadelphia, 1949.

Spuler, Bertold. *The Muslim World, A Historical Survey, II: The Mongol Period*. Translated by F. R. C. Bagley. Leiden, 1960.

Steen de Jehay, le Comte Frédéric van den. *De la situation légale des sujets ottomans non-Musulmans*. Brussels, 1906.

Steinschneider, Moritz. *Die hebräischen Übersetzungen des Mittelalters und die Juden als Dolmetscher*. Berlin, 1893.

Stern, S. M. "Arabic Poems by Spanish-Hebrew Poets." In *Romanica et Occidentalia: Etudes dédiées à la mémoire de Hiram Peri (Pflaum)*. Edited by Moshé Lazar. Jerusalem, 1963.

———. *Fatimid Decrees*. All Souls Studies, vol. 3. London, 1964.*

———. "A Petition to the Fāṭimid Caliph al-Mustanṣir Concerning a Conflict within the Jewish Community," *REJ* 128 (1969).

Stillman, Norman A. "Aspects of Jewish Life in Islamic Spain," *Aspects of Jewish Culture in the Middle Ages*. Edited by Paul E. Szarmach. Albany, 1979.

———. "Charity and Social Service in Medieval Islam," *Societas* 5, vol. 2 (Spring 1975).

———. "The Eleventh-Century Merchant House of Ibn ᶜAwkal (A Geniza Study)," *JESHO* 16, pt. 1 (1973).

———. "Joseph Ibn ᶜAwkal: A Jewish Communal Leader in Eleventh Century Egypt," *The Eleventh Century*. Edited by Stanley Ferber and Sandro Sticca. Acta of the Center for Medieval and Early Renaissance Studies. State University of New York, Binghamton, 1974.

———. "Khilᶜa," *EI²* 5.

———. "The Moroccan Jewish Experience: A Revisionist View." *The Jerusalem Quarterly* 9 (1978).

———. "Muslims and Jews in Morocco: Perceptions, Images, Stereotypes," *Proceedings of the Seminar on Muslim-Jewish Relations in North Africa*. New York, 1975.

———. "New Attitudes toward the Jew in the Arab World," *Jewish Social Studies* 37, nos. 3–4 (1975).

———. "Quelques renseignements biographiques sur Yōsēf Ibn ᶜAwkal, médiateur entre les communautés juives du Maghreb et les Académies d'Irak," *REJ* 132, fasc, 4 (1973).

———. "Recent North African Studies in Israel: A Review Article," *IJMES* 8, no. 3 (July 1977).

———. "Two Accounts of the Persecution of the Jews of Tetouan in 1790," *Michael* 5 (1978).*

———. "Un témoignage contemporain de l'histoire de la Tunisie Ziride," *Hespéris-Tamuda* 13 (1972).*

Stillman, Yedida K. "The Costume of the Jewish Woman in Morocco,"

Aspects of Jewish Folklore. Edited by Dov Noy. Cambridge, Mass.: Association for Jewish Studies (forthcoming).
———. "Libās," *EI*² 5 (forthcoming).
Strauss [–Ashtor], Eliyahu. *A History of the Jews in Egypt and Syria under the Rule of the Mamlūks*. 3 vols. Jerusalem, 1944–70 [Hebrew].
———. "The Social Isolation of Ahl Adh-Dhimma." In *Etudes orientales à la mémoire de Paul Hirschler*. Edited by O. Komlós. Budapest, 1950.
Suriano, Fra Francesco. *Treatise on the Holy Land*. Translated by T. Bellorini and E. Hoade. Publications of the Studium Biblicum Franciscanum, no. 8. Jerusalem, 1949.
al-Suyūṭī. *Ḥusn al-Muḥāḍara fī Ta'rīkh Miṣr wa 'l-Qāhira*. 2 vols. Edited by Muḥammad Abu 'l-Faḍl Ibrāhīm. Cairo, 1968.
al-Ṭabarī. *Ta'rīkh al-Rusul wa 'l-Mulūk [Annales quod scripsit Abu Djafar Mohammed Ibn Djarir at-Tabari]*. 3 pts. 16 vols. Edited by M. J. de Geoje et al. Reprint. Leiden, 1964–65.
Talmage, Frank Ephraim, ed. *Disputation and Dialogue: Readings in the Jewish-Christian Encounter*. New York, 1975.
Terrasse, Henri. *Histoire du Maroc des origines à l'établissement du Protectorat français*. 2 vols. Casablanca, 1949–50.
al-Thaᶜālabī. *ᶜArā'is al-Majālis*. Cairo, 1313/1894–95.
Tobi, Yosef. *The Jews of Yemen in the 19th Century*. Tel Aviv, 1976 [Hebrew].
Toledano, Jacob. *Nēr ha-Maᶜarāv: Hū Tōledōt Yisrā'ēl be-Mārōqqō*. Jerusalem, 1911.
Torrey, Charles Cutler. *The Jewish Foundation of Islam*. New York, 1933.
Tritton, A. S. *The Caliphs and their Non-Muslim Subjects: A Critical Study of the Covenant of ᶜUmar*. Reprint. London, 1970.
———. "Islam and the Protected Religions," *JRAS* n.v. (1927, 1928, and 1931). 3 pts.
Turki, A. "Situation du ⟨⟨Tributaire⟩⟩ qui insulte l'Islam, au regard de la doctrine et de la jurisprudence musulmanes," *Studia Islamica* 30 (1969).
Tyckoczynski, Ḥayyim. "Bustānay Rōsh ha-Gōlā," *Devir* 1 (1923).
al-ᶜUmarī. *al-Taᶜrīf bi 'l-Muṣṭalaḥ al-Sharīf*. Cairo, 1312/1894–95.*
Usque, Samuel. *Consolation for the Tribulations of Israel*. Translated by Martin A. Cohen. Philadelphia, 1965.
Vajda, Georges. *Introduction à la pensée juive du Moyen Age*. Paris, 1947.
———. "Le milieu juif à Baġdād," *Arabica* 9 (1962).
———. ed. and trans. *Recueil de textes historiques judéo-marocains*. Collection Hespéris, no. 12. Paris, 1951.*
Veccia Vaglieri, L. "Fadak," *EI*² 2.
———. "Ḥarra," *EI*² 3.
Vicaire, A., and Le Tourneau, R. "La fabrication du fil d'or à Fès," *Hespéris* 24 (1937).

———. "L'industrie du fil d'or au Mellah de Fès," *Bulletin Economique du Maroc* 3 (1936).
Voinot, L. *Pèlerinages judéo-musulmans du Maroc*. Paris, 1948.
al-Wansharīsī. *Kitāb al-Mi^{c}yār al-Mughrib wa 'l-Jāmi^{c} al-Mu^{c}rib ^{c}an fatāwī ^{c}Ulamā' Ifrīqiya wa 'l-Andalus wa 'l-Maghrib*. 12 vols. Fez, 1314–15/1896–98.
———. "La pierre de touche des Fétwas de Aḥmad al-Wanscharānsī," Abridged French translation by E. Amar. *Archives Marocaines* 12–13 (1908–09).
al-Wāqidī. *Kitāb al-Maghāzī*. 3 vols. Edited by Marsden Jones. London, 1966.*
Watt, W. Montgomery. "Ḥanīf," *EI*^{2} 3.
———. "The Condemnation of the Jews of Banū Qurayẓah: A Study in the Sources of the Sīrah," *Muslim World* 42, no. 3 (July 1952).
———. "al-Ḥudaybiyya," *EI*^{2} 3.
———. *Muhammad at Mecca*. Oxford, 1953.
———. *Muhammad at Medina*. Oxford, 1956.
Wellhausen, Julius, ed. and trans. *Muhammed in Medina: Das ist Vakidi's Kitab al-Maghazi in verkürzter deutscher Wiedergabe*. Berlin, 1882.
———. *Skizzen und Vorarbeiten* 4. Berlin, 1889.
Wellsted, Lieut. J. R., F.R.S. *Travels in Arabia*. Vol. 1. London, 1838.*
Wensinck, Arent Jan. *Muhammad and the Jews of Medina*. Translated and edited by Wolfgang Behn. Berlin, 1975.
———, and Ansari, A. S. Bazmee "Baḳī^{c} al-Gharḳad." *EI*^{2} 1.
Widengren, Geo. "The Status of the Jews in the Sasanian Empire," *Iranica Antiqua* 1 (1961).
Wiet, Gaston. "Bilbays," *EI*^{2} 1.
Yaari, Avraham, ed. *Letters from the Land of Israel*. Ramat Gan, 1971 [Hebrew].*
Yāqūt. *Mu^{c}jam al-Buldān [Jacut's geographisches Wörterbuch]*. 6 vols. Edited by Ferdinand Wüstenfeld. Leipzig, 1866–70.
Yellin, David. "Jewish Jerusalem Three Hundred Years Ago." *Yerushalayim: Journal of the Jewish Palestine Exploration Society* 1 (1928) [Hebrew].
Yerushalmi, Yosef Hayim. "Professing Jews in Post-Expulsion Spain and Portugal," *Salo Wittmayer Baron Jubilee Volume*. Edited by Saul Lieberman, with Arthur Hyman. Jerusalem, 1975.
Zafrani, Haïm. *Etudes et recherches sur la vie intellectuelle juive au Maroc de la fin du 15e au debut du 20e siècle: Première partie. Pensée juridique et environment social, économique et religieux [= Les Juifs du Maroc: Vie sociale, économique et religieuse]*. Paris, 1972.
al-Zawzanī. *Sharḥ al-Mu^{c}allaqāt al-Sab^{c}*. Beirut, n.d.

INDEX

Aaron b. Amram, 36, 176, 259, 267
Aaron b. Baṭash, 79, 81, 281–86
Aaron b. Sarjado, 39
Aaron Ma^{c}afī, 265
^{c}Abbādids, 220
al-^{c}Abbās, 30
Abbasid(s) 29, 30, 33, 34, 35, 41, 68, 242, 275
^{c}Abd Allāh b. ^{c}Abd Allāh b. Ubayy, 134
^{c}Abd Allāh b. Abī Bakr, 124
^{c}Abd Allāh b. Abī Madyan, 279f.
^{c}Abd Allāh b. Abī Najīḥ, 146
^{c}Abd Allāh b. Buluggīn, 217, 225
^{c}Abd Allāh b. Ja^{c}far b. al-Miswar, 122, 129
^{c}Abd Allāh b. Mughīth, 124
^{c}Abd Allāh b. Ruwāḥa, 124
^{c}Abd Allāh b. Sahl, 146
^{c}Abd Allāh b. Salām, 12f., 113–14, 120, 134, 256
^{c}Abd Allāh b. Ṣayf, 119f.
^{c}Abd Allāh b. Sūriyā al-A^{c}war, 119
^{c}Abd Allāh b. Ubayy, 13, 14, 123, 132, 133, 134, 140
^{c}Abd Allāh Aghā Zāde, 392
^{c}Abd Allāh Pasha, 338
^{c}Abd al-^{c}Azīz, 99
^{c}Abd al-Bāsiṭ, 81, 285, 286, 288
^{c}Abd al-Hādī, 342
^{c}Abd al-Ḥaqq b. Abī Sa^{c}īd (Merinid sultan), 79, 81, 281–86
^{c}Abd al-Majīd I, 96, 97, 99, 106,
^{c}Abd al-Malik, 39, 242
^{c}Abd al-Malik b. ^{c}Umayr, 143
^{c}Abd al-Mu'min, 240
^{c}Abd al-Nabi' b. Mahdī, 234, 240
^{c}Abd al-Raḥmān III, 55
^{c}Abd al-Raḥmān b. Ghanam, 157
^{c}Abd al-Raḥmān b. al-Lamghānī, 181
^{c}Abdalīs, 350
Abecasis, Aaron, 367
Abenetar Pimentel, Jacob, 310
^{c}abīd al-Bukhārī, 308, 309
al-Ābilī, 279
Abitbol family, 368–69, 370
Abitbol, M., 370
Abolafia, Moses, 393–95, 396
Abood, Fatholla, 374
Abraham (biblical), 165, 268, 296, 328
Abraham Ibn Daud, 56, 213
Abraham b. Eliezer ha-Levi, 88
Abraham b. Ezra, 41, 76
Abraham b. Muhājir, 57
Abraham b. Zamiro, 81f.
Abū ^{c}Abd Allāh Muḥammad III, 288
Abū ^{c}Abs b. Jabr, 125
Abū ^{c}Alī b. al-Maṣīḥī, 180
Abū ^{c}Awn, 122
Abū Bakr, 14, 130, 131, 143, 147, 231
Abu 'l-Baqā' Yaḥyā b. ^{c}Abbās. *See* Judah b. Abūn
Abu 'l-Barakāt Hibat Allāh b. ^{c}Alī, 229
Abu 'l-Faraj b. Qusāsā, 209
Abu 'l-Faraj b. Ra'īs al-Ru'asā', 254
Abu 'l-Fatḥ al-Baṣrī, 229
Abū Ḥafṣ al-Dimashqī, 153
Abu 'l-Ḥasan b. al-Naqqāsh, 230
Abu 'l-Ḥasan al-Daskarī, 229, 230
Abu 'l-Ḥusayn the Goldsmith, 196

Abū Ibrāhīm b. Sahl al-Tahertī, 183
Abū cImrān al-Fāsī, 63
Abū cImrān Mūsā b. al-Majjānī, 183, 196
Abū cĪsā of Isfahan, 242
Abū Isḥāq of Elvira, 59, 216
Abu 'l-Khayr the Moneychanger, 196
Abu 'l-Khayr al-Tahertī, 184, 185
Abū Laylā al-Māzinī, 134
Abū Lubāba b. cAbd al-Mundhir, 15, 138, 139
Abū Manṣūr al-Tustarī, 195
Abū Muḥammad al-Qāsim, 190–91
Abū Mūsā Hārūn the Jahbadh, 197
Abu 'l-Muẓaffar al-Shahrazūrī, 229
Abū Naṣr, 248
Abū Naṣr Faḍl (Ḥesed) al-Tustarī, 52, 62, 194, 195, 207
Abu 'l-Qāsim b. al-cArīf, 211–12
Abu 'l-Rabīc b. al-Maṭūnī, 221
Abu 'l-Rabīc Sulaymān (Merinid sultan), 79
Abū Rāfic Sallām b. Abi 'l-Ḥuqayq, 17, 134, 135
Abū Sacd Ibrāhīm al-Tustarī, 51, 52, 62, 195, 204, 207
Abū Sacd b. Wahb, 135
Abū Sacīd the Muqqadam, 208
Abū Ṭāhir Abraham, 252
Abū Ṭalḥa, 145
Abū cUbayda b. al-Jarrāḥ, 231
Abū Yacqūb Yusūf, 279–80
Abū Yāsir, 119
Abū Yūsuf, 161, 162
Abū Zikrī Judah, 188
Abū Zikrī Judah b. Sighmār, 195
Abulafia, Ḥayyīm Nissīm, 334–35
Abyssinia, 70, 349
accusation: of blasphemy, 103, 104, 325, 385–87; that Jews sell unfit food to Muslims, 215, 366
Acre, 336, 338, 342, 345, 354
Aden, 247–50, 349–52
Adhricat, 13
cAdiya b. Menasseh, 200
cadleeyeh (*cadliyya*) [coin], 326
cadliyya. *See* cadleeyeh
Adrianople, 89
advisory councils, 98
Afghans, 347
Aghlabid(s), 41
Aghmat (Morocco), 217
cAhd al-Amān (Covenant of Security), 98, 416
ahl al-dhimma, 25, 65, 70, 159–61, 162, 167–68, 257, 269f., 271, 272. *See also dhimmī*(s); People of the Book
Aḥmad b. Taymiyya, 69
Aḥmad al-Ghazzāl, 307
Aḥmad Jazzār Pasha, 338f.
Aḥmad Tawfīq, Ra'īs Pasha, 388
Aḥmad al-Wansharīsī, 83
Ahwaz, 164
cĀ'isha, 142
cAkkāra, 410
Alans, 253
cAlawid(s), 81, 84, 304–5
Alberoce (cloak) [*al-burnus*], 312
alcoholism, 85
Aleppo, 105, 318–21, 338
Alexander Dhu 'l-Qarnayn (Alexander the Great), 230, 253
Alexandria, 35, 38, 63, 74, 105f., 292, 346, 400, 407, 423, 426
Algeria, 77, 78, 96, 99, 305, 416
Algiers, 77, 305, 414, 416
Alhambra, 220, 224
The Alhambra, 53
cAlī b. Abi 'l-Fatḥ, 254
cAlī b. Abī Ṭālib, 7, 30, 31, 130, 137, 145, 159, 256–58
Allah, 7, 14, 15, 19, 20, 25, 59, 71, 113, 114, 115, 116, 118, 119, 120, 121, 122, 123, 124, 125, 126, 127, 128, 129, 130, 131, 132, 133, 134, 135, 137, 138, 139, 140, 141, 142, 143, 144, 145, 146, 147, 148, 149, 150, 151, 153, 157, 158, 159, 161, 165, 169, 170, 176, 178, 179, 181, 182, 189, 190, 217, 218, 219, 220, 222, 223, 229, 230, 231, 232, 255, 256, 257, 258, 271, 272, 273, 274, 275, 276, 280, 281, 282, 283, 284, 286, 288, 301, 329, 357, 371, 392
Alliance Israélite Universelle, 100–1, 409, 410, 411–12, 418, 421
Allūf, 192, 193
Almería, 219
Almohad(s), 61, 76, 77, 78, 240
Almoravid(s), 59f., 78, 217
Almuñecar, 219, 224
Alqama b. Waqqāṣ al-Laythī, 141
Amalek, 235
amān, 25, 255–58
American(s), 105, 330, 353
Ammi, 293
Amidah, 172
Amon, 205
Amoraim, 31, 32, 335
cAmr b. Jaḥḥāsh, 119
cAmr b. Jiḥāsh, 130, 132, 135
cAmr b. Sucdā al-Quraẓī, 139f.
cAmr b. Umayya, 129
cAmram Gaon, 41
cAnan b. David, 32
Anas b. Mālik, 145
al-Andalus. *See* Spain
Andalusian, romanticism in Europe, 53f.

Andrae, Tor, 8, 16
The Annals of Ṭabarī, 230
al-Anqā', 230
ᶜAntar, 230
Ante Atlas mountains, 61
Anti-Christian sentiment, diffused into anti-*dhimmī*, 70, 75
anti-*dhimmī*: decrees, 52, 69, 70, 71, 72, 73, 92, 273–74; propaganda, 72, 106–7, 110, 151, 275–76; sentiment, 66, 69, 70, 71, 73, 75, 76; violence, 69, 70, 73, 75, 76, 103, 104, 390
anti-Jewish: sentiment, 51, 59, 66, 102, 340–41, 388; violence, 51, 59, 66, 75, 76, 77, 79, 80, 81, 87, 101f., 103, 105, 106, 181, 201, 205–6, 213, 225, 235, 251, 254, 263, 278, 281–86, 305, 308–9, 310, 316, 340–41, 342–46, 399–400, 410, 411–12, 417, 427
anti-Semitism, 63, 104f., 106–7, 110, 187, 201f., 249, 251, 263, 291, 305, 325, 403, 426–27
Antioch, 38, 163
Apocalyptic attitudes, 23, 242
Aqaba, Gulf of, 19
al-ᶜAqaba (near Mecca), 9, 10
al-Aqṣā Mosque, 301
Arab conquests, 19, 20, 21, 22–25, 26, 27, 29, 30, 35, 42, 58, 152, 153, 156, 157–58
Arab historians, 28, 71, 81, 85, 100, 230
Arab-Israeli conflict, xvi, xvii, 107, 110, 330
Arabia, 3, 4–17, 19, 21, 23, 24, 99, 113, 115, 117–20, 121, 123, 124, 125, 127, 130, 131, 132, 134, 135, 136, 137, 138, 140, 141, 144, 145, 150, 169, 170, 216, 233–46, 247–48, 249–50, 253, 255–58, 271, 322–23, 347, 348, 349–52
Arabian Peninsula. *See* Arabia
Arabic language, xv, xvi, xviii, xxi, 4, 6, 7, 8, 9, 20, 26, 40, 41, 44, 47, 49, 54, 55, 58, 59, 61, 62, 63, 65, 66, 77, 78, 81, 87, 90, 101, 104, 157, 158, 163, 229, 231, 234–45, 246, 264, 277, 289, 310, 312, 316, 317, 318–19, 320, 326, 342, 351, 392, 409, 418
Arabic literature, 72, 104, 124, 211, 214–16
Arabic poetry, 4, 13, 14, 46, 51, 55, 58, 59, 61, 66f., 71f., 124, 125, 146, 214–16, 275
ᶜArāgī, 322, 323
Aragon, 80
Aramaic language, xviii, xxi, 5, 9, 31
Arari, Aron, 393–98
Arari, David, 393–98
Arari, Isaac, 393–98
Arari, Joseph, 393–98
Arari, Salomon, 393–94
Arbil, 182
Arghūn Khān, 65, 66, 262–63
Armenia(n), 22, 253, 361, 375, 390, 393
Asad b. ᶜUbayd, 139
Asfar, Fatholla, 374
Asfar, Yoosef, 374
aṣḥāb al-khilaᶜ, 50
Ashi, 233
Ashjaᶜ, 132
Ashkenazi, Abraham, 90
Ashkenazi, Eliezer, 90
Ashkenazīm(ic), 85f., 89, 90, 329, 331, 365–66
Ashloma, 165
al-Ashraf Qānṣūh al-Ghūrī, 264
Ashtor, Eliyahu, 54
ᶜAshūrā', 11
Asi, 293
Asia Minor, 330
ᶜĀṣim b. ᶜUmar b. Qatāda, 122, 124, 141
Aslam, 140
asper (Ottoman coin), 293
Asser of Lisbon, 395
astrology, 227, 229, 239–40, 245
Asveh, 253
Atabeg, 249
ᶜAtīka b. al-ᶜĪs b. Umayya, 124
ᶜAṭiyya al-Quraẓī, 143
Atlantic Ocean, 30
Atlas mountains, 315
Attal, Jacob, 316
Augsburg, 330
Australia, 103, 347
Austria(n), 105f., 365, 404, 409, 413
Autevi, Jacob, 393–94
Aws. *See* Banū Aws
ᶜAyn Zaytūn, 344
Ayyūb b. ᶜAbd al-Raḥmān, 143
Ayyubid(s), 50, 52, 61, 67, 68, 74
Azerbayjan, 232
Azuelos, Hm., 367
ᶜAzzāl b. Samaw'al, 143
ᶜAzzāl b. Shamwīl, 120
al-ᶜAzīz (Fatimid Caliph), 200

Bāb al-Mandab, 349
Bāb al-Nūbī, 182, 254
bābūj (slippers), 318
Babylonia (Bāvēl), 29, 31f., 45, 46, 268. *See also* Iraq
Babylonian academies, 29, 31–33, 34, 35, 36, 37, 45, 46, 47, 53, 55f., 171–74, 178–79, 180, 181, 182, 192

Babylonian Jews, 29, 31–33, 34, 45, 48, 185
badges, 26, 63, 68f., 167, 243, 251, 264, 270, 273, 347
*al-Badī*ᶜ, 230
Bādīs (Zirid amir of Ifriqiya), 46
Bādīs b. Ḥabbūs, 212, 214, 217, 218, 219, 220, 221, 222, 223, 224, 225
Badr, Battle of, 13, 122, 124, 230, 231
Badr al-Jamālī, 49
Baer, Abraham Dov, 343–46
Baghdad, 29, 31, 34, 35, 37, 41, 42, 43, 45, 64, 66, 101, 103, 160, 164, 171–75, 176–77, 179, 187, 210, 229, 242, 251, 252–54, 263, 291, 338, 347, 374, 375, 377–83, 388, 389–92
Bahar, Dawood, 374
Bahar, Yoosef, 374
Bahrayn, 19
Baḥrī b. ᶜAmr, 120, 135
Baḥsīta, 318
al-Balādhurī, 153
Balearic Islands, 77
Balḥārith b. al-Khazraj, 136
Balkh, 164
banking, 34, 35, 36, 37, 195, 197, 254, 282, 319, 338, 375, 376, 395, 398, 413–15
Banū ᶜAbd al-Ashhal, 124, 125, 141, 144
Banu Abi 'l-Ḥuqayq, 145f.
Banū ᶜAdī b. al-Najjār, 143
Banū ᶜĀmir, 129
Banū ᶜAmr b. ᶜAwf, 113, 115, 120, 138
Banū ᶜAmr b. Qurayẓa, 143, 144
Banū ᶜAwf, 115, 117
Banū Aws, 9, 13, 15, 115, 118, 119, 130, 132, 138, 140
Banu 'l-Aws, 115, 117
Banū Hadl, 139
Banu 'l-Ḥārith, 115, 117
Banū Ḥāritha, 120, 125, 146, 148
Banū Hārūn. *See* Sons of Aaron
Banū Jarrāḥ, 205–6
Banū Jusham, 115, 117
Banū Kaᶜb b. Qurayẓa, 143
Banū Khazraj, 9, 13, 15, 119, 123, 130, 140
Banū Nabhān, 119, 124
Banu 'l-Nabīt, 115
Banū 'l-Naḍīr, 9, 13, 14, 15, 16, 17, 18, 119, 124, 129–36, 138, 139, 147
Banu 'l-Najjār, 115, 117, 120, 141
Banū Qaynuqā', 9, 13, 15, 119f., 122–23
Banū Qurayẓa, 9, 13, 14, 15, 16, 17, 120, 127, 134, 137–44
Banū Sabtī, 279
Banū Sāᶜida, 115, 117
Banū Shuṭayba, 117
Banū Taghlib, 159
Banū Thaᶜlaba, 117, 119
Banū Umayya b. Zayd, 127
Banū Umm al-Qawm, 139
Banū Zurayq, 120
Bar Hebraeus, xviii–xix, 263
Barbary. *See* Maghreb and North Africa
Barekhū, 193
Barmecide(s), 219
Baron, Salo W., 16, 18, 30, 45
Bartlett, W. H., 333
Bashīr b. ᶜAbd al-Mundhir, 123
Basra, 34, 160, 164, 229, 321
Bassola, Moses. *See* Moses Bassola d'Ancona
Baṭlānīm, 252f.
al-Baṭṭāl, 230
Battle of the Trench, 15, 17, 138, 140
Bavaria, 330
Baybars, 68
Bayezid II, 87
Bechara, Bassiouni, 426
bedel-i askeri (military substitution tax), 97
Bedouin, 14, 15, 17, 18, 19, 23, 44, 47, 205, 410, 414, 418
Beglerbeg 298, 299, 300
Beirut, 107, 395, 403, 404, 405
Bell, Richard, 8
Beluches, 347
Ben Berechiah family, 185, 188
Ben Ezra Synagogue, 74
Ben Guidalla family, 368–69
Ben Nahory, 369
Benaim, Joseph, 364
Benaim, Shalum, 364
Benamor, Solomon, 367
Benghazi, 406, 407
Benider, Jacob, 306
Benjamin al-Nehāwandī, 33
Benjamin of Tudela, 31, 252–54
Benzaquen, Joseph, 367
Benzaquen, Moses, 367
Berab, Jacob, 89
berāt, 93f., 358
beratlıs, 93f.
Berber(s), 54, 56, 57, 61, 78, 79, 81, 86, 211, 212, 213, 214, 223, 234, 304
berberiscos, 81
Berlin, 413, 414, 415
Bēt Dīn, 330, 351f., 382
Bible, 4, 32, 41, 74, 114, 119, 130, 131, 138, 149, 150, 153, 165, 173–74, 203, 209, 213, 226, 229, 233, 234, 236, 237, 239, 244, 252, 254, 257, 259–60, 267, 268, 269, 303, 305, 318, 330, 338–39, 349, 350f., 352, 378, 380, 422

biblical exegesis, 11, 41, 229, 239, 241f., 243, 245, 246, 269, 352
biblical quotations, xviii, 31, 186, 202, 226, 233, 234, 235, 237, 238, 239, 240, 241, 242, 243, 244, 245, 246, 250, 253, 338, 377, 378
Biddulph, William, 318
Bilbays, 277
Bint al-Ḥārith, 141
Bi'r al-ᶜAzab, 322
Bi'r Maᶜūna, 129
Bishr b. Aaron, 36
Bishr b. al-Barā', 148
Bismark, Prince von, 414, 415
Black Death, 73
blood libel, 72, 105–6, 276, 393–402, 426–27
Bohemia, 339
Bombay, 351, 374
boneta (conical hat), 92
Book of Beliefs and Opinions, 41
Book of Comfort, 45
Book of Common Prayer, 377
"bourgeois revolution," 29
Bowen, Harold, 91
Britain (British), 96, 99, 102, 103, 106, 306, 307, 310–11, 316, 317, 341, 349–52, 354–55, 356, 362, 363, 364, 365–66, 367, 368, 370, 371, 375, 377–83, 384, 385–87, 389–92, 399–400, 404, 405, 406–8, 409, 415, 421f.
Buᶜāth, 127, 142
Buharon, David, 406–8
Buharon, Nissim, 406
Buluggīn b. Bādīs, Sayf al-Dawla, 217–19
Buluggīn b. Ḥabbūs, 212
Bulwer, Sir H. L., 362, 389, 405
Bunino, Mōrī Menahem, 352
Burckhardt, John Lewis, 339
al-Burhānī Ibrāhīm, 189–91
al-burnus (cloak), 312
Bustanay b. Ḥaninay, 30
Byzantine Empire, 5, 18, 22, 23, 24, 26, 27, 29, 33, 38, 42, 55, 152, 153, 163, 164, 231, 237f.
Byzantium. *See* Byzantine Empire; Constantinople

Cabra, 219
Cabrera, 224
Caesarea, 23
Caiffa. *See* Haifa
Cairo, 47, 48, 62, 68, 70, 74, 75, 106, 194, 207, 248, 249, 264–66, 277, 285, 324–27
Cairo, Geniza documents, 47f., 52, 56, 154–55, 183–85, 186–88, 189–91, 192–93, 194, 195–97, 198–99, 201–3, 204, 208–10, 247–48, 249–50, 251
Calcutta, 374
caliphate, 25, 28, 29, 30, 33, 38, 42, 43, 51, 54f., 56, 64, 68, 161, 174–75, 178–79, 198–99, 242f., 249, 250, 252, 271, 273
Camondo, Abraham de, 395
Canning, Stratford, 356, 377, 379. *See also* Stratford de Redcliffe
capitulations, 25, 93, 95f.
çapraz (metal whip), 298
caravan travel, 185, 277, 321
Cardozo, Aaron Nuñez, 367
Carmona, 395
Caspian Sea, 164
Castelnuovo, Baron, 421
Castile, 80
catholicos, 29, 30, 165
Cattaoui, Jacques Menache 426–27
Caucasus, 68
census, 299
Chapman, W. D., 407
charitable trust(s), 147, 190, 208–210, 296, 302, 390
charity and social service, 48, 74, 192–93, 195–97, 208–10, 278, 305, 319, 337, 350, 421
China, 34, 90, 143, 163, 164, 347
Chosroes Anushirvan, 231
Christian(s), 5, 6, 8, 10, 12, 18, 19, 20, 21, 22, 23, 24, 25, 27, 34, 35, 50, 54, 55, 59, 61, 62, 65, 68, 69, 70, 71, 74, 77, 80, 82, 84, 90, 93, 94, 96, 98, 99, 101, 102, 103, 104, 105, 106, 110, 149, 150, 151, 153, 154, 157–58, 159–61, 165, 167, 169–70, 180, 200, 231, 253, 259, 260, 262, 263, 264, 266, 271, 272, 273, 277, 278, 287, 294, 301, 308, 318, 319, 321, 325, 333, 336, 338, 354–55, 356, 357–60, 361, 368, 374, 375, 376, 384, 387, 388, 390, 393, 394, 399, 401, 403, 404, 418, 421f., 426
Christian Europe, 38, 47, 53f., 69, 75, 93
Christian influence on Muḥammad, 5, 6, 7, 8
Christianity, 6, 20, 23, 66, 267, 278, 377–83, 422
Church of England Mission to the Jews, 377–83, 421f. *See also* missionaries
Circassian, 70
Civil rights for non-Muslims, 96–101, 109, 357–60, 361, 371–73, 416–17
Clement VII, 291
Clenardus, Nicholas, 80, 287
clothing 20, 26, 50, 62, 63, 68f., 71,

clothing (*continued*)
76, 83, 85, 92, 109, 122, 123, 132, 136, 137, 141f., 157–58, 167, 179, 201, 251, 253, 257, 263, 264, 270, 272, 273, 290, 304, 308–9, 312, 313, 318, 320, 321, 322f., 324, 327, 332, 334, 351, 353, 367, 418, 424
Coen, Aron, 393
Cohen, Abraham, 364
Cohen, Coçio, 391
Cohen, Deborah O., 364
Cohen, Mark R., xvii, 49
Cohen, Mōrī Isaac, 351f.
colonialism, xvi, 93
Commercial Revolution, 29
Conorte, Abram, 393
Constantinople, 22, 23, 33, 88, 90, 91, 96, 97, 102, 106, 163, 291, 337, 358, 360, 362, 364, 365, 374, 377–83, 384, 385, 386, 387, 388, 389, 401, 402, 403, 405, 406, 407, 408
"Constitution of Medina," 11, 115–18
consular correspondence, xviii, 354–55, 356, 365–66, 368, 370, 377–83, 384, 385–87, 389–92, 399–400, 403–5, 406–7, 409, 413–15
consuls, 95f., 98, 102f., 104, 105, 106, 304, 310–11, 317, 341, 345f., 354–55, 356, 362, 363, 364, 365–66, 368, 370, 375, 377–83, 384, 385–87, 389–92, 399, 400, 403–5, 406–8, 409, 413–15, 416, 417
consuls, Jews as, 409
conversion to Christianity, 13, 22f., 390, 421f.
conversion to Islam, 10, 13, 16, 20, 27, 28, 43, 50, 66, 73, 74, 89, 103f., 105, 113–114, 119, 128, 134, 135, 139, 144, 157, 229–32, 247–48, 249–50, 257, 261, 264, 268, 271, 273, 278, 288, 369, 395
conversos. *See* Marranos
Coptic patriarchate, 49, 70, 74
Copts, 39, 49, 70, 73, 75, 325
Corcos, David, 79
Cordova, 53, 56, 57, 60, 156, 211, 212, 245, 292
Corneilhan, Georges, 107
Cornwallis, Charles, 306
corruption of the Scripture, 12, 150, 165f., 239, 269
corsairs, 370, 417
corveé labor, 304, 372
Courbash. *See kırbaç*
court Jew(s). *See* Jewish courtiers
Crémieux, Adolphe, 106, 400, 404, 411
Crusades(ers), 61, 64, 68, 75, 84, 93, 216, 263, 294
Ctesiphon, 29
cultural assimilation, 41, 53f., 58, 78, 104, 107, 110, 312, 313–14, 416
Cyprus, 295, 296–97

dahir, 100, 371–73
Daᶜī, 189–91
Dallata, 342
Damanhur, 426–27
Damascus, 29, 49, 65, 101, 104, 105–6, 164, 200, 289, 293, 296, 298–99, 300, 338, 341, 353, 393–405
Damascus Affair, 105–6, 393–402, 404
Damietta, 337, 423
Daniel (biblical), 165, 235, 237, 238, 239, 241f., 246, 267
Daniel b. Elazar b. Hibat Allāh, 178–79
Daniel b. Ḥasday, 31, 252–53
Daniel b. Samuel Ibn Abi 'l-Rabīᶜ, 181
Daniel, "Foundation of the Yeshiva," 252
Daniel al-Qūmisī, 33
Dār al-Islam (the Domain of Islam), 26, 28, 30, 31, 38, 54, 60, 162, 242, 257, 273
dār al-makhzan (government administrative center), 79
Dār al-Nāqa, 208–10
Darb al-Nabbādhīn, 189–91
Dā'ūd Pasha, 103, 347
David (biblical), 30, 57, 165, 241, 242, 259, 319, 338
David, House of, 29, 30, 36, 50, 176, 243, 252–53
David b. Daniel, 50
David b. Zakkay, 36, 39
David al-Ḥamr, 265
David Ibn Abī Zimra, 91
Dayr al-Qamar, 106
dayyān(īm), 49, 179, 248, 252f.
Dayyān, Mōrī Samuel, 352
de Vidas, Elijah, 352
Declaration of the Rights of Man, 96
decree of ᶜAbd al-Majīd I, 106, 401–2
decree of Muḥammad IV, 100, 371–73
Décret Crémieux, 416
Defterdār Efendi, 299, 301
dei Rossi, David, 292
dei Rossi, Elijah, 291
dei Rossi, Sarah, 292
della Valle, Pietro, 318
Dennett, Daniel, 25
deportation of Jews, 295, 296–97
Derby, Earl of, 413
dhimma, 25, 68, 99, 167–68, 255–58, 270

dhimmīs, 25, 26, 27, 28, 34, 38, 39, 40, 43, 50, 52, 62, 63, 65, 68, 69, 70, 71, 72, 73, 75, 76, 77, 81, 83, 85, 91, 92, 93, 95, 96, 97, 101, 103, 108, 109, 167–68, 180, 251, 255–58, 261, 270, 271–72, 273–74, 288, 304f., 324f., 367, 373
Dhu 'l-Himma, 230
Dhu 'l-Jadar, 132
Dhū Nuwās. *See* Yūsuf Asᶜar Dhū Nuwās
Diḥya b. Khalīfa al-Kalbī, 146
dinar, 20, 37, 74, 135, 175, 184, 188, 195, 196, 197, 200, 207, 209, 210, 243, 248, 251, 277
diplomacy, Jews in 55, 306, 307, 367, 370
dirham, 73, 159, 160, 161, 162, 175, 208, 215, 277, 298
discriminatory tariffs, 27, 34, 43f., 73, 264, 296
Diyar Bakr, 253
Djerba, 410
Docetist heresy, 259
Dombay, Franz von, 309
Dome of the Rock, 296
Draᶜ Valley, 243
dragomans, 264, 310–11, 317, 326, 368f.
Drummond Hay, J. R., 406, 409
Druze, 104, 342–46, 399
ducat, 264, 265, 277
Dukkāla, 368
Dūnash b. Labrāṭ, 55
Dūnash b. Tamīm (Abū Sahl), 44

Ebionites, 7
economic life, 27f., 29, 34–37, 40, 43, 44, 50, 52, 61, 65, 67f., 73, 79, 82, 85f., 89, 92, 93, 99, 101, 110, 122, 160–61, 194, 195–97, 198, 211, 247f., 254, 262, 290, 294, 296, 297, 304, 315, 319, 322, 325, 327, 340, 347, 349, 356, 404, 416, 417, 418, 424
education, 31, 45, 56, 60, 100f., 168, 226–28, 229, 246, 257, 289, 319, 329–31, 337f., 359, 378f., 418, 421
Egypt, 5, 22, 33, 34, 37, 41, 42, 43, 44, 46–53, 54, 61, 62, 67, 68, 70, 71, 73, 74, 75, 76, 81, 87, 88, 98f., 101, 106, 107, 164, 194, 195–97, 201–3, 204, 207, 208–10, 213, 229, 249, 264–66, 267–68, 269–70, 271–72, 273–74, 275–76, 277, 281, 283, 285, 290, 292, 324–27, 329, 347, 349, 351, 355, 371, 420, 426–27
Elazar b. Hilāl b. Fahd, 178
Elazar b. Ṣemaḥ, 252
Elazar the Ḥaver, 252
Eldridge, George J., 405
Elḥanan b. Shemarya, 48f.
Eli b. Zechariah, 182
Eliezer b. ᶜArakh, 289
Elijah (biblical), 289
Elijah b. R. Eli the Ḥāvēr, 208
elitism of Andalusian Jewry, 57, 58–59, 60, 61, 81
Elliot, H. G., 406, 407
Elvira, 156
Emesa. *See* Ḥimṣ
Emicho, 263
Emigrants (*Muhājirūn*), 14, 115, 129, 141, 169, 258
England, 105, 328, 330, 332, 349, 370, 378, 416
English. *See* British
English language, xviii, 310, 316, 317, 350, 378, 379
Ephraim (the *ḥāvēr*), 48
Epistle of Sherīa Gaon, 45
Ethiopia(n), 4, 70, 88, 170, 290, 349, 351. *See also* Abyssinia
ethos of Andalusian Jewish elite, 57, 58, 59, 60, 61, 81
Euclid, 230
Euphrates, 163f.
Europe(an, -s), xv, xvi, xviii, 42, 44, 45, 54, 64, 69, 74, 75, 79, 84, 85, 86, 89, 93, 95–107, 109, 304, 308, 312, 318, 345f., 365, 367, 373, 374, 393–405, 409, 410, 413–15, 416–22, 423, 427
European: interference, 95–107; intervention on behalf of non-Muslims, 96, 103, 104, 109, 389–92, 399–400, 403–5
Examination into the Inquiries of the Three Faiths, 66, 259–60, 261
exilarch (*rēsh galūthā*), xxiii, 29, 30–31, 32, 35, 36, 39, 171–75, 176–77, 189–91, 252–54
exilarchate, xxiii, 29, 30–31, 32, 38, 39, 171–75, 176–77, 252–54
The Experiences of the Nations, 230
Expulsion from Spain and Portugal, 75, 81f., 87, 88, 315
ᶜEyn Yaᶜaqōv, 352
Ezekiel's tomb, 389–92
Ezion-Geber, 349
Ezra (biblical), 151, 165, 259
Ezra, "Counsel of the Yeshiva," 252
Ezrah, Moshi, 374
Ezrah, Yamīn, 375
Ezrah, Yoosef, 375

Fabri, Félix, 74
Fadak, 17, 18, 147, 148
al-Faḍl b. al-Rabīᶜ, 165
Faḍl al-Kōhēn b. al-Shaykh Abu 'l-Karam b. Saᶜdān, 208
Falmouth, 306
Famagusta, 295
faqīh (jurist), 63
Faraj, 376
al-Faramā (Pelusium), 163
Farḥī, Ḥayyīm, 338
Farḥi, Mordohai, 395
Farḥi, Raphael, 395
Farḥī, Saul, 338
Farḥī family, 319, 338
Farnese, Alexander (Pope Paul III), 291
Fars, 164
Father Thomas, 393, 404
Fāṭima, 147
Fatimid(s), 33, 42–53, 74, 198–99, 200, 201–3, 204, 207
Fatimid Empire, 33, 42–53, 198–99, 200, 201–3, 204, 207
fatwā (legal opinion), 83, 284, 302, 386, 387
Fazāra, 15
Ferdinand (Spanish king), 87
Ferrara, 293
feudalism, Middle Eastern, xvi, 64, 68, 96
Fez, 78, 80, 81, 83, 229, 243f., 279, 281–86, 287, 304–5
Fez Jdīd. *See* New Fez
Fi 'l-Zawāya Khabāya, aw Kashf Asrār al-Yahūd (Clandestine Things in the Corners, or Secrets of the Jews Unmashed), 107
Finn, James, 356, 365
Firuz-Shapur, 31
Flemish, 80, 287
Florence, 264, 265, 277
flori, 296
folklore, 19, 45, 79, 86, 106, 290
food, 215, 268, 319, 324, 334, 365–66
forasteros, 81
forced conversion to Islam, 76, 149, 247–48, 359
Fourth Lateran Council, 69
France (French), 96, 99, 100, 104, 105, 106, 107, 163, 164, 245, 318, 361, 363, 389, 399, 400, 404, 414, 416–22
Franco, Abraham, 310
Franco, David, 310
Franco, Jacob, 310
Franco, Joseph, 310
francos, 93, 318
franjīs. See *francos*
Frankish, 163
Frankl, Ludwig August, 335
Franks, 163, 164, 245, 327
French language, 101, 264, 316, 409, 418
Fu'ād Pasha, 403–4
funduq, 80
funeral processions, 26, 158, 201, 304, 313
Fustat, 37, 43, 47, 48, 74, 184, 185, 187, 188, 192–93, 200

Gabbay, Ezekiel, 347
Gabbay, Yūsuf Nissīm, 347
Gabes, 188
Gabriel (angel), 7, 137
Galen, 72
Galician Jews, 329
Galilee, 291, 346
gālūt, 27, 61, 84
Gandersheim, 53
gaon (*geonim*), 31–33, 34, 36, 37, 38, 45, 47, 48, 52, 171–74, 178–79, 180, 181, 182, 183, 184, 185, 187, 192–93, 233f., 252, 254
gaonate, 31–33, 35, 37, 38, 41, 45, 49, 50, 56, 171–74, 178–79, 181, 182
garrison towns, 27, 42
Garsin, Solomon, 410
Gaza, 24, 89
Geiger, Abraham, 8
Gelibite, 294
Georgia, 253
geraldito (skirt), 313
German(s), 53, 329, 331, 335, 339, 342–46, 353, 413–15
German language, 264, 339, 366
Germany, 330
Ghalla, Shawool, 391
gharāma (tribute), 304
Ghaṭāfān, 15, 133, 138
ghetto, 80, 421
ghifāra (cloak), 419
ghiyār (differentiation), 65, 77, 83f., 92, 157–58, 251, 264, 273
Gibb, H. A. R., 91
Gibraltar, 317, 337, 364, 367
Gihon, 253
Ginzberg, Louis, 31
Girgashites, 253
Giṭṭīn, 343
Goitein, S. D., xvii, 8, 10, 29, 46
Goliath, 267
Golz, Count von der, 403
Gourgee, Yussif, 391
government, intervention in Jewish communal affairs, 38–39, 198–99
Graetz, Heinrich, 53f.

Granada, 57, 59, 64, 81, 156, 211, 212, 213, 214–16, 217–25
Great Assembly, 32
Great Synagogue (Synagogue of the Palestinians), 203
Greece, 88, 152, 163, 236, 237f., 278, 361
Greek language, 163, 264
Greek Orthodox(y), 22, 38–39, 106, 153, 404
Green, James, 367
Guadix, 218, 219, 224
Guedalla, Haim, 99f.
Guide of the Perplexed, 41, 237
guilds, 64, 82, 85
Guinea, 370
Gurgan (Gurganites), 164, 253
Gwyn, Peter, 370

Ḥabbūs b. Māksan, 211–212
Hadadrimmon, 205
ḥadith, 17, 271, 338
Hadrian, 235
Ḥafṣids, 67, 77
Haggai the Nasi, 252
Haick. See *ḥā'ik*
Haifa, 345, 354–55, 364
ḥā'ik (enveloping wrap), 312, 313
al-Ḥajjāj b. ᶜAmr, 119
Hajjy Suliman Agha, 384
ḥakam, 9
al-Ḥakam II, 55, 210
ḥākhām bāshī, 38, 97, 289, 318, 319, 321, 334, 335
Ḥākhām Shushan, 342
al-Ḥākim, 52, 63, 201–3
halakha. See Jewish law
"Halbanon" (Hebrew newspaper), 362–63
Hallel, 203
Ham (biblical), 206
Haman, 267
Hamon, Joseph, 92
Hamon, Moses, 92
Ḥananel b. Ḥushiel, 45
Hananiah, Provost of the Levites, 252
Ḥanbalite, 69
ḥanīf(s), 6, 7, 132
Ḥanokh b. Moses, 56, 211
Hanukka, 268
al-Ḥāra al-Kabīra, 410
al-Ḥāra al-Ṣaghīra, 410
ḥārat al-Yahūd, 364, 419
al-Ḥārith b. Aws, 125, 126f.
al-Ḥarīzī. *See* Judah al-Ḥarīzī
Ḥarrat al-ᶜUrayḍ, 127
Harūn al-Rashīd, 165, 219, 275
al-Hārūnī, 275–76
Ḥasan b. Ibrāhīm al-Tustarī, 50
Ḥasday b. Shaprūṭ, 55–56, 210, 211
Ḥasday, "Glory of the Scholars," 252
Hashemite, 6
Hasney Bey, 384
Hatchuel, Sol, 103f.
ḥāvēr (Fellow of the Academy), 48, 252
Hay Gaon, 46, 57, 184, 213
Hayim, Abdolla Faraj, 374
Hayim, Faraj, 374
Hayim, Hiskiel Dawood, 374
Hayta Bashi, 384
Hazael (biblical), 289
ḥazzān(īm), 253f.
Heads of the Yeshivot. *See gaon* (*geonim*); gaonate
Hebrew grammar and lexicography, 41, 44, 55, 226, 238
Hebrew language, xv, xvi, xviii, xxi, 5, 31, 41, 44, 47, 49, 54, 55 57–58, 63, 89, 101, 226, 233–34, 245f., 264, 312, 319, 351, 352, 362–63, 366, 382–83, 408, 411, 418
Hebrew literature, 23, 44, 47, 53f., 55, 56, 57, 58, 60, 61, 213, 226, 229, 330, 338, 362–63, 377, 401
Hebrew poetry, 41, 53f., 55, 57, 58, 60, 61, 76, 192, 205–6, 226, 229
Hebrew printing, 89f., 226, 229, 319, 337, 362–63
Hebron, 23, 152, 291, 296, 331, 336
Hellenic sciences, 29, 36, 40, 71f., 226–28
Hellenism(istic), 29, 35, 54, 61, 64, 109
hellenistic world, 10
Helpers (*anṣār*), 14, 115, 129, 141, 169, 258
Henderson, 406
henna, 313
Heraclius, 22–23, 153
ḥerem (ban), 377–83
Hesse-Wartegg, Chevalier de, 422
Hiba b. Abī Ghālib al-Ṣā'igh, 208
Hijaz, xxiii, 19, 24, 119, 250
Hijra, 8, 129, 230f.
Ḥimṣ (Emesa), 23, 153
Ḥimyar, 4
Ḥīra, 159
Hirschberg, H. Z., 16
Hodges, G. Lloyd, 400
Holland, 330
Host desecration, 79, 105
Hroswitha of Gandesheim, 53
Huammar Pasha, 403f.
al-Ḥudaybiyya, 18, 145
Hülagü Khān, 64

Hürben, 330
Ḥusayn b. ^{c}Alī, 30
Ḥusayn b. Qāsim al-Manṣūr, 322
Ḥushiel b. Elḥanan, 45, 47
Ḥuwayyiṣa b. Mas^{c}ūd, 128
Ḥuyayy b. Akhṭab, 15, 17, 119, 129–32, 133, 134, 135, 137, 138, 141, 142, 143
Hypocrites (*Munāfiqūn*), 11, 13, 119, 123, 132
Hyslop, J. M., 388, 390

Iberian Peninsula. *See* Spain; Portugal
Ibn ^{c}Abbās, 122
Ibn Abī ^{c}Āmir, 211
Ibn Abī Ḥabība, 129
Ibn Abī Turāb, 229f.
Ibn Arieh, 60, 245
Ibn al-^{c}Arīf, 211–212
Ibn Arqam, 222, 223
Ibn al-Athīr, 200
Ibn al-Fuwaṭī, 180, 181, 182, 254
Ibn al-Ḥājj, 72
Ibn Ḥazm, 59
Ibn Hishām, 114, 118, 120, 121, 123, 127, 128, 137, 142, 144, 146, 149
Ibn ^{c}Imrān (the physician), 195
Ibn Isḥāq, 113, 119, 121, 122, 123, 124, 128, 145
Ibn Kammūna. *See* Sa^{c}d b. Kammūna
Ibn Khaldūn, 280
Ibn Khurradādhbih, 164
Ibn Mahdī, 234, 240
Ibn al-Sā^{c}ī, 179
Ibn Salmūn, 248
Ibn Salūbā, 119
Ibn Sanā' al-Mulk, 71f.
Ibn Shāhīn. *See* Jacob b. Nissīm and Nissīm b. Jacob
Ibn Shihāb al-Zuhrī, 142
Ibn Shuway^c, 210
Ibn al-Shuwayḥ, 180
Ibn Sunayna, 128
Ibn Taghrī Birdī, 71
Ibn al-Ukhuwwa, 272
Ibn Umm Maktūm, 137
Ibrāhīm b. ^{c}Aṭā', 46, 57, 63, 183–85, 186–88, 213
Ibrāhīm b. Waqqāṣa, 279, 280
Ibrāhīm Pasha, 388
Ibrāhīm Pasha (son of Muḥammad ^{c}Alī), 104, 329, 342, 355
Ifrīqiya, 41, 42–46, 47, 48, 54, 57, 164, 213. *See also* Tunisia
Ikhshidid(s), 43
^{c}Ikrima, 122
i^{c}lām (decree), 385
Ilkhanid Empire, 65, 66, 68, 81, 262–63
illegitimate Jewish children, 176
Imām, 42, 43, 160, 189, 322, 347
imperialism, xvi, 96, 109
imtiyāzāt. See capitulations
India(n, -s), xv, 3, 44, 47, 96, 103, 163, 164, 229, 247–48, 253, 290, 291, 347, 348, 349, 351, 352, 362, 374
India trade, 3, 44, 163–64, 247–48, 290–92, 349, 351, 374
Indus River, 30, 163
Inquisition, 82, 88
interfaith relations, 62, 63, 65, 86, 104, 149, 169–70, 354–55, 389–92
international trade, 34, 40, 42, 44, 81, 92, 93, 95f., 109, 163–164, 247–48, 249–50, 265, 277, 290, 292, 310, 315–16, 321, 322, 349, 367, 374, 423–24
irade (imperial order), 358
Iran. *See* Persia. *See also* Sasanian Empire
Iraq, 5, 28, 29, 30, 31, 32, 33, 34, 37, 41, 44, 45, 47, 48, 52, 53, 56, 64, 65, 66, 67, 77, 87, 102, 103, 104, 110, 159, 171–75, 176–77, 179, 184, 185, 187, 211, 229, 251, 252–54, 262–63, 347, 374, 375, 377–83, 388, 389–92
Irving, Washington, 53
^{c}Īsā b. Nestorius, 200
Isaac (biblical), 165
Isaac b. Abraham ha-Levi, 229
Isaac b. Leon, 212
Isaac b. Samuel the Spaniard, 208
Isaac b. Sāsōn, 248, 249
Isaac b. Sheshet Perfet, 77
Isaac Gaon, 31
Isaac al-Fāsī, 60, 243
Isaac Ḥāvēr, 289
Isaac Israeli, 44
Isaac Mas^{c}ūd, 289
Isaiah (biblical), 234
Isfahan, 242, 243
Islam, 9, 10, 13, 16, 19, 20, 27, 28, 29, 40, 43, 50, 58, 61, 63, 65, 66, 68, 69, 71, 73, 74, 76, 89, 103f., 105, 108, 113–14, 119, 120, 122, 123, 128, 131, 134, 135, 139, 144, 157, 167, 181, 229–32, 238, 247–48, 261, 264, 269, 271, 273, 276, 282, 284, 288, 312, 325, 361
Islamic civilization, xv, 33, 40, 41, 54, 58, 61, 64, 92, 109f.
Islamic law, 18, 20, 43, 54, 63, 65, 69, 72, 83, 96, 98, 103, 109, 178, 181, 182, 189–91, 201, 249–50, 261, 274, 278, 284, 299, 302, 321, 369, 371, 372, 385–87

Islamic tolerance, 18f., 44, 62, 63, 64, 68f., 77, 78, 91, 108f., 115–18, 157–58, 161, 321, 324f., 338, 347, 357–60, 361, 371–73, 387
Ismāᶜīl b. Barhūn al-Tahertī, 184
Ismaᶜili sect, 42–46
isolation (social, cultural) of Jews, 78, 80f., 87, 322–23, 347
Israel (patriarch), 165, 176
Israel, Joseph, 367
Israel, State of, xvi
Israel al-Nakawa, 352
Istanbul, 92. *See also* Constantinople
Italian, 45, 56, 90, 105, 264–66, 290–92, 353, 413, 415
Italian language, 264, 316, 409, 418
Italy, 33, 42, 75, 89, 163, 164, 211, 291, 292, 318, 330, 352, 409, 413, 415
izār, 167, 273
Izzet Pasha, 365f.

Jabaliyya, 136
Jābir b. ᶜAbd Allāh, 146
al-Jābiya, 163f.
Jacob (biblical), 238, 336
Jacob b. ᶜAwkal, 37
Jacob b. Ḥabīb, 352
Jacob b. Nathaniel Fayyūmī, 233
Jacob b. Nissīm b. Shāhīn, 45
Jacob b. Samuel, 265
Jacob al-Ṭabawiyya, 265
Jaen, 224
Jaffa, 328, 399, 423
Jafna clan, 117
jahbadh(s), 36, 197
al-Jāḥiẓ, 170
Jalfon (Ḥalfon), Azaria, 393–94
Jaqmaq, 71
al-Jār, 163
Jawbar, 289
al-Jawbarī, 72
Jawhar, 43
al-Jazira, 384
Jeremiah (biblical), 267
Jericho, 268
Jerusalem, 11, 25, 38, 58, 74, 88, 89, 92, 98, 101, 106, 144, 154–55, 185, 192–93, 198–99, 213, 245, 264, 267, 269, 278, 291, 292, 301–302, 328, 329–31, 332–33, 334–35, 336, 346, 356, 362, 363, 365–66, 377, 420
Jesus, 13, 151, 165, 232, 236, 238, 259f., 268
Jethro (biblical), 267
Jevdet Pasha, 361
Jewish: apostates, 12f., 89, 103, 113–114, 229–32, 234–45, 247–48, 256–58, 264, 369; collaboration with Muslim invaders, 22–24, 30, 54, 152, 153, 156; communal officials, 38, 43, 46, 48, 49, 50, 52, 55–60, 74, 77, 82f., 97, 99, 154, 171–75, 176–77, 178–79, 180, 181, 182, 183–85, 186–88, 189–93, 198, 200, 201, 208, 233, 247, 248, 249, 252–54, 256, 265, 269–70, 304, 321, 334–35, 347, 358, 361, 395, 398; communal organization, 4, 16, 27, 28, 32, 35f., 37–39, 42, 44, 45f., 49, 52, 55, 56, 58, 67, 74, 81, 90f., 94, 97, 109, 171–75, 176–77, 252–54, 264–66, 304, 357–60, 361; communal strife, 9, 10f., 36, 39, 40, 49, 52, 60, 61, 62, 74, 198–99, 337, 365–66; community moral decline, 74; courtiers, 30, 36, 43, 46, 49–52, 55–60, 61, 62, 63, 65f., 71, 78, 79, 81, 82f., 90, 91, 92, 171–75, 176–77, 189–91, 194, 211–16, 217–25, 262–63, 279–80, 281–86, 288, 316, 319, 322, 338, 395, 413, 418, 425; historiography, 53; homes described, 353; influence on Muḥammad, 6, 7, 8; law, xv, 31, 32–33, 41, 45, 46, 48, 58, 89, 151, 181, 182, 210, 235, 236, 237, 244, 245, 248, 249, 250, 265, 268, 269, 278, 291, 339, 351f., 365–66, 382, 401, 410, 427; merchants, 5, 6, 33, 34, 36, 37, 44, 47, 51, 57, 62, 128, 211, 247, 290, 296, 310, 319, 322, 327, 336, 349, 351, 364, 367, 368, 370, 371, 374, 375, 380, 391, 418, 423–24; merchant class, 34–35, 36f., 81, 99, 198; quarter(s), 24, 59, 62, 79, 154–55, 263, 284, 287, 292, 298, 301, 304, 308–9, 315–16, 318, 322–23, 324–27, 328, 336–39, 364, 368, 378, 388, 393–94, 397, 403, 410, 417, 419, 421; renegades. *See* Jewish apostates; scholars and teachers, 8, 11, 32, 35, 36f., 41, 44f., 47, 48, 50, 53, 56, 57, 60, 65, 76, 81, 89, 91, 113–14, 119, 120, 154, 171–74, 211, 229, 233–46, 252, 292, 336f., 351; tribes, 9, 11, 12 (map), 13, 14, 15, 16, 17, 113, 115, 117, 118, 119–20, 122–24, 127, 129–36, 137–44, 165, 255–58, 268; women described, 313–14, 320f., 332–33, 353, 424
Jews: in agriculture, 3, 9, 19, 28, 86, 134, 147; in government service, 30, 37, 44, 46, 50–52, 54, 55–60, 61, 62, 65f., 79, 81, 168, 200, 211–13, 214–16, 217–25, 262–63, 281–86, 292, 306, 307, 316, 338, 350, 418; in the vizierate, 50, 57f., 65f., 79, 81, 212–213, 214–16, 217–25, 262–63, 281–86

Jews' oath, 72f., 165–66, 267–68. *See also More Judaico*
Jidda, 163
jihād (holy war), 84, 116, 255–58, 283, 284, 286
jinn, 7, 259
Jisr Banāt Ya^c^qūb, 342
jizya, 19, 20, 25, 28, 73, 77, 91, 97, 149, 159–61, 162, 180, 251, 257, 368–69
Joakhin, 260
John the Baptist, 165, 267
Joseph (biblical), 268
Joseph b. Abītūr, 206
Joseph b. Adret (Ibn Ardut), 293–94
Joseph b. Berechiah, 185, 188
Joseph b. Jacob b. ^c^Awkal, 185, 188, 196
Joseph b. Judah Ibn ^c^Aqnīn, 228
Joseph b. Megash, 60, 212, 243f.
Joseph b. Naghrēla (ha-Nagid), 59, 60, 81, 211–13, 217–25
Joseph b. Phinehas, 36
Joseph ha-Kohen, 294
Josiah (biblical), 205
Jubayl, 204
Juda, Moses Benar, 393
Judah (biblical kingdom), 29, 31, 253
Judah b. Abūn, 229
Judah b. Arikha, 265
Judah b. Sa^c^adya, 49f.
Judah b. Samuel, 36
Judah b. Shushan, 77
Judah al-Ḥarīzī, 58
Judah ha-Levi, 60f.
Judaism, xv, 4, 6, 20, 27, 34, 40, 65, 85, 88, 108, 144, 249–50, 264, 268, 278, 282, 312, 367, 382
Judayy b. Akhṭab, 133, 134
Judea, 4, 292
Judeo-Arabic, 4f., 17, 47, 62, 85, 312, 318–19, 352
Judeo-Christian sects, 7
judería(s), 80
Juifs et opportunistes, 107
Jūkhā, 34
Jurjān. *See* Gurgan; Gurganites

Ka^c^b b. Asad, 14, 120, 133, 138, 141, 143
Ka^c^b b. al-Ashraf, 13, 119, 124–27
Ka^c^ba, 7, 58
Kaddish, 173
kāhin(s), 7
al-kāhinān, 9
Kalfun, Abraham, 364
Karaite(s), 32–33, 48, 52, 189, 198–99, 208, 265
Kārim, 248
al-Karkh, 254
al-Karkhī, 230
Karo, Joseph, 89, 352
Kashf al-Asrār (*Unveiled Secrets*), 72
kashrut, 4, 365–66, 423
al-Katība, 147
Katterm, 395
Kaza (district), 98
Kedar, 241
Khadīja, 7
Khālida b. al-Ḥāritha, 113, 114
Khalīfa b. Waqqāṣa (the Elder), 78f., 279–80
Khalīfa the Younger, 78f., 279, 280
Khallād b. Suwayd, 142
Khamlīj, 164
khān, 65, 296
Khanishu (Nestorian patriarch), 39
kharāj, 25, 28, 161, 162, 339, 376
al-Khaṭāra, 277
Khaṭṭ-i Humayun, 97, 98, 99, 357–60, 361
Khaṭṭ-i Sherif of Gülhane, 96–97, 98, 99, 357, 371, 401
Khaybar, 14, 17, 18, 19, 119, 134, 138, 145–49, 230
Khaybarī Jews, 14, 17, 18, 19, 24, 119, 134, 138, 145–49
Khazars, 164
Khazraj. *See* Banū Khazraj
Khorasan, 243, 253
Khurshīd Effendī, 404
Kināna b. al-Rabī^c^ b. Abi 'l-Ḥuqayq, 119, 146, 147
Kināna b. Ṣuwayrā', 120, 130, 134
Kinglake, Alexander William, 341
kırbaq (leather whip), 298, 396, 397
Kirman, 164
Kirmanshah, 36
Kitāb al-Mi^c^yār al-Mughrib, 83
kölemen (Mamluk governors), 347
Koran, 4, 8, 10, 20, 24f., 26, 43, 58f., 83, 119, 149–51, 157, 231, 236, 239, 259, 260, 268, 271, 273, 276, 282, 325, 338, 373
koranic quotations, 7f., 20, 76, 122, 144, 149–51, 259, 268, 272, 276, 282, 325
Kufa, 160, 164
kunya, 271f.
Kurds, 102, 347, 384
Kuzarī, The, 60f.

Labi, Saul, 409
Labīd b. A^c^ṣam, 120
La Faye, Jean Baptiste, 305
Ladino, 313, 318
Lagnado, Joseph, 393, 397

Laḥj, 350
lamentations, 205–6
Landauer, 330
Lane, Edward William, 327
Lateran Council. *See* Fourth Lateran Council
Latin, 44, 54
Layard, A. H., 409
Lebanon, 52, 106, 204
Leghorn. *See* Livorno
Lempriere, William, 314, 315, 316, 317
letter(s) of appointment, 38, 178–79, 182, 269–70, 306
Levant, 43, 46, 68, 75, 88, 93, 104, 105, 109, 110, 354–55
Leven, Narcisse, 100f.
Levi, Aron, 395
Levi, Nathan, 395
Libya, 406–8, 409
Light, Henry, 328
Liniado, Shaool, 374
Lip-Bril, Jechiel Judah, 362–63
Lisbon, 306
Livorno, 352, 409, 413
Loewe, Louis, 346
Løkkegaard, Frede, 25
London, 310, 337, 370, 371, 405, 421f.
Lost Tribes, 290
Lucena, 243
Luria, Isaac, 89
Lurian, I., 391
Lyons, Lord, 365–66

Machpelah, 152
Macnin family, 368–69
maḍbaṭa (report), 392
madīna, 86
al-Madīna al-Bayḍā' (New Fez), 78
Madīnat al-Salām. *See* Baghdad
Madkhal al-Shar[c] *al-Sharīf* (Introduction to the Noble Religious Law), 72
Maḍmūn b. David, 247–48, 249–50
Maḍmūn b. Jacob, 250
madrasa, 65
Mafṭīr, 174
Maghreb, 44, 75, 76–87, 90, 101, 102, 183, 184, 188, 207, 213, 234, 240, 244, 281–86, 304–5, 306, 307, 308–9, 310–11, 312–14, 315–16, 317, 330, 336, 364, 367, 370, 371–73, 406–8, 409, 410, 411–12, 413–15, 416–422
al-Maḥalla, 194
Mahdī, 42
al-Mahdī al-[c]Abbās, 322
Mahdids, 234, 240
al-Mahdiyya, 42, 47
maḥfal (gathering place), 392
maḥkama (Muslim court), 318, 385
Maḥmūd b. Maslama, 145, 147
Maḥmūd b. Sayḥān, 119
maḥya (brandy), 85
Maimon b. Joseph, 244f.
Maimonides, Moses, 41, 50, 53, 71f., 77, 233–46, 248, 249, 250, 276, 289, 291
Mainz, 263
Maksān b. Ḥabbūs, 217, 219, 220, 221
Malabar, 291
Malaga, 156, 211f., 220, 288
al-Malik al-Mu'ayyad, 70, 277
al-Malik al-Mu[c]izz, 240, 249
al-Malik al-Mu[c]izz Ismā[c]īl, 234–45
al-Malik al-Nāṣir, 273
al-Mālik al-Nāṣir Ayyūb, 249
al-Malik al-Ṣāliḥ, 69f., 273–74
Maliki(ism), 63, 78, 85f.
Ma[c]mar b. Rāshid, 129
Mamluk(s), 49, 67–76, 77, 87, 88, 267–68, 269–70, 277, 281, 347
Mamluk Empire, 49, 67–76, 77, 85, 87, 267–68, 269–70, 277
al-Ma'mūn, 275
al-Manṣūr, 29, 71, 183, 240, 242
Maqāmāt of al-Ḥarīrī, 58
Maqna[c], 19
al-Maqrīzī, 71
Mar [c]Uqba, 36
Marāgha, 232
Marḥab, 146, 147
Ma'rib, 9
Markar, Avit, 374
Maronites, 104, 106
Marrakesh, 304, 312, 315–16, 371
Marranos, 82, 88, 90
martyrdom, 77, 103–4, 303
Marwān II, 242
Marwān b. [c]Uthmān b. Abī Sa[c]īd, 148f.
Mary, 151, 165, 259f., 267, 268
Masqat, 103, 347–48, 349
Massignon, Louis, 34
Maṭraḥ. *See* Muttrah
mawālī, 27, 29, 36
Mawlāy Muḥammad. *See* Muḥammad IV
Mawlāy al-Shaykh, 303
Mawlāy Yazīd, 308–9
Mawza[c], 322
Maxims and proverbs, 17, 240, 303, 325, 416
Mecca, 5–12, 18, 19, 124, 130, 131, 138, 144, 145, 170, 236, 290, 420
Meccans, 7, 13, 15, 17, 124, 130, 138, 141, 145, 257
Medicine, Jews in, 44, 46, 49f., 55, 57, 62, 63, 65, 71f., 189–91, 195, 210, 222, 229, 230, 233–46, 247, 249, 250, 262–63, 265, 276, 288, 289, 292

medieval Christian Europe, compared with medieval Islam, 75, 79–80, 85f.
Medina (Yathrib), 8–17, 19, 24, 113, 115, 117, 118, 119–20, 121, 123, 124, 125, 127, 130, 131, 132, 134, 135, 136, 137, 138, 140, 141, 150, 169, 216
Medinese, 9, 10, 12, 13, 14, 15, 16, 18, 115
Mediterranean, 6, 40–63 passim, 64, 88, 163, 183–254 passim, 423
Mehmed Fātiḥ, 358
Meknes, 282
mellāḥ, 79, 80, 81, 83, 86, 284, 287, 304, 308–9, 315–16, 368
Menaḥem b. Sarūq, 55
Menasseh b. Abraham Ibn al-Qazzāz, 200
Mendes, Gracia, 90
Menōrat ha-Mēʾōr, 352
Merinids, 78–81, 84, 279–80, 281–86, 287
Meshed, 76
Meshullam da Volterra, 74f., 266, 277
Mesopotamia, 102, 253
messianism, 23, 42, 60, 85, 88f., 90, 151, 234–45, 247–50, 259, 268, 328, 334, 336, 340, 346
Meᶜullēh, 209–210
Mevorakh b. Saᶜadya, 50
Mez, Adam, 40
Mezwār al-Shurafā', 283–86
Midian, 267
miḥrāb, 301, 392
Mikveh Israel Agricultural School, 101
Milan, 264
military service for *dhimmīs*, 97, 325, 359
millet system, 90, 97, 109, 358, 361
minhag (customary practice), 77, 198
minṭaqa, 167
minting, 315
al-Miqdād b. al-Aswad al-Kindī, 275
Mishnah, 31, 213, 226
Mishne Torah, 41, 250, 291
Miskawayh, 230
missionaries, 101, 104f., 377–83, 422
mithqāl, 162, 257, 303. *See also* dinar
mixed tribunals, 360
mjahdīn (holy warriors), 84
modernization, 95, 97f., 378f., 416
Mogodore, 317, 337, 368–69
Mohammed Damoor, 340–41
Mokha, 322
moneychanging and assaying, 93, 254, 282, 326, 347, 424
moneylending, 85, 93, 151, 193, 254, 292, 417. *See also* banking
Mongol(s), 64, 65, 66, 68, 262–63
Mongolian language, 65
Monophysite(s), 22, 23, 153
Montefiore, Sir Moses, 99f., 106, 371–73, 400, 404
Morpurgo, 413
More, Noel Temple, 362, 366
More Judaico (Jews' oath), 73
Morocco, xv, 60, 61, 76, 77, 78–87, 95, 99, 100, 101, 102, 103f., 217, 229, 243f., 279–80, 281–86, 304–5, 306, 307, 308–9, 310–11, 312–14, 315–16, 364, 367, 370, 371–73, 416f.
Moses (biblical), 32, 113, 131, 165, 166, 176, 232, 233, 240, 243, 252, 257, 267, 268, 269, 334, 338
Moses, Mōrī Menahem, 351
Moses b. Ezra, 58
Moses b. Ḥanokh, 56, 211
Moses b. Jacob b. Isaac al-Isrāʾīlī, 189–91
Moses b. Mevorakh, 50
Moses b. Samuel Ibn Ashqar, 288
Moses Bassola d'Ancona, 289
Moses al-Darᶜī, 243f., 245
Moses Ḥanokh ha-Levi, 352
Moses Marin de Villa Reale, 265
Mosul, 102, 384, 385, 386, 387
Mouette, Germaine, 305
Mount Atlas. *See* Atlas mountains
Mount Lebanon, 104
Mount of Olives, 193
Mozarab(s, -ic), 54
Mu'ayyad al-Dīn Muḥammad b. al-ᶜAlqamī, 181
mu'ayyadī (coin), 277, 298
Mughīth, 156
Muḥammad (Prophet), 3, 4, 5, 6, 7, 8, 9, 10, 11, 12, 13, 14, 15, 16, 17, 18, 19, 20, 21, 22, 25, 30, 84, 113–114, 115, 116, 117, 118, 119, 120, 121, 122, 123, 124, 125, 126, 127, 128, 129, 130, 131, 132, 133, 134, 135, 137, 138, 139, 140, 141, 142, 143, 144, 145, 146, 147, 148, 149, 159, 161, 169, 170, 178, 179, 182, 216, 230, 232, 236, 237f., 239, 241, 253, 255–58, 259, 260, 261, 271, 272, 275, 279, 281, 282, 288, 296, 301, 325, 329, 338, 347, 385–87
Muḥammad IV, 99f., 371, 372
Muḥammad Agha, 301
Muḥammad ᶜAlī, 99, 101, 104, 105–6, 329, 355, 399
Muḥammad Amīn ᶜAlī Pasha, 357–60
Muḥammad Beg, 98
Muḥammad b. ᶜAbd Allāh b. Muhammad b. Rajā, 191
Muḥammad b. Aḥmad b. ᶜĪsā al-ᶜUtbī, 191

Muḥammad b. ᶜImrān al-Sharīf, 281–86
Muḥammad b. Jaᶜfar b. al-Zubayr, 142
Muḥammad b. Maslama, 124–27, 131f., 135, 139f., 146, 147
Muḥammad b. ᶜUmar al-Madā'inī, 165
Muḥammad b. Yaḥyā b. Sahl, 129
Muḥammad al-Ḍuᶜayyif al-Ribāṭī, 309
Muḥammad al-Ṣādiq Beg, 411
Muḥayyiṣa b. Masᶜūd, 128, 148
Muḥtasib (market inspector), 70, 271–72, 324f.
Muḥyi 'l-Dīn Muḥammad b. Faḍlān, 180
al-Muᶜizz (Fatimid caliph), 43
al-Muᶜizz b. Bādīs (Zirid Amir of Ifriqiya), 46, 63
al-Muᶜizz b. Buluggīn, 217, 221, 222
Mukhayrīq, 119, 120, 121
Mulla Muḥammad (*al-Mōsēr*), 103
al-Munfatil, 58f.
Muqātil b. Yaḥyā, 220
al-Muqtadī, 251
Murabṭīn (marabouts), 84
Murad, Shelumo, 391
Murād III, 92
muruwwa, 4, 13, 14, 283
Mūsā b. al-Sabtī, 279, 280
muṣādara (shaking down), 216
al-Musakkan b. Ḥabbūs al-Maghralī, 224
Musellim, 342
music, 14, 136, 153, 227, 254, 320
Muslim religious brotherhoods, 64
Muslim scholars, 43, 59, 63, 65, 69, 70. *See also ᶜulamā'*
Muṣṭafā Muḥammad, 346
Muṣṭafā Nūrī Pasha, 388, 389–92
Muṣṭafā Rashīd Pasha, 96
al-Mustanṣir (Fatimid caliph), 51, 207
Mustaᶜrabīm (Moriscos), 90, 289
al-Mustaᶜṣim, 64
al-Muᶜtaḍid b. ᶜAbbād, 219
al-Muṭallib b. Abī Wadāᶜa b. Dubayra al-Sahmī, 124
al-Muᶜtaṣim b. Sumādiḥ, 219, 222, 223, 224
al-Mutawakkil, 167–68
Muttrah (Maṭraḥ), 347–48
Muwallad(s), 54
mysticism, 44, 85, 89, 352

Nafīsa b. Abī Naṣr al-Dāwūdī, 229
nāgīd, 38, 46, 48, 49, 57, 58, 59, 63, 82, 183–85, 186–88, 213, 233, 264, 265, 269–70, 304
Nahḍa (Revival), 104
Naḥmanides Synagogue, 92, 301–2
Nā'ib Zāde Aḥmad Efendī, 392
Nāᶜim, 145
Najīb al-Ḥājj, 107
Najran, 19, 159
Namias, Rachel, 310–11
Namias, Salom, 310–11
Naqīb al-Ashrāf, 283
nāsī, 29, 55, 56, 252, 347
Nasi, Joseph, 90, 92, 293–94
al-Nāṣir, 178–79
al-Nāṣirī, 100, 373
Nāṣir-i Khosraw, 207
Naṭāh, 147
Nathan ha-Bavlī, 45, 171, 175
Nathaniel Fayyūmī, 233
nationalism, Arab, xvi, 107, 110
nationalism, Jewish, xvi, 107
naturalization, of *dhimmīs* by foreign powers, 96, 413–15
Naûm, Salomon, 364
al-Nāya, 219, 220, 222, 223
Nebuchadnezzar, 165, 235, 267
Negev, 23
Negīd ha-Gōla, 46. *See also nagīd*
Negri, Behor, 395
Nehemiah Ishkafa, 212
Nejd, 19, 144
Nejib Pasha, 380, 381, 382–83
Nessim, Khakham, 391
Nestorian(s) 23, 29, 39
Neṭīra, 35, 36, 171
New Fez, 78, 79, 80, 81, 281–86, 287, 304–5
Newcastle, Duke of, 310
Niebuhr, Carsten, 323
Nissīm b. Berechiah, 185, 188
Nissīm b. Jacob Ibn Shāhīn, 45
Nistārōt shel Rabbī Shimᶜon b. Yoḥay, 23
Normans, 64
North Africa, xvi, 33, 34, 42–53, 55, 60, 61, 64, 75, 76–87, 90, 95, 99, 100, 101, 102, 183, 184, 188, 207, 213, 217, 234, 240, 244, 281–86, 304–5, 306, 307, 308–9, 310–11, 312–14, 315–16, 317, 364, 367, 370, 371–73, 406–8, 409, 410, 411, 413–15, 416–422
Numayla b. ᶜAbd Allāh, 145

Obadiah da Bertinoro, 74, 75, 265
Obadiah the Proselyte, 251
Obediya, Khakham, 391
Old Fez, 78, 79, 80, 287
Oman, 164, 347–48
Ömer, 301
Oppenheim & Co., 413

Ottoman(s), 68, 75, 87–94, 95, 96, 97, 98, 99, 101, 109, 110, 290–92, 293, 295, 296–97, 298–99, 300, 324–27, 334, 336, 337f., 339, 354–55, 356, 357–60, 361, 362, 363, 364, 371–73, 377–83, 384, 385–87, 388, 389–92, 393–405, 406–8, 413–15, 417–22, 426–27
Ovruch, 343
Oxus, 253
Ozer, Yusef, 374

Pacheco da Silva, Michael, 310
Pact of ᶜUmar, 25–26, 62, 63, 69, 85, 157–58, 179, 214, 215, 270, 273–74, 279, 284, 304f.
Padua, 264
Palestine, 5, 11, 19, 22, 25, 29, 33, 34, 38, 47, 48, 49, 52, 53, 58, 60, 61, 68, 74, 75, 85, 88, 89, 90, 91, 92, 98, 101, 106, 144, 154–55, 185, 192–93, 198–99, 205–6, 211, 213, 244, 245, 264, 267, 269, 277, 278, 290–92, 293–94, 295, 296–97, 298–99, 300, 301–2, 328, 329–31, 332–33, 334–35, 336–39, 340–41, 342–46, 352, 356, 362–63, 365–66, 420
Palestian Academy (Tiberian Academy), 33, 47, 48, 49, 50, 53, 184, 201, 211, 213, 252
Palestinian Jews, 24, 30, 33, 34, 49, 89f., 91, 154–55, 185, 192–93, 198–99, 205–6, 278, 293–94, 295, 296–97, 298–99, 300, 328, 329–31, 332–33, 334–35, 336–39, 340–41, 342–46, 356, 365–66
Palmerston, Viscount, 381
pāra, 298
Paret, Rudi, 16, 76
Paris, 100, 400, 409
Party Kings, 56f., 59, 211–13
Passover, 105, 244, 334, 393–402, 426–27
patriarch (*nāsī*), 29, 30, 33
patriarchate (Greek Orthodox), 38, 154, 358
patronage of the arts, 55, 57, 58, 213
The Pen and the Inkwell, 165
People of the Book, 20, 25, 149, 157–58, 159–61, 162, 167–68, 279
persecution of Jews, 63, 73f., 76, 77, 78, 84, 91, 102, 103, 105–6, 109, 241, 247–48, 251, 298–99, 308–9, 310, 316, 323, 347, 350, 369, 393–405, 416
Persia, 32, 36, 65, 66, 76, 101, 102f., 164, 237f., 253, 262–63, 291, 347, 348, 349, 378
Persian(s), 24, 29, 30, 35, 36, 44, 87, 99, 231, 236, 347, 375
Persian Empire, 18, 22, 23, 24, 27. *See also* Sasanian Empire
Persian Gulf, 347, 349
Persian language, xviii, 22, 65, 163
Peters, F. E., 35
petitions, 194, 204, 298–99, 310–11, 362–63, 364, 367, 381, 382–83, 407–8
philosophy, 41, 44, 53f., 60, 66, 226–27, 228, 229, 261
piastres, 353, 417. *See also qirsh*
Piha, Ibrāhīm, 426–27
pilgrimage, Jewish, 391, 420
pious foundation(s). *See* charitable trust(s)
poetry. *See* Arabic poetry; Hebrew poetry
Poland, 330, 336
polarization, between Muslims and non-Muslims, 59, 65–87 passim, 101
polemics, 12f., 66f., 70, 72, 114, 119, 150–51, 214–16, 236, 259–60, 272, 275–76
Polish Jews, 329, 330, 336, 337, 339
political psychology, 79
poll tax, 19, 20, 21, 24, 25, 52, 162, 180, 194, 195–97, 208, 247, 249, 292, 296, 299, 301, 368–69
Polveroso, 265
population estimates, 47f., 54, 74f., 89, 252, 264, 265, 287, 289, 299, 318, 324, 336, 348, 350, 356, 416, 419, 423, 424
population movements, 28, 34, 42, 56, 75, 350
Port Said, 423–25
Portello de Quiras (the Widow), 310
Portugal (Portuguese), 81f., 84, 87, 88, 291, 331
al-pōshēᶜa (renegade), 238, 247
prayerbook, xv, 41, 350
precious metal and stone work(men), 122f., 196, 265, 290, 322, 327, 349
Priego, 219
Prime, William C., 353
prostitution, 74, 267, 327, 424
protection by foreign powers, 93f., 95f., 356, 367, 371, 374, 375, 380, 405, 406–7, 413–15, 416
proto-Zionism, 60–61
Provence (Provençal), 54
Provincial Reform Laws, 97f.
Prussia(n, -s), 346, 365, 403–5, 413–15
Psalms, 319, 338
Pumbeditha, 29, 31–33, 34, 35, 36, 37, 45, 46, 47, 55f., 171–74
Putiel the Ḥazzān, 201

Qā^cat al-Yahūd, 322–23
qāḍī, 69, 103, 181, 182, 189, 190, 191, 201, 208f., 249, 276, 295, 298, 300, 301, 366, 385, 386, 387, 401, 402
Qāḍī al-Fāḍil, 276
qafṭān (caftan), 312
al-qā'id, 220, 315, 368
qalansuwa (conical cap), 157, 167
al-Qalqashandī, 166, 270
al-Qamūṣ, 145f.
Qanāt, 129
Qarawī family, 218–19
Qarawiyyīn Mosque, 283
al-Qāsim b. Ibrāhīm, 177
Qayrawan, 44f., 47, 62, 183, 196
Qays, 135
Qedūsha, 192f.
qibla, 144, 269
qirsh (Turkish piastre), 346, 353, 417
Qubā', 113, 129, 132
al-Qulzum, 163
Quraysh, 6, 18, 115, 116, 118, 122, 124, 130, 138, 141, 145, 257

ra^cāyā (subject population), 97, 359, 361
Rabbanite(s), 33, 48, 49, 52, 60f., 189, 190, 193, 198–99, 208, 269
al-Rabī^c b. al-Rabī^c, 119
Radd ^calā Ahl al-Dhimma, 72, 275–76
Rādhān, 34
Rādhānites, 34, 35, 163–64
Ragusa (Dubrovnik), 291
ra'īs al-Yahūd (head of the Jews), 49, 74, 269–70
Rakakh, Jacob, 265
Ramle, 43, 48, 164, 198–99
Ra's al-Aḥmar, 342
Rassam, Charles, 102f., 384, 386, 387
Ratti-Menton, 105
rāv rōsh (chief scholar), 48f., 56
Rawlinson, H. C., 377, 381
Rayḥāna b. ^cAmr b. Khunafa, 144
receipt for taxes, 28, 369
Reconquista, 59, 64
Red Sea, 349
redemption of captives, 56, 211, 370
Reiyo, 156
Relations between Muslims and Jews. *See* interfaith relations
"Renaissance of Islam," 40
renascence of Hellenistic culture, 29, 109
Representative of the Merchants (*Wakīl al-Tujjār*), 43
representatives of the academies, 32, 37, 47, 48, 173, 183–85, 186–88
Rēshīt ha-Ḥokhma, 352
responsa (*teshūvōt*), 32, 41, 45, 56
restrictions, 25, 26, 33, 38, 68f., 72, 73, 75, 76, 83, 84f., 92, 109, 157–58, 167, 251, 264, 265f., 269f., 271–72, 273–74, 302, 304, 312, 318, 325, 367, 417
Reubenī, David, 88
Rhodes, 401
Rifā^ca b. Qays, 120
Rifā^ca b. Samaw'al al-Quraẓī, 144
Riley, James, 369
Rochford, Earl of, 306, 307
Rome, xv, 4, 237f., 264
Rooben, Hiskiel, 374
Rosales, Jacob, 81f.
Rosetta, 264
Rōsh Kalla (Reshē Kallōt), 174, 192
rōsh ha-qehillōt (head of the congregations), 46, 233
Rōsh Sēder, 252
Rothchild, 371
Rufayda, 140
Russell, Alexander, 321
Russian Jews, 329, 356, 404
Rustum, 231
Rute, Jacob, 81f.
Rute family, 82
al-Ruwā^c b. ^cUmayr, 135

Sa^cadian(s), 81–83, 84
Sa^cadya Gaon, 36, 37, 39, 41, 239, 351
Saba' (biblical Sheba), 3, 233, 253, 259
Sabaeans, 159–61
Sabbatay Ṣevi, 89
Sabbath, 4, 14, 59, 121, 129, 138, 165, 171–74, 213, 214, 224f., 256–57, 268, 276, 292, 298, 304, 309, 319f., 321, 334, 342–43, 349, 350, 377, 378, 421, 423–25
Sabbatianism, 89
Saboraim, 32
Sa^cd b. Abī Waqqāṣ, 231
Sa^cd b. Ḥunayf, 119
Sa^cd b. Kammūna, 66, 260, 261
Sa^cd b. Mu^cādh, 15, 130, 140, 141
Sa^cd b. ^cUbāda, 130, 134
Sa^cd b. Zayd al-Anṣārī, 144
Sa^cd al-Dawla, xviii, 65f., 81, 262–63
ṣadaqa (charity), 162
Ṣadaqa b. Yūsuf al-Fallāḥī, 50
Safavid(s), 87, 291
Safed, 89f., 91, 92, 290–92, 293, 295, 296–97, 298–99, 300, 331, 336, 339, 340–41, 342–46, 352, 356
Ṣaffayn, 196
Safi, 81
Safir, Jacob, 352

Ṣafiyya b. Ḥuyayy, 119, 135, 146, 255
"sages of Qayrawan," 44f.
Sahara, 86
Sahl b. Neṭīra, 36
Ṣāᶜid al-Andalusī, 56, 210
Saᶜīd b. ᶜAbd al-ᶜAzīz, 153
Saᶜīd b. ᶜAwād, 303
Saᶜīd b. Jubayr, 122
Saladin. *See* Ṣalāḥ al-Dīn
Ṣalāḥ al-Dīn, 216, 240, 249, 301
Ṣalāl al-Ṣabbār, 392
Sale, 310
Ṣāliḥ b. Abī Umāma, 124
al-Ṣāliḥiyya, 277
Salīṭ b. Qays, 143f.
Sallām b. Mishkam, 119, 130, 133, 134, 135, 148
Salmā b. Qays Umm al-Mundhir, 143f.
Salomon, Moses, 426
Salonika, 352
Samaritan(s), 23, 69, 159–61, 189, 265, 268, 273
Samarqand, 253
al-Samaw'al b. ᶜAdiyā', 4
al-Samaw'al al-Maghribī, 229–32
al-Sāmirī, 268
Samuel, Sydney Montagu, 425
Samuel b. ᶜAlī Ibn al-Dastūr, 179
Samuel b. ᶜAṭīl, 265
Samuel b. Hoshaᶜna, 201, 203
Samuel b. Isaac, 208
Samuel b. Naghrēla (ha-Nagid), 57f., 60, 211–13
Samuel Gaon, 252–53
Sanᶜa (Sana), 322–23, 347, 351, 352
Sandwith, Thomas B., 364
Sandys, George, 320
Ṣanhāja, 214, 223, 225
Sanhedrin, reconstitution of, 89
sanjaq (subprovince), 98, 299
Sanjaq-Beg, 295, 298
"Saracen(s)," 74, 278
Saragossa, 57, 211
ṣarrāf (banker), 327, 338
Sasanian Empire, 5, 22, 23, 27, 29, 30
Sasone, Benyamin, 391
Sasone, Khakham, 391
Sassoon, David S., 351
Sassoon, Sassoon David, 351
Sassoon family, 103, 351
Saul (biblical), 267
Saul b. Baṭash, 283–84
Sawād, 159, 161
Sayf al-Dīn Sunqur, 249
Sayf al-Islām, 249
ṣayrafī (moneychanger), 326
Schwarz, R. Joseph, 331
science, 55, 62, 71f., 210, 227–28, 288
Sebbagh, Haï, 413–15
Second Temple, 3f., 108
Sefardim, 77, 81, 86, 87, 89f., 90, 289, 329, 342, 365–66
Sēfer Eliyāhū, 23
Sēfer ha-Yeṣīra, 44
Selim the Grim, 87f., 94
Seljuq(s), 49
Sennacherib, 235
Sequerry, S., 367
Seraglio, 319
Serussi, Moussa, 427
Seth, Gregor, 374
Seville, 57, 212, 219
Sfez, Batto, 104
Shāfiᶜī, 189–91
shāᶜir(s), 7
shamla (wrap), 132
Shams al-Dīn, 194
Shamwīl b. Zayd, 120
Shaqq, 147
Sharīf(s, -an), 84, 99, 100, 279, 281, 282, 284, 285, 286, 293
shāsh (turban cloth), 318
al-Shaykh al-Imām al-Sharīf, 284
Shaykh al-Islām, 189, 386, 387
shaykh al-Yahūd, 38, 82, 304
Shaykh Yaḥyā, 303
Sheba. *See* Saba'
Shem Tov al-Furanī, 289
Shemarya b. Elḥanan, 47, 48
Sherif Pasha, 393, 396, 399
Sherira Gaon, 37, 45
sheshia, 418
Shiᶜb al-ᶜAjūz, 126
shield of David, 334, 423
Shiᶜite, 33, 35, 42–46, 65, 176–77
Shuᶜba b. al-Ḥajjāj, 143
Shujaᶜ b. Aslam, 230
Shukur, Isaac, 374
Shukur, Ruben, 374
Shulḥān ᶜArūkh, 89, 352
Siberia, 253
Sicilians, 289
Sicily, 64, 75, 213
Sīdī Abū ᶜAbd Allāh Muḥammad, 283
Sīdī Abū ᶜAbd Allāh Muḥammad al-Qawrī, 284
Sīdī Muḥammad b. ᶜAbd Allāh, 307, 308, 316
Sīdnā ᶜUmar Mosque, 301
Sidon, 354–55, 399
Sijilmasa, 188
Silkān b. Salāma, Abū Nā'ila, 125–26
Silsila b. Barhām, 120
Silwan, 154
Sima, Yacoob, 374
Simon b. Ṣemaḥ Duran, 77
Simsār, 375
Sinai, 23, 165, 238, 257, 267

Sind, 163, 164
sin'ūth ("anti-Semitism"), 63, 187
Sinyēl (Shinkali?), 291
Sīra, 20, 113–14, 115–18, 119–20, 121, 122–23, 124–27, 128, 137–44, 145–49
Sisera, 235
Sitt al-Ahl b. Faḍl al-Kōhēn, 208
Slav(s), 54, 56, 164
Slavonic, 163
Sodom, 268
Sofer, Shelumo, 391
Solicofre, John Leonard, 310
Solomon (biblical), 3, 245, 259
Solomon b. Danān, 303
Solomon b. Joseph, 265
Solomon b. Judah (the Younger), 193
Solomon Ibn Yaᶜīsh, 90, 92
Solyman Hallak, 396
"Songs of Zion," 60
Sons of Aaron (Banū Hārūn), 9, 36, 37, 130, 133
Sons of Neṭīra, 36, 37
Soomekh, Ibrahim, 375
Sophronios, 25
Sowdai, Dawood, 391
Spain, 24, 34, 41, 42, 44, 53–61, 64, 75, 77, 81f., 87, 88, 156, 164, 185, 210, 211–13, 214–16, 217–25, 234, 240, 243f., 245, 264, 288, 294, 308, 332, 336, 352, 371, 417
Spain, Christian, 55, 61, 75, 81f., 87, 88
Spaniard(s), Spanish, 31, 53–61, 76, 264, 335, 337, 370, 416
Spanish language, 81, 163, 312, 313, 315f., 334
Spanish-Moroccan War, 371
St. Jeremiah (Abu Ghosh), 328
Steinschneider, Moritz, 53f.
stereotypes, 79, 80
Stern, the Rev. Mr., 378, 379
Sternshuss, the Rev. Mr., 378, 379
Stratford de Redcliffe, 384, 385, 386, 387
su-başı, 299
Sublime Porte (Ottoman court), 91f., 96, 97, 295, 300, 301, 358, 359, 362, 363, 378, 380, 381, 385–87, 388, 402, 407, 414
Sudan(-ese), 51
Suez Canal, 423
Sufi, 84, 291
suftajas, 37
Sukkot, 187, 268
al-Sulālim, 146, 147
Sulaymān Pasha, 338
Sulaymān the Magnificent, 291, 293
sumptuary laws, 26, 63, 68f., 71, 76, 83, 85, 92, 109, 157–58, 167, 243, 251, 264, 273, 304, 312, 318, 367
sunna, 25, 373
sūq al-zahra (jewel bazaar), 418
Sura, Academy of, 29, 31–33, 34, 36, 37, 45, 46, 47, 55f., 171–74
Surat, 374
Suriano, Fra Francesco, 278
Sūs, 164, 315
Sutayt b. Faḍl al-Kōhēn, 208
Suwayd b. al-Ḥārith, 120
synagogue(s): closed by government, 301–2; confiscation of, 92f., 167, 204, 301–2; construction of, 152, 300, 350, 358f.; destruction of, 69, 167, 206, 293, 323
Synagogue of the Rabbanites, 189–91
Syria, xxv, xxvi, xxvii, 5, 7, 13, 22, 29, 34, 61, 65, 68, 73, 75, 87, 88, 104, 105–6, 107, 157–58, 200, 236, 277, 289, 293, 296, 298–99, 300, 318–21, 329, 336, 337, 338, 339, 341, 347, 353, 354–55, 393–405
Syro-Lebanese Christians, 5, 22, 34, 61, 65, 68, 104f., 107, 110, 151f., 157–58, 200, 236, 354–55, 399–400

al-Ṭabarī, 168, 230
Taghrī Birdī, 264
Tahertī family, 183, 184, 188
Taḥkemōnī, 58
Tahmāsp, 291, 292
Ṭā'if, 19
Tales of ᶜAntar, 230
Ṭalḥa, 130
ṭālib (petty-grade scholar), 369
Talmud, 28, 29, 31, 34, 45, 213, 246, 254, 330, 331, 336, 337, 338, 343, 346
Talmudic commentaries, 41, 45, 343
Talmudic Judaism, 29, 31, 34
Talmudic quotations, 209, 226, 246, 346
Tangier, 101, 103f., 164, 312, 317
Tannaim, 32, 335
Tanzimat (reforms), 97, 98, 100, 109f., 357–60, 361, 399, 401
tanzimatçılar (reformers), 96
ṭarḥa (shawl), 181, 182
al-Taᶜrīf, 269–70
tariffs. *See* discriminatory tariffs
Ṭāriq b. Ziyād, 156
Tarudant, 312, 315
Taurel, M. I., 367
Tawfīq, Khedive of Egypt, 99
tax farming, 93, 292, 296
taxation and tribute, 18, 19, 20, 24f., 27–28, 38, 39, 43f., 73, 97, 98, 99, 148, 149, 153, 159–61, 162, 176, 180, 192–93, 194, 195–97, 251, 257,

taxation and tribute (*continued*) 261, 264, 277, 287, 292, 298, 304, 305, 315–16, 328, 339, 360, 410, 414, 417, 420
ṭaylasān, 167
Ṭayyi', 119, 124
Taza, 285
Temple Mount, 154, 192f., 267, 332
Tent of Meeting, 267
Terrasse, Henri, 84
Tetouan, 101, 308–9, 312, 371
Thābit b. Qays, 142–43
Thaclaba b. Sacya, 139, 144
Theodosius (Byzantine emperor), 30
Tiberias, 33, 89, 90, 91, 155, 293–94, 331, 336–39, 340–41, 356
Tibet, 253
Tigris, 29, 164, 254
Tiqva ha-Kōhēn b. R. Nathan, 208
Titus, 235
Tlemcen, 77, 280, 281, 288
Toledano, Jaime, 307
Toledo, 211, 352
Torah, 4, 74, 114, 119, 130, 131, 138, 153, 165, 173–74, 203, 209, 213, 226, 229, 233, 239, 244, 252, 257, 267, 268, 269, 303, 338, 349, 350f., 352, 424
Torrey, Charles Cutler, 3
Tower of Hippicus, 332
Transoxania, 164, 243
ṭrēfa, 215
Tripoli (Lebanon), 52, 204
Tripoli (Libya), 290, 406–8, 409, 416f.
tschibuk (pipe), 334, 335
Tüfenqjī-bāshī (police chief), 403
Tughuzghuzz, 164
Tulunid(s), 41
Tunis, 104, 316, 413, 416–22
Tunisia, 41, 42–46, 76, 77, 78, 98f., 104, 164, 183–85, 186–88, 411–12, 413–15, 416–22, 424
Tūrānshāh, 240
Turk(s), 35, 49, 67–76, 77, 79, 85, 87–94, 95, 96, 97, 98, 99, 101, 102, 106, 109, 110, 253, 267–70, 277, 281, 290–92, 293, 295, 296–97, 298–99, 300, 305, 318, 319, 320f., 324–27, 334, 336, 337f., 339, 354–55, 356, 357–60, 361, 362, 363, 364, 371–73, 377–83, 384, 385–87, 388, 389–92, 393–405, 406–8, 413–15, 417–22, 427
Turkey, 88, 96, 99, 293, 322, 330, 352
Turkish language, xviii, xxi, 65, 67, 264, 277, 326, 392
al-Ṭurṭūshī, 158
Tustarī(s), 52, 194, 195, 204
Tyre, 49, 354–55

cUbayd Allāh al-Mahdī, 42
Ubulla, 164
Uḥud, Battle of, 13, 14, 121, 122
cUkāẓ, 5
culamā', 68, 259–60, 274, 279, 284, 302, 337f., 366, 385, 386, 387
cUmar b. cAbd al-cAzīz, 25
cUmar b. cAbd al-Azīz b. Khalaf, 191
cUmar b. al-Khaṭṭāb, 19, 25, 130, 154–55, 157–58, 159, 162, 231, 271, 273, 301
al-cUmarī, 268
Umayyad(s), 28–29, 33, 39, 41, 54f., 242f.
Umm Bishr b. al-Barā', 148f.
Umm Salama, 139
Umma, 18, 19, 21, 25, 62, 115, 159f., 256, 270
cUnb, 289
ūqiyya (coin), 303
cUrwa b. al-Zubayr, 142
Usayd b. Ḥuḍayr, 130, 135
Usayd b. Sacya, 139
Usayr (Yusayr) b. Zārim, 17
Usque, Samuel, 88
usury, 86, 151
cUzayr, 259, 260. *See also* Ezra
cUzayr b. Abī cUzayr, 119

Valley of Jehosaphat, 332
Vekil Kharj (tax agent), 375
Venice, 264, 294, 296, 319, 337, 338
Vicars, the Rev. Mr., 379–81
Victor Emmanuel, 421
Vienna, 338, 413
vilayet (province), 98, 102, 103
Visigoth(s, -ic), 24, 54

Wādi 'l-Qurā, 5, 18
Wakkāra, 285f.
wālī(s) (governors), 103, 325, 388, 391
waqf. See charitable trusts
al-Wāqidī, 136
Waqqāṣa family, 78f., 279–80
Warghamma, 410
warrior elite(s), 67f.
Wars of Ridda, 21
al-Wāsiṭī (mathematician), 230
al-Wāsiṭī (polemicist), 72, 276
al-Waṭīḥ, 146, 147
Watt, W. Montgomery, 10, 16, 20
Waṭṭāsid(s), 81–83, 84, 281, 282
wedding ceremonies, 313, 338
Wellsted, Lieut. J. R., 348

westernization of non-Muslims, 95, 97f., 109, 416, 418
Wetzstein, Johann Gottfried, 405
Wissenschaft des Judentums, 53f.
Wood, Richard, 415
Wrench (Mr.), 405
Writ of appointment, 38, 178–79, 181, 182, 254, 269–70

Yaḥyā b. Ifrān, 224
Yaḥyā b. Yaḥyā al-Waṭṭāsī, 281
Yamama, 19
Yamīn b. ᶜUmayr, 135
Yaᶜqūb b. ᶜAbd al-Ḥaqq, 279
Yaᶜqūb b. Killis, 43, 50
Yaᶜqūb b. Yūsuf (Merinid sultan), 80
Yaᶜqūb al-Manṣūr, 76
Yarmuk, 153
Yathrib. *See* Medina
Yazīd b. ᶜAbd Allāh b. Qusayṭ, 139
Yemen, 4, 5, 9, 19, 20, 24, 99, 132, 233–46, 247–48, 249–50, 253, 255–58, 291, 322–23, 347, 349–52
Yequtiel b. Ḥasan, 57
yeshiva, 31, 45, 47, 56, 60, 90, 171–74, 178–79, 180, 181, 182, 183, 184, 185, 187, 192, 193, 201, 211, 213, 243, 252, 289, 329–31, 338
Yoḥannan b. Zakkay, 289, 329
Yom Kippur, 11, 410
Yoosef, Saleh, 375
Youda, Saleh, 391
Young, W. L., 355
Yurt, 164
Yūsuf Asᶜar Dhū Nuwās, 4
Yūsuf b. Yaᶜqūb (Merinid sultan), 78, 279

Zabid, 234
al-Zabīr b. Bāṭā al-Quraẓī, 142–43
Zacharias, 165
Zagury family, 368–69
zakāt (alms tax), 160, 162
Zakkay b. Bustanay the Nasi, 252
zaptiye (gendarmerie), 417
Zayd b. Ḥāritha, 7, 124
Zayd b. al-Laṣīt, 119
Zayd b. Thābit, 122
Zayn al-Dīn ᶜAlī b. Ṣāᶜid, 66
Zaynab b. al-Ḥārith, 148
Zayyanids, 67, 77, 288
Zelkha, Nessim, 391
Zenāta, 78, 79
Zion, yearning for, 60f., 85, 90, 292, 328, 334
Zion Synagogue, 329
Zionism (religious), 85
Zirid(s), 46, 63, 211–13, 214, 217–25
Zohar, 352
Zoroastrian(s), 21, 24, 25, 27, 159–61, 169, 231
Zuᶜar, 285f.
al-Zubayr b. al-ᶜAwwām, 130, 147
al-Zubayr b. Bāṭā b. Wahb, 120
al-Zuhrī, 137
Zunnār (belt), 158, 167, 251, 257, 273
Zunz, Leopold, 53f.
Zuwayla Quarter, 189–91